ESSENTIAL PAPERS IN PSYCHOANALYSIS

Essential Papers on Borderline Disorders
Edited by Michael D. Stone, M.D.

Essential Papers on Object Relations
Edited by Peter Buckley, M.D.

Essential Papers on Narcissism
Edited by Andrew P. Morrison, M.D.

Essential Papers on Depression
Edited by James C. Coyne

Essential Papers on Psychosis
Edited by Peter Buckley, M.D.

Essential Papers on Countertransference
Edited by Benjamin Wolstein

Essential Papers on Character Neurosis and Treatment
Edited by Ruth F. Lax

Essential Papers on the Psychology of Women
Edited by Claudia Zanardi

Essential Papers on Transference
Edited by Aaron H. Esman, M.D.

Essential Papers on Dreams
Edited by Melvin R. Lansky, M.D.

Essential Papers on Literature and Psychoanalysis
Edited by Emanuel Berman

ESSENTIAL PAPERS ON LITERATURE AND PSYCHOANALYSIS

Edited by
Emanuel Berman

NEW YORK UNIVERSITY PRESS
NEW YORK AND LONDON

NEW YORK UNIVERSITY PRESS
New York and London

Library of Congress Cataloging-in-Publication Data
Essential papers on literature and psychoanalysis / edited by Emanuel Berman.
p. cm.
Includes bibliographical references and index.
ISBN 0-8147-1184-7 (cloth).—ISBN 0-8147-1185-5 (pbk.)
1. Psychoanalysis and literature. I. Berman, Emanuel, 1946-
PN56.P92E87 1992 92-28361
801'.92—dc20 CIP

New York University Press books are printed on acid-free paper, and their binding materials are chosen for strength and durability.

Manufactured in the United States of America

c 10 9 8 7 6 5 4 3 2 1
p 10 9 8 7 6 5 4 3 2 1

To Ronit Matalon,
my literary counterpart

Contents

Introduction

Emanuel Berman

1.

A few years ago, I asked my undergraduate psychology students, in the first meeting of a seminar on psychology and literature, to write a brief analysis of the following text:

> The Truth about Sancho Panza
>
> Without making any boast of it Sancho Panza succeeded in the course of years, by devouring a great number of romances of chivalry and adventure in the evening and night hours, in so diverting from him his demon, whom he later called Don Quixote, that his demon thereupon set out in perfect freedom on the maddest exploits, which, however, for the lack of a pre-ordained object, which should have been Sancho Panza himself, harmed nobody. A free man, Sancho Panza philosophically followed Don Quixote on his crusades, perhaps out of a sense of responsibility, and had of them a great and edifying entertainment to the end of his days.

I offered no information regarding the text, and no one guessed the author. (The analysis was ''blind.'')

What characterized the analyses offered by these talented students? Most were written as case studies: ''the case of Sancho.'' The explicit statement in the text, that Don Quixote represents an aspect of Sancho's personality, was reformulated by using psychological jargon. Various mechanisms were offered to explain the process described: projection, sublimation, denial, identification with the aggressor, rationalization, projective identification, displacement, repression (or its failure). Don Quixote was identified by many students as representing the id, but others saw him in the role of the superego, the object, the drive or the shadow (Jungian version). Dramatic differences of opinion evolved regarding the ''patient's'' mental health: Some students saw him as a model of healthy integration, who found the magic solution for handling inner conflict, whereas others doubted his sanity or even diagnosed him as psychotic, or as a case of multiple personality.

In comparison to this richness of dynamic and diagnostic formulations, only three out of twenty students used the word *humor* or *irony* in their responses. Most treated the text very sternly and some relied on the title as proof of its truthfulness. Most students did not refer to the earlier connotations of the names used in the text. (Indeed, I suspect many would have offered the same analysis to a text describing how Dick Jones succeeded in diverting from himself his demon, whom he later called Harry Smith). Only three answers referred to the way the text reverses the traditional images of Quixote and Sancho. Only four discussed literary characteristics of the text: its unique syntax; the different voices present in it; the contrasts, paradoxes and turnabouts that startle and confuse the reader; its exploration of the creative process; the literary figure as an artifact and as an emotional reality; the parallels between the actual author of the text and its protagonist-author, and their "alliance" in dismissing another author (Cervantes).

This little experiment has intrigued me because my students—eager, undoubtedly, to satisfy what they imagined to be the expectations of a psychoanalyst-teacher—duplicated unknowingly almost all the pitfalls that characterized the psychoanalytic discussion of literature for many decades.

Generations of psychoanalysts treated literary characters as patients seeking treatment, and analyzed their pathology and dynamics. They often accepted biographical statements as an ultimate truth, forgetting that biography (and autobiography) is also a form of fiction. They neglected the study of the literary traditions and genres in which novels and stories arose, and missed many of their allusions to earlier literary works. In their enthusiastic search for psychological explanations they risked missing the irony and subtlety of texts, risked disregarding the complex interplay of writer and reader.

This experiment demonstrates, in my eyes, the futility of reductionistic approaches that bypass basic literary understanding. Most interpreters here exchanged the profound psychological insights of the text itself for jargon-laden formulations that were at best equivalent and at worst impoverished. The result was an unintended self-parody.

Only those students who were tuned to the unique qualities of the text as a work of literature, and noticed the surprising and amusing interplay it creates between the writer, an unmentioned earlier writer (Cervantes), an even earlier literary generation (authors of the romances of chivalry, already ridiculed by Cervantes), two highly loaded figures, and the perplexed reader, only they could approach a serious psychoanalytic reading. Such a reading requires an abandonment of the pretentious attitude of therapists and diagnosticians toward "disturbed" figures (or authors), and a greater willingness to let literature be our therapist, that is, to allow it to teach us new ways of looking at ourselves. "The Truth about Sancho Panza" is a good example, because it has the potential to teach us a lot about reality, fantasy, and the intermediate space between them; about self, other, and all that is not easily delineated as belonging to self or to the other; about the subtle interrelation of dominance and submission, anxiety and playfulness, freedom and commitment.

When we discussed the interpretations in the next meeting of the seminar, one student guessed the text was written by Borges. We could argue, indeed, that Borges toiled all his life on writing "The Truth about Sancho Panza," just as his protagonist Pierre Menard toiled on writing *Don Quixote*. But "The Truth about Sancho Panza" had also been written before, by Franz Kafka (1946).

2.

A paper by the eminent psychoanalyst Paul Schilder ([1937] 1938) has stirred an enormous turmoil in the U.S. literary community, especially when its presentation in a conference of the American Psychoanalytic Association was reported by the *New York Times*. Schilder studied *Alice in Wonderland*. After discussing Lewis Carroll's "narrow and distorted life," and analyzing sadistic and cannibalistic elements in the story, its distortion of space, time, and language, and the lack of any tenderness in its anxiety-ridden atmosphere, he concluded:

> Carroll appears to the writer of this essay as a particularly destructive writer. I do not mean this in the sense of a literary criticism, which does not concern us here. We may merely ask whether such a literature might not increase destructive attitudes in children beyond the measure which is desirable. . . . One may be afraid that without the help of the adult, the child may remain bewildered, and, alone, may not find his way back to a world in which it can appreciate love relations, space and time and words.

Schilder's aggressive exposition of Carroll's aggression aroused intense aggression in its turn, including a recommendation to treat him as Father William (a protagonist of *Alice*) treated an inquisitive youth: "Be off, or I'll kick you downstairs!" (Greenacre 1955, p. 259). Reacting to Schilder's rescue fantasy of saving innocent children from a perverted writer, many literary critics and scholars responded with the fantasy of rescuing innocent literature from a perverted psychoanalyst. Joseph Wood Krutch (1937) stated vehemently: "Personally I have never heard of a child who confessed to being dangerously terrified by 'Alice' or of an adult who attributed his downfall to a trauma received from the book in infancy." And several critics quoted Carroll's own statement: "The thought of the many English firesides where happy faces have smiled her a welcome, and of the many English children to whom she has brought an hour of (I trust) innocent amusement, is one of the brightest and pleasantest thoughts of my life" (1871; in Phillips 1971, p. xxiii).

Here we witness the full price of a historical polarization. One pole is represented by the self-confident and single-minded psychoanalyst, who reads literature as a series of case studies, searching for the psychopathology of figures and authors. The other, by the defensive counterattack of literary loyalists who cling to manifest content or to the declared intentions of the author, accepting them at face value and depriving the work of its emotional complexity.

Some early psychoanalytic studies of literature may bring to mind an enlightened anthropologically minded military governor, who spends long evenings by the fire, listening with fascination to the tales of the elders of the tribe, but will not hesitate to use force if his authority is questioned by any tribespeople. Similarly, early analysts are intrigued by literature and are attracted to it, but take it for granted that they have an exclusive capacity to master it. "While literature is considered as a body of *language—to be interpreted*—psychoanalysis is considered as a body of *knowledge,* whose competence is called upon *to interpret*" (Felman 1982, p. 5). This colonialist invasion is met with fierce animosity by local liberation movements with xenophobic views, such as New Criticism, which wish to expel psychoanalysts, Marxists, existentialists, theologians, and all other dangerous invaders of literature's homeland.

From today's perspective we may notice that in the first decades of this century both psychoanalysts and literary scholars faced a similar dilemma, which may have contributed to rigidity and dogmatism on both sides: competition with the growing prestige of the natural sciences and their positivistic foundations. Jane Tompkins (1980) describes how literature people, who during the Renaissance shaped their theories in order to survive a struggle with moralistic Puritan objections, were forced to meet in the twentieth century the pressures of the empiricist–objectivist norms that became dominant in the academic world. Formalist criticism walled itself off from neighboring fields in order to establish disciplinary autonomy, and ruled out the discussion of personal feelings and experiences in order to emulate scientific objectivity and rigor.

A good example of this attempt "to beat science in its own game" is Wimsatt and Beardsley's struggle against "the Affective Fallacy" (1949, p. 21): "The Affective Fallacy is a confusion between the poem and its results. . . . It begins by trying to derive the standard of criticism from the psychological effects of a poem and ends in impressionism and relativism."

Psychology becomes an enemy. Such a view may have more personal sources as well. T. S. Eliot, in his discussion of poetry, emphasized the need to keep emotion under control, to eliminate the "chaotic" and "irregular" from experience (Tompkins 1980, p. 220). He concluded that "poetry is not a turning loose of emotion, but an escape from emotion; it is not the expression of personality, but an escape from personality" (Kermode 1975, pp. 42–43).

Freud found himself under a similar pressure. In attempting to legitimize the revolutionary and controversial insights of psychoanalysis, an appeal to scientific respectability was essential. Freud's own background as a researcher in neurology added to his tendency to couch his models in scientific terms, to define a "metapsychology," to claim objectivity. His image of the analyst as an impartial observer in the analytic situation, who overcomes his subjective distortions (countertransference) and becomes an honest mirror to the analysand, is an outgrowth of this emphasis. The scientific claims of psychoanalysis were emphasized in Strachey's English translation of Freud's work (Bettelheim 1982), and became a weapon in the struggle of U.S. psychoanalysis to take over psychiatry (a struggle in which it won a temporary—and pyrrhic—victory) and to obtain footing within academic psychology (Hale 1978). The claim for scientific objectivity made psychoanalysis more authoritative—and authoritarian?—vis-à-vis patients, and also vis-à-vis literature, art, and history.

Clinical psychoanalysis was expected to offer a definite, veracious interpretation, which according to the early theory of technique would be therapeutic. The expectation to find a clear causal answer regarding the patient's problems can be related to Freud's fascination with archeology. Spence (1987) described it in literary terms, calling it "the Sherlock Holmes tradition": "The genre is familiar to all. It features a master sleuth (therapist) who is confronted by a series of bizarre and disconnected events (symptoms) reported by a somewhat desperate and disorganized client (patient). The sleuth listens, watches, and ponders, never prejudging, never despairing, almost never surprised, always confident that when all the facts are in, the mystery will disappear and truth will emerge'' (Spence 1987, p. 114).

In this model, we may notice, transference and interpretation are sharply separated. Transference is attributed to the patient, and is seen as subjective and mostly distorted; the analysand sees the analyst through displacements from past figures, mostly parents, and past impressions are now arbitrarily attributed to the analyst. Interpretation, on the other hand, belongs to the analysts, and is part of their capacity to look at analysands objectively and understand their problems within the framework of theory, which at that point tended to be somewhat reductionistic.

Any exchange of roles appeared in this framework to be problematic. Attempts by the analysand to interpret the analyst's behavior were understood as part of the distortion, as serving resistance. Transference by the analyst (countertransference) was seen as a failure to maintain the desired neutrality, maybe a reason to return for further analysis to overcome the difficulty.

We can see that the paternalistic attitude toward literature in the early practice of ''applied'' psychoanalysis was an outgrowth of attitudes and assumptions present at the time in psychoanalytic theory and in clinical practice. The reductionistic understanding of patients was mirrored in a reductionistic look at literature, as described so sarcastically by a disenchanted psychoanalytic critic, Frederic Crews: ''It must be admitted that Freudian criticism too easily degenerates into a grotesque Easter-egg hunt: find the devouring mother, detect the inevitable castration anxiety, listen, between the syllables of verse, for the squeaking bedsprings of the primal scene'' (Crews 1975, p. 166).

3.

To understand the gradual change in the encounter between literature and psychoanalysis, we must follow some developments within psychoanalysis during this century. One development has been continuous: Reductionism has necessarily decreased with the expansion of psychoanalytic understanding to more aspects of emotional life. With more explanatory models available (oedipal and pre-oedipal, drive related and pertaining to separation-individuation, focusing on conflict or on developmental arrest, rooted in object relations or in self integration, etc.) the need to reduce clinical or literary phenomena to one hypothetical source decreases, and more respect can be guaranteed to the uniqueness of each person or work of art.

This trend can be traced to Freud's ([1900] 1953, p. 283) notion of overdetermination, and was strengthened by Waelder's (1936) concept of multiple function. The latter is already a part of ego psychology, an outgrowth of its increasing emphasis on the multiplicity of human needs mediated by the regulating functions of the ego. This new emphasis added complexity to the psychoanalytic theory of motivation. At the same time, the emphasis on regulation may have moderated some of the more subversive, revolutionary elements of Freud's thought (Wright 1984).

Ego psychology (e.g., Anna Freud, Hartmann, Kris, Erikson) has also contributed to the erosion of Freud's initial dichotomy between manifest and latent (in the dream, and in other aspects of personality), to the abandonment of the view of observable phenomena as merely a shell that needs to be cracked and thrown away. Erikson's (1954) re-analysis of Freud's "dream specimen," the dream of Irma's injection, is a good example. It is actually a patient literary analysis of the dream's text, in which Erikson derives much insight from the narrative qualities of the manifest dream, and then relates it to more latent aspects that can be deciphered only with the help of Freud's own associations and additional knowledge about his life at the time.

The attention to the visible, and the interest of ego psychology in individual differences based on defensive structure, paves the way to a psychoanalytic consideration of issues of style and artistic devices, issues that were out of place in Freud's own content-focused thinking. Questions of sentimentality and dryness, sarcasm and involvement, laconic and expansive treatment of experiences, are all crucial in determining the atmosphere and emotional impact of works of literature. The possibilities of exploring the dynamic (and defensive) significance of form materialize in Holland's (1968) now classical work, *The Dynamics of Literary Response.*

Kris's (1952) concept of "regression in the service of the ego" freed psychoanalysis from a simplistic equation of regression and pathology. We may notice that the lack of such a concept was felt in Schilder's alarmist view of *Alice in Wonderland,* and its incorporation made it possible for a later psychoanalyst, Martin Grotjahn (1947, p. 41), to reach a completely different view of Carroll's book: "Such books . . . lead to an artistic and testing regression; they open a temporary guilt-free and relatively anxiety-free communication to the unconscious. Necessary repression and sublimation are achieved easier and with healthier results when the communication with the creative unconscious is kept alive, free and open.''

A central contribution of object relations models in psychoanalysis is the deepening of our understanding of self–other (''self–object'') relations—an issue crucial to the understanding of author–figure, author–story, reader–figure, and reader–story relations, and in a less direct but no less meaningful way, author–reader relations.

All object relations models (British and American like) cast doubt on any simplistic dichotomous division between object and subject, self and other. Margaret Mahler (influenced both by ego psychology and by object relations models), in studying ''the psychological birth of the human infant,'' teaches us how much the separate, individuated existence of one's personality is not given, but is rather a developmental challenge; how much obstacles in the separation–individuation process may sabotage or distort the achievement of this goal. In completely different terms, Melanie Klein emphasizes the fluidity of the experiential boundary between self and other, its vulnerability to constant processes of introjection and projection that may lead us to ''locate'' our contents in the other (''divert from us our demon,'' in Kafka's words), or ''locate'' within us experiences of the other. The development of the idea of projective identification (by Bion, Ogden, and others) as not merely an inner fantasy, but an actual interpersonal process, may make it particularly valuable in understanding the emotional undercurrents of writing and reading.

A similar goal is achieved in Heinz Kohut's Self Psychology through the concept of the selfobject, which could be understood as an aspect of the other (parent, initially), which becomes a building block of the self. (For more extensive explorations of the relevance of Self Psychology to literature, see Layton and Schapiro 1986; Wolf 1980).

The most profound erosion of the object–subject dichotomy is inherent in the work of D. W. Winnicott, which gives a central role to transitional objects (mostly in childhood) and transitional phenomena (throughout life) that create an intermediate space in-between self and other, reality and fantasy. ''The place where cultural experience is located is in the *potential space* between the individual and the environment (originally the object). The same can be said of playing. Cultural experience begins with creative learning first manifested in play'' (Winnicott 1971, p. 118). Winnicott's thinking has indeed inspired many applications to literature, although not all questions regarding such an application have been fully resolved (see Skura 1981, pp. 185–190).

It is not surprising that object relations models led to a reformulation of the dynamics of the analytic situation, and eroded the distinction between interpretation and transference, objectivity and subjectivity. There is now a strong trend toward conceptualizing the analytic process "primarily as an encounter between two people, rather than as a setting whose purpose is the examination of the intrapsychic process of one of them" (Abrams & Shengold 1978, p. 402).

The more modest and self-critical contemporary approach to interpretation is expressed in Winnicott's comment regarding the need for interpretations: "If I make none the patient gets the impression that I understand everything. In other words, I retain some outside quality by not being quite on the mark—or even by being wrong" (Winnicott 1965, p. 167). Another radical challenge to traditional interpretation is Lacan's view "that the lack of meaning—the discontinuity in conscious understanding—can and should be interpreted as such, without necessarily being transformed into meaning" (Felman, chap. 13, this volume).

Skepticism regarding omniscient interpretation goes hand-in-hand with the growing realization that countertransference is omnipresent and unavoidable, that the analyst's emotional life is no less influential than the analysand's. Starting with the pioneering work of Winnicott, Paula Heimann, and Margaret Little, the question of overcoming countertransference gave way to the question of understanding it and attempting to draw on it.

Heinrich Racker ([1968] 1982) in his now classical book on transference and countertransference, says:

> The first distortion of truth in "the myth of the analytic situation" is that analysis is an interaction between a sick person and a healthy one. The truth is that it is an interaction between two personalities, in both of which the ego is under pressure from the id, the superego and the external world; each personality has its internal and external dependencies, anxieties, and pathological defenses; each is also a child with his internal parents; and each of these whole personalities—that of the analysand and that of the analyst—responds to every event in the analytic situation. . . . The analyst's objectivity consists mainly in a certain attitude towards his own subjectivity and countertransference. (p. 132)

This view of analyst and analysand as undergoing parallel experiences naturally leads to the question: If the analyst's interpretive task is colored by (counter)transference, doesn't the analysand's transference to the analyst involve potentially valid interpretive observations?

Merton Gill's (1982) book on transference goes in this direction, and objects to defining transference in terms of distortion. Gill casts doubt on the analysts' pretense to be able to judge what is the truth about themselves, in order to define what is distortion. He believes transference inevitably combines accurate observations and projections, influences of the past and perceptions of the present. Rather than dismiss the analysand's responses as unrealistic, the analyst accepts their potential realistic dimension, while trying to elucidate their personal meaning in the analysand's life.

4.

The possibility that transference and interpretation are inseparable and form one cohesive experience is particularly important to us. It may be enormously useful in defining the position of the reader, attempting to understand (interpret) a work of literature while having emotional transference toward it. This may be experienced as a therapist's transference, when figures, book, or author are experienced as needing to be explained, and at the extreme end as being pathological. Alternately, the reader's emotional set may be closer to an analysand's countertransference, when figures, text, or writer are experienced as valuable and a source of insight for the reader. Felman (1982, pp. 7–8) suggests that the difficulty to choose one response or the other characterizes being a literary critic: "Therefore, submitting psychoanalysis to a *literary* perspective would necessarily have a subversive effect on the clear-cut polarity through which psychoanalysis handles literature as its other, as the mere object of interpretation."

The return of subjectivity into psychoanalysis brings the experience of the reader into the psychoanalytic study of literature, and this shift coincides with the return of the reader into general literary criticism, under the title of Reader Response Criticism. In both psychoanalysis and literary scholarship this legitimization of subjectivity marks an end to the attempt to emulate the natural sciences.

Reader Response Criticism "deprives science of its privileged position in relation to other forms of knowledge by declaring that the objectivity on which science bases its superiority is a fiction"; this move makes it possible to reintroduce into literary criticism "all the idiosyncrasy, emotionality, subjectivity and impressionism that had made the literary enterprise vulnerable to attack by science and that the New Critics had worked so hard to eliminate from critical practice'' (Tompkins 1980, p. 224).

Cary Nelson's (1977) essay, ''Reading Criticism,'' expresses the new trend forcefully. Nelson states:

> If we can forgo the collective professional illusion of objectivity and learn to be somewhat iconoclastic about what we write, the practice and evaluation of criticism will become unashamedly exciting. . . . For the study of criticism is necessarily also the study of ourselves as critics, just as the study of literature is also the study of ourselves as readers. Those critics who can (or must) risk themselves in their writing not only give us a glimpse of their own inwardness, they also let us see ourselves from a new vantage point. (p. 813)

These developments in psychoanalysis and literary studies were combined in the work of Norman Holland. Whereas his earlier work focused on identifying ''core fantasies'' in books, or in the whole literary output of authors (and was at times accused of reductionism), his later work turned to the significance of subjective individual interpretation of literature, to the influence of (independently assessed) ''identity themes'' of readers on their understanding and re-creation of a story (Holland 1975), or to the sources of his own personal experience in reading a story (Holland 1980). ''*All* readers create from the fantasy seemingly 'in' the work fantasies to suit their several character structures'' (Holland, chap. 14, this volume).

This realization leads him to a radical redefinition of goals: ''Instead of subtracting readings as to narrow them down or cancel some . . . let us use human differences to add response to response, to multiply possibilities, and to enrich the whole experience. . . . We can restore stories to their rightful owners . . . you and me and all of you and me, our emotional as well as our intellectual selves . . . by recovering reading as a personal transaction'' (Holland 1980, p. 370).

Whereas the exploration of individual meaning can lead each reader in a self-analytic direction, the interest in the responses of readers can also lead to a study of their combined significance to the meta-understanding of a work of literature. This would be similar to the attempt of a clinical team to figure out how divergent countertransference reactions to one patient could lead to a better understanding of that patient's dynamics (e.g., Hartman 1971). Such attempts proved quite fruitful to the study of literature in the hands of Felman (1982) and Reed (see p. 371, this volume).

Of course, legitimizing the importance of subjective reading raises numerous new dilemmas: Are all readings of equal value? Do we have criteria to favor one reading over the other, or even to consider some as distortions? Is there an objective text stimulating the different readings, or is the text created (recreated?) in each reading? Will careful readings lead to a crystallization of meaning, or to its disappearance in a deconstructive process? Coen (1982) surveys some of the debates surrounding these intriguing issues, and central participants—Bleich, Culler, Fish, Iser, Riffatterre, Todorov—are represented in Tompkins (1980) and in Suleiman and Crosman (1980).

Can such an emphasis on the experience of reading, on the interconnectedness of transference and interpretation, shed a new light on the Schilder–Krutch controversy regarding *Alice in Wonderland?* Clearly, we no longer need to take sides. In noticing the peculiarities and blind spots of each interpretation of *Alice,* we could—following in Holland's (1975) footsteps—study its relation to the personality structure of each critic. Of course, our knowledge of them is limited, and the endeavor may lead us to a slippery ethical ground. Still, it would be reasonable to suggest that responses to a book like *Alice* will vary (among professional readers and amateurs alike) according to the place the book touches in the inner world of the readers, according to the nature of the readers' object relations and self-experiences, according to their own ways of handling anxiety, aggression, and fear regarding disintegration.

Actually, both Schilder and Krutch appear to be defending against the regressive potential of the book. Krutch (himself an author of a study of Poe emphasizing psychopathology; Felman, chap. 13, this volume) does it by denying this regressive potential and clinging to a forced naive view overlooking any anxiety. Schilder does it by projecting and externalizing (only a disturbed author could imagine such crazy scenes, they are very far from "our" sane world), as well as by seeking mastery through the role of the rescuer. Indeed, both interpretations have a strong transferential quality.

At the same time—in the footsteps of Felman and Reed—we could attempt to study the characteristics of Carroll's work through the collective response of many different (and divergent) critics. What do we learn about the book's ambivalence regarding its protagonist, about its subtle game of touching and not touching, of frightening and pacifying, of uncovering horrors and covering them up whimsically, of being cynical and innocent?

I do not attempt an actual analysis here, but hint at its possible usefulness. In order to undertake it, however, we may have to overcome our skepticism: Could the argument among specific critics half a century ago be so meaningful and indicative of qualities actually existing in the book? To answer this challenge, I quote the first minutes of a spontaneous discussion held in my psychology and literature seminar, after all its participants read *Alice in Wonderland* (but no critical discussion of the book).

HANNA (after a short silence in class): It was really fun to read this book! I never read it before. I felt like a young girl.

RACHEL: I laughed a lot, all these jokes. I identified with Alice, recalled scenes from my childhood. It was very moving.

JUDITH (hesitant): I saw it as very frightening. A lot of things are unintelligible, unexpected. I wouldn't read it to my kids!

REBECCA: Yes, I never liked it as a child, and I don't like it now. The figures are unpleasant. There is no continuity, words are "shot" without any connection. When I read it as a child, Alice sounded so miserable.

DAVID: I had a feeling the author doesn't like Alice. He ridicules her as vicious—how she torments the mice with the story about her cat—it's not innocent at all!

REUBEN: Yes, she hurts people all the time!

DIANA: But she tries to relate, even if in the world she goes into people are not related. I am not sure the author ridicules her—maybe he allows her to recognize her limitations?

MYRA: Yes, there are many crazy things in this book, but that's why it's so fascinating. As a child I was very enthusiastic abut Alice—about her being so adventurous, never deterred, trying everything, then disengaging and running on . . .

SAUL: I realize now I must have been awfully scared by this book. Yesterday I fell asleep right after reading about Alice's fall, at the very beginning. Earlier I went to fetch it from friends, and only when I returned I recalled I have it. The kids reminded me we saw the movie together a few months ago—I forgot all about it. Now I start understanding my fear. What goes on there? A fall, disappearance, drowning, helplessness—everything is so slippery . . .

RUTH: Really, it has a lot of cruel elements.

MYRA (excited): I am getting annoyed with those who don't like Alice. What's the matter with you, why do you present it as so cruel? It has such a moving sense of adventure, and Alice's experience is not of helplessness and misery, but of curiosity and courage!

As the discussion went on, every single one of the major critical assessments of *Alice in Wonderland* (Phillips 1971) was unknowingly represented by one of the participants, and the class as a group continued to recreate the whole debate.

5.

Finally, we must mention the most profound challenge to the domineering tradition of "applying psychoanalysis to literature": the realization that—

just as in the analytic situation—interpretation can be mutual. Literature can be understood (fruitfully) in psychoanalytic terms, whereas psychoanalysis can be understood (no less fruitfully) as a form of literature.

Freud was aware of this possibility, and apparently ambivalent about it. In "Studies on Hysteria" (Breuer and Freud [1895] 1955, p. 160) he states:

> I have not always been a psychotherapist. Like other neuropathologists, I was trained to employ local diagnoses and electro-prognosis, and it still strikes me myself as strange that the case histories I write should read like short stories and that, as one might say, they lack the serious stamp of science. I must console myself with the reflection that the nature of the subject is evidently responsible for this, rather than any preference of my own.

As the preoccupation with achieving "the serious stamp of science" has subsided, the possibility of viewing psychoanalysis as literature became more acceptable. Stolorow and Atwood (1979) showed us convincingly how much the metapsychological interpretations regarding human nature (of Freud, Jung, Rank, Reich) are shaped by the life of the theorists and their personal emotional concerns, by "their own stories." The proliferation of biographical studies of Freud and other psychoanalytic pioneers during the last decade added support to this point of view, which may enable us to explore the relationship of psychoanalysts and their writings, as basically similar to the relationship of writers and their works of fiction.

Attempts to reformulate psychoanalytic theory as a hermeneutic discipline (e.g., Steele 1979) also contributed to our awareness that psychoanalytic formulations are not factual discoveries but rather narrative ways of organizing and illuminating experience. Schafer's work (chap. 15, this volume) emphasizes that the analyst is offering a story (a construction, a plot) in exchange to the analysand's story and the interaction between these two narratives makes it possible for analysands to reach a more flexible and rich view of their lives. Analyst and analysand may be now seen as co-authoring a new text (Schafer 1985, p. 280).

No wonder that psychoanalytic case studies could be subjected to literary analysis, yielding new insights about the way analyses are presented, and even conducted (e.g., Marcus, chap. 2, and Mahony, chap. 3, this volume). A perspective based on Reader Response Criticism may help us in evaluating the effectiveness of psychoanalytic interpretations (Priel 1990).

Literary analysis need not be limited to case histories. A literary line of inquiry can be extended to theoretical psychoanalytic papers. An influential example is Derrida's ([1980] 1987) study of "Beyond the Pleasure Principle." This extension is part of a more general cultural trend, at times described as central to post-modernism: The basic similarity of different texts and their accessibility to similar kinds of reading is emphasized beyond their unique attributes. A poem, an advertisement, a political speech, a booklet of instructions for the users of a refrigerator, all can be subjected to the same semiotic analysis, to the same exploration of style, of rhetoric, of social prejudices, of values, of poetics. Note, for example, Schor's paper, "Fiction as Interpretation, Interpretation as Fiction" (Suleiman and Crosman 1980).

The literary study of Freud—who was, let us not forget, a recipient of the Goethe Prize for Literature in 1930—has benefitted from the re-examination of Strachey's translation of *The Standard Edition,* and has influenced it in turn.

The re-examination itself is not new. Brandt wrote in 1961 (p. 50): "Freud's English translators have rather consistently replaced affect-laden German terms by neutral English words and dynamic, active constructions by static, passive ones. In this way, something Freud described as a process became in English translation a structure."

However, this concern gained little attention when it was first voiced, probably because the conceptualization of psychoanalysis in the language of objective structures was so dominant that the critical examination of its origins was inhibited. In contrast, within today's *zeitgeist,* the elaboration of this critical re-examiniation (e.g., Bettelheim 1982; Ornston 1985) becomes central in psychoanalytic discourse. We now realize that a more personal, more ambivalent, more tormented (and therefore more literary) Freud may be hidden behind his ossified portrait, and a return to the original, or new translations, are needed if we want to enliven our contact with him.

My sense is that the exploration of psychoanalytic writing (theory and case studies alike) as a form of literature may make it more accessible and more meaningful to contemporary readers, rather than alienate or disappoint them as was feared by earlier generations. Its ambiguity, subtlety, inner contradictions, and imaginative power give this literature a more lasting place in cultural history than the texts of most other psychological theories can ever achieve.

6.

This volume follows the encounter between literature and psychoanalysis during the past century. Its twenty chapters document many divergent points —and turning points—of this encounter.

Choosing was not easy. Many thousands of papers and books have been published in this area (see Kiell 1982), as well as several anthologies (e.g., Felman 1982; Kurzweil and Phillips 1983; Rimmon-Kenan 1987; Tennenhouse 1976). In structuring the present collection, an attempt was made to present the history of literature and psychoanalysis—from Freud to the present—emphasizing the basic conceptual and methodological difficulties inherent in this area. These difficulties became clearer in the past two decades, and the ways of handling them became more sophisticated, so recent literature receives more space than older work.

My approach, as expressed in this introduction, views literature and psychoanalysis as equal partners with potential mutual contributions. Still, more work has been devoted to the psychoanalytic exploration of literature than to the literary exploration of psychoanalysis, and this uneven proportion is reflected in this selection as well.

Although the understanding of psychoanalysis from the perspective of literary theory is represented, we were not able to include yet another relevant literary point of view: the depiction of psychoanalysis in works of fiction. Berman (1987), who studied this aspect extensively, reminds us that this is also a part of the ambivalent interaction of the two domains: "Psychiatric journals still publish articles on neurotic or narcissistic artists and novelists still portray rigid, repressive, or reductive analysts" (p. 32).

Most authors in this volume are practicing psychoanalysts, a substantial minority are literary critics and teachers of literature. The emphasis on newer contributions made it possible to include many authors who combine (in scholarship, and at times in formal training as well) impressive credentials in both literature and psychoanalysis. The impact of writers with this combined perspective (much rarer in the past) undoubtedly shapes the present more integrative phase in the literature–psychoanalysis encounter.

Some of these contemporary authors were also helpful in advice and encouragement. I would like to acknowledge the help of Francis Baudry, Patrick Mahony, Gail Reed, Bennett Simon, Meredith Ann Skura, and David Werman.

Let me close this introduction with my favorite lines from Lionel Trilling (quoted by Eckardt 1977, p. 528):

> I have been read by Eliot's poems and by *Ulysses* and by *Remembrance of Things Past* and by *The Castle,* for a good many years, since early youth. Some of these books first rejected me. I bored them. But as I grew older and they knew me better, they came to have more sympathy with me and to understand my hidden meanings.

REFERENCES

Abrams, S., and L. Shengold. 1978. Some reflections on the topic of the 30th Congress: Affects and the psychoanalytic situation. *International Journal of Psycho-Analysis* 59: 395–407.

Berman, J. 1987. *The talking cure: Literary representations of psychoanalysis*. New York: New York University Press.

Bettelheim, B. 1982. *Freud and man's soul*. New York: A. A. Knopf.

Brandt, L. W. 1961. Some notes on English Freudian terminology. *Journal of the American Psychoanalytic Association* 9: 331–39.

Breuer, J., and S. Freud [1895] 1955. Studies on hysteria. *Standard Edition,* vol. 2. London: Hogarth.

Coen, S. J. 1982. Essays on the relationship of author and reader: Transference implications for psychoanalytic literary criticism. Introduction. *Psychoanalysis and Contemporary Thought* 5: 3–15.

Crews, F. 1975. *Out of my system*. New York: Oxford University Press.

Derrida, J. [1980] 1987. *The post card. From Socrates to Freud and beyond*. Chicago: University of Chicago Press.

Eckardt, M. H. 1977. Reply to Shainess and Arieti. *Journal of the American Academy of Psychoanalysis* 5: 527–28.

Erikson, E. H. 1954. The dream specimen of psychoanalysis. *Journal of the American Psychoanalytic Association*. 2: 5–56.

Felman, S., ed. 1982. *Literature and psychoanalysis. The question of reading: Otherwise*. Baltimore: Johns Hopkins University Press.

Freud, S. [1900] 1953. The interpretation of dreams. *Standard Edition,* vol. 4. London: Hogarth.

Gill, M. 1982. *Analysis of transference*. New York: International Universities Press.

Greenacre, P. 1955. *Swift and Carroll*. New York: International Universities Press.

Grotjahn, M. 1947. About the symbolization of Alice's Adventures in Wonderland. *American Imago* 4: 32–41.

Hale, N. 1978. From Berggasse XIX to Central Park West: The Americanization of Psychoanalysis. *Journal of the History of Behavioral Sciences*. 14: 299–315.

Hartman, J. G. 1971. The case conference as a reflection of unconscious patient–therapist interaction. *Contemporary Psychoanalysis* 8: 1–17.

Holland, N. N. 1968. *The dynamics of literary response*. New York: Oxford University Press.

———. 1975. *Five readers reading*. New Haven and London: Yale University Press.

———. 1980. Recovering "The purloined letter": Reading as a personal transaction. In *The reader in the text: Essays on audience and interpretation,* edited by S. R. Suleiman and I. Crosman. Princeton: Princeton University Press.

Kafka, F. 1946. *The great wall of china: Stories and reflections.* New York: Schocken.

Kermode, F., ed. 1975. *Selected Prose of T. S. Eliot.* New York: Harcourt.

Kiell, N. 1982. *Psychoanalysis, psychology and literature: A bibliography,* 2nd ed. Metuchen, N.J.: Scarecrow.

Kris, E. 1952. *Psychoanalytic explorations in art.* New York: International Universities Press.

Krutch, J. 1937. Psychoanalysing Alice. *The Nation* CXLIV (Jan. 30): 124–30.

Kurzweil, E., and W. Phillips, eds. 1983. *Literature and psychoanalysis.* New York: Columbia University Press.

Layton, L., and B. A. Schapiro, eds. 1986. *Narcissism and the text: Studies in literature and the psychology of the self.* New York: New York University Press.

Nelson, C. 1977. Reading criticism. *PMLA* 92 (March): 311.

Ornston, D. 1985. Freud's conception is different from Strachey's. *Journal of the American Psychoanalytic Association* 33: 379–412.

Phillips, R., ed. 1971. *Aspects of Alice.* New York: Vanguard.

Priel, B. 1990. The effectiveness of interpretations: A reader-response perspective on psychoanalytic cure. *Psychoanalysis and Contemporary Thought* 13: 535–50.

Racker, H. [1968] 1982. *Transference and countertransference.* London: Maresfield.

Rimmon-Kenan, S., ed. 1987. *Discourse in psychoanalysis and literature.* London: Methuen.

Schafer, R. 1985. Wild analysis. *Journal of the American Psychoanalytic Association* 33: 275–99.

Schilder, P. [1937] 1938. Psychoanalytic remarks on Alice in Wonderland and Lewis Carroll. *Journal of Nervous and Mental Disease* 87: 159–68.

Skura, M. A. 1981. *The literary use of the psychoanalytic process.* New Haven: Yale University Press.

Spence, D. 1987. *The Freudian metaphor: Toward paradigm change in psychoanalysis.* New York: Norton.

Steele, R. S. 1979. Psychoanalysis and hermeneutics. *International Review of Psycho-Analysis* 6: 384–411.

Stolorow, R. D., and G. E. Atwood. 1979. *Faces in a cloud: Subjectivity in personality theory.* New York: Aronson.

Suleiman, S. R., and I. Crosman, eds. 1980. *The reader in the text: Essays on audience and interpretation.* Princeton: Princeton University Press.

Tennenhouse, L., ed. 1976. *The practice of psychoanalytic criticism.* Detroit: Wayne State University Press.

Tompkins, J. P., ed. 1980. *Reader response criticism: From formalism to post-structuralism.* Baltimore: Johns Hopkins University Press.

Waelder, R. 1936. The principle of multiple function. *Psychoanalytic Quarterly* 5: 45–62.

Wimsatt, W. K., Jr., and M. Beardsley. 1949. *The verbal icon: Studies in the meaning of poetry.* Lexington: University Press of Kentucky.

Winnicott, D. W. 1965. *The maturational processes and the facilitating environment.* London: Hogarth.

Winnicott, D. W. 1971. The location of cultural experience. *Playing and reality.* London: Tavistock.

Wolf, E. S. 1980. Psychoanalytic psychology of the self and literature. *New Literary History* 12: 41–60.

Wright, E. 1984. *Psychoanalytic criticism.* London: Methuen.

PART I

FREUD ON LITERATURE, FREUD AS LITERATURE

INTRODUCTION

In a draft attached to a letter to his friend and confidante Wilhelm Fliess (31 May 1897), Freud develops an idea: "The mechanism of fiction is the same as that of hysterical fantasies." He supports this thought with a brief analysis of the biographical sources of Goethe's *Werther*, and concludes with the comment: "So Shakespeare was right in juxtaposing fiction and madness (fine frenzy)" (Masson 1985, p. 251).

A few months later, on 15 October 1987, he mails Fliess a detailed account of childhood experiences unearthed by his self-analysis. One point appears to him as particularly important.

> I have found, in my own case too, being in love with my mother and jealous of my father, and I now consider it a universal event in early childhood. . . . If this is so, we can understand the gripping power of *Oedipus Rex* . . . the Greek legend seizes upon a compulsion which everyone recognizes because he senses its existence within himself. Everyone in the audience was once a budding Oedipus and each recoils in horror from the dream fulfillment here transplanted into reality. . . . Fleetingly the thought passed through my head that the same thing might be at the bottom of *Hamlet* as well. I am not thinking of Shakespeare's conscious intention, but believe, rather, that a real event stimulated the poet to his representation, in that his unconscious understood the unconscious of his hero. (Masson 1985, p. 272).

These two letters contain the seeds of most of Freud's work relating to literature. We may notice the equation of pathology and literature on the one hand, and the search for universal human motives on the other. Freud is intrigued by the relation of art to fantasy (an issue developed in "Creative Writers and Daydreaming," Freud [1908] 1959), by the impact of the author's life on his works of fiction (as studied in "*Dostoyevsky and Parricide,*" Freud [1928] 1957), and specifically by the relation of writers and their protagonists. At the same time he is also concerned with the impact of fiction and drama on the emotions of the readers or the spectator.

While comparing, in the 15 October letter, the effectiveness of Sophocles to the ineffectiveness of later "dramas of fate," Freud raises the question of audience response as a path to understanding the unique characteristics of particular works. Audience response is further studied by Freud in his work on jokes (Freud [1905] 1960), which can give us—alongside clinical studies of transference—a model for exploring the rhetorical-interactional dimension of literature (see Skura 1981, particularly pp. 178–85).

Oedipus and Hamlet may be said to be treated in these letters as imaginary patients, as were to be treated later the heroes of Jensen's *Gradiva* (Freud [1907] 1959), or Richard III, Lady Macbeth, and Ibsen's Rebecca Gamvik (Freud [1916] 1957). We must keep in mind, however, that Oedipus and Hamlet were put on Freud's couch only after he put himself on it; "analyzing" them was not an expression of condescending superiority, but rather of a sense of identification and shared destiny, of inspiration and confirmation. The formulation of the "Oedipus complex" model was for Freud both a theoretical and clinical turning point (supplying him with a substitute to the seduction theory, about which he developed doubts), and an achievement in his own self-analytic search for insight and relief from his most personal anxieties, depressive moods, and neurotic symptoms. Oedipus, Hamlet, the archeologist Norbert Hanold (Jensen's protagonist) and numerous other literary figures, were Freud's fantasized brothers in this search.

Of course, our present understanding of the interrelatedness of transference and interpretation gives us an added perspective on Freud's remarks. We may notice that his reading of *Oedipus Rex* is highly selective. He focuses on the impulses of Oedipus, while bypassing the murderous impulses of Laius (Ross 1982, speaks in this context of "the Laius complex"). This bias can be easily related to the shift of responsibility for neurosis from the parent (in the "seduction theory") to the child (in the Oedipus complex model), and to the emphasis on the distorting transference of the patient while disregarding the analyst's actual personality and countertransference, and its impact on the analysand's experience. Such personal biases are unavoidable, of course; taking them into account may reduce our tendency to treat interpretations as discoveries of definitive truth.

Freud's excitement with literature was lifelong. We can find in his writings references to all of Shakespeare's plays, as well as to dozens of other writers of his own and earlier generations. Grinstein (1968), in his thorough exploration of Freud's dreams, demonstrates time after time the depth of the influence of books Freud read and how their emotional impact can be discerned in aspects of his dreams that go far beyond his own conscious associations to these books.

Freud's works are easily accessible, but I felt this anthology would not be complete without at least one item by Freud. I chose *"The Theme of the Three Caskets,"* written in 1913, as one of the most revealing and profound discussions of literature in Freud's work. Here he is loyal to his warning in the last line of the *Gradiva* paper: "But we must stop here, or we may really forget that Hanold and Gradiva are only creatures of their author's mind" (Freud [1907] 1959, p. 93). Neither authors nor figures are treated as patients here. Literary themes are explored with the hope of understanding the deeper layers of human reality. The highly personal nature of this exploration for Freud himself (fifty-seven at the time of writing) is most directly expressed in the moving final paragraph.

Marcus's study of Freud's Dora case remains the most influential literary discussion of one of Freud's works. Marcus is a professor of English and Comparative Literature at Columbia University. His essay, which later appeared in an extended form in *Representations* (Marcus 1975), effectively demonstrates the potential contribution of artistic sensitivity to the elucidation of a clinical report, and the reported clinical process itself. The failed treatment of Dora has attracted numerous other commentators, starting with Erikson and Lacan, and leading to several contemporary literary and feminist explorations (many included in Bernheimer and Kahane 1985), as well as more strictly psychoanalytic discussions (see Jennings 1986).

Suleiman (1987) in a study comparing Dora to André Breton's *Nadja* and to Marguerite Duras' *Lol V. Stein,* suggested an additional literary dimension:

> . . . Freud's love story for Dora was inspired not only by putting himself in Herr K.'s place but also by his putting himself in the place of an omniscient narrator who, having a limited number of "characters" to work with, must find the most plausible and psychologically motivated solution to their entanglements. In other words, it was the desire for narrative coherence *as such* . . . that may have been a driving force. Freud's own transference, then, was not only to Herr K. but to Balzac . . . he desired to possess the authority of a Balzacian narrator (pp. 129–30).

Mahony's investigation of Freud's writings lays the groundwork for a literary study of Freud's work as a consistent whole. In *Freud as a Writer* (Mahony 1982), he follows the pioneering studies of Walter Muschg (1930/1959) and François Roustang ([1980] 1983), and analyzes Freud's stylistic uniqueness and complexity. His major samples are *Totem and Taboo,* Part 4;

and *Beyond the Pleasure Principle,* where he follows and develops Derrida's attempt to apply Freud's thinking to his own text by demonstrating the role of repetition and detour in the paper itself. Later on he studies Freud's continuous appeals to his audience and his constant sensitivity to audience receptivity, analyzes the varying proportions of certainty and ambiguity in Freud's text, and demonstrates the richness and playfulness of his figurative language. The final chapter, "Theory Is Also the Man," emphasizes aggression and a quest for Woman as latent forces that puncutate Freud's writing. Mahony is a literary scholar and psychoanalyst residing in Quebec.

In the chapter included here, Mahony applies his method to another work, Freud's case of "the Rat Man" (Freud [1909] 1955). This later book combines literary, historical, biographical, and psychoanalytic scholarship. Mahony compares the published case, Freud's unpublished process notes, references to the case in Freud's correspondence, and independent information he managed to obtain about this patient (Ernst Lanzer), his origins, and his life. This combined approach, which Mahony applied to "the Wolf Man" as well (Mahony 1984), leads to an insightful critical re-examination of the cases, including Freud's technique and Freud's countertransference.

This chapter demonstrates once more the importance of linguistic nuances that got lost in the existing English translation. Mahony contrasts Strachey's "stilted, reserved language" with Freud's "vivid, experiential language and his general intimacy with his wide audience" and concludes: "The elimination of lexical traces of Freud's personal and temporal nearness to his patient and reader reveals Strachey's heroic enterprise to be to some degree a translating-acting out and a monumental displacement" (Mahony 1986, p. 220).

The chapter we reproduce here is followed by a study of Part 2 of the case history, later accorded the title "Theoretical." Mahony (1986) summarizes the overriding organization of Freud's paper:

> Beginning with apologies for textual fragmentariness offset by the claim that he had completely restored Dr. Lanzer, Freud moved in Part One to a defensively definitive closure with its rapidly repeated claim about therapeutic resolution. In contrast, Part Two begins with a lexical clarification that is thereafter undone, and likewise proceeds to take up expository stances that undergo repeated undoings right up to the conclusion. Here it seems as if Freud hesitated between retaining and eliminating, a dual gesture comprehending both ends of the anal phase and elliptically leaving the impression that there was more to say of both. (p. 211)

For literary studies of other works of Freud—not case studies—intriguing examples are Derrida ([1980] 1987), Cixous (1976), or Mehlman (1975).

The final chapter in this section is an example of the theoretical reformulation that becomes possible when literary dimensions of Freud's work are recognized. In his earlier book *Narrative Truth and Historical Truth,* Donald Spence (1982) cast doubt on "the archeological model" of Freud. He suggested we move "away from the interpretation as a literal proposition and emphasize instead what might be called its rhetorical presence" (p. 285), called for a more relativistic view of truth, and warned analysts against "pseudo confirmations," which may make them mistake their hypothetical constructions for actual reconstructions. Spence, a psychoanalyst, is on the faculty of the R. W. Johnson Medical College in New Jersey.

The chapter included here is the opening chapter of Spence's *The Freudian Metaphor* (1987), which describes central psychoanalytic concepts, such as the unconscious, as metaphors, and defines seeing psychoanalysis as a science as a metaphor too. We rarely notice, he argues, how much theory supplies us the meaning that we "discover" in clinical data, how much psychoanalytic literature "represents a compromise between observation and speculation" (p. 113). Spence's harsh criticisms of "the myth of the innocent analyst" and of "the Sherlock Holmes tradition" in psychoanalysis add to the controversial nature (see Gehrie 1990) of this intriguing work.

REFERENCES

Bernheimer, C., and C. Kahane, eds. 1985. *In Dora's case: Freud—hysteria—feminism.* New York: Columbia University Press.

Cixous, H. 1976. Fiction and its phantoms: A reading of Freud's *Das Unheimliche. New Literary History* 3: 525–48.

Derrida, J. [1980] 1987. *The postcard. From Socrates to Freud and beyond.* Chicago: University of Chicago press.

Freud, S. [1905] 1960. Jokes and their relation to the unconscious. *Standard Edition,* vol. 8. London: Hogarth.

———. [1907] 1959. Delusions and dreams in Jensen's *Gradiva. Standard Edition,* vol. 9. London: Hogarth.

———. [1908] 1959. Creative writers and day-dreaming. *Standard Edition,* vol. 9. London: Hogarth.

———. [1909] 1955. Notes upon a case of obsessional neurosis. *Standard Edition,* vol. 10. London: Hogarth.

———. [1916] 1957. Some character types met with in psychoanalytic work. *Standard Edition,* vol. 14. London: Hogarth.

———. [1928] 1957. Dostoevsky and parricide. *Standard Edition,* vol. 21. London: Hogarth.

Gehrie, M. J. 1990. Review of Spence's "The Freudian metaphor." *Journal of the American Psychoanalytic Association* 38: 821–28.

Grinstein, A. 1968. *On Sigmund Freud's dreams.* Detroit: Wayne State University Press.

Jennings, J. L. 1986. The revival of "Dora": Advances in psychoanalytic theory and technique. *Journal of the American Psychoanalytic Association* 34: 607–35.

Mahony, P. 1982. *Freud as a writer.* New York: International Universities Press.

———. 1984. *The cries of the Wolf Man.* New York: International Universities Press.

———. 1986. *Freud and the Rat Man.* New Haven and London: Yale University Press.

Marcus, S. 1975. *Representations: Essays on literature and society.* New York: Random House.

Masson, J. M., ed. 1985. *The complete letters of Sigmund Freud to Wilhelm Fleiss: 1887–1904.* Cambridge and London: Harvard University Press.

Mehlman, J. 1975. How to read Freud on jokes: The critic as Schadchen. *New Literary History* 4: 439–61.

Muschg, W. 1930. Freud als Schriftsteller. *Die Psychoanalytische Bewegung* 2: 467–509. (Freud écrivain. 1959. *La Psychoanalyse* 5: 69–124).

Ross, J. M. 1982. Oedipus revisited: Laius and the Laius complex. *Psychoanlytic Study of the Child* 37: 169–200.

Roustang, F. [1980] 1983. Freud's style. In *Psychoanalysis never lets go.* Baltimore and London: Johns Hopkins University Press.

Skura, M. A. 1981. *The literary use of the psychoanalytic process.* New Haven and London: Yale University Press.

Spence, D. 1982. *Narrative truth and historical truth: Meaning and interpretation in psychoanalysis.* New York and London: Norton.

———. 1987. *The Freudian metaphor: Toward paradigm change in psychoanalysis.* New York and London: Norton.

Suleiman, S. R. 1987. Nadja, Dora, Lol V. Stein: Women, madness and narrative. In *Discourse in psychoanalysis and literature,* edited by S. Rimmon-Kenan. London and New York: Methuen.

1. The Theme of the Three Caskets

Sigmund Freud

I

Two scenes from Shakespeare, one from a comedy and the other from a tragedy, have lately given me occasion for posing and solving a small problem.

The first of these scenes is the suitors' choice between the three caskets in *The Merchant of Venice*. The fair and wise Portia is bound at her father's bidding to take as her husband only that one of her suitors who chooses the right casket from among the three before him. The three caskets are of gold, silver and lead: the right casket is the one that contains her portrait. Two suitors have already departed unsuccessful: they have chosen gold and silver. Bassanio, the third, decides in favour of lead; thereby he wins the bride, whose affection was already his before the trial of fortune. Each of the suitors gives reasons for his choice in a speech in which he praises the metal he prefers and depreciates the other two. The most difficult task thus falls to the share of the fortunate third suitor; what he finds to say in glorification of lead as against gold and silver is little and has a forced ring. If in psycho-analytic practice we were confronted with such a speech, we should suspect that there were concealed motives behind the unsatisfying reasons produced.

Shakespeare did not himself invent this oracle of the choice of a casket; he took it from a tale in the *Gesta Romanorum*,[1] in which a girl has to make the same choice to win the Emperor's son.[2] Here too the third metal, lead, is the bringer of fortune. It is not hard to guess that we have here an ancient theme, which requires to be interpreted, accounted for and traced back to its origin. A first conjecture as to the meaning of this choice between gold,

Reprinted by permission of Sigmund Freud Copyrights, The Institute of Psycho-Analysis, The Hogarth Press and Basic Books, Inc., a division of Harper Collins Publishers, for permission to quote from *The Standard Edition of the Complete Psychological Works of Sigmund Freud*, translated and edited by James Strachey, vol. 13, [1913] 1958.

silver and lead is quickly confirmed by a statement of Stucken's,[3] who has made a study of the same material over a wide field. He writes: "The identity of Portia's three suitors is clear from their choice: the Prince of Morocco chooses the gold casket—he is the sun; the Prince of Arragon chooses the silver casket—he is the moon; Bassanio chooses the leaden casket—he is the star youth.' In support of this explanation he cites an episode from the Estonian folk-epic 'Kalewipoeg', in which the three suitors appear undisguisedly as the sun, moon and star youths (the last being 'the Pole-star's eldest boy') and once again the bride falls to the lot of the third.

Thus our little problem has led us to an astral myth! The only pity is that with this explanation we are not at the end of the matter. The question is not exhausted, for we do not share the belief of some investigators that myths were read in the heavens and brought down to earth; we are more inclined to judge with Otto Rank[4] that they were projected on to the heavens after having arisen elsewhere under purely human conditions. It is in this human content that our interest lies.

Let us look once more at our material. In the Estonian epic, just as in the tale from the *Gesta Romanorum,* the subject is a girl choosing between three suitors; in the scene from *The Merchant of Venice* the subject is apparently the same, but at the same time something appears in it that is in the nature of an inversion of the theme: a *man* chooses between three—caskets. If what we were concerned with were a dream, it would occur to us at once that caskets are also women, symbols of what is essential in woman, and therefore of a woman herself—like coffers, boxes, cases, baskets, and so on.[5] If we boldly assume that there are symbolic substitutions of the same kind in myths as well, then the casket scene in *The Merchant of Venice* really becomes the inversion we suspected. With a wave of the wand, as though we were in a fairy tale, we have stripped the astral garment from our theme; and now we see that the theme is a human one, *a man's choice between three women.*

This same content, however, is to be found in another scene of Shakespeare's, in one of his most powerfully moving dramas; not the choice of a bride this time, yet linked by many hidden similarities to the choice of the casket in *The Merchant of Venice.* The old King Lear resolves to divide his kingdom while he is still alive among his three daughters, in proportion to the amount of love that each of them expresses for him. The two elder ones, Goneril and Regan, exhaust themselves in asseverations and laudations of their love for him; the third, Cordelia, refuses to do so. He should have recognized the unassuming, speechless love of his third daughter and rewarded it, but he does not recognize it. He disowns Cordelia, and divides the kingdom between the other two, to his own and the general ruin. Is not this once more the scene of a choice between three women, of whom the youngest is the best, the most excellent one?

There will at once occur to us other scenes from myths, fairy tales and literature, with the same situation as their content. The shepherd Paris has to choose between three goddesses, of whom he declares the third to be the most beautiful. Cinderella, again, is a youngest daughter, who is preferred by the prince to her two elder sisters. Psyche, in Apuleius's story, is the youngest and fairest of three sisters. Psyche is, on the one hand, revered as Aphrodite in human form; on the other, she is treated by that goddess as Cinderella was treated by her stepmother and is set the task of sorting a heap of mixed seeds, which she accomplishes with the help of small creatures (doves in the case of Cinderella, ants in the case of Psyche).[6] Anyone who cared to make a wider survey of the material would undoubtedly discover other versions of the same theme preserving the same essential features.

Let us be content with Cordelia, Aphrodite, Cinderella and Psyche. In all the stories the three women, of whom the third is the most excellent one, must surely be regarded as in some way alike if they are represented as sisters. (We must not be led astray by the fact that Lear's choice is between three *daughters;* this may mean nothing more than that he has to be represented as an old man. An old man cannot very well choose between three women in any other way. Thus they become his daughters.)

But who are these three sisters and why must the choice fall on the third? If we could answer this question, we should be in possession of the interpretation we are seeking. We have once already made use of an application of psycho-analytic technique, when we explained the three caskets symbolically as three women. If we have the courage to proceed in the same way, we shall be setting foot on a path which will lead us first to something unexpected and incomprehensible, but which will perhaps, by a devious route, bring us to a goal.

It must strike us that this excellent third woman has in several instances certain peculiar qualities besides her beauty. They are qualities that seem to be tending towards some kind of unity; we must certainly not expect to find them equally well marked in every example. Cordelia makes herself unrecognizable, inconspicuous like lead, she remains dumb, she 'loves and is silent'.[7] Cinderella hides so that she cannot be found. We may perhaps be allowed to equate concealment and dumbness. These would of course be only two instances out of the five we have picked out. But there is an intimation of the same thing to be found, curiously enough, in two other cases. We have decided to compare Cordelia, with her obstinate refusal, to lead. In Bassanio's short speech while he is choosing the casket, he says of lead (without in any way leading up to the remark):

'Thy paleness[8] moves me more than eloquence.'

That is to say: 'Thy plainness moves me more than the blatant nature of the other two.' Gold and silver are 'loud'; lead is dumb—in fact like Cordelia, who 'loves and is silent'.[9]

In the ancient Greek accounts of the Judgement of Paris, nothing is said of any such reticence on the part of Aphrodite. Each of the three goddesses speaks to the youth and tries to win him by promises. But, oddly enough, in a quite modern handling of the same scene this characteristic of the third one which has struck us makes its appearance again. In the libretto of Offenbach's *La Belle Hélène,* Paris, after telling of the solicitations of the other two goddesses, describes Aphrodite's behaviour in this competition for the beauty-prize:

La troisième, ah! la troisième . . .
La troisième ne dit rien.
Elle eut le prix tout de même . . .[10]

If we decide to regard the peculiarities of our 'third one' as concentrated in her 'dumbness', then psycho-analysis will tell us that in dreams dumbness is a common representation of death.[11]

More than ten years ago a highly intelligent man told me a dream which he wanted to use as evidence of the telepathic nature of dreams. In it he saw an absent friend from whom he had received no news for a very long time, and reproached him energetically for his silence. The friend made no reply. It afterwards turned out that he had met his death by suicide at about the time of the dream. Let us leave the problem of telepathy on one side:[12] there seems, however, not to be any doubt that here the dumbness in the dream represented death. Hiding and being unfindable—a thing which confronts the prince in the fairy tale of Cinderella three times, is another unmistakable symbol of death in dreams; so, too, is a marked pallor, of which the 'paleness' of the lead in one reading of Shakespeare's text is a reminder.[13] It would be very much easier for us to transpose these interpretations from the language of dreams to the mode of expression used in the myth that is now under consideration if we could make it seem probable that dumbness must be interpreted as a sign of being dead in productions other than dreams.

At this point I will single out the ninth story in Grimm's *Fairy Tales,* which bears the title 'The Twelve Brothers'.[14] A king and a queen have twelve children, all boys. The king declares that if the thirteenth child is a girl, the boys will have to die. In expectation of her birth he has twelve coffins made. With their mother's help the twelve sons take refuge in a hidden wood, and swear death to any girl they may meet. A girl is born, grows up, and learns one day from her mother that she has had twelve brothers. She decides to seek them out, and in the wood she finds the youngest; he recognizes her, but is anxious to hide her on account of the brothers' oath. The sister says: 'I will gladly die, if by so doing I can save my twelve brothers.' The brothers welcome her affectionately, however, and she stays with them and looks after their house for them. In a little garden beside the house grow twelve lilies. The girl picks them and gives one to each brother. At that moment the brothers are changed into ravens, and disappear, together with the house and garden. (Ravens are spirit-birds; the killing of the twelve brothers by their sister is represented by the picking of the flowers, just as it is at the beginning of the story by the coffins and the disappearance of the brothers.) The girl, who is once more ready to save her brothers from death, is now told that as a condition she must be dumb for seven years, and not speak a single word. She submits to the test, which brings her herself into mortal danger. She herself, that is, dies for her brothers, as she promised to do before she met them. By remaining dumb she succeeds at last in setting the ravens free.

In the story of 'The Six Swans'[15] the brothers who are changed into birds are set free in exactly the same way—they are restored to life by their sister's dumbness. The girl has made a firm resolve to free her brothers, 'even if it should cost her her life'; and once again (being the wife of the king) she risks her own life because she refuses to give up her dumbness in order to defend herself against evil accusations.

It would certainly be possible to collect further evidence from fairy tales that dumbness is to be understood as representing death. These indications would lead us to conclude that the third one of the sisters between whom the choice is made is a dead woman. But she may be something else as well—namely, Death itself, the Goddess of Death. Thanks to a displacement that is far from infrequent, the qualities that a deity imparts to men are ascribed to the deity himself. Such a displacement will surprise us least of all in relation to the Goddess of Death, since in modern versions and representations, which these stories would thus be forestalling, Death itself is nothing other than a dead man.

But if the third of the sisters is the Goddess of Death, the sisters are known to us. They are the Fates, the Moerae, the Parcae or the Norns, the third of whom is called Atropos, the inexorable.

II

We will for the time being put aside the task of inserting the interpretation that we have found into our myth, and listen to what the mythologists have to teach us about the role and origin of the Fates.[16]

The earliest Greek mythology (in Homer) only knew a single *Μοῖρα,* personifying inevitable fate. The further development of this one Moera into a company of three (or less often two) sister-goddesses probably came about on the basis of other divine figures to which the Moerae were closely related —the Graces and the Horae [the Seasons].

The Horae were originally goddesses of the waters of the sky, dispensing rain and dew, and of the clouds from which rain falls; and, since the clouds were conceived of as something that has been spun, it came about that these goddesses were looked upon as spinners, an attribute that then became attached to the Moerae. In the sun-favoured Mediterranean lands it is the rain on which the fertility of the soil depends, and thus the Horae became vegetation goddesses. The beauty of flowers and the abundance of fruit was their doing, and they were accredited with a wealth of agreeable and charming traits. They became the divine representatives of the Seasons, and it is possibly owing to this connection that there were three of them, if the sacred nature of the number three is not a sufficient explanation. For the peoples of antiquity at first distinguished only three seasons: winter, spring and summer. Autumn was only added in late Graeco-Roman times, after which the Horae were often represented in art as four in number.

The Horae retained their relation to time. Later they presided over the times of day, as they did at first over the times of the year; and at last their name came to be merely a designation of the hours *(heure, ora).* The Norns of German mythology are akin to the Horae and the Moerae and exhibit this time-signification in their names.[17] It was inevitable, however, that a deeper view should come to be taken of the essential nature of these deities, and that their essence should be transposed on to the regularity with which the seasons change. The Horae thus became the guardians of natural law and of the divine Order which causes the same thing to recur in Nature in an unalterable sequence.

This discovery of Nature reacted on the conception of human life. The nature-myth changed into a human myth: the weather-goddesses became goddesses of Fate. But this aspect of the Horae found expression only in the Moerae, who watched over the necessary ordering of human life as inexorably as do the Horae over the regular order of nature. The ineluctable severity of Law and its relation to death and dissolution, which had been avoided in the charming figures of the Horae, were now stamped upon the Moerae, as though men had only perceived the full seriousness of natural law when they had to submit their own selves to it.

The names of the three spinners, too, have been significantly explained by mythologists. Lachesis, the name of the second, seems to denote 'the accidental that is included in the regularity of destiny'[18]—or, as we should say, 'experience'; just as Atropos stands for 'the ineluctable'—Death. Clotho would then be left to mean the innate disposition with its fateful implications.

But now it is time to return to the theme which we are trying to interpret—the theme of the choice between three sisters. We shall be deeply disappointed to discover how unintelligible the situations under review become and what contradictions of their apparent content result, if we apply to them the interpretation that we have found. On our supposition the third of the sisters is the Goddess of Death, Death itself. But in the Judgement of Paris she is the Goddess of Love, in the tale of Apuleius she is someone comparable to the goddess for her beauty, in *The Merchant of Venice* she is the fairest and wisest of women, in *King Lear* she is the one loyal daughter. We may ask whether there can be a more complete contradiction. Perhaps, improbable though it may seem, there is a still more complete one lying close at hand. Indeed, there certainly is; since, whenever our theme occurs, the choice between the women is free, and yet it falls on death. For, after all, no one chooses death, and it is only by fatality that one falls a victim to it.

However, contradictions of a certain kind—replacements by the precise opposite—offer no serious difficulty to the work of analytic interpretation. We shall not appeal here to the fact that contraries are so often represented by one and the same element in the modes of expression used by the unconscious, as for instance in dreams.[19] But we shall remember that there are motive forces in mental life which bring about replacement by the opposite in the form of what is known as reaction-formation; and it is precisely in the revelation of such hidden forces as these that we look for the reward of this enquiry. The Moerae were created as a result of a discovery that warned man that he too is a part of nature and therefore subject to the immutable law of death. Something in man was bound to struggle against this subjection, for it is only with extreme unwillingness that he gives up his claim to an exceptional position. Man, as we know, makes use of his imaginative activity in order to satisfy the wishes that reality does not satisfy. So his imagination rebelled against the recognition of the truth embodied in the myth of the Moerae, and constructed instead the myth derived from it, in which the Goddess of Death was replaced by the Goddess of Love and by what was equivalent to her in human shape. The third of the sisters was no longer Death; she was the fairest, best, most desirable and most lovable of women. Nor was this substitution in any way technically difficult: it was prepared for by an ancient ambivalence, it was carried out along a primaeval line of connection which could not long have been forgotten. The Goddess of Love herself, who now took the place of the Goddess of Death, had once been identical with her. Even the Greek Aphrodite had not wholly relinquished her connection with the underworld, although she had long surrendered her chthonic role to other divine figures, to Persephone, or to the triform Artemis-Hecate. The great Mother-goddess of the oriental peoples, however, all seems to have been both creators and destroyers—both goddesses of life and fertility and goddesses of death. Thus the replacement by a wishful opposite in our theme harks back to a primaeval identity.

The same consideration answers the question how the feature of a choice came into the myth of the three sisters. Here again there has been a wishful reversal. Choice stands in the place of necessity, of destiny. In this way man overcomes death, which he has recognized intellectually. No greater triumph of wish-fulfilment is conceivable. A choice is made where in reality there is obedience to a compulsion; and what is chosen is not a figure of terror, but the fairest and most desirable of women.

On closer inspection we observe, to be sure, that the original myth is not so thoroughly distorted that traces of it do not show through and betray its presence. The free choice between the three sisters is, properly speaking, no free choice, for it must necessarily fall on the third if every kind of evil is not to come about, as it does in *King Lear*. The fairest and best of women, who has taken the place of the Death-goddess, has kept certain characteristics that border on the uncanny, so that from them we have been able to guess at what lies beneath.[20]

So far we have been following out the myth and its transformation, and it is to be hoped that we have correctly indicated the hidden causes of the transformation. We may now turn our interest to the way in which the dramatist has made use of the theme. We get an impression that a reduction of the theme to the original myth is being carried out in his work, so that we once more have a sense of the moving significance which had been weakened by the distortion. It is by means of this reduction of the distortion, this partial return to the original, that the dramatist achieves his more profound effect upon us.

To avoid misunderstandings, I should like to say that it is not my purpose to deny that King Lear's dramatic story is intended to inculcate two wise lessons: that one should not give up one's possessions and rights during one's lifetime, and that one must guard against accepting flattery at its face value. These and similar warnings are undoubtedly brought out by the play; but it seems to me quite impossible to explain the overpowering effect of *King Lear* from the impression that such a train of thought would produce, or to suppose that the dramatist's personal motives did not go beyond the intention of teaching these lessons. It is suggested, too, that his purpose was to present the tragedy of ingratitude, the sting of which he may well have felt in his own heart, and that the effect of the play rests on the purely formal element of its artistic presentation; but this cannot, so it seems to me, take the place of the understanding brought to us by the explanation we have reached of the theme of the choice between the three sisters.

Lear is an old man. It is for this reason, as we have already said, that the three sisters appear as his daughters. The relationship of a father to his children, which might be a fruitful source of many dramatic situations, is not turned to further account in the play. But Lear is not only an old man: he is a dying man. In this way the extraordinary premiss of the division of his inheritance loses all its strangeness. But the doomed man is not willing to renounce the love of women; he insists on hearing how much he is loved. Let us now recall the moving final scene, one of the culminating points of tragedy in modern drama. Lear carries Cordelia's dead body on to the stage. Cordelia is Death. If we reverse the situation it becomes intelligible and familiar to us. She is the Death-goddess who, like the Valkyrie in German mythology, carries away the dead hero from the battlefield. Eternal wisdom, clothed in the primaeval myth, bids the old man renounce love, choose death and make friends with the necessity of dying.

The dramatist brings us nearer to the ancient theme by representing the man who makes the choice between the three sisters as aged and dying. The regressive revision which he has thus applied to the myth, distorted as it was by wishful transformation, allows us enough glimpses of its original meaning to enable us perhaps to reach as well a superficial allegorical interpretation of the three female figures in the theme. We might argue that what is represented here are the three inevitable relations that a man has with a woman—the woman who bears him, the woman who is his mate and the woman who destroys him; or that they are the three forms taken by the figure of the mother in the course of a man's life—the mother herself, the beloved one who is chosen after her pattern, and lastly the Mother Earth who receives him once more. But it is in vain that an old man yearns for the love of woman as he had it first from his mother; the third of the Fates alone, the silent Goddess of Death, will take him into her arms.

NOTES

1. [A mediaeval collection of stories of unknown authorship.]
2. Brandes (1896).
3. Stucken (1907, 655).
4. Rank (1909, 8 ff.).
5. [See *The Interpretation of Dreams* (1900), *Standard Ed.*, 5, 354.]
6. I have to thank Dr. Otto Rank for calling my attention to these similarities. [Cf. a reference to this in Chapter XII of *Group Psychology* (1921), *Standard Ed.*, 18, 136.]
7. [From an aside of Cordelia's, Act I, Scene 1.]
8. 'Plainness' according to another reading.
9. In Schlegel's translation this allusion is quite lost; indeed, it is given the opposite meaning: 'Dein schlichtes Wesen spricht beredt mich an.' ['Thy plainness speaks to me with eloquence.']
10. [Literally: 'The third one, ah! the third one . . . the third one said nothing. She won the prize all the same.'—The quotations is from Act I, Scene 7, of Meilhac and Halévy's libretto. In the German version used by Freud 'the third one' *'blieb stumm'*—'remained dumb'.]
11. In Stekel's *Sprache des Traumes,* too, dumbness is mentioned among the 'death' symbols (1911, 351). [Cf. *The Interpretation of Dreams* (1900), *Standard Ed.*, 5, 357.]
12. [Cf. Freud's later paper on 'Dreams and Telepathy' (1922).]
13. Stekel (1911), loc. cit.
14. ['Die zwölf Brüder,' Grimm (1918, 1, 42).]
15. ['Die sechs Schwäne.' Grimm (1918, 1, 217, No. 49.)]

16. What follows is taken from Roscher's lexicon [1884–1937], under the relevant headings.
17. [Their names may be rendered: 'What was', 'What is', 'What shall be'.]
18. Roscher [ibid.]. quoting Preller, ed. Robert (1894).
19. [Cf. *The Interpretation of Dreams* (1900), *Standard Ed., 4, 318.*]
20. The Psyche of Apuleius's story has kept many traits that remind us of her relation with death. Her wedding is celebrated like a funeral, she has to descend into the underworld, and afterwards she sinks into a death-like sleep (Otto Rank).—On the significance of Psyche as goddess of the spring and as 'Bride of Death', cf. Zinow (1881).—In another of Grimm's Tales ('The Goose-girl at the Fountain' ['Die Gänsehirtin am Brunnen', 1918, 2, 300], No. 179) there is, as in 'Cinderella', an alternation between the beautiful and the ugly aspect of the third sister, in which one may no doubt see an indication of her double nature—before and after the substitution. This third daughter is repudiated by her father, after a test which is almost the same as the one in *King Lear*. Like her sisters, she has to declare how fond she is of their father, but can find no expression for her love but a comparision with salt. (Kindly communicated by Dr. Hanns Sachs.)

REFERENCES

Brandes, G. (1896) *William Shakespeare*, Paris,

Freud, S. (1900) *Die Traumdeutung*, Vienna. *G.S.*, 2–3; *G.W.* 2–3. [*Trans.: The Interpretation of Dreams*, London and New York, 1955; *Standard Ed.*, 4–5.]

———. (1921) *Massenpsychologie und Ich-Analyse*, Vienna. *G.S.*, 6, 261; *G.W.*, 13, 73. [*Trans.: Group Psychology and the Analysis of the Ego*, London, 1922; New York, 1940; *Standard Ed.*, 18, 67.]

———. (1922) 'Traum und Telepathie', *G.S.*, 3, 278; *G.W.*, 13, 165. [*Trans.:* 'Dreams and Telepathy', *C.P.*, 4, 408; *Standard Ed.*, 18, 197.]

Grimm, Brothers (1918) *Die Märchen der Brüder Grimm* (complete ed.), Leipzig.

Preller, L., ed. Robert, C. (1894) *Griechische Mythologie* (4th ed.), Berlin.

Rank, O. (1909) *Der Mythus von der Geburt des Helden*, Leipzig and Vienna. [*Trans.: The Myth of the Birth of the Hero*, New York, 1914.]

Roscher, W. H. (1884–1937) *Ausführliches Lexikon der griechischen und römischen Mythologie*, Leipzig.

Stekel, W. (1911) *Die Sprache des Traumes*, Wiesbaden.

Stucken, E. (1907) *Astralmythen der Hebraeer, Babylonier und Aegypter*, Leipzig.

Zinow, A. (1881) *Psyche und Eros*, Halle.

2. Freud and Dora: Story, History, Case History

Steven Marcus

I

It is generally agreed that Freud's case histories are unique. Today more than half a century after they were written they are still widely read. Even more, they are still widely used for instruction and training in psychoanalytic institutes. One of the inferences that such a vigorous condition of survival prompts is that these writings have not yet been superseded. Like other masterpieces of literature or the arts, these works seem to possess certain transhistorical qualities—although it may by no means be easy to specify what those qualities are. The implacable "march of science" has not—or has not yet—consigned them to "mere" history. Their singular and mysterious complexity, density, and richness have thus far prevented such a transformation and demotion.

This state of affairs has received less attention than it merits. Freud's case histories—and his works in general—are unique as pieces or kinds of writing, and it may be useful to regard them from the standpoint that this statement implies. I shall undertake, then, to examine one of Freud's case histories from the point of view of literary criticism, to analyze it as a piece of writing, and to determine whether this method of proceeding may yield results that other means have not. The assumption with which I begin, as well as the end that I hope to demonstrate, is that Freud is a great writer and that one of his major case histories is a great work of literature—that is to say, it is both an outstanding creative and imaginative performance and an intellectual and cognitive achievement of the highest order. And yet, as we shall see, this triumphant greatness is in part connected with the circumstance that it is about a kind of failure, and that part of the failure remains in fact unacknowledged and unconscious.[1]

"Fragment of an Analysis of a Case of Hysteria," better known to future

Reprinted by permission of the author and the *Partisan Review*, 41 (1974).

readers as the case of Dora, is Freud's first great case history—oddly enough, he was to write only four others. It may be helpful for the reader if at the outset I refresh his or her memory by briefly reviewing some of the external facts of the case. In the autumn of 1900 Dora, an 18-year-old young woman, began treatment with Freud. She did so reluctantly and against her will, and, Freud writes, "it was only her father's authority which induced her to come to me at all." (22)[2] Neither Dora nor her father was a stranger to Freud. He had made separate acquaintance with both of them in the past, during certain episodes of illness that characterized their lives if not the life of the family as a whole. (Freud knew other members of the family as well.) Dora's father was a man "of rather unusual activity and talents, a large manufacturer in very comfortable circumstances." (18) In 1888 he had fallen ill with tuberculosis, which had made it necessary for the family to move to a small town with a good climate in some southern part of Austria; for the next ten years or so that remained their chief place of residence. In 1892 he suffered a detached retina which led to a permanent impairment of his vision. Two years later he fell gravely ill—it was "a confusional attack, followed by symptoms of paralysis and slight mental disturbances." (19) He was persuaded by a friend to come to Vienna and consult with Freud, who was then a rising young neurologist and psychiatrist. Freud settled upon the diagnosis of "diffuse vascular affection," a meningeal disturbance associated with the tertiary stage of syphilis; and since the patient admitted to having had a "specific infection" of syphilis before he married, Freud prescribed "an energetic course of anti-luetic treatment, as a result of which all the remaining disturbances passed off." (19) By 1899 his constitution had sufficiently recovered from the tuberculosis to justify the family's leaving the health resort and moving to "the town in which his factory was situated"; and in 1900 they moved again and settled permanently in Vienna.

Despite this long and protracted history of illness—he also at one time had apparently been infected with gonorrhea, which he may have passed onto his wife—Dora's father was clearly a dominating figure: vigorous, active, energetic, enterprising, and intelligent. Nothing of the sort could be said of Dora's mother, who from the accounts received of her by Freud appeared to his imagination as

> an uncultivated woman and above all as a foolish one, who had concentrated all her interests upon domestic affairs, especially since her husband's illness and the estrangement to which it led. She presented the picture, in fact, of what might be called the "housewife's psychosis." She had no understanding of her children's more active

interests, and was occupied all day long in cleaning the house with its furniture and in keeping them clean—to such an extent as to make it almost impossible to use or enjoy them. (20)

The immediate family circle was completed by a brother, a year and a half older than Dora, who hardly figures in the account rendered by Freud and who seems to have escaped from his childhood and family experiences without severe disablements. In adult life he became a leading figure in Socialist politics and apparently led an active, successful, and distinguished career up to his death many years later.

As for Dora herself, her afflictions, both mental and physical, had begun in early childhood and had persisted and flourished with variations and fluctuating intensities until she was presented to Freud for therapy. Among the symptoms from which she suffered were to be found dyspnea, migraine, and periodic attacks of nervous coughing often accompanied by complete loss of voice during part of the episode. Dora had in fact first been brought by her father to Freud two years earlier, when she was 16 and suffering from a cough and hoarseness; he had then "proposed giving her psychological treatment," but this suggestion was not adopted, since "the attack in question, like the others, passed off spontaneously." (22) In the course of his treatment of Dora, Freud also learned of further hysterical—or hysterically connected—productions on her part, such as a feverish attack that mimicked appendicitis, a periodic limp, and a vaginal catarrh or discharge. Moreover, during the two-year interval between Dora's first visit and the occasion on which her father brought her to Freud a second time, and "handed her over to me for psychotherapeutic treatment" (19), "Dora had grown unmistakably neurotic" in what today we would recognize as more familiar manifestations of emotional distress. Dora was now "in the first bloom of youth—a girl of intelligent and engaging looks." (23) Her character had, however, undergone an alteration. She had become chronically depressed and was generally dissatisfied with both herself and her family. She had become unfriendly towards the father, whom she had hitherto loved, idealized, and identified with. She was "on very bad terms" with her mother, for whom she felt a good deal of scorn. "She tried to avoid social intercourse, and employed herself—so far as she was allowed to by the fatigue and lack of concentration of which she complained—with attending lectures for women and with carrying on more or less serious studies."[3] (23) Two further events precipitated the crisis which led to her being delivered to Freud. Her parents found a written note in which she declared her intention to commit suicide because "as she said, she could no longer endure her life." Following this there occurred one day "a slight passage of words" between Dora and her father, which ended with Dora suddenly losing consciousness—the attack, Freud believed, was "accompanied by convulsions and delirious states," although it was lost to amnesia and never came up in the analysis.

Having outlined this array of affections, Freud dryly remarks that such a case "does not upon the whole seem worth recording. It is merely a case of *'petite hystérie'* with the commonest of all somatic and mental symptoms. . . . More interesting cases of hysteria have no doubt been published . . . for nothing will be found in the following pages on the subject of stigmata of cutaneous sensibility, limitation of the visual field, or similar matters." (24) This disavowal of anything sensational to come is of course a bit of shrewd disingenuousness of Freud's part, for what follows at once is his assertion that he is going to elucidate the meaning, origin, and function of every one of these symptoms by means of the events and experiences of Dora's life. He is going, in other words, to discover the "psychological determinants" that will account for Dora's illnesses; among these determinants he lists three principal conditions: "a psychical trauma, a conflict of affects, and . . . a disturbance in the sphere of sexuality." (24) And so Freud begins the treatment by asking Dora to talk about her experiences. What emerges is the substance of the case history, a substance which takes all of Freud's immense analytic, expository, and narrative talents to bring into order. I will again very roughly and briefly summarize some of this material.

Sometime after 1888, when the family had moved to B——(The health resort where the father's tuberculosis had sent them), an intimate and enduring friendship sprang up between them and a couple named K. Dora's father was deeply unhappy in his marriage and apparently made no bones about it. The K.'s too were unhappily married, as it later turned out. Frau K. took to nursing Dora's father during these years of his illness. She also befriended Dora, and they behaved towards one another in the most familiar way and talked together about the most intimate subjects. Herr K., her husband, also made himself a close friend of Dora's—going regularly for walks with her and giving her presents. Dora in her turn befriended the K.'s two small children, "and had been almost a mother to them." What begins to be slowly if unmistakably disclosed in that Dora's father and Frau K. had established a sexual liaison and that this relation had by the time of Dora's entering into treatment endured for many years. At the same time Dora's father and Frau K. had tacitly connived at turning Dora over to Herr K., just as years later her father "handed her over to me [Freud] for psychotherapeutic treatment." And Dora had herself, at least at first, behaved towards Frau K.'s children in much the same way that Frau K. had behaved towards her. Up to a certain point, then, the characters in this embroilment were virtually behaving as if they were walking in their sleep. In some sense everyone was conspiring to conceal what was going on; and in some yet further sense everyone was conspiring to deny that anything was going on at all. What we have here, on one if its sides, is a classical Victorian domestic drama, that is at the same time a sexual and emotional can of worms.

Matters were brought to a crisis by two events that occurred to Dora at two different periods of her adolescence. When she was 14 Herr K. contrived one day to be alone with her in his place of business; in a state of sexual excitement, he "suddenly clasped the girl to him and pressed a kiss on her lips." (28) Dora responded with a "violent feeling of disgust," and hurried away. This experience, like those referred to in the foregoing paragraph, was never discussed with or mentioned to anyone, and relations continued as before. The second scene took place two years later in the summer when Dora was 16 (it was just after she had seen Freud for the first time). She and Herr K. were taking a walk by a lake in the Alps. In Dora's words, as they come filtered to us through Freud, Herr K. "had the audacity to make her a proposal." Apparently he had begun to declare his love for this girl whom he had known so well for so long. "No sooner had she grasped Herr K.'s intention than, without letting him finish what he had to say, she had given him a slap in the face and hurried away." (46) The episode as a whole will lead Freud quite plausibly to ask: "If Dora loved Herr K., what was the reason for her refusing him in the scene by the lake? Or at any rate, why did her refusal take such a brutal form, as though she were embittered against him? And how could a girl who was in love feel insulted by a proposal which was made in a manner neither tactless nor offensive?" (38) It may occur to us to wonder whether in the extended context of this case that slap in the face was a "brutal form" of refusal; but as for the other questions posed by Freud, they are without question rhetorical in character.

On this second occasion Dora did not remain silent. Her father was preparing to depart from the Alpine lake, and she declared her determination to leave at once with him. Two weeks later she told the story of the scene by the lake to her mother, who relayed it—as Dora had clearly intended—to her father. In due course Herr K. was "called to account" on this score, but he

> denied in the most emphatic terms having on his side made any advances which could have been open to such a construction. He had then proceeded to throw suspicion upon the girl, saying that he had heard from Frau K. that she used to read Mantegazza's *Physiology of Love* and books of that sort in their house on the lake. It was most likely, he had added, that she had been over-excited by such reading and had merely "fancied" the whole scene she had described. (26)

Dora's father "believed" the story concocted by Herr—and Frau—K., and it is from this moment, more than two years before she came to Freud for treatment, that the change in Dora's character can be dated. Her love for the K.'s turned into hatred, and she became obsessed with the idea of getting her father to break off relations with them. She saw through the rationalizations and denials of her father and Frau K., and had "no doubt that what bound her father to this young and beautiful woman was a common love-affair. Nothing that could help to confirm this view had escaped her perception, which in this connection was pitilessly sharp." (32) Indeed, "the sharp-sighted Dora" was an excellent detective when it came to uncovering her father's clandestine sexual activities, and her withering criticisms of her father's character—that he was "insincere . . . had a strain of baseness in his character . . . only thought of his own enjoyment . . . had a gift for seeing things in the light which suited him best" (34)—were in general concurred in by Freud. As he also agreed that there was something in her embittered if exaggerated contention that "she had been handed over to Herr K. as the price of his tolerating the relations between her father and his wife."[4] (34) Nevertheless, the cause of her greatest embitterment seems to have been her father's "readiness to consider the scene by the lake as a product of her imagination. She was almost beside herself at the idea of its being supposed that she had merely fancied something on that occasion." (46) And although Freud was in his customary way skeptical about such impassioned protestations and repudiations—and surmised that something in the way of an opposite series of thoughts or self-reproaches lay behind them—he was forced to come to "the conclusion that Dora's story must correspond to the facts in every respect." (46) If we try to put ourselves in the place of this girl between her sixteenth and eighteenth years, we can at once recognize that her situation was a desperate one. The three adults to whom she was closest, whom she loved the most in the world, were apparently conspiring—separately, in tandem, or in concert—to deny her the reality of her experience. They were conspiring to deny Dora her reality and reality itself. This betrayal touched upon matters that might easily unhinge the mind of a young person; for the three adults were not betraying Dora's love and trust alone, they were betraying the structure of the actual world. And indeed, when Dora's father handed her over to Freud with the parting injunction "Please try and bring her to reason" (26), there were no two ways of taking what he meant. Naturally, he had no idea of the mind and character of the physician to whom he had dealt this leading remark.

Two other persons round out the cast of characters of this late-Victorian romance. And it seems only appropriate that they should come directly from the common stock of Victorian literature and culture, both of them being governesses. The first of these was Dora's own governess, "an unmarried woman, no longer young, who was well read and of advanced views." (36) This woman "used to read every book on sexual life and similar subjects, and talked to the girl about them," at the same time enjoining Dora to secrecy abut such conversations. She had long since divined the goings-on between Dora's father and Frau K. and had in the past tried in vain to turn Dora against both Frau K. and her father. Although she had turned a blind eye to this side of things, Dora very quickly penetrated into the governess's real secret: she, too, was in love with Dora's father. And when Dora realized that this governess was actually indifferent to her—Dora's—welfare, she "dropped her." At the same time Dora had dimly to realize that there was an analogy between the governess's behavior in Dora's family and Dora's behavior in relation to the children of the K.'s and Herr K. The second governess made her appearance during Dora's last analytic hour; the appearance was brilliantly elicited by Freud, who remarked that Dora's decision to leave him, arrived at, she said, a fortnight beforehand, " 'sounds just like a maid servant or governess—a fortnight's warning.' " (105) This second governess was a young girl employed by the K.'s at the time of Dora's fateful visit to them at the Alpine lake some two years before. She was a silent young person, who seemed totally to ignore the existence of Herr K. Yet a day or two before the scene at the lake she took Dora aside and told her that Herr K. had approached her sexually, had pleaded his unhappy cause with her, had in fact seduced her, but had quickly ceased to care for her. He had, in short, done to her what in a day or two he was going to try to do again with Dora. The girl said she now hated Herr K., yet she did not go away at once, but waited there hoping that Herr K.'s affections would turn again in her direction. Dora's response at the lake and afterward was in part a social one—anger at being treated by Herr K. as if she were a servant or governess; but it was also in part a response by identification, since she, too, did not tell the story at once but waited perhaps for something further from Herr K. And when, after the two-week interval, she did tell the story, Herr K. did not renew "his proposals but . . . replied instead with denials and slanders" (108) in which he was aided and abetted by Dora's father, and Frau K. Dora's cup of bitterness was full to overflowing, as the following two years of deep unhappiness and deepening illness undeniably suggest.

II

Dora began treatment with Freud sometime in October 1900, for on the fourteenth of that month Freud writes Fliess that "I have a new patient, a girl of eighteen; the case has opened smoothly to my collection of picklocks." According to this statement the analysis was proceeding well, but it was also not proceeding well. The material produced was very rich, but Dora was there more or less against her will. Moreover, she was more than usually amnesic about events in her remote past and about her inner and mental life—a past and a life towards which Freud was continually pressing her—and met many or even most of his interpretations with statements such as "I don't know" and with a variety of denials, resistances, and grudging silences. The analysis found its focus and climax in two dreams. The first of these was the production by Dora of a dream that in the past she had dreamed recurrently.[5] Among the many messages concealed by it, Freud made out one that he conveyed to his patient: " 'you have decided to give up the treatment,' " he told her, adding, " 'to which, after all, it is only your father who makes you come.' " (70). It was a self-fulfilling interpretation. A few weeks after the first dream, the second dream occurred. Freud spent two hours elucidating it, and at the beginning of the third, which took place on December 31, 1900, Dora informed him that she was there for the last time. Freud pressed on during this hour and presented Dora with a series of stunning and outrageously intelligent interpretations. The analysis ended as follows: "Dora had listened to me without any of her usual contradictions. She seemed to be moved; she said good-bye to me very warmly, with the heartiest wishes for the New Year, and—came no more." (109) Dora's father subsequently called on Freud two or three times to reassure him that Dora was returning, but Freud knew better than to take him at his word. Fifteen months later, in April 1902, Dora returned for a single visit; what she had to tell Freud on that occasion was of some interest, but he knew that she was done with him, as indeed she was.

Dora was actuated by many impulses in breaking off the treatment; prominent among these partial motives was revenge—upon men in general and at that moment, Freud in particular, who was standing for those other men in her life who had betrayed and injured her. He writes rather ruefully of Dora's "breaking off so unexpectedly, just when my hopes of a successful termination of the treatment were at their highest, and her thus bringing those hopes to nothing—this was an unmistakeable act of vengeance on her part." And although Dora's "purpose of self-injury" was also served by this action, Freud goes on clearly to imply that he felt hurt and wounded by her behavior. Yet it could not have been so unexpected as all that, since as early as the first dream, Freud both understood and had communicated this understanding to Dora that she had already decided to give up the treatment.[6] What is suggested by this logical hiatus is that although Dora had done with Freud, Freud had not done with Dora. And this supposition is supported by what immediately followed. As soon as Dora left him, Freud began writing up her case history—a proceeding that, as far as I have been able to ascertain, was not in point of immediacy a usual response for him. He interrupted the composition of the *Psychopathology of Everyday Life* on which he was then engaged and wrote what is substantially the case of Dora during the first three weeks of January 1901. On January 25 he wrote to Fliess that he had finished the work the day before and added, with that terrifying self-confidence of judgement that he frequently revealed, "Anyhow, it is the most subtle thing I have yet written and will produce an even more horrifying effect than usual." (4) The title he had at first given the new work—"Dreams and Hysteria"—suggests the magnitude of ambition that was at play in him. This specific case history, "in which the explanations are grouped round two dreams . . . is in fact a continuation of the dream book. It further contains solutions of hysterical symptoms and considerations on the sexual-organic basis of the whole condition." As the provisional title and these further remarks reveal, it was to be nothing less than a concentrated synthesis of Freud's first two major works, *Studies on Hysteria* (1895) and *The Interpretation of Dreams* (1900), to which there had been added the new dimension of the "sexual-organic basis," that is, the psychosexual developmental stages that he was going to represent in fuller detail in the *Three Essays on the Theory of Sexuality* (1905). It was thus a summation, a new synthesis, a crossing point and a great leap forward all at once. Dora had taken her revenge on Freud, who in turn chose not to behave in kind. At the same time, however, Freud's settling of his account with Dora took on the proportions of a heroic inner and intellectual enterprise.

Yet that account was still by no means settled, as the obscure subsequent history of this work dramatically demonstrates. In the letter of January 25, 1901, Freud had written to Fliess that the paper had already been accepted by Ziehen, joint editor of the *Monatsschrift für Psychiatrie und Neurologie,* by which he must mean that the acceptance did not include a reading of the piece, which had only been "finished" the day before. On February 15, in another letter to Fliess, he remarks that he is now finishing up *The Psychopathology of Everyday Life,* and that when he has done so, he will correct it and the case history—by which he apparently means that he will go through one last revision of the mss. and then "send them off, etc." That "etc." is covering considerable acreage. About two months later, in March 1901, according to Ernest Jones, Freud showed "his notes of the case"—whatever *that* may mean—to his close friend Oscar Rie. The reception Rie gave to them was such, reports Freud, that "I thereupon determined to make no further effort to break down my state of isolation."[7] That determination was less unshakable, and on May 8, 1901, Freud wrote to Fliess that he had not yet "made up his mind" to send off the work. One month later he made up his mind and sent it off, announcing to Fliess that "it will meet the gaze of an astonished public in the autumn." (4) But nothing of the sort was to occur, and what happened next was, according to Jones, "entirely mysterious" and remains so. Freud either sent it off to Ziehen, the editor who had already accepted it and then having sent it, asked for it back. Or he sent it off to another magazine altogether, the *Journal für Psychologie und Neurologie,* whose editor, one Brodmann, refused to publish it, basing his outright rejection, it has been surmised, on the grounds of the improprieties and indiscretions that would be perpetrated by such a publication (Jones, *Life and Work of Sigmund Freud,* Vol. II, pp. 255 f.). The upshot of all those circlings and countercirclings was that Freud returned the manuscript to a drawer for four more years. And when he did at last send it into print, it was in the journal that had accepted it in the first place.

But we are not out of the darkness and perplexities yet, for when Freud finally decided in 1905 to publish the case, he revised the work once again. As James Strachey remarks, "there is no means of deciding the extent" of these revisions, meaning no certain, external, or physical means. Strachey nonetheless maintains that "all the internal evidence suggests . . . that he changed it very little." According to my reading, Strachey is incorrect, and there is considerable internal evidence that intimates much change. But this is no place to argue such matters, and anyway, who can say precisely what Strachey means by "little" or what I mean by "much"? There is one further touch of puzzlements to top it all off. Freud got the date of his case wrong. When he wrote or rewrote it, either in January 1901, or in 1905, he assigned the case to the autumn of 1899 instead of 1900. And he continued to date it incorrectly, repeating the error in 1914 in the "History of the Psychoanalytic Movement" and again in 1923 when he added a number of new footnotes to the essay on the occasion of its publication in the eighth volume of his *Gesammelte Schriften.* Among the many things suggested by this recurrent error is that in some sense he had still not done with Dora, as indeed I think we shall see he had not. The modern reader may be inclined to remark that all this hemming and hawing about dates and obscurities of composition, questions of revision, problems of textual status, and authorial uncertainties of attitude would be more suitable to the discussion of a literary text—a poem, play, or novel—than to a work of "science." If this is so, one has to reply to this hypothetical reader that he is barking up the wrong discourse, and that his conception of the nature of scientific discourse—particularly the modes of discourse that are exercised in those disciplines which are not preponderantly or uniformly mathematical or quantitative—has to undergo a radical revision.

The final form into which Freud casts this material is as original as it is deceptively straightforward. It is divided into five parts. It opens with a short but extremely dense and condensed series of "Prefatory Remarks." There follows the longest section of the work, called "The Clinical Picture" *(Der Krankheitszustand).* In this part Freud describes the history of Dora's family and of how he got to know them, presents an account of Dora's symptoms and how they seemed to have been acquired, and informs the reader of the process by which she was brought to him for treatment. He also represents some of the progress they had made in the first weeks of the treatment. Throughout he intersperses his account of Dora's illness and treatment with excursions and digressions of varying lengths on an assortment of theoretical topics that the material of the case brought into relevant prominence. The third part of the essay, "The First Dream," consists of the reproduction in part of the analysis of Dora's recurrent dream. Part of it is cast in dramatic dialogue, part in indirect discourse, part in a shifting diversity of narrative and expository modes, each of which is summoned up by Freud with effortless mastery. The entire material of the case up to now is reviewed and reenacted once more: new material ranging from Dora's early childhood through her early adolescence and down to the moment of the analysis is unearthed and discussed, again from a series of analytic perspectives and explanatory levels that shift about so rapidly that one is inclined to call them rotatory. The fourth part, "The Second Dream," is about the final three sessions of the treatment, and Freud invents yet another series of original compositional devices to present the fluid mingling of dramatic, expository, narrative, and analytic materials that were concentrated in the three hours. The final part of the essay, "Postscript," written indeed after the case was officially "closed" but at an utterly indeterminate set of dates, is true to its title. It is not a conclusion in the traditional sense of neatly rounding off through a final summary and group of generalizations the material dealt with in the body of the work—although it does do some of that. It is rather a group of added remarks, whose effect is to introduce still further considerations, and the work is brought to its proper end by opening up new and indeterminate avenues of exploration; it closes by giving us a glimpse of unexplored mental vistas in whose light presumably the entire case that has gone before would be transfigured yet again.

The general form, then, of what Freud has written bears certain suggestive resemblances to a modern experimental novel. Its narrative and expository course, for example, is neither linear nor rectilinear; instead, its organization is plastic, involuted, and heterogeneous, and follows spontaneously an inner logic that seems frequently to be at odds with itself; it often loops back around itself and is multi-dimensional in its representation of both its material and itself. Its continuous innovations in formal structure seem unavoidably to be dictated by its substance, by the dangerous, audacious, disreputable, and problematical character of the experiences being represented and dealt with, and by the equally scandalous intentions of the author and the outrageous character of the role he has had the presumption to assume. In content, however, what Freud has written is in parts rather like a play by Ibsen, or more precisely, like a series of Ibsen's plays. And as one reads through the case of Dora, scenes and characters from such works as *Pillars of Society, A Doll's House, Ghosts, An Enemy of the People, The Wild Duck,* and *Rosmersholm* rise up and flit through the mind. There is, however, this difference. In this Ibsen-like drama, Freud is not only Ibsen, the creator and playwright; he is also and directly one of the characters in the action, and in the end suffers in a way that is comparable to the suffering of the others.

What I have been reiterating at excessive length is that the case of Dora is first and last an extraordinary piece of writing, and it is to this circumstance in several of its most striking aspects that we should direct our attention. For it is a case history, a kind of genre of writing—a particular way of conceiving and constructing human experience in written language—which in Freud's hands became something that it never was before.[8]

III

The ambiguities and difficulties begin with the very title of the work, "Fragment of an Analysis of a Case of Hysteria." In what sense or senses is this piece of writing that the author describes as "a detailed report of the history of a case" a fragment? (7) Freud himself supplies us with a superabundant wealth of detail on this count. It is a fragment in the sense that its "results" are "incomplete." The treatment was "broken off at the patient's own wish," at a time when certain problems "had not been attacked and others had only been imperfectly elucidated." It follows that the analysis itself is "only a fragment," as are "the following pages" of writing which present it. (12) To which the modern reader, flushed with the superior powers of his educated irony, is tempted to reply: how is it that this fragment is also a whole, an achieved totality, an integral piece of writing called a case history? And how is it, furthermore, that this "fragment" is fuller, richer, and more complete than the most "complete" case histories of anyone else? But there is no more point in asking such questions of Freud—particularly at this preliminary stage of proceedings—than there would be in posing similar "theoretical" questions to Joyce or Proust. And indeed Freud has barely begun.

The work is also fragmentary, he continues, warming to his subject, because of the very method he has chosen to pursue; on this plan, that of non-directional free association, "everything that has to do with the clearing-up of a particular symptom emerges piecemeal, woven into various contexts, and distributed over widely separate periods of time." Freud's technique itself is therefore fragmentary; his way of penetrating to the micro-structure—the "finer structure," as he calls it—of a neurosis is to allow the material to emerge piecemeal. At the same time these fragments only *appear* to be incoherent and disparate; in actuality they eventually will be understood as members of a whole. Still, in the present instance the results were more than usually unfinished and partial, and to explain what in the face of such difficulties he has done, he resorts to one of his favorite metaphorical figures:

> I had no choice but to follow the example of those discoverers whose good fortune it is to bring to the light of day after their long burial the priceless though multilated relics of antiquity. I have restored what is missing, taking the best models known to me from other analyses; but, like a conscientious archaeologist, I have not omitted to mention in each case where the authentic facts end and my constructions begin. (12)[9]

Here the matter has complicated itself one degree further. The mutilated relics or fragments of the past also remain fragments; what Freud has done is to restore, construct, and reconstruct what is missing—an activity and a group of conceptions that introduce an entirely new range of contingencies. And there is more of this in the offing as well.

Furthermore, Freud goes on, there is still another "kind of incompleteness" to be found in this work, and this time it has been "intentionally introduced." He has deliberately chosen not to reproduce "the process of interpretation to which the patient's associations and communications had to be subjected, but only the results of that process." That is to say, what we have before us is not a transcription in print of a tape recording of eleven weeks of analysis but something that is abridged, edited, synthesized, and constructed from the very outset. And as if this were not enough, Freud introduces yet another context in which the work has to be regarded as fragmentary and incomplete. It is obvious, he argues, "that a single case history, even if it were complete and open to no doubt, cannot provide an answer to all questions arising out of the problem of hysteria." One case of hysteria, in short, cannot exhaust the structure of all the others. And so in this sense too the work is a particle or component of a larger entity or whole. It nevertheless remains at the same time a whole in itself and has to stand by itself in its own idiosyncratic way—which is to be simultaneously fragmentary and complete. Thus, like a modernist writer—which in part he is—Freud begins by elaborately announcing the problematical status of his undertaking and the dubious character of his achievement.

Even more, like some familiar "unreliable narrator" in modernist fiction, Freud pauses at regular intervals to remind the reader of this case history that "my insight into the complex of events composing it [has] remained fragmentary," that his understanding of it remains in some essential sense permanently occluded. This darkness and constraint are the result of a number of converging circumstances, some of which have already been touched on and include the shortness of the analysis and its having been broken off by Dora at a crucial point. But it also includes the circumstance that the analysis—any analysis—must proceed by fragmentary methods, by analyzing thoughts and events bit by discontinuous bit. Indeed, at the end of one virtuoso passage in which Freud demonstrates through a series of referential leaps and juxtapositions the occurrence in Dora's past of childhood masturbation, he acknowledges that this is the essence of his procedure. "Part of this material," he writes, "I was able to obtain directly from the analysis, but the rest required supplementing. And, indeed, the method by which the occurrence of masturbation in Dora's case has been verified has shown us that material belonging to a single subject can only be collected piece by piece at various times and in different connections." (80) The method is hence a fragmentary construction and reconstruction which in the end amount to a whole that simultaneously retains its disjointed character—in sum it resembles "reality" itself, a word that, as writers today like to remind us, should always be surrounded by quotation marks.

At the same time, however, Freud protests too much in the opposite direction, as when he remarks that "it is only because the analysis was prematurely broken off that we have been obliged in Dora's case to resort to framing conjectures and filling in deficiencies." (85) At an earlier moment he had asserted that "if the work had been continued, we should no doubt have obtained the fullest possible enlightenment upon every particular of the case." (19) We shall return later to these and other similar remarks, but in the present connection what they serve to underscore is Freud's effort to persuade us, and himself, of how much more he could have done—an effort which, by this point in the writing, the reader is no longer able to take literally.[10] And this tendency to regard such assertions with a certain degree of skepticism is further reinforced when at the end of the essay—after over 100 pages of dazzling originality, of creative genius performing with a compactness, complexity, daring, and splendor that seem closer to incomparable in their order—he returns to this theme, which was, we should recall, set going by *the very first word* of his title. He begins the "Postscript" with a statement whose modesty is by now comically outrageous. "It is true," he writes, "that I have introduced this paper as a fragment of an analysis; but the reader will have discovered that it is incomplete to a far greater degree than its title might have led him to expect." (112) This disclaimer is followed by still another rehearsal of what has been left out. In particular, he writes, he has "in this paper entirely left out of account the technique," and, he adds, "I found it quite impracticable . . . to deal simultaneously with the technique of analysis and with the internal structure of a case of hysteria." In any event, he concludes, "I could scarcely have accomplished such a task, and if I had, the result would have been almost unreadable." (112) And if the reader is not grateful for these small mercies, Freud goes on a few pages later to speak of this essay as a "case of whose history and treatment I have published a fragment in these pages." In short, this fragment is itself only a fragment of a fragment. If this is so—and there is every reason to believe that Freud is seriously bandying about with words—then we are compelled to conclude that in view of the extreme complexity of this fragment of a fragment, the conception of the whole that Freud has in mind is virtually unimaginable and inconceivable.

We are then obliged to ask—and Freud himself more than anyone else has taught us most about this obligation—*what else* are all these protestations of fragmentariness and incompleteness about? Apart from their slight but continuous unsettling effect upon the reader, and their alerting him to the circumstances that there is an author and a series of contingencies behind the solid mass of printed matter that he is poring over, plowing through, and browsing in, as if it were a piece of nature and not a created artifact—apart from this, what else do these protestations refer to? They refer in some measure, as Freud himself indicates in the postscript, to a central inadequacy and determining incompleteness that he discovered only after it was too late—the "great defect" (118) of the case was to be located in the undeveloped, misdeveloped, and equivocal character of the "transference," of the relation between patient and physician in which so much was focused. Something went wrong in the relation between Freud and Dora or—if there are any analysts still reading—in the relation between Dora and Freud. But the protestations refer, I believe, to something else as well, something of which Freud was not entirely conscious. For the work is also fragmentary or incomplete in the sense of Freud's self-knowledge, both at the time of the actual case and at the time of his writing it. And he communicates in this piece of writing a less than complete understanding of himself, though like any great writer, he provides us with the material for understanding some things that have escaped his own understanding, for filling in some gaps, for restoring certain fragments into wholes.

How else can we finally explain the fact that Freud chose to write up this particular history in such extensive detail? The reasons that he offers in both the "Prefactory Remarks" and the "Postscript" aren't entirely convincing—which doesn't of course deny them a real if fractional validity. Why should he have chosen so problematic a case, when presumably others of a more complete yet equally brief kind were available? I think this can be understood in part through Freud's own unsettled and ambiguous role in the case; that he had not yet, so to speak, "gotten rid" of it; that he had to write it out, in some measure, as an effort of self-understanding—an effort, I think we shall see, that remained heroically unfinished, a failure that nonetheless brought lasting credit with it.

IV

If we turn now to the "Prefactory Remarks," it may be illuminating to regard them as a kind of novelistic framing action, as in these few opening pages Freud rehearses his motives, reasons, and intentions and begins at the same time to work his insidious devices upon the reader. First, exactly like a novelist, he remarks that what he is about to let us in on is positively scandalous, for "the complete elucidation of a case of hysteria is bound to involve the revelation of intimacies and the betrayal of . . . secrets." (8) Second, again like a writer of fiction, he has deliberately chosen persons, places, and circumstances that will remain obscure; the scene is laid not in metropolitan Vienna but "in a remote provincial town." He has from the beginning kept the circumstance that Dora was his patient such a close secret that only one other physician—"in whose discretion I have complete confidence"—knows about it. He has "postponed publication" of this essay for "four whole years," also in the cause of discretion, and in the same cause has "allowed no name to stand which could put a nonmedical reader on the scent." (8) Finally, he has buried the case even deeper by publishing it "in a purely scientific and technical periodical" in order to secure yet another guarantee against unauthorized readers." He has, in short, made his own mystery within a mystery, and one of the effects of such obscure preliminary goings-on is to create a kind of Nabokovian frame—what we have here is a history framed by an explanation which is itself slighly out of focus.[11]

Third, he roundly declares, this case history is science and not literature: "I am aware that—in this city, at least—there are many physicians who (revolting though it may seem) choose to read a case history of this kind not as a contribution to the psychopathology of neuroses, but as a *roman à clef* designed for their private delectation." (9) This may indeed be true; but it is equally true that nothing is more literary—and more modern—than the disavowal of all literary intentions. And when Freud does this again later on towards the end of "The Clinical Picture," the situation becomes even less credible. The passage merits quotation at length.

> I must now turn to consider a further complication to which I should certainly give no space if I were a man of letters engaged upon the creation of a mental state like this for a short story, instead of being a medical man engaged upon its dissection. The element to which I must now allude can only serve to obscure and efface the outlines of the fine poetic conflict which we have been able to ascribe to Dora. This element would rightly fall a sacrifice to the censorship of a writer, for he, after all, simplifies and abstracts when he appears in the character of a psychologist. But in the world of reality, which I am trying to depict here, a complication of motives, an accumulation and conjunction of mental activities—in a word, overdetermination—is the rule. (59 f).

In this context it is next to impossible to tell whether Freud is up to another of his crafty maneuverings with the reader or whether he is actually simply unconscious of how much of a modern and modernist writer he is. For when he takes to describing the difference between himself and some hypothetical man of letters and writer of short stories he is in fact embarked upon an elaborate obfuscation. That hypothetical writer is nothing but a straw man; and when Freud in apparent contrast represents himself and his own activities, he is truly representing how a genuine creative writer writes. And this passage, we must also recall, came from the same pen that only a little more than a year earlier had written passages about Oedipus and Hamlet that changed for good the ways in which the civilized world would henceforth think about literature and writers.[12] What might be thought of as this sly unliterariness of Freud's turns up in other contexts as well.

If we return to the point in the "Prefatory Remarks" from which we have momentarily digressed, we find that Freud then goes on to describe other difficulties, constraints, and problematic circumstances attaching to the situation in which he finds himself. Among them is the problem of "how to record for publication" (10) even such a short case—the long ones are as yet altogether impossible. We shall presently return to this central passage. Moreover, since the material that critically illuminated this case was grouped about two dreams, their analysis formed a secure point of departure for the writing. (Freud is of course at home with dreams, being the unchallenged master in the reading of them.) Yet this tactical solution pushes the *entire problematic* back only another step further, since Freud at once goes on to his additional presupposition, that only those who are already familiar with "the interpretation of dreams"—that is, *The Interpretation of Dreams* (1900), whose readership in 1901 must have amounted to a little platoon indeed—are likely to be satisfied at all with the present account. Any other reader "will find only bewilderment in these pages." (11) As much as it is like anything else, this is like Borges—as well as Nabokov. In these opening pages Freud actively and purposefully refuses to give the reader a settled point of attachment, and instead works at undercutting and undermining his stability by such slight manipulations as this: i.e., in order to read the case of Dora which the reader presumably has right in front of him, he must also first have read the huge, abstruse, and almost entirely unread dream book of the year before. This off-putting and disconcerting quality, it should go without saying, is characteristically modern; the writer succumbs to no impulse to make it easy for the reader; on the contrary, he is by preference rather forbidding and does not extend a cordial welcome. But Freud has not yet finished piling Pelion upon Ossa, and he goes on to add for good measure that the reader really ought to have read *Studies on Hysteria* as well, if only to be confounded by the differences between this case and those discussed at much briefer length there. With this and with a number of further remarks about the unsatisfactory satisfactory character of what he has done and what is to come, Freud closes this frame of "Prefatory Remarks," leaving what audience he still has left in a bemused, uncertain, and dislocated state of mind. The reader has been, as it were, "softened up" by his first encounter with this unique expository and narrative authority; he is thoroughly off balance and is as a consequence ready to be "educated," by Freud. By the same token, however, if he has followed these opening few pages carefully, he is certainly no longer as prepared as he was to assert the primacy and priority of his own critical sense of things. He is precisely where Freud—and any writer—wants him to be.

At the opening of Part I, "The Clinical Picture," Freud tells us that he begins his "treatment, indeed, by asking the patient to give me the whole story of his life and illness," and immediately adds that "the information I receive is never enough to let me see my way about the case." (16) This inadequacy and unsatisfactoriness in the stories his patients tell is in distinct contrast to what Freud has read in the accounts rendered by his psychiatric contemporaries, and he continues by remarking that "I cannot help wondering how it is that the authorities can produce such smooth and exact histories in cases of hysteria. As a matter of fact the patients are incapable of giving such reports about themselves." There is an immense amount beginning to go on here. In the first place, there is the key assumption that everyone—

that every life, every existence—has a story, to which there is appended a corollary that most of us probably tell that story poorly. There follows at once Freud's statement of flat disbelief in the "smooth and exact" histories published by his colleagues who study hysteria. The implications that are latent in this negation are at least twofold: (1) these authorities are incompetent and may in some sense be "making up" the histories they publish; (2) real cases histories are neither "smooth" nor "exact," and the reader cannot expect to find such qualities here in the "real" thing. Furthermore, the relations at this point in Freud's prose between the words "story," "history," and "report" are unspecified, undifferentiated, and unanalyzed and in the nature of the case contain and conceal a wealth of material.

Freud proceeds to specify what it is that is wrong with the stories his patients tell him. The difficulties are in the first instance formal shortcomings of *narrative:* the connections, "even the ostensible ones—are for the most part incoherent," obscured and unclear; "and the sequence of different events is uncertain." In short, these narratives are disorganized, and the patients are unable to tell a coherent story of their lives. What is more, he states, "the patients' inability to give an ordered history of their life in so far as it coincides with the history of their illness is not merely characteristic of the neurosis. It also possesses great theoretical significance." (16) Part of this significance comes into view when we regard this conjecture from its obverse side, which Freud does as once in a footnote.

Another physician once sent his sister to me for psychotherapeutic treatment, telling me that she had for years been treated without success for hysteria (pains and defective gait). The short account which he gave me seemed quite consistent with the diagnosis. In my first hour with the patient I got her to tell me her history herself. When the story came out perfectly clearly and connectedly in spite of the remarkable events it dealt with, I told myself that the case could not be one of hysteria, and immediately instituted a careful physical examination. This led to the diagnosis of a not very advanced stage of tabes, which was later on treated with Hg injections . . . with markedly beneficial results. (16 f).

What we are led at this juncture to conclude is that Freud is implying that a coherent story is in some manner connected with mental health (at the very least, with the absence of hysteria), and this in turn implies assumptions of the broadest and deepest kind about both the nature of coherence and the form and structure of human life. On this reading, human life is, ideally, a connected and coherent story, with all the details in explanatory place, and with everything (or as close to everything as is practically possible) accounted for, in its proper causal or other sequence. And inversely, illness amounts at least in part to suffering from an incoherent story or an inadequate narrative account of oneself.

Freud then describes in technical detail the various types and orders of narrative insufficiency that he commonly finds; they range from disingenuousness both conscious and unconscious to amnesias and paramnesias of several kinds and various other means of severing connections and altering chronologies. In addition, he maintains, this discomposed memory applies with particular force and virulence to "the history of the illness" for which the patient has come for treatment. In the course of a successful treatment, this incoherence, incompleteness, and fragmentariness are progressively transmuted, as facts, events, and memories are brought forward into the forefront of the patient's mind.

> The paramnesias prove untenable, and the gaps in his memory are filled in. It is only towards the end of the treatment that we have before us an intelligible, consistent, and unbroken case history. Whereas the practical aim of the treatment is to remove all possible symptoms and to replace them by conscious thoughts, we may regard it as a second and theoretical aim to repair all the damages to the patient's memory. (18).

And he adds as a conclusion that these two aims "are coincident"—they are reached simultaneously and by the same path.[13] Some of the consequences that can be derived from these tremendous remarks are as follows. The history of any patient's illness is itself only a sub-story (or a sub-plot), although it is at the same time a vital part of a larger structure. Furthermore, in the course of psychoanalytic treatment, nothing less than "reality" itself is made, constructed, or reconstructed. A complete story—"intelligible, consistent, and unbroken"—is the theoretical, created end story. It is a story, or a fiction, not only because it has a narrative structure but also because the narrative account has been rendered in language, in conscious speech, and no longer exists in the deformed language of symptoms, the untranslated speech of the body. At the end—at the successful end—one has come into possession of one's own story. It is a final act of self-appropriation, the appropriation by oneself of one's own history. This is in part so because one's own story is in so large a measure a phenomenon of language, as psychoanalysis is in turn a demonstration of the degree to which language can go in the reading of all our experience. What we end with, then, is a fictional construction which is at the same time satisfactory to us in the form of the truth, and as the form of the truth.

No larger tribute has ever been paid to a culture in which the various narrative and fictional forms had exerted for centuries both moral and philosophical authority and which had produced as one of its chief climaxes the great bourgeois novels of the nineteenth century. Indeed, we must see Freud's writings—and method—as themselves part of this culmination, and at the same moment, along with the great modernist novels of the first half of the twentieth century, as the beginning of the end of that tradition and its authority. Certainly the passages we have just dealt with contain heroic notions and offer an extension of heroic capabilities if not to all men then to most, at least as a possibility. Yet we cannot leave this matter so relatively unexamined, and must ask ourselves how it is that this "story" is not merely a "history" but a "case history" as well. We must ask ourselves how these associated terms are more intimately related in the nexus that is about to be wound and unwound before us. To begin to understand such questions, we have to turn back to a central passage in the "Prefatory Remarks." Freud undertakes therein "to describe the way in which I have overcome the *technical* difficulties of drawing up the report of this case history." (9) Apparently "the report" and the "case history" referred to in this statement are two discriminable if not altogether discrete entities. If they are, then we can further presume that, ideally at any rate, Dora (or any patient) is as much in possession of the "case history" as Freud himself. And this notion is in some part supported by what comes next. Freud mentions certain other difficulties, such as the fact that he "cannot make notes during the actual session . . . for fear of shaking the patient's confidence and of disturbing his own view of the material under observation." (9) In the case of Dora, however, this obstacle was partly overcome because so much of the material was grouped about two dreams, and "the wording of these dreams was recorded immediately after the session" so that "they thus afforded a secure point of attachment for the chain of interpretations and recollections which proceeded from there." Freud then writes as follows:

The case history itself was only committed to writing from memory after the treatment was at an end, but while my recollection of the case was still fresh and was heightened by my interest in its publication. Thus the record is not absolutely—phonographically—exact, but it can claim to possess a high degree of trustworthiness. Nothing of any importance has been altered in it except in some places the order in which the explanations are given; and this has been done for the sake of presenting the case in a more connected form. (10)

Such a passage raises more questions than it resolves. The first sentence is a kind of conundrum in which case history, writing, and memory dance about in a series of logical entwinements, of possible alternate combinations, equivalences, and semi-equivalences. These are followed by further equivocations about "the record," "phonographic" exactitude, and so forth—the ambiguities of which jump out at one as the terms begin to be seriously examined. For example, is "the report" the same thing as "the record"; and if "the record" were "phonograpically" exact, would it be a "report"? Like the prodigious narrative historian that he is, Freud is enmeshed in an irreducible paradox of history: that the term itself refers to both the activity of the historian—the writing of history—and to the objects of his undertaking, what history is "about." I do not think, therefore, that we can conclude that Freud has created this thick context of historical contingency and ambiguity out of what he once referred to as Viennese *schlamperei*.

The historical difficulties are further compounded by several other sequential networks that are mentioned at the outset and that figure discernibly throughout the writing. First, there is the virtual Proustian complexity of Freud's interweaving of the various strands of time in the actual account; or, to change the figure, his geological fusing of various time strata—strata which are themselves at once fluid and shifting. We observe this most strikingly in the palimpsest-like quality of the writing itself; which refers back to *Studies on Hysteria* of 1895; which records a treatment that took place at the end of 1900 (although it mistakes the date by a year); which then was written up in first form during the early weeks of 1901; which was then exhumed in 1905 and was revised and rewritten to an indeterminable extent before publication in that year; and to which additional critical comments in the form of footnotes were finally appended in 1923. All of these are of course held together in vital connection and interanimation by nothing else than Freud's consciousness. But we must take notice as well of the co-presence of still further different time sequences in Freud's presentation—this co-presence being itself a historical or novelistic circumstance of some magnitude. There is first the connection established by the periodically varied rehearsal throughout the account of Freud's own theory and theoretical notions as they had developed up to that point; this practice provides a kind of running applied history of psychoanalytic theory as its development is refracted through the embroiled medium of this particular case. Then there are the different time strata of Dora's own history, which Freud handles with confident and loving exactitude. Indeed, he is never more of a historical virtuoso than when he reveals himself to us as moving with compelling ease back and forth between the complex group of sequential histories and narrative accounts with divergent sets of diction and at different levels of explanation that constitute the extraordinary fabric of this work. He does this most conspicuously in his analytic dealings with Dora's dreams, for every dream, he reminds us, sets up a connection between two "factors," an "event during childhood" and an "event of the present day—and it endeavors to reshape the present on the model of the remote past." (71). The existence or re-creation of the past in the present is in fact "history" in more than one of its manifold senses. And such a passage is also one of Freud's many analogies to the following equally celebrated utterance.

> Men make their own history, but they do not make it just as they please; they do not make it under circumstances chosen by themselves, but under circumstances directly encountered, given and transmitted from the past. The tradition of all the dead generations weighs like a nightmare on the brain of the living. And just when they seem engaged in revolutionising themselves and things, in creating something that has never yet existed, precisely in such periods of revolutionary crisis they anxiously conjure up the spirits of the past to their service and borrow from them names, battle cries, and costumes in order to present the new scene of world history in this time-honored disguise and this borrowed language.[14]

And just as Marx regards the history-makers of the past as sleepwalkers, "who required recollections of past world history in order to drug themselves concerning their own content," so Freud similarly regards the conditions of dream-formation, of neurosis itself, and even of the cure of neurosis, namely, the analytic experience of transference. They are all of them species of living past history in the present. If the last of these works out satisfactorily, then a case history is at the end transfigured. It becomes an inseparable part of an integral life history. Freud is of course the master historian of those transfigurations.[15]

V

We cannot in prudence follow Freud's written analysis of the case in anything like adequate detail. What we can do is try to trace out the persistence and development of certain themes. And we can try as well to keep track of the role—of some of the roles—played by Freud in the remainder of this case out of whose failure this triumph of mind and of literature emerged. At the very beginning, after he had listened to the father's account of "Dora's impossible behavior," Freud abstained from comment, for, he remarks, "I had resolved from the first to suspend my judgement of the true state of affairs till I had heard the other side as well." (26) Such a suspension inevitably recalls an earlier revolutionary project. In describing the originating plan of *Lyrical Ballads,* Coleridge writes that it "was agreed that my endeavours should be directed to persons and characters supernatural, or at least romantic; yet so as to transfer from our inward nature a human interest and a semblance of truth sufficient to procure for these shadows of imagination that willing suspension of disbelief for the moment, which constitutes poetic faith."[16] We know very well that Freud had a more than ordinary capacity in this direction, and that one of the most dramatic moments in the prehistory of psychoanalysis had to do precisely with his taking on faith facts that turned out to be fantasies. Yet Freud is not only the reader suspending judgment and disbelief until he has heard the other side of the story; and he is not only the poet or writer who must induce a similar process in himself if he is to elicit it in his audience. He is also concomitantly a principal, an actor, a living character in the drama that he is unfolding in print before us. Moreover, that suspension of disbelief is in no sense incompatible with a large body of assumptions, many of them definite, a number of them positively alarming. I think that before we pursue any further Freud's spectacular gyrations as a writer, we had better confront the chief of these presuppositions.

They have to do largely with sexuality and in particular with female sexuality. They are brought to a focus in the central scene of Dora's life (and case), a scene that Freud "orchestrates" with inimitable richness and to which he recurs thematically at a number of junctures with the tact and sense of form that one associates with a classical composer of music (or with Proust, Mann, or Joyce). Dora told this episode to Freud towards the beginning of their relation, after "the first difficulties of the treatment had been overcome." It is the scene between her and Herr K. which took place when she was 14 years old—that is, four years before the present tense of the case—and that acted, Freud said, as a "sexual trauma." The reader will recall that on this occasion Herr K. contrived to get Dora alone "at his place of business" in the town of B——, and then without warning or preparation "suddenly clasped the girl to him and pressed a kiss upon her lips." Freud then asserts that "this was *surely* just the situation to call up a *distinct* feeling of sexual excitement in a *girl* of *fourteen* who had *never before* been approached. But Dora had at that moment a violent feeling of disgust, tore herself free from the man, and hurried past him to the staircase and from there to the street door.'' [all italics are mine] 28. She avoided seeing the K.'s for a few days after this, but then relations returned to ''normal''—if such a term survives with any permissible sense in the present context. She continued to meet Herr K., and neither of them ever mentioned ''the little scene.'' Moreover, Freud adds, ''according to her account Dora kept it a secret till her confession during the treatment,'' and he pretty clearly implies that he believes this.

This episode preceded by two years the scene at the lake that acted as the precipitating agent for the severe stage of Dora's illness; and it was this later episode and the entire structure that she and others had elaborated about it that she had first presented to Freud, who continues thus:

> In this scene—second in order of mention, but first in order of time—the behavior of this child of fourteen was already entirely and completely hysterical. I should without question consider a person hysterical in whom an occasion for sexual excitement elicited feelings that were preponderantly or exclusively unpleasurable; and I should do so whether or no the person were capable of producing somatic symptoms. (28)

As if this were not enough, he proceeds to produce another rabbit out of his hat. In Dora's feeling of disgust an obscure psychical mechanism called the ''reversal of affect'' was brought into play; but so was another process, and here Freud introduces—casually and almost as a throw away—one more of his grand theoretical-clinical formulations, namely, the idea of the ''*displacement* of sensation,'' or, as it has more commonly come to be referred to, the ''displacement upwards.'' ''Instead of the genital sensation which would certainly have been felt by a healthy girl in such circumstances, Dora was overcome by the unpleasurable feeling which is proper to the tract of mucous membrane at the entrance to the alimentary canal—that is by disgust.'' Although the disgust did not persist as a permanent symptom but remained behind residually and potentially in a general distaste for food and poor appetite, a second displacement upward was the resultant of this scene ''in the shape of a sensory hallucination which occurred from time to time and even made its appearance while she was telling me her story. She declared that she could still feel upon the upper part of the body the pressure of Herr K.'s embrace.'' Dipping into the hat once again, and taking into account certain other of Dora's ''inexplicable''—and hitherto unmentioned—''peculiarities'' (such as her phobic reluctance to walk past any man she saw engaged in animated conversation with a woman), Freud ''formed in my own mind the following reconstruction of the scene. I believe that during the man's passionate embrace she felt not merely his kiss upon her lips but also his erect member against her body. The perception was revolting to her; it was dismissed from her memory, repressed, and replaced by the innocent sensation of pressure upon her thorax, which in turn derived an excessive intensity from its repressed source.'' (30) This repressed source was located in the erotogenic oral zone, which in Dora's case had undergone a developmental deformation from the period of infancy. And thus, Freud concludes, ''the pressure of the erect member probably led to an analogous change in the corresponding female organ, the clitoris; and the excitation of this second erotogenic zone was referred by a process of displacement to the simultaneous pressure against the thorax and became fixed there.'' (30)

This passage of unquestionable genius contains at the same time something questionable and askew. In it Freud is at once dogmatically certain and very uncertain. He is dogmatically certain of what the normative sexual response in young and other females is, and asserts himself to that effect. At the same time he is, in my judgement, utterly uncertain about where Dora is, or was, developmentally. At one moment in the passage he calls her a ''girl,'' at another a ''child''—but in point of fact he treats her throughout as if this 14-, 16- 18-year-old adolescent had the capacities for sexual response of a grown woman—indeed, at a later point he conjectures again that Dora either responded, or should have responded, to the embrace with specific genital heat and moisture. Too many determinations converge at this locus for us to do much more than single out a few of the more obvious influencing circumstances. In the first instance, there was Freud's own state of knowledge about such matters at the time, which was better than anyone else's but still relatively crude and undifferentiated. Second, we may be in the presence of what can only be accounted for by assuming that a genuine historical-cultural change has taken place between then and now. It may be that Freud was expressing a legitimate partial assumption of his time and culture when he ascribes to a 14-year-old adolescent—whom he calls a ''child''—the normative responses that are ascribed today to a fully developed and mature woman.[17] This supposition is borne out if we consider the matter from the other end, from the standpoint of what has happened to the conception of adolescence in our own time. It begins now in pre-puberty and extends to—who knows when? Certainly its extensibility in our time has reached well beyond the age of 30. Third, Freud is writing in this passage as an advocate of nature, sexuality, openness, and candor—and within such a context Dora cannot hope to look good. The very framing of the context in such a manner is itself slightly accusatory. In this connection we may note that Freud goes out of his way to tell us that he knew Herr K. personally and that "he was still quite young and of prepossessing appearance."[18] If we let Nabokov back into the picture for a moment, we may observe that Dora is no Lolita, and go on to suggest that *Lolita* is an anti-*Dora*.

Yet we must also note that in this episode—the condensed and focusing scene of the entire case history—Freud is as much a novelist as he is an analyst. For the central moment of this central scene is a "reconstruction" that he "formed in my own mind." This pivotal construction becomes henceforth the principal "reality" of the case, and we must also observe that this reality remains Freud's more than Dora's, since he was never quite able to convince her of the plausibility of the construction; or, to regard it from the other pole of the dyad, she was never quite able to accept this version of reality, of what "really" happened. Freud was not at first unduly distressed by this resistance on her side, for part of his understanding of what he had undertaken to do in psychoanalysis was to instruct his patients—and his readers—in the nature of reality. This reality was the reality that modern readers of literature had also had to be educated in. It was conceived of as a *world of meanings*. As Freud put it in one of those stop-you-dead-in-your-tracks footnotes that he was so expert in using strategically, we must at almost every moment "be prepared to be met not by one but several causes —by *overdetermination*." (31) Thus the world of meanings is a world of multiple and compacted causations; it is a world in which everything has a meaning, which means that everything has more than one meaning. Every symptom is a concrete universal in several senses. It not only embodies a network of significances but also "serves to represent several unconscious mental processes simultaneously." (58) By the same token, since it is a world almost entirely brought into existence, maintained and mediated through a series of linguistic transactions between patient and physician, it partakes in full measure of the virtually limitless complexity of language, in particular its capacities for producing statements characterized by multiplicity, duplicity, and ambiguity of significance. Freud lays particular stress on the ambiguity, is continually on the lookout for it, and brings his own formidable skills in this direction to bear most strikingly on the analyses of Dora's dreams. The first thing he picks up in the first of her dreams is in fact an ambiguous statement, with which he at once confronts her. While he is doing so, he is also letting down a theoretical footnote for the benefit of his readers.

I laid stress on these words because they took me aback. They seemed to have an ambiguous ring to them. . . . Now, in a line of associations ambiguous words (or as we may call them, 'switch-words') act like points at a junction. If the points are switched across from the position in which they appear to lie in the dream, then we find ourselves on another set of rails; and along this second track run the thoughts which we are in search of but which still lie concealed behind the dream. (65).[19]

As if this were not sufficient, the actual case itself was full of such literary and novelistic devices or conventions as thematic analogies, double plots, reversals, inversions, variations, betrayals, etc.—full of what the "sharp-sighted" Dora as well as the sharp-sighted Freud thought of as "hidden connections"—though it is important to add that Dora and her physician mean different things by the same phrase. And as the case proceeds Freud continues to confront Dora with such connections and tries to enlist her assistance in their construction. For example, one of the least pleasant characteristics in Dora's nature was her habitual reproachfulness—it was directed mostly towards her father but radiated out in all directions. Freud regarded this behavior in his own characteristic manner. "A string of reproaches against other people," he comments, "Leads one to suspect the existence of a string of self-reproaches with the same content." (35) Freud accordingly followed the procedure of turning back "each simple reproach on the speaker herself." When Dora reproached her father with malingering in order to keep himself in the company of Frau K., Freud felt "obliged to point out to the patient that her present ill-health was just as much actuated by motives and was just as tendentious as had been Frau K.'s illness, which she had understood so well." (42) At such moments Dora begins to mirror the other characters in the case, as they in different degrees all mirror one another as well.

Yet the unity that all these internal references and correspondences points to is not that of a harmony or of an uninflected linear series. And at one moment Freud feels obliged to remark that

my experience in the clearing-up of hysterical symptoms has shown that it is not necessary for the various meanings of a symptom to be compatible with one another, that is, to fit together into a connected whole. It is enough that the unity should be constituted by the subject-matter which has given rise to all the various phantasies. In the present case, moreover, compatibility even of the first kind is not out of the question. . . . We have already learned that it quite regularly happens that a single

> symptom corresponds to several meanings *simultaneously*. We may now add that it can express several meanings *in succession*. In the course of years a symptom can change its meaning or its chief meaning, or the leading role can pass from one meaning to another. (53)

To which it may be added that what is true of the symptom can also be true of the larger entity of which it is a part. The meaning in question may be a contradictory one; it may be constituted out of a contradictory unity of opposites, or out of a shifting and unstable set of them. Whatever may be the case, the "reality" that is being both constructed and referred to is heterogeneous, multi-dimensional and open-ended—novelistic in the fullest sense of the word.

Part of that sense, we have come to understand, is that the writer is or ought to be conscious of the part that he—in whatever guise, voice, or persona he chooses—invariably and unavoidably plays in the world he represents. Oddly enough, although there is none of his writings in which Freud is more vigorously active than he is here, it is precisely this activity that he subjects to the least self-conscious scrutiny, that he almost appears to fend off. For example, I will now take my head in my hands and suggest that his extraordinary analysis of Dora's first dream is inadequate on just this count. He is only dimly and marginally aware of his central place in it (he is clearly incorporated into the figure of Dora's father) comments on it only as an addition to Dora's own addendum to the dream, and does nothing to exploit it. (73 f.) Why he should choose this course is a question to which we shall shortly return. Instead of analyzing his own part in what he has done and what he is writing, Freud continues to behave like an unreliable narrator, treating the material about which he is writing as if it were literature but excluding himself from both that treatment and that material. At one moment he refers to himself as someone "who has learnt to appreciate the delicacy of the fabric of structures such as dreams" (87), intimating what I surmise he incontestably believed, that dreams are natural works of art. And when in the analysis of the second dream, we find ourselves back at the scene at the lake again; when Dora recalls that the only plea to her of Herr K. that she could remember is "You know I get nothing out of my wife"; when these were precisely the same words used by Dora's father in describing to Freud his relation to Dora's mother; and when Freud speculates that Dora may even "have heard her father make the same complaint . . . just as I myself did from his own lips" (98, 106)—when a conjunction such as this occurs, then we know we are in a novel, probably by Proust. Time has recurred, the repressed has returned, plot, double plot, and counterplot have all intersected, and "reality" turns out to be something that for all practical purposes is indistinguishable from a systematic fictional creation.

Finally, when at the very end Freud turns to deal—rudimentarily as it happens—with the decisive issue of the case, the transferences, everything is transformed into literature, into reading and writing. Transferences, he writes, "are new editions of facsimiles" or tendencies, fantasies, and relations in which "the person of the physician" replaces some earlier person. When the substitution is a simple one, the transferences may be said to be "merely new impressions or reprints": Freud is explicit about the metaphor he is using. Others "more ingeniously constructed . . . will no longer be new impressions, but revised editions." (116) And he goes on, quite carried away by these figures, to institute a comparison between dealing with the transference and other analytic procedures. "It is easy to learn how to interpret dreams," he remarks, "to extract from the patient's associations his unconscious thoughts and memories, and to practise similar explanatory arts: for these the patient himself will always provide the text." The startling group of suppositions contained in this sentence should not distract us from noting the submerged ambiguity in it. The patient does not merely provide the text; he also *is* the text, the writing to be read, the language to be interpreted. With the transference, however, we move to a different degree of difficulty and onto a different level of explanation. It is only after the transference has been resolved, Freud concludes, "that a patient arrives at a sense of conviction of the validity of the connections which have been constructed during the analysis." (117) I will refrain from entering the veritable series of Chinese boxes opened up by that last statement, and will content myself by proposing that in this passage as a whole Freud is using literature and writing not only creatively and heuristically—as he so often does—but defensively as well.

The writer or novelist is not the only partial role taken up unconsciously or semi-consciously by Freud in the course of this work. He also figures prominently in the text in his capacity as a nineteenth-century man of science and as a representative Victorian critic—employing the seriousness, energy, and commitment of the Victorian ethos to deliver itself from its own excesses. We have already seen him affirming the positive nature of female sexuality, "the genital sensation which would certainly have been felt by a healthy girl in such circumstances" (37), but which Dora did not feel. He goes a good deal further than this. At a fairly early moment in the analysis he faces Dora with the fact that she has "an aim in view which she hoped to gain by her illness. That aim could be none other than to detach her father from Frau K." Her prayers and arguments had not worked; her suicide letter and fainting fits had done no better. Dora knew quite well how much her father loved her, and, Freud continues to address her,

> I felt quite convinced that she would recover at once if only her father were to tell her that he had sacrificed Frau K. for the sake of her health. But, I added, I hoped he would not let himself be persuaded to do this, for then she would have learned what a powerful weapon she had in her hands, and she would certainly not fail on every future occasion to make use once more of her liability to ill-health. Yet if her father refused to give way to her, I was quite sure she would not let herself be deprived of her illness so easily. (42)

This is pretty strong stuff, considering both the age and her age. I think, moreover, that we are justified in reading an overdetermination out of this utterance of Freud's and in suggesting that he had motives additional to strictly therapeutic ones in saying what he did.

In a related sense Freud goes out of his way to affirm his entitlement to speak freely and openly about sex—he is, one keeps forgetting, the great liberator and therapist of speech. The passage is worth quoting at some length.

> It is possible for a man to talk to girls and women upon sexual matters of every kind without doing them harm and without bringing suspicion upon himself, so long as, in the first place, he adopts a particular way of doing it, and, in the second place, can make them feel convinced that it is unavoidable. . . . The best way of speaking about such things is to be dry and direct; and that is at the same time the method furthest removed from the prurience with which the same subjects are handled in "society," and to which girls and women alike are so thoroughly accustomed. I call bodily organs and processes by their technical names. . . . *J'appelle un chat un chat.* I have certainly heard of some people—doctors and laymen—who are scandalized by a therapeutic method in which conversations of this sort occur, and who appear to envy either me or my patients the titillation which, according to their notions, such a method must afford. But I am too well acquainted with the respectability of these gentry to excite myself over them. . . . The right attitude is: "*pour faire une omelette il faut casser des oeufs.*" (48 f.)

I believe that Freud would have been the first to be amused by the observation that in this splendid extended declaration about plain speech (at this point he takes his place in tradition coming directly down from Luther), he feels it necessary to disappear not once but twice into French. I think he would have said that such slips—and the revelation of their meanings—are the smallest price one has to pay for the courage to go on. And he goes on with a vengeance, immediately following this passage with another in which he aggressively refuses to moralize in any condemnatory sense about sexuality. As for the attitude that regards the perverse nature of his patient's fantasies as horrible—

> I should like to say emphatically that a medical man has no business to indulge in such passionate condemnation. . . . We are faced by a fact; and it is to be hoped that we shall grow accustomed to it, when we have learned to put our own tastes on one side. We must learn to speak without indignation of what we call the sexual perversions. . . . The uncertainty in regard to the boundaries of what is to be called normal sexual life, when we take different races and different epochs into account, should in itself be enough to cool the zealot's ardor. We surely ought not to forget that the perversion which is the most repellent to us, the sensual love of a man for a man, was not only tolerated by a people so far our superiors in cultivation as were the Greeks, but was actually entrusted by them with important social functions. (49 f.)

We can put this assertion into one of its appropriate contexts by recalling that the trial and imprisonment of Oscar Wilde had taken place only five years earlier. And the man who is speaking out here has to be regarded as the greatest of Victorian physicians, who in this passage is fearlessly revealing one of the inner and unacknowledged meanings of the famous "tyranny of Greece over Germany."[20] And as we shall see, he has by no means reached the limits beyond which he will not go.

How far he is willing to go begins to be visible as we observe him sliding almost imperceptibly from being the nineteenth-century man of science to being the remorseless "teller of truth," the character in a play by Ibsen who is not to be deterred from his "mission." In a historical sense the two roles are not adventitiously related, any more than it is adventitious that the "truth" that is told often has unforeseen and destructive consequences and that it can rebound upon the teller. Sometimes we can see this process at work in the smallest details. For instance, one day when Freud's "powers of interpretation were at a low ebb," he let Dora go on talking until she brought forth a recollection that made it clear why she was in such a bad mood. Freud remarks of this recollection that it was "a fact which I did not fail to use against her." (59) There can be no mistaking the adversary tone, however slight, of this statement. It may be replied that Freud is writing with his customary dry irony; yet this reply must be met by observing that irony is invariably an instrument with a cutting edge. But we see him most vividly at this implacable work in the two great dream interpretations, which are largely "phonographic" reproductions of dramatic discourse and dialogue. Very early on in the analysis of the first dream, Freud takes up the dream element of the "jewel-case" and makes the unavoidable symbolic interpretation of it. He then proceeds to say the following to this Victorian maiden who has been in treatment with him for all of maybe six weeks:

> So you are ready to give Herr K. what his wife withholds from him. That is the thought which has had to be repressed with so much energy, and which has made it necessary for every one of its elements to be turned into its opposite. The dream confirms once more what I had already told you before you dreamt it—that you are summoning up your old love for your father in order to protect yourself against your love for Herr K. But what do all these efforts show? Not only that you are afraid of Herr K., but that you are still more afraid of yourself, and of the temptation you feel to yield to him. In short, these efforts prove once more how deeply you love him. (70)

He immediately adds that "naturally Dora would not follow me in this part of the interpretation," but this does not deter him for a moment from pressing on with further interpretations of the same order; and this entire transaction is in its character and quality prototypical for the case as a whole. The Freud we have here is not the sage of the Berggasse, not the master who delivered the incomparable *Introductory Lectures* of 1916–17, not the tragic Solomon of *Civilization and Its Discontents.* This is an earlier Freud, the Freud of the Fliess letters, to certain passages of which I would now like to turn.

In May 1895 Freud writes to Fliess to tell him why he has not been writing to him. Although he has been overburdened with work, patients, and so on, he is aware that such excuses are in part pretexts.

> But the chief reason was this: a man like me cannot live without a hobby-horse, a consuming passion—in Schiller's words a tyrant. I have found my tyrant, *and in his service I know no limits.* My tyrant is psychology; it has always been my distant, beckoning goal and now, since I have hit on the neuroses, it has come so much the nearer. [italics mine]

Three weeks later he writes to Fliess to inform him that he has started smoking again after an abstinence of fourteen months "because I must treat that mind of mine decently, or the fellow will not work for me. I am demanding a great deal of him. Most of the time the burden is superhuman." In March of the next year he tells Fliess that "I keep coming back to psychology; it is a compulsion from which I cannot escape." A month later he communicates the following:

When I was young, the only thing that I longed for was philosophical knowledge, and now that I am going over from medicine to psychology I am in the process of attaining it. I have become a therapist against my will; I am convinced that, granted certain conditions in the person and the case, I can definitely cure hysteria and obsessional neurosis.[21]

And in May 1897 he writes: "No matter what I start with, I always find myself back again with the neuroses and the physical apparatus. It is not because of indifference to personal or other matters that I never write about anything else. Inside me there is a seething ferment, and I am only waiting for the next surge forward." This is the Freud of the case of Dora as well. It is Freud the relentless investigator pushing on no matter what. The Freud that we meet with here is a demonic Freud, a Freud who is the servant of his *daimon*. That *daimon* in whose service Freud knows no limits is the spirit of science, the truth, or "reality"—it doesn't matter which; for him they are all the same. Yet it must be emphasized that the "reality" Freud insists upon is very different from the "reality" that Dora is claiming and clinging to. And it has to be admitted that not only does Freud overlook for the most part this critical difference; he also adopts no measures for dealing with it. The demon of interpretation has taken hold of him, and it is this power that presides over the case of Dora.

In fact, as the case history advances, it becomes increasingly clear to the careful reader that Freud and not Dora has become the central character in the action. Freud the narrator does in the writing what Freud the first psychoanalyst appears to have done in actuality. We begin to sense that it is his story that is being written and not hers that is being retold. Instead of letting Dora appropriate her own story, Freud became the appropriator of it. The case history belongs progressively less to her than it does to him. It may be that this was an inevitable development, that it is one of the typical outcomes of an analysis that fails, that Dora was under any circumstances unable to become the appropriator of her own history, the teller of her own story. Blame does not necessarily or automatically attach to Freud. Nevertheless, by the time he gets to the second dream he is able to write: "I shall present the material produced during the analysis of this dream in the somewhat haphazard order in which it recurs to my mind." (95) He makes such a presentation for several reasons, most of which are legitimate. But one reason almost certainly is that by this juncture it is his *own* mind that chiefly matters to him, and it is *his* associations to her dream that are of principal importance.

At the same time, as the account progresses, Freud has never been more inspired, more creative, more inventive; as the reader sees Dora gradually slipping further and further away from Freud, the power and complexity of the writing reach dizzying proportions. At times they pass over into something else. We have already noted that at certain moments Freud permits himself to say such things as: if only Dora had not left "we should no doubt have obtained the fullest possible enlightenment upon every particular of the case" (13); or that there is in his mind "no doubt that my analytic method" can achieve "complete elucidation" of a neurosis (32); or that "it is only because the analysis was prematurely broken off that we have been obliged . . . to resort to framing conjectures and filling in deficiencies." (85) Due allowance has always to be made for the absolutizing tendency of genius, especially when as in the case of Dora the genius is writing with the license of a poet and the ambiguity of a seer. But Freud goes quite beyond this. There are passages in the case of Dora which, if we were to find them, say, in a novel, would prompt us to conclude that either the narrator or the character who made such an utterance was suffering from *hubris;* in the context of psychoanalysis one supposes that the appropriate term would be *chutzpah.* For example, after elucidating the symbolism of the jewelcase and Dora's reticule, Freud goes on to write:

> There is a great deal of symbolism of this kind in life, but as a rule we pass it by without heeding it. When I set myself the task of bringing to light what human beings keep hidden within them, not by the compelling power of hypnosis, but by observing what they say and what they show, I thought the task was a harder one than it really is. He that has eyes to see and ears to hear may convince himself that no mortal can keep a secret. If his lips are silent, he chatters with his finger-tips; betrayal oozes out of him at every pore. And thus the task of making conscious the most hidden recesses of the mind is one which it is quite possible to accomplish. (77f.)

This, we are forced to recall, is from the Freud who more than anyone else in the history of Western civilization has taught us to be critically aware of fantasies of omniscience, and who on other occasions could be critical of such tendencies in himself. But not here where the demon of interpretation is riding him, riding him after Dora, whom it had ridden out. And it rides him still further, for he follows the passage I have just quoted with another that in point of mania quite surpasses it. Dora had complained for days on end of gastric pains. Freud quite plausibly connected these sensations with a series of other events and circumstances in her life that pointed to a repressed history of childhood masturbation. He then continues:

It is well know that gastric pains occur especially often in those who masturbate. According to a personal communication made to me by Wilhelm Fliess, it is precisely gastralgias of this character which can be interrupted by an application of cocaine to the "gastric spot" discovered by him in the nose, and which can be cured by the cauterization of the same spot.

At this juncture we have passed beyond interpretation and are in the positive presence of demented and delusional science. This passage was almost certainly written in 1901 as part of the first draft of the text; but it must remain a matter of puzzlement that neither in 1905, when he published the revised version, nor at any time thereafter did Freud think it necessary to amend or strike out those mythological observations.[22]

Anyone who goes on like this—and as Freud has gone on with Dora—is, as they say, asking for it. *Chutzpah*'s reward is poetic justice. When Dora reports her second dream, Freud spends two hours of inspired insight in elucidating some of its meanings. "At the end of the second session," he writes, "I expressed my satisfaction at the results." (105) The satisfaction in question is in large measure self-satisfaction, for Dora responded to Freud's expression of it with the following words uttered in "a depreciatory tone: 'Why, has anything so remarkable come out?' " That satisfaction was to be of short duration, for Dora opened the third session by telling Freud that this was the last time she would be there—it was December 31, 1900. Freud's remarks that "her breaking off so unexpectedly, just when my hopes of a successful termination of the treatment were at their highest, and her thus bringing those hopes to nothing—this was an unmistakable act of vengence of her part" (109) are only partly warranted. There was, or should have been, nothing unexpected about Dora's decision to terminate; indeed, Freud himself on the occasion of the first dream had already detected such a decision on Dora's part and had communicated this finding to her. Moreover, his "highest" hopes for a successful outcome of the treatment seem almost entirely without foundation. The case, as he himself presents it, provides virtually no evidence on which to base such hopes—Dora stonewalled him from the beginning right up to the very end. In such a context the hopes of success almost unavoidably become a matter of self-reference and point to the immense *intellectual* triumph that Freud was aware he was achieving with the material adduced by his patient. On the matter of "vengeance," however, Freud cannot be faulted; Dora was, among many other things, certainly getting her own back on Freud by refusing to allow him to bring her story to an end in the way he saw fit. And he in turn is quite candid about the injury he felt she had caused him. "No one who, like me," he writes, "conjures up the most evil of those half-tamed demons that inhabit the human breast, and seeks to wrestle with them, can expect to come through the struggle unscathed."(109)

This admission of vulnerability, which Freud artfully manages to blend with the suggestion that he is a kind of modern combination of Jacob and Faust, is in keeping with the weirdness and wildness of the case as a whole and with this last hour. That hour recurs to the scene at the lake, two years before, and its aftermath. And Freud ends his final hour with the following final interpretation. He reminds Dora that she was in love with Herr K.; that she wanted him to divorce his wife; that even though she was quite young at the time she wanted "to wait for him, and you took it that he was only waiting till you were grown up enough to be his wife. I imagine that this was a perfectly serious plan for the future in your eyes.' " But Freud does not say this in order to contradict it or categorize it as a fantasy of the adolescent girl's unconscious imagination. On the contrary, he had very different ideas in view, for he goes to tell her:

> You have not even got the right to assert that it was out of the question for Herr K. to have had any such intention; you have told me enough about him that points directly towards his having such an intention. Nor does his behaviour at L——contradict this view. After all, you did not let him finish his speech and do not know what he meant to say to you.

He has not done with her yet, for he then goes on to bring in the other relevant parties and offers her the following conclusion:

> Incidentally, the scheme would by no means have been so impracticable. Your father's relation with Frau K. . . . made it certain that her consent to a divorce could be obtained; and you can get anything you like out of your father. Indeed, if your temptation at L——had had a different upshot, this would have been *the only possible solution for all the parties concerned.* (108) [italics mine]

No one—at least no one in recent years—has accused Freud of being a swinger, but this is without question a swinging solution that is being offered. It is of course possible that he feels free to make such a proposal only because he knows that nothing in the way of action can come of it; but with him you never can tell—as I hope I have already demonstrated. One has only to imagine what in point of ego-strength, balance, and self-acceptance would have been required of Dora *alone* in this arrangement of wife-and-daughter swapping to recognize at once its extreme irresponsibility, to say the least.[23] At the same time we must bear in mind that such a suggestion is not incongruent with the recently revealed circumstance that Freud analyzed his own daughter. Genius makes up its own rules as it goes along—and breaks them as well. This "only possible solution" was one of the endings that Freud wanted to write to Dora's story; he had others in mind besides, but none of them was to come about. Dora refused or was unable to let him do this; she refused to be a character in the story that Freud was composing for her, and wanted to finish it herself. As we now know, the ending she wrote was a very bad one indeed.[24]

VI

Let us move rapidly to a conclusion long overdue. In this extraordinary work Freud and Dora often appear as unconscious, parodic refractions of each other. Both of them insist with implacable will upon the primacy of "reality," although the realities each has in mind differ radically. Both of them use reality, "the truth," as a weapon. Freud does so by forcing interpretations upon Dora before she is ready for them or can accept them. And this aggressive truth bounds back upon the teller, for Dora leaves him. Dora in turn uses her version of reality—it is "outer" reality that she insists upon—aggressively as well. She has used it from the outset against her father, and five months after she left Freud she had the opportunity to use it against the K.'s In May 1901 one of the K.'s children died. Dora took the occasion to pay them a visit of condolence—

> and they received her as though nothing had happened in the last three years. She made it up with them, she took her revenge on them, and she brought her own business to a satisfactory conclusion. To the wife she said: 'I know you have an affair with my father'; and the other did not deny it. From the husband she drew an admission of the scene by the lake which he had disputed, and brought the news of her vindication home to her father. Since then she had not resumed her relations with the family.(121)

She told this to Freud fifteen months after she had departed when she returned one last time to visit him—to ask him, without sincerity, for further help, and "to finish her story." (120). She finished her story, and as for the rest, Freud remarks, "I do not know what kind of help she wanted from me, but I promised to forgive her for having deprived me of the satisfaction of affording her a far more radical cure for her troubles."(122)

But the matter is not hopelessly obscure, as Freud himself has already confessed. What went wrong with the case, "Its great defect, which led to its being broken off prematurely," was something that had to do with the transference; and Freud writes that "I did not succeed in mastering the transference in good time." (118) He was in fact just beginning to learn about this therapeutic phenomenon, and the present passage is the first really important one about it to have been written. It is also in the nature of things heavily occluded. Instead of trying to analyze at what would be tedious length its murky reaches, let me state summarily my sense of things. On Dora's side the transference went wrong in several senses. In the first place, there was the failure on her part to establish an adequate positive transference to Freud. She was not free enough to respond to him erotically—in fantasy—or intellectually—by accepting his interpretations: both or either of these being prerequisites for the mysterious "talking cure" to begin to work. And in the second, halfway through the case a negative transference began to emerge, quite clearly in the first dream. Freud writes that he "was deaf to this first note of warning," and as a result this negative "transference took me unawares, and, because of the unknown quantity in me which reminded Dora of Herr K., she took her revenge on me as she wanted to take her revenge on him, and deserted me as she believed herself to have been deceived and deserted by him." This is, I believe, the first mention in print of the conception that is known as "acting out"—out of which, one may incidentally observe, considerable fortunes have been made.

We are, however, in a position to say something more than this. For there is a reciprocating process in the analyst known as the countertransference, and in the case of Dora this went wrong too. Although Freud describes Dora at the beginning of the account as being "in the first bloom of youth—a girl of intelligent and engaging looks," almost nothing attractive about her comes forth in the course of the writing. (31) As it unwinds, and it becomes increasingly evident that Dora is not responding adequately to Freud, it also becomes clear that Freud is not responding favorably to this response, and that he doesn't in fact like Dora very much.[25] He doesn't like her negative sexuality, her inability to surrender to her own erotic impulses. He doesn't like "her really remarkable achievements in the direction of intolerable behavior." (91) He doesn't like her endless reproachfulness. Above all, he doesn't like her inability to surrender herself to him. For what Freud was as yet unprepared to face was not merely the transference, but the countertransference as well—in the case of Dora it was largely a negative countertransference—an unanalyzed part of himself.[26] I should like to suggest that this cluster of unanalyzed impulses and ambivalences was in part responsible for Freud's writing of this great text immediately after Dora left him. It was his way—and one way—of dealing with, mastering, expressing, and neutralizing such material. Yet the neutralization was not complete; or we can put the matter in another way and state that Freud's creative honesty was such that it compelled him to write the case of Dora as he did, and that his writing has allowed us to make out in this remarkable Fragment a still fuller picture. As I have said before, this Fragment of Freud's is more complete and coherent than the fullest case studies of anyone else. Freud's case histories are a new form of literature—they are creative narrative that include their own analysis and interpretation. Nevertheless, like the living works of literature that they are, the material they contain is always richer than the original analysis and interpretation that accompany it; and this means that future generations will recur to these works and will find in them a language they are seeking and a story they need to be told.

NOTES

1. The empirical rule that literary criticism generally follows is to trust the tale and not the teller; indeed, it was the empirical rule pursued by Freud himself.
2. All quotations have been drawn from *The Standard Edition of the Complete Psychological Works of Sigmund Freud.* Vol. VII, pp. 3–122. Numbers in parentheses represent pages from which quotations have been taken. The Strachey translation has been checked against the text in *Gesammelte Werke,* Vol. V, pp. 163–286. In a few places the translation has been corrected.
3. It is worth noting that Freud tells us nothing more about these activities.
4. Later on, Freud adds to this judgement by affirming that "Dora's father was never entirely straightforward. He had given his support to the treatment so long as he could hope that I should 'talk' Dora out of her belief that there was something more than a friendship between him and Frau K. His interest faded when he observed that it was not my intention to bring about that result." (109)
5. Since this dream will be referred to frequently in what is to come, it may be helpful to the reader if I reproduce its wording: "A house was on fire. My father was standing beside my bed and woke me up. I dressed quickly. Mother wanted to stop and save her jewel-case; but Father said: 'I refuse to let myself and my two children be burnt for the sake of your jewel-case.' We hurried downstairs and as soon as I was outside I woke up." (64)
6. It is also permissible to question why Freud's hopes for a successful termination were at that moment at their highest—whether they were in fact so, and what in point of fact his entire statement means. We shall return to this passage later.
7. Ernest Jones, *The Life and Work of Sigmund Freud,* 3 Vols. (New York, 1953–57), Vol. 1, p. 362. Oscar Rie was a pediatrician who had earlier worked as Freud's assistant at Kassowitz's Institute for Children's Diseases; he became a member of Freud's intimate

circle, was a partner at the Saturday night tarok games, and was at the time the Freud family physician.

8. Freud's chief percursors in this, as in so much else, are the great poets and novelists. There are a number of wórks of literature that anticipate in both form and substance the kind of thing that Freud was to do. I shall mention only one. Wordsworth's small masterpiece "Ruth" can in my judgement be most thoroughly understood as a kind of proto-case history, as a case history, so to speak, before the fact.
9. From almost the outset of his career, images drawn from archaeology worked strongly in Freud's conception of his own creative activity. In *Studies on Hysteria* Freud remarks that the procedure he followed with Fräulein Elisabeth von R. was one "of clearing away the pathogenic psychical material layer by layer, and we liked to compare it with the technique of excavating a buried city." In a closely related context, he observes that he and Breuer "had often compared the symptomatology of hysteria with a pictographic script which has become intelligible after the discovery of a few bilingual inscriptions." And his way of representing the "highly involved trains of thought" that were determinants in certain of the hysterical attacks of Frau Cäcilie was to compare them to "a series of pictures with explanatory texts." (*Standard Edition,* Vol. II, pp. 139, 129, 177).
10. In later years, and after much further experience, Freud was no longer able to make such statements. In *Inhibitions, Symptoms and Anxiety* (1926) he writes: "Even the most exhaustive analysis has gaps in its data and is insufficiently documented." (*Standard Edition,* Vol. XXI, p. 107).
11. One is in a position now to understand rather better the quasi-meretricious fits of detestation that overtake Nabokov whenever Freud's name is mentioned. That "elderly gentleman from Vienna" whom Nabokov has accused of "inflicting his dreams upon me" was in fact a past master at all the tricks, ruses, and sleights-of-hand that Nabokov has devoted his entire career to. The difference is this: that in Freud such devices were a minor item in the immense store of his literary resources.

    Nabokov's revenge has been such cuties as "Dr Sig Heiler," "Sigismund Lejoyeux," and one "Dr Froit of Signy-Mondieu-Mondieu." At an entirely different level an analogous relation existed between Charlie Chaplin and W.C. Fields. The latter often tried to get his own back on the comic genius by calling him "that god-damned juggler" along with similar phrases of endearment.
12. Some years earlier Freud had been more candid and more innocent about the relation of his writing to literature. In *Studies on Hysteria* he introduces his discussion of the case of Fräulein Elisabeth von R. with the following disarming admission:

    > I have not always been a psychotherapist. Like other neuropathologists, I was trained to employ local diagnosis and electro-prognosis, and it still strikes me myself as strange that the case histories I write should read like short stories and that, as one might say, they lack the serious stamp of science. I must console myself with the reflection that the nature of the subject is evidently responsible for this, rather than any preference of my own. The fact is that local diagnosis and electrical reactions lead nowhere in the study of hysteria, whereas a detailed description of mental processes such as we are accustomed to find in the works of imaginative writers enables me, with the use of a few psychological formulas, to obtain at least some kind of insight into the course of that affection. Case histories of this kind are intended to be judged like psychiatric ones; they have, however, one advantage over the latter, namely, an intimate connection between the story of the patient's sufferings and the symptoms of his illness—a connection for which we still search in vain in the biographies of other psychoses. (*Standard Edition,* Vol. II, pp. 160f.)

13. There is a parodic analogue to this passage of some contemporary significance. It is taken from the relatively esoteric but influential field of general systems theory, one of whose

important practitioners suffered from severe disturbances of memory. Indeed, he could hardly remember anything. He nonetheless insisted that there was nothing wrong with his memory; in fact, he went on to argue, he had a perfect memory—it was only his retrieval system that wasn't working. In the light of such a comment, it is least open to others to wonder whether other things as well weren't working.

14. K. Marx, *The Eighteenth Brumaire of Louis Bonaparte,* pt I. (Chicago, 1913).
15. Erik H. Erikson has waggishly observed that a case history is an account of how someone fell apart, while a life history is an account of how someone held together.
16. *Biographia Literaria,* ch. 14.
17. Freud may at this point be thinking within an even more historically anachronistic paradigm than the one that normally applied in the late-Victorian period or in the Vienna of the time. In both pre- and early-industrial Europe sexual maturity was commonly equated—especially for women—with reproductive maturity, and both were regarded as conterminous with marriageability. Ironically it was Freud more than any other single figure who was to demonstrate the inadequacy and outmodedness of this paradigm. See John H. Gagnon and William Simon, *Sexual Conduct: the Social Sources of Human Sexuality* (Chicago, 1973), p. 296.
18. There is a fourth influencing circumstance that deserves to be mentioned. Freud appears to have worked in this case with a model in mind, but it turned out that the model either didn't fit or was the wrong one. In the case of "Katharina" in *Studies on Hysteria,* Freud had performed a kind of instant analysis with a fair degree of success. Katharina was the 18 year-old daughter of the landlady of an Alpine refuge hut that Freud had climbed to one summer's day. This "rather sulky-looking girl" had served Freud his meal and then approached him for medical advice, having seen his signature in the Visitor's Book. She was suffering from various hysterical symptoms—many of which resembled those that afflicted Dora—and the story that came out had to do with attempted sexual seductions by her father, followed by her actually catching her father in the act with a young cousin—a discovery that led to the separation and divorce of the parents. The symptoms and the experiences seemed very closely connected, and as Freud elicited piecemeal these stories from her she seemed to become "like someone transformed" before his eyes. He was very pleased and said that he "owed her a debt of gratitude for having made it so much easier for me to talk to her than to the prudish ladies of my city practice, who regard whatever is natural as shameful." (*Standard Edition,* Vol. II, pp. 125–34). The circumstances of her case and of Dora's are analogous in a number of ways, but Dora was no rustic Alpine *Jungfrau* who spoke candidly and in dialect (which Freud reproduces); she was in truth one of the prudish ladies of his city practice who was frigid then and remained so all her life.
19. Such a passage serves to locate Freud's place in a set of traditions in addition to those of literature. It is unmistakable that such a statement also belongs to a tradition that includes Hegel and Marx at one end and Max Weber and Thomas Mann somewhere near the other. It was Weber who once remarked that "the interests of society are the great rails on which humanity moves, but the ideas throw the switches." *Gesammelte Aufsätze zur Religionssoziologie* (Tübingen, 1922) Vol. I, p. 252. And Mann for his part regularly gave off such observations as: "Relationship is everything. And if you want to give it a more precise name it is ambiguity." *Doctor Faustus,* ch. VII.
20. "When the social historian of the future looks back to the first half of the twentieth century with the detachment that comes with the passage of time, it will by then be apparent that amongst the revolutionary changes to be credited to that period, two at least were of vital importance to the development of humanism: the liberation of psychology from the fetters of conscious rationalism, and the subsequent emancipation of sociology from the more

primitive superstitions and moralistic conceptions of crime. It will also be apparent that this twin movement towards a new liberalism owed is impetus to the researches of a late-Victorian scientist, Sigmund Freud, who first uncovered the unconscious roots of that uniquely human reaction which goes by the name of 'guilt'.'' Edward Glover, *The Roots of Crime* (New York, 1960), p. ix.

21. One might have thought that such a passage would have at least slowed the endless flow of nonsense about Freud's abstention from philosophical aspirations. To be sure, Freud is himself greatly responsible for the phenomenon. I am referring in part to the famous passage in *Inhibitions, Symptoms and Anxiety* (1926):

> I must confess that I am not at all partial to the fabrication of *Weltanschauungen*. Such activities may be left to the philosophers, who avowedly find it impossible to make their journey through life without a Baedeker of that kind to give them information on every subject. Let us humbly accept the contempt with which they look down on us from the vantage-ground of their superior needs. But since *we* cannot forgo our narcissistic pride either, we will draw comfort from the reflection that such ''Handbooks to Life'' soon grow out of date and that it is precisely our short-sighted, narrow, and finicky work which obliges them to appear in new editions, and that even the most up-to-date of them are nothing but attempts to find a substitute for the ancient, useful and all-sufficient Church Catechism. We know well enough how little light science has so far been able to throw on the problems that surround us. But however much ado the philosophers may make, they cannot alter the situation. Only patient, persevering research, in which everything is subordinated to the one requirement of certainty, can gradually bring about a change. The benighted traveller may sing aloud in the dark to deny his own fears; but, for all that, he will not see an inch beyond his nose.

This is splendid and spirited writing; but I cannot resist suggesting that Freud is using philosophy here as a kind of stalking horse and that the earlier passage is in some senses closer to his enduring meaning. What Freud meant there by ''philosophical knowledge'' was knowledge or comprehension of the veritable nature of reality itself, and I do not believe he ever abandoned his belief in such knowledge. In any case, too much has been made—on both sides—of the ''antagonism'' between psychoanalysis and philosophy.

22. It is pertinent to the present discussion to add that on at least one occasion in 1895 Freud directly addressed Fliess as ''Demon'' or ''You Demon.'' (*Daimonie* warum schreibst Du nicht? Wie geht es Dir? Kummerst Du ich gar nicht mehr, was ich treibe?) Futhermore, the treatment described by Freud in the foregoing paragraph was administered by Fliess to Freud himself on several occasions during the 1890s. Throughout that decade Freud suffered at irregular intervals from migraine headaches and colds. He applied cocaine locally (one supposes that he took a healthy sniff), permitted Fliess to perform a number of nasal cauterizations, and at one point seems to have undergone minor surgery of the turbinate bone in the nasal passage at Fliess's hands.

The pertinence of the displacement of Freud's relation to Fliess into the case of Dora becomes clearer if we recall that in this friendship—certainly the most important relation of its kind in his life—Freud was undergoing something very like a transference experience, without wholly understanding what was happening to him. In this connection, the case of Dora may also be regarded as part of the process by which Freud began to move towards a resolution of his relation with Fliess—and perhaps vice versa as well.

That relation is still not adequately understood, as the documents that record it have not been fully published. As matters stand at present, one has to put that relation together from three sources: (1) *The Origins of Psychoanalysis*, ed. Ernst Kris (New York, 1950); this volume contains some of Freud's letters to Fliess, many of them in fragmentary or excerpted form, plus drafts and notes of various projects; (2) Ernest Jones, *The Life and Work of Sigmund Freud* (New York, 1953–57); (3) Max Schur, *Freud: Living and Dying* (New

York, 1972). The last work provides the fullest account yet available, but does not stand by itself and must be supplemented by material drawn from the other two sources.

23. Fifteen years later, when Freud came to write about Ibsen, the character and situation that he chose to analyze revealed the closest pertinence to the case of Dora. In "Some Character-Types Met with in Psycho-Analytic Work" he devotes a number of pages to a discussion of Rebecca West in *Rosmersholm.* Rebecca, the new, liberated woman, is one of those character-types who are "wrecked by success." The success she is wrecked by is the fulfillment—partly real, partly symbolic—in mature life of her Oedipal fantasies, the precise fulfillment that Freud, fifteen years earlier, had been capable of regarding as the "only solution" for Dora, as well as everyone else involved in the case (see *Standard Edition,* Vol. XIV, pp. 324–31).

24. For what happened to Dora in later life, see Felix Deutsch, "A Footnote to Freud's 'Fragment of and Analysis of a Case of Hysteria,' " *Psychoanalytic Quarterly,* XXVI (1957), pp. 159–67. The story is extremely gruesome. For some further useful remarks, see Erik H. Erikson, "Psychological Reality and Historical Actuality," *Insight and Responsibility* (New York, 1964), pp. 166–74.

25. Dora seems indeed to have been an unlikeable person. Her death, which was caused by cancer of the colon, diagnosed too late for an operation, "seemed a blessing to those who were close to her." And Dr Deutsch's informant went on to describe her as " 'one of the most repulsive hysterics' he had ever met."

26. That the counter-transference was not entirely negative is suggested in the very name that Freud chose to give to his patient in writing this case history. Freud's favorite novel by Dickens was *David Copperfield.* Like David, Freud was born with or in a caul—an augury of a singular destiny. On at least one occasion, Freud described his father as a Micawber-like figure. The first book he sent as a gift to Martha Bernays shortly after they had met was a copy of *David Copperfield.*

    Dora, of course, was David Copperfield's first love and first wife. She is at once a duplication of David's dead mother and an incompetent and helpless creature, who asks David to call her his "child-wife." She is also doomed not to survive, and Dickens kills her off so David can proceed to realize himself in a fuller way. One could go on indefinitely with such analogies, but the point should be sufficiently clear: in the very name he chose, Freud was in a manner true to his method, theory, and mind, expressing the overdeterminations and ambivalences that are so richly characteristic of his work as a whole.

    For the relevant biographical material, see Jones, *Life and Work of Sigmund Freud,* Vol. 1, pp. 2, 4, 104, 174.

3. The Art and Strategy of Freud's Exposition

Patrick J. Mahony

Yf they smell a ratt
The grisely chide and chatt.

—John Skelton, "The Image of Hypocrisy"

The case history stands as the most adequate representation of clinical treatment, and yet, of all the genres in psychoanalytic literature, it is the most difficult to write. This is one reason—there are others—that our discipline has such a limited body of verifiable primary source material of a sustained narrative nature. Those who want to maintain that psychoanalysis is a science rather than a discipline must then contend with the uneasy reflection that among the sciences psychoanalysis would be the one with the least amount of verifiable data narratively corresponding to the nature of the laboratory experiment (the clinical situation). From any point of view, however, there reigns a textual vacuum at the center of psychoanalysis. But can it be otherwise?

Whether on first or successive readings, this question is disconcerting, for the analytic situation resists satisfactory representation. Upon even slight consideration one could advance many reasons supporting Freud's belief that "a real, complete case cannot be narrated but only described' (Freud, 1974, p. 141). Language is quintessentially linear—one word coming after another —and can only falter in the task of adequately representing both the sequentiality or simultaneity of external events and the kaleidoscopic complexities of endopsychic life, such as repression, deferred effect, partial or full regression, and so forth. Language is further defied by the various orders in psychoanalytic treatment, among which number the order of the patient's fantasying and remembering, the order of his narration of what he remembers

Reprinted by permission of Yale University Press from *Freud and the Rat Man,* by Patrick J. Mahony, 1986.

or might even experience somatically at the time of his narration, the order of his repeating rather than recalling his past life in the transference, the order of his understanding and his cure, the order of imparting or withholding that knowledge through memories or dreams or spontaneous associations, and the order of the analyst's understanding and his communication of that understanding to the patient. Finally, there is the order of exposition, its footnotes, anticipatory and retrospective remarks, and diverse work drafts of that exposition.

No wonder Freud could lament after he attempted to write up the reimbursement episode in his process notes: ''Not well reproduced; many of the characteristic beauties of the case are omitted, effaced'' (Hawelka, 1974, p. 62; my translation—the comment itself is ''omitted'' in the published case!). As Freud was writing up the case, he complained to Jung:

> I am finding it very difficult; it is almost beyond my powers of presentation; the paper will probably be intelligible to no one outside our immediate circle. How bungled our reproductions are, how wretchedly we dissect the great art works of psychic nature! (letter of 6/30/09; Freud, 1974, p. 238)

Jung, a prolific author in his own right, read Freud's manuscript shortly thereafter and concurred about the expository obstacle:

> I understand perfectly your impressions of your own paper. This is something that also holds me back from presenting my cases. We just cannot do things as beautifully and as truly as Nature does. (letter of 7/13/09; Freud, 1974, pp. 240–41)[1]

Shortly after this exchange of correspondence, from August 20 to September 21 to be precise, Freud and Jung made their famous trip to the United States, and it is tempting to speculate on how they resumed discussion of the Rat Man and his case history. We do at any rate have a letter from Freud shortly after his return home, expressing dissatisfaction with his corrections of the Rat Man proofs and asking somewhat anxiously about Jung's reaction:

> I am sure you will approve of what I did yesterday (Sunday). I corrected the Rat Man. I still didn't like it. Let me know as soon as you have seen it if you get a different impression. (letter of 10/4/09; Freud, 1974, p. 249)

Jung's buoyant approval was not long in coming:

> Your Rat Man has filled me with delight, it is written with awesome intelligence and full of the most subtle reality. Most people, though, will be too dumb to understand it in depth. Splendid ingenuities! I regret from the bottom of my heart that I didn't write it. (letter of 10/14/09; Freud, 1974, p. 251)[2]

Three days later, Freud replied: "You are the first critic of the Rat Man. . . . I am overjoyed at your praise" (Freud, 1974, p. 254).

Up to now I have been concerned with Freud's general success as a writer of case history in spite of its formidable intrinsic difficulties. Now I turn momentarily to the circumspect aspects of Freud's endeavor, keeping in mind meanwhile that no other analyst has ever composed a more impressive case history. I should also make clear at the outset that my somewhat reserved attitude toward Freud's case history does not extend in the same way to his oral delivery at the Salzburg congress in 1908. Even though Freud feared that he would utter there "a potpourri of particular observations and general remarks" (Freud, 1974, p. 141), his performance was a memorable triumph, according to the reports of such listeners as Jones and Jung. My guess is that the physical presence and commanding personality of Freud as speaker were able to counteract the disconnected or "potpourri" nature of his remarks.

When he began afterward to write up the case, he again was aware of its disconnectedness and twice considered qualifying it by putting "Aphorisms" in the general title (Freud, 1974, pp. 145, 159), but finally decided for the more modulated label "Notes upon a Case of Obsessional Neurosis." Going beyond Freud's self-criticism, one reader has insightfully appraised the Rat Man case as "one of the richest, most complex and opaque pieces" in the Freudian corpus, the piece "most difficult to read and the most resistant to serial interpretative schematization." The clinical text in particular he found to be lacking in "the coherence, expository fullness, narrative virtuosity, and sustained sinuosity of episodic, incremental development" of the other major cases (Marcus, 1984, pp. 87, 89, 164).

How are we to explain such deficiencies of the Rat Man case, which at times moves like an ill-coordinated puppet before our eyes? In justifying the disconnected fragmentariness, Freud brought up the ethical need for discretion, his limited literary talents, and his relative ignorance of obsessional neurosis; yet those reasons, slightly adapted, could apply equally to his other, more skillfully written cases. We are left to venture the answer that the Rat Man's obsessionality influenced not only Freud's clinical focus but also his understanding and exposition of the material. For instance, in spite of the importance accorded by the Rat Man to dreams in his life and in spite of the many dreams reported during the treatment, Freud was guided by a therapeutic rationale that appeared to some extent to redirect his interventions. He even said at one point: "The dream was not interpreted. For it is in fact only a more distinct version of the obsessional idea which he did not dare to become aware of during the day'' (1909b, p. 267; cf. p. 274). In retrospect, it seems that after having given major semiotic importance to dreams in the Dora case, Freud went on to extend his interest to verbal lapses and faulty actions in *The Psychopathology of Everyday Life* and then concentrated on the wording of obsessions in the Rat Man case. Upon his entrance into this clinical territory, the indefatigable Freud focused on the aphoristic nature and dynamics of obsessional acts and sayings, bringing them into consciousness when the patient did not know their wording and filling in their ellipses, thereby attempting to reconstruct them into larger units of discourse. The noted fragmentation and disconnectedness of the Rat Man's associations and Freud's therapeutic attentiveness to that factor might have rubbed off on his attempts to present a synthetic picture of his patient's life story and obsessional neurosis.

A supplementary explanation for the disarticulateness of the Rat Man's case history as compared to Freud's other writings is that Freud's own obsessionality was countertransferentially activated, leaving traces on his expository control. That is, Freud's expression was infected by its contents, obsessional neurosis, which, by severing causal connections by defensive isolation, is after all a pathology that affects the contiguity of psychic material as well as the verbal expression of that material. Perhaps in that sense, instead of encountering the familiar Freud, with his consistent expository and theoretical articulateness, we come upon an author who confuses precipitating causes; who elaborated but little on the oedipal links among the heterosexual object choices in the patient's oedipal and postoedipal life; who did not firmly enmesh the clinical and theoretical considerations as much as he did in his other cases; who did not integrate his principal explantory perspectives (in this instance, anality, ambivalence, and economic theory); and who did not succeed in neatly tying together child and adult symptomatology. A consideration of Freud's case history of the Wolf Man can enlighten us at this juncture. With the childhood animal phobia of the Wolf Man, Freud established a forward-moving coherence in his narrative, whereas he was unable to do that in the reverse direction with Dr. Lanzer's rat symptomatology erupting in childhood. At the risk of forcing the issue, we might say that Freud did not sufficiently trace the ratlines, the symbolic lineage, of his patient's symptoms back to childhood. In this and other ways, isolation is analytically enacted as well as described, inscribed in Freud's very text, with the result that the text is a mixture of literary failure and overwhelming achievement.

It is that mixture we shall now analyze as we follow the course of the case history. The style of its sections varies in formalistic features and intrinsic merit so that we shall change our examination correspondingly—now dealing with noteworthy verbal usage, now with more general organizational pattern. We shall also discover the functioning of time in Freud's style, some of whose richness is unimaginable if we rely only on Strachey's translation.

In turning to Freud's Introduction (1909b, pp. 155–57) to his case history, we are struck by the contrast he draws between his consummate therapeutic results and limitation of various sorts. There is the sharp contrast between the heralded removal of the Rat Man's inhibitions *(Hemmungen)* by the treatment and the persistence of external and internal inhibitions, which affects Freud himself in his desire to give a representative account of the case. A second contrast, this time of more pronounced proportions, obtains between the proclamation about a *complete* restoration of Dr. Lanzer's personality and the sundry repeated references to the fragmentary, the disconnected or isolated or individual or detail (these last four terms being *[das] einzeln[e]* in German): Freud proposes to furnish in Part One some ''fragmentary extracts'' of clinical material; in Part Two he will theoretically share some ''isolated, aphoristic'' *(einzelne, aphoristische)* statements; he is impeded from going ''into detail'' *(im einzelnen)* about his patient's life.[3] Up to now the psychoanalytic investigation of obsessionality has managed to have but ''isolated'' *(einzelne)* results; Freud hopes that his work as an individual *(einzelnen)* may contribute to the common scientific enterprise. Curiously, the diverse references to the limited and the disconnected make Freud's claim about effecting a complete restoration of personality stand out as an even greater and yet ''isolated'' accomplishment. There are other strategic artifices involved in Freud's claim, but they must await a retrospective clarification toward the end of our stylistic analysis.

The German language lets one appreciate other differences and nuances in Freud's discourse in the Introduction. He tells us that obsessional language, by surpassing hysterical language in its resemblance to the expressive forms of our conscious thought, yields more easily to our empathy (*Einfühlung,* which Strachey periphrastically translates as ''find our way about.''). In his unique way, Freud continues his clinical empathy into the writing of his text, constructing his expository vocabulary partly out of references to sight and military life, thus subtly preparing us for the voyeurism and soldierly life of his patient in the pages ahead. Thus, after signaling the ''burdensome attention'' *(belästigende Aufmerksamkeit)* that his private practice draws in Vienna, Freud admits having never been able to ''see through'' *(durchschauen)* a severe case of obsessional neurosis; furthermore, even if he had, he still would not be able to render the psychoanalysis of its structure visible *(sichtbar)* to others. Freud's martial allusions are even more pronounced:

> Obsessional neurotics of a severe caliber [*Kalibers*] present themselves [*stellen sich*—also a military verb, meaning ''to enlist''] for analytic treatment far less seldom than do hysterics. . . . just as with the chronic infectious disease, we can point to a file [*Reihe*] of brilliant healing successes in light and severe cases of obsessional neurosis when combated [*bekämpften*] early. . . . The crumbs [*Brocken,* also slang for military clothes or uniform] of knowledge here . . . may in themselves prove less satisfying. (1909b,157/383; my translation)[4]

What emerges clearly from this passage is Freud's tendency to let his critical language be infiltrated by the everyday language of its subject matter, an infiltration undone by Strachey, who, along with most psychoanalytic writers, wished to impose a ''scientific'' policy of lexical apartheid between critical commentary and clinical material. (Their invention of such a rigid lexical borderline, one surmises, often implies the conception of a more ''purified'' and autonomous ego than Freud would have been ready to grant.)

In the case history proper, Freud's expository maneuvers in presenting the clinical material are fascinating. Part One, ''Extracts from the Case History,'' opens with the preliminary interview followed by a series of labeled sections, the first four of which report and comment on the first seven analytic sessions. Schematically, Part One looks like this:

The Preliminary Interview
(A) The Beginning of the Treatment
(B) Infantile Sexuality (session 1)
(C) The Great Obsessive Fear (sessions 2 and 3)
(D) Initiation into the Nature of the Treatment (sessions 4 to7)
(E) Some Obsessional Ideas and Their Translation
(F) The Precipitating Cause of the Illness
(G) The Father Complex and the Solution of the Rat Idea

The schematic outline, however, is not so coherent as it appears on first glance, prompting us to wonder about the peremptory and even unconscious factors underlying the expository organization. On closer look, for example, we may be drawn to ask why there are seven general sections instead of six, since ''Some Obsessional Ideas and Their Translation'' might well have gone into the theoretical Part Two. Equally pertinent is the question as to why

Freud chose to give seven day-to-day reports. As far as patients directly treated by Freud are concerned, the only other case history containing the organizational device of a day-to-day report is that of Emmy von N., a patient with a rodent phobia to whom Freud recounted the rat story of Bishop Hatto (Freud, 1893–95, pp. 51–53, 62–63, 73).[5] But whatever the value of the associative link between the cases of Emmy von N. and the Rat Man, we might find it more profitable to note the heptadic pattern throughout Freud's works: *The Interpretation of Dreams, Jokes and Their Relation to the Unconscious,* "The Unconscious," *New Introductory Lectures, Beyond the Pleasure Principle,* and *The Question of Lay Analysis* each has seven chapters; *The Introductory Lectures* are twenty-eight in number; the first two of the *Three Essays on the Theory of Sexuality* have seven sections each, as does Freud's personal favorite among all his writings, Part Four of *Totem and Taboo* (Freud, 1913, p. xi). Relatedly, Freud thought his life was marked by seven-year cycles; he specifically linked seven to a prediction of death and the effort of his seven internal organs to usher his life to an end; and he eventually visited the forbidden city of Rome and its seven hills for a total of seven times after having phobically avoided it for years (Mahony, 1982, pp. 66–67). *Pace* Freud's contention, the presentation of the first seven sessions does not constitute "the expository portion of the treatment" (p. 186), for the published account of the fifth to the seventh sessions contains little new in relation to the preceding and subsequent ones. To account, therefore, for the not altogether successful heptadic pattern in Freud's case history, we must be ready to recognize the persistent influence of his superstition, which might have been activated by the treatment of the Rat Man, who himself was remarkably superstitious. So much for the overall compositional structure of "Extracts from the Case History"; let us now proceed to its analysis, section by section.

Freud's abrupt presentation of the initial interview disarms us, propels us into the immediate scene, an immediacy unfortunately lost in Strachey's translation. The larger fact is that Strachey characteristically turned into the past tense the present tense which Freud often used for narration, more often to convey patients' associations, and invariably to transcribe their dreams. Here, then, is a sampling of Freud as he dramatically lifts the curtain on his initial contact with the Rat Man:

A youngish man of academic education introduces himself with the statement that he suffers from obsessional ideas since his childhood, but with particular intensity since four years ago. The principal contents of his suffering are *fears* that something might happen to two persons whom he loves very much—his father and a lady he reveres. Besides this he feels *compulsive impulses*—for example, cutting his throat with a straight-razor; he further produces *prohibitions,* which deal also with unimportant things. (Freud, 1909b, *G.W.*, p. 384; my translation)

Here is Strachey:

A youngish man of university education introduced himself to me with the statement that he had suffered from obsessions ever since his childhood, but with particularly intensity for the last four years. The chief features of his disorder were *fears* that something might happen to two people of whom he was very fond—his father and a lady whom he admired. Besides this he was aware of *compulsive impulses*—such as an impulse, for instance, to cut his throat with a razor; and further he produced *prohibitions,* sometimes in connection with quite unimportant things. (Freud, 1909b, p. 158)

In passing we can appreciate Freud's intimate talking of the patient's *suffering,* a verbal form of everyday use which we may heuristically compare with Strachey's technical substantive, *disorder.*

But Strachey's Olympian stance toward time is heuristically even more revealing for us; it is as if he resorted to the past tense in order to control, to contain the living present by inserting an antiseptic distance between it and himself, and as if his idea of scientific objectivity demanded the guise of a chronological remove in the very reporting. Freud does not need such posturing; he quickly opens the door to let us into the consultation room. But wait an instant—is that true? Or is it rather that he invites us into his study where he is writing up his process notes at night?[6] Not quite either, for the interview account is a slight revision of the process notes and therefore comes from a different moment of writing. What then? The fact is that, with a majestic daring never attempted by any other analyst, Freud uses the present tense to merge three different temporal scenes—the clinical scene and two separate scenes of Freud as note taker and revisionist. Fused with a dreamlike vividness into the present tense, clinical event and its successive descriptions become one. We arrive then at a precious conclusion about the psychological makeup of Freud's creative genius: he could relive the past intensely and dramatically express that experience in the immediate present in which all dreams take place; likewise, he had the ability to bypass the conscious perception of time as discrete units in order to express his unconscious perception of it as duration. This extraordinary feature, manifest in his German text, counters to some extent his aphoristic disconnectedness, which we have previously discussed.

We pass on the first analytic session to read how Freud makes a bold gesture: he starts out under the heading "The Beginning of the Treatment," and then, where the Rat Man is proceeding without any apparent transition, Freud scriptively intrudes to give the indented label "Infantile Sexuality" to the subsequent associations. In effect, Freud expositorily benefits from the Rat Man's packaging, which, however, is not interpreted as such. The fact of the matter is that, despite the Rat Man's love affair with words he usually has problems giving a long narrative unit (the first analytic session and those of December 23, 27, and 28 are exceptions). Freud, in sum, is confronted by two stylistic factors: Dr. Lanzer fits into the category of patients who have a greater aptitude for the lyric style of association by similarity than for the epic style of association by contiguity (Rosen, 1977, pp. 138–39); and in a pathological sense, owing to the considerable disruption of casual connections by defensive isolation, he cannot give a sustained narrative either of his own "real" life or of that subtending his personal myth.

Nevertheless, in Freud's discussion of the first session, he masterfully infiltrates his expository language with visual references, a lexical element suggesting an empathically analytic stance to his scopophilic patient. Freud begins by announcing that we "see" little Ernst driven by the pleasure of looking (I have translated somewhat literally in order to bring out the visual references):

> We *see* the child under the domination of a sexual drive-component, the *desire to look,* whose result is the ever recurrent wish of great intensity to *see naked* female persons who please him. . . . As often as he wishes something of this kind, he must fear something dreadful would happen. This dreadful thing already *clothes* itself in a characteristic indeterminateness which hence forth will never be lacking from the expressions of the neurosis. Yet in a child it is not hard to find out what is *veiled* by such indeterminateness. If one can come to learn an example from any one of the blurred generalities of the obsessional neurosis, then one can be sure that the example is the original and actual thing itself which must be *hidden away* by the generalization. . . . The distressing affect [of the obsessional neurosis] *clearly* takes on the *tinge* of the uncanny, the superstitious. . . . We shall scarcely go astray if we perceive in this childlike quest for *enlightenment* an inkling of those remarkable psychic processes which we call unconscious and which we cannot dispense with [*entraten*] in the scientific *illumination* of the *dark* circumstances. (1909b, 162–64/388–89; italics mine)

Freud and Ernst, drive and defense, analysis and exposition, all meet in the eye. Another example of Freud's typical flair for permitting a conflictual theme to invade his very exposition of it concerns little Ernst's lascivious wishes and his defensive reaction; in his clinical comment Freud says that one can hardly "resist" *(stäuben)* qualifying sexual experiences as especially consequential.

We should also remark that three times Freud speaks of "our patient," which Strachey rendered as "the patient." The discrepancy is far-reaching in that Freud pronominally conjoins us with him and thereby turns us as readers into cotherapists in the analysis. Thus a fourth track announces itself in Freud's stereophonic prose—the analytic treatment, the writing of the process notes, their revision, and the public reading experience are now copresent. But the alert German reader detects even a fifth track, for Freud (1909b) discusses Ernst's life in childhood as also transpiring in the present. As a way of contrastively highlighting this effect, I shall first cite Freud, then Strachey's Freud:

> *Wollen wir noch als ein wahrscheinlich nicht gleichgültiges Zusammentreffen betonen, dass die Kindheitsamnesie unseres Patienten gerade mit dem 6. Jahre ihr Ende erreicht.* (Yet we want to emphasize a coincidence which is probably no accident: *our* patient's amnesia about his childhood end*s* precisely with the sixth year). (p. 390; my translation and italics) . . . stress may be laid on the fact, which is probably more than a mere coincidence, that the patient's infantile amnesia ended precisely with his sixth year. (pp. 164–65)

The temporal and pronominal indicators of Freud's closeness to Ernst and his readership were displaced by Strachey, who interposed his scientific ideology of clinical reportage between Freud and his patient, between Freud and us, and between us and Ernst. Let us further note the diametric opposition of the fictive simultaneity of Freud's five-track stereophonic prose to the pathological simultaneity of the Rat Man's fear, expressed in the first session, that his already dead father might die.

Countering the potentially monotonous typography found in the presentation of the clinical material, Freud precedes the second session with the title "The Great Obsessive Fear." He then sets out by citing his patient at length; Lanzer interrupts himself, we read in the second paragraph, and several sentences later we come upon the most unusual stylistic irregularity in the entire case history and, I would risk saying, in the Freudian corpus. Freud's stereophonic style breaks down next to our very ears as he inconsistently switches to the past tense, thereby expressing a defensive reaction to the interpersonal intrication and his intrusive interventions marking the exchange. By such temporal withdrawal, Freud (1909b) tries to undo the rat penetration which has already been enacted in and through his enunciatory interplay with Lanzer (my italics stress the significant irregularities in the use of tense):

> Here he breaks off, stands up and asks me to spare him the description of the details. I assure him that I myself have no inclination whatever for horror and certainly have no desire to torment him, but that naturally I cannot grant him something over which I have no ordinance. He may just as well ask me to grant him two comets. The overcoming of resistances is a precept of the treatment which we could in no way disregard. (I *had expounded* on the concept of "resistance" to him at the beginning of this hour, when he said that he had many things in himself to overcome if he were to relate his experience.) I *continued:* but what I could do is to guess fully, from something hinted by him, about what ought to happen. *Is* he perhaps thinking of impalement?—"No, not that, but the condemned *is being* tied up"—(he *expressed* himself so indistinctly that I could not immediately guess in what position)—"over his buttocks a pot *is* turned upside down, in which then rats *are* let in, and they"—he *was* again standing up and *gave* all signs of horror and resistance—"*bored* in." —"Into the anus," I *permitted* myself to complete it. (166/391–92; my translation)

Freud then brings us into his presence: "At all the more important moments one notes on him [*merkt man an ihm*] a very strange composite facial expression." Soon thereafter, although one shifts tense more freely in German, we can find no reason for Freud's inconsistent use of past and present in his exposition (relative to his customary practice), unless we see projection in Freud's account that the Rat Man is "confused" and "bewildered." Seemingly the Rat Man's disowning of his obsessions as "foreign," his enticing reluctance to narrate the torture, and Freud's guessing *(erraten)* his way into the narration all indicate disturbances of intrapsychic and analytic space, overflowing into the irregular temporal nearness and distancing of Freud's account that significantly starts with the antiphonal construction of the rat story.

Freud's report of the third session has three long paragraphs. In the first, he resumes the description of the Rat Man's madness, starting from near the end of maneuvers to his arrival in Vienna, where he and Dr. Palatzer finally dispatched the famous payment. Thankful for this last detail, Freud says in the second paragraph that he can begin to straighten out the distortions in the Rat Man's story—that is, Ernst must really have known for some time his actual creditor at the post office. Freud then clarifies the imbroglio over the payment for the rest of the second paragraph and, in the third one, traces the Rat Man's life from Dr. Palatzer's consoling companionship to the consultation on Berggasse.

We must note first that the sequence of events in paragraphs one and two is reversed in the process notes, which begin with clarifications in which Freud's moment of clear perception occurs not with the final detail about Dr. Palatzer in Vienna but with an earlier detail concerning a medical officer during maneuvers.[7] Now why, one may ask, does Freud reorganize the sequence? The answer is readily found in his own qualification of the Rat Man's actions as a "comedy" *(Komödie),* with the result that, with appropriate artistry, Freud restructures the session like a comedy. Thus he eliminates clarifications at the beginning; a partial denouement is saved for the middle; and in a final remark, he maintains the traditional open-endedness of comedy by alluding to the Rat Man's subsequent temptation to resume his maddening quest. Also, like a typical comic dramatist, Freud depicts his questful protagonist as ensnared in a maze of both fate and fortune—obsessive wishes, a demand for cure "woven up" *(verwoben)* into a delirium, and a "chance" discovery of Freud's book on chance *(The Psychopathology of Everyday Life),* with the effect of directing the Rat Man's "choice" to Freud. We should note, however, that Freud did not present his drama but narrated it; with few exceptions as this juncture, he set the action in the past, the distancing effect of which is nevertheless offset by his thrice referring to Ernst Lanzer as "our patient."

As opposed to the previous session, with its narrated comedy, the fourth is mostly a dramatic presentation of the Rat Man, with the changing turns of the speakers signaled in the present: "he asks," "he says," "I reply," and so on. This dramatic effect befits Freud's aim, stated at the outset of the sessions, to eschew omniscient remarks in order to sustain the reader's curiosity just as he and Ernst Lanzer do in pursuing free association:

> Let no one expect to hear so soon what I have to bring forward in the clarification of these strange, senseless obsessional representations (about rats); correct psychoanalytic technique requires the physician to suppress his curiosity and leaves the patient the free ordering of the sequence of themes during the work. I therefore received the patient in the fourth session with the question: "How are you going to start off now?" (1909b, 173–74/398; my translation)

It might also be noted, incidentally, that Freud inconsistently carries out his advocacy of suppressed curiosity, for midway through the session he instructs his patient in basic psychoanalytic principles instead of letting him curiously discover them for himself.

I have little to say about the next three sessions except that Freud enters further into a dramatic style; accordingly, the reader is seldom addressed, and the change in speaker is indicated by a dash, thereby enabling the report of the sessions to be laid out like a theatrical text. I should mention, however, one of those rare instances in which Freud turns from his patient to address us: in the main text Freud asserts, "I take the opportunity of urging my case" (p. 185) and then self-reflectively adds in a footnote, "I only produce these arguments so as once more to demonstrate to myself their inefficacy" (Strachey, of course, translated *take* and *produce* in the past). This is another superb example of how Freud's stereophonic style in German creates the impression that the scenes of the ongoing treatment and his subsequent write-up and self-reflection all take place concomitantly on the same dramatic stage.

In the last three sections of Part One of his case history, Freud (1909b) adopted a new expressive mode. In the references to former events he largely left behind the dramatic present for the narrative past tense (two notable exceptions are the renditions of the Rat Man's dream [p. 193] and fantasy [pp. 194–95], both transcribed in the present tense and hence in conformity with Freud's firm contention that the intrapsychic activities of dreaming and fantasying are preeminently and intrinsically occurrences of the present). Section E is interesting for some verbal complexity, starting with a spatial referent in its title: "Some Obsessional Ideas and Their Translation." The last word in German *(Übersetzung)* also means "carrying over"—in translating unconscious ideas, the analyst also effects a carrying over from the unconscious to the conscious and "brings" *(bringt)* obsessional ideas into a temporal connection with the patient's experiences; in that way he finds out the pathological "derivation" (*Abkunft*, literally, coming away). Later on Freud playfully voiced the hope that his explanation of an obsessional idea *(Zwangsidee)* is itself not "forced" *(gezwungen)*, a humorous self-reflection set in motion by the *zwang* and *gezwungen*, which are respectively the past and past participle of the main verb *zwingen*. Freud also let a note of compulsion enter his exposition when, after expounding on the obsession for protecting, he wrote, "and it bore other fruit besides this"; the English here does not capture the German *Blüten trieb* (literally, put forth flowers), especially in that as a noun *Trieb* means drive. In a more amusing wordplay, Freud (1909b) compared his patient to Balaam, the self-defeating biblical soothsayer, and then to an incantatory alchemist. Lanzer saw,

> like an inverted Balaam, that something always inserted itself into his pious formulas, which turned them into the opposite. . . . In such affliction he found the way out by putting aside the prayers and replacing them by a short formula that was brewed together [*zusammengebraut*] out of initial letters or syllables of different prayers. (193/415; my translation)

Both the beginning and the end of Section E mention Ernst's ambivalence toward Gisela's absence (pp. 187, 195), and as a matter of fact, Freud resorted to a complex use (and nonuse) of language to deal with that ambivalence. When we hunt up the source in the process notes for Freud's initial assertion that Ernst's suicidal obsessions were occasioned by Gisela's absence (187/410), we are forced to give the following rereading:

> He lost several weeks through the *presence* of the lady, who went off when her very old grandmother became ill. (Hawelka, 1974, p. 92; my translation and italics)[8]

In his terminal remark (195/417), Freud expressed his patient's feelings of affection and revenge toward Gisela this way:

> These impulses were silent mostly in her presence and came out of her absence. (my translation)[9]

But within the main part of his elaboration, Freud made more involved distinctions: Ernst's obsession for protecting took place during Gisela's presence at his summer resort, whereas his obsession for understanding broke out after her departure. Both obsessions, though, derived from a common circumstance. When he was taking his leave of Gisela before departing for the summer resort, she said something that he understood as her repudiating him before "the present company" (190/412). During her belated stay at the country resort, Gisela cleared up that misunderstanding; prior to that clarification, according to Freud, Ernst's obsession to protect must have broken out. On the other hand, Freud linked the obsession to understand (which occurred after Gisela's departure) to Ernst's ambivalence, which was exemplified by his removing and subsequently replacing the stone in the road several hours before his lady's departure. Yet that replacing, in Freud's words, would be incorrectly classified as a critical repudiation of a pathological action: since putting the stone back was accompanied by a sense of compulsion, that very act was part of the original pathological action. Hence the first stage of the compulsive act was not "neutralized" (as Strachey [p. 192] would have it) by the second stage but rather was both "annulled and conserved" (*aufgehoben,* p. 414). Through his brilliant use of this primal word of antithesis, therefore, Freud showed that the first stage was annulled by what followed and was also conserved in that the compulsion continued into the second stage. In this context, then, the perceptual difference betwen Gisela's presence and absence was collapsed in the Rat Man's ambivalence and compulsion.

From the foregoing, one is driven to conclude that Gisela's fate was to move with equal ease in and out of Ernst's life, and in and out of both Freud's and Strachey's texts. Let us give another example: Ernst uttered two juxtaposed, ambivalent statements about Gisela's presence and absence in his very first analytic session (p. 255); yet those statements are absent from Freud's published report of the first session (p. 158) as well as from Strachey's generalizing account that Freud published the first third of the process notes "almost verbatim" (p. 254). In sum, the matter of absence and presence appears like a series of Chinese boxes, during the unpackaging by which, nuisance turns to new sense as one discovers that by virtue of a dwindling absence, the containers themselves are the only presents.

The outstanding feature of the next section, "The Precipitating Cause of the Illness," revolves around time. Freud settled on Mrs. Lanzer's plan for her son's marriage as the one precipitating cause of illness, seeming to forget for the moment the other explanations: Gisela's infertility and Ernst's aunt's death. In support of his thesis, Freud drew all his clinical material on the Rat Man from the process notes of one session, December 8, whose brevity, however, went against Freud's narrative concerns. As a countermeasure, he opted for the following strategy. In the first of the section's six paragraphs, Freud began in his storylike way with the most traditional of epithets, "One day," and alluded briefly to the Rat Man's unwitting mention of the immediate cause of his illness. Then for the next two paragraphs Freud dropped the Rat Man and took up the mechanisms of isolation and displacement in obsessionality, digressing at length on a former case[10] (meanwhile we are thinking about the displacements in Freud's own diagnosis and exposition). Returning to his main story in the fourth paragraph, Freud brought up the decisive marriage plan and, in doing so, made the first and only substantial mention of his patient's mother in the main text of the whole case history; the fifth and last paragraphs further explain the cause of illness but do not refer to her. In retrospect, we can think of perhaps three reasons for Freud's deferred reference to Mrs. Lanzer: he was uneasy and reluctant to discuss her, and when he did, it was as a deus ex machina; the deferment figures in Freud's expository concern to make the treatment appear longer; and from an artistic point of view, Freud's dilatory tactic mimicked his subject's habit of postponing decisions.

In analyzing the last and longest section of Part One, "The Father Complex and the Solution of the Rat Idea," we may initially study several instances of Freud's engaging wordplay and then the more important overall structure of his exposition. After bringing up the debt incurred by Heinrich Lanzer in his military days as a gambler (*Spielratte,* literally, a play-rat), Freud claimed that Ernst must have heard a paternal reference in the cruel captain's reimbursement request. Thus Freud:

The captain's words, "You must pay back the 3.80 kronen to Lieutenant A." had sounded to his [Ernst's] ears like an allusion to this unpaid debt of his father's. (p. 211)

What is startling is that not only the captain's words "sounded" *(klangen)* like an allusion to the gambling father *(Spielratte)* but also that the very term *allusion (Anspielung)* means as well as enacts itself by virtue of its identical root with *Spielratte;* consequently the difference between language and metalanguage is deftly subverted. In this way Freud blended his expository language with a principal signifier in his patient's story. A double instance of this lexical maneuver is found in the following footnote:

Since the patient had done everything to confuse the little incident of the repayment of the charges for the pince-nez, perhaps my presentation also did not succeed in making it transparent [*durchsichtig,* literally, looked through] without default [*Rückstand*]. (212*n*/431*n*; my translation)

Just as vision and payment dominate the Rat Man's story, so also do those themes enter into the self-reflectiveness of Freud's narrative.[11]

A slightly humorous example of narrative self-reflectiveness occurs in a watery context about the rat:

The rat is a dirty animal, feeding upon excrement and living in drains that carry waste [*Kanälen die den Abfall führen*]. It is rather superfluous [*überflüssig,* literally, overflowing] to point out that . . . (214/433; my translation)[12]

There is also an instance of perhaps unintentional comic effect accompanied by more successful verbal play. In the course of describing his patient's masturbation upon hearing a postilion illegally blowing his horn or upon reading a poignantly amorous passage in Goethe, Freud labeled those occasions as "uplifting" *(erhebenden)* and continued the spatial reference, which disappears when rendered in fluent English:

But I could not help stressing [*herausheben,* literally, to lift out] what was common in these two examples: the prohibition and a defiance of [*Sichhinaussetzen über,* literally, putting oneself outside and over] a command. (204/425; my translation)[13]

Then Freud resonantly went on to mention the Rat Man's ritual of midnight masturbation which would begin by his defiantly opening the front door as if his father were standing outside. In this way, Freud's phraseology skillfully united father and son as being outside, one in a perceptually external space, the other in the intrapsychic space of moral defiance.

Freud (1909b) saved some of his most extensive punning, however, to depict his patient's itinerary "along the painful road of transference." I shall use Strachey's translation this time:

> "How can a gentleman like you, sir" he used to ask, "let yourself be abused in this way by a low, good-for-nothing fellow [*hergelaufenen Kerl,* literally, a runabout fellow] like me? You ought to turn me out; that's all I deserve." While he talked like this, he would get up from the sofa and roam about [*herumlaufen*] the room. . . . If he stayed on the sofa he behaved like someone in desperate violence; he would bury his head in his hands, cover his face with his arm, jump up suddenly, rush [*lief,* past tense of *laufen,* to run] away, his features distorted with pain, and so on. He recalled his father had had a passionate temper, and sometimes in his violence had not known where to stop [*gehen,* literally, to go]. (209/429)

We cannot fail to marvel at how this text runs together Ernst's self-evaluation (a runabout fellow), his expression of fear (running about the room), and his father's expression of anger (not knowing where to go). Although it is an open question as to how much Freud himself contributed to the pertinent chain of signifiers, his condensed recording of them is in itself a response to the poetry of the unconscious.

In terms of the larger focus of thematic organization, we find that Freud enlivened the pace of his discourse by constantly referring to events as mediated by tales, by literal hearsay. He saw his first reconstruction confirmed by a tale his patient heard but could not remember (p. 205); the Rat Man's obsessions were activated by the captain's two speeches (p. 210); it seemed as if fate, when the captain told the torture tale, had "called out" (*zugerufen,* 216/435) a "complex stimulus-word" to the Rat Man; the Rat Man identified with his father in his novel about marriage (*Eheroman,* 211/431);[14] parallel to the captain's erroneous remark that was transformed into paternal infallibility in one of the Rat Man's obsessional sayings is the king's magical utterance. As Freud states, "The king cannot be mistaken; if he addresses one of his subjects by a title which is not his, the subject bears that title ever afterwards" (p. 218).[15] It is precisely through further reflection on this tale that we are enabled to make a surprising discovery about Ernst's mother. In the main text of the case history, she is given limited, mediating status as the bearer of a tale or arranger of marriage, whereas it is only in the subjected typography of a footnote that she acquires a fully oedipal role;

curiously, it is also in the important footnote, running for three pages (pp. 206–08), that we find Freud's only considerable treatment of the oedipal (nuclear) complex in the case, albeit largely in general terms.[16]

The time is now ripe for us to outline the structure of the section under consideration, which is as follows: some clinical material, taken from the opening sessions of the analysis, about the conflict between Ernst and his father (pp. 200–04); Freud's construction of an early conflictual scene between Ernst and his father, and the emergence of that conflict within the transference (pp. 205–09); the ensuing solution of the rat obsession and Freud's "restoration of the context" (*Herstellung des Zusammenhanges,* 209–10/429–30). The last subject itself has three parts: a summary account of the deliria during the military exercises (pp. 210–12); the emergence of the rat associations during the analysis (pp. 213–17); and the explanation of the process and the general context informing the nascent rat obsession (pp. 217–20). Even a cursory examination of the foregoing outline shows how it sets in relief the narrative thrust and vitality we familiarly encounter in Freud's prose. The narrative thrust is further strengthened by the frequent usage of such words as *way, course, follow, turn, lead,* and *reach.* Even though these words compose a family of dead metaphors, their original meanings may be reset in motion by a surrounding narrative context and thereby enhance in turn the narrative flow, as we can pursue in the following:

> From the precipitating cause of the patient's illness in his adult years there was a thread leading back to his childhood. . . . To this impeachable body of evidence we shall be able to add fresh material, if we turn to the history of the masturbatory side of our patient's sexual activities. . . . Starting from these indications and from other data of a similar kind, I ventured to put forward a construction. . . . To my great astonishment the patient then informed me. . . . And so it was only along the painful road of transference that he was able to reach a conviction. . . . A quantity of material information which had hitherto been withheld became available. . . . In elucidating the effects produced by the captain's rat story we must follow the course of the analysis more closely. . . . Yet, in spite of all this wealth of material, no light was thrown upon the meaning of his obsessional idea until one day. . . . It was only then that it became possible to understand the inexplicable process by which his obsessional idea had been formed. . . . Let us, further, picture to ourselves the general conditions under which the formation of the patient's great obsessional idea occurred.

These extracts help us see that, thanks partly to Freud's lexical choices, his exposition takes on a narrative quality, a quality further reinforced by the metaphor of the journey coursing through his prose (Mahony, 1982). Briefly, even in the etymological sense, the conquistadorial prose of Freud is ambitious (Latin *ambulare,* to walk).

Indeed, the virtuosity of Freud's vivid discourse is so captivating that we must beware of being distracted from the recognition of crucial organizational discrepancies. There is one that is as important as anything we have analyzed stylistically up to now. The matter concerns the two main topics of the section at hand—Ernst's relation to his father and the rat phobia. On one hand, the construction given on October 12 about little Ernst's outburst of anger toward his father was supposedly worked through in the transference, a working through that Freud described solely with material drawn from the period of November 21 to December 8. On the other hand, the *subsequent* solution (p. 209) of the rat idea was based on material drawn essentially from the period of November 18 to January 7 (pp. 210–16); but this time, as our outline plainly shows, Freud did not record any working through in the treatment. Instead, he merely imparted to the reader the reconstructed formation of the rat idea (pp. 217– 19) and then concluded with an intellectualizing assertion that when he and his patient had reached (not worked through) the solution given to the reader, the rat delirium disappeared. A bare, bold claim with no demonstration, no further explanation.

It is now that the overall structure of Part One of Freud's case history suddenly becomes clearer to us. In his opening remarks, Freud repeatedly apologized for the fragmentary nature of his report; in both substance and repetition, those apologies starkly contrast with the single, succinctly worded claim by Freud that he effected a *complete* restoration of his patient's personality and a removal of his inhibitions. Gone is any reference to fragmentariness at the end of Part One, for at this late hour any such avowal would spotlight the transparency of Freud's contention. Like a good rhetorician who may resort to aesthetic and other devices, especially in the area where his logical demonstration is weakest, Freud combines dramatic staging and the typographical strategy of a concluding blank space to give the impression of definitiveness and to distract from the defensive closure of his narration. By a stylistic sleight of hand, the father complex in its full recapitulation was apparently tucked under the rat idea, and now, at the final moment, the disappearance of the delirium is announced. Exit rats, exit father complex, and offstage, somewhere, a fully restored man is walking, we are told.

NOTES

1. Cf. Jung's letter of January 3, 1908, to Abraham: "Seldom in my analytical work have I been so struck by the 'beauty' of neurosis as with this [hysterical] patient. The construction and course of the dreams are of a rare aesthetic beauty" (Jung, 1973, p. 5).
2. Cf. Jung's horse of a different color when he addressed Ferenczi: "Freud's paper on obsessional neurosis is marvellous but *very hard to understand.* I must soon read it for the third time. Am I particularly stupid? Or is it the style? I plump cautiously for the latter. Between Freud's speaking and writing there is a 'gulf fixed' which is very wide. Most of all I have disputed with Freud 'the symptoms of *omnipotence*' (!) because the term is too clinical. Naturally he is right, and the term is artistic too. But if you have to *teach* that kind of thing in a systematic context, you get goose pimples and take to swearing" (letter of 12/25/09; Jung, 1973, p. 14).
3. Although Freud asserts that the revelation of the patient's most intimate secrets is less likely to violate discretion than is the disclosure of harmless facts, little data of any sort appear in the case history about his patient's mother.
4. Cf. Strachey's translation of *Kalibers* (degree), *Reihe* (number), and *bekämpften* (taken in hand).
5. Cf. Freud's diagnostic appraisals of the symptomatic reactions of Fräulein Elisabeth and the Rat Man: "if one pressed or pinched the hyperalgesic skin and muscles of her legs, her face assumed a peculiar expression, which was one of pleasure rather than pain. . . . it could only be reconciled with the view that her disorder was hysterical" (Freud, 1893–95, p. 137); "At all the more important moments while he was telling his story [of the rat torture] his face took on a very strange, composite expression. I could only interpret it as one of *horror at pleasure of his own of which he himself was unaware*" (Freud, 1909b, pp. 166–67).
6. In his process notes on the interview Freud terminates by mentioning the patient's return on the next day and his acceptance of the practical conditions; hence at least part of the write-up occurred on the following day. One can find other such discrepancies, including deferred addenda, which undercut Freud's initial declaration about writing down notes at the end of each day (cf. 1909b, p. 159*n*).
7. On the other hand, and to Freud's credit, the number of male personnel in the original account (nine) is trimmed by two, thus facilitating the comprehensibility of the published version.
8. Yet that very word *presence* (clearly *Anwesenheit* in my copy of the holograph) was silently changed by Strachey into *absence* (which is *Abwesenheit* in German; p. 259)—presence itself was textually sent into exile!
9. Cf. Strachey's rendering: "These impulses were mostly in abeyance when she was there, and only appeared in her absence." Perhaps in a moment of absentmindedness Strachey unwarrantably inserted an "only" before the last verb, thereby giving rise to a nonsequitur.
10. Strachey's translation does not capture Freud's wordplay in the description of this self-justifying elderly man who left alone neither little girls nor his own self-reproach (the latter was conveniently displaced): thus, on one hand, he sexually molested girls entrusted in his charge by going into their adjacent room and masturbating them; on the other hand, "if he left alone the [self-] reproach where it belonged, he would have had to renounce a sexual satisfaction to which he was probably pushed by strong infantile determinants" (198/419).
11. *Rückstand* is commonly used in the sense of arrears, a financial reference missing in

Strachey's translation: "perhaps my own account of it may also have failed to clear it up entirely."

12. The richness of Freud's text is blotted out by Strachey, who translated *Kanälen die den Abfall führen* simply by sewers, and *überflüssig* by unnecessary (p. 214).
13. Cf. Strachey's translation on page 204. In passing, I might briefly allude to Freud's portrayal of the Rat Man's efforts to bring military colleagues "into his combination" (*Kombination,* 212/431). The richer German term also carries the meanings of reasoning, deduction, conjecture, and guesswork, all applicable to the present context.
14. Freud mentioned a series of identifications that the Rat Man established with his father that had different bases: marital choice, military life, money, and punishment/victimization; but rather than be expressed in one condensed passage, the identifications are strewn out in the narration, which thereupon approximates associative flow.
15. The implications of Freud's observation are far-reaching when considered in the light of speech theorists' distinction between constative and performative discourse. Constative discourse merely describes an event, whereas performative discourse not only discloses an utterance of its speaker but, through the very act of its enunciation, accomplishes the action. Thus, given the necessary felicitous circumstances, such utterances as "I bid hearts" and "I promise" or "I do" perform and accomplish actions in themselves; the imperial enunciation given by Freud is also of such an order. What Freud is saying on a deeper level, however, is that obsessional wording assumes the character of performative discourse for the obsessional, who becomes the enunciated victim of his compulsions and omnipotent wishes.
16. In the footnote, Freud discussed at length the thorny difficulty of ascertaining the historical or psychic reality of infantile sexuality. The discussion is a choice illustration of those times when Freud resorted to an expressive mode in which doubts, qualifications, and assertions loop back upon each other; in resuming the topic of the Wolf Man case, Freud wrote similarly (Freud, 1918, pp. 67–70, 102–03).

REFERENCES

Freud, S. (1893–95). *Studies on hysteria.* S.E., 2.

———. (1909a). Analysis of a phobia in a five-year-old boy. S.E., 10: 3–145.

———. (1909b). Notes upon a case of obsessional neurosis. S.E., 10: 155–320. Also in *Gesammelte Werke* (vol. 7, pp. 379–463). Frankfurt am Main: Fischer Verlag, 1941; and *Collected Papers* (Vol. 3, pp. 291–383). London: Hogarth Press, 1957.

———. (1913). *Totem and taboo. S.E.,* 13 : 1–162.

———. (1918). From the history of an infantile neurosis. S.E., 17: 3–122.

———. (1974). *The Freud/Jung letters* (W. McGuire, Ed.). Princeton: Princeton University Press. [*Briefwechsel* (1906–16) (W. McGuire & W. Sauerlander, Eds.) Frankfurt am Main: S. Fischer Verlag].

Hawelka, E. (1974). (Ed. & transl.) *L'Homme aux rats. Journal d'une analyse.* Paris: Presses Universitaires de France.

Jung, C. (1973). *Letters* (1906–1950). (Vol. 1., G. Alder, Ed., and R. Hall, Trans.). Princeton, N.J.: Princeton University Press.

Marcus, S. (1984). *Freud and the culture of psychoanalysis.* London: Allen & Unwin.

Mahony, P. (1982). *Freud as a writer.* New York: International Universities Press.

Rosen, V. (1977). *Style, character and language* (S. Atkins and M. Jucovy, Eds.). New York: Jason Aronson.

4. The Metaphorical Nature of Psychoanalytic Theory

Donald P. Spence

To mention both metaphor and Freud in the same breath may seem somewhat unusual—but certainly not unappreciative. I use the word *metaphor* in the spirit of Max Black and believe that it is a necessary first step along the way to a rigorous theory. At the same time, however, we must recognize that much of psychoanalytic theory is still hypothetical and therefore a piece of undeveloped metaphor.* Many of Freud's conventions were intentional uses of figurative language, which allow us to see clinical happenings in a new and different manner, but have no necessary connection with reality. Much of this figurative usage has been lost in the Strachey translation (the so-called Standard Edition of Freud), as recent writers have pointed out (see Bettelheim, 1983, and Ornston, 1985), and as we are more and more distanced from the poetry of the original German, we are in increasing danger of losing sight of the metaphor as well. The pseudo-scientific language invented by Strachey contributes to this danger.

Not only is metaphorical language becoming more respectable, but it is also increasingly clear that it represents a critical means of representing the world. "Metaphor," we are told, "is one of our most important tools for trying to comprehend partially what cannot be comprehended totally. . . . These endeavors of the imagination are not devoid of rationality; since they use metaphor, they employ an imaginative rationality" (Lakoff and Johnson, 1980, p. 193).

Building on a line of thought first expressed by Vico in the eighteenth century, metaphor has come to be seen (in the words of Isaiah Berlin) as a

*For a somewhat different discussion of the role of metaphor in Freud's writings, see J. Edelson, 1983.

fundamental category through which at a given stage of development men cannot help viewing reality—which is for them reality itself, neither mere embellishment, nor a repository of secret wisdom, nor the creation of a world parallel to the real world, nor an addition to, or distortion of, reality, harmless or dangerous, deliberate or involuntary: but is the natural, inevitably transient, but, at the time of its birth or growth, the only possible way of perceiving, interpreting, explaining, that is open to men of that particular time and place, at that particular stage of their culture. (1976, p. 104)

Only a century before Vico, the use of metaphor was generally frowned upon in educated circles; it carried connotations of a pre- or anti-scientific state of mind.

Thomas Sprat, one of the founders of the Royal Society, declared that "specious tropes and figures" should be banished "out of all Civill societies as a thing fatal to peace and good manners"; the Royal Society should avoid "myths and uncertainties," and return to "a close, naked, natural way of speaking . . . as near the Mathematical plainness as they can." So, too, Hobbes banished metaphor from all writings aimed at "the rigorous search for truth." Locke, Hume, and Adam Smith say much the same, although Hume allows that rigid adherence to "geometrical truth . . . might have a disagreeable effect upon the reader." (Berlin, 1976, p. 104)

We can see now that the widespread fear of metaphor reflected by such philosophers as Locke, Hobbes, and Hume contained its own metaphor—an underlying belief in "geometrical truth" or in what Lakoff and Johnson call the myth of objectivity. The attacks on metaphorical thinking contained their own metaphorical pitfalls: all the time the critical philosophers were attacking this or that figure of speech, they were applying an objective metaphor to the world and thus committing the very crime they were attacking.

What does it mean to speak of the Freudian metaphor? In the first place, such usage highlights the poetic nature of Freud's language and underscores his revolutionary campaign to put the unspeakable and the unthinkable into words. These attempts, as he has made clear in many passages, were often groping, tentative, and exploratory: first approximations to phenomena and experience which, even now, have a way of slipping between our fingers. It is partly because it remains hard to capture that the experience tends to be replaced by the metaphor. But the experience may disappear in the process. The word—no matter how experimental or tentative or metaphoric—tends to replace the thing being described and we lose sight of the fact that the word is often more poetic than otherwise. A return to the original German (see Bettelheim, 1983) might repair some of the damage, but it would not solve the problem. To the extent that the language becomes more fanciful and romantic, it may only make it worse.

More specifically, the Freudian metaphor tempts us to believe in the idea of a dynamic unconscious which is actively and continuously influencing the contents of consciousness. It tells us that the contents of this unconscious "proliferate in the dark" where they develop "with less interference and more profusely" than in the light of conscious thought. It strongly suggests that evenly suspended attention, in conjunction with free association, provides the analyst with the opportunity to uncover the contents of the key happenings in the patient's past—the historical truth of his early life. And finally, the Freudian metaphor trains us to see the transference as a faithful replication of critical past experiences.

Each of these assumptions can be seen as a critical part of Freudian theory, and for some, they have the status of established axioms. But they are also metaphors. Once we lose sight of their metaphoric nature, we are in danger of turning psychoanalytic theory into a blueprint of the mind—or rather, into what we think is a blueprint. In actual fact, however, the reified metaphor is probably closer to a kind of mythology which acquires its own reality and which deludes us into believing that now, at last, we understand. This is the worst kind of metaphor; because of its figurative, poetic nature, it resists falsification and turns into what Black has called "self-certifying myth." Metaphor of this kind quickly turns into stereotype. If we are indeed living with a Freudian mythology, we have lost touch with science.

The central issue facing us at the present time is not one of confirmation or disconfirmation—a metaphor, after all, can never be validated—but rather, which metaphors to choose and whether they facilitate or interfere with the discovery of clinical wisdom. Whatever metaphors we finally adopt, it is important to realize that they are functioning primarily as models, as a kind of extended sensory apparatus (see Lakoff and Johnson, 1980) which allows us to see certain sorts of phenomena and certain kinds of causal relationships that would otherwise go unnoticed. But the paradox is this: Their power as an aid to comprehension is directly proportional to our awareness of their metaphoric nature.

To keep alive the Freudian metaphor—that is the challenge of the moment. To keep it uppermost in our awareness and prevent it from becoming transparent allows us to keep its metaphorical nature clearly in mind, to avoid the trap of projecting its terms onto the clinical domain and finding things that are not really there. But to take the Freudian approach for granted, to deaden the metaphor and rule out other approaches, is to reduce our options to only one and mistakenly transform the theory into pseudo-science and the practice into a certain kind of religion.

Metaphor works, it would appear, by

> transferring the associated ideas and implications of the secondary [figurative] system to the primary system [domain of observation]. These select, emphasize, or suppress features of the primary; new slants on the primary are illuminated; the primary is seen through the frame of the secondary. In accordance with the doctrine that even literal expressions are understood partly in terms of the set of associated ideas carried by the system they describe, it follows that the associated ideas of primary are changed to some extent by the use of the metaphor, and that therefore even its original literal description is shifted in meaning. The same applies to the secondary system, for its associations come to be affected by assimilations to the primary. Men are seen to be more like wolves after the wolf-metaphor is used [''man is a wolf''] and wolves seem to be more human. (Hesse, 1980, p. 114)

So it comes about that for the committed Freudian, a certain kind of unexpected outburst by the patient is literally *seen* as a piece of the unconscious which has remained too long in the dark and acquired an unexpected and frightening face. What is metaphoric in the original Freud becomes transformed into a literal description in the case report. When the Freudian metaphor is operating insistently (and invisibly), almost any piece of the clinical material can be seen in the literal language of the initial formulation. Under these conditions, however, the metaphor is no longer being used metaphorically; distorted perceptions of the analyst are projected onto the clinical material and there is no sense in which a particular model has been chosen or—what is just as distorting—that a set of alternatives has been excluded. As Hesse and other writers make clear, metaphors both emphasize and suppress: To see man as a wolf is to not see him as a grown child; to see all events as determined by an actual unconscious is to exclude the view that some events are random happenings.

When the Freudian metaphor operates in completely transparent fashion, it has shifted its status from alive to dead.

> Once such literalization has occurred and a ''live'' metaphor has been regressively transformed into a ''dead'' one, one no longer compares the ''leg'' of a table, let us say, to the leg of a person . . . but *literally* thinks of the supports of a table as its legs. (Carveth, 1984, p. 496)

On the other hand, to step outside the reigning metaphor and see it as one possibility among many is to carry out what Carveth calls a process of ''deliteralization.'' By this means

We are capable of achieving . . . the cognitive flexibility to intentionally diversify and alternate our conceptual frameworks and languages such that reality may be approached first from one angle and then from another. (Carveth, 1984, p. 509)

To carry out this goal and step outside the reigning metaphor is part of a central theme in modern philosophy.

It would seem that we must abandon our quixotic attempts to discover *the* meaning (as opposed to a range of *complementary* meanings) of anything, not least ourselves. A great deal of the very best thinking in various fields of modern thought suggests that our grandiose positivist aspirations to godlike omniscience must be relinquished and replaced by a principle of uncertainty—a sacrifice through which, from conceit of knowledge, we might possibly advance toward a rudimentary knowledge of our conceit. (Carveth, 1984, p. 512)

To see the Freudian metaphor more clearly does not make it disappear and need not reduce it to triviality (as in saying, "Well, it's only a metaphor"). Because metaphors are central aspects of our understanding, we will always continue to use them; by the same token, we should not be used *by* them. But we will never step out from under the reigning metaphor unless we have a metaphor to take its place.

Once we see more clearly into the metaphorical nature of psychoanalytic theory, we begin to see the possible limits of validation and verification. Both metaphor and empirical laws carry explanatory force, but the kind of explanation provided by the first is significantly different from that provided by the second. The explanatory force of the Freudian metaphor of the unconscious is not diminished by the fact that it is seen as a manner of speaking; indeed, its credibility may even by strengthened. To become aware of its metaphoric foundation does, however, sensitize us to the fact that the Freudian system is not a lawful set of axioms which calls for explicit testing —either inside or outside the clinical arena. Its overthrow (or confirmation) will not come from experimental evidence precisely because of its heavy reliance on metaphorical explanation; for this reason, calls by Grünbaum (1984), Edelson (1983), and Holzman (1985) for systematic testing of psychoanalytic concepts seem more than a little misplaced. It might even be argued that calls for such testing represent a serious literalization of the Freudian metaphor and a mistaken belief that the critical psychoanalytic concepts possess a testable reality. To test the Freudian system as if it contained a set of falsifiable propositions is to overlook its essential metaphorical nature and to seriously concretize its most important concepts.

To keep alive the Freudian metaphor would seem to go beyond the argument of hermeneutics vs. science or truth vs. illusion; instead, it looks for different kinds of truth depending on what questions are being asked and what metaphors are being assumed. To make the fullest use of the Freudian metaphor requires a flexibility in approach which raises questions as to the conditions in which it seems relevant and a guide to understanding—and the conditions which call out for some other approach. To identify the Freudian metaphor as a description for a certain approach and a certain set of assumptions opens the way to specifying other metaphors which would illuminate other parts of the clinical picture and thus enlarge and further our understanding.

To keep the Freudian approach alive as metaphor is to extract its fullest potential and to make the greatest use of other options when the need requires. To speak metaphorically in full awareness of this fact is to be reminded that we are using language figuratively and tentatively—but at the same time, extending its use in significant ways. But to take the Freudian system for granted—to deaden the metaphor and rule out other approaches—is to reduce our options to only one and mistakenly transform metaphor into pseudo-science. To use it in this way is to diminish the poetry of Freud's original inspiration and, in the long run, to miss the spirit of the whole adventure.

FREUD'S USE OF METAPHOR

Freud was well acquainted with the explanatory power of metaphor. At the start of his paper on instincts, he had this to say about the language of science:

> We have often heard it maintained that sciences should be built up on clear and sharply defined basic concepts. In actual fact, no science, not even the most exact, begins with such definitions. The true beginning of scientific activity consists rather in describing phenomena and then in proceeding to group, classify, and correlate them. Even at the stage of description it is not possible to avoid applying certain abstract ideas to the material in hand, ideas derived from somewhere or other but

> certainly not from the new observations alone. Such ideas—which will later become the basic concepts of the science—are still more indispensable as the material is further worked over. They must at first necessarily possess some degree of indefiniteness; there can be no question of any clear delimitation of their content. So long as they remain in this condition, we come to an understanding about their meaning by making repeated references to the material of observation from which they appear to have been derived, but upon which, in fact, they have been imposed. Thus, strictly speaking, they are in the nature of conventions although everything depends on their not being arbitrarily chosen but determined by their having significant relations to the empirical material, relations that we seem to sense before we can clearly recognize and demonstrate them. It is only after more thorough investigation of the field of observation that we are able to formulate its basic scientific concepts with increased precision, and progressively so to modify them that they become serviceable and consistent over a wide area. (Freud, 1915a, p. 117)

It can be seen that Freud was well aware of the distinction between explanatory concepts which opened up a field of investigation and provided the initial (although possibly erroneous) glimpses into an unexplored domain, and later models which are more closely fitted to emerging observations and which may differ in both form and content from the earlier concepts. He was perhaps less sensitive to the underside of metaphorical usage—less concerned about the fact that the concept which sensitizes us to one part of the domain will blind us to another, and that if the wrong metaphor is chosen in the first place, it may never be possible to refine the "basic scientific concepts with increased precision, and . . . modify them that they become serviceable and consistent over a wide area."

It should not be assumed that the idea of replacement was unfamiliar; only the year before, he had discussed the way in which science begins its work with "nebulous, scarcely imaginable basic concepts, which it hopes to apprehend more clearly in the course of its development, or which it is even prepared to replace by others" (1914, p. 77). But then he goes on: "For these ideas are not the foundation of science, upon which everything rests; that foundation is observation alone. They are not the bottom but the top of the whole structure, and they can be replaced and discarded without damaging it" (p. 77).

As Freud developed and extended his theory, his metaphors tended to become more reified and less tentative, and this tendency made it all the more unlikely that they would either be influenced by new findings or replaced by more fitting models. Elsewhere we look in some detail at the unconscious; it will appear that Freud's 1915 model was extraordinarily specific on a variety of levels. With the advent of the structural theory, however, the topographic unconscious was turned into the id; many of the original details specified in the original (1915c) paper were never referred to again; and they were replaced by such figures as "a chaos, a cauldron full of seething excitations" (1932, p. 73). A seething cauldron can hardly be falsified by the data, no matter how careful the observations; as a result, it tends to become uncoupled from the clinical observations and exist in a protected domain where it is free of influence and yet always available for rhetorical mischief. Not only is the use of these "free-floating" metaphors epistemologically empty, but so long as they remain in circulation, they interfere with the formation of other kinds of models and may actually reduce or totally eliminate our awareness of certain clinical happenings. Protected by its vagueness, the free-floating metaphor can never be falsified and therefore always exists as a kind of presumptive explanation, a working hypothesis which invites us to believe that validation is just around the corner. Here is Freud's extended description of the id:

> It is filled with energy reaching it from the instincts, but it has no organization, produces no collective will, but only a striving to bring about the satisfaction of the instinctual needs. . . . Wishful impulses which have never passed beyond the id . . . are virtually immortal; after the passage of decades they behave as though they had just occurred. (1932, pp. 73–74)

BREADTH VS. DEPTH

We have seen how Freud was in the habit of using figures of speech to capture the phenomena which he wanted to study, and we have seen how he was quite deliberate in this attempt and well aware that the metaphor was being brought in from the outside. To the extent that it represents a convention, a certain way of thinking about the phenomenon under investigation, the metaphor has no necessary connection to the observations. In this regard, metaphor in psychoanalysis operates no differently from metaphor in physics. The early theory of the atom, for example, represented the atom as a miniature "solar system" in which electrons were represented as revolving around the nucleus. Since it could never be visualized concretely, it could never be tested directly.

But the Bohr model was not *merely* a metaphor—and that fact makes all the difference. The "solar system" metaphor led to a number of testable hypotheses; it could predict, for example, the spectrum of light emitted by a specific element. Results of these tests could be used to further refine the metaphor, elaborate the underlying model, and arrive at a clarified conception of the "solar system" which would be even more relevant to the nature of the atom.

Psychoanalytic metaphors, by contrast, have not generated testable predictions in ways that lead to specific alterations of the model. As is discussed elsewhere, we know very little more at the present time about the form and content of the unconscious than was proposed by Freud (1915b) in his original paper (some might say a good idea less). As is the case with any number of Freud's innovative figures of speech, the metaphor of an unknowable, timeless, and content-rich unconscious which "proliferates in the dark" has neither given rise to new observation nor led to a better understanding of earlier findings. The same criticism could be leveled against the metaphor of psychic structure or psychic energy. We have no precise way of visualizing either the structure or its energy; we cannot even propose a plan of study which could make this possible.

Cut off from systematic elaboration, unrelated to the clinical findings, the central (free-floating) metaphors of psychoanalysis have tended, as we have seen, to take on a life of their own; they have become reified prematurely and treated as something more than figures of speech. The desire to make psychoanalysis into a science may accelerate this process. It seems closer to science to speak of psychic structure in place of pieces of the mind, or of diminished libido in place of reduced interest in sex. To speak of a specific unconscious fantasy with knowable content and predictable derivatives takes on its own kind of reality. The models then become doubly misleading; they support Freud's original aim to capture phenomena in concrete images while also enhancing the metaphor of psychoanalysis as a science.

Something else happens as well. The more sanctified its use and the more established it becomes in the literature, the more we are tempted to assume that the free-floating metaphor is literally true. Given that assumption, the more likely we are to see the world through its eyes, and the more we are cut off from other models and other ways of seeing. Consider Freud's philosophical heritage from Descartes and Brentano, the foundation for many of his favorite models. As part of this tradition, he carried forward the idea that the mind is a set of mental states, with each of these states presumed to have a content, to be *about* something: This is Brentano's intentional conception of the mind. By this metaphor, elaborated by Freud's concept of the unconscious, the mind can be represented as a set of mental states, some in awareness and some not. (I am indebted to Dreyfus and Wakefield, 1988, for this way of representing Freud's epistemology.)

The view of the mind as a layered collection of representations leads directly to Freud's well-known archeological metaphor, to the model of *depth* psychology, and to the family of tropes representing the mind as a storehouse of memories and conflicts. It leads to the model of neurotic distress as somehow situated *in* the mind. By contrast, as Dreyfus and Wakefield (1988) have made clear, the problems of the patient and his difficulties with the world could just as well be represented by a *breadth* psychology in which the mind is not mentioned at all. In this view (inspired in particular by Heidegger and Merleau-Ponty), there is no need to believe that the objects in the world have a fixed representation in the mind, taking a library or an archive as the model. In their theory:

> The shared practices into which we are socialized provide a background understanding of what counts as objects, what counts as human beings, and ultimately what counts as real, on the basis of which we can direct our mind toward particular things and people. (Dreyfus and Wakefield, 1988, p. 275)

This background understanding or clearing *(Lichtung)* can be compared to the illumination in a room.

> The illumination allows us to perceive objects, but is not itself an object towards which the eye can be directed. [Merleau-Ponty] argues that this clearing can be correlated with our bodily skills and thus with the bodily stance we take towards people and things.

The metaphor of the clearing (breadth) may not necessarily be superior to the metaphor or archeology (depth), but that is not the point. What seems clear is how difficult it is to believe in both at the same time. If we think of the mind as a collection of representations of the world, each idea having a fixed meaning, then it is tempting to see therapy as an attempt to rearrange this collection and change their relation to awareness (the metaphor of therapy as ''shrinking'' tries to capture this attempt). It is also tempting to see the world as a fixed reality through which we move and in which we live. The view of the world as a given set of objects, each having a fixed meaning, leads naturally to Freud's metaphor of free association in which the patient is represented as as passenger on a train, reporting the changing scene (the contents of his mind) to his seatmate, the analyst.

If, on the other hand, the world is not a collection of fixed objects but a shifting set of meanings, the names of which depend on who is looking, then the patient's view through the train window is not so easy to either capture or understand. If the world depends for its description on who is looking, then the representations in your head may be significantly different from the representations in mine. The meaning and usefulness of empathy are immediately brought into question. And if problems in living are a function of problems in categorization, then attention should be focused on how the world is seen rather than how it is stored. If the meaning of an object depends on who is looking and his sense of what it is used for, then it follows that experiences will always be colored by issues of time and place. The absence of early memories, for example, could be seen, using this metaphor, as the problem of having access to specific codes—not as the outcome of repression.

The well-known theory of Ernst Schachtel (1947) makes use of this alternative model. According to this formulation, infantile experiences are registered in a language which is more responsive to the emotional, nonverbal, sensual, and positional correlates of experience. Many of these experiences impinge on the child before his language is well developed. As he moves into an adult world, he acquires new categories of meaning and classification, categories which "are not suitable vehicles to receive and reproduce experience of the quality and intensity typical of early childhood" (1947, p. 4).

We begin to see in more detail how metaphor can contract as well as enlarge our view of the world. Steeped in the archeological metaphor and trained to believe in a real unconscious which has both depth and content, we may be somewhat shocked to be told that these are only figures of speech and that alternative metaphors are also available which might make even better sense of the clinical findings. The die is cast when we lose sight of the metaphoric nature of the theory. A dead metaphor, as noted, comes close to being confused with what we are trying to describe. Despite Freud's sensitivity to this issue, he frequently overlooked the distinction between model and observation and tended to treat his metaphor as if it were a confirmed piece of reality. Many of his followers have made the same mistake.

The danger of reification becomes all the greater when we are working with free-floating metaphors—the kind that psychoanalysis contains in abundance. Uncoupled from the clinical observation, unresponsive (because of their global nature) to subtle changes in observation, the central Freudian images threaten to completely dominate our view of the discipline and fool us into thinking that precise explanation is just over the horizon, that our main task is one of validation, not discovery, and that the main outlines of the theory have long since been settled. In his 1979 Presidential address, Kaplan states that "it is becoming much more evident that any progress in psychoanalysis must include our evaluation of the psychoanalytic process . . . with the hope of verifying the data of observation" (1981, p. 19). Kaplan's address emphasizes confirmation over disconfirmation and carries the implicit message that Freud's guiding metaphors are largely correct. Psychoanalysis is represented as a science which has now entered its final phase.

From a more skeptical point of view, prospects are not quite so bright. We still seem to be in the early stages of choosing the right metaphor; many of our favorite models have not developed much beyond their early formulations; and most sobering of all, we have no metaphor which has been turned into algebra. When the metaphor becomes free-floating and uncoupled from the clinical observation, the danger becomes all the greater. Shielded from elaboration or emendation, the chosen mataphor becomes all that more easily reified, and instead of a provisional model, we are left with a fully formed structure which masquerades as science.

REFERENCES

Berlin, I. (1976). *Vico and Herder: Two Studies in the History of Ideas.* New York: Viking.

Bettelheim, B. (1983). *Freud and Man's Soul.* New York: Knopf.

Carveth, D. (1984). The analyst's metaphors: A deconstructionist perspective. *Psychoanalysis and Contemporary Thought* 7: 491–560.

Dreyfus, H., and Wakefield, J. (1988). Alternative philosophical conceptualizations of psychopathology. In *Hermeneutics and Psychological Theory: Interpretive Perspectices on Personality, Psychotherapy, and Psychopathology,* edited by B. Messer et al. New Brunswick: Rutger University Press.

Edelson, J. (1983). Freud's use of metaphor. *The Psychoanalytic Study of the Child* 38: 17–59.

Freud, S. (1914). On Narcissism. *Standard Edition* 14: 73–102. New York: Norton, 1957.

———. (1915a). Instincts and their vicissitudes. *Standard Edition* 14: 109–140. New York: Norton, 1957.

———. (1915b). Repression. *Standard Edition* 14: 141–158. New York: Norton, 1957.

———. (1915c). The unconscious. *Standard Edition* 14: 161–215. New York: Norton, 1957.

———. (1932). The dissection of the psychical personality (New introductory lectures on psycho-analysis). *Standard Edition* 22: 57–80. New York: Norton, 1964.

Grünbaum, A. (1984). *The Foundations of Psychoanalysis.* Berkeley: University of California Press.

Hesse, M. (1980). *Revolutions and Reconstructions in the Philosophy of Science*. Bloomington.: Indiana University Press.

Holzman, P. S. (1985). Psychoanalysis: Is the therapy destroying the science? *Journal of the American Psychoanalytic Association* 33: 725–770.

Kaplan, A. (1981). From discovery to validation. *Journal of the American Psychoanalytic Association* 29: 3–26.

Lakoff, G., and Johnson, M. (1980). *Metaphors We Live By*. Chicago: University of Chicago Press.

Ornston, D. (1985). Freud's conception is different from Strachey's. *Journal of the American Psychoanalytic Association* 33: 379–412.

Schachtel, E. (1947). On memory and childhood amnesia. *Psychiatry* 10: 1–26.

PART II

THE CLASSICAL CONTRIBUTION AND ITS CRITICAL EVALUATION

INTRODUCTION

When Freud discussed the first attempts to develop psychoanalytic studies of literature (using revealing expressions such as "the regions into which psycho-analysis might penetrate," and "these attempted invasions"), he noted, "Among the strictly scientific applications of analysis to literature, Rank's exhaustive work on the theme of incest easily takes the first place" (Freud [1914] 1957, p. 37). Indeed, Otto Rank—initially Freud's young secretary-assistant and later on the first prominent nonmedical analyst—was outstanding in the early analytic circle in his systematic scholarship in literature and in cultural history.

The chapter included here is the concluding section of Rank's essay, *The Double (Der Doppelgänger),* originally published in *Imago*—edited by Freud—in 1914. Some of the questions it raises are further explored in Freud's "The 'Uncanny' " *(Das unheimliche* [1919] 1955).

Rank introduces numerous examples of the double in literature: works of Heinz Ewers, E.T.A. Hoffmann, Oscar Wilde, Edgar Allan Poe, Fyodor Dostoyevsky, and many others. He studies the biographies of some of these authors, describing them as "decidedly pathological personalities who, in more than one direction, went beyond even that limit of neurotic conduct otherwise allowed to the artist" (Rank [1914] 1971, p. 35). He discusses anthropological theories regarding the double in numerous cultures, developed by Frazer and others (we may notice an old-fashioned condescending attitude to "the primitives," widespread at the time), and concludes with the theoretical explication we reproduce.

Although written at a time when Rank was a loyal disciple of Freud, we may notice in his formulations first glimpses of his more original, later views regarding the centrality of narcissism (foreshadowing Kohut in separating it from a drive-defence model), the power of splitting as distinct from repression (a notion that disappeared and later reappeared in Freud's work; see Berman 1981) and the quest for immortality.

Jones's essay, "Hamlet and Oedipus," is a thorough exploration of Freud's oedipal interpretation, first mentioned in the 1897 letter to Fliess and spelled out in *The Interpretation of Dreams* (Freud [1900] 1953, pp. 264–66). Jones developed his study of *Hamlet* from a 1910 paper, through several revisions and expansions, to a book published in 1949. We include here two central segments of this book, appearing in the chapters "The Psycho-analytical Solution" and "Tragedy and the Mind of the Infant."

Jones represents the classical tradition at its best, thanks to his thorough knowledge and use of all studies of Shakespeare available at the time; this enables him to go, in many points, beyond Freud's intuitive impression. Still, the basic conception is identical, and it invited many critical and polemical evaluations throughout the years. One may mention questions regarding the artificiality of reducing Hamlet's matricidal impulse to a theory-derived patricidal core (see Wertham, in Faber 1970), or the risk that a narrow emphasis on Hamlet's personal pathology may blind us to his insights into the surrounding social pathology (see Friedman and Jones 1963).

Dan Jacobson (1989) questions the basic assumptions of Jones regarding the hidden a priori "meaning" of works of literature and their direct relation to the unconscious mind of the author:

> By contrast, the author argues that works like *Hamlet* actually subvert the distinctions we ordinarily make between conscious and unconscious intention, between manifest and latent content, even between language and the material world. It is suggested that *Hamlet* itself is peculiarly concerned with the problems and dangers arising from the attempts by Shakespeare's characters to interpret each other's acts and words. Every such interpretation is shown to be ultimately an act of self-revelation. This, the argument concludes, is true not only for the characters in the play, but for each of its readers. (p. 271.)

This is an excellent example of the more mutual image of analyst–analysand interaction, as related to literature: We may turn to the play to better understand our dilemmas as interpreters; Shakespeare may interpret us. The centrality of mutual interpretations (and misinterpretations) within drama was also studied by Simon (1985).

The paper by Kris is another lucid and thoughtful example of the classical tradition, basically interpreting literary figures as patients. Still, we may notice—especially in the last part—the sophistication and caution of the author, whose original training in art history made him well-equipped to challenge and change psychoanalytic notions of aesthetics (Kris 1952), developing the understanding of art as communication, as "an invitation to common experience in the mind" (p. 39), and giving the needed weight to the centrality of ambiguity. His call to avoid an exclusive focus on plot and character is not sufficiently fulfilled in the paper itself, but—alongside his warning against shortcuts in equating biographical data and themes in the writer's work—helps prepare the stage for the more mature stages in psychoanalytic studies of literature.

Phyllis Greenacre surpasses most analytic authors in the thoroughness of biographical scholarship, though she appears to fully succumb to the temptation—against which Kris warns us, p. 164 in this volume—"to detect a neat connection between the artist and one of his characters." Her study of Swift and *Gulliver,* reproduced here, and its counterpart study of Carroll and *Alice* (both incorporated in Greenacre 1955), were followed by papers exploring the impact of talent on the childhood of artists, the family romance of the artist (studying Gogol, Rilke, and others), and the relation of the impostor to the artist (e.g., Thomas Mann and his protagonist Felix Krull; all in Greenacre 1971).

A thoughtful critique of Greenacre's work on Swift and *Gulliver* is offered by Reed (1976), who attempts to demonstrate how Greenacre's "conventions of reading involve a leap from the fictional to the real" (p. 186):

> Gulliver has become part of the patient Swift, detachable from his text, material for a case presentation. Ironically, the conventions which equate fiction with fantasy and consider Gulliver part of Swift, create a new fiction, Gulliver-Swift as the patient, a fiction which obliterates the very text to which the literary critic listens. (Reed 1976, p. 187)

Greenacre's overconfident interpretations may be discerned when she "invents" biographical events that would fit into her theoretical scheme (e.g., "his own nurse had a baby during the time of his stay with her, of whom he was inordinately jealous"). She also uses uncritically Swift's autobiography, written at age 70, assuming it represents a truthful account of his childhood, and not considering the possibility that some events in it (e.g., his kidnapping) may represent a personal myth, an expression of failing memory (as Reed suggess), or of the emotional needs of the author at the time of writing (I would add). Autobiography, after all, is also a kind of fiction, and cannot provide an independent basis for interpretation. (For a different view of *Gulliver,* see Freedman 1991).

Of the critical work evaluating classic psychoanalytic studies of literature—

including Baudry (1984) and Reed (1985), who are represented in this collection by their own original work—I chose three poignant articles.

Bonime and Eckardt, who are both psychoanalysts practicing in N.Y.C., persuasively discuss the pitfalls in the "literary figure as patient" tradition, also criticized by Slochower (1971, p. 109: "To treat characters in literature as living people is to confuse the esthetic and symbolic with the factual and the existent"), Skura (1981, pp. 29–57), and others. One may question, however, Bonime and Eckardt's emphasis on this approach as "not a legitimate contribution." Such a superego-based judgment overlooks the emotional (transferential) need of so many readers (not only analysts) to imagine literary figures as real persons, and to try and understand them on this level. This tendency cannot be outlawed, though their arguments suggest the need to supplement such an imaginary exercise with a more sober critical analysis, and integrate it into a higher level interpretation that will recognize the significance of figures as "part of a state of mind which pervades the work" (Skura 1981, p. 56).

A point missing in their discussion is the lack of a dynamic analyst–analysand interaction when fictional figures are "put on the couch." This issue is discussed by Werman, psychoanalyst on the faculty of the Duke University Medical Center in Durham, N.C., whose meta-analysis of psychoanalytic readings of *Antigone* elegantly demonstrates the risks of naive, overzealous, and overconfident readings that bypass the full appreciation of the cultural and literary context of the work, and do not pay sufficient attention to the subjective emotional dimension of reader/spectator response. (For additional readings of *Antigone,* see Almansi 1991, and Simon 1985).

Spitz's chapter deals primarily with the visual arts, but is very relevant to the psychoanalytic study of literature. She focuses on Freud, but her comments are relevant to generations of analysts who followed in his footsteps in developing the pathographic tradition, the "author as patient" model (e.g., Greenacre). Spitz teaches aesthetics in psychiatry at the Cornell University Medical College.

When Spitz expanded this into a chapter in her book (Spitz 1985), she added a useful discussion of Greenacre's and Niederland's developmental models, derived from their experiences in analyzing artists. She also drew some valuable conclusions regarding the limits of pathography. "Pathography presents an artist-as-patient paradigm of psychoanalytic interpretation. It assumes that creative activity does not represent for the artist a real 'working through' of basic conflict . . . This view severely limits the pathographer's capacity to deal with aspects of creating that are relatively conflict-free and prejudices him in favor of the Romantic notion of the artist as deeply troubled, as limited in some way'' (Spitz 1985, p. 51).

Later on Spitz adds: ''Pathography does not sufficiently take into account the countertransferential aspects of the interpretative process'' (p. 51). The lack of an examination of the critic's own emotional needs may make him blind to his biases. Also, pathography ''fails to deal with those aspects of the artist's intention that arise in response to the reality of the developing work itself, which has an existence in a medium, in a tradition, and in a reality external to the psyche of the artist'' (p. 52).

Although classical pathography may be rare today, we may notice (with Ellsworth 1980) that the ''author as patient''equation may reappear in newer work, equating the literary text and the analytic text without recognizing the substantial differences in the context of their creation and in the goals of writer and analysand.

Finally, let me add one comment: The narrow focus of traditional psychoanalytic scholars on the author as patient or on the figure as patient, and at times on the figure as a thinly disguised author (still a patient), prevented so far a serious exploration of the complex dynamics in the relationship of authors to their figures. Rank hints at the possibility of the protagonist experienced by the writer as his double, and at the splits such an experience may undergo; Kris mentions the author's potential identification with numerous figures.

We may assume that the source of each figure is the author's representational world—self-representations and object representations. Self-representations, as Freud suggested, are often based on the internalization of objects, so these two levels are inseparable. Such representations undergo very complex unconscious processes—splits, condensations, displacements, reversals —which are similar to those creating dream figures and dissociated self-identities (Berman 1981, 1982). Spontaneous potential figures may appear in the author's imagination as a consequence of such unconscious processes, and then they undergo conscious elaborations influenced by many aspects of the author's goals, values, literary preferences, need for privacy, and so forth. Of course, only a thorough and rich information regarding the process in which a book or story was created makes it possible to begin such a study, and when such information is limited the risk of projective speculation is intensified.

Giving up the search for causes in the author's childhood or in the figure's pseudo-childhood may be difficult for psychoanalysts, traditionally dependent on "originology" ("the habitual effort to find the 'causes' of a man's whole development in his childhood conflicts," Erikson 1969, p. 98). However, as recent contributions in clinical psychoanalysis demonstrate, thorough work in the "here and now" (e.g., the reader's experience of the text) may provide a better pathway to the unconscious than a speculative discussion of "then and there."

REFERENCES

Almansi, R. J. 1991. A psychoanalytic study of Sophocles' *Antigone*. *Psychoanalytic Quarterly* 60: 69–85.

Baudry, F. 1984. An essay on method in applied psychoanalysis. *Psychoanalytic Quarterly* 53: 551–81.

Berman, E. 1981. Multiple personality: Psychoanalytic perspectives. *International Journal of Psycho-Analysis* 62: 283–300.

———. 1982. "Collective figures" and the representational world. *Psychoanalytic Review* 70: 553–57.

Ellsworth, P. 1980. Regarding the author as patient. *New Literary History* 12: 187–97.

Erikson, E. H. 1969. *Gandhi's truth*. New York: Norton.

Faber, M. D. 1970. *The design within: Psychoanalytic approaches to Shakespeare*. New York: Science House.

Freud, S. [1900] 1953. The interpretation of dreams. *Standard Edition*, vol. 4. London: Hogarth.

———. [1914] 1957. On the history of the psychoanalytic movement. *Standard Edition*, vol. 14. London: Hogarth.

———. [1919] 1955. The "uncanny." *Standard Edition*, vol. 17. London: Hogarth.

Freedman, W. 1991. Gulliver's voyage to the country of the Houyhnhnms: Adolescent asceticism, idealization, and ideology. *International Review of Psycho-Analysis* 18: 527–39.

Friedman, N., and R. M. Jones. 1963. On the mutuality of the Oedipus complex: Notes on the Hamlet case. *American Imago* 20: 107–31.

Greenacre, P. 1955. *Swift and Carroll*. New York: International Universities Press.

———. 1971. *Emotional growth*. New York: International Universities Press.

Jacobson, D. 1989. Hamlet's other selves. *International Review of Psycho-Analysis* 16: 265–72.

Kris, E. 1952. *Psychoanalytic explorations in art*. New York: International Universities Press.

Rank, O. [1914] 1971. *The double*. Chapel Hill: University of North Carolina Press.

Reed, G. 1976. Dr. Greenacre and Captain Gulliver. Notes on conventions of reading and interpretation. *Literature and Psychology* 26: 175–90.

———.1985. Psychoanalysis, psychoanalysis appropriated, psychoanalysis applied. *Psychoanalytic Quarterly* 54: 234–69.

Simon, B. 1985. "With cunning delays and evermounting excitement": or, what thickens the plot in psychoanalysis and tragedy? In *Psychoanalysis: The vital issues*, edited by J. Gedo and G. Pollock, vol. II. New York: International Universities Press.

Skura, M.A. 1981. *The literary use of the psychoanalytic process*. New Haven and London: Yale University Press.

Slochower, H. 1971. The psychoanalytic approach to literature: Some pitfalls and promises. *Literature and Psychology* 21: 107–10.

Spitz, E. H. 1985. *Art and psyche: A study in psychoanalysis and aesthetics*. New Haven and London: Yale University Press.

5. Narcissism and the Double

Otto Rank

It is the phantom of our own Self, whose intimate relationship with, and deep effect upon, our spirit casts us into hell or transports us into Heaven.

—E. T. A. Hoffmann

By no means can psychoanalysis consider it as a mere accident that the death significance of the double appears closely related to its narcissistic meaning —as also noted elsewhere in Greek legend. Our reason for not being satisfied with Frazer's account lies in the fact that his explanation of the Narcissus fable only shifts the problem to the question of the origin and significance of the underlying superstitious ideas. If we accept the basis of Frazer's assumption and look first for an explanation of why the idea of death in the Narcissus legend, associated with the sight of the double, should have been masked especially by the theme of self-love, [1] then we are compelled next to think of the generally effective tendency to exclude with particular stubbornness the idea of death, which is extremely painful to our self-esteem. To this tendency correspond the frequent euphemistic substitute-ideas, which in superstition gradually come to overlie the original death meaning. In the myth of the Fates, in the changed forms of which the goddess of love takes the place of the goddess of death, Freud has shown that this tendency aims at establishing an equivalent as distant and pleasant as possible—the reason being an understandable endeavor to compensate.[2] This development of the motif, however, is not capricious. It only refers to an old, original identity of these two figures. This identity is consciously based upon the conquest of death by a new procreation and finds it deepest foundation in the relationship to the mother.

That the death meaning of the double likewise tends to be replaced by the love meaning can be seen from manifestly late, secondary, and isolated traditions. According to these traditions, girls are able to see their sweethearts in the mirror under the same conditions in which death or misfortune also reveal themselves.[3] And in the exception that this does not apply to vain girls we may recognize a reference to narcissism, which interferes with the choice of a love object. Similarly, in the Narcissus legend there is a late but psychologically valid version which reports that the handsome youth thought he saw his beloved twin sister (his sweetheart) in the water. Besides this plainly narcissistic infatuation, the death meaning too has so much validity that the close association and deep relationship of both complexes are removed from any doubt.

The Narcissus meaning by its nature is not alien to the motif of the double, which exhibits meanings of the spirit and of death in the folklore material. This observation is shown not simply from the cited mythological traditions of creation by self-reflection, but above all by the literary treatments which cause the Narcissus theme to appear in the forefront along with the problem of death, be it directly or in pathological distortion.

Along with fear and hate of the double, the narcissistic infatuation in one's own image and self is most strongly marked in Oscar Wilde's *Dorian Gray.* "The sense of his own beauty came on him like a revelation" at the first view of his portrait, when he "stood gazing at the shadow of his own liveliness."[4] At the same time, the fear seizes him that he could become old and different—a fear closely associated with the idea of death: "When I find that I am growing old, I shall kill myself" (p. 42). Dorian, who is directly characterized as Narcissus,[5] loves his own image and therefore his own body: "Once, in boyish mockery of Narcissus, he had kissed . . . those painted lips that now smiled so cruelly at him. Morning after morning he had sat before the portrait, wondering at its beauty, almost enamoured of it, as it seemed to him at times" (p. 126). "Often . . . he himself would creep upstairs to the locked room . . . and stand with a mirror in front of the portrait . . . looking now at the evil and aging face on the canvas, and now at the fair young face that laughed back at him from the polished glass. . . . He grew more and more enamoured of his own beauty . . ." (p. 150).

Tied in with this narcissistic attitude is his imposing egoism, his inability to love, and his abnormal sexual life. The intimate friendships with young men, for which Hallward reproaches him, are attempts to realize the erotic infatuation with his own youthful image.[6] From women he is able to obtain only the crudest sensual pleasures, without being capable of a spiritual relationship. Dorian shares this defective capacity for love with almost all double-heroes.[7] He himself says in a significant quotation that this deficiency arises from his narcissistic fixation on his own ego " 'I wish I could love,' cried Dorian Gray, with a deep note of pathos in his voice. 'But I seem to have lost the passion, and forgotten the desire. *I am too much concentrated on myself* [Rank's emphasis]. My own personality has become a burden to me. I want to escape, to go away, to forget' " (p. 232). In a particularly clear *defensive form, The Student of Prague* shows how the *feared* self obstructs the love for a woman; and in Wilde's novel it becomes clear that fear and hate with respect to the double-self are closely connected with the narcissistic love for it and with the resistance of this love. The more Dorian despises his image, which is becoming old and ugly, the more intensive does his self-love become: "The very sharpness of the contrast used to quicken his sense of pleasure. He grew more and more enamoured of his own beauty . . ." (p. 150).

This erotic attitude toward one's own self, however, is only possible because along with it the defensive feelings can be discharged by way of the hated and feared double. Narcissus is ambivalent toward his ego for something in him seems to resist exclusive self-love. The form of defense against narcissicism finds expression principally in two ways: in fear and revulsion before one's own image, as seen in Dorian and most of the characters of Jean Paul; or, as in the majority of cases, in the loss of the shadow-image or mirror-image.[8] This loss, however, is no loss at all, as the persecutions show. On the contrary, it is strengthening, a becoming independent and superiorly strong, which in its turn only shows the exceedingly strong interest in one's own self. Thus the apparent contradiction—the loss of the shadow-image or mirror-image represented as pursuit—is understood as a representation of the opposite, the recurrence of what is repressed in that which represses (see the concluding paragraph of this chapter).

This same mechanism is shown by the dénouement of madness, almost regularly leading to suicide, which is so frequently linked with pursuit by the double, the self. Even when the depiction does not measure up to Dostoyevsky's unsurpassable clinical exactitude, it does become clear that it is a question of paranoid ideas of pursuit and influencing to which the hero is prey by reason of his double. Since Freud's psychoanalytic clarification of paranoia, we know that this illness has as a basis "a fixation in narcissism," to which corresponds typical megalomania, the sexual overrating of oneself.[9] The stage of development from which paranoids regress to their original narcissism is sublimated homosexuality, against the undisguised eruption of which they defend themselves with the characteristic mechanism of projection. On the basis of this insight, it can easily be shown that the pursuit of the ill person regularly proceeds form the originally loved persons (or their surrogates).

The literary representations of the double-motif which describe the persecution complex confirm not only Freud's concept of the narcissistic disposition toward paranoia, but also, in an intuition rarely attained by the mentally ill, they reduce the chief pursuer to the ego itself, the person formerly loved most of all, and now direct their defense against it.[10] This view does not contradict the homosexual etiology of paranoia. We know, as was already mentioned, that the homosexual love object was originally chosen with a narcissistic attitude toward one's own image.

Connected with paranoid pursuit is yet another theme which deserves emphasis. We know that the person of the pursuer frequently represents the father or his substitute (brother, teacher, etc.), and we also find in our material that the double is often identified with the brother. It is clearest in Musset but also appears in Hoffmann *(The Devil's Elixirs, The Doubles)*, Poe, Dostoyevsky, and others. The appearance for the most part is as a twin and reminds us of the legend of the womanish Narcissus, for Narcissus thinks that he sees in his image his sister, who resembles him in every respect. That those writers who preferred the theme of the double also had to contend with the male sibling complex follows from the not infrequent treatment of fraternal rivalry in their other works. So Jean Paul, in the famous novel *The Twins,* has treated the theme of twin brothers who compete with each other, as has Maupassant in *Peter and John* and the unfinished novel *The Angelus,* Dostoyevksy in *The Brothers Karamasov,* and so on.[11]

Actually, and considered externally, the double is the rival of his prototype in anything and everything, but primarily in the love for woman—a trait which he may partly owe to the identification with the brother. One author expresses himself about his relationship in another connection: "The younger brother is accustomed, even in ordinary life, to be somehow similar to the elder, at least in external appearance. He is, as it were, a reflection of his fraternal self which has come to life; and on the account he is also a rival in everything that the brother sees, feels, and thinks."[12] What connection this identification might have with the narcissistic attitude may be shown by another statement by the same author: "The relationship of the older to the younger brother is analogous to that of the masturbator to himself."

From this fraternal attitude of rivalry toward the hated competitor in the love for the mother, the death wish and the impulse toward murder against the double becomes reasonably understandable,[13] even though the significance of the brother in this case does not exhaust our understanding. The theme of the brothers is not precisely the root of the belief in the double, but rather only an interpretation—well-determined, to be sure—of the doubtlessly purely subjective meaning of the double. This meaning is not sufficiently explained by the psychological statement that "the mental conflict creates the double," which corresponds to a "projection of inner turmoil" and the shaping of which brings about an inner liberation, an unburdening, even if at the price of the "fear of encounter." So "fear shapes from the ego-complex the terrifying phantom of the double," which "fulfills the secret, always suppressed wishes of his soul."[14] Only after determining this formal meaning of the double do the real problems arise, for we aim at an understanding of the psychological situation and of the attitude which together create such an inner division and projection.

The most prominent symptom of the forms which the double takes is a powerful consciousness of guilt which forces the hero no longer to accept the responsibility for certain actions of his ego, but to place it upon another ego, a double, who is either personified by the devil himself[15] or is created by making a diabolical pact. This detached personification of instincts and desires which were once felt to be unacceptable, but which can be satisfied without responsibility in this indirect way, appears in other forms of the theme as a beneficient admonitor (e.g., *William Wilson*) who is directly addressed as the "conscience" of the person (e.g., Dorian Gray, etc.). As Freud has demonstrated, this awareness of guilt, having various sources, measures on the one hand the distance between the ego-ideal and the attained reality; on the other, it is nourished by a powerful fear of death and creates strong tendencies toward self-punishment, which also imply suicide.[16]

After having stressed the narcissistic significance of the double in its positive meaning as well as in its various defensive forms, it still remains for us to understand more about the meaning of death in our material and to demonstrate its relationship to the meaning already gained. What the folkloric representations and several of the literary ones directly reveal is a tremendous thanatophobia, which refers to the defensive symptoms heretofore discussed to the extent that, in these, fear (of the image, of its loss, or of pursuit) formed the most prominent characteristic.

One motif which reveals a certain connection between the fear of death and the narcissistic attitude is the wish to remain forever young. On the one hand, this wish represents the libidinous fixation of the individual onto a definite development stage of the ego; and on the other, it expresses the fear of becoming old, a fear which is really the fear of death.[17] Thus Wilde's Dorian says, "When I find that I am growing old, I shall kill myself" (p. 42). Here we are at the significant theme of suicide, at which point a whole series of characters come to their ends while pursued by their doubles. Of this motif, apparently in such contradiction to the asserted fear of death, it can be shown precisely from its special application in this connection that it is closely relevant not only to the theme of thanatophobia, but also with narcissism. For these characters and their creators—as far as they attempted suicide or did carry it out (Raimund, Maupassant)—did not fear death; rather, the *expectation* of the unavoidable destiny of death is unbearable to them. As Dorian Gray expresses it: "I have no terror of Death. It is only *the coming* [Rank's emphasis] of Death that terrifies me" (p.231). The normally unconscious thought of the approaching destruction of the self—the most general example of the repression of an unendurable certainty—torments these unfortunates with the conscious idea of their eternal, eternal *[sic]* inability to return, an idea from which release is only possible in death. Thus we have the strange paradox of the suicide who voluntarily seeks death in order to free himself of the intolerable thanatophobia.

It could be objected that the fear of death is simply the expression of an overly strong instinct for self-preservation, insisting upon fulfillment. Certainly the only too-justified fear of death, seen as one of the fundamental evils of mankind, has its main root in the self-preservation instinct, the greatest threat to which is death. But this motivation is insufficient for pathological thanatophobia, which occasionally leads directly to suicide. In this neurotic constellation—in which the material to be repressed and against which the individual defends himself is finally and actually realized—it is a question of a complicated conflict in which, along with the ego-instincts serving self-preservation, the libidinous tendencies also function, which are merely rationalized in the conscious ideas of fear. Their unconscious participation explains fully the pathological fear arising here, behind which we must expect a portion of repressed libido. This, along with other already-known factors,[18] we believe we have found in that part of narcissism which feels just as intensely threatened by the idea of death as do the pure ego-instincts, and which thereupon reacts with the pathological fear of death and its final consequences.

As proof that the pure ego-interests of self-preservation cannot explain the pathological fear of death satisfactorily to other observers either, we cite the testimony of a researcher who is completely unprejudiced psychologically. Spiess, from whose work[19] we have borrowed many a documentation, expressed the view that "man's horror of death does not result merely from the natural love of life." He explains this with the following words:

> That, however, is not a dependency upon earthly existence, for man often hates that. . . . No, it is the love for the personality peculiar to him, found in his conscious possession, the love for his self, for the central self of his individuality, which attaches him to life. This *self-love* is an inseparable element of his being. In it is founded and rooted the instinct for self-preservation, and from it emerges the deep and powerful longing to escape death or the submergence into nothingness, and the hope of again awakening to a new life and to a new era of continuing development.[20] The thought of losing oneself is so unbearable for man, and it is this thought which makes death so terrible for him. . . . This hopeful longing may be criticized as childish vanity, foolish megalomania; the fact remains that it lives in our hearts; it influences and rules over our imagination and endeavors. (p.115)

This relationship is evident in all of its desirable clarity—indeed, downright plasticity—in literary material, although narcissistic self-assertion and self-exaggeration generally prevail there. The frequent slaying of the double, through which the hero seeks to protect himself permanently from the pursuits of his self, is really a suicidal act. It is, to be sure, in the painless form of slaying a different ego: an unconscious illusion of the splitting-off of a bad, culpable ego—a separation which, moreover, appears to be the precondition for every suicide. The suicidal person is unable to eliminate by direct self-destruction the fear of death resulting from the threat to his narcissism. To be sure, he seizes upon the only possible way out, suicide, but he is incapable of carrying it out other than by way of the phantom of a feared and hated double, because he loves and esteems his ego too highly to give it pain or to transform the idea of his destruction into the deed.[21] In this subjective meaning, the double turns out to be a functional expression of the psychological fact that an individual with an attitude of this kind cannot free himself from a certain phase of his narcissistically loved ego-development. He encounters it always and everywhere, and it contains his actions within a definite direction. Here, the allegorical interpretation of the double as a part of the ineradicable past gets its psychological meaning. What attaches the person to the past becomes clear, and why this assumes the form of the double is evident.[22]

Finally, the significance of the double as an embodiment of the soul—a notion represented in primitive belief and living on in our superstition—has close relevance to the previously discussed factors. It seems that the development of the primitive belief in the soul is largely analogous to the psychological circumstances demonstrated here by the pathological material—an observation which would seem to confirm anew the "agreement in the psychology of aborigines and of neurotics." This circumstance would also explain how the primitive conditions are repeated in the later mythical and artistic representations of the theme, specifically with particular emphasis on the libidinous factors which do not so clearly emerge in the primeval history but which nonetheless allowed us to form a conclusion about the less transparent primal phenomena.

Freud, by pointing out the animistic view of the world based on the power of thoughts, has justified our thinking of primitive man, just as of the child,[23] as being exquisitely narcissistic.[24] Also, the narcissistic theories of the creation of the world which he cites, just like the later philosophical systems based on the ego (e.g., Fichte), indicate that man is able to perceive the reality surrounding him mainly only as a reflection, or as a part, of his ego.[25] Likewise, Freud [see n. 24] has pointed out that it is death, ANANKE the implacable, which opposes the primitive man's narcissism and obliges him to turn over a part of his omnipotence to the spirits. Linked to this fact of death, however, which is forced upon man and which he constantly seeks to deny, are the first concepts of the soul, which can be traced in primitive peoples as well as those of advanced cultures.

Among the very first and most primitive concepts of the soul is that of the shadow, which appears as a faithful image of the body but of a lighter substance. It is true that Wundt contends that the shadow provided an original motif for the concept of the soul.[26] He believes that the "shadow-soul," the *alter ego,* as distinct from that of the body, "as far as we can tell has its sole source in dreams and visions."[27] But other researchers—Tylor, for example—have shown by a wealth of material that among primitive peoples designations of images or shadows predominate;[28] and Heinzelmann, who finds support in the most recent investigations, objects to Wundt on this point by showing in an abundance of examples "that here, too, it is a question of quite constant and extensively recurring views" (*loc. cit.*, p. 19 *[sic]*). Just as

Spencer justly asserts in the case of the child,[29] primitive man considers his shadow as something real, as a being attached to him, and he is confirmed in his view of it as a soul by the fact that the dead person (who is lying down) simply no longer casts a shadow.[30] From the experience of dreaming, man may have taken the proof for his belief that the viable ego might exist even after death; but only his shadow and his reflected image could have convinced him that he had a mysterious double even while he was alive.

The various taboos, precautions, and evasions which primitive man uses with regard to his shadow show equally well his narcissistic esteem of his ego and his tremendous fear of its being threatened. Primitive narcissism feels itself primarily threatened by the ineluctable destruction of the self. Very clear evidence of the truth of this observation is shown by the choice, as the most primitive concept of the soul, of an image as closely similar as possible to the physical self, hence a true double. The idea of death, therefore, is denied by a duplication of the self incorporated in the shadow or in the reflected image.

We have seen that among primitives the designations for shadow, reflected image, and the like, also serve for the notion "soul," and that the most primitive concept of the soul of the Greeks, Egyptians, and other culturally prominent peoples coincides with a double which is essentially identical with the body.[31] Then, too, the concept of the soul as a reflected image assumes that it resemble an exact copy of the body. Indeed, Negelein speaks directly of a "primitive monism of body and soul," by which he means that the idea of the soul originally coincided completely with that of a sound body. As proof he cites the fact that the Egyptians made images of the dead in order to protect them from eternal destruction.[32] Such a material origin, then, does the idea of the soul have. Later, it became an immaterial concept with the increasing reality-experience of man, who does not want to admit that death is everlasting annihilation.

Originally, to be sure, the question of a belief in immortality was of no concern; but the complete ignorance of the idea of death arises from primitive narcissism, as it is evidenced even in the child. For the primitive, as for the child, it is self-evident that he will continue to live,[33] and death is conceived of as an unnatural, magically produced event.[34] Only with the acknowledgement of the idea of death, and of the fear of death consequent upon threatened narcissism, does the wish for immortality as such appear. This wish really restores the original naive belief in an eternally continuing existence in partial accommodation to the experience of death gained in the meantime. In this way, therefore, the primitive belief in souls is originally nothing else than a kind of belief in immortality which energetically denies the power of death;[35] and even today the essential content of the belief in the soul—as it subsists in religion, superstition, and modern cults—has not become other, nor much more, than that.[36] The thought of death is rendered supportable by assuring oneself of a second life, after this one, as a double. As in the threat to narcissism by sexual love, so in the threat of death does the idea of death (originally averted by the double) recur in this figure who, according to general superstition, announces death or whose injury harms the individual.[37]

So, then, we see primitive narcissism as that in which the libidinous interests and those serving self-preservation are concentrated upon the ego with equal intensity, and which in the same way protect against a series of threats by reactions directed against the complete annihilation of the ego, or else toward its damage and impairment. These reactions do not result merely from the real fear which, as Visscher says, can be termed the defensive form of an exceedingly strong instinct for self-preservation. They arise also from the fact that the primitive, along with the neurotic, exhibits this "normal" fear, increased to a pathological degree, which "cannot be explained from the actual experiences of terror."[38] We have derived the libidinous component, which plays a part here, from the equally intensively felt threat to narcissism, which resists the utter immolation of the ego just as much as it resists its dissolution in sexual love. That it is actually primitive narcissism which resists the threat is shown quite clearly by the reactions in which we see the threatened narcissism assert itself with heightened intensity: whether it be in the form of pathological self-love as in Greek legend or in Oscar Wilde, the representative of the modern esthete; or in the defensive form of the pathological fear of one's self, often leading to paranoid insanity and appearing personified in the pursuing shadow, mirror-image, or double. On the other hand, in the same phenomena of defense the threat also recurs, against which the individual wants to protect and assert himself. So it happens that the double, who personified narcissistic self-love, becomes an unequivocal rival in sexual love; or else, originally created as a wish-defense against a dreaded eternal destruction, he reappears in superstition as the messenger of death.[39]

NOTES

1. Friedrich Wieseler, *Narkissos* (Götingen, 1856) conceives of Narcissus as a malign spirit of death (pp. 76 ff.), but also relates the myth to cold egoism (pp. 37, 74).
2. S. Freud, "Das Motiv der Kästchenwahl," *Imago,* II (1913), 257–66 ["The Theme of the Three Caskets," chap. 1, this volume].
3. Also when the meaning of death, as we have seen, has changed into a general indication of the future, the transition to a meaning of happiness (love, wealth) is easily provided. The wish-fantasies of a promising expectation take the place of an unavoidable gloomy future.
4. [Wilde, *The Picture of Dorian Gray* (Cleveland and N.Y., 1946), pp. 40–41.]
5. Hallward had previously painted him like this also: "You had leant over the still pool of some Greek woodland, and seen in the water's silent silver the marvel of your own face" [Wilde, *op. cit.*, pp. 135–36.]
6. On the significance of narcissism for the homosexual predilection and its choice of love-object, see my "Beitrag zum Narzissimus," *Jahrbuch für Psychoanalytische und Psychopathologische Forschungen,* III (1912), 401–26, as well as the works of Freud, Sadger, and others, on which it is based. Sadger has already called attention to the relationship of the double to narcissism and to various sexual fantasies; see "Psychiatrisch-Neurologisches in psychoanalytischer Beleuchtung," *Zentralblatt f. d. Gesamtgeb. d. Medizin* (1908), Nos. 7 and 8. A pathologically distinct narcissism is found in the interesting self-observation of a man who likes to talk a great deal with his second self: "Especially in the evening I take a chair and mirror and for almost an hour contemplate my face. . . . Then I lie in bed, take the mirror, smile at myself, and think: what a pity it is that no one sees you now . . . you are a girl, completely so. Then I kiss myself in the mirror; that is, I slowly move the mirror to my lips, gazing at myself therein. In this way, I kiss my second self and admire his good appearance." Also, he calls his second self a "sorry fellow" *(Zentralblatt für Psychoanalyze,* IV [1914], 415).
7. It seems a subtle poetic touch when Lenau gives a narcissistic justification to the Swedish legend of the connection of the loss of one's shadow with infertility:

   By the lake stands Anna, dreaming,
   Gazing at the waters bright,
   Sees her beauty at her gleaming,
   Self-reflected, feels delight.

   Speaks: "O beauty of the rarest,
   Wondrous virgin, canst reply,
   Sweden's maids of all the fairest,
   Am I thou? and art thou I?"

   From the lake's green borders bending
   Downward to her image near,
   From her breast her garments rending,
   Anna sees her bosom bare.

   Downward does she gaze, admiring,
   Doubting, blissful, at the sight;
   And the form, herself desiring,
   Stares, transported with delight.

With the gestures so enraptured,
Anna sees her beauty grow,
Which her image now has captured,
And to her enthralled, doth show.

"Would that thus I be forever!"
Cries she, self-enamoured, vain,
"Would that th'imaged self go never!"
Hark! the rushing winds bring rain!

And her likeness now is vanished
In the foaming water's swirl;
Like a dream, to nothing banished,
Sees herself the hapless girl.

Then the old woman appears, and warns her of the danger to her beauty from bearing children:

"Oh, then do they *shadow* query [Rank's emphasis]:
Art thou mine, ye cheeks so wan?
These my eyes, so hollow, weary?
And thou'lt weep into the pond."

She demands of the old woman that her beauty never pass away, and does enjoy this favor for fully seven years:

Oft, with bolted door's protection,
Is she all unseen alone,
Darts her gaze to her reflection,
Feasts upon herself so shown.

[See *Lenaus Werke,* ed. C., A. von Bloedau (Leipzig, n.d.), Part 1, pp. 315–26.]

8. What forms the defensive attitude toward the mirrored self can assume is shown by a trial which took place in 1913 in London. The following is cited from a report of the trial in a daily newspaper (December 9, 1913). A young lord had locked up his beautiful, unfaithful sweetheart for eight days' punishment in a room whose walls consisted of panes of plate glass. These had the purpose "of constantly offering her countenance to the young lady so that she might contemplate it, and vow to improve her ways in the sight of herself. In the course of the days and nights which the young girl spent partly awake, she felt such a horror of the everrecurrent image of her own face that her reason began to be confused. She continually attempted to avoid the reflection; yet from all sides her own image grinned and smiled at her. One morning, the old serving-woman was called in by a terrible rumpus: Miss R. was striking the reflecting walls with both fists; fragments were flying around and into her face, but she paid no heed to them; she kept on smashing, with only the purpose of no longer seeing the image of which she had conceived such a horror. The physician who was called in stated that a frenzy had broken out in her which probably had become incurable, and attributed the cause to the solitude in the room, in which the young girl had had nothing to look at except her mirrored image." The terrible result of this punishment indicates how greatly she was affected psychologically.

Eduard Fuchs, in the supplementary volume, *The Aging of Gallantry,* of his *Illustrierte Sittengeschichte* (Munich, 1909–1912) states that places devoted to amorous activities were lavishly provided with mirrors, and he refers also the testimony of Casanova. In contrast to the [aforementioned] report, the following passage is cited from Fuchs: "She was surprised by the marvel of seeing, without moving, her charming person in a thousand different ways. Her likeness was multiplied by the mirrors—thanks to an ingenious arrangement of the candles—and offered her a new spectacle, from which she was unable to avert her gaze" (*ibid.* p. 16).

In a variant of the Snow White fairy tale from Rumanian Transylvania, the foster-mother finally is locked up for punishment (of her vanity) in a room, the walls of which consist of nothing but mirrors.—Ernst Böklen, *Schneewittchen-Studien* [in *Mythologische Bibliothek* (Leipzig, 1915), Vol. VII, fasc. 3] p. 51.

9. S. Freud, "Psychoanalytische Bemerkungen über einen autobiographisch beschriebenen Fall von Paranoia (Dementia paranoides)," 1911 ["Psychoanalytic Notes on an Autobiographical Account of a Case of Paranoia," *S.E.*, Vol. 12].
10. The significance of the pursuer's possibly being of the other sex in the picture of paranoia cannot be discussed here. A counterpart to paranoid illness as a consequence of defending narcissism is shown by Raimund's presentation of Rappelkopf's cure of his paranoid delusion by deliberately introducing the double. Also, Rappelkopf's ideas of being influenced proceed primarily from his wife, by whom he feels persecuted and from whom he flees in order "tenderly to make a wife" of solitude. But here the author succeeds in reversing the projection: instead of loving herself and hating others, the hero learns to love others and to hate himself.
11. Besides these, cf. the play *Brüder* (1902) by J. E. Poritzky, the author of several stories of the double; cf. also the play of the same title by Paul Lindau (after the novel by the same author), who likewise gave particular interest to the theme of the double. The comedy of mixed identities based on the motif of twins permits the humorous resolution of tragic fraternal rivalry.
12. J. B. Schneider, "Das Geschwisterproblem," *Gerschlecht und Gesellschaft,* VIII (1913), 381.
13. So also does the sympathy which makes of the rival a sort of protective spirit *(William Wilson),* or even a person who sacrifices himself for the welfare of his double—e.g., as in Dickens' *Tale of Two Cities,* in which the doubles love the same girl (rivalry), and one of them permits himself to be executed for the other. In this way, the original death wish, even though in altered form, is realized, after all, by the elimination of the rival.
14. Emil Lucka, "Dostojewski und der Teufel," *Literarisches Echo,* XVI (December 15, 1913), 6.
15. Dostoyevsky's *The Brothers Karamasov,* Jean Paul's *Confession,* or in *Satan's Memoirs,* cited by J. Sadger, "Psychiatrisch-Neurologisches in psychoanalytischen Beleuchtung," *Zenterblatt f.d. Gesamtgeb. d. Medizin* (1908), Nos. 7 and 8.
16. S. Freud, "Zur Einführung des Narzissmus," 1914 ["On Narcissism: An Introduction," S.E., vol. 14].
17. Cf. Adolf Wilbrandt's *[Der] Meister von Palmyra* [Stuttgart, 1889] for a representation of this theme, which has an interesting relationship to the love for a woman. [Cf. also Th. C. van Stockum, "Ein vergessenes deutsches Drama: Adolf Wilbrandts *Der Meister von Palmyra,*" in *Von Friedrich Nicolai bus Thomas Mann: Aufsätze zur deutschen und vergleichenden Literaturgeschichte* (Groningen, 1961), pp. 254–73.]
18. The defense against death wishes, originating in the libido (jealousy), toward closely related competitors (e.g., a brother) takes the form of turning against oneself (self-punishment). In a case of severe attacks of thanatophobia, the intermediate stage of death wishes directed against closely related persons could easily be demonstrated: the patient declares that these severe fears of death first applied to those members of his family nearest to him (mother, brother) before they attacked himself.

19. Edmund Speiss, *Entwicklungsgeschichte der Vonstellungen vom Zustande nach dem Tode* (Jena, 1877).
20. Here, taphephobia may be recalled, which Poe, Dostoyevsky, and other writers reveal. Merezhkovsky has shown this pathological fear of death to be the most important factor for the understanding of Tolstoy's transformation and personality; see *Tolstoi und Dostojewski*, tr. Carl von Gütschov (Leipzig, 1903), p. 27 f. Toward the close of the 1870's such an "onset of the fear of death," according to Merezhkovsky, "almost drove him to suicide" (p. 30). Merezhkovsky finds the source of this overwhelming fear of death logically in its reverse aspect—a strong love of life, manifested in the form of a boundless love for his body. He does not tire of emphasizing this love for his own self as being Tolstoy's most essential trait of character, even from the dim memory of his earliest childhood. Tolstoy mentions a bath when he was three or four years old as one of his happiest impressions: "For the first time I caught sight of my small body with the ribs visible on my chest, and grew fond of it." Merezhkovsky established that from this moment on, this attitude toward his body never left him for the remainder of his life (pp. 52 f.). Of Tolstoy's activity as a teacher, Merezhkovsky says: "An eternal Narcissus, he took pleasure in the reflection of his ego in the minds of the children. . . . In the children, too, he loved . . . only himself, himself alone" (p. 15). As a counterpart to Jean Paul's well-defined fear of seeing his own limbs, and as one example of several, we may refer to the passage in *Anna Karenina* where Vronsky complacently observes his "elastic calf," which he injured shortly before: "Earlier, too, he had felt the joyful awareness of his physical life, but never before had he loved himself—his body—so much" (p.53). "The love of oneself—everything begins and ends with this. Love or hate of oneself, only of oneself: these are the principal and only hubs—now apparent, now concealed—around which everything turns and moves in the first and perhaps most honest works of L. Tolstoy" (p. 12).
21. The narcissistic element of forbearance in the suicide of the double is shown very nicely by Gautier in the duelling scene of his already-mentioned short story *The Exchange of Souls:* "Each one actually had his own body before him and was compelled to plunge the steel into flesh which still had belonged to him two days previously. The duel developed into a kind of unforeseen suicide; and although Octave and the Count were both brave, they felt an instinctive terror when, with the daggers in their hands, they found themselves facing their own selves, ready to attack each other" (p.136). Such a situation is also indicated in Arthur Schnitzler's story *Casanova's Homecoming,* (N.Y.: Seltzer, 1923), in which Casanova, slipping away in the dawn from a purchased night of love, is challenged by his young twin and rival with whom, from the first moment, he feels strangely congenial. Casanova has thrown nothing but a coat around his naked body and, so that he be at no disadvantage confronting his opponent, the latter undressed also. "Lorenzi stood opposite him, as splendidly naked as a young god. 'If I should cast down my dagger,' though Casanova. 'If I embraced him?' " (p. 177).

Similarly, the writer creates for himself even in the main character a double whom he allows to die for himself. In primitive form this is evident in the well-known stories of the double life of one and the same person—e.g., in Stevenson's *The Strange Case of Doctor Jekyll and Mr. Hyde;* H.G. Wells' *Love and Mr. Lewisham;* Kipling's *At the End of the Passage,* and Wiedmann's *A Double Life*. With these are associated the related descriptions of [August Hoffmann von] Vestenhof's *The Man with the Three Eyes* [Munich, 1913] (a dual existence in one body) and the last book of the elder Rosny [J. Henri], *The Enigma of Givreuse,* which treats the duplication of one person (scientifically) and combines this with the rivalry of the two doubles for one girl. Most recently, the theme of the double has again been brought to the stage in George Kaiser's symbolic play *The Coral,* in which the multimillionaire flees into the soul of his double, his secretary, in order to partake of the latter's blissful childhood and guiltlessness. He murders the secretary and assumes his identity, although he is then considered to be the murderer of the multimillionaire and can prove his true identity only by means of the coral.

22. In his fragmentary work *Funeral Rites* (*Dziady,* 1823–32), Adam B. Mickiewicz has dealt with the problem of the double by having the suicide Gustav awaken at the moment of his death to a new, second life. In this new life he really experiences his first life up to the point of death, since he cannot live beyond this definite point (kind communication from Dr. [Paul?] Federn). We find this psychological mechanism typified in a *literal* way, from our point of view, in the song of the petrified youth, sung by a child as an interlude. Once a knight, von Twardow, takes an old castle by assault and finds, in a closed vault, a young man in chains standing before a mirror; little by little he is turning to stone through a magic spell. In the course of two centuries he is already petrified up to his chest; yet his face is still youthful and lively! The knight, knowing of the spell, is about to shatter the mirror, thereby liberating the youth, but the latter wishes to have the mirror in order to release himself from the curse:

   Took it, and signed—and paling, he gazes
   Into it with weeping and moan:
   And then for a kiss the mirror he raises—
   And turned all into stone.

   (See *Totenfeier,* translated into German by Siegfried Lipiner [Leipzig, 1887], p. 9.)

23. See Fritz Wittels, "Das Ich des Kindes," in *Die sexuelle Not* (Vienna, 1909), p. 109. Here Wittels describes very charmingly the awakening of the child's awareness of himself and its connection with egotism: "When I was still a small boy, I woke up one day with the overwhelming realization that I was an 'I,' that I looked externally, to be sure, like other children but nonetheless was fundamentally different and tremendously more important. I stood before the mirror, observed myself attentively, and often repeatedly addressed my image by my first name. In doing so, I evidently intended to create a bridge from the image in the external world over to me, across which I might penetrate into my unfathomable self. I do not know if I kissed my reflection, but I have seen other children kissing theirs; they come to terms with their ego by loving it." While correcting proof, I see by chance the last book of this author, *Über den Tod . . .* (Vienna, 1914), which reduces the problem of death to that of the fear of death [c.f. Rank's "The Double As Immortal Self"].
24. S. Freud, "Animismus, Magie und Allmacht der Gedanken," *Imago,* II (1913), 1–21 [this is the title of the third part of the paper "Totem and Taboo", S.E., vol. 13].
25. Cf. J. Frazer, "The Belief in Immortality," p.19. "He is a boundless egoist," says Heinzelmann (G. [Gerhard] Heinzelmann, *Animismus und Religion . . .* ([Gutersloh], 1913), p. 14), after H. Visscher, *Religion und soziales Leben bei den Naturvölkern* (Bonn, 1911), I, 117; II, 243 ff.
26. W. M. Wundt, *Vökerpsychologie . . .* [4th ed.; Stuttgart, 1912], Vol. 11, Part 2.
27. For emphasis placed upon the dream as the main source for the belief in the survival of the soul after death, see Frazer, "The Belief. . .," pp. 57, 140, 214; see also Paul Radestock, *Schlaf und Traum* (Leipzig, 1878 [1879])., p. 251. It should not be forgotten that one sees oneself in dreams.
28. E. B. Tylor, *The Beginnings of Culture* [*Primitive Culture* (3rd ed.; London, 1891)], I, 43 ff.
29. Cf. also the poem by Richard Dehmel, modeled after R. L. Stevenson:

The funniest thing about him is the way he likes to grow—
Not at all like proper children, which is always very slow;
For he sometimes shoots up taller like an india-rubber ball,
And he sometime gets so little that there's none of him at all.

30. See Herbert Spencer, *Prinzipien der Sociologie,* tr. into German by B. Vetter [Stuttgart, 1877–97], II, 426; see also J. v. Negelein, "Ein Beitrag zum indischen Seelenwanderungs-glauben," in *Arch. f. Rel.-Wiss.*, 1901.
31. According to Rohde, the primary concept of the soul leads to a duplication of the person, to the formation of a second self. "The soul which has disappeared at death is the exact copy of the person here below" (Heinzelmann, *op. cit.*, p. 20). I can add to these citations a reference to the book by Rudolf Kleinpaul, *Volkspsychologie* (Berlin, 1914), which also gives evidence of a double as the most primitive concept of the soul (pp. 5 f., 131, 171).
32. Cf. mirrors as burial-gifts in the oldest Grecian times (Goerg Friedrich Creuzer, *Symbolik und Mythologie der alten Volker, besonders der Griechen* [3rd ed.; Leipzig and Darmstadt, 1836–1843], IV, 196), and among the Mohammedans (K. Haberland, "Der Spiegel im Blauben und Brauch der Volker," *Zeitschrift fur Volkerpsychologie,* XIII [1882]).
33. Frazer, "The Belief . . .," pp. 33, 35, 53, and *passim.* Characteristic of this naive view is the remark of the anthropologist K. von den Steinen, who gave a Bakairi-Indian the sentence, "All men must die," to translate into the latter's language. To his great amazement, it turned out that the man was unable to grasp the meaning of this sentence, since he had no idea of the necessity of death (*Unter den Naturvölkern Zentral-Brasiliens* [Berlin, 1894], pp. 344, 348; according to Frazer, "The Belief . . .," p. 35).
34. Frazer [?], *op. cit.*, pp. 84 ff.
35. Primitive man, in fact, does not know any belief in immortality in our sense. Also, many primitive peoples think of the shadowy life of the mind as gradually fading away, significantly often simultaneously with the body's decomposition; or else they have the view that man dies several times in the underworld until he is finally and definitively dead. This idea agrees largely with the infantile attitude, which lacks the concept of "being dead" in our sense and which considers it to be a matter of passing away by degrees (cf. the corresponding communications under the heading "Kinderseele" in *Imago*).
36. This belief is shown best by the current spiritism, which maintains that the souls of deceased persons return in their human form (spirit), and by the occult meaning of the double. According to this meaning, the soul leaves the body and takes on a material form which becomes visible under favorable conditions (exteriorization of the soul). It appears, further, that the soul originally was identified with the consciousness of oneself which passes away in death. Our modern scientific way of looking at the world has not yet rid itself of this idea, as the affective resistance to accepting a psychology of the unconscious teaches us. The Belgian writer M. Maeterlinck has followed up these problems, merely touched upon here, to the outermost limits of imaginability in a profound book, *Concerning Death* (translated into German by F. von Oppeln-Bronikowski [Jena, 1913]).
37. Turgenev writes to a friend:"Love is one of the passions which destroy our own egos" (after Merezhkovsky, *op. cit.*, p. 65). How the male's narcissism seeks to come to terms with this problem is indicated by a passage, typical of Strindberg's whole attitude toward woman, from *Legends:* "We begin to love a woman by depositing with her our souls, bit by bit. We duplicate our personality; and the beloved woman who formerly was indifferent and neutral begins to assume the guise of our other self, becoming our double" (p. 293). In Villiers de L'Isle-Adam's short story *Vera,* the husband is satisfied to hallucinate his young deceased wife—to incorporate her, as it were, in his own individuality, and he feels happy

in this duple life. There are narcissistic fantasies and mirror-fantasies in the same author's short story *Be a Man.*

38. G. Heinzelmann, *op. cit.*, p. 60.
39. This fundamental trait of the double-problem is further clarified in Freud's essay "Das Unheimliche," 1919 ["The 'Uncanny,' " S.E., Vol. 17]

6. Hamlet and Oedipus

Ernest Jones

What we are essentially concerned with is the psychological understanding of the dramatic effect produced by Hamlet's personality and behaviour. That effect would be quite other were the central figure in the play to represent merely a "case of insanity." When that happens, as with Ophelia, such a person passes beyond our ken, is in a sense no more human, whereas Hamlet successfully claims our interest and sympathy to the very end. Shakespeare certainly never intended us to regard Hamlet as insane, so that the "mind o'erthrown" must have some other meaning than its literal one. Robert Bridges[1] has described the matter with exquisite delicacy:

Hamlet himself would never have been aught to us, or we
To Hamlet, wer't not for the artful balance whereby
Shakespeare so gingerly put his sanity in doubt
Without the while confounding his Reason.

I would suggest that in this Shakespeare's extraordinary powers of observation and penetration granted him a degree of insight that it has taken the world three subsequent centuries to reach. Until our generation (and even now in the juristic sphere) a dividing line separated the sane and responsible from the irresponsible insane. It is now becoming more and more widely recognized that much of mankind lives in an intermediate and unhappy state charged with what Dover Wilson[2] well calls "that sense of frustration, futility and human inadequacy which is the burden of the whole symphony" and of which Hamlet is the supreme example in literature. This intermediate plight, in the toils of which perhaps the greater part of mankind struggles and suffers, is given the name of psychoneurosis, and long ago the genius of Shakespeare depicted it for us with faultless insight.

Extensive studies of the past half century, inspired by Freud, have taught us that a psychoneurosis means a state of mind where the person is unduly, and often painfully, driven or thwarted by the ''unconscious'' part of his mind, that buried part that was once the infant's mind and still lives on side by side with the adult mentality that has developed out of it and should have taken its place. It signified *internal* mental conflict. We have here the reason why it is impossible to discuss intelligently the state of mind of anyone suffering from a psychoneurosis, whether the description is of a living person or an imagined one, without correlating the manifestations with what must have operated in his infancy and is *still operating*. That is what I propose to attempt here.

For some deep-seated reason, which is to him unacceptable, Hamlet is plunged into anguish at the thought of his father being replaced in his mother's affections by someone else. It is as if his devotion to his mother had made him so jealous for her affection that he had found it hard enough to share this even with his father and could not endure to share it with still another man. Against this thought, however, suggestive as it is, may be urged three objections. First, if it were in itself a full statement of the matter, Hamlet would have been aware of the jealousy, whereas we have concluded that the mental process we are seeking is hidden from him. Secondly, we see in it no evidence of the arousing of an old and forgotten memory. And, thirdly, Hamlet is being deprived by Claudius of no greater share in the Queen's affection than he had been by his own father, for the two brothers made exactly similar claims in this respect—namely, those of a loved husband. The last-named objection, however, leads us to the heart of the situation. How if, in fact, Hamlet had in years gone by, as a child, bitterly resented having had to share his mother's affection even with his own father, had regarded him as a rival, and had secretly wished him out of the way so that he might enjoy undisputed and undisturbed the monopoly of that affection? If such thoughts had been present in his mind in childhood days they evidently would have been ''repressed,'' and all traces of them obliterated, by filial piety and other educative influences. The actual realization of his early wish in the death of his father at the hands of a jealous rival would then have stimulated into activity these ''repressed'' memories, which would have produced, in the form of depression and other suffering, an obscure aftermath of his childhood's conflict. This is at all events the mechanism that is actually found in the real Hamlets who are investigated psychologically.[3]

The explanation, therefore, of the delay and self-frustration exhibited in the endeavour to fulfil his father's demand for vengeance is that to Hamlet the thought of incest and parricide combined is too intolerable to be borne. One part of him tries to carry out the task, the other flinches inexorably from the thought of it. How fain would he blot it out in that "bestial oblivion" which unfortunately for him his conscience condemns. He is torn and tortured in an insoluble inner conflict.

We are now in a position to expand and complete the suggestions offered earlier in connection with the Hamlet problem.[4] The story thus interpreted would run somewhat as follows.

As a child Hamlet had experienced the warmest affection for his mother, and this, as is always so, had contained elements of a disguised erotic quality, still more so in infancy. The presence of two traits in the Queen's character accord with this assumption, namely her markedly sensual nature and her passionate fondness of her son. The former is indicated in too many places in the play to need specific reference, and is generally recognized. The latter is also manifest: Claudius says, for instance (Act IV, Sc. 7), "The Queen his mother lives almost by his looks." Nevertheless Hamlet appears to have with more or less success weaned himself from her and to have fallen in love with Ophelia. The precise nature of his original feeling for Ophelia is a little obscure. We may assume that at least in part it was composed of a normal love for a prospective bride, though the extravagance of the language used (the passionate need for absolute certainty, etc.) suggests a somewhat morbid frame of mind. There are indications that even here the influence of the old attraction for the mother is still exerting itself. Although some writers,[5] following Goethe,[6] see in Ophelia many traits of resemblance to the Queen, perhaps just as striking are the traits contrasting with those of the Queen. Whatever truth there may be in the many German conceptions of Ophelia as a sensual wanton[7]—misconceptions that have been questioned by Loening[8] and others—still the very fact that it needed what Goethe happily called the "innocence of insanity" to reveal the presence of any such libidinous thoughts demonstrates in itself the modesty and chasteness of her habitual demeanour. Her naïve piety, her obedient resignation, and her unreflecting simplicity sharply contrast with the Queen's character, and seem to indicate that Hamlet by a characteristic reaction towards the opposite extreme had unknowingly been impelled to choose a woman who should least remind him of his mother. A case might even be made out for the view that part of his courtship originated not so much in direct attraction for Ophelia as in an unconscious desire to play her off against his mother, just as a disappointed and piqued lover so often has resort to the arms of a more willing rival. It would not be easy otherwise to understand the readiness with which he later throws himself into this part. When, for instance, in the play scene he replies to his mother's request to sit by her with the words "No, good mother, here's metal more attractive" and proceeds to lie at Ophelia's feet, we seem to have a direct indication of this attitude; and his coarse familiarity and bandying of ambiguous jests with the woman he has recently so ruthlessly jilted are hardly intelligible unless we bear in mind that they were carried out under the heedful gaze of the Queen. It is as if his unconscious were trying to convey to her the following thought: "You give yourself to other men whom you prefer to me. Let me assure you that I can dispense with your favours and even prefer those of a woman whom I no longer love." His extraordinary outburst of bawdiness on this occasion, so unexpected in a man of obviously fine feeling, points unequivocally to the sexual nature of the underlying turmoil.

Now comes the father's death and the mother's second marriage. The association of the idea of sexuality with his mother, buried since infancy, can no longer be concealed from his consciousness. As Bradley[9] well says: "Her son was forced to see in her action not only an astounding shallowness of feeling, but an eruption of coarse sensuality, 'rank and gross,' speeding post-haste to its horrible delight." Feelings which once, in the infancy of long ago, were pleasurable desires can now, because of his repressions, only fill him with repulsion. The long "repressed" desire to take his father's place in his mother's affection is stimulated to unconscious activity by the sight of someone usurping this place exactly as he himself had once longed to do. More, this someone was a member of the same family, so that the actual usurpation further resembled the imaginary one in being incestuous. Without his being in the least aware of it these ancient desires are ringing in his mind, are once more struggling to find conscious expression, and need such an expenditure of energy again to "repress" them that he is reduced to the deplorable mental state he himself so vividly depicts.

There follows the Ghost's announcement that the father's death was a willed one, was due to murder. Hamlet, having at the moment his mind filled with natural indignation at the news, answers normally enough with the cry (Act I, Sc. 5):

Haste me to know 't, that I with wings as swift
As meditation or the thoughts of love,
May sweep to my revenge.

The momentous words follow revealing who was the guilty person, namely a relative who had committed the deed at the bidding of lust.[10] Hamlet's second guilty wish had thus also been realized by his uncle, namely to procure the fulfilment of the first—the possession of the mother—by a personal deed, in fact by murder of the father. The two recent events, the father's death and the mother's second marriage, seemed to the world to have no inner causal relation to each other, but they represented ideas which in Hamlet's unconscious phantasy had always been closely associated. These ideas now in a moment forced their way to conscious recognition in spite of all "repressing forces," and found immediate expression in his almost reflex cry: "O my prophetic soul! My uncle?" The frightful truth his unconscious had already intuitively divined, his consciousness had now to assimilate as best it could. For the rest of the interview Hamlet is stunned by the effect of the internal conflict thus re-awakened, which from now on never ceases, and into the essential nature of which he never penetrates.

One of the first manifestations of the awakening of the old conflict in Hamlet's mind is his reaction against Ophelia. This is doubly conditioned by the two opposing attitudes in his own mind. In the first place, there is a complex reaction in regard to his mother. As was explained [earlier], the being forced to connect the thought of his mother with sensuality leads to an intense sexual revulsion, one that is only temporarily broken down by the coarse outburst discussed [previously]. Combined with this is a fierce jealousy, unconscious because of its forbidden origin, at the sight of her giving herself to another man, a man whom he had no reason whatever either to love or to respect. Consciously this is allowed to express itself, for instance after the prayer scene, only in the form of extreme resentment and bitter reproaches against her. His resentment against women is still further inflamed by the hypocritical prudishness with which Ophelia follows her father and brother in seeing evil in his natural affection, an attitude which poisons his love in exactly the same way that the love of his childhood, like that of all children, must have been poisoned. He can forgive a woman neither her rejection of his sexual advances nor, still less, her alliance with another man. Most intolerable of all to him, as Bradley well remarks, is the sight of sensuality in a quarter from which he had trained himself ever since infancy rigorously to exclude it. The total reaction culminates in the bitter misogyny of his outburst against Ophelia, who is devastated at having to bear a reaction so wholly out of proportion to her own offence and has no idea that in reviling her Hamlet is really expressing his bitter resentment against his mother.[11] "I have heard of your paintings too, well enough; God has given you one face, and you make yourselves another; you jig, you amble, and you lisp, and nickname God's creatures, and make your wantonness your ignorance. Go to, I'll no more on 't: it hath made me mad" (Act III, Sc. 1). On only one occasion does he for a moment escape from the sordid implication with which his love has been impregnated and achieve a healthier attitude towards Ophelia, namely at the open grave when in remorse he breaks out at Laertes for presuming to pretend that his feeling for her could never equal that of her lover. Even here, however, as Dover Wilson[12] has suggested, the remorse behind his exaggerated behaviour springs not so much from grief at Ophelia's death as from his distress at his bad conscience that had killed his love—he acts the lover he fain would have been.

Hamlet's attitude towards Ophelia is still more complex. Dover Wilson[13] has adduced good evidence for thinking that Hamlet is supposed to have overheard the intrigue in which Polonius "looses" his daughter to test her erstwhile lover, a suggestion which had previously been made by Quincy Adams.[14] This is probably an echo of the old (Saxon) saga in which the girl is employed by the king to test his capacity for sexual love and so decide whether he is an imbecile or a cunning enemy. It certainly helps to explain the violence with which he attacks her feminine charms and treats her worse than a paid prostitute. He feels she is sent to lure him on and then, like his mother, to betray him at the behest of another man. The words "Get thee to a nunnery"[15] thus have a more sinister connotation, for in Elizabethan, and indeed in later, times this was also a term for a brothel; the name "Covent Garden" will elucidate the point to any student of the history of London.

The underlying theme relates ultimately to the splitting of the mother image which the infantile unconscious effects into two opposite pictures: one of a virginal Madonna, an inaccessible saint towards whom all sensual approaches are unthinkable, and the other of a sensual creature accessible to everyone. Indications of this dichotomy between love and lust (Titian's Sacred and Profane Love) are to be found later in most men's sexual experiences. When sexual repression is highly pronounced, as with Hamlet, then both types of women are felt to be hostile: the pure one out of resentment at her repulses, the sensual one out of the temptation she offers to plunge into guiltiness. Misogyny, as in the play, is the inevitable result.

The intensity of Hamlet's repulsion against woman in general, and Ophelia in particular, is a measure of the powerful "repression" to which his sexual feelings are being subjected. The outlet for those feelings in the direction of his mother has always been firmly dammed, and now that the narrower channel in Ophelia's direction has also been closed the increase in the original direction consequent on the awakening of early memories tasks all his energy to maintain the "repression." His pent-up feelings find a partial vent in other directions. The petulant irascibility and explosive outbursts called forth by his vexation at the hands of Guildenstern and Rosencrantz, and especially of Polonius, are evidently to be interpreted in this way, as also is in part the burning nature of his reproaches to his mother. Indeed, towards the end of his interview with his mother the thought of her misconduct expresses itself in that almost physical disgust which is so characteristic a manifestation of intensely "repressed" sexual feeling.

Let the bloat king tempt you again to bed,
Pinch wanton on your cheek, call you his mouse,
And let him for a pair of reechy kisses,
Or paddling in your neck with his damn'd fingers,
Make you to ravel all this matter out. (Act III, Sc. 4)

Hamlet's attitude towards Polonius is highly instructive. Here the absence of family tie and of other similar influences enables him to indulge to a relatively unrestrained extent his hostility towards what he regards as a prating and sententious dotard.[16] The analogy he effects between Polonius and Jephthah[17] is in this connection especially pointed. It is here that we see his fundamental attitude towards moralizing elders who use their power to thwart the happiness of the young, and not in the over-drawn and melodramatic portrait in which he delineates his father: "A combination and a form indeed, where every god did seem to set his seal to give the world assurance of a man."

It will be seen from the foregoing that Hamlet's attitude towards his uncle-father is far more complex than is generally supposed. He of course detests him, but it is the jealous detestation of one evil-doer towards his successful fellow. Much as he hates him, he can never denounce him with the ardent indignation that boils straight from his blood when he reproaches his mother, for the more vigorously he denounces his uncle the more powerfully does he stimulate to activity his own unconscious and "repressed" complexes. He is therefore in a dilemma between on the one hand allowing his natural detestation of his uncle to have free play, a consummation which would stir still further his own horrible wishes, and on the other hand ignoring the imperative call for the vengeance that his obvious duty demands. His own "evil" prevents him from completely denouncing his uncle's, and in continuing to "repress" the former he must strive to ignore, to condone, and if possible even to forget the latter; *his mortal fate is bound up with his uncle's for good or ill.* In reality his uncle incorporates the deepest and most buried part of his own personality, so that he cannot kill him without killing himself. This solution, one closely akin to what Freud[18] has shown to be the motive of suicide in melancholia, is actually the one that Hamlet finally adopts. The course of alternate action and inaction that he embarks on, and the provocations he gives to his suspicious uncle, can lead to no other end than to his own ruin and, incidentally, to that of his uncle. Only when he has made the final sacrifice and brought himself to the door of death is he free to fulfil his duty, to avenge his father, and to slay his other self—his uncle.

There are two moments in the play when he is nearest to murder, and it is noteworthy that in both the impulse has been dissociated from the unbearable idea of incest. The second is of course when he actually kills the King, when the Queen is already dead and lost to him for ever, so that his conscience is free of an ulterior motive for the murder. The first is more interesting. It is clear that Hamlet is a creature of highly charged imagination; Vischer,[19] for instance, quite rightly termed him a "Phantasie-mensch." As is known, the danger then is that phantasy may on occasion replace reality. Now Otto Rank,[20] who uses the same term, has plausibly suggested that the emotionally charged play scene, where a nephew kills his uncle(!), and when there is no talk of adultery or incest, is in Hamlet's imagination an equivalent for fulfilling his task.[21] It is easier to kill the King when there is no ulterior motive behind it, no talk of mother or incest. When the play is over he is carried away in exultation as if he had really killed the King himself, whereas all he has actually done is to warn him and so impel him to sign a death warrant. That his pretext for arranging the play—to satisfy himself about Claudius' guilt and the Ghost's honesty—is specious is plain from the fact that *before* it he had been convinced of both and was reproaching himself for his neglect. When he then comes on the King praying, and so to speak finds him surprisingly still alive, he realizes that his task is still in front of him, but can only say "Now *might* I do it" (not "will"). He then expresses openly the unconscious thoughts of his infancy—the wish to kill the man who is lying with his mother ("in th' incestuous pleasure of his bed")—but he knows only too well that his own guilty motive for doing so would always prevent him. So there is no way out of the dilemma, and he blunders on to destruction.

The call of duty to kill his stepfather cannot be obeyed because it links itself with the unconscious call of his nature to kill his mother's husband, whether this is the first or the second; the absolute "repression" of the former impulse involves the inner prohibition of the latter also. It is no chance that Hamlet says of himself that he is prompted to his revenge "by heaven and hell."

In this discussion of the motives that move or restrain Hamlet we have purposely depreciated the subsidiary ones—such as his exclusion from the throne where Claudius has blocked the normal solution of the Oedipus complex (to succeed the father in due course)—which also play a part, so as to bring out in greater relief the deeper and effective ones that are of preponderating importance. These, as we have seen, spring from sources of which he is quite unaware, and we might summarize the internal conflict of which he is the victim as consisting in a struggle of the "repressed" mental processes to become conscious. The call of duty, which automatically arouses to activity these unconscious processes, conflicts with the necessity of "repressing" them still more strongly; for the more urgent is the need for external action the greater is the effort demanded of the "repressing" forces. It is his moral duty, to which his father exhorts him, to put an end to the incestuous activities of his mother (by killing Claudius), but his unconscious does not want to put an end to them (he being identified with Claudius in the situation), and so he cannot. His lashings of self-reproach and remorse are ultimately because of this very failure, i.e. the refusal of his guilty wishes to undo the sin. By refusing to abandon his own incestuous wishes he perpetuates the sin and so must endure the stings of torturing conscience. And yet killing his mother's husband would be equivalent to committing the original sin himself, which would if anything be even more guilty. So of the two impossible alternatives he adopts the passive solution of letting the incest continue vicariously, but at the same time provoking destruction at the King's hand. Was ever a tragic figure so torn and tortured!

Action is paralysed at its very inception, and there is thus produced the picture of apparently causeless inhibition which is so inexplicable both to

Hamlet[22] and to readers of the play. This paralysis arises, however, not from physical or moral cowardice, but from that intellectual cowardice, that reluctance to dare the exploration of his inmost soul, which Hamlet shares with the rest of the human race. "Thus conscience does make cowards of us all."

NOTES

1. Robert Bridges: *The Testament of Beauty* (New York: Oxford University Press, 1930), I, p. 577.
2. Dover Wilson: *What Happens in Hamlet* (Cambridge: Cambridge University Press, 1925), p. 261.
3. See, for instance, Wulf Sachs: *Black Hamlet* (London: Bles, 1937).
4. Here, as throughout this essay, I closely follow Freud's interpretation ["Interpretation of Dreams," *Standard Edition,* Vol. IV, pp. 264–266]. He there points out the inadequacy of the earlier explanations, deals with Hamlet's feelings towards his mother, father, and uncle, and mentions two other matters that will presently be discussed, the significance of Hamlet's reaction against Ophelia and of the probability that the play was written immediately after the death of Shakespeare's own father.
5. For example, Georg Brandes: *William Shakespeare* (London: Heinemann, 1898), remarks that Hamlet's talk to Ophelia could be translated as "You are like my mother; you could behave like her" (vol. II, p. 48).
6. Johann Wolfgang von Goethe: *Wilhelm Meister* (Boston, Niccolls, 1901) IV, 14: "Her whole being hovers in ripe, sweet voluptuousness." "Her fancy is moved, her quiet modesty breathes loving desire, and should the gentle Goddess Opportunity shake the tree the fruit would at once fall" (pp. 306-7).
7. For instance, D. B. Storffrich: *Psychologische Aufschlüsse über Shakespeares Hamlet* (Bremen: Kauhtman, 1859), p. 131; Karl Dietrich: *Hamlet, der Konstabel der Vorsehung; eine Shakespeare-Studie* (Hamburg: Nolte, 1883), p. 129; Ludwig Tieck: *Dramaturgische Blätter, 2: 1826, pp. 85 ff.*
8. Richard Loening: *Die Hamlet Tragödie Shakespeares* (Stuttgart: Cotta, 1893), p. 245.
9. A. C. Bradley: *Shakespearean Tragedy* (London: Macmillan, 1905), p. 118.
10. It is not maintained that this was by any means Claudius' whole motive, but it was evidently a powerful one and the one that most impressed Hamlet.
11. His similar tone and advice to the two women show plainly how closely they are identified in his mind. Cp. "Get thee to a nunnery: why wouldst thou be a breeder of sinners?" (Act III, Sc. 2) with "Refrain to-night; And that shall lend a kind of easiness To the next abstinence" (Act III, Sc. 4).

    The identification is further demonstrated in the course of the play by Hamlet's killing the men who stand between him and these women (Claudius and Polonius).
12. Op. cit., p. 270.
13. Op. cit., p. 128, etc.
14. J. Q. Adams: "Commentary" in his edition of *Hamlet, Prince of Denmark,* Boston, 1929, p. 255.
15. This exhortation (with its usual connotation of chastity) may be equated with the one addressed later to his mother, "Go not to my uncle's bed," indicating Hamlet's identification of the two women in his feelings.

16. It is noteworthy how many producers and actors seem to accept Hamlet's distorted estimate of Polonius, his garrulity being presumably an excuse for overlooking the shrewdness and soundness of his worldly wisdom. After all, his diagnosis of Hamlet's madness as being due to unrequited love for Ophelia was not so far from the mark, and he certainly recognized that his distressful condition was of sexual origin.
17. What Shakespeare thought of Jephthah's behaviour towards his daughter may be gathered from a reference in *Henry VI, Part III,* Act V, Sc. 1. See also on this subject Charles Wordsworth: *On Shakespeare's Knowledge and Use of the Bible* (London: Elder, 1864), p. 67.
18. Freud: "Trauer and Melancholie" ["Mourning and Melancholia," *Standard Edition,* Vol. XIV].
19. F. T. Vischer: "Hamlet, Prinz von Dänemark," in *Shakespeare Vorträge.* Bd. I, 1899.
20. Otto Rank: "Das Schauspiel in Hamlet," *Imago,* Jahrg. IV, S. 45.
21. There is a delicate point here which may appeal only to psychoanalysts. It is known that the occurrence of a dream within a dream (when one dreams that one is dreaming) is always found when analysed to refer to a theme which the person wishes were "only a dream," i.e. no true. I would suggest that a similar meaning attaches to a "play within a play," as in *Hamlet.* So Hamlet (as nephew) can kill the King in his imagination since it is "only a play" or "only in play."
22. The situation is perfectly depicted by Hamlet in his cry (Act IV, Sc. 4):

I do not know
Why yet I live to say "this thing's to do,"
Sith I have cause, and will, and strength, and means,
To do't.

With greater insight he could have replaced the word "will" by "pious wish," which, as Loening (op. cit., p. 246) points out, it obviously means. Oddly enough, William Rolfe (*Introduction to Karl Werder, The Heart of Hamlet's Mystery.* [New York: Putnam, 1907], p. 23) quotes this very passage in support of Werder's hypothesis that Hamlet was inhibited by the thought of the external difficulties of the situation, which shows to what straits the supporters of this untenable hypothesis are driven.

7. Prince Hal's Conflict

Ernst Kris

For well over a century some of Shakespeare's critics have pointed to inconsistencies in the character of Henry, Prince of Wales (later King Henry V), occasionally explained by the poet's lack of interest, whose attention, it is said, was concentrated mainly on the alternate but 'true' hero, Falstaff. This seemed the more plausible since most of the puzzling passages or incidents occur in *King Henry IV, Parts I* and *II* of the trilogy; however, closer examination of three inconsistencies, to which critics are wont to refer as typical of others, seems to throw new light on the psychological conflict with which Shakespeare has invested the hero of the trilogy.[1]

Prince Hal's first appearance on the stage as Falstaff's friend and Poins's companion is concluded by the soliloquy in which he reveals his secret intentions. While he has just made plans to riot with the gang and to rob the robbers, his mind turns to the future.

I know you all, and will awhile uphold
The unyok'd humour of your idleness:
Yet herein will I imitate the sun,
Who doth permit the base contagious clouds
To smother up his beauty from the world,
That, when he please again to be himself,
Being wanted, he may be more wonder'd at,
By breaking through the foul and ugly mists
Of vapours that did seem to strangle him.
If all the year were playing holidays,
To sport would be as tedious as to work;
But when they seldom come, they wish'd-for come,
And nothing pleaseth but rare accidents.
So, when this loose behaviour I throw off,

Reprinted by permission of the author's estate and *the Psychoanalytic Quarterly*, 17 (1974).

And pay the debt I never promised,
By how much better than my word I am,
By so much shall I falsify men's hopes,
And, like bright metal on a sullen ground,
My reformation, glittering o'er my fault,
Shall show more goodly and attract more eyes
Than that which hath no foil to set it off.
I'll so offend, to make offence a skill;
Redeeming time when men think least I will.[2]

Some critics feel that this announcement deprives the play of part of its dramatic effect: the change in the Prince's behavior should surprise the audience as it does the personages on the stage. The anticipation, we are told, was forced on the poet as a concession to the public. Henry V appeared to the Elizabethans as the incarnation of royal dignity and knightly valor. His early debauches had therefore to be made part of a morally oriented plan; but some critics find the price of justification too high, since it leaves a suspicion of hypocrisy on the Prince's character.

The second inconsistency is seen in the course of the Prince's reformation which proceeds in two stages. In Part I, Prince Hal returns to his duties when the realm is endangered by rebels; at Shrewsbury, he saves the King's life and defeats Percy Hotspur in combat; but while the war against other rebels continues, we find him back in Eastcheap feasting with his companions. His final reformation takes place at the King's deathbed. Critics usually account for this protracted and repeated reformation by assuming that the success of the Falstaff episodes in Part I suggested their continuation in Part II, an argument supported by the widely accepted tradition that Falstaff's revival in *The Merry Wives of Windsor,* after the completion of the trilogy, was at the special request of Queen Elizabeth. It has nevertheless been emphasized that the concluding scenes of Part II follow in all essential details existing tradition.

The third and most frequently discussed inconsistency is King Henry V's treatment of his former companions with merciless severity. Falstaff, who waits to cheer the new King, is temporarily arrested and, while he hopes that Henry will revoke in private his public pronouncement, we later hear that he has hoped in vain. The King's harshness has broken his heart. In the 'rejection of Falstaff',[3] who has won the audience's heart, the dramatist has 'overshot his mark'; the King's reformation could have been illustrated by gentler means, and some critics suggest how this could have been achieved without offending the Old Knight. The formula of banishment, however, is only partly Shakespeare's invention since it paraphrases traditional accounts.

This tradition originated soon after Henry V suddenly died in Paris, at the age of thirty-five, crowned the King of England and France (1421). The tradition grew in chronicles and popular accounts, hesitantly at first, more rapidly later, when Henry's striving for European leadership and hegemony in the Channel appeared as an anticipation of the political goals of Tudor England. In Shakespeare's time, fact and legend had become firmly interwoven.[4]

Prince Henry (of Monmouth, born 1387) was early introduced to affairs of state. He was twelve years old when, in 1399, his father succeeded Richard II. At fifteen he took personal control of the administration of Wales and of the war against the Welsh rebels. He had shared in this task since 1400, initially guided by Henry Percy, Hotspur, who at that time was thirty-nine, three years older than the Prince's father. In 1405 Hotspur led the rebellion of the Percies and attacked the Prince's forces at Shrewsbury. Supported by the King and his army, Henry of Monmouth carried the day. The rebellion and the pacification of Wales kept the Prince busy until 1408 or 1409. He then entered politics as leader of the parliamentary opposition against the King's council. Repeated illnesses complicated Henry IV's negotiations with Parliament that at the time of his uprising against Richard II had vested royal power in him. Since 1406 rumors concerning his abdication had been spreading. In 1408 he was thought to have died in an attack of seizures 'but after some hours the vital spirits returned to him'. From January, 1410 to November, 1411 the Prince governed England through the council, supported by the King's half brothers, Henry and Thomas Beaufort. In November, 1411 Henry IV took over again and dismissed the Prince from the council. One of the reasons for the Prince's dismissal was his desire for an active policy in France. It seems that, initially without the King's consent, he had arranged for a small expeditionary force to be sent to the continent in support of Burgundy against the Royal House of France; later the King agreed to the expedition but the Prince had to renounce his intention to lead the forces.

The circumstances that led to Henry of Monmouth's removal from the council are not entirely clear. It seems that Henry IV was motivated by the suspicion that the Prince intended to depose him. The Prince issued public statements denying such intention, and demanded the punishment of those who had slandered him. He finally forced an interview on the King, during which a reconciliation took place. The struggle between father and son was terminated by Henry IV's death in 1413.

According to the chronicle of the fifteenth and sixteenth centuries, Henry of Monmouth's character changed after his accession to the throne. The early chronicles do not state in detail wherein the conversion consisted. They familiarize us, however, with two areas in which the Prince's attitude was different from that of the later King. The first of these areas is less well defined than the second: during the conflict with his father, the Prince appeared twice at court 'with much peoples of lords and gentles'. This show of strength was meant to exercise pressure on King and council. During his reign Henry V never used similar methods; no appeal to forces outside 'government' is attributed to him, neither in his dealings with Parliament nor with the baronage. Within the framework of his age he was a rigorously constitutional monarch. Somewhat better defined is the change of the Prince's attitude to the Church. The noble leader of the Lollards, Sir John Oldcastle, was the Prince's personal friend, and at least by tolerance, the Prince seems vaguely to have favored the cause for which he stood. Shortly after Henry V's accession to the throne the persecution of the Lollards was intensified. Sir John was arrested and asked to abandon his error. He refused any compromise, succeeded twice in escaping, but he was finally, in 1417, executed after Parliament had determined on the extirpation of Lollardy as heresy.

The legendary versions of the Prince's reformation elaborated these incidents later on; in their earliest formulation they simply stated: 'that the Prince was an assiduous center of lasciviousness and addicted exceedingly to instruments of music. Passing the bounds of modesty he was the fervent soldier of Venus as well as of Mars; youthlike, he was tired with her torches and in the midst of the worthy works of war found leisure for excess common to ungoverned age'.[5] Later sources place the Prince's reformation in relation to the conflict with his father: the baronage that had adopted the Prince as leader becomes a group of irresponsible delinquents. Amongst this group the name of Sir John Oldcastle appears. The fanatic leader of a religious sect thus underwent the transformation into Sir John Falstaff, whose name was substituted by Shakespeare only after Oldcastle's descendants had complained of what seemed a vilification of their ancestor; but various traces of the original name are extant in Shakespeare's text. The banishment of Falstaff then may be considered as an elaboration of Henry V's persecution of the Lollards whom he once had favored. Other elements of the legendary tradition are inserted with clearly moralistic intentions: the Prince's reformation is used to exemplify the nature of royal responsibility. Thus Sir Thomas Elliott in his treatise, *The Book Called the Governor* (1536), introduced the tale of Prince and Chiefjustice according to which the King confirms that Chiefjustice in office who, in the royal name, had once arrested the riotous Prince. The image of Henry V was thus idealized into that of the perfect Renaissance ruler.[6]

Shakespeare borrowed these and similar incidents of his trilogy from a variety of sources, but mainly from the second edition of Raphael Holinshed's *Chronicles of England, Scotland and Ireland* (1587).[7] In addition to historical sources he relied upon a popular play produced a few years earlier. So closely does he follow *The Famous Victories of Henry V* that it seems as if he had set himself the task to retain as many as possible of the incidents familiar to his audience in spite of the total transformation of the context. Without commenting in detail upon this transformation—though such a comparison would permit one to support the hypothesis here to be proposed—it suffices to point to its general direction. The historical facts concerning the conflict between Henry IV and his son and 'heir apparent', Henry of Monmouth, had been blurred by legend. The conversion of the Prince became the dominant theme, a conversion modeled after that of the life of the saints. Shakespeare returns to the core of this tradition, or rather rediscovers that core, in the sources accessible to him. He centers his attention on the conflict between father and son which is made to account for both the Prince's debauchery and his reformation.

The conflict between father and son appears in Part I of *Henry IV* in three versions, each time enacted by one central and two related characters.[8] The theme is manifestly stated by the King in the introductory scene of the trilogy, when he compares Henry of Monmouth to Henry Percy.

Yea, there thou makest me sad and makest me sin
In envy that my Lord Northumberland
Should be the father to so blest a son,
A son who is the theme of honour's tongue;
Amongst a grove, the very straightest plant;
Who is sweet fortune's minion and her pride:
Whilst I, by looking on the praise of him,
See riot and dishonour stain the brow

Of my young Harry. O! that it could be prov'd
That some night-tripping fairy had exchang'd
In cradle-clothes our children where they lay,
And called mine Percy, his Plantagenet!
Then would I have his Harry, and he mine.[9]

The position of the Prince between Falstaff and the King is almost as explicitly stated; he has two fathers, as the King has two sons. When he enacts with Falstaff his forthcoming interview with his father, the theme is brought into the open.[10] It is not limited to court and tavern, the centers of the 'double plot', as W. Empson calls it,[11] but extends to the rebel camp. Henry Percy stands between a weak father, Northumberland, who is prevented by illness from participating in the decisive battle, and a scheming uncle, Worcester, who plans the rebellion, conceals from Percy that the King offers reconciliation and drives him thus to battle and to death.

The three versions of the father–son conflict compelled Shakespeare to deviate from his sources and thereby to enrich the stage: he sharpened the report of the chronicles on the rebellion of the Percies in order to create the contrast of Worcester and Northumberland; he reduced Henry Percy's age from a slightly older contemporary of Henry IV to a somewhat older contemporary of the Prince—and he invented Falstaff.

The triangular relationships are not only similar to each other, since they all contain variations of the theme of good and bad fathers and sons, but within each triangle the parallel figures are closely interconnected; thus the two Harrys, whom Henry IV compares, form a unit; Hotspur's rebellion represents also Prince Hal's unconscious parricidal impulses.[12] Hotspur is the Prince's double. Impulses pertaining to one situation have thus been divided between two personages;[13] but though in the triangles the characters are paired and contrasted, each of the play's personages transcends the bondage to his function in this thematic configuration. They have all outgrown the symmetry which they serve, into the fullness of life.

To appraise Falstaff as a depreciated father figure is to grasp the superficial aspect of a character who, more than any other of Shakespeare, has enchanted readers and audiences since his creation. Franz Alexander finds two principal psychoanalytic explanations for this universal enchantment: Falstaff's hedonism, he says, represents the uninhibited gratification of an infantile and narcissistic quest for pleasure, a craving alive to some extent in everyone of us; this hedonism, moreover, is made acceptable by contrast: one turns with relief from the court or the rebel camp to the tavern.[14] In accordance with the last is the traditional antithesis of 'tragic King and comic people' (Empson) used by Shakespeare to emphasize a moral antithesis. From Prince Hal's point of view, Falstaff is a contrast to the King, who represents another version of the unsatisfactory paternal image. Henry IV succeeded his cousin Richard II by rebellion and regicide. The feeling of guilt that overshadowed his life becomes manifest when on his deathbed, in addressing the Prince, he reviews the sorrows that the unlawfully acquired crown inflicted on him.

How I came by the crown, O God forgive;
And grant it may with thee in true peace live![15]

In this great scene Prince Henry's mood accords with his father's; he too is burdened with guilt. In the preceding scene he finds his father sleeping, and believes him to be dead. Shakespeare, adapting this scene from the chronicle play, has added a prop device: the crown which lies next to the Kings' bed.[16] The crown inspires the Prince with awe and apprehension. He longs to possess it, but 'the best of gold' is 'the worst of gold'; it endangers the bearer. He wages 'the quarrel of a true inheritor', controls his desire and, in a mood of contemplation, concludes that royal responsibility is a heavy burden. He has overcome the hostile impulse against the dying King and can now reply to his father:

You won it, wore it, kept it, gave it me;
Then plain and right must my possession be;[17]

It is an attempt to reassure: 'Since I have come guiltless into the possession of the crown, since I refrained from regicide and parricide, I shall rightfully be King'; yet in the greatest crisis of his life, the Prince, now King Henry V, reveals that his apprehension has not been vanquished. The night before the battle of Agincourt, when his outnumbered army is weakened by disease, and confidence is more than ever required, he turns to prayer to avert divine retaliation for his father's crime that, with the crown, seems to have moved to his shoulders.

O God of battles! steel my soldiers' hearts;
Possess them not with fear; take from them now
The sense of reckoning, if the opposed numbers
Pluck their hearts from them! Not to-day, O Lord!

O, not to-day, think not upon the fault
My father made in compassing the crown!
I Richard's body have interred anew;
And on it have bestow'd more contrite tears
Than from it issu'd forced drops of blood:
Five hundred poor I have in yearly pay,
Who twice a day their wither'd hands hold up
Toward heaven, to pardon blood; and I have built
Two chantries, where the sad and solemn priests
Sing still for Richard's soul. More will I do;
Though all that I can do is nothing worth,
Since that my pentinence comes after all,
Imploring pardon.[18]

The essential passages of this prayer follow Holinshed's *Chronicles* wherein it is reported that after his succession to the throne Henry V had King Richard's body ceremoniously interred in Westminister Abbey and made specified donations in commemoration. Reference to this incident and the place in which it is made invite comment. By reintroducing the theme of the tragic guilt attached to the House of Lancaster, Shakespeare establishes a downfall of the Lancastrian Kings *(Henry VI, Richard III)*. The victory of Agincourt and the life of Henry V are thus made to appear as a glorious interlude in a tragic tale of crime and doom; however, the King's prayer before the battle reveals the structure of the conflict which Shakespeare embodied in his character: the desire to avoid guilt and to keep himself pure of crime is paramount in *Henry V*. In one passage of the prayer the King recalls the tears he shed on Richard's coffin, a detail not recorded by Holinshed, and yet obviously suggested by other passages of the Chronicle. It may well be considered a hint—the only one we find in the trilogy—that there ever existed a personal relationship between Richard II and the son of his banished cousin Henry of Lancaster—Henry of Monmouth. During the last months of his rule King Richard II sailed for Ireland to quell a local rebellion and he took Henry of Monmouth with him. The young Prince seems to have attracted the King's attention. The Prince was knighted by King Richard, Holinshed records, 'for some valiant act that he did or some other favourable respect'. Shakespeare was undoubtedly familiar with this account and very probably familiar with reports of the Prince's reaction to the news of his father's rebellion. Young Henry of Monmouth is said to have replied to a question of Richard's that he could not be held responsible for his father's deed.

In Shakespeare's *King Richard II* no direct reference is made to the relationship between Prince Hal and Richard,[19] but the theme to which we refer is present and clearly emphasized: one entire scene is devoted to it, the first in which the Prince is mentioned. Henry IV, newly enthroned, meets with his Lords—but his son is absent.

Can no man tell of my unthrifty son?
'Tis full three months since I did see him last:
If any plague hang over us, 'tis he.
I would to God, my lords, he might be found:
Inquire at London, 'mongst the taverns there,
For there, they say, he daily doth frequent,
With unrestrained loose companions,
Even such, they say, as stand in narrow lanes,
And beat out watch, and rob our passengers;[20]

The Prince has dissociated himself from the court that his father won by treason. In silent protest he has turned to the tavern rather than to participate in regicide.[21] Regicide dominates the scene that starts with Henry IV's quest for his absent son. The last of Richard's followers and the new King's cousin, the Duke of Aumerle, confesses to Henry IV that he has plotted against his life. Before Aumerle can complete his confession, the Duke of York, his father and uncle of Henry IV, forces his way into their presence. He doubts whether the purpose of Aumerle's audience be murder or repentance and is prepared to surrender his son.[22] This is the environment from which the Prince withdraws, to which he prefers the vices of Eastcheap and the freedom of Falstaff's company.

In *King Henry IV, Part II,* the contrast between court and tavern is re-emphasized in a scene in which Falstaff's carefree vice is juxtaposed with John of Lancaster's virtuous villainy. This younger brother of Prince Hal is in command of the campaign against the still surviving rebels. Falstaff serves in his inglorious army. Lancaster promises the rebels pardon; they accept his offer and he breaks his word to send them to the gallows. We have just witnessed this monstrous performance—taken directly from Holinshed's *Chronicles*—when Lancaster and Falstaff meet. The 'sober blooded youth' provokes Falstaff's soliloquy in praise of Sherristack and of Prince Hal, whose valor has not made him addicted to 'thin potations'.

Falstaff's loving praise of the Prince, and what others say when they refer to the Prince in the latter part of Part II of *Henry IV* remind us once more of how well he has succeeded in deceiving the world. His conversion upon his accession to the throne comes as a surprise to the court and to the tavern. Only the audience, having been in his confidence from his first soliloquy, are enabled to understand the contradictions in his behavior as being a part of his paramount conflict.

When Shakespeare familiarized himself with the youth of Henry V this conflict must have imposed itself upon his mind as one that would unify the various traits and incidents reported. The tendentious accounts in the *Chronicles* had not fully obliterated the traces of antagonism in the relationship between the Prince and the King. This antagonism, the legends of the Prince's debauchery and conversion, and other elements that the dramatist found in his sources, he wove into a plausible character. The Prince tries to dissociate himself from the crime his father had committed; *he avoids contamination with regicide because the impulse to regicide (parricide) is alive in his unconscious. When the King's life is threatened he saves the King and kills the adversary, who is his alter ego.* In shunning the court for the tavern he expresses his hositility to his father and escapes the temptation to parricide. He can permit himself to share Falstaff's vices because he does not condone the King's crime; but hostility to the father is only temporarily repressed. When finally he is in possession of the crown, *he turns against the father substitute;* hence the pointed cruelty of Falstaff's rejection. Both paternal figures between which the Prince oscillates have less meaning to him than appears at first. What he opposes to them is different and of an exalted nature: his ideals of kingship, royal duty and chivalry. These ideals are with him when he first appears on the stage; they grow in and with him throughout the tragedy, and they dominate throughout the five acts of *King Henry V*.

These ideals, one might speculate, may have been modeled on an idealization of Richard II, the murdered King, whom Prince Hal as a boy had accompanied to Ireland and whose favor he had won. Richard, however, was hardly fit to serve as model of a great king. Shakespeare has drawn him as a weak and irresponsible man, who depended presumptuously on the trappings of royalty for his kingship, on that ceremony that meant so little to Henry V and for which he substituted royal duty. One may conjecture this to have been a further reason why Shakespeare did not explicitly refer to the existence of a personal relationship between Prince Henry and King Richard. But all this is speculative. Opposed to it is solid evidence of the importance of moral conflicts in the personality of Henry V; it would be easy to demonstrate from metaphors and puns alone, with which the poet speaks through the hero, his proclivity to such conflicts. His major actions and interests all indicate too the Prince's search for moral justification.

While living the roistering life of the tavern, his thirst for glory won in battle—but only battle with a moral purpose—and chivalry was great; hence the Prince's bitter caricature of Hotspur.

> . . . I am not yet of Percy's mind, the Hotspur of the North; he that kills me some six or seven dozen of Scots at a breakfast, washes his hands, and says to his wife, 'Fie upon this quiet life! I want work.' 'O my sweet Harry,' says she; 'how many hast thou killed to-day?' 'Give my roan horse a drench,' says he; and answers, 'Some fourteen' an hour after; 'a trifle, a trifle.'[23]

There is jubilant relief when Percy turns to rebellion and the Prince can finally fight an envied rival, and in the service of a just cause liberate and use his own aggressive impulses; hence also, before the invasion of France, the preoccupation with legal points; and finally, on the night before Agincourt, the protracted debate with Williams, the soldier. Assuming that his partner in discussion is 'Harry le Roy' an English commoner, the soldier argues

> . . . There are few die well that die in a battle; for how can they charitably dispose of anything, when blood is the argument? Now, if those men do not die well, it will be a black matter for the king that led them to it. . . .[24]

Henry goes to great lengths to refute this thesis. He contends that the King is answerable only for the justice of his cause and cannot be answerable for 'the particular endings of his soldiers', since 'every subject is the King's, but every subject's soul is his own'. The moving subtleties of this theological discourse[25] lead to the King's soliloquy on ceremony and royal destiny:

> Upon the King! let us our lives, our souls,
> Our debts, our careful wives,
> Our children, and our sins lay on the king!
> We must bear all. O hard condition,
> Twin-born with greatness, subject to the breath
> Of every fool, whose sense no more can feel
> But his own wringing! What infinite heart's-ease
> Must kings neglect that private men enjoy!
> And what have kings that privates have not too,
> Save ceremony,—save general ceremony?
> And what art thou, thou idol ceremony?[26]

Summoned to battle, the King kneels in prayer in which he disclaims any complicity in his father's crime; thus prepared, the hero can conquer.

Henry V's preoccupation with morals is not glorified by Shakespeare nor presented as the dominant virtue of 'a Christian soldier'; it is shown in its dynamic interplay with opposite tendencies, and occasionally—with a slightly ironical smile—exposed as a pretense. While the King is urging the clergy to establish his claim to the throne of France, the audience knows that he has forced the support of the Church by political pressure. The bishops, who have accepted the deal and supplied the garbled justification, are well aware of the King's burning desire for conquest. We are left in doubt as to whether it is political shrewdness or self-deception which prompts the King to pose the question:[27]

May I with right and conscience make this claim?[28]

Ambiguities and schisms of motivation are characteristic of the King. He flees to the tavern to escape from the evils of the court—but he becomes a past master of licentious living. He strives for humane warfare, and protects the citizens of conquered Harfleur;[29] but when the French break the laws of warfare in attacking the English encampment and killing the boys, Henry has every French prisoner's throat cut. The 'friction between flesh and spirit' (Traversi), between impulse and inhibition, is fully resolved only when from moral scrutiny Henry proceeds to heroic venture, when as leader of men who are determined to fight with a clear conscience against overwhelming odds, he feels himself one among peers:

We few, we happy few, we band of brothers.[30]

The inconsistencies in Prince Hal's character that some of Shakespeare's critics thought to have detected are not inconsistencies but attempts to resolve a conflict which is in some of its elements similar to Hamlet's. In *Hamlet* the oedipus is fully developed, centering around the queen. In Shakespeare's historical dramas women are absent or insignificant. Prince Hal's struggle against his father appears therefore in isolation, enacted in male society. Hamlet stands between a murdered father and a murderous uncle. Prince Hal's father murdered his second cousin—and predecessor—to whom the Prince had an attachment. Thus the crime is in both cases carried out by the father or by his substitute—the King in *Hamlet*—while both heroes are battling against the murderous impulse in their own hearts.

The psychological plausibility of Prince Hal as a dramatic character is not inferior to that of Hamlet, whatever the difference in depth and dramatic significance of the two plays may be. While only one part of the oedipal conflict is presented, the defenses which Prince Hal mobilizes in order to escape from his internal predicament are well known from the clinical study of male youths. In our analysis of the Prince's character we have implicitly referred mainly to two mechanisms: first, to the formation of the superego; second, the displacement of filial attachment onto a father substitute.

The Prince, in his thoughts, compares the King, his father, with an ideal of royal dignity far superior to the father himself. This ideal, derived from paternal figures but exalted and heightened, is his protection in the struggle against his parricidal impulses and against submission to the King. This mechanism operates in some form or other in every boy's development at the time of the resolution of the oedipal conflict. During this process the superego acquires part of its severity and some of its autonomy. It is a process subject to many vicissitudes, as illustrated by a clinical example.

A boy of eight approached his father, a distinguished judge, with a request for advice. He held two one dollar bills and wanted to know whether he might keep them. They had been acquired by the sale to neighbors of pencils which a mail order house had sent him on his request. Upon the receipt of the two dollars he was to be sent a premium to which he now preferred the money. The judge asked to see the advertisement to which the boy had responded and the letter of the mail order house. After reading both he ruled: 'You may keep the money; they have no right to make such contracts with minors'.

When thirty-five years later the incident was recalled in analysis it appeared that he had not only lost confidence in all authority since that time, but also that when he had asked his father's advice he was testing him. He had grown suspicious that the father did not live up to the principles—sexual and moral—he advocated, and when in his own conflict he sought the father's advice, he had hoped that the father would support his own hesitant moral views. When this expectation was disappointed, he acquired a cynical independence. The compulsion to live up to his ideal became part of a complex neurotic symptomatology.

In one detail only did this patient resemble Prince Hal: his own moral standards assured his independence from all paternal figures and were used as aggressive reproach in every contact with them. Prince Hal uses not only his ideal of moral integrity as reproachful contrast against his father, but also his own playful depravity. The second mechanism of defense the Prince mobilizes is no less common than the first. He adopts an extrafamilial substitute who, true to a pattern frequently observed, is the antithesis of the father. Falstaff is closer to the Prince's heart than the King; he satisfies the libidinal demands in the father–son relation through his warmth and freedom. Yet the Prince proves superior to Falstaff in wit and royal reveling: he triumphs over both father and father substitute.[31] He is paramount in licence as he will be paramount in royal dignity.

Literary critics seem of late weary of the intrusion of psychoanalysis. However politely, they assert—and rightly so—their independence.[32] This essay is a psychological analysis which attempts only to underline a few universal, unconscious mechanisms, and is not intended as literary criticism. It suggests that Shakespeare had puzzled about the nature of Henry V's personality, and that already, while writing the last act of *Richard II,* was aware of the conflict on which he intended to center the character development of the King. Shakespeare's plan, suggested in this case by the nature of the tradition about the subject, must have been one of the trends of thought that, on various levels of awareness, directed him in writing the trilogy. It is not suggested that the plan was complete from the beginning; it might have manifested itself to the poet during his work, i.e., it might have been preconscious before. Moreover, some elements we here consider part of this plan probably never reached consciousness. What answer Shakespeare might have given if asked why Henry V kills Falstaff by his harshness is comparatively irrelevant. What counts is that he had the King do so, and he surely must have known that this could hardly be popular with an audience. Such internal consistency, the final parricide, can only have been conceived by one who in creating had access to his own unconscious impulses.

If investigations similar to the one here attempted, but more complete and authoritative, were carried out systematically, if they were to comprehend all of Shakespeare's work and, at least for purposes of comparison, the works of other Elizabethans; if conflicts and their varied or preferred solutions, and those omitted by one author, one group of authors, one period, or one cultural area were collated, such an application of psychoanalysis might be integrated with the work of the literary historian or critic.

Plot and character are clearly not the only, and not always the most important, tools of the dramatic poet. Psychoanalysis suggests other approaches for the study of poetic language, its metaphors and hidden meanings.[33] Systematic investigation in this area may lead to other types of integration than the study of plot or character. The combination of various sequences of such systematic studies might finally lead to a topic in which critics and psychoanalysts are equally interested and about which they are both, each in his own field, almost equally ignorant: the nature of the artist's personality, a question that must be studied in its cultural variations before generalizations can be made.

Psychoanalysis has frequently attempted short cuts, mostly by correlating one of the artist's works with an occurrence noted by his biographers,[34] assumptions that can rarely be verified.

Clinical analysis of creative artists suggests that the life experience of the artist is sometimes only in a limited sense the source of his vision; that his power to imagine conflicts may by far transcend the range of his own experience; or, to put it more accurately, that at least some artists possess the particular gift to generalize from whatever their own experience has been. One is always tempted to look for a cue that would link this or that character to its creator's personality. Falstaff, it has been said, is clearly Shakespeare himself. Why not Percy or Richard II? Are they not equally alive, equally consistent? Could not for each of these characters that very same psychological plausibility be claimed, that we here claim for Prince Hal? Such a quest seems futile and contrary to what clinical experience with artists as psychoanalytic subjects seems to indicate.[35] Some great artists seem to be equally close to several of their characters, and may feel many of them as parts of themselves. The artist has created a world and not indulged in a daydream.

This writer is not exempt from the temptation to detect a neat connection between the artist and one of his characters. I therefore record my own venture in this direction, with appropriate reservations. At the time Shakespeare was working on *Richard II,* and studying the life of Prince Hal, he reestablished the prestige of the Shakespeare family (which had been lost through his father's bankruptcy) by purchasing a coat of arms. The motto chosen is one that might well have been used to characterize Prince Hal's striving for the crown: 'Non sanz droict'.

NOTES

1. It is generally assumed that Part I of *King Henry IV* was written in 1596 or 1597, immediately or soon after the completion of *King Richard II,* and Part II in 1597 or 1598. *King Henry V* must have been completed shortly before or some time during 1599. *Cf.*

Spencer, Hazelton: *The Art and Life of William Shakespeare*. New York: Harcourt, Brace & Co., 1940.

2. *King Henry IV, Part I,* Act 1, Sc. 2.
3. *Cf.* Bradley, A. C.: The Rejection of Falstaff, in *Oxford Lectures on Poetry*. London: Macmillan & Co., 1934. Bradley's censure of Shakespeare is moderate compared to that of Hazlitt, William: *Characters of Shakespeare's Plays*. 4th ed., London: C. Templeman, 1848.
4. For the legend of Prince Hal see especially Kabel, P.: *Die Sage von Heinrich V, bis zur Zeit Shakespeares,* Palaestra, LXIX, Berlin, 1908: and Bowling, W. G.: *The Wild Prince Hal in Legend and Literature*. Washington Studies, Humanist Ser., XIII, 1925–1926, pp. 305–334. For summaries of historical facts see mainly Kingsford, C. L.: *Henry V, The Typical Medieval Hero*. New York: G. P. Putnam Sons, 1901; and McFarlane, K. B.: The Lancastrian Kings, in *The Cambridge Medieval History*. Cambridge, England: Cambridge University Press, VIII, 1936, pp. 363–416.
5. Kingsford, C. L.: *Op. cit.* p. 12.
6. *Cf.* Spencer, Theodor: *Shakespeare and the Nature of Man*. New York: Macmillan & Co., 1942.
7. *Cf.* Ax, Herman: *The Relation of Shakespeare's King Henry IV to Holinshed's Chronicle*. Freiburg I. Breisgau: D. Lauber, 1912.
8. That the repetition of one theme in various configurations indicates its central position was pointed out by Jekels, Ludwig: *Das Problem der doppelten Motivgestaltung*. Imago, XIX, 1933, pp. 15–26.
9. *King Henry IV, Part I,* Act 1, Sc. 1.
10. The idea of the travestied interview itself is borrowed from *The Famous Victories of Henry the Fifth*. London: Thomas Creede, 1898. There the Prince and his companion enact the Prince's subsequent interview with the Chiefjustice.
11. Empson, W.: *Some Versions of the Pastoral*. London: Chatto & Windus, 1935, pp. 43–46.
12. This point was made by Alexander, Franz: *A Note on Falstaff*. Psychoanalytic Q., II, 1933, pp. 592–606; and by Empson, W.: *Op. cit.*, p. 43.
13. Ernest Jones speaks in a similar connection of decomposition; see A Psychoanalytic Study of Hamlet, in *Essays in Applied Psycho-Analysis*. London: Int. Psa. Library, No. 5, 1923.
14. Alexander, Franz: *Op. cit.*
15. *King Henry IV, Part II,* Act IV, Sc. 5.
16. The very crown that literally he had taken from Richard II. *Cf. Richard II,* Act IV, Sc. 1.
17. *King Henry IV, Part II,* Act IV, Sc. 5.
18. *King Henry V,* Act IV, Sc. 1.
19. One might conjecture that Shakespeare preferred not to refer to the personal relationship between Prince Hal and King Richard since he needed a more mature Prince, not a boy of twelve.
20. *King Richard II,* Act V, Sc. 3.
21. Only once Henry V states openly his disapproval of his father's actions, and then in a highly restrained fashion. When wooing, somewhat abruptly, Katherine of France he says

> . . . I dare not swear thou lovest me; yet my blood begins to flatter me that thou dost, notwithstanding the poor and untempering effect of my visage. *Now beshrew my father's ambition! He was thinking of civil wars when he got me*. . . . (Italics added.)

22. York himself had plotted against Richard II and seeks his son's punishment out of a displaced feeling of guilt. Some of the complexities of this relationship were elucidated by Taylor, M. P.: *A Father Pleads for the Death of His Son*. Int. J. of Psa., VIII, 1927, pp. 53–55.

23. *King Henry IV, Part I,* Act II, Sc. 4.
24. *King Henry V,* Act IV, Sc. 1.
25. Canterbury says of the newly enthroned Henry V (Act I, Sc. 1):

    Hear him but reason in divinity
    And, all admiring, with an inward wish
    You would desire the King were made a prelate.

26. *King Henry V,* Act IV, Sc. 1.
27. A somewhat similar analysis of this passage has been given by Traversi, D. A.: *Henry V,* Scrutiny. IX, No. 4, March, 1941, pp. 352–374, who in a remarkable essay stresses the importance of 'cool reasoning' and 'self-domination' in the King's character.
28. *King Henry V,* Act I, Sc. 2.
29. Traversi notes that when the King presents his ultimatum to Harfleur his passion rises, and that in accepting the surrender he regains self-control. *Op. cit.*
30. *King Henry V,* Act IV, Sc. 3.
31. The son's superiority over the father occurs also in other connections in the trilogy. Hotspur is superior to both Worcester and Northumberland and Aumerle is superior to his father, York, who first betrays King Richard before he betrays his own son.
32. *Cf.* Trilling's excellent essay, *Freud and Literature.* Horizon, XVI, No. 92, 1947, pp. 182–200; or Knights, L. C.: *Explorations.* London: Chatto & Windus, 1946, especially the essay, Prince Hamlet, pp. 66–77.
33. *Cf.* Sharpe, Ella Freeman: *From King Lear to the Tempest.* Int. J. Psa., XXVII, 1946, pp. 19–30. *Cf.* also Kaplan, Abraham and Kris, Ernst: *Æsthetic Ambiguity.* Philosophy and Phenomenological Research, VIII, No. 3, March, 1948, pp. 415–435.
34. This procedure was initiated in 1900 by a remark of Freud who envisaged the possibility that Shakespeare's choice of Hamlet as a topic and the treatment of the conflict might have to do with the death of Shakespeare's son Hamnet.
35. *Cf.* Kris, Ernst: *Probleme der Æsthetik.* Int. Ztschr. f. Psa., u. Imago, XXVI, 1941, pp. 142–178; for clinical aspects *cf.* Bergler, Edmund: Psychoanalysis of Writers and of Literary Production, in *Psychoanalysis and the Social Sciences.* I. Edited by Géza Róheim. New York: International Universities Press, 1947, pp. 247–296.

8. The Mutual Adventures of Jonathan Swift and Lemuel Gulliver: A Study in Pathography

Phyllis Greenacre

This study has emerged from an interest in distortions in the body image involving sensations of change in size, either of the entire body or some part of the body, sensations which I believe to be of particular significance in fetishism. It is extracted from a book in preparation about Dean Swift and Lewis Carroll, with special reference to their lives in connection with their famous literary masterpieces, Gulliver's Travels and Alice's Adventures in Wonderland, in both of which such distortions of the body play a noteworthy role.

I. SWIFT'S LIFE

Swift was a remarkable man of picturesque contradictions. He was secretive, enigmatic, touchy, inordinately power-driven and active; always in the public eye, he was conspicuously afraid of gossip, and had many hiding places. He was a political power in his day in both England and Ireland, and in his activities swung like a pendulum between the two countries during much of his adult life. He rarely wrote or talked directly of his own experiences; yet he celebrated himself flagrantly in poetry and was never modest. He became known for his satirical prose and his obscene verses; yet in speech he was generally charming, immaculate, and witty. He wrote often under pseudonyms, a not uncommon practice of the time; he would wait until he could see the success of his anonymous pamphlet and when it was attributed to someone else, would come forth and angrily claim it, seemingly after having sat back and laughed at the commotion it had caused. He was known as a great practical joker too. His political writings especially revealed his unpar-

Reprinted by permission of the author's estate and *the Psychoanalytic Quarterly,* 24 (1955).

alleled courage and his great timidity, together with his fierce resentment at what he had himself provoked. Of himself he wrote: 'A person of great honor in Ireland . . . used to say that my mind was like a conjured spirit that would do mischief if I would not give it employment'. The 'person of great honor' seems to have been Swift himself *(10)*.

He came of a Yorkshire family. In his one autobiographical account *(8, 22)*—which petered out after a few pages—he was inclined to stress the aristocracy of his English forebears, and showed especial admiration for his English clergyman grandfather, in whose honor he erected a tombstone. He had not known his grandfather, nor his father either. The father, also named Jonathan Swift, had come to Ireland with several brothers, and had proved the least successful of them all. This Jonathan died in the spring of 1667, seven and a half months before the birth of his only son on November thirtieth of that year. Swift always spoke of having been 'dropped', not born, on Irish soil, and rather exhibitionistically mentioned that he was wont to read the third chapter of the Book of Job on his birthday—the chapter in which Job curses the day he was conceived. Yet Swift always celebrated his birthday with poetry and festivity as well as curses.

His mother, Abigail, was an Englishwoman of simple background, some eight to ten years older than her husband. They had married three years before Jonathan's birth, and he had a sister Jane, less than two years older. Some considered that Jonathan was illegitimate, others that he was really the posthumous child of the elder Jonathan. Whatever the facts, these two accounts of his birth must have been the gossip of the time and have contributed to the fantasies of the growing boy. The father died leaving many debts, and the records of the time indicate that the mother made great efforts to collect certain money due her husband in order to pay these debts. One is surprised to learn that in spite of this impoverishment the family had an English nurse for the two children, possibly furnished by the paternal uncle Godwin, a successful barrister and prolific husband and father. He married successively four wealthy wives and had in all eighteen children.

The events of Swift's infancy were more than dramatic and seem to have set an indelible pattern for his restless, driven, divided life. Swift wrote of himself that he had been a frail baby, and that when a year old he had been kidnaped by his nurse 'without the knowledge or consent' of his mother or his uncle, and had been taken by the nurse to the town of Whitehaven in England; further, that his mother, on discovering his abduction and after some delay in learning his whereabouts, sent word that he was not to be returned until he was sufficiently sturdy to bear easily the trip across the Irish Sea. This was accomplished three years later, when young Jonathan was between four and five. The nurse, he says, had been so devoted and careful that she had taught him to read and write so well that he could read any chapter in the Bible. The immediate cause and circumstances of his return are nowhere described. It is rather striking, too, that a few months after his return his mother left him in Ireland with his uncle Godwin and herself returned to her home in England, where she continued to live unmarried the rest of her life, depending on a small annuity of which the source is unclear.

The mysteries of this early career are more baffling in that, while Swift in the autobiographical fragment records the nurse's devotion to him and attributes to her his early literacy, he mentions her nowhere else, and seems generally to have consigned her to anonymity, which was his way in later life with those who displeased him. (We shall rediscover the nurse in Gulliver's account of *his* life.) The mother, who had apparently deserted Swift twice before he was five years old, was on the other hand described by Swift's second cousin, grandson of uncle Godwin, as 'a woman greatly beloved and esteemed by all the family of Swifts. Her conversation was so exactly polite, cheerful and agreeable, even to the young and sprightly.' He further remarked on her generosity, her decorum, her industrious reading and needlework. Whether this was sincere or a 'face' for the world is difficult to say.

When Swift came to know his mother later in life, he was fond of her and visited her whenever he went to England. According to some accounts, the mother maintained a playful relationship with him, so that when she visited him unexpectedly once in Ireland and found him absent, she succeeded in persuading his landlady that he was her lover. She died when Swift was forty-three. He then wrote that with her passing he had lost the barrier between himself and death, and he put this memorandum away between the pages of an account book.

Swift's relationship to his sister Jane is obscure. She presumably stayed with her mother. The same second cousin who wrote amiably of Abigail Swift noted that she was equally fond of both her children, between whom disagreements often existed. This must have been in their young adulthood, for they did not know each other after the earliest months until then. After his mother's return with Jane to England, Jonathan was placed under the care of his uncle Godwin, who presently sent him to school at Kilkenny, which was considered the Eton of Ireland. At school he was with two of his cousins, while vacations may have been spent among the eighteen children in Godwin Swift's household. Certainly from age five or six until twenty-two the young Jonathan lived an institutional existence which he hated. He later referred to these school years as comprising 'the education of a dog', and described himself as 'discouraged and sunk in spirit'. He was a poor student both at Kilkenny and at Trinity College in Dublin, where finally he got his degree only by a special dispensation at eighteen. He seems to have been compliant and inhibited in his work.

Swift later wrote to Lord Bolingbroke of an incident in his early days at Kilkenny—undoubtedly a screen memory of considerable significance:

> I remember when I was a little boy, I felt a fish at the end of my line which I drew up almost to the ground, but it dropped in and the disappointment vexes me to this day and I believe it the type of all my future disappointments.

This incident is told in other terms in the first voyage of Gulliver, in which he loses his hat in the water because the cord has been broken *(11)*. The hat is later retrieved and, attached by hooks on cords, is dragged in by five horses. This screen memory and its later literary elaboration, which we should regard as a corrective or restitutive version of the original screen memory, seems extremely significant, the two forming a picture not unlike the famous screen memory described by Freud.

Swift described another incident from his student days, which he repeated to impecunious young people seeking to marry without adequate savings *(8)*. He so much wanted a horse that he invested his entire capital in a worn-out nag which was the only horse he could afford, only to find that he had no money with which to buy feed for it. The horse finally solved the problem by lying down and dying. That Swift connected this story with marriage is significant, the tired horse quite possibly representing his own improvident father who also lay down and died. The horse was an important figure to both Swift and Gulliver, as we shall observe later.

Only after the attainment of his degree, disgraceful as it was, did the young man rebel, and as a graduate student at Trinity he became known as the writer of a scurrilous harangue which is described by one biographer as showing 'the will and capacity to wound and above all a directness in insolence, a mercilessness in savage laughter' *(10)*. Thenceforward he seemed more or less freed from his intellectual serfdom and from his depressions, which now rather appeared in the form of savage laughter turned to high moral purpose whenever possible. He left Trinity without a higher degree, ostensibly because of the illness and increasing dementia of his uncle Godwin, whom he hated and whose illness consequently made a deep impression on him. Swift then, at the age of twenty-two, turned to England and his mother, and embarked on his first flirtation with a rather undistinguished young woman named Betty Jones, who subsequently married a tavern keeper. Whatever this affair amounted to, it provoked some self-examination, for he wrote afterward to a friend that 'his own cold temper and unconfined humor were the greatest hindrance to any kind of folly'. He seems also to have turned to power and pride, for at the same time he wrote: 'I hope my carriage will be so as my friends need not be ashamed of the name'.

After a short time he obtained, through his mother and uncle, a position as a kind of secretary or literary steward in the home of Sir William Temple, who had previously been ambassador to Holland and active in affairs of state but was now retired and wanted the younger man to help him in the editing and sorting of his papers. Swift spent ten years in this household, the decade punctuated by several interruptions and some discontent. During his first year he developed symptoms of dizziness, deafness, and headache, probably Ménière's disease, which was to stalk him the rest of his life. He attributed it to eating too much 'stone fruit' in the Temple garden and sought to cure it by returning to his native Ireland.

The onset of this illness seems to have precipitated a wealth of hypochondriacal fears to counteract which he intensified by compulsive walking and exercising, keeping track of the amount of his daily walking and interrupting his work at regular intervals to keep up his pedal score. This continued throughout his life. His return to Ireland lasted only three months, after which he was back in the Temple household, this time not only editing and doing routine secretarial work but also attempting to write poetry. In this he was discouraged by his distant cousin Dryden, but he succeeded at this time in writing some of his famous satires, The Battle of the Books and The Tale of the Tub, which were not to be published until some years later.

Swift's second interruption of his sojourn in the Temple household occurred at twenty-seven, when he decided to enter the church. He had certainly been restless and resentful, and obviously felt unappreciated. He had obtained his Master's degree at Oxford at twenty-five without difficulty, much to his surprise, and had been busy with his own literary enterprises, but had not yet really tasted the heady wine of publication. The significance of his step in the direction of the church is not clear. He had already attacked religion like an atheist. But he was without a real home or family, and his position with the Temples was not well-defined. His sister Jane was also a member of the Temple ménage, but he seemed not to care much for her, and she remains throughout Swift's life a shadowy, drab, and disappointing figure at best. It is possible he looked to the church to take the place of a family. (It will be remembered that the ancestor he most admired was a clergyman grandfather.) This position in the church also offered him an excellent rationalization for his neurotic fear of gossip and exposure. But he was again to be disappointed: the prebend of Kilroot which was granted him was a dreary country place near Belfast.

During his stay with the Temples, Swift had become acquainted with a Mrs. Johnson, widow of Sir William's steward. As a lady-in-waiting she was also part of the establishment, together with her little daughter Hester, who was eight years old when Jonathan first came there. The lonely young man took an interest in the child and taught her so effectively to read and write that her evenly formed letters were almost a replica of his own. This little girl was to play an important part in his life and in a most engimatic relationship which has been puzzling and provocative of fantasy to students of literature throughout the more than two hundred and fifty years since then.

At Kilroot, however, he fell in love with a young lady, Jane Waring, the sister of a college classmate. He wanted to marry her, but his infatuation for her he likened to distemper, and he hoped the marriage would cure him. He renamed her Varina—a Latinized version of her last name—and she became the first of the three important women of his adult life: little Hester Johnson, the second, was to become the Stella who was most in his confidence and his companion until her death; and the third was another Hester whom he nicknamed Vanessa, again condensing her first name Hester with her last one, Van Homrigh. The two Hesters were the daughters of widows; whether this was true of Jane Waring is not known.

The courtship of Varina was an odd affair, in which the tortured man was by turns suspicious and peremptory, obviously frightened, yet driven toward marriage, while the girl wavered irresolutely. Swift's letters to her, of which he seems to have kept careful copies, were strange mixtures of philosophizing and violence *(14)*. Finally, at twenty-nine, he left and again returned to the Temples. Three years later, when at thirty-two he again visited Ireland, Varina got in touch with him. Hinting then that he felt she valued him for his better worldly standing, he wrote her an angry offer of marriage, in which he adjured her to be cleanly and obedient. This seems to have been the end of his relationship with Varina, and he did not mention her again.

His demand for cleanliness, and especially his fear of dirtiness in a woman, spoke loudly of the core of his neurosis *(7)*. Characteristically he used the word slut as a term of endearment, while he called his cook 'sweetheart' when she displeased him with overdone roasts. He was himself more than scrupulously clean at a time when to be so was a luxury and an achievement, and there are stories of his refusing to give alms to old women with unclean hands. In his repeated attacks on whatever seemed corrupt or evil, whether in a woman's body or in a matter of state, his language was itself so violent and foul that presently the stench seemed to come from him rather than from the object of his attack.

Just before his rupture with Varina, he wrote a series of pathetic 'Resolutions when I come to be old'—seventeen resolutions for self-protection and self-strengthening *(7)*. One was not to marry a young woman; another, not to harken to flatterers or conceive 'that I can be loved by a young woman', and another, 'not to be fond of children or let them come near me hardly'. Yet he remained the devoted tutor of little Hester Johnson (Stella).

Swift's thirty-second year (1699) was momentous: Sir William Temple died; Jane Swift married; Jonathan Swift made a final break with Jane Waring (Varina). This seems to have been the closing of an emotional epoch for him. Subsequently he became more cautious, negativistic, and aggressively touchy. He may have realized that he could not love, but was rather one who can feel that he is a person only if he opposes; the more so because he could thus save himself from the counterdemand of his nature, which was to lose himself completely in another, in the unconditional love of infancy.

His relationship with the Temple family and with his sister Jane fell apart completely. He sought preferment in the church, and being disappointed wrote two of his bitterest and foulest poems, The Discovery *(27)* and The Problem *(27)*, which caused one of his biographers to remark that he had behaved like an animal that relieves itself on the despised carcass of an adversary *(10)*. At this time too some of his writings, for example, Meditations Upon a Broomstick and Digression on Madness *(23)*, showed an unmistakable preoccupation with sexual inversion. He soon obtained a small country church at Laracor, a few miles from Dublin.

Swift had a theory that girls should be trained to be as much like boys as possible, and that only thus could they hope for a secure marriage. His education of Hester Johnson was continued in this way. He demanded great accuracy in spelling, reading, and writing, and he warned continuously against the frivolities of interest in dress, social chatter, or flirtations. He was training the first Hester to be a second version of himself. Two years after the death of Sir William, he persuaded Stella, who was living with a nurse-chaperon, Rebecca Dingley, to join him in Ireland. The great rationalization was that they would have more money because living was cheaper there. It is interesting that this move, referred to as the abduction of Stella, occurred at almost exactly the same interval after Sir William's death as Swift's own abduction by his nurse, traveling in the opposite direction, had occurred after the death of his father.

The life of Stella and Dingley in Ireland was unusual. They lived in a tiny cottage a discreet half mile or so from the rectory at Laracor, and when Swift was Dean of St. Patrick's in Dublin they lived near him there. He schooled them relentlessly to be discreet, meaning secretive. When he went to England they stayed behind in Ireland, but moved into his quarters, and Stella carried on his routine business for him, like a Junior Dean. It is said that he never saw her except in Dingley's presence. For twenty-seven years this strange triangle continued, with Swift complaining openly of Dingley's stupidity, but keeping her always as a guardian.

Stella's inner relationship with Swift, like so much else, is unclear. Her father had been a steward in Sir William Temple's household. (His father had been steward of the King's Inns.) We do not know the time of her father's death, nor her feeling for him. By some it was said that she was not his child. She was sickly till the age of fifteen, and later developed tuberculosis. Until her death in middle age, she lived in this synthetic family with the brilliant Jonathan Swift as her 'father' (her platonic lover in fact), and Dingley as a nurse-mother. Her own mother remained in England until her death. Swift quarreled with his sister Jane about her marriage, but when she was widowed a few years later he dutifully helped to support her although he did not wish to see or hear much of her, and sent her to live with Stella's mother. It seems amply clear that the Swift-Stella-Dingley ménage was a condensed version of Swift's own early life, with Mrs. Johnson playing the part of Abigail Swift with her daughter Jane in keeping. The real Abigail continued to live in Leicester until her death.

There was nothing to indicate a sexual relationship between Swift and Stella, and much to suggest that for Swift the idea was loathsome and perhaps impossible. He addressed Stella as 'Young Sir'; wrote to her, 'Why are you not a young fellow and then I might prefer you?', and again declared that Stella and Dingley were not women. Swift pictured her as a stern and exacting idealist like himself *(14);* she was as prudent and frugal with money as he. When another clergyman sought Stella in marriage, Swift was pushed to a declaration 'in conscience and in honor', in which he told 'the naked truth', but proceeded to an appraisal of Stella's fortune and intellect such that the poor man retreated—for Swift seemingly supported the suit of his rival but ended with the pretense that the gentleman would presently be obliged to marry Stella in order to satisfy gossip. Swift's letter on the occasion is extraordinarily cold.

At the time of Swift's mother's death when he was forty-three (1710), he was at the height of his political power in England. He knew himself to be a genius, and savored his influence with arrogance and sometimes with revenge. Just then he began his famous Journal to Stella, a series of letters always frequent and sometimes daily, which continued for three years (1710–1713). This Journal is fascinating, for side by side with his account of his political and literary achievements are long chronicles of his complaints and illnesses, together with barely decipherable personal communications written in a kind of baby talk pig Latin, with many abbreviations known between Swift and Stella as the 'little language' *(26)*.

It was in 1710 too that the third goddess, the second Hester, appeared on the scene—the girl who was to be Vanessa *(9)*. Her father had been Lord Mayor of Dublin, and Swift met the widow and her children on the boat from Ireland to England. The new Hester was about seven years younger than the first. Swift frequently and seemingly carelessly misstated the ages of the two Hesters, often making them two or three years younger than they were. It is interesting to note that this is the difference in age between himself and his sister Jane. Hester van Homrigh was older when Swift met her, more worldly, but as direct and intolerant of deception as he had trained Stella to be. Swift once wrote to Vanessa's cousin about her in such terms that it provoked the young woman to protest that he sounded as though he were describing a hermaphrodite. This Hester was said actually to resemble Swift. She was, however, not as docile as Stella, and she was developed as a woman. While she reverenced his genius, she fell in love with him—a state which became distressing to all three and caused Swift finally to turn on her in coldness and destroy her.

For a time Swift kept up visits and correspondence with the two Hesters, often with amazingly similar expressions. One was in England, the other in Ireland, and for a long time they did not know each other. In these letters he addressed Vanessa as 'agreeable bitch', Stella as 'brat'. His disappointing cook he addressed as 'sweetheart'. There is no doubt that his affection for

Stella was more consistent than that for Vanessa. It was Vanessa however who elicited from him an attempt at a passionate response, which he 'half revealed and all concealed' in his famous poem Cadenus and Vanessa. What remains of her letters to him is filled with the urgency of her desire to see him and her disappointment at his constantly broken promises. On his side, however, every expression of warm feeling for her is followed by one of coldness and desire to flee.

In 1711 Swift's satirical pamphlets were so successful that his Conduct of the Allies *(18)* was credited with ending the war between France and England. In 1713 he became Dean of St. Patrick's Cathedral in Dublin. But by this time he was caught in the decline of the Tory power, was personally unpopular, and began to complain of being old and to write his epitaphs. Now too Vanessa unfortunately returned to Ireland to live on her family's estate at Celbridge, also a few miles from Dublin. The two young women heard rumors of each other. Swift's relationship to Vanessa progressively declined, and had throughout a desparate, tantalizing quality. Swift, often placating, sometimes sentimentally tender, treated her with what Scott described as 'cruelty under the mask of mercy' *(17)*, and Vanessa complained that he kept her in 'a languishing death' *(9)*. He even twitted her with behaving as though she were in love. Stella however remained generally steadfast but possibly more demanding.

In the years 1713–1718 Swift seems to have written only once to Vanessa, and his correspondence with Stella was not kept. The famous Journal stopped in 1713. Swift was personally uncourageous and seemed always afraid of being caught in scandal. In 1716 some event occurred which gave rise to stories that Swift had married or almost married Stella, but with the proviso that they should continue to live apart. There were evidently rumors that the marriage had not been finally accomplished, but the official version for nearly seventy-five years was that it had. Later investigations revealed no documentary evidence of any kind that it had occurred, and some indications that it had not. And so the secretive man who was always so afraid of the nasty tattle of the town succeeded in setting up a mystery that has stimulated the scoptophilia of students of English literary history every since.

The marriage is said to have occurred in the garden of the Deanery in Dublin. Stella was ill and jealous. The reports come mostly from two clergymen friends, one of whom was said to be the officiating churchman. Just as the marriage ceremony was to have been performed someone, whose identity is not stated, revealed that it could not continue, as Swift and Stella were actually brother and sister, the natural children of Sir William Temple. The occurrence of any marriage was later denied by Dingley and by Stella's executor. That the rumors represent some sort of fantasy—with what grain of truth?—is obvious; but like the stories concerning Swift's birth it is not clear whose fantasies predominated. One may well ask whether it is conceivable that these fantasies sprang primarily from Swift himself, representing some older longing of his own, and were advanced and 'confessed' by him in a way to block the marriage and let the situation remain as it had been. The facts already presented rather clearly suggest Swift's fixation on and identification with the fantasied sister of his childhood, Jane, the child who was absent with the mother and who was actually so disappointing to him in the materialization. Swift's first love affair was with Jane Waring, sister of his school friend. It is my further suggestion that one of the many determinants in the choice of the two Hesters was the name itself, so alliteratively close to the word 'sister'. Both were the children of widowed mothers; one the daughter of a steward, and the other of a more distinguished sire, the Mayor of Dublin.

Eleven years after the supposed marriage, Swift was again writing to a young woman to prepare her for marriage and stressing the need for rational love and intellectual companionship. Always he emphasized cleanliness and avoidance of gossip, and warned the girl not to be sentimental or rapturous, or to taunt a man about his physical deformity or his lack of a family fortune. Of love itself, or of spirituality, he said nothing *(7)*.

A few of Vanessa's letters remain, betraying a pathetic, growing disillusionment and hatred for the man who besought her to be sincere and was himself so indirect. Her idolatry turned to bitterness. When she wrote to him of the approaching death of her sister, of whom he had seemed to be fond, he advised her to get her friends around her but himself stayed away, writing, 'I want comfort and can give little'. One feels that he could not tolerate being called upon for personal help or being confronted with suffering. Then he felt worse himself, whether out of identification or guilt it is hard to say; but he stayed away, plagued and hypochondriacal, and considered the suffering of others as due to 'unhappy imagination'!

Vanessa died in 1723 at the age of thirty-six. On hearing of her death, he hastened a southern trip which he had planned for some time and, leaving that very night, he stayed away for some months, traveling more than five hundred miles on horseback seeking 'companionship among those of least consequence and most compliance'. He gave no indication of conscious grief or guilt, but spent his energy in riding, even as earlier he had required his compulsive walking. He could not go to England because of his unpopularity. True to the pattern of his earlier life, he climbed out of this period by becoming again politically active, and that in the interest of a noble cause. The next year he was writing the famous Drapiers Letters *(7, 23),* satire which was so successful that it forced the rescinding of a law permitting special coinage for Ireland in a way that would have ruined Irish trade. His popularity in Ireland now rose to new heights. It seems then that what he could not do for Vanessa, who had been emotionally closer to him than anyone else in his life, he did on a grand scale for the suffering people of Ireland. Presently, however, he was playing a practical joke which showed his contempt for these same Irish he had just rescued.

It seems probable that Swift thought much about Gulliver's Travels, but especially of the fourth (and last) voyage, while he was on this journey of concealed mourning. It is known that he had long had the main ideas for the Travels, and had already written much, but the fourth voyage is but scantily mentioned in the earlier drafts. In 1726 Gulliver's Travels was published.

On the whole Swift seems to have been esteemed and feared by his contemporaries. His wit and his intellect won him social recognition and his periodic forays into politics brought great admiration. He could seldom sustain friendships of close intimacy with men, perhaps because of his possessiveness but also because of the interplay between his great charm and his implacably fierce principles. To be sure, Addison wrote of him as 'the most agreeable companion, the truest friend, and the greatest genius of his age'—remarks on the flyleaf of a presentation copy of one of Addison's own books (1705), indicative of considerable enthusiastic respect. Charles Ford was the one man, however, with whom Swift maintained a close and confidential relationship over many years. The full extent of this relationship was probably not recognized by early biographers, as many of the letters between the two men did not come to light until 1896 *(19).*

Charles Ford was Dublin born and of almost exactly the same age as Stella. Swift probably came to know him about 1707, when Ford was taking his Master's degree and was about to marry. The marriage never took place, however, and as the friendship between the two men grew, Ford became a real confidant, who knew about Vanessa and Stella and offered solace and help rather generally. He is described as gay, joyous, and bright, but never profound. He had Stella and Dingley visit him for months after Vanessa's death, while Swift was galloping along the South coast of Ireland. Sometime later, however, Ford seems gradually to have removed himself from Ireland and Swift, and he spent his last years in London.

The publication of Gulliver's Travels reinstated and increased Swift's fame, and somewhat counteracted the ill feeling aroused by the poem, Cadenus and Vanessa, publication of which had been vengefully ordered in Vanessa's will but might well have been stopped by Swift. Characteristically he preferred to pretend that it meant nothing to him and was only a bit of a frolic among women, ignoring how much suffering its publication must have caused the faithful Stella.

Stella began to fail in health. Swift absented himself often and began to speak as though she were already dead. He was aware of his profound distaste for seeing her ill and found great difficulty in overcoming this enough to go to see her and comfort her during the last months of her life. He narrowly missed being present at her death in January 1727; she died while he was entertaining friends at dinner. He had been overwhelmingly afraid that she would die in the Deanery. He could not bear to go to her funeral, and sat in an adjacent room writing a long eulogy of her during the service.

By 1730 both Stella and Vanessa were dead and Charles Ford had settled in London. Swift became increasingly lonely and resentful. He spent much time with the erratic and rather dirty but charming Sheridan, grandfather of the playwright, and began to write many things for which he had had ideas for years. He incessantly reviled the body, especially the body of woman; he expressed his resentment of children as dirty nuisances who cluttered the world. Under the strange guise of a savage attack upon conditions of poverty in Ireland, he wrote one of his most dreadful and fierce satirical essays, entitled A Modest Proposal for Preventing the Children of Poor People being a Burden to their Parents *(7, 23)*, in which he suggested that infants one year old be roasted and served at the tables of the rich. He wrote both fair and filthy verse, became pugnacious in espousing the causes of the distressed, and took on the minor problems of people who had little or no claim upon him.

During the next decade, he suffered increasingly from attacks of rage and from progressive failure of his memory *(25)*. In 1742, it was necessary to have him declared to be mentally incompetent and to appoint a guardian. He was silent for almost one year. It is reported that before his capacity to think had become quite clouded, he would look at himself in a pierglass and mutter, 'Poor old man. Poor old man', and again, as though childishly philosophizing to himself, 'I am what I am. I am what I am.' He died in

Dublin at seventy-eight, on October 19, 1745. He left his fortune to found a hospital for fools and madmen.

II. GULLIVER'S TRAVELS

This book is manifestly an adventure story burlesquing the reports of world explorations at a time when new areas of the strange world were being discovered and the explorer was a romantic storyteller, a conqueror, and a kind of amateur reporter of anthropological mysteries *(11)*. Sometimes, as by Defoe, the book of travel was used as an allegorical medium. Gulliver's Travels contains bold satirical attacks upon the political policies of the day, but its enduring popularity as a fairy tale classic for children is obviously not based on its political significance but upon its closeness to profound and unconscious problems of mankind.

Gulliver's Travels was written between 1721 and 1725 and published in 1726. The outline of the voyages had long been cast, having been written but not fully published by Swift as early as 1711–1714, under the title of the Memoirs of Scriblerus *(7)*. But the fourth and last voyage seems to have been largely a product of a later time, and its elaboration may have been influenced by the prolonged emotional strain which Swift suffered, culminating with Vanessa's death in 1723. The first voyage was to Lilliput, the land of tiny folks; the second to Brobdingnag, the land of the giants; the third to five places: Laputa, Balnibarbi, Glubdubdrib, Luggnagg, and Japan; the fourth was to the country of the strangest creatures of all, the Houyhnhnms.

Lemuel Gulliver, the traveler, is a young man of Nottinghamshire, England, the third among five sons, recently apprenticed to a surgeon, Mr. James Bates. He has always had an interest in travel, having prepared himself for it by studying navigation, mathematics and two years of physics at Leyden. Bates, his master, recommends him as surgeon on a ship, the Swallow,[1] where he serves for three years on voyages to the Levant. Later, again under the influence of Bates, he settles down to the practice of his profession in London and marries a woman who brings him a modest dowry. But his good master Bates dying in two years, Gulliver finds himself failing in his profession and has so strong a conscience that he cannot imitate the corrupt practices of his colleagues. He returns to the sea, where his maritime career continues more than fifteen years (1699–1715).[2]

It is interesting to compare the lives of Lemuel Gulliver and Jonathan Swift, his creator, both as to sequence of events and the occurrences at specific dates in the two lives. There are no very full nor reliable accounts of either. Gulliver was born a few years before Swift. Both men were travelers. Though Swift never traveled far, he was a constant voyager between Ireland and England, sometimes dividing the year between the two countries, and many times made plans for foreign travel. Swift was a clergyman, preoccupied with the ills of his own body and with the political ills of the state, but could hardly bear to consider the bodies of others. Gulliver was a surgeon's apprentice who went on to explore the topography of foreign lands and peoples. Gulliver went to Cambridge at fourteen; Swift at the same age had gone to Trinity. While Gulliver was being apprenticed to Mr. Bates, Swift at a corresponding time was doing graduate work for his Master's degree. Both left their native soil at the age of twenty-one, Gulliver going to Leyden to prepare for travel, Swift to England to find his mother. At twenty-seven, Gulliver married and attempted to settle down in London. At the same age, Swift was wishing to marry Jane Waring and settle into the life of a clergyman. Both men lost their benefactors, Mr. Bates and Sir William Temple respectively, at the age of thirty-two. Gulliver then returned to the sea, and Swift to the church. The actual year 1699, in which Gulliver set out on the first recorded voyage, was a landmark in the life of Swift, being the time of Sir William Temple's death, of Swift's rupture with Jane Waring, and of the unapproved marriage of Jane Swift. The date, December 1715, of Gulliver's return from his last voyage, in a state of abhorrence toward his wife, was only a few months before Swift's supposed marriage to Stella.

If one may summarize the qualities of the voyages in a phrase or two apiece, it may be said that the first two are concerned with size of the body; while in the third, changes of size, and especially the movement of inanimate objects in a land of abstract geometric fantasies not subject to reality testing, are the striking factors. The land of the fourth voyage is inhabited by ideal creatures and foul creatures, and the interrelation of these, and their relation to the traveler, compose the climax of the travels.

The first and best known voyage to Lilliput took three years. The ship, headed for the East Indies, was wrecked and Gulliver was the only survivor. He found himself in a land of very tiny people who, having caught him napping, pinned him to the ground with lacings of rope, attempting so to hold him down. Later they conveyed him to a temple which had been profaned by the murder of a man. There he was placed on view, tethered by a chain. Unable to escape, he defecated once within the temple, but later went into the open air for this purpose. Gulliver tells all this in meticulous detail, much as a child who is striving to be good in a new and strange place. He resembles Swift in his preoccupation with involuntary moral guilt and unavoidable physical dirtiness.

I would not have dwelt so long upon a circumstance which . . . may appear not very momentous, if I had not thought it necessary to justify my character in point of cleanliness to the world, which I am told some of my maligners have been pleased . . . to call into question. (p. 14)*

The most pervasive motif of the first voyage is the disparity in size between Gulliver and the Lilliputians who are afraid that Gulliver's need for food and clothing will impoverish them. This seems to reproduce something of Swift's first year of life to which he returns in his horrible satire, A Modest Proposal . . . , in which he proposes that the child be roasted at the age of one, the age at which he was kidnaped and taken to England. In Lilliput, Gulliver pretends to eat up the little folk. Most conspicuous of all is the awesomeness and offensiveness to the Lilliputians of Gulliver's mountainous body: his sneeze produces a tornado, his urination creates a torrent of 'noise and violence', his defecation causes a national problem of health. He brandishes his sword and the sunlight on the blade causes them to kneel down in blinded awe. When he shoots his pistol into the air a hundred men fall from shock. One cannot but think that these experiences correspond in reverse to Swift's own infantile experiences when, still in an era of primary identification, he was transported on *his* first voyage to England, where his stay also lasted three years.

Threads, ropes, and cords play an important part, in many variations, in the game of Gulliver and the Lilliputians, reminding one strongly of the importance of ropes and thongs among fetishists. The interest, awe, and revulsion aroused by the human body is represented actively and passively by both Gulliver and the Lilliputians, with reciprocal exhibitionism and scoptophilia, with great attention to the excretory functions. Gulliver plays with the King's cavalry[3] like a child playing with toy soldiers, and in turn is directed by the Emperor to stand, like a colossus, with his legs apart while the soldiers parade under the arch thus formed, stealing covert glances at the torn crotch of the giant's pants.

The problem of size reappears in the Lilliputian religious and political problems, for the country is split into factions: the High-Heelers against the

*[All quotes from *Gulliver's Travels* are from The Pocket Library edition. New York: Pocket Books, 1957].

Low-Heelers, and the Big-Endians against the Little-Endians (who dispute the question, which end of a boiled egg is preferred). The Emperor's son wears heels of uneven height, so that he hobbles in compromise, and the country is in danger of being conquered by a neighboring country. But the giant Gulliver rescues Lilliput by dragging the enemy fleet out of the channel, like a child manipulating toys.

His visit to the Lilliputians culminates in his famous exploit of putting out a fire in the Queen's chamber by urinating upon it; but the Queen reacts in revenge rather than gratitude.

The system of education among the Lilliputians was certainly founded by the infant Swift. It is based on the principle that parents beget children from purely biological drives and therefore should not be permitted to educate them, nor to visit them for more than two hours in a year. Boys and girls are educated separately, but girls are educated to be as much like boys as possible, on the principle that a wife 'should always be a reasonable and agreeable companion, since she cannot always be young'. Throughout the story morals are valued higher than abilities. Consequently Gulliver finds himself impeached because his abilities are recognized and feared, and he finds it ultimately necessary to escape and return home. Thus ends the first voyage of Lemuel Gulliver and Jonathan Swift.

The second voyage is soon undertaken. Again the ship loses its course and after a year of wandering lands upon a new continent. Gulliver becomes separated from his companions and finds himself among giants in the land of Brobdingnag. This voyage seems but a continuation and reversed version of the first. Gulliver is now afraid of being trampled or eaten. The appearance of the nurse as an important figure is significant. She appears in two forms. In one she is the revolting adult nurse who bares her dry nipple to quiet the baby by suckling it, and in so doing reminds Gulliver that the Lilliputians had found his skin revolting, with its oversized pores and stumps of hairs. In the other she is the little girl nurse who teaches him the language and calls him her manikin. The impression of the disgusting adult woman is later re-enforced by the sight of a woman with cancerous holes in her breast, so large that Gulliver might have crawled into one. The traveler himself suffers passive exhibition, being carried in a kind of doll cage dangling from a cord around the waist of the little girl nurse when she shows him at county fairs.

Ultimately he is protected by the Queen, who prepares a little closet in which he can go riding on horseback strapped to the belt of the rider. It is of interest that he is unimpressed by the tallest tower in the land, computing its height to be less than that of Salisbury Cathedral. He suffers exposure and mutual exhibitionism at the hands of the Maids of Honor, who use him for their erotic amusement, balance him astride their nipples, and disgust him by their copious urination and the odor of their bodies. This indeed is the first voyage in reverse. Finally he suffers the typical lesson of being brought to witness the beheading, with a dramatic spurt of blood, of a murderer. The Queen now makes a little boat for him, which is propelled down a water-filled trough by the breeze from the ladies' fans.

The common symbolism of the man-in-the-boat as the clitoris suggests the identification with the female phallus thought to be characteristic of the male transvestite. A further incident confirming this occurs when one of the ladies lifts him up between her thumb and forefinger to put him into his little boat, but he slides through and plunging downward is caught by a corking pin in the lady's stomacher. The head of the pin passing between his skin and his waistband, he is suspended in this way more or less attached to the lady's stomacher until rescued by his little nurse.

The theme of the kidnaping appears also, for Gulliver is carried away three times: by a dog, by a kite, and by a monkey. The monkey holds him 'as a nurse does a child she is about to suckle'. The further description of this event specifies that the monkey is a male, who crams food into Gulliver's mouth, squeezing it out from his chaps. This whole experience sickens Gulliver terribly, and the food has to be picked out again by the child nurse. Surely this is a fantasy of fellatio—of being at the mercy of a bisexual adult. Gulliver is forced to recognize his insignificance when the King chaffs him about this disgusting experience. Finally, when the King wishes to find him a mate, it is time for the traveler, who has been away two years, to return home. He cannot bear to propagate a race so diminutive as to be laughable. He escapes by being kidnaped again, this time by an eagle which carries him off in his box, then drops the box with its occupant into the sea. It is noteworthy that, after he is picked up by sailors, his return voyage takes exactly nine months, during which he suffers severe sensory feelings of unreality in trying to reconcile himself to the normal size of those around him. He has difficulty in focusing his vision.

After this homecoming, his wife begs Gulliver never to leave again, but he has an insatiable thirst for seeing the world and soon is off again. Many critics have thought the third voyage out of place; they feel it does not belong in this sequence.To me it seems an essential link. On this trip, his ship is attacked by pirates and he is cast adrift in a canoe. This leads to his discovery of a peculiar, exactly circular island suspended in the air over the body of a continent, and resting so delicately on a lodestone that a little child's hand can manipulate it; and its inhabitants can thus move it at will 'to raise or sink, or put it in progressive motion'. This is the Island of Laputa, and might be described as the Island of Abstract Fantasy without Reality Testing. The movement of the island, directed by the King, depends much upon mathematics and music. Ideas are expressed in geometrical figures, although there is great contempt for practical geometry. The Laputans are chronically anxious and fearful of total destruction of the earth, the planets, everything. Peculiar marital relations prevail, and the women are mostly restless and unsatisfied, a condition which reminds Gulliver of his home in England. Through the intervention of the stupidest man on the island, Gulliver succeeds in getting away to the adjacent Island of Balnibarbi, a place once rich and substantial, but recently ruined by the infiltration of smatterings of mathematics from the Laputans, which has produced too great a volatility of spirit. The Balnibarbians have attempted to put the ideas of the Laputans to practical tests, and consequently have impoverished their people. Their Institute of Scientific Exhibits, however, would be well worth a visit in our own day. It must have resembled a display of patents. In one place, words are mixed in a kind of grinding machine and then used for poetry, politics, law, and theology. In another, words are abolished, as each word uttered diminishes the lungs by corrosion. Following this, words are supplanted by things, in a kind of symbolic realization, and only the women rebel and insist upon using their tongues; moreover, a kind of lobotomy is performed, but with the advantage of an exchange of amputated lobes between individuals. In this progressive country, Gulliver recommends the establishment of a governmental department of spies, informers, discoverers, accusers, and witnesses, so that it can first be agreed who shall be accused; the papers of the accused can then be seized, and the anagrammatic method used for evaluating the evidence. This country makes Gulliver homesick for England and he feels, prophetically, that it may perhaps extend to America and the land of California. (Swift only missed using the name McCarthy.)

There is still another island, Glubdubdrib, inhabited by sorcerers and magicians, where the servants are ghosts, changing each twenty-four hours and being made to evaporate into thin air by a flick of the Governor's finger. Another stop is at Luggnagg, where he is met by a male interpreter, a contrast to his previous experiences of having been nursed and taught by girls, women, princesses, and queens. Here Gulliver has to lick the dust before the royal footstool and utter words which mean 'my tongue is in the mouth of my friend!'. He makes a final stop in the vicinity of the eerie Struldbrugs, variant creatures, human but undying, and finds them a dejected, opinionated, covetous group of immortals.

After a short stop at home, during which his wife enters her third pregnancy, Gulliver again leaves on the ship Adventure, not as a ship's surgeon this time, but as a sailing captain. There is a mutiny, and he is left on a strange, desolate island inhabited by strangely evil and by noble creatures. The evil ones are dirty, hairy, nightmarish animals that scamper about and climb trees, persecuting and tormenting the traveler by letting excrement drop on his head. In contrast to these are reasonable, gentle horses, the natural aristocrats of the land. Soon a pair of the gentle horses take him in hand, teach him the language, and give him a home. From them he learns that they are Houyhnhnms, and that the foul creatures are called Yahoos. From the way the Houyhnhnms look at his face and hands he realizes that they regard him as a special Yahoo, unexpectedly clean and teachable. When they see him at night, partly undressed and with the lower part of his body uncovered, they are sure that he is a Yahoo, and a complete examination of his body brings them to the opinion that he is a perfect specimen of Yahoo—a characterization which greatly displeases him. When he tries to explain to them the laws and customs of his native England, they feel even more strongly confirmed in their diagnosis, but feel also that Gulliver is not quite so hardy as their local members of the species. After a time he decides never to return home, but to stay permanently with the Houyhnhnms. They explain to him that the Yahoos hate each other more than they do any creatures of other species, the reason for this being the odiousness of their shapes which all can see in each other but none in himself. The Yahoos are greedy, lacking in discrimination, and foul in their sexuality, and their system of medicine is founded upon coprophagic practices. Gulliver himself, studying the Yahoos, confirms their unteachability but interestingly attributes it to a perverse, restive disposition rather than to inherent defect.

After three years in this country, Gulliver becomes convinced of his own indubitable Yahoo origin when a Yahoo maiden falls in love with him as she sees him bathing, and is so energetic in her advances that he has to be rescued by his devoted sorrel nag. In contrast to the Yahoos, the Houyhnhnms are reasonable, just, and friendly. In their education of children they depend upon reason rather than love; the marital relationship is one of mutual benevolence and friendship of a standardized communal variety. They train their youth after a Swiftian rule by having them run up and down hills in competitive races.

In this country, the Houyhnhnms embody equable reason and impersonal good will, while the Yahoos are creatures of primordial hate and passion. The former are minute and exact in their descriptions and 'just' in their similes. When they die, by a process of gradual fading, there is no emotion, no mourning. The dead person is said 'to have returned to his first mother', and before taking this final step he pays a last ceremonial call upon his friends, being sure to repay all past visits.

After Gulliver's discovery of his true Yahooness he settles down to stay in this strange country, hating himself in a way unique among them, and trying hard to emulate the behavior of the Houyhnhnms. After five years residence, he finds himself banished by the General Council of Houyhnhnms, who consider him dangerous, perhaps because he is mixing customs so much. He builds a boat and gets away. Ultimately picked up by a Portuguese ship, he is at first judged deranged because of his accounts of his experiences. He wants to isolate himself for the rest of his life on an island. He returns home, however, and finds that he cannot bear his wife for he is still under the influence of Houyhnhnm ideals and cannot endure the thought of having cohabited with a Yahoo and produced Yahoo children. It is more than a year before he can bear to be in the same room with his wife, and never afterward can he bring himself to drink from the same cup as his family or to be touched by one of them. In memory of the good Houyhnhnms he buys a pair of horses with whom he lives in amiable friendship, the smell of their stable being sufficient to revive his sagging spirits.

No account of Gulliver and Swift can be tolerably complete unless it links with these two names that of Martin Scriblerus, later known as Tim. The Scriblerus Club, originally the Tory Club, consisted of Swift, Pope, Gay, Oxford, Parnell, and Arbuthnot, and Swift proposed that all write in collaboration a comprehensive satire on the abuses of learning. They produced the Memoirs of Scriblerus, the major part of which was supposed to have been written by Swift. It was openly admitted, furthermore, that Swift himself was identified with Scriblerus, and Swift was temporarily nicknamed 'Dr. Martin' for, as he explained in his Journal to Stella, surely a Martin was a kind of Swift, and both were swallows. (Swallow was the name of one of the ships on which Gulliver traveled.) In the early Scriblerus writings, Swift revealed certain fantasies regarding his birth, his grandiose dreams, and his attitudes toward his own genius. He projected the Travels (not to be published for another fifteen years) as consisting of four voyages: first to the pygmies; second to the giants; third to the mathematicians and philosophers; and fourth, one in which a 'vein of melancholy proceeds almost to a disgust of his species'. At this time he was preoccupied with his conservative plan of using cannibalism for the relief of the conditions of the poor. It was certainly a long-standing preoccupation, for the Modest Proposal was not published until 1729.

III. CLINICAL DISCUSSION

Swift's problems of identity and identifications, inherent in the strange circumstances of his birth, were again evident at the end of his life, when he addressed the old man in the mirror as 'poor old man', and philosophized 'I am what I am. I am what I am.' The complications of his kidnaping and the return to his mother, followed by her apparent desertion at the very height of the œdipal period, furnished in reality a fateful family romance that might otherwise have been a powerful fantasy. His living almost entirely in institutions from this time until his majority really completed the punishment of fate. Even his vacations were presumably spent among the eighteen children of uncle Godwin, and it is of interest that he mentions no girl among them.

His one attempt to write an autobiography petered out after a few pages, and about the kidnaping nurse we have only the barest statement that she prematurely taught him to read the Bible. Gulliver tells us more, as I have indicated, and splits the image of the nurse into two, the evil, repulsive, gaping old nurse, and the gentle, prepubertal little girl nurse, who protected him and kept him dangling in his cage attached to her belt. I have already indicated, in relating the histories of Dean Swift and Dr. Gulliver, that it is my belief that the infant Swift must have been in close bodily contact with the kidnaping nurse, and almost surely somehow built up a complementary fantasy of the sister from whom he had been separated at the age of one; and that he made a deep identification of himself with both by a direct primary bodily identification with the actual nurse, and with a sustaining ideal image of the sister, which seems to have been a phallic image whereby he became predominantly identified with the sister's phallus. (Recall the child nurse who has him dangling from her waist, the Maids of Honor who blow him in his little boat down a trough of water, and the incident of his getting impaled on the stomacher of the lady-in-waiting.) That the young adult Swift first sought a girl of his sister's name, Jane, and then formed attachments to two girls named Hester (sister), and that he broke with Jane Waring in bitter disillusionment at the same time that he practically banished sister Jane because he disapproved of her marriage, are not pure accidents. Furthermore, his mutual identification between himself, his sister, and the nurse is consistently reenacted in his arrangement of his own life as tutor to the two Hesters, whom he would also turn into boys by his education of them. All this seems to me so clinically clear as to need little further elucidation in this presentation.

Swift's physical health and symptoms are worthy of notice. He was said to have been a frail, premature infant, and certainly his mother was under stress during the pregnancy and throughout his first year. One cannot avoid the conclusion that her attitude toward this baby, whose birth caused so many complications in her life, must have been disturbed; but in just what direction is unclear. Swift had two mothers, in fact; and that he had two fathers is indicated by the reports of illegitimacy and remarks that his father never even knew of his conception. This question of paternity was to reappear in the never-solved mystery story of how Swift's marriage to Stella was stopped by the rumor that they actually were brother and sister. It seems to me important that Swift, whether or not he furthered the rumor, must have known of it, and certainly made no move to correct or deny it. It either sprang from his fantasy or closely corresponded to a latent fantasy and served this purpose for him.

In the Memoirs of Scriblerus Swift shows again his enormous anality—so evident in his character—and gives a clear picture of the anal birth of genius. Martin Scriblerus's mother, having difficulty in conceiving, was advised to take seven sheets of paper and write upon each with seven alphabets of seven languages in such a way that no letter would stand twice in the same posture (surely a fantasy of a polymorphously perverse conception); then to clip all letters apart and put them into a pillow which she was to use to support her in a certain position favorable to fecundity. This proved helpful and Scriblerus was conceived. But on the eve of his birth his mother dreamed that she had given birth to a monster in the shape of an inkpot spurting black liquid in rivulets throughout the room. These were interpreted by a sorceress as being symbols of the infant's genius, signifying the variety of the productions of human learning; the spout of the inkpot signified that the child would be a son. When he was born, the infant enjoyed the rattling of paper and dabbling in ink. When the child was thought to say 'Papa' it was determined by the nurse that he had really said 'paper'. Thus was launched the Genius of the Age.

Swift does not seem to have been a sickly child after his infancy. Yet by adolescence he had instituted walking rituals as a way of preserving his health and of showing his strength. In adulthood he was a man of unusually fine physique, but from the age of twenty-two he frequently complained of ill health, weakness, pains, stomach-aches, nausea, and rather diffuse bodily pains. He developed Ménière's disease, which caused him many attacks of dizziness and deafness, and his account of its origin from eating stone fruit in the Temple garden suggests a strong homosexual conflict, which was to appear also in his Meditations Upon a Broomstick. He was extremely fearful of insanity from an early age ('dying at the top' he said, likening himself to a fir tree), and his constant reiteration of his defiance of death seems an overprotestation. In the third voyage of Gulliver, his meeting with the Struldbrugs condenses these fears.

Swift suffered from severe chronic anxiety and diffuse hypochondriasis of the type that so often accompanies an inordinately severe castration complex, to which his early life inevitably predisposed him. This hypochondriasis always increased when he saw the suffering of another. While some of these situations suggested guilt, so that he turned away in seeming callousness, there is the further question whether the sight of suffering did not cause him to take it unto himself through a primary identification. In his Life and Character of Dr. Swift (1731), Swift states:

> I could give instances enough that Human Friendship is but stuff.
> . . .
> True friendship in two breasts requires the same aversions and desires;
> My friend should have when I complain, a Fellow feeling for my pain. *(27)*

What was writ large, vividly, and constantly in Swift's letters was his preoccupation with the lower bowel. He suffered from hemorrhoids, and complained of them in letters to Charles Ford *(19),* but in general he was personally reticent about this part of his body. Gulliver's concern with the excretions is noteworthy, and Swift's character contained juxtaposed gratification and reaction-formation against gratification from this primitive source. That all sexuality was dirty and confused with excretory functions is amply evident. The fourth voyage of Gulliver portrays the conflicts and attempt at resolution vividly. It is quite clear that the Yahoos represent the dirty, unrestrained sexual parents, while the Houyhnhnms are the idealized, gentle reasonable ones, the superego ones, possessing all the reaction-formations against the primitive animal instincts. In the second voyage, it is the older nurse who is described as the most loathsome of creatures, with foul and gaping bodily apertures. It should be noted that the sweet, charming, protective little girl nurse was at prepuberty, a period when actually the little girl's body more closely resembles that of the boy than at any other time. Swift made the resemblance closer by endowing her with a phallus, through the diminutive Gulliver. Swift's actual hatred of the adult nurse is large and is nowhere more clear than in the paragraph devoted to nurses in his Essay on Directions to Servants in General *(7)*. This, together with certain passages in Gulliver, suggests strongly that his own nurse had a baby during the time of his stay with her (ages one to four), of whom he was inordinately jealous. The constant intermingling of literary learning and toilet functioning seems to indicate the severe and simultaneous training in these lines that was to leave a permanent mark upon his character and abilities. In the Memoirs of Scriblerus are invectives against the 'accursed nurse' who, among other things, made the infant's ears 'lie forever flat and immovable'—surely a reference to the impotence, both genital and auditory, of the writer *(7)*.

Another theme, so often found in Swift's writing and life, is the confusion, determinedly rationalized, between the sexes. It occurs in his frank attempts to make boys of Stella and Vanessa, in his treatises on education, in his descriptions of the bodies of men and women. This naturally was associated with the opposite, a polarization of characteristics between the sexes, so that women became the completely emotional, dirty, unreliable ones, and men were reasonable, just, temperate, and cleanly. In the land of the fourth voyage, the Houyhnhnm horses are both male and female, and so are the Yahoos, yet in spirit the horses are good male, and the Yahoos dirty, seducing female. In a letter Swift even referred to Stella as a Yahoo.

The alternating scoptophilia and exhibitionism so much described in the first two voyages (they are inevitably great in a posthumous child), seem to have formed the basis of many of Swift's most charming and penetrating capacities. Physically he was well built and rather handsome, with clear, blue eyes, of which he was so proud that he would never permit himself to wear spectacles, much to the disgust of Samuel Johnson, who wrote one of the biographies of Swift.

Perhaps the most fascinating problem of Swift's development was the configuration of his œdipus complex. He had no real father on whom to play out his œdipal development. Indeed his œdipal crime was accomplished seemingly by his very conception, after which the father died, while the son lived, and possessed his mother, at least in fantasy. Whether he found a substitute father during those years with the nurse in Whitehaven is not clear, but he was again confronted with his actual fatherlessness exactly at the œdipal period. It is apparent that there was an attempt to find a father through his interest in his English clergyman grandfather, and later in his decade of wavering allegiance to Sir William Temple. The feeling of his œdipal crime may well be expressed in the second voyage of Gulliver, in which he is given as a place to stay a deserted temple which has long ago been defiled by the murder of a man. Gulliver's recalling of the heroic ancestors of history on the Island of Glubdubdrib also belongs here.

Just at the height of the œdipal period Swift's mother left him and he was from then until young manhood almost entirely in a homosexual environment. This may well have heightened and directed his postœdipal idealism by increasing his feelings of guilt and his hostilities in a mutually re-enforcing way. Much of his conflict was played out in his relation to the church, which he seems to have adopted and then to have fought with personal disillusion and bitterness; yet he fell back on it time and again, and finally made it the substance of his career. It is no wonder that having 'killed' his father by being conceived, and lost mothers three times before the age of six, he should have accepted the protection of school with a chronic suppressed rage, low-spirited compliance, and some difficulty in formal learning. This difficulty of learning was further aggravated by the fact that his learning inevitably acquired its pattern from his toilet functions, as is shown by the life stories of Gulliver and Scriblerus. The early death of the father, a prehistoric event for the child, inescapably increased the fear of death for himself—a fear which he met by the repeated denial that life was worth having.

That the lonely and disappointed child should have suffered from worries over masturbation was also inevitable. Swift, the man, wrote seldom of genital sexuality, though through Scriblerus and Gulliver he made extensive expositions of his masturbatory concern and fantasies. Dr. Martin Scriblerus treated a young nobleman for distempers of the mind evident in his affectations of speech and his tendency to talk in verse, to show a whimsicality of behavior, and to choose odd companions. Scriblerus diagnosed his condition as that of being in love, and since no woman was involved he must be in love with himself. 'There are people', says Swift through Scriblerus, 'who discover from their youth a most amorous inclination to themselves . . . [they] are so far gone in this passion, they keep a secret intrigue with themselves and hide it from all the world. . . . This patient has not the least care of the Reputation of his Beloved, he is downright scandalous in his behavior with himself.' Scriblerus then prescribes the remedies which Swift applied to himself and offered to others: to give up extravagance, travel in hardship, look at 'the naked truth and purge himself' weekly. If these did not avail, nothing was left but for the sufferer to marry himself, and when he tired of himself he might drown himself in a pond. What a complete version of Narcissus!

The other traveling surgeon, Lemuel Gulliver, had had his training under a master named Bates. To repeat a quotation from Gulliver:

> My good Master Bates, dying in two years after, and I having few friends, my business began to fail, for my conscience would not suffer me to imitate the bad practice of too many among my brethren. (p. 4)

Swift's peculiar relation to words and to punning lends support to the notion that this might be a sly and even conscious trick of self-revelation. The greatest exposition of the masturbation fantasies appears, however, in the third voyage. After a glorious start, Gulliver was much reduced by pirates, set adrift in a canoe, and he fell into a great despondency. He then came to a small, perfectly round island, already described as floating in the air, rising and falling above the body of the continent from which it sometimes shut out the sun. Many of the people here were so absorbed in speculation that they forgot to speak or pay attention to those around them. Consequently they kept 'flappers' who tapped them on the mouth, eyes, or ears, with blown bladders attached like flails to short sticks. These bladders held small quantities of dried peas or pebbles. This island was balanced so delicately on a lodestone that the tenderest hand could move it up and down to a height of four miles. It also somewhat controlled the fate of the continent, Balnibarbi, beneath it; and since it was a place of intense speculation without reality, it had a deleterious effect on the Balnibarbians, who engaged in feats of scientific magic and concocted marvelous inventions of great intricacy and incompleteness, while the country itself was impoverished and wasted, and the senators suffered from 'redundant, ebullient, and peccant humors, with many diseases, of head and heart'.

Swift's early life certainly predisposed him to a stunting bisexuality which is apparent in the man's later life. That his genitality was impaired and degraded by its amalgamation with anal drives is also indicated in his character and his writings. He moreover tended to absorb friends into his service in a demanding and possessive way,—the infantile oral quality of these relationships being partly obscured by his real genius, which could fascinate and command others so that they wanted to be absorbed by him, only to find themselves intolerably burdened. Two additional developments are of special interest: first, the influence of his special anal character on the texture of the family romance, which determined in reality and stimulated in fantasy; second, the special nature of his relationship to his sister, which left a strong mark on his relations with other women.

There can be little doubt that the young child was aware that he was not the son of the nurse during his early stay in England, and must have had some fantasies about his own family. On returning to his mother and sister in Ireland, he had memories and thoughts about the family in England. Within a few months he had neither of these families, and only memories of both, when he became the peripheral and special child in the enormous family of his uncle Godwin. Later he repeated this in the decade spent with Sir William Temple.

The anal stamp on his character, which must have come from the period with the nurse in Whitehaven, appeared compellingly throughout his life. It is quite clear, too, that to Swift the spoken word and the written word were miles apart. The spoken word was airy, pure, and of the spirit. The vowels, especially, were 'airy little creatures, all of different voice and features' *(27)*. The written word was discharged in secret and disclaimed until it had proved itself, and was in danger of appearing 'fathered by another' as he once wrote. The spoken word was oral-respiratory; the written word was genito-anal. The consonants too seemed anal in contrast to the airy vowels, and the proper names in Gulliver's Travels are heavy with repeated consonants and duplicated syllables: Glubdubdrib, Luggnagg, Traldragdribh, Glumdalclitch, Clumeging, to name a few. These words suggest an onomatopoeic derivation from the sounds of drippings and droppings, possibly owing to the overly intense toilet preoccupation, which seemed to engulf and then to color the important infantile philosophies of the little child Jonathan.

Swift always played with words, with clang and pun, which concealed and revealed simultaneously. The original Journal to Stella (1710–1713), which has suffered too much later editing, reveals Swift's language in its most infantile oral qualities, in terms of endearment in which 'you' is 'oo' 'dearest' is 'dealest'; r's and l's get strangely mixed up, and the effect is of a lisping child saying good night. For example, he writes to Stella: 'Nite dealest richar M.D. Sawey dealest M.D. M.D. M.D. F.W. F.W. F.W. M E,

Poo Pdfr. Lele, lele, lele.' Swift himself said 'When I am writing in our language, I make up my mouth just as if I were speaking it'. *'Our richar Gangridge'* is our little language. *M.D.* is 'my dears'; *F.W.* is 'farewell foolish wench'; *M E* is (myself and) Madame Elderly—i.e. Dingley; *Pdfr.* is 'poor dear foolish rogue', Swift. The 'little language', as it was called, was baby talk, simple code, and hog-Latin contrivances, the latter so characteristic of prepubertal years. It is possible that the names Yahoo and Houyhnhnm are nonsense words, peculiarly condensing in function, having profoundly to do with Gulliver's efforts to find himself, that is, to achieve some integration of his own identity, and that 'Yahoo' signifies 'Who are you?'; and 'Houyhnhnm', the sound of which is so close to 'human', contains also suggestions of the pronouns *you, him,* and *who,* in a jumbled hog-Latin fashion. It is on this voyage that Gulliver is forced to admit his attraction to the primitive and dirty, but attempts to save himself through adopting the rationality of the Houyhnhnms, and subsequently suffers a powerful increase in his neurosis.

The family romance has been regarded as occurring in sexually active and imaginative children especially attached to the parents, who suffer severe retaliatory resentment toward the parents, especially in the œdipal relationship, when the parents prohibit the child's sexual practices and the child subsequently recognizes that the parents themselves indulge in the very sexuality they have condemned. The child then repudiates the parents and adopts new, lofty and asexual ones, in a revengeful reversal of the situation; but as Freud remarked in his early paper on the subject, the ennoblement of the adopted parents really represents the original estimate of the child's own parents.

It is my belief that the family romance appears in a severe and sometimes malignant form in those children who not only fulfil the conditions stated but also have a special distortion and degradation of genitality and the œdipal situation through severe anal fixations, and also in those who have had such overpowering (usually anxious) mothers that the development of the early ego has been possible only through an organization by opposition, resulting in a diffuse negativism. In many instances this early ego-by-opposition combines with the anal fixation in a constitutionally strong and well-endowed child.

Children with emphatic theories of anal birth and with nursery ethics of approval (counterfeit of love) focused on toilet functions frequently utilize their interest in the stool (the visible material dirt) and its smell or gaseous image (thought or memory) as representatives of such opposites as good and bad, dirty and godly, black and white, and low and high. This dichotomizing joins directly with the family romance. The foundling is either the abandoned child of the gypsies or the royal infant stolen by them. Swift rarely wrote or spoke of his father except to remark that the father lived long enough to secure the mother's reputation, a fantasy of bastardy masked by humor. The father had been unsuccessful and had abandoned the family through death and poverty. Neither did Swift write of the nurse, except indirectly as cited. On the other hand, Sir William Temple, ambassador and man of the world, emerges quite clearly as the materialization of the noble, illustrious father, with Swift's grandfather as an earlier, less satisfactory version.

Swift's relationship to his mother, once re-established after its long suspension, remained cordial, and he visited her frequently at considerable expense of effort. The one personal anecdote—her pretending to his landlady that he was her lover—is an indication of her reversed œdipal attachment to him. He rarely mentions her in his writings. But the year of her death, when he was forty-two, marked the beginning of his Journal to Stella, with its chronicling of events in the world and its feeling expressed in the 'little language' of infancy.

Jane Swift too is very shadowy in the writings of her brother. One of Swift's cousins mentions a chronic hostility between brother and sister, and commends the mother's attitude of fairness. But some fantasied image of the sister, probably from the years of separation following the first year of intimacy, influenced Swift in his selection of and attitudes toward the three women who played such important parts in his life. It is not necessary to repeat the indications that they represented both himself and his sister. He gave them all names of goddesses, and he could not touch them in any intimate way—which to him would clearly have been a despoiling.

Swift showed marked anal characteristics (his extreme personal immaculateness, secretiveness, intense ambition, pleasure in less obvious dirt, stubborn vengefulness in righteous causes), which indicate clearly that early control of the excretory functions was achieved under great stress and perhaps too early. It seems justified to conclude that the kidnaping nurse, however devoted, was in some way overly conscientious and harsh in his early toilet training, and left this stamp of chamber pot morality forever on his character. That she was also ambitious for his intellectual development is clear as well. He must have been a very special child. A kind of linking of the written or printed word with the excretory functions has already been noted. This seemed to extend further into an animation of the word and its endowment with magic personalized meanings. In this setting, then, the functions of speech, reading, and writing tend to become overly emotional and full of conflicts. In Swift the emotional battleground was shifted largely to the written or printed word—the deposited word, one might say. 'I am very angry', wrote Swift to Arbuthnot in 1714; 'I have a mind to be very angry and to let my anger break out in some manner that will not please them, at the end of a pen'. When Swift was angry but trying hard to please, at Kilkenny and Trinity, he did not break out with a pen, but was compliant and depressed and even thought to be a little dull. Later in life, when he sent his manuscripts to the publisher he disowned them to the extent of having them copied by someone else, and sent them by another—often Charles Ford—to be dropped at night. One gets the feeling that he was acting out both his own birth and early toilet accidents of spite.

That the infant Jonathan lived in such close and continuous bodily intimacy with the nurse as to produce a tendency to overidentify with the woman, is strongly indicated; the problem of anatomical differences was never solved in any stable way, but obvious attempts were made to meet the situation by masculinizing the girl. His castration fear of the woman was overwhelming. Every bodily aperture became a threatening vagina-anus. In unconscious or preconscious fantasy Swift tended to phallicize the woman and identify the child, himself, with the female phallus; this is indicated in the passages from the Travels already quoted. While we have no knowledge of transvestite tendencies in Swift, it is possible that his accepting the robes of the Anglican priest included such a hidden tendency in an acceptable way that could be integrated into his life.

He was continually obsessed with body imagery which formed the almost too constant backdrop for his moralizing satire. The quotation given by Bullitt at the beginning of his book on Swift's satire *(3)* is characteristic:

> To this End I have some time since, with a world of Pains and Art, dissected the carcass of Human Nature and read many useful Lectures upon the several Parts, both containing and contained; till at last it smelt so strong I could preserve it no longer. Upon which I have been at great expense to fit up all the Bones with exact Contexture and in due Symmetry; so that I am ready to show a very compleat Anatomy thereof to all the curious Gentlemen and others.

It is appropriate that Bullitt's book is subtitled The Anatomy of Satire. Again Swift wrote satirically to prove that the stomach is the seat of honor.

In the course of the intimacy between the infant Jonathan and the unnamed nurse there was a marked turn for the worse, described rather vividly in the second voyage of Gulliver. He is now no longer the oversized, important, threatening figure, but small, helpless, and endangered among giants. In Brobdingnag the disgusting nurse appears. To quote Gulliver:

> . . . the nurse came in with a child of a year . . . who immediately spied me and began to squall . . . after the usual oratory of infants, to get me for a plaything. The mother out of pure indulgence, took me up and put me toward the child who presently . . . got my head in his mouth where I roared so loud that the urchin was frighted and let me drop, and I should . . . have broken my neck if the mother had not held her apron under me. The nurse . . . was [finally] forced to apply the last remedy by giving it suck. . . . No object ever disgusted me so much as the sight of her monstrous breast. . . . It stood prominent six foot and [was] sixteen in circumference. The nipple was about half the bigness of my head; the hue of that and the dug so varified with spots, pimples, and freckles that nothing could appear more nauseous: I had a near sight of her, she sitting down . . . and I standing on the table. This made me reflect upon the fair skins of our Irish ladies who appear so beautiful to us only because they are of our own size, and their defects not to be seen but through a magnifying glass, where we find by experiment that the smoothest and whitest skins look rough and coarse, and ill colored. (p. 82)

It was after this that he was adopted and protected by the little girl nurse, not yet at puberty, who carried him everywhere with her.

Thus Gulliver bitterly finds the tables turned and himself displaced by the infant who was just the age Swift had been when he was kidnaped, and the age at which in the Modest Proposal infants of the poor should be eaten by the rich. The picture of the breast certainly contains elements of awe and envy turned to loathing with the aim of degrading it. It seems likely that the nurse became pregnant after her return to England, and this pregnancy, together with the subsequent suckling of the child upset the little boy Jonathan and aroused in him intensest jealousy, biting resentment, and cannibalistic feelings toward the infant—projected by Gulliver as felt toward him by the infant.

The image of the nurse's breast carried with it fear and a sense of its similarity to the pregnant abdomen and to an adult phallus. This combined image is then rendered less dangerous by being made into the female phallus and degraded or fecalized. The word *dug* used by Swift in this context is itself close to the word *dung*. Later in the second voyage the bad nurse reappears in male form as the evil kidnaping monkey who carries the small Gulliver as though suckling an infant and does actually cram his mouth full of vile stuff which must be picked out by the amiable little girl nurse. Here we have clearly the turn to the fully homosexual fantasy of fellatio, the reverberation of which appears in Swift's own life in his sickness from 'too much stone fruit'. In the story the monkey is executed. In the Travels two other assaults on the helpless Gulliver are made by male creatures; one by a deformed dwarf encountered in the Queen's garden, who there knocks Gulliver flat by shaking the apple tree so that the fruit falls on his head, and the second by a huge frog which hops into his little boat and, jumping over him, deposits its odious slime upon his face and clothing. Gulliver finally rids himself of this disgusting animal. At about the same time Gulliver seizes a linnet the size of a swan by the neck with both his hands, causing the enraged bird to beat him around the head with its wings until it is finally subdued and ultimately served for dinner.

IV. CONCLUSION

It has been my intention to give the story of Swift based on the known facts and as it is revealed in Gulliver's Travels, and not primarily to make a clinical study of Swift's neurosis. Since I begin however with references to changes in body image and to fetishism, and since, in the course of presenting the combined biographies of Gulliver and of Swift, I unavoidably include some pertinent clinical data, it seems appropriate to make a few concluding remarks.

Swift does not seem to have been an overt fetishist, although in the structure of his personality there is much that he shares with the fetishist. One gets the impression that the anal fixation was intense and binding, and the genital demands so impaired or limited at best that there was a total retreat from genital sexuality in his early adult life, probably beginning with the unhappy relationship with Jane Waring, the first of the goddesses. After this, Swift never again seems willingly to have considered marriage, and his expressed demands were that the women who were closest to him should be boys. His genital demands were probably partly sublimated through his writings, but these too bear the stamp of a strongly anal character. He did not need a fetish because he resigned from physical genitality. In a sense, converting the women of his choice into 'boys' fulfilled his fetishistic need.

Lemuel Gulliver went a step further than his creator. He was a married man, but one who was continually escaping from his marriage which was predominantly disgusting to him, though his periodic sojourns at home sufficed sometimes for the depositing of a child with his wife. The Travels seem to be largely the projection into activity of Lemuel's masturbatory fantasies which, like the character of Swift, are closely interwoven with anal problems and ambitions rather than with exclusively genital ones.

The problems of changes in body size (based on phallic functioning)[4] are characteristically reflected onto the total body, and much re-enforced by the theme of the reversal of generations. There is much less substitution of different parts of the body for the phallus than is to be found in Alice's Adventures in Wonderland, for example; although there are some disguised references in the third voyage, in which the phallic problems are expressed in the medium of thought rather than that of the body itself. A further discussion of the problems of distortions of body image and changes of size will be more fruitful when it can be combined with a study of Alice and Lewis Carroll.

NOTES

1. Swift liked to pun on the names Swift, Martin, and Swallow, all being birds.
2. After the publication of Gulliver's Travels Pope wrote humorously to Swift that one Jonathan Gulliver had turned up in Boston as a member of the local parliament; Swift replied in kind, that a Lemuel Gulliver had actually appeared in England, had the reputation of being a liar, but that he, Swift, considered this a coincidence *(28)*.
3. When King William encountered the young Swift in the Temple household, he taught him to eat asparagus and offered him a post in the cavalry.
4. Greenacre, Phyllis: Certain Relationships Between Fetishism and the Faulty Development of the Body Image. In: *The Psychoanalytic Study of the Child, Vol. VIII*. New York: International Universities Press, Inc., 1953, p. 79.

BIBLIOGRAPHY

(The following sources were used in preparing this paper.)

1. Asworth, Bernard: *Swift. London:* Eyre & Spottiswoode, 1947.
2. Ball, F. Elrington, Editor: *The Correspondence of Jonathan Swift*. London: G. Bell & Sons Ltd., 1914.
3. Bullitt, John M.: *Jonathan Swift and the Anatomy of Satire*. Cambridge: Harvard University Press, 1953.
4. Craik, Henry: *The Life of Jonathan Swift*. London: John Murray, 1882.
5. Davis, Herbert: *The Satire of Jonathan Swift*. New York: The Macmillan Co., 1947.
6. ———: *Stella. A Gentlewoman of the 18th Century*. New York: The Macmillan Co., 1942.
7. Eddy, William A., Editor: *Satires and Personal Writings of Jonathan Swift*. Reprinted. London: Oxford University Press, 1951.

8. Forster, John: *The Life of Jonathan Swift*. New York: Harper & Brothers, 1876.
9. Freeman, Martin, Editor: *Vanessa and Her Correspondence With Jonathan Swift*. London: Selwyn & Blount, Ltd., 1921.
10. Hardy, Evelyn: *The Conjured Spirit*. London: The Hogarth Press, 1949.
11. Heilman, Robert B.: Introduction to the Modern Library Edition of *Gulliver's Travels*. New York: Random House, 1950.
12. Johnson, Samuel: *The Poetical Works of Dr. Jonathan Swift, With the Life of the Author*. Lives of the English Poets. Edinburgh: Apollo Press, 1778.
13. Johnston, Denis: Personal communications.
14. Lane-Poole, Stanley, Editor: *Swift's Letters and Journals*. London: Kegan Paul, Trench & Co., 1885.
15. Orrery, John, Earl of Orrery: *Remarks on the Life and Writings of Dr. Jonathan Swift*. Dublin: George Faulkner, 1752.
16. Quintana, Ricardo: *The Mind and Art of Jonathan Swift*. Reprinted. London: Methuen & Co., Ltd, 1953.
17. Scott, Sir Walter: *Memoirs of Jonathan Swift, D.D.* Edinburgh: Robert Cadell, 1841.
18. Scott, Temple, Editor: *Prose Works of Jonathan Swift* (12 vols.). London: G. Bell & Sons Ltd., 1913.
19. Smith, David Nichol, Editor: *The Letters of Jonathan Swift to Charles Ford*. Oxford: Clarendon Press, 1935.
20. Sheridan, Thomas: *The Life of the Reverend Dr. Jonathan Swift*. Dublin: Luke White, 1785.
21. Stephen, Sir Leslie: *Swift*. English Men of Letters Series. London: Macmillan & Co., 1889.
22. Swift, Dean: *Essay Upon the Life, Writings and Character of Dr. Swift*. London, 1755.
23. Swift, Jonathan: *The Works of Jonathan Swift, D.D., D.S.P.D.* Dublin: George Faulkner, 1735.
24. Van Doren, Carl: *Swift*. New York: Viking Press, 1930.
25. Wilde, W. R.: *The Closing Years of Dean Swift's Life*. Second edition. Dublin: Hodges and Smith, 1849.
26. Williams, Harold, Editor: *Jonathan Swift. Journal to Stella* (2 vols.). Oxford: Clarendon Press, 1948.
27. ———: *The Poems of Jonathan Swift* (3 vols.). Oxford: Clarendon Press, 1937.
28. Wilson, C. H.: *Swiftiana* (2 vols.). London: Richard Phillips, 1804.

9. On Psychoanalyzing Literary Characters

Florence Bonime and Marianne H. Eckardt

SUMMARY

Minds met and a collaborative paper was born. For a long time Florence Bonime had questioned the validity of psychiatric dissection of literary characters. She found in Marianne Eckardt a responsive listener who had, for an equally long time, objected to the inappropriate application of our psychoanalytic understanding to nonclinical matters. The present format evolved spontaneously: Part 1, a presentation by Bonime regarding some dramatic techniques which distinguish written characters from alive human beings who have acquired individuality from the spontaneous play of natural forces. Part 2, Eckardt's argument emphasizes the psychoanalyst's traditional attraction to, as well as misuse of, the dramatic medium.

I

"We tend to forget," Albert Hutter wrote (1975), "that Hamlet is not a living being, that he exists only through language and our imaginative interaction with that language." Hutter's statement is hardly arguable. No matter how many actors play the part, and no matter how their portrayals differ, Hamlet exists initially, and irreducibly, through Shakespeare's language.

Nevertheless, a massive amount has been written on Hamlet's pathology, and his neuroses have been copiously analyzed as if he were "a living being" who was born and who then grew up to be the character we discover in the play (Barnett 1975; Shainess 1975; Lidz 1975; Eissler 1969; Holland 1966, 1976). Not only Hamlet, but many other literary characters (Raskolnikov, Von Aschenbach, and King Lear among others) have been analyzed as if they were living beings. In these writings an invented character is dealt with

Reprinted by permission of the *Journal of the American Academy of Pychoanalysis,* 5, no. 2 (1977).

as a person, the writer by-passing all questions as to the kinds of connections and distinctions that exist between art and reality. The character is assumed to be a true reflection of a living and psychoanalyzable person.

One exception is Eissler (1969, p. 14), who says that ". . . literary reality often gives the impression of being real reality." He rejects the notion that Shakespeare copied nature, but goes on then to assert that Shakespeare's characters are ". . . *more* human than living people" (italics mine). He argues that "analysis along the lines of psychological content can produce its best results when it treats Shakespeare's plays *as if they were full fledged human reality*" (p. 11, italics mine). Eissler acknowledges a problem, but then sets it aside and proceeds with his analytic method on an "as if" basis.

Similarly, Bartlett (1976) comments on Raskolnikov's schizophrenia:

> In *Crime and Punishment* Dostoyevsky has left us an illuminating portrayal of schizophrenic consciousness as it exists and develops in the actual process of living. Such examples are not easy to come by. An artist, bringing to life a fictitious character in a world of imaginary people is able to do what no analysis of an actual case can do. . . . Dostoyevsky, picturing the succession of concrete events, the particular, complex, moment-by-moment interplay between Raskolnikov and other characters equally well known to us, shows us a man's consciousness perceptibly changing through the multiplicity of daily experiences.

Here, too, the character is acknowledged to be fictitious, yet the moment-by-moment interplay is dealt with as if it were reality on display. The legitimacy of this practice is not questioned by Eissler or Bartlett, nor by the mainstream of psychoanalyst-writers.

Holland (1975) addresses the problem from a different viewpoint. He deplores ". . . the familiar kind of slambang symbol-twirling or shot-from-the-hip diagnoses that people commonly associate with psychoanalytic criticism" (p. 133), and is critical of ". . . diagnoses of characters as though they had walked out of the pages of fiction into a psychiatric clinic" (p. 164). Holland has developed a mode of literary study in which he uses a psychoanalytic approach to his students' anxieties and resistances in order to bring them subjectively closer to the books they are reading. Holland remains committed to all the formal qualities of literature, to the style or essence of the work, and to the language. He says (p. 175) that ". . . the great thing psychoanalysis brings to the study of literature is a way to understand a writer's choice of words."

Thus Hutter and Holland both stress the primary importance in any approach to literature of imaginative interaction with language. I would like to extend this concept beyond language, to some of the writer's dramatic devices, and also to our conventions of novel-reading and play-going—that is, to our own conventional acceptances, by means of which we interact with the writer's devices. It is this interaction that creates the illusion of the real-life existence of fictive characters.

We may ask of psychoanalysts: If the lifelike quality of literary characters is illusory, then is psychoanalyzing these characters a legitimate practice? In pursuit of an answer, I will call attention to some readily recognizable aspects of dramatic technique which contribute to the illusion of reality.

The words *devices* and *techniques* are used in daily life and sometimes in psychoanalysis with derogatory manipulative connotations. Journalist-debunkers of political rhetoric, or of deceptive salesmanship, use these words contemptuously. In literary theory, however, the words are simply denotative and contain no value judgments. Langer (1953, p. 245) comments:

> Literary composition, however 'inspired,' requires invention, judgment, often trial and rejection, and long contemplation. An air of unstudied spontaneous utterance is apt to be as painstakingly achieved as any other quality in the poetic fiction. . . . There are countless devices for creating the world of [a literary work] and for articulating the elements of its virtual life, and almost every critic discovers some of these means and stands in wondering admiration of their 'magic.'

It is in this sense, as a reference to the writer's ways and means, that *devices* and *techniques* will be used in these pages.

Such devices are countless, but I will focus on only one, in three of its common and visible manifestations. I will call attention to compression, as it affects the portrayal of *time, space,* and *character*.

The conventional acceptances to be discussed are those related to these specific compressions. Our conventions are so familiar, so completely assimilated by us and obvious to us, that they seem scarcely worth mentioning. We interact with minuscule verbal clues and linguistic devices. William Gass, for example (1971, p. 51) calls attention to a moment in a Henry James story: "Their friend, Mr. Grant-Jackson, a highly preponderant pushing person, great in discussion and arrangement, abrupt in overture, unexpected, if not perverse, in attitude etc." and Gass comments that "Mr. Grant-Jackson is a preponderant pushing person because he's been made by *p*'s."

When we go beyond linguistic devices into a consideration of complete novels and plays, we contend with some large facts that have become invisible because we have no reason to keep them in mind. With a novel, for example, there is a first line and a last line. The action opens, unfolds, and stops. With a play in performance the curtain (if there is one) goes up, and later goes down. Curtain and lights may be lowered and raised several times during the evening, but within the allotted time the play ends. We enter the characters' lives at a point designed by the writer, and when his planned culmination is reached, we leave these invented lives. We do not cry out, "Wait! What happened next?" We accept the circumscribed, finite nature of the action-span that is laid before us. There is no tomorrow and, as I will point out later, there is no yesterday, unless we invent it ourselves. The boundaries are determined by the formal necessities of the artist's conception. The boundaries do not frustrate or outrage us because, by convention, we know that literary works do not begin and end in a life-like manner. Literary works have been created by artistry; they are shaped and finite.

By accepting the boundaries, we lend ourselves to the artist's formal arrangements and contrivances. In the course of a play or novel we may find ourselves, imaginatively, in many places, and we may live through any desired span of time, from an hour to centuries. The time and space of the story are contained within book-covers, or within the dimensions of the stage and the duration of the performance. We experience framed time and framed space, and through our imaginative interaction with these devices we feel at ease with them, scarcely notice them, and can translate them into a meaningful semblance of life.

In films, each frame is a device—a fact that we seldom think about. "The pictured space," says Rudolf Arnheim (1957, p. 17), "is visible to a certain extent, but then comes the edge which cuts off what lies beyond. It is a mistake to deplore this restriction as a drawback. . . . On the contrary it is just such restrictions which give film its right to be called an art."

Arnheim referred (at that point) only to space. If we turn our attention to compression of time, we can recall instances when a line in the program reads: "Scene Two, a year later." We wait calmly during the two minutes it takes for the year to pass. We may supply, hardly aware of doing so, a sense of the passage of time, a sense of relationships building up or wearing down —but these are our own imaginative contributions.

Many playgoers, though not all, can participate emotionally in the illusion while still remaining aware that it *is* an illusion. As Peter Brook expresses this dual consciousness (1968, p. 69), ". . . it is sufficient for an actor of power to speak a powerful text for the spectator to be caught up in an illusion, although of course he will still know that he is at every instant in a theatre.'' He goes on: ''. . . the illusion is composed by the flash of quick and changing impressions [which] keep the dart of the imagination at play.''

By convention, and to the degree that we are able to release our imaginations, we allow this dart to play, and we absorb the writer's time/space compressions.

These compressions can produce effective distortions and juxtapositions which, in turn, become devices for establishing an audience's reaction to a character. As a hypothetical example, a crude but usefully transparent example, let us suppose that the curtain rises on a white-haired woman waiting at a window. A few yards away across the stage, we see a teen-aged girl in cap and gown receiving her high school diploma. The two sides of the stage have been given different lighting. A modern audience will quickly recognize the device, and will know that there are not two characters: there is one character at two different stages of life.

Is this the same as ordinary memory? In life we recall old scenes, but two scenes do not simultaneously appear, fully fleshed, before our eyes. On the stage they can both be vividly present, dramatically illuminated and juxtaposed. The girl may dream aloud or act out her plans for the future. The older woman may do any of a hundred different things—shout up the stairs, make a phone call, soliloquize about her situation. This time-compression can achieve various effects, deliver a sense of the scene as tragic, comic, ironic, absurd—or whatever the writer intends. It is obviously an artifice, but it is also a familiar convention in the theatre, and playgoers may have strong emotional responses to the character. If the artifice is successful, well-written, and well-staged, it is the writing and staging that we absorb and forget, and our own responses that we retain. These interactions with the writer's devices contribute to our total interaction with the total illusion of the play.

This hypothetical example is simple and limited. Numerous and more intricate devices come into being when the writer is dealing with complex characters in tangled situations which must unravel or reach some kind of culmination or resolution within the confines of a play or novel. Henry James remarked (1934, p. 5) that ''Really, universally, relations stop nowhere, and the exquisite problem of the artist is eternally to draw the circle within which they shall appear to do so.''

The disparity between life and art is nowhere more visible than it is in the artist's compression of time as he advances his characters toward a crisis. Our own life-crises arrive circuitously. They disappear and return; we see them differently as time passes; we grow weary, the situation becomes boring, and then becomes acute and painful. Eventually the crisis erupts—but even then it is not ended. All the convolutions leave residues which, at later times, we may re-evaluate.

But in facing a play or novel we do not have a long, undulating developmental process. We face immediate or imminent crisis. We discover the characters rapidly, and are caught up in the galloping action. Langer (1953, p. 310) writes on the distinctions between dramatic action and life events, between dramatic characters and living people:

> Since stage action is not, like genuine action, embedded in a welter of irrelevant doings and divided interests, and characters on the stage (however complex they may be) have no unknown complexities, it is possible there to see a person's feelings grow into passions, and those passions issue in words and deeds. We know, in fact, so little about the personalities before us at the opening of a play that their every move and word, even their dress and walk, are distinct items for our perception. Because we are not involved with them as with real people, we can view each smallest act in its context, as a symptom of character and condition. We do not have to find out what is significant; the selection has been made—whatever is there is significant, and it is not too much to be surveyed *in toto*. A character stands before us as a coherent whole. It is with characters as with their situations: both become visible on the stage, transparent and complete, as their analogues in the world are not.

That Hamlet is either transparent or complete would of course be unacceptable to a psychoanalyst who has discussed Hamlet's neuroses. Beginning with Freud and Jones (1949) and continuing into the recent books of Eissler (1969) and Lidz (1975) and with all the intervening and later papers (see Holland 1966, 1976), analysts have expressed the view that only invisible and unconscious motivations could possibly explain Hamlet's behavior. Since unconscious motivations originate in childhood experience, a childhood must be posited. Lidz (1975) exemplifies this approach. Throughout his book there is repeated reference to Hamlet's childhood, development, and hypothetical future life. For example (page 26), ". . . we witness how the youth is kept . . . from becoming the man we know he could become." (Page 52), "Like every child, Hamlet had internalized something of his mother . . ." (Page 59), "This is not the world Hamlet was raised to live on." And so on through many references to Hamlet's early childhood and later development. Yet (page 240) Lidz states: ". . . Hamlet had no childhood, but emerged full grown as a youth or young adult from Shakespeare's imagination." (On p. 199), ". . . we know nothing of Hamlet's childhood," and, in a footnote, these acknowledgments come late, after much of the book's argument has been based upon forces in Hamlet's unconscious that developed during his childhood.

An imaginative interaction so intense that it causes someone to fully invent an unwritten childhood commands respect for the intellectual activity involved, but it also indicates insufficient awareness of the artifact quality of literary characters.

Theorists of literature in great measure concur with Langer's view of the selectivity, the stripping-down that must be practiced in the portrayal of fictitious characters. Rawdon Wilson comments (1976, p. 194) that "the distinction between characters and actual persons is an absolute one." He quotes Price's earlier statement (1975) that one could ". . . make long lists of all the attributes of characters that are never supplied," and that we do not miss; and he cites Gass (p. 45): "Characters are mostly empty canvass."

The empty canvas and the missing attributes do not become irritating, or even noticeable, for several reasons. One of them, given by Wilson (p. 195), is that "characters provide a range of evidence that is, inevitably, more significant because it is not random, not cluttered, not mind-bogglingly vast." Secondly, readers and play-goers so quickly supply, through imaginative interaction, whatever is uncomfortably missing, that they do not become aware of the sparseness of the evidence, nor of their own contribution.

Compression in character-portrayal contributes to the intensity of the play or novel. On the connection between compression and intensity, Langer says (1953, p. 324): ". . . in the theatre . . . the import of every little act is heightened. . . . What we see . . . is not behavior, . . . but action and passion; and as every act has exaggerated importance, so the emotional responses . . . are intensified. Even indifference is a concentrated and significant attitude." Later (p. 356) she writes, "Tragic drama is so designed that the protagonist spends himself in the course of one dramatic action. . . . This is, of course, *a tremendous foreshortening of life* [italics mine]: instead of undergoing the physical, psychical, many-sided long process of an actual biography, the tragic hero lives and matures in some particular respect; his entire being is concentrated in one aim, one passion, one conflict and ultimate defeat. . . . His character, the unfolding situation, the scene, even though ostensibly familiar and humble, are all exaggerated, charged with more feeling than comparable actualities would possess." This exaggerated intensity, partly achieved by compression, is conventionally accepted as lifelike during a theatre experience, and provides a means of achieving, from highly compressed and distorted scenes and characters, a powerful illusion of reality.

At times one or two elements in a characterization produce in us a particular response because they seem to be mirror-images of the same elements in a known living person. Viewers can and do build large structures of illusion around fragments of a characterization, ignoring the total design of the character and the part it plays in the total design of the play or novel. If someone, says, "But she's exactly like Margaret!" that is an expression of personal response, which requires no validation, but establishes no objective truth.

The way we attend to character, and involve ourselves in actions, will determine what any character becomes for us. Objectively, we hold a book in hand and know it to be paper. Subjectively, we read our way into an invented world, and live there for framed periods of time, with characters who seem intensely real for the duration.

A character on the stage, or on the page, without genetic endowment, without a childhood, with no relationships in the larger outside world, without a future life, with no possibility for unplanned change or for later altered memory of the past—with all these human attributes and capacities missing, the character yet seems radiantly alive. In large part we feel this aliveness because our learned conventions of novel-reading and play-going make possible our imaginative interaction with language and with dramatic techniques.

The interaction takes place in varying degrees. In psychoanalytically oriented people the interaction may induce the invention of a childhood, which is a developmental organic process and not, certainly, an artistic process. The two processes are more than different, they are totally incompatible.

Commenting on the distinction Langer says (1953, p. 312), "Literally, 'organic process' is a biological concept; 'life,' 'growth,' 'development,' 'decline,' 'death'—all of these are strictly biological terms. They are applicable to organisms. In art they are lifted out of their literal context and forthwith, in place of organic processes we have dynamic forms."

In pursuit of dynamic form, the artist utilizes all the devices—not only those I have mentioned, but countless subtler techniques. Fundamentally, all techniques exist in the service of the embodiment of the artist's poetic conception. The poetic conception requires integration of the work into a single web of illusion—which then seems to us "more alive than life itself."

Caught up in the illusion, the play-goer to some degree remains aware that he is sitting in a theatre. If the second awareness is acute, the playgoer may also notice some of the playwright's artistry, and may respond to that with a separate excitement. The dual experience is richer than a simple surrender to the illusion, and can at times produce the rare, sought-after, profound inner stir that is possible in the theatre, and possible when reading a novel. Most of us at some time, and not only in youth, have felt this profound, inexpressible stir, which is not achievable by way of intellectual analysis, and is likely to come as a complete surprise. As described by Charles Morgan (1933):

> The order of [the playgoer's] experience is always the same—a shock, and after the shock an inward stillness, and from that stillness an influence emerging, which transmutes him. Transmutes *him*—not his opinions. . . . Dramatic art has . . . a double function—first to still the preoccupied mind, to empty it of triviality, to make it receptive and meditative; and to impregnate it. Illusion is the impregnating power.

An experience so profound cannot be frequent, but when it comes, or when the more usual experience of good theatre or good novel comes, it is made possible by the cumulative effect of our moment-by-moment interaction, our "darting, flickering" imaginative interaction with the artist's language and devices.

At every moment of a literary work artistry is practiced. In these pages I have discussed only compression. Our reactions, which exist within ourselves, may cause us to infer, deduce, and invent much that does not exist in the literary work *per se*. If we invent a childhood and then analyze that childhood, it is a personal illusion that we analyze. The play or novel has activated the illusion, but does not itself contain the illusion—perhaps that is the distinction that requires more attention and definition if we attempt to answer the question: Can literary characters legitimately be psychoanalyzed?

II

Psychoanalytic interpretation of literary characters, authors, artists, religious leaders, religions, tribal rituals, or of primitive societies has been a serious pastime of psychoanalysts ever since psychoanalysis became a discipline in its own right. Freud the many-sided genius set the tone. He was fascinated by, and drew much inspiration from myths, anthropological data, and literature. They reflected and affirmed his equally dramatic vision of mankind's basic passions, conflicts, and their impact on character formation and life events.

This interest became a formalized venture for psychoanalysis with the founding of the journal *Imago,* a periodical designed for the nonmedical application of psychoanalysis. Freud had great admiration for outstanding writers and artists. Ernest Jones (1957, Vol. III, p. 419) quotes Freud as writing: "One may heave a sigh at the thought that it is vouchsafed to a few, with hardly an effort, to salve from the whirlpool of their emotions the deepest truths, to which we others have to force our way, ceaselessly groping amid torturing uncertainties." In a letter to Arthur Schnitzler (p. 443), Freud writes in 1922: "I think I have avoided you from a kind of reluctance to meet my double . . . whenever I get deeply absorbed in your beautiful creations I invariably seem to find beneath their poetic surface the very presuppositions, interests and conclusions which I know to be my own. . . . So I have formed the impression that you know through intuition—or rather from detailed self-observation—everything that I have discovered by laborious work on other people."

Psychoanalytic writing generally is enlivened and illustrated by ample quotes from novels or plays. These quotes either serve as an elaboration of the analyst's theme, or as an interpretation of the artist's writing. Theodore Lidz (1975, p. 3) beautifully expresses the analyst's attraction to great plays as well as his psychoanalytic involvement with the play and its riddles:

> Hamlet again! I return to Hamlet as one participates in a mystery—to regain vitality after descending into its depth, to skirt madness with its hero, to find release from anguish with its heroine in her hebephrenia, to slough disillusion with the treacherous world onto a scapegoat who carries the burden to his destruction. I also return to sun in lines that light the world in beauty, to absorb nurture from genius beyond envy. . . . I listen in awe because here, so much that psychoanalysts have laboriously learned flows in measured profusion—as if the Muses had whispered in the poet's ear all that Apollo's Pythoness had learned from her countless suppliants.

Thus Lidz expresses his understandable attraction. But then he proceeds to what appears to him a most natural step, namely, to the psychoanalyst's professional involvement with the play (p. 7). "Hamlet . . . attracts the psychiatrist because it is a play that directly challenges his professional acumen. He can join the characters in the play in seeking the cause of Hamlet's antic behavior."

It is exactly this step of joining the characters in the play to seek out the cause of Hamlet's antic behavior which Bonime and I regard as an intriguing, entertaining pastime but not a legitimate contribution to the understanding of the character Hamlet. We have the lines of the play only and, as we know, actors and producers have envisioned the play and its characters in many a light. There are no facts available about the past personality or interrelationships of the characters.

Lidz, however, continues to be persuasive about the similarities of concern between the playwright and the psychoanalyst. He writes (page 6), "The drama is a direct derivative of the ritual and its accompanying myth. The playwright carries on, to varying degrees, the process of dramatizing tales of the impact of unrestrained impulsions upon human lives and upon society and the turmoil brought about by breaches in the bonds of kinship that form the warp and woof of society and lay the foundations for dependable relationships everywhere. . . . The psychoanalyst . . . works with the conflicts between passionate drives and the controls required by social living, and he studies basic configurations of human relationships to unravel what has gone awry in them and undermined a person's emotional balance. . . . Through his absorption with the dynamics of mental disorders, the psychoanalyst attains an ability to grasp the essentials in myths and the salient transactions in the drama."

Lidz writes with an elegant pen. This very elegance, however, obscures facile generalizations and veils reasoning which in this instance is used to justify his professional exploration of Hamlet. His generalizations about the meaning of drama and the intent of the playwright are as debatable as are his formulations of the psychoanalyst's activities. It is true that psychoanalytic theories are using dramatic conceptions—many a myth is the foundation of an aspect of theory—but myths as well as our theoretical dramas are each separate and individual expressions of the manifold manifestations of human conflicts and struggles. The words "basic," "fundamental," and "deepest" are unfortunately central in the psychoanalyst's vocabulary and thus restrict his vision and his ability to grasp the infinite variations of man's interactions with society and with himself.

It is true that our absorption as psychoanalysts in mental disorders develops in us a skill for recognizing dynamics or evolving patterns, but in actual practice we are required to attend to the unique manifestations, rather than to the more general attributes of human nature. Thus our special ability to grasp the "essentials" in myths and drama may be in question, mainly because we do not know whether there is "the essential" in a myth or drama, or whether both myth and great drama have the wondrous characteristic of reflecting, like hidden mirrors, our own perceptions.

I am stressing the exciting, rewarding, and to me important attraction which drama, myth, religion, societal structure, and anthropological findings held and hold for psychoanalysts. This revitalizing attraction has to be kept in mind to understand the enthusiastic trespassing of psychoanalytic imaginations beyond the reasonable limits of their knowledge, into the open fields mentioned [earlier]. The trespass, while understandable, causes psychoanalysts to operate with two different professional standards. Freud's clinical explorations were marked by careful observations, attention to minute details and corroboration which gradually developed into a standardized yet ever-evolving technique as well as theory of psychoanalysis.

Psychoanalysis, when applied to other fields, lacks all of these safeguards. Speculation is free-wheeling and often takes off from a minimum of facts. Speculation easily leads into the language of certainty. A letter by Freud (1960) designed to be playfully speculative demonstrates this easy linguistic transition. Writing to Thomas Mann in response to Mann's novel based on the Joseph legend, he prefaces his own speculative remarks about the role of the Joseph myth in the life of a historical figure, namely Napoleon, with a comment that he himself does not take this experiment very seriously. He then describes the dynamic forces driving and shaping Napoleon's life.

Napoleon, Freud postulates, probably suffered from severe rivalry with his older brother Joseph—a hatred which, through the process of reversal, turned to love—resulting in his infatuation with Josephine (which "undoubtedly" was brought about by her name). The repressed hatred then led to the campaign in Egypt, where he was driven to outdo his brother Joseph (by identification with the legendary Joseph). Thus overcompensation became the source of Napoleon's aggression against hundreds of thousands of unknown individuals who had to atone for the fact that the little tyrant had spared his first enemy.

The word "undoubtedly" reflects the easy way in which this elaborate fancy drifts into a sense of certainty.

The application of psychoanalysis to nonclinical fields has aroused much controversy. What has disturbed the scientific and the psychiatric community about this continuing exercise is not the activity of speculation, but the lack of respect for the reasonable limits of our knowledge, the lack of discrimination as to what can be considered relevant fact, the glib misuse of our professional tools in the setting of another profession—and the lack of appreciation of our natural propensity to inter-relate facts into a meaningful whole, not because they necessarily belong together, but because our minds seek meaning and find it only when items are placed in a larger coherent context.

The perturbance of psychiatrists is expressed in an American Psychiatric Association Task Force Report (1976) summarized in the *Psychiatric News* of July 16. The report urged the A.P.A. to use whatever means were available to inform psychiatrists of the risks inherent in writing psychohistory, psychobiography, or in psychiatric profiling done without personal contact, especially of living persons. The first part of this report deals with questions of ethics, the second part deals with questions of competence and thus validity. The news item states:

> The most common mistake of the psychiatrist or psychoanalyst turned historian is a frequent reliance upon secondary or even tertiary sources instead of primary sources, resulting in an inadequate perception and presentation of the socio-cultural matrix in which the subjects function. Freud (the report notes) makes these mistakes in his study of Leonardo da Vinci.

The major concern emerging from Bonime's paper, from the Task Force Report, and from my own remarks, points to the psychoanalyst's traditional lack of cognizance of the limits of his professional good judgment. There are may historical reasons for this. There is first of all Freud's search for, and then belief in, his discovery of the basic dynamic forces leading to man's inner and outer conflictual existence. In Freud's view these basic forces remained mostly unconscious. The analyst became the only qualified discerner of the true wellsprings of life. ''Depth''—that is, the analytic perception of ''depth''—was defined as knowing more about the real truth of human beings. As these basic forces were fundamental to all human existence, they could be divined in the great designs of most human manifestations. Freud's emphasis was on the universal, rather than in the delight or explication of the rich variation or the unique adaptation of each human being to his own cultural milieu.

The psychoanalyst's indebtedness to myths, great poems, dramas, and novels is as great as Freud and Lidz have described; they enlighten us and enlarge our vision. We need our love affair with literature. We need its enrichment and its language, but we need not claim that it is ''real life.''

Our theories are not real life, either. They are abstractions and in a sense highlighted drama. Our theoretical language is not literary—it is abstract, and so coded that it invariably requires translation.

Literature (like our more poetic patients) provides us through its language with the beauty of nuances, the shadings of mood and meaning, and a sense of the rich complexity of relationships. We feel that literature expresses vividly what we dimly sense. Its rich tapestry of projected human life allows us to conceive of relations that have a particular meaning for ourselves. In all these ways we are enriched by the artist.

Bonime has pointed out that attention to dramatic devices, or even moderate awareness that they exist, allows us to distinguish the character, the artistic product, from an alive person.

Our competence as psychoanalysts is in the treatment of the emotionally troubled person. Our more far-flung extravaganzas are akin to play, to an imaginative dance, to a dialogue with the artist or any of his characters. It is revitalizing play, but let us remember that our imaginative involvement can seduce, and we are seduceable; it can bewitch our sense so that imagination conceived becomes the truth and the real.

REFERENCES

A.P.A. Task Force Report on Psychohistory (1976), A review, *Psychiatric News,* 11, 14.

Arnheim, R. (1957), *Film as Art,* Univ. California Press, Los Angeles.

Barnett, J. (1975), Hamlet and the family ideology, *J. Amer. Acad. Psychoanal,* 3(4), 405–417.

Bartlett, F. H. (1976), Unpublished paper, private communication.

Brook, P. (1968), *The Empty Space,* Atheneum, New York.

Eissler, K. R. (1969), *Discourse on Hamlet and HAMLET,* International Universities Press, New York.

Freud, E. L. (1960), *Letters of Sigmund Freud,* Basic Books, New York.

Gass, W. H. (1971), *Fiction and the Figures of Life,* Knopf, New York; Random Vintage ed., 1972.

Holland, N. N. (1975), *Poems in Persons,* Norton Library, New York.

Holland, N. N. (1966), *Psychoanalysis and Shakespeare,* McGraw-Hill, New York; Octagon Books, New York, 1976. This book is complete up to 1964, and summarizes books and articles. There are 91 listings on *Hamlet* alone, and roughly 190 listings on the other plays.

Hutter, A. D. (1975), The language of Hamlet, *J. Amer. Acad. Psychoanal.,* 3(4), 429–438.

James, H. (1934), *The Art of the Novel,* Scribner, New York.

Jones, E. (1949), *Hamlet and Oedipus,* W. W. Norton, New York, A development of Freud's earlier writing on this subject.

Jones, E. (1957), *The Life and Work of Sigmund Freud,* Basic Books, New York.

Langer, S. K. (1953), *Feeling and Form: A Theory of Art,* Scribner, New York.

Lidz, T. (1975), *Hamlet's Enemy,* Basic Books, New York.

Morgan, C. (1933), The nature of dramatic illusion, in *Essays by Divers Hands* (London), Vol, 12, pp. 61–77 of Transactions of the Royal Society of Literature in England. Cited in Langer's *Feeling and Form,* pp. 309 and 399.
Price, M. (1975), People of the book: Character in Forster's *A Passage to India, Critical Inquiry,* 1(3), Chicago.
Shainess, N. (1975), The coup that failed, *J. Amer. Acad. Psychoanal.,* 3(4), 383–403.
Wilson, R. (1976), On character, A reply to Martin Price, *Critical Inquiry,* 2(1), Chicago.

10. Methodological Problems in the Psychoanalytic Interpretation of Literature: A Review of Studies on Sophocles' *Antigone*

David Werman

Ever since Freud discovered psychic function, applied psychoanalysis has been closely related to the main body of psychoanalytic theory. This relationship was a natural consequence of Freud's classical education and his fascination and preoccupation with literature as a derivative of man's mental life. In art and literature Freud found illustrations of the theoretical concepts he was organizing out of his clinical experience; at the same time, art and literature presented a convincing body of data to corroborate and demonstrate his ideas.

Although Freud and others such as Abraham and Rank made extensive and often brilliant excursions into a number of cultural areas, recasting them in the light of psychoanalysis, their efforts were limited by methodological difficulties which were evident to the writers themselves. The inherent problem is that the psychoanalytic interpretation of a cultural phenomenon lies outside of the therapeutic process in which an interpretation can be inserted and become a "mutative" element. Ricoeur (1970) likens applied psychoanalysis to data about the analysand that might be supplied to the analyst by a third party. Despite the claim of some authors, such as Greenacre, that "the study of the works of a prolific artist offers material as usable for psychoanalytic investigation as the dreams and free associations of the patient" (1955, p. 13), this assumption has been disputed.

This essay will present some of the methodological problems encountered in the psychoanalytic study of literature. For my purpose I shall examine selected aspects of a number of psychoanalytic studies of Sophocles' *Antigone*. I shall also indicate methods of approaching the work based on textual

Reprinted by permission of the author and International Universities Press from *JAPA*, 27 (1979).

analysis and on subjective response—procedures that appear complementary to the usual methods of psychoanalytic explication of literary works.

It might be appropriate to begin by reviewing the mythological background to the *Antigone*. Following Oedipus' death, his sons agreed to rule Thebes during alternate years. But at the end of his year on the throne, Eteocles refused to step down. His brother, Polyneices, with his father-in-law, raised an army and attacked Thebes, but their attempt ended in a disastrous rout. At the foot of the walled city the two brothers killed each other, and Creon, the former regent and uncle of the brothers, became king. Although he buried the Theban dead, he denied sepulcher to the enemy, including Polyneices. According to the myth, Antigone managed to bury her proscribed brother. The foregoing is all we possess of the mythological context of the play, and it is presumed that the events occurring in Sophocles' tragedy are largely his invention or that of his contemporaries.

The play opens on the day following the deaths of the brothers and Creon's assumption of the throne. Antigone tells her sister, Ismene, of Creon's edict that Polyneices' body must go unmourned and unburied, "a tasty meal for vultures," and that whoever violates his decree shall be stoned to death. Pleading fraternal love and the laws of the gods, Antigone announces her determination to bury Polyneices even if she must forfeit her life. The more Ismene insists that the idea is madness and bound to fail, that as women they must be obedient, the more hardened does Antigone become in her resolve.

When she attempts to carry out the funeral rites, she is seized and brought before Creon, to whom she avows her act but evokes "unwritten laws"—divine laws—that are timeless and universal, that transcend the edicts of any man. Creon proclaims his rule and law, asserting that enemies must be treated differently from friends, even though they be blood relatives. Antigone responds that she loves both her brothers. The king rejects this view and condemns her to death, absurdly and spitefully including Ismene in this sentence. Although Ismene pleads to be permitted to die with her sister, Antigone spurns her offer, desiring neither help nor a partner to share her sacrifice.

Creon's son, Haemon, appears before him and asks that Antigone be pardoned. Although he is engaged to marry her, his plea is free of emotion; he is logical and tactful, dealing with issues of justice and what he perceives are his father's profound errors. The scene ends with father and son exploding with rage and pain, and Creon poised to kill Antigone before Haemon's eyes.

Nevertheless, the king decides not to carry out the sacrilegious execution and orders that Antigone be immured in a cave with "enough fodder only to defend the country from the filth of a curse" (Braun, 1973, 936–937).[1] In her last appearance Antigone chants of her pain in departing from life, of never having been a bride, and never having nursed a baby.

She is succeeded on stage by the prophet Tiresias who describes a series of strange omens symbolic of the gods' anger with Creon's impious decree. It is clear that Polyneices must be buried at once. Creon incredibly accuses the seer of selling him out for money; Tiresias replies that the king is a sick tyrant who is committing a "crime of violence" and will be pursued by the "furies of death and deity." Although he repudiates the prophet, Creon is frightened and turns to the Chorus for counsel; they advise him to immediately release Antigone from the cave and to build a tomb for Polyneices. When he sets off to rescind his edict, the dramatic action rushes toward its ineluctable tragic end: Eurydice, his wife, learns that just before Creon reached the cave, Antigone had hanged herself. Haemon, in a frenzy of rage and anguish, attempts to kill his father, fails, and plunges the sword into himself.

Creon enters, bearing Haemon's shrouded body, lamenting his folly and violence; but his punishments are not yet at an end, for a messenger reveals that Eurydice, cursing her husband, has stabbed herself. Torn with grief and guilt, Creon yearns for oblivion, and the play ends.

From his studies on "neurotic virginity and old maidenhood," Weissman (1964) sought to demonstrate that Antigone is a typical "old maid" reflecting a specific psychosexual development. He found that the fixation of the old maid is not "truly Oedipal," but a fixation on the preoedipal mother—a wish for unification with her; and by displacement these disturbed object relations lead to the wish for unification with other family members—father and siblings—which results in an "indiscriminate devotion and loyalty to various members of the immediate family" (p. 32).

In support of his thesis Weissman cites Antigone's passionate desire to bury her brother as a demonstration of her "irrational devotion to the family unit" (p. 34). Similarly, Antigone's request that Ismene join her in the burial is regarded as an "unconscious motive" to unite all the family members in death. Since the pivot of the tragedy consists of Antigone's unrelenting drive to secure Polyneices' burial, Weissman does not lack for quotations to buttress his point of view. But at no point does he suggest an alternative interpretation of these actions, such as the sacred import of burial in ancient (and even modern) times. For the ancient Greeks, failure to bury the dead was an unspeakable crime. Bowra (1944) wrote that, although Sophocles' audience might, at most, have disagreed with Antigone, they would have readily understood her need to bury Polyneices. The dead have undeniable rights: to justice, to vengeance, and especially to proper burial. Without sepulcher the body lies unsanctified and homeless.[2] Through powerful images the dramatist makes us see the degradation of Polyneices' corpse: "ripped for food by dogs and vulture," "the body was oozing," "the mangled body lay . . . where the dogs had dragged it," "the eagles ripped him for food," and so on. Clearly, the poet forces us to experience the horror of this uncared-for body. The omission of the issue of burial seriously weakens Weissman's thesis.

He stresses Antigone's "irrationalism," indicating that it comes from her unconscious wish for reunion with her mother; logically, her defiance of Creon's edict is "irrational," since it will lead to the death she unconsciously seeks. Weissman quotes an exchange with Creon wherein she declares that Hades makes no distinction between the brothers. But Creon retorts, "Not even death can metamorphose hate to love." To which Antigone responds: "No, nor decompose a love to hate" (p. 34).[3] To this affirmation of the power of Eros, Creon, the "rational" protagonist, exclaims, "Curse you! Find the outlet for love down there [in Hades]" (p. 34).

To further establish Antigone's irrationality, Weissman presents Ismene not only as a standard of rationality, but as the "loyal mature mate or daughter," who "gives evidence . . . of a mature oedipally derived love . . ." (p. 40). His evidence for this characterization is that Ismene, unlike Antigone, did not wish to die when their father, Oedipus, died. Furthermore, during Oedipus' lifetime, Ismene did not "become his eyes or his single prop, or his partner in pain" (p. 39). Her maturity is illustrated by her "see[ing] no sense in Antigone's wish to die for her dishonorable brother. Her wish is to live, to be forgiven, and perhaps fulfill her own life" (p. 40). (Goethe described Ismene as a "beautiful standard of the commonplace" [Eckermann, 1836, p. 185].)

Finally, Weissman's interpretation of an ambiguous passage is of particular significance. He asserts that the following speech of Antigone gives us a

> climactic portrayal of [her] psychosexual development toward old maidenhood, her preoedipal attachments, her devaluation and incapacity for a finalizing heterosexual relationship and having her own child. She explains to Creon:

On what principle do I assert so much?
Just this: A husband dead, another can be found,
A child, replaced; but a brother lost
(Mother and father buried too)
No other brother can be born or grows again.
That's my principle, which Creon stigmatized
As criminal—my principal for honoring
You my dearest brother. So taken
So I am led away; a spinster still
Uncelebrated, barren and bereft of joys;
No children to my name. [pp. 34–35]

While Weissman's broad interpretation of these verses seems challenged by the last three lines, his choice of this passage is of special interest because these lines (904–920 in the original version) have been the focus of a long-standing, unresolved controversy among scholars regarding their very authenticity. At this point it will be useful to make a detour in order to review another psychoanalytic study which is based entirely on the foregoing speech.

Van der Sterren's (1952) thesis is succinct and his methodology explicitly described: "I have used Freud's views on the psychology of the dream as my starting-point . . . myth and poetical productions come into being in the same way and have the same meaning . . . [except that] the secondary elaboration is much further developed. . . . I hold, *a priori,* that this conception is the correct one, and the close study of these plays of Sophocles has shown me once more that this approach alone is able to solve the various problems and is moreover, a fruitful method" (p. 343). Van der Sterren seeks to demonstrate Antigone's neuroticism by asserting that by the time she speaks these lines (904–920) she has "lost the esteem of everyone." Clearly, if this allegation is correct it would totally undermine our acceptance of Antigone as a heroine. However, the evidence to support it is flimsy: Ismene rejects helping in Polyneices' burial only because it means risking her life; the Chorus, a group of timid old men, indeed at first support Creon's edict, but by the time of Antigone's final confrontation with the king they proclaim to her: "You go with fame and in glory / to the hidden place of the dead . . . Your doom is worth grand fame; for living and dying, both you share / the heritage of the gods' equals" (972–973, 988–990). Tiresias flatly calls Creon "stupid" and "criminal." Haemon declares that "the whole nation denies [that Antigone did wrong]" (882). Creon himself, far from disputing these assertions, retorts: "Will the nation tell me what orders I can give?" (883).

And the denouement of the tragedy is Creon's destruction, working as a counterpoint to the paean of praise to Antigone.

Van der Sterren castigates critics who have questioned the validity of the speech; they are attempting to cover up its "real motive," he notes, and they "make false translations" (p. 349). In this context, he ambiguously quotes Goethe. Inasmuch as Weissman (1964) and Seidenberg and Papathomopoulos (1962) also refer to Goethe's comments, it would be instructive to examine them. According to Eckermann (1836), Goethe observed that: ". . . Creon by no means acts from political virtue, but from hatred towards the dead. Polyneices . . . did not commit such a monstrous crime against the state that his death was insufficient, and that further punishment of the innocent corpse was required. . . . Creon . . . *has everybody in the play against him*" (p. 177–178; emphasis added). As for the disputed passage, Goethe did regard it as a "blemish," but stated he "would give a great deal for an apt philologist to prove that it is interpolated and spurious." In short, he believed the "passage . . . very far-fetched" (p. 178).

Although Jebb (1898) observed that "few problems of Greek Tragedy have been more discussed than the question whether those verses, or some of them, are spurious" (p. 164), only Seidenberg and Papathomopoulos utilize this literature. This apparent lack of familiarity with the work carried out by nonanalytic scholars, as well as the not infrequent neglect of primary sources, often justifies the criticism of amateurism leveled against studies in applied psychoanalysis.

One might agree with Weissman's thesis that "neurotic virginity and old maidenhood" may mask a deeper attachment to the preoedipal mother; such a psychological schema may be an important factor in some women's avoidance of marriage; but we have little basis for assuming that Antigone had such an attachment to her mother. In fact, we do know that she is betrothed and deeply in love with Haemon; that she yearns for marriage and children; and that, far from "welcoming" death, she goes toward it with suffering and reluctance. At the end she chants: "No wedding song has been sung for this bride. I never nursed a child; and with those I love gone, I go alone and desolate" (1072–1074). These do not sound like the words of a woman in search of death fleeing from life, love, and men. We are overwhelmed by her death because it is a denial of all she desires. The poet obliges us to perceive Antigone as *especially* rich with the promise of life, precisely so that we experience the tragedy of her death rather than regard it as senseless, paltry, and banal.

Seidenberg and Papathomopoulos have dealt with Antigone in two communications. The first (1962) presents literary examples of "daughters who tend their fathers"; the second (1974) overlaps the earlier paper, but deals entirely with the "enigma" of Antigone. Their thesis is that Oedipus bound Antigone into caring for him, an "enslavement" which she dutifully accepted. "Although she is unable to fight on the battlefield, she seeks *arete* [virtue] in the capacity of a rebel, against the humiliation which her uncle demanded" (1962, p. 154); she prefers honor and *arete* to marriage and motherhood; in agreement with Van der Sterren they believe her defiant act represents an "abandonment of the feminine role," and is perhaps a defense against incestuous wishes toward Polyneices; that her defiance of Creon's edict represents an identification with her brothers; and that she has "at last succeeded in playing a role in the battlefield." They believe that "in the age of misogyny" Sophocles apparently realized the "hidden desires of certain women who did not conform to the general role . . . of homemaking and child rearing" (p. 155). Thus, while Antigone perhaps lamented being deprived of marriage and children she "secretly gives them up in favor of . . . a nobler destiny" (pp. 155–156).

Why Antigone "secretly" means the opposite of what she says is not demonstrated. Indeed, if Sophocles intends her words to be false, the drama would cease to be a tragedy and Antigone a heroine. Their speculation (also made by other writers) of her incestuous yearnings for Polyneices cannot be faulted. But much more prominent is the special role of women, in ancient societies, of attending to the sacred burial rites. If one views Antigone's behavior in terms of the values and mores current in Sophocles' time, one tends to accept this as a motive rather than a desire to shed her enslaved feminine self. Curiously, while Van der Sterren's argument is that Antigone is neurotically unhappy being a woman, Seidenberg and Papathomopoulos refer to him in support of their position that she is secretly and *appropriately* unhappy being a woman—because she is oppressed.

Seidenberg and Papathomopoulos demonstrate another methodological error in treating Antigone and other fictional characters re-created by the artist (despite their mythological antecedents), as if they are historical figures, treating Euripides' Antigone to explain Sophocles' Antigone.

In their 1974 paper these authors again "confirm" Weissman's contention that Antigone is "a pre-oedipal old maid whose basic drive is to return to her nurturing mother." Through unification with her mother, Antigone "would make herself and create unto herself all those things which her mother lacked, strength, loyalty, convictions, in order to win mother, to be loved and be united with her. With good authority, Antigone would become irresistible to such a mother, for mother could never resist authority'' (p. 202). Seidenberg and Papathomopoulos arrive at these conclusions in the following manner: Robert Graves, they note, ''feels'' that the name of Antigone in Greek means ''in place of a mother'';[4] '' 'in place of mother' . . . might . . . mean identification with mother; it is more likely the name represents the life that a woman might lead apart from motherhood with the confinements and passivity it engenders. The ancient Greeks in their wisdom knew that all women did not submit to the role of inferiority that the culture ruthlessly demanded'' (p. 202). Such linguistic ''evidence'' is unconvincing, and, furthermore, does not explain the contradiction between what is described as a ''ruthlessly'' misogynistic society and the wise ancient Greeks who inhabited it. Through the same need to establish an aura of *universal* misogyny, they cite, correctly, Creon's depreciation of women. Yet they observe that Antigone was ''esteemed'' by the ''whole'' city. Actually, Sophocles seems primarily intent on the aesthetic task of polarizing Antigone and Creon in every plausible way. Undoubtedly, the growing regard for women in fifth-century Greece had some impact on him. But his artistic imperative is to stress the conflict between Creon and Antigone, and this is expressed in their respective imagery, the rhythms of their speech, their age and their sex—in order to make the drama work as theatre. Accordingly, Creon is the *only* male character who demeans women. Seidenberg and Papathomopoulos, along with the authors reviewed here, minimize aesthetic considerations.

The conclusion of their article reiterates their feminist interpretation of the *Antigone* through a series of speculations, of which I shall quote but one: ''Had Antigone been a male youth and had been similarly disobedient, there would have been at most talk of generational gap, oedipal conflict, primal horde, but not deformity'' (p. 204). One cannot disagree with the authors' impassioned denunciation of the oppression of women, but one must challenge the correctness of their interpretation of Antigone, its ahistoric viewpoint, and their concept that the *Antigone* concerns the subjugation of women.

Along with others, Kanzer (1948, 1950) regards the *Oedipus Tyrannus,* the *Oedipus at Colonus,* and the *Antigone* as an Oedipus Trilogy, which ''dramatize[s] three stages in the development and resolution of the oedipus complex'' (1950, p. 571). Kanzer's focus is on Oedipus, and his remarks on

Antigone for the most part relate to her relation to him. For example, he interprets the blinded Oedipus' dependence on Antigone as her playing the "role of the mother." Similarly, he regards her defiance of Creon's ban on the burial of Polyneices as a displacement of "her loyalty from her father to her brother"; thus, her behavior is seen primarily as a manifestation of her unresolved oedipal conflict. While this interpretation is plausible from the perspective of the total "trilogy," it loses cogency when considered within the reduced frame of the *Antigone* where the oedipal dynamics do not appear central to the drama and in which more acute and gripping issues occupy the stage.

By maintaining an oedipal interpretation of the *Antigone,* Kanzer is led to interpret Creon as a figure complementary to Oedipus; as the latter partially identified with his rejecting father, Laius, and hence expelled his sons, so, in the *Antigone,* Creon is the castrator of the sons: Haemon, Polyneices, and Eteocles. "It is the force of this castration anxiety," Kanzer writes, "effecting the resolution of the oedipus complex, which is the unconscious content of the Antigone" (p. 566). But are the sons Creon's victims? In the first instance it is his niece, Antigone, whom he destroys. His son and wife kill themselves, admittedly because of what Creon has done. But Polyneices and Eteocles destroy each other, and the former is victimized by Creon only by being denied reunion with the other dead in the family. In the broadest sense, Creon's victims are all the citizens of Thebes who quickly found themselves under his yoke. Even Creon's clash with Haemon is unconvincing as an oedipal father–son battle because the element of jealousy is totally lacking. Only by hypothesizing a series of displacements can Creon be plausibly described as essentially a "castrating father." As I shall show later on, his behavior seems more understandable when viewed in terms of narcissistic considerations.

Perhaps because Kanzer was not satisfied with his interpretation of the *Antigone,* he concludes his essay by focusing on the Athenian society of Sophocles' time, which he presents as a necessary background for understanding the tragedies. He suggests that Antigone's behavior might represent a love of family. But he does not integrate the psychoanalytic and sociologic interpretations beyond noting that "social forces impinge on and are transmitted into the idiom of individual experience" (Kanzer, 1950, p. 571).

Wolman (1965) has related Antigone's sacrifice of her life to Freud's description of self-sacrificing love: an overflowing of narcissistic libido onto the object. The latter becomes increasingly precious "until at last it gets possession of the entire self-love of the ego, whose self-sacrifice thus follows as a natural consequence" (Freud, 1921, p. 113). Wolman calls such self-sacrificial love the Antigone Principle and describes it in terms of valorous acts in battle, rites of passage, martyrdom, and resistance to religious persecution. Since he makes no distinction between heroism in general, heroism in Greek tragedy, courage, martyrdom and self-sacrifice, he is able to place in his Pantheon of heroes the youth of Sparta, Jan Huss, Londoners under the Blitz, and Israeli soldiers. Wolman concludes that, since "not every suffering is heroic," the true heroes are "men who *willingly* suffer for others" (p. 193). How one might determine willingness to suffer, the degree of pain endured, and what Wolman means by "a better future for others," is unclear. Antigone, he asserts, was a normal individual, not a masochist; she loved life, but her "love for justice was stronger than the love for herself" (p. 200). This abstract "love for justice," however, is different from Antigone's piety, from her moral imperative, from her powerful sense of family bonds, and from her outrage at Creon's violation of the unwritten laws.

Furthermore, Wolman does not use the meaning of the hero in the specific sense in which it was understood in ancient Greece, particularly in Greek tragedy. What makes Antigone a heroine in the classic mold, what distinguishes her from ordinary mortals, are, it seems to me, superior powers: her burning emotions, her keener insight, her capacity *both* to give and to experience pain, and her endurance of suffering. The hero may rise above common men by his mastery in battle or statecraft, in athletics, in prophesy, or in dance or song. He demands respect, inspires love, and is recognized as noble—as befits "a strange being neither man nor god but both" (Bowra, 1944, p. 315). This delineation of the classic hero has little in common with many of Wolman's heroes, who are measured by other scales; but it is the very essence of the Antigone of Sophocles, who forges her character precisely so that she becomes a heroine in this sense. To misconstrue Antigone's heroism reduces the *Antigone,* at best, to a brilliantly constructed tale of martyrdom and a one-dimensional view of Creon-as-villain.

Erich Fromm's remarks on Antigone appear in the context of a general discussion of the Oedipus complex and the Oedipus myth (1949). He asserts that the Oedipus myth is "a symbol not of the incestuous love between mother and son but of the rebellion of the son against the authority of the father in a patriarchal society" (p. 338). Like Kanzer (who has critically reviewed Fromm's essay) he leans heavily on regarding the three Oedipus plays as a unity. Although much of their respective theses depends on this hypothesis, the evidence remains inconclusive.[5] In a scholarly discussion of this question, Jebb (1898) presents internal evidence in support of the view that the plays do not constitute a connected trilogy, and that the *Antigone* was actually part of another trilogy, of which the other two plays are lost (of the over 120 written by Sophocles, only seven remain). He concludes that "in nothing is the art of Sophocles more characteristically seen than in the fact that each of these three masterpieces—with their common thread of fable, and with all their particular affinities—is still, dramatically and morally, an independent whole" (xlix-1). Disagreement with Jebb—and other likeminded scholars—is hardly a breach of critical rigor, but such differences should be acknowledged even if not evaluated.

Again, like Kanzer, Fromm interprets the conflict between Creon and Haemon as analogous to the clash between Oedipus and Polyneices in the *Oedipus at Colonus,* where the unforgiven son is cast out. But where Kanzer interprets this conflict as fueled by the son's incestuous strivings in a headlong encounter with the castrating potential of the father, Fromm explains it in terms of a conflict between a matriarchal principle incarnated by Oedipus, Haemon, and Antigone, and a patriarchal principle represented by Creon. These principles were formulated by J. J. Bachofen, between 1859 and 1870, and emerged from his detailed scholarly work on "mother right." Since Fromm reviews this work, and it is also alluded to by Kanzer, only a brief exposition of it is required here.

Bachofen studied the symbols found in the myths, art, and artifacts of ancient Greece, Rome, Egypt, and other areas of the Mediterranean basin. He conceptualized a nomadic, hetaeristic, primitive world governed by unbridled sexuality, which was slowly replaced by an agricultural, socioreligious culture, in which mother right dominated. Ultimately, this era was superseded by a patriarchal society which brought the "liberation of the spirit from the manifestation of nature, a substitution of human existence over the law of material life . . ." (Bachofen, 1859–1870, p. 109). Bachofen stressed that elements of the old often coexisted with the new, or re-emerged after periods of oblivion.

During the era of mother right, there was an "emphasis on maternal property and the name of the maternal line, the closeness of maternal kinship . . . and the inexpiability of matricide" (p. 71). There was greater love for sisters than for brothers, loyalty to mothers, and ". . . the divine principle of love, of union, of peace'' (p. 79). Matriarchal love is more intense, and unlike the patriarchal principle, which is ''inherently restrictive, the matriarchal principle, is universal.'' It is the basis of freedom, equality, and hospitality. ''Devotion, justice, and all the qualities that embellish man's life are known by feminine names . . .'' (p. 91). The rise of patriarchy saw the emergence of spiritual over corporeal existence, of the Apollonian over the chthonian-maternal principle. Laws, rationality, monogamy, authority, a hierarchical order in society, and inequality became the hallmarks of the new epoch.

Against all objections to Bachofen, Fromm finds the theory of matriarchy ''established beyond any doubt,'' and thus he explicates the Oedipus ''trilogy'' as a clash between the matriarchal and patriarchal principles. The slow, painful, and often violent passage of matriarchal into patriarchal society, and the continued presence of aspects of the earlier period in the later is represented, according to Fromm, in the conflict in the *Antigone*. Antigone herself embodies the importance of the human being, of natural law and love, in contrast to Creon who proclaims the state, man made laws, and obedience. Ismene is the prototype of the woman who accepts patriarchal domination and the defeat of women. For Creon, his son is mere property whose unique purpose is to serve; the king's defeat brings to an end the ''principle of authoritarianism, of man's domination over the people'' (p. 353).

Fromm thus projects onto the *Antigone* his social ideology, but, despite undoubted relevances, his formulation seems strangely external to the passions of the drama itself; its approach to the play is with an ideological yardstick that reductively interprets this (or any) work of art, in which the protagonists are in conflict over such issues as authority, law, conscience, and religious standards, as representing a conflict between the matriarchal and patriarchal principles.

Fromm appends to the foregoing interpretation of the *Antigone* an auxiliary but unintegrated view which attempts to relate the drama to the ''specific political and cultural situation of Sophocles' time.'' He identifies Sophocles as an adversary of the Sophists, whom he describes as seeking to establish a despotism of the intellectual elite and ''upholding unrestricted selfishness as a moral principle'' (p. 354), and he equates Creon with the Sophists, a view shared by Kanzer. While both authors urge us to accept Sophocles' straightforward antagonism to Sophism, Fromm interprets the trilogy as specifically expressing not only Sophocles' opposition to the Sophists, but his sympathy for the old, nonolympian, religious traditions of the matriarchy, when love, equality, and justice were valued. These assertions are questionable if we look at Sophocles' place in Athenian society. Bowra (1944), Kirkwood (1958), Kitto (1956), Whitman (1951), and other scholars mentioned here, have made authoritative contributions in this area. I shall only touch on some of the sociologic issues raised by Fromm and Kanzer.

There is, in fact, little difficulty in identifying aspects of the *Antigone* with matters that were prominent in Sophocles' lifetime. That he himself was totally a part of this era, if not an active partisan of positions, is attested to by even the scant knowledge we have of him: a total of perhaps four pages of uncertain biographic data. Letters (1953) sums up some of this material: "Sophocles was not only one of Athens' 'lofty, grave tragedians,' he was an active citizen, man about town, lover of food, wine and company, musician, conversationalist, wit, homosexual, actor, literary dictator, juror, admiral, priest and copious writer of Rabelaisian farces . . ." (p. 2). It is not then surprising that the play brilliantly reflects issues such as divine and human justice, the nature of the unwritten laws, the position of women in society, the individual vis-a-vis the state, the role of the king, and fate versus free will. Much of the critical literature seeks to establish which of these questions is what the Antigone "is about." And yet, the only certain conclusions one can reach is that the drama is as remarkably free of open partisanship on these issues as it is thoroughly penetrated with the social, philosophical, political, and religious issues of its day.

The *Antigone,* on one level, demonstrates that unreason, impiety (even if religion is only a projection made by man—as the Sophists averred), and pride *(hubris)* are among the greatest dangers for man. These themes are characteristic of that "impact of society" on the drama to which Kanzer alluded, and they reach us on conscious and preconscious levels of apprehension. But there exists another dimension to the poet's work, of which he himself may have been unaware, and which we may deeply experience even if without intellectual understanding: the resonance of the drama with our unconscious, which has only the most intricate, indirect, and long-term relation to society.

If we seek a psychoanalytic understanding of the *Antigone,* or any other work of art, we must turn to the text, with as few a priori ideas about it as possible, as the source best embodying the data to be studied (the analogy of listening to the patient, rather than studying documents from other people, seems valid). It is my impression that the first and most striking observation about the drama, as an aesthetic entity, is that it is a tissue of contrasts. The structure is built up through a series of confrontations: of Antigone and Ismene, of Creon and the sentry, then with Ismene, Haemon, Antigone, and Tiresias. Light and dark episodes alternate, as do life and death, hope and despair, authority and revolt, justice and injustice, man's law and divine law, piety and impiety, free will and fate, democracy and autocracy, the individual and the state, reason and passion, flexibility and rigidity—the list of antinomies could be continued. And affectively, as scene follows scene, we swing between states of tension and relaxation, until we are finally swept to the horrifying denouement.

The poet uses all his craft to suggest contrast. As mentioned earlier, the very language used by each character, the cadences of their speech, the imagery—everything builds the atmosphere of conflict. The details of how this is done, e.g., Creon's repeated use of animal images, has been elucidated by Goheen (1951).

Although the superstructure of the tragedy consists of contrasting elements welded into an aesthetic whole, and the chief polarities of that conflict are represented by Antigone and Creon, these characters are not simple conduits for contrasting beliefs; on the contrary, they are concrete as well as generic individuals, whose personalities reverberate in our unconscious. It is because Creon and Antigone are not mere standard-bearers, engaged in abstract verbal exchanges, but are plausible flesh-and-blood individuals, that the drama "works" on the affective as well as cognitive levels. The poet engages us in a powerful enterprise of empathy.

To experience the play is also to recognize that Antigone and Creon transcend simple opposition, for each serves to define the other. If "Antigone is the balance in which Creon is weighed and found wanting" (Whitman, 1951, p. 80), then Creon must be the crucible in which Antigone becomes tempered so that she may achieve the grandeur that death bestows upon her. Creon's behavior leads Antigone to heroism. To experience the *Antigone* obliges us to enter Creon's inner world.

What manner of man is this ruler? Some authors, such as Kitto (1956), assert that he is the central character in the *Antigone;* in fact, a third of the drama takes place after Antigone's final appearance. For the Athenian audience, to whom Sophocles spoke, Creon is a tyrant. He first appears with homage to the gods on his lips, asserting that the worst ruler is one who "fails to embrace the best man's counsels" (218). But he swiftly reveals his duplicity, and by the end of his first speech his authoritarianism is revealed in his decree that brutally violates all tradition. Each succeeding confrontation of his power progressively exposes him as stubborn, arrogant, violent, and irrational. At one point his sense of reality is so overwhelmed by rage that he forgets that it is only Antigone, and not Ismene as well, whom he has condemned to death! The more his authority is challenged or even questioned, the more his self-esteem is threatened and the more are ignoble qualities brought to light. His piety is a sham; he courts the gods only when they serve him and denigrates them when they no longer meet his needs. When he fears their anger at his decree of death for Antigone he changes only the letter of his command by ordering that she be permitted to die of starvation. From wherever the source, whatever the validity, he intemperately rejects all criticism—even the timid questions of the old men in the Chorus.

Repeatedly, Sophocles shows us that Creon values individuals only as possessions to be utilized and manipulated for his own aggrandizement. His view of love is mostly limited to its physical aspect: when Ismene asks him if he means to "kill the girl you promised your own son would marry" (701–702) he crassly responds that "there are other fields to furrow" (703). Of utmost importance are the growing distortions in his thinking: he levels totally unjustified accusations of corruption by bribery against those who oppose him: the unknown individuals who first attempt to bury Polyneices "were seduced by money" (372); the sentry who reports the deed is told that "for money—you sold your soul" (402); even the saintlike Tiresias has it flung in his face that he "and his kind, for a long time now, have been selling me out . . ." (196–197). This almost delusional thinking is scarcely surprising, for early in the play Creon complains of "certain men in the city . . . [who] mutter about me" (366–368). When Tiresias aptly states "you are a sick man" (1216), we concur that Creon indeed exhibits paranoid thoughts. His narcissistic hunger pervades all his behavior, his thoughts and feelings, domestic as well as public, and leads to his resentment of youth and women and to his voracious yearnings for power. "Nations," he pronounces, "belong to the men with power. That's common knowledge" (888–889).

And yet, beyond all expectations, at his downfall, after we have witnessed the blood bath he has brought about, we do not cast this prototypical tryant into darkness, but instead feel, as Bonnard put it (1951), "only tenderness and pity." Creon is a figure of "human error" whom Sophocles has given us, not as a warning, but as a fraternal being; too much *a part of us* to condemn him from the heights of our own abstract principles. Within his character Creon is ''right'' and must act as he does so that the drama will confront us with our divided self and the real world in which it must act. Through Creon the poet awakens sleeping aspects of ourselves, illuminating our complexity. His childlike tyranny acts not only on the people around him but on himself because he is in bondage to his instinctual impulses and primitive modes of response. In contrast, Antigone is more autonomous and object-seeking, and through her death she escapes the very solitude that finally descends on Creon. His need for power becomes impotence; he fears and despises Eros for it would make him vulnerable to the world, and with the loss of narcissistic objects his world collapses. But his late-learned wisdom echoes our yearning to be free from the imperious reign of our own infantilism—thus we rejoice in his tragic growth as we do in Antigone's tragic and heroic death.

This brings us to consider the feelings we experience at the conclusion of the drama. I believe that this subjective dimension, the experience of the spectator, is a critical aspect of the psychoanalytic investigation of literature, and yet, more frequently than not, it is neglected in favor of more ''objective'' criteria. The ''evenly suspended attention'' of the analyst in the analytic situation, his brief identifications with the patient, the scrutiny and analysis of his own fantasies, dreams, and feelings are processes that do not often occur in applied psychoanalysis. Paradoxically, the *Antigone* leaves us with a special sense of pleasure, which suffuses us at the conclusion of the tragedy. The universality of this experience may be open to question, but its widespread occurrence is readily observed. ''Tragic pleasure'' is more than a simple experience of evasion and disengagement, or a vicarious brush with Antigone's pain from which we escape unscathed. Bonnard (1951) described it as ''the price of our active participation in the poet's work. It manifests our commitment to this enterprise of recreation of the world'' (p. 71). The tragic poet's classical vocation was educative and formative, and his drama, in which we participate, becomes an apprenticeship in pain that leads to a mastery of the human condition through a process of self-elucidation—a process reminiscent of psychoanalysis.

The contradiction between our pain and our pleasure is only apparent once we recognize that Creon and Antigone represent profound aspects of our self. As Creon acts out before us his infantile wishes for omnipotence, omniscience, approval and admiration, and total license, we cannot reject him because too much of him resonates with elements that once were in us—and may still reside in only relative silence; we see in him our ''negative ego ideal''; he incarnates all that we would project on to the other. Antigone, on the other hand, embodies what we would become. Her tragic end represents the expression of our yearnings, of our ideal ego; with her we triumph over blind fate, over our infantile self, and we identify with her victory.

Antigone might be perceived as embodying many facets of our ego ideal: courageous, passionate, loyal to her kin, eloquent, loved and loving, generous, competent, and possessing ''superior powers''; in short, the qualities described by Bibring (1953) as constituting our narcissistic aspirations. Although we are aware of her arrogance, irrationality, and stubbornness, it is her positive characteristics that engage us. On the other hand, while Creon is stubborn, increasingly irrational, arrogant, misogynistic, unloved, and not truly loving, he feels pain, bereavement, fear, shame, and in some manner he loves his wife, his children, and his subjects, and yearns to be approved of by the city. His downfall brings us no pleasure, for we experience his despair.

Somewhat analogous to the two levels of experiencing the *Antigone* which I have described, Holland (1968) hypothesized two paths of experiencing a work of art: one tests reality, is intellectual, is generally characterized by other aspects of secondary-process thinking, and is in connection with the ''central theme'' of the work; the other is characterized by the introjection of the work, the experience of the nuclear fantasy and the formal management of that fantasy as if it were our own. We analogize the work to our own fantasies which become more acceptable to us, and the work itself takes on an intellectual meaning. Our identification with a character would be due to a complicated mixture of the introjection of that character's drives and defenses and our projection onto him of elements within ourself. We can identify with certain characters chiefly on the basis of their instinctual drives, and with others mostly because of their defenses. From this perspective, some of the pleasure of literature would derive from various combinations of limited gratification of drive and other fantasies, and the defensive management of those fantasies, leading to pleasure in the totality of the work. Holland's conceptualization further explains the pleasure we experience from the *Antigone*.

This dimension of aesthetic pleasure appears to promise much in furthering a psychoanalytic view of literature. Despite studies by Freud (1905), Kris (1952), Lesser (1957), Rose (1964), Waelder (1965), Coltrera (1965), Within (1969), and Ricoeur (1970), among others, the subject remains far from resolved. The analysis of the aesthetic response offers the advantage of obliging us to consider the work as an artistic unity, rather than as a collection of isolated characters and events. It becomes a part of the task of viewing the work as the creation of a given poet in a particular culture, which is being experienced by concrete individuals at the same time and other times and places. Such a holistic view necessarily leads to interdisciplinary studies.

Regarding the expression I have used here, "the psychoanalytic interpretation of literature," it must be avowed that the term is imprecise because interpretations made in the analytic situation cannot be equated with those made in applied psychoanalysis. Loewenstein (1951) succinctly defined interpretation: "In psychoanalysis this term is applied to those explanations, given to patients by their analyst, which add to their knowledge about themselves" (p. 4); these explanations are given piecemeal and ultimately encompass ego and id elements. This definition applies specifically to the clinical psychoanalytic situation. A number of authors have discussed the differences between interpretation in analysis compared with other settings. Kohut (1960) observed that in applied psychoanalysis there is no free association, no therapeutic alliance, no emotional tie to the therapist, no reverbatory dreams that might follow an interpretation, and no motivation (and, one might add, there is no patient). Ricoeur (1970) noted that "the psychoanalytic interpretation of art is fragmentary because it is analogical" (p. 164). What is lacking is the *process* of interchange, on many levels, between patient and analyst, involving fluctuating levels and varieties of resistance, the vicissitudes of transference and the integration of insight—in a word, the flux of a human relationship in the analytic setting.

CONCLUSIONS

The problems inherent in the psychoanalytic interpretation of literature, not to speak of other areas of applied psychoanalysis, have led at times to skepticism that scholarly work can be accomplished in a field so fraught with pitfalls. Such a position is counterproductive because it is only through many efforts and repeated critiques that more rigorous approaches will be developed.

Great works of art, such as the *Antigone*, offer different levels of meaning. They are ambiguous in that the elements within them are highly overdetermined—a concept explored by Kris and Kaplan (Kris, 1952). It is natural that exclusive attention to selected aspects, or levels of meaning, of a literary work, can be carried out for research purposes, but these must ultimately be integrated into the work as a whole lest serious distortions occur. Similarly, while it may be useful to isolate a character from a work, to explore him "independently," that character must be reinserted into the network of his dynamic relations with the other characters and with the writer's overarching aesthetic conception. Perhaps the greatest weakness in the psychoanalytic studies of literature is that they rarely acknowledge that several interpretations may all plausibly reveal something about a work of art.

It must be stressed that psychoanalytic interpretations of literature, just as interpretations in the analytic situation, must not only be logical and internally consistent, but must be supported by the text. The more of the work that can be reasonably explained and the fewer the exceptions and contradictions, the sturdier will be the interpretation. The text itself is the final arbiter: other data—such as information about the author and his motives—can at best be used to support and confirm interpretations based on the text, its style, form, and content.

To seek to understand some literature through a purely "psychological" approach appears as untenable as the reverse of that coin—a purely "sociological" approach. It has become increasingly apparent, especially for certain literary works, that it is not possible to understand them unless the web of relations of the work to society are carefully explored. Similarly, certain works will remain an enigma unless brought into relation with the author's life if useful data about it are available. In still other works, biographical data and information about the social setting may be relatively unimportant for our understanding, and the text itself remains the crucial datum.

Despite the hazards that confront psychoanalysis when it attempts to understand literature, despite the shortcomings and the reductionism, there is little doubt that psychoanalysis has made valuable and unique contributions. Psychoanalysis, of all disciplines, remains the only one able to explore the unconscious and all its derivatives. The cultural products of man are therefore a most fitting subject for psychoanalytic investigation, and if the difficulties are vast, the process itself is its own reward.

SUMMARY

Through a critical review of several studies dealing with Sophocles' drama, the *Antigone,* I have explored some of the prominent methodological problems encountered in the psychoanalytic interpretation of literature. Foremost among these is the inherent difficulty that the interpretation of literature is unable to benefit from the process of the analytic situation. Divorced from the realities of the therapeutic process, the drama itself is often used to corroborate an author's theoretical bias or to advance some special interest, with consequent distortion or blurring of the text. Although data about the artist's life and sociocultural environment may be of crucial significance, it is the text itself that must be the ultimate object of study. Through a re-examination of the *Antigone* as an aesthetic totality I have sketched out what appears to be an alternative manner of approaching the drama, and suggested that works of art reach us on both unconscious and conscious levels. I have stressed the need to analyze our emotional response to a work as affording a valuable source of insight into the work itself.

Throughout, I have drawn attention to the need for greater scholarly rigor and the value of interdisciplinary collaboration. An open recognition of the problems in the psychoanalytic study of literature should serve to minimize dilettantism and raise the level of scholarship.

NOTES

1. All quotations are taken from Braun (1973) unless otherwise indicated. I should like to thank Professor Braun, as well as the Oxford University Press, for their kind permission to quote from his translation. Numbers correspond to lines in this edition.
2. Sophocles also dealt with this issue in the *Ajax*.
3. This line is usually translated as: "I was born not to hate but to love." See translations of Braun (1973), Fitts and Fitzgerald (1939), and Wyckoff (1973)
4. Braun notes: "Sophocles took their [names'] meaning seriously, for he created an Antigone who, 'born to oppose,' relies on innate courage in facing tyranny . . ." (1973, p. 7).
5. The three plays were actually written over a forty-year span, with the *Antigone* written first, the *Oedipus Tyrannus* at least thirteen years later, and the *Oedipus at Colonus* over twenty-two after that, when Sophocles was close to ninety years old.

REFERENCES

Bachofen, J. J. (1859–1870), *Myth, Religion and Mother Right*. Trans. R. Manheim. Princeton: Princeton University Press, 1967.

Bibring, E. (1953), The mechanism of depression. In: *Affective Disorders*, ed. P. Greenacre, New York: International Universities Press, pp. 13–48.

Bowra, C. M. (1944), *Sophoclean Tragedy*. New York: Oxford University Press.

Bonnard, A. (1951), *La Tragédie et l'Homme*. Paris: A la Baconnière.

Braun, R. E., trans. (1973), Sophocles, *Antigone*. New York: Oxford University Press.

Coltrera, J. T. (1965), On the creation of beauty and thought: The unique as vicissitude. *JAPA*, 13: 634–703.

Eckermann, J. P. (1836), *Conversations with Goethe*. Trans. J. Oxenford. London: Dent, 1930.

Eissler, K. R. (1959), The function of details in the interpretation of works of literature. *Psychoanal. Quart.*, 28: 1–20.

——— (1968), The relation of explaining and understanding in psychoanalysis: Demonstrated by one aspect of Freud's approach to literature. *The Psychoanalytic Study of the Child*, 23: 141–177. New York: International Universities Press.

Fitts, D. & Fitzgerald, R., trans. (1939), Sophocles, *The Oedipus Cycle*. New York: Harcourt, Brace & World.

Freud, S. (1905), Psychopathic characters on the stage. *Standard Edition*, 7: 305–310.

——— (1921), Group psychology and the analysis of the ego. *Standard Edition*, 18:67–143.

Fromm, E. (1949), The Oedipus complex and the Oedipus myth. In: *The Family: Its Function and Destiny*, ed. R. N. Anshen. New York: Harper, pp. 334–358.

Gedo, J. E. (1970), Thoughts on art in the age of Freud. *JAPA*, 18: 19–245.

Goheen, R. E. (1951), *The Imagery of Sophocles' Antigone*. Princeton: Princeton University Press.

Greenacre, P. (1955), *Swift and Carroll: A Psychoanalytic Study of Two Lives*. New York: International Universities Press.

Holland, N. (1968), *The Dynamics of Literary Response*. New York: Oxford University Press.

Jebb, R. (1898), *Sophocles: The Plays and Fragments*. Part III, *The Antigone*. Cambridge: Cambridge University Press, 1972.

Kanzer, M. (1948), The passing of the oedipus complex in Greek drama. *Internat. J. Psycho-Anal.*, 29:131–134.

——— (1950), The Oedipus trilogy. *Psychoanal. Quart.*, 19: 561–573.

Kirkwood, G. M. (1958), *A Study of Sophoclean Drama*. Ithaca: Cornell University Press.

Kitto, H. D. F. (1956), *Form and Meaning in Drama: A Study of Six Greek Plays and of Hamlet*. London: Methuen.

Kohut, H. (1960), Beyond the bounds of the basic rule. *JAPA*, 8:567–586.

Kris, E. (1952), *Psychoanalytic Explorations in Art*. New York: International Universities Press.

Lesser, S. O. (1957), *Fiction and the Unconscious*. Boston: Beacon Hill Press.

Letters, F. J. H. (1953), *The Life and Work of Sophocles*. London: Sheed & Ward.

Loewenstein, R. M. (1951), The problem of interpretation. *Psychoanal. Quart.*, 20: 1–14.

Ricoeur, P. (1970), *Freud and Philosophy*. New Haven: Yale University Press.

Rose, G. J. (1964), Creative imagination in terms of ego "care" and boundaries. *Internat. J. Psycho-Anal.*, 45: 75–85.

Seidenberg, R. & Papathomopoulos, E. (1962), Daughters who tend their fathers. A literary survey. *The Psychoanalytic Study of Society*, 2: 135–160. New York: International Universities Press.

——— (1974), The enigma of Antigone. *Internat. Rev. Psycho-Anal.*, 1:197–205.

Van der Sterren, H. A. (1952), The "King Oedipus" of Sophocles. *Internat. J. Psycho-Anal.*, 33: 343–350.

Waelder, R. (1965), *Psychoanalytic Avenues to Art*. New York: International Universities Press.

Weissman, P. (1964), Antigone—a preoedipal old maid. *J. Hillside Hosp.*, 13: 32–42.

Whitman, C. H. (1951), *Sophocles: A Study of Heroic Humans*. Cambridge: Harvard University Press.

Within, P. (1969), The psychodynamics of literature. *Psychoanal. Rev.*, 56: 556–585.

Wolman, B. (1965), The Antigone principle. *Amer. Imago*, 22: 186–201.

Wyckoff, E., trans. (1973), Sophocles, *Antigone*, ed. D. Greene & R. Lattimore. New York: Washington Square Press.

11. A Critique of Pathography: Freud's Original Psychoanalytic Approach to Art

Ellen Handler Spitz

Freud's psychoanalytic investigations growing initially out of his dissatisfaction with the use of hypnosis as a method for treating neurotic patients in the last decade of the 19th century[1] have given rise to widespread cultural changes in our actual institutions and overt behavior as well as in our mental life itself, i.e., in the ways in which we think about many aspects of human functioning. Insights into the structure and workings of the psyche gleaned from psychoanalysis have in our time been applied to nearly every aspect of human experience and, with respect to art, the influences have been pervasive, not only on art itself but on artists, audiences, and critics.

To attempt the task of tracing the myriad paths by which Freud's ideas have found their way into the aesthetic realm in and since his own time would thus be rather like trying to trace the fluff of a dandelion after a child has blown it from its stem. Within the field of literary criticism, for example, Freud's ideas on parapraxes and jokes, dream symbolism, myth of the primal horde, Oedipus complex, and concept of overdetermination have all been used by critics at various times as ways of approaching poems and novels. In this paper I am concerned with one model of the Freudian approach to art. This is the model that Freud himself developed in his book *Leonardo da Vinci and a Memory of his Childhood* (1910) and to which he gave the name "pathography." Clearly, Freud did not limit his applications of psychoanalysis outside the clinical setting to just this model. He also, for example, applied his ideas directly to the texts of certain of Shakespeare's major plays (including *Hamlet, King Lear,* and *Macbeth*) as well as to myths, nursery rhymes, fairy tales, etc. These intratextual applications of psychoanalytic theory will not be considered here. I will be concerned solely with the

Reprinted by permission of the author and the Analytic Press, Inc. from *Psychoanalytic Perspectives on Art,* vol. 1, edited by M. M. Gedo, 1985.

pathographic paradigm, *which treats each work of art as an outgrowth of the internal and external biography of its creator.*

It is important to realize at the outset that Freud's tastes in art were limited and conservative, albeit enthusiastic. He did not enjoy music, for example (Freud, 1914a), and took no interest in the stirring avant-garde movements of his time in visual arts, music, theater, or dance. He ignored such contemporary geniuses as Kandinsky, Picasso, Schoenberg, Joyce, Isadora Duncan, and likewise avoided 20th-century European philosophy. Thus, supremely gifted, original, and daring as he was in developing within his own bailiwick, his cultural preferences were derived from the world of the 19th century.

My first task here will be to show a continuity between Freud's model of pathography and the 19th-century critical tradition to which he was heir. Needless to say, the parallel point, namely, that Freud was importantly successor to a specific 19th-century medical and scientific tradition, has been much stressed elsewhere. After demonstrating important links between pathography and Romantic criticism, I turn to a discussion of pathography in terms of the ongoing debate in aesthetics on problems of intention and expression. Finally, I shall suggest that psychoanalysts have much to gain by considering their projects from both the relevant historical and philosophical perspectives and that to do so is to enrich pathography as a mode of psychoanalytic criticism as well as to bring it more focally into the mainstream of critical inquiry.

FREUD AND THE ROMANTIC CRITICAL TRADITION

The views on art that formed the background for Freud's work have been characterized as the Romantic or expressive critical tradition. Although Abrams (1953) opines that to fix a *terminus a quo* for this tradition would be tantamount to determining the precise point at which yellow turns to orange on the rainbow, nevertheless, he offers the year 1800, which is among other things the year of publication of Wordsworth's *Preface to the Lyrical Ballads,* generally considered the prototypic document of Romantic criticism.[2] In this work Wordsworth defines poetry as "the spontaneous overflow of powerful feelings,"—feelings, that is, *of the poet*—thereby shifting dramatically the focus of critical attention from audience or work of art to the psyche of the artist who created it.

My claim is that Freud's approach, pathography, may be seen as emerging from this larger context. Seen in this manner, rather than as an isolated phenomenon, we can perhaps better understand some of the possibilities and limitations attendant upon it. In describing this Romantic context, Abrams (1953) points out that, when art is viewed as "the expression or uttering forth of feeling" (as John Stuart Mill put it in his essay on poetry of 1833), certain questions and notions follow from this. A critic will want to ask, for example, how and to what extent a particular work yields insights into the psyche of its creator: whether it be genuine, spontaneous, sincere.[3] Furthermore, if the external world is depicted in art or described in poetry, it must under this approach be seen primarily as a *projection* of the artist's state of mind, an idea that eventually finds its most felicitous formulation in T. S. Eliot's notion of the "objective correlative" (1932). Aspects of works of art as externalizations of psychic states paved the way for the advent of late 19th-century Symbolism and a host of other styles including Post-Impressionism, Expressionism, Fauvism, Surrealism, and Abstract Expressionism,[4] the relevant question for the critic in each case being: what is the underlying feeling, psychic state, conflict, or desire that is finding expression here, possibly disguised? A model such as this necessarily implies an interpretative mode that involves a "looking through." Abrams's metaphor for this is that the mirror that the artist had formerly held up to nature, in the Romantic model becomes transparent (1953), thus enabling an audience to look through this tinted glass to the mind and heart of the artist himself.

This Romantic viewpoint, with its attention centered on the way in which an artist's inner life of feeling finds expression in his works, informed the climate into which Freud's first writings were released, and it may have played a role in shaping both the reception of his ideas and their development. Kris (1952) reports, for example, the intriguing phenomenon that, when Freud first published his *Studies on Hysteria* in 1895, reviews from the scientific and medical communities were mixed; *one* reviewer only, not a clinician but a literary critic and poet—Alfred von Berger, director of the Imperial Theater in Vienna—recognized the significance of the new work and saw it as a "herald" of a new psychology. Kris believes it no accident that the greatness of Freud's discoveries should thus have been first recognized by a literary rather than a scientific scholar since "Freud's predecessors in the study of man were not the neurologists, psychiatrists and psychologists, from whom he borrowed some of his terms, but rather the great intuitive teachers of mankind [i.e., the artists]" (1952, p. 265). Yet, and this is a point I want to emphasize here, Kris further states that "their influence [i.e., the influence of Freud's discoveries] on the literary mind would be inexplicable had not the previous development of literature turned in a direction which created favorable predispositions for this influence'' (p. 270).

Thus, the Romantic tradition that Freud inherited not only provided fertile soil for the reception of his ideas but also nourished, it seems, the growth of these very ideas, particularly as Freud began to apply them directly to the arts.

This Romantic or expressive mode which found its way in various guises into European fine arts, literature, music, and criticism of the 19th century, gave rise by its focus on the artist to myths and cults of the artist,[5] to views of the artist as different from others, as hypersensitive, fragile, ''possessed,'' etc., thus reviving in modern times Plato's notion of the artist's madness. Indeed it is not uncommon today for psychoanalysts (and others) to regard artists as persons with particularly intense or persistent conflicts, as the very term ''pathography'' connotes.

Actually, after coining this term in his study of Leonardo da Vinci and promising to ''stake out in a quite general way the limits which are set to what psycho-analysis can achieve in the field of biography'' (1910), Freud in fact defines pathography only by making exclusions. He says, for example, that ''we should be glad to give an account of the way in which artistic activity derives from the primal instincts of the mind if it were not just here that our capacities fail us'' (p. 132), and that ''pathography does not in the least aim at making the great man's achievements intelligible.'' He tells us what pathography cannot (yet) do and what psychoanalysis cannot (yet) explain. Hence, in the absence of a clear, positive account of either his aims or the supposed value of his work, we must fall back on the obvious connotations of the word. A less inclusive term than biography, pathography seems to imply writing about suffering, illness, or feeling, with important overtones of empathic response on the part of the author for his subject. It suggests *selected* aspects of a life, precisely in fact those aspects pertaining to (mental) disease, to intrapsychic conflict, its symptoms, and their etiology. My point here is that the conception of the artist implicit in Freud's term grows solidly out of the Romantic tradition in which artistic creativity is variously associated with moments of intense emotion, altered states of consciousness, and pain.

Such a view of the artist as uniquely endowed emotionally, as chosen or cursed, can be seen as leading to speculations about what possible therapeutic value the making of art might have for its creator. Psychoanalysts in recent years have debated this issue, and the very term "art therapy" betokens a positive side to the controversy. Most pathographers tend, however, to see the solution of artistic problems as contributing little of lasting value to the resolution of intrapsychic conflict; in fact, this viewpoint is fundamental to their interpretative method, which depends on the repetition, the reappearance of certain persistent motifs throughout the artist's lifespan. For example, Liebert says:

> We expect that the underlying forces [of conflict] will be expressed repeatedly as a reflection of continuous internal pressure within the artist. This expectation grows out of the view that the manifest solution of the latent and unconscious conflict in the artist, the work of art, does *not* have the effect of "working through"—that is, of permanently altering the central mental representation of himself and others and bringing about basic changes in other aspects of his internal psychological organization and outlook. Thus, as each artistic endeavor inevitably fails in this respect, the underlying conflict will reappear. Each new artistic solution to it will be somewhat different from the previous one, but still motivated toward a similar end (1982)

A further discussion of the issues involved in this controversy would be out of place at this point. Suffice it to say that the entire matter presupposes a view of art and artists that derives from the Romantic critical tradition.

Abrams offers one passage in which he attempts to characterize the overall approach common to this tradition. One is struck by its similarity to Freud's views which, I propose, take Romanticism as their point of departure, going on then to develop and refine it by offering hypotheses concerning the nature and origin of "perceptions, thoughts, and feelings."[6] Abrams's summary follows:

> A work of art is essentially the internal made external, resulting from a creative process operating under the impulse of feeling, and embodying the combined product of the poet's *perceptions, thoughts and feelings*. The primary source and subject matter of a poem, therefore, are the attributes and actions of the poet's own mind; or if aspects of the external world, then these only as they are converted from fact to poetry by the feelings and operations of the poet's mind. (1953, p. 22, my italics)

Freud's pathographic approach—minimally (or only secondarily) concerned with the ways in which art either mirrors the outside world per se or affects its audience or possesses its own internal formal structure, but maximally concerned with the narrative of an artist's inner life as it can be inferred from a careful study of his works (and other biographical material)—thus represents a final flowering in the 20th century of Romantic criticism. Before asking how pathography has furthered, advanced, or contributed to this particular mode of criticism, I would like to spend another moment on Freud's predecessors and then turn to a discussion of the way in which pathography poses problems that coincide with problems aestheticians have considered under the categories of intention and expression in art.

Although Romantic critics generally viewed the work of art as an expression of the artist's feeling, it is interesting to note that, even before Freud's seminal work of the 1890s, there were literary critics who understood that works of art may function not merely to express feelings but also to disguise and conceal them. One such critic was John Keble, a leader in the Oxford movement and holder of the Oxford Chair of Poetry; in the 1840s Keble had formulated a theory of poetry which—dedicated appropriately to Wordsworth, who can also be seen as proto-Freudian in his developmental thinking—embodies the notion that art is an *indirect* expression of "some overpowering emotion, or ruling taste, or feeling, the direct indulgence whereof is somehow *repressed*" (Abrams, 1953, p. 145). Keble speaks of art as giving "healing relief to secret mental emotion" (p. 145), of art as "paint[ing] all things in the hues which the mind itself desires" (p. 147), and as "a safety-valve, preserving man from actual madness" (p. 146). Thus, for Keble, art involves not simply the direct, spontaneous expression of feeling but rather internal *conflict* between the artist's need to give utterance to his emotions and his "instinctive delicacy which recoils from exposing them openly" (p. 147).

Although my research has not unearthed any *perfectly* parallel passage in Freud's oeuvre to juxtapose with the [aforementioned] quotations, it must be clear to any reader of Freud how close Keble's (and other Romantics')[7] views are to those of classical psychoanalysis. I offer the following excerpts from Freud which at least presuppose Keble's views and are perspicuously consonant with the Romantic theory of art:

> Creative writers are valuable allies and their evidence is to be prized highly, for they are apt to know a whole host of things between heaven and earth of which our philosophy has not yet let us dream. [Freud's point is underscored by his literary paraphrase from Act I, scene 4 of *Hamlet.*] In their knowledge of the mind they are far in advance of us everyday people, for they draw upon sources which we have not yet opened up for science. (1907, p. 8, my insert)

Here Freud indicates his agreement with the Romantics that artists are uniquely endowed with an ability to tap into the powerful emotions and hidden secrets of the human heart.

> In my opinion, what grips us so powerfully can only be the artist's *intention,* in so far as he has succeeded in *expressing* it in his work and in getting us to understand it. . . . what he aims at is to awaken in us the same emotional attitude, the same mental constellation as that which in him produced the impetus to create . . . [Freud goes on to say that a work of art should admit of the application of psychoanalysis] if it really is *an effective expression of the intentions and emotional activities of the artist* (1914a, p. 212, my italics).

Here Freud agrees with the Romantic position that the work of art is the result of an artist's need or intent to express some aspect of his emotional life or a certain intrapsychic "constellation."

In the [previous] passages, Freud indicates that what the artist finally creates is a compromise resulting from his inner conflict between wanting to express certain feelings directly and not being permitted to do so. His mode of compromise is to express his fantasies in altered form in his works of art, a mode which, although Freud does not indicate it here, he considered less than entirely satisfying. The parallel with Keble's views is apparent; although Keble seemed to feel by contrast that poetry possesses for the poet a healing power akin to prayer.

In the second passage quoted [earlier], Freud uses the words "intention" and "expression." If we acknowledge that pathography emanates from the matrix of Romantic criticism, as I have tried to demonstrate, then we may expect it will admit of the same sort of philosophical critique as does that approach to art. Before considering this critique as it is found in some aesthetician's arguments against intention and expression, I would like to pause to (1) distinguish pathography from Romantic criticism on the one hand and (2) argue that pathography *can* function as a critical mode on the other. For it is clear that unless we can establish pathography as at least potentially a critical mode, the arguments of the aestheticians will be irrelevant to it.

First I must acknowledge having blurred certain distinctions between pathography and romantic criticism in the foregoing pages in order to establish parallels between the two. However, whereas the romantic critic employs biographical and other information in order to interpret the work of art, his prime object of inquiry, in pathography the movement is reversed: according to Freud, the works of art or aspects thereof are taken as starting points "for discovering what determined [the artist's] mental and intellectual development" (1910, pp. 130–131). Thus, in pathography, the psyche is the prime object of inquiry. As such it might be possible to rule out pathography as a critical mode entirely, to see it as a purely psychological study, as the search for a man. In mocking a quest of this sort and dismissing it as not only extraneous to critical inquiry but also as quite absurd, the aestheticians Wimsatt and Beardsley (1954) offer a mischievous quote from Thomas Hardy: " 'He's the man we were in search of, that's true,' says Hardy's rustic constable, 'and yet he's not the man we were in search of. For the man we were in search of was not the man we wanted' " (p. 295).

I want, however, to argue that pathography *may* be seen as a viable critical mode. My reasons seem to fall spontaneously into metaphoric language. While in pursuit of pearls, because he is looking so intently about him, a diver may discover many beautiful coral reefs and underwater flora. Arnold Isenberg (1944), arguing for a somewhat different point, uses a similar figure (which may have been my inspiration): "It is as if we found both an oyster and a pearl when we had been looking for a seashell because we had been told it was valuable. It *is* valuable, but not because it is a seashell" (p. 163).

The idea is that, in order to *do* pathography, one must *look* carefully and read slowly. One must dwell on detail. One must attend with utmost sensitivity. Since something of the artist has found its way into each work of art (and this is granted even by Wimsatt & Beardsley, 1954), then to seek the former, we must deal with the latter. Hence, if my analogy holds, pathography in its effort to penetrate to certain sorts of psychic meaning in works of art is bound to attend to these works aesthetically and—if well done—even to contribute to our awareness and understanding of them. I am suggesting that, in other words, although the directions of emphasis are different, the lines do run parallel and, since works of art are perceived as wholes, since what the artist meant by the poem *is* in some sense the poem, the pathographer-psychoanalyst may be considered as partaking in critical inquiry, as contributing (even if he conceives this as only a minor or secondary function) to the critical enterprise.[8]

It is also worth noting that, contrary to Freud's formulation in the *Leonardo* (as quoted [earlier]), in actual practice, pathography works both ways; works of art are used to penetrate the psyche of the artist, but hypotheses about the artist's inner life are also used to interpret his works. In the latter case, certainly, the analyst can be seen as speaking with a critical voice. One important way of judging the value of such remarks is to return to the works of art in question and reexperience them in the light of the proferred psychoanalytic interpretation. Such a reexperiencing or "second moment" is fundamental to the concept of criticism held by at least some philosophers (cf. Isenberg, 1944), and its centrality to the pathographic approach is manifest by the usual inclusion in pathographic texts of reproduction of the works of art under consideration. Note the inclusion of at least several plates in Freud's *Leonardo*. More tellingly, however, with respect to literature, Freud specifically instructs his readers "to put aside this little essay and instead to spend some time in acquainting themselves with *Gradiva* . . . so that what I refer to in the following pages may be familiar to them" (1907, p. 10). We might compare this passage with the following from Isenberg: "Reading criticism otherwise than in the presence, or with direct recollection, of the objects discussed, is a blank and senseless employment" (1944, p. 164).

A counter-argument to my claim that pathography be considered at least potentially capable of functioning as a critical mode could be made by citing differences between psychoanalysts and critics with respect to their techniques of listening, looking, or reading. Such differences certainly do exist, and the issue bears further study. I want to maintain, however, that such variations are no different in kind from those one might encounter among individual critics or representatives of particular schools. For example, it might be argued that a psychoanalyst approaches a text with an eye or ear for only certain sorts of psychosexual allusions, for certain sorts of gaps or inconsistencies. Yet, similarly, the formalist critic may approach a painting oblivious of its iconography, his eye attuned merely to nuances of line, shape, and color, to perhaps a "steeply rising and falling curve" (Isenberg, 1944, p. 162). A drama critic may be principally concerned with language rather than with psychological subtlety or dramatic fulfillment. One music reviewer may listen for the guest conductor's particular interpretation of tempo and dynamics and attend to his rapport with the orchestra; whereas another critic attending the same concert may have score in hand, intently listening for the balance of sound, his focus on the internal arrangement of voices within the music. In each case, and I include the psychoanalytic, what is seen, read, or heard will be somewhat different but may, under particular circumstances and for a particular audience, become critically relevant.

The circumstances under which remarks become critically relevant can be highly variable. For example, even an art dealer's pronouncement about the relative worth of two seemingly fine impressions from the same lithographic plate *could* become critically relevant to the prospective buyer if such a pronouncement spurred him to look more carefully and "critically" at the two prints in question. On the other hand, comments on the monetary value of works of art are generally taken to be critically irrelevant and usually are. As we mentioned earlier, such factors as conscious and unconscious need and motive, knowledge, familiarity, and curiosity all play a role. The best definition I have encountered for what actually happens when a remark does become critically relevant is to be found in Isenberg, where he says that the essential condition of the aesthetic experience is that attention should rest on a certain content (1944). Any remark that contributes to this, which serves "to expand the field on which attention rests," would seem to me critically relevant.

Thus, I can find no better reason for excluding any one of these approaches (i.e., the formal, historical, psychoanalytic, etc.) than any other. It even seems plausible that under most circumstances, except in the case of normative criticism, these modes would come into conflict only when exponents of one or another claim to have exclusive or prior hegemony over a work or works of art, to possess, in other words, "The *true* interpretation."[9]

INTENTION, EXPRESSION, AND PATHOGRAPHY

Granted then what we can, at least under some circumstances, consider pathography a critical mode with respect to art, we must now raise the issues that have been advanced by modern aestheticians with respect to romantic theories of art. Broadly speaking, the critique falls into two parts: (1) It accuses romantic criticism of incorporating the so-called "intentional fallacy," that is, of assuming unjustifiably that knowledge of the artist's intentions is (a) available and (b) desirable as a standard for how a work of art should be interpreted, read, responded to; and (2) it claims that Romantic theory takes a wrong-headed view of the expressive qualities of art. In what follows, I shall draw upon the work of Wimsatt and Beardsley as representatives of the first of these critiques (with Cioffi as their principal opponent), and Bouwsma, Tormey, and Kivy as exponents of the second critique.

The psychoanalyst writing on art using Freud's *Leonardo* as a model may be unaware of the ways in which such aestheticians have called into question the validity of his enterprise. If, in addition to advancing or illustrating some aspect of psychoanalytic theory for an audience of peers, he seeks to make an interdisciplinary contribution to our understanding of the works discussed and be taken seriously outside his own domain, the analyst is bound to entertain the arguments of such philosophers as the [aforementioned]—not so much with the end of refuting them as of understanding and attempting to incorporate the valid insights they possess.

My aim in this section, therefore, will be to summarize some of the arguments and counter-arguments that bear on issues already in part discussed. My own view is that the anti-intentionalist arguments have sufficient weight to be taken seriously; they offer (at least) good reasons why intentionalist critics (pathographers) cannot pretend to have both necessary and sufficient claims on the way in which works of art ought be read. By insisting on the autonomy of the art object, they provide an important caveat for the pathographer and point out at least one direction in which he might look for what he senses might be missing in his approach. On the other hand, the arguments in favor of intention and expression are strong enough to establish these modes as viable, critically relevant ways of approaching works of art.

The first charge that is made against the intentionalist critic is that an artist's intention, defined as other than or more than, in some sense, the resultant work of art, is ultimately unknowable and hence a rather poor criterion on which to hang an interpretation. This charge bears on the problem of freedom and determinism in human behavior, an issue on which Freud, as we have seen, wavered, though usually holding to the view that even if intention could not be entirely explained by current theory, it is determinate and hence susceptible of full explanation at some future time.[10] In the *Leonardo,* which came under heavy attack when first published and which has provoked periodic attacks ever since, he demurs, however, on this point:

> But even if the historical material at our disposal were very abundant, and if the psychical mechanisms could be dealt with with the greatest assurance, there are important points at which a psycho-analytic enquiry would not be able to make us understand how inevitable it was that the person concerned should have turned out in the way he did and in no other way. . . . We must recognize here a degree of freedom which cannot be resolved any further by psycho-analytic means. Equally, one has no right to claim that the consequence of [a particular] wave of repression was the only possible one. (1910, p. 135)

Yet, further on in the same work he stresses an opposite claim, namely, that a person's fate is ultimately determined by "the accidental circumstances of his parental constellation." In any case, his ambivalence aside, Freud would certainly have argued, against Wimsatt and Beardsley, that we can know *something* about the artist's intentions from sources external to the work of art and that this "something" will be not only relevant but central to our understanding of the work in question.

Wimsatt and Beardsley, however, want to define intention in terms of the work the artist has created. They justify this by pointing out that a work of art is usually defined by what it excludes as well as by what it contains (1954). Therefore, intention must be equated with result and, if so, we are free to deal exclusively with the latter on its own terms. If, however, pursuing some alternative chimera of intention, we are driven outside the work into a morass of conflicting, incomplete, and altogether troublesome data, none of this will have critical bearing on the work of art which, by definition, we have already claimed as the embodiment of intention.

Thus, Wimsatt and Beardsley seek to argue, whereas a designing intellect caused the work of art to come into being, we cannot turn back and make that designing intellect (or whatever we can fathom of it) into the standard by which we interpret the work. The poem must "work" like a pudding they claim: all lumps have to be stirred out before the dish is served and, to elaborate on their image, I would add that to offer the lumps or the recipe or some information about the past personal circumstances and present humor of the chef would not improve the flavor of the pudding. They draw a sharp line between what they call "personal and poetic studies," between "internal and external evidence." Internal evidence is public and discoverable through *reading* the poem;[11] therefore, it is admissible; whereas, external evidence is private and not a part of the work itself (it may be found in journals, letters, etc.) To follow it is to be led away from the work of art and thus to make extra-critical judgments that devalue the existing body of the work as a sufficiently rich source of immanent consistent suggestive meanings. To do pathography as criticism, would be for these authors to violate the given boundaries of the work of art, to fail to respect it as a realized whole.

Wimsatt and Beardsley clearly base their anti-intentionalist protest on the grounds that to do pathography is to reduce the work of art to a window, or to tamper with its frame, or to treat it as if it were an ordinary message, thus to deprive it of its special ontological status in the culture. I believe it important for psychoanalysts to confront this particular issue and to recognize that for most aestheticians and art critics, even amateurs of art, and above all for artists, the work represents an end and not a means. It is importantly bracketed or framed. Consequently, there is a necessity in doing pathography for returning frequently to the work of art. For example, one must return to

Leonardo's *Madonna, Child, and St. Anne* to reexperience the painting in the light of Freud's hypothesis about the artist's two mothers. One must test the interpretation by seeing whether the painting *looks* different, whether new aspects of it come into focus, whether in Wimsatt and Beardsley's jargon it *works* differently. In this sense the anti-intentionalist argument must be taken seriously by the pathographer: his interpretations must bear the test of a second moment of aesthetic experience or else he cannot claim, whatever else he may be doing, to be making critical statements about works of art.

An intriguing point to consider here is whether what "works" aesthetically is sometimes, always, or never what "works" psychodynamically. My hunch is that the aesthetic solution must work psychologically, but that a given work may admit of more psychological possibilities than aesthetic ones. I am not prepared to argue this point here, and whether or not I am correct, it is clear that the anti-intentionalists make sense when they challenge us to show the *coincidence* of aesthetic and psychological needs. We need to question, for example, the relationship between the psychological and aesthetic demands which a piece in progress places on the artist as he works. When a pathographer attempts to discuss intention, he must not neglect this aspect of intention, that is to say, the needs, dictates, strictures, and seductions of the work of art itself—its form, its own internal structure. The pathographer must, in short, remember that the artist is after all an artist, and that in the process of creation, the created work enters into its own dialogue with its creator. Moreover, as Gay (1976) points out, in some cases the imperatives of "craft" take precedence over other (psychic) considerations.

Returning to Wimsatt and Beardsley, their distinction between internal and external may be difficult to uphold. They reluctantly admit to cases where it is hard to draw lines between the public history of a word or phrase and the usage or associations of that word for a particular author. Rebutting them, Cioffi (1964) points out that when we know something (biographical) about a poem, we often tend to read it into the poem; the intended meaning thus seems to inhere in the poem (work of art). Likewise, when we learn that something was *not* intended, we are apt to reject an interpretation that ignores this even though such an interpretation may previously have seemed legitimate.[12] In other words, what we know about a given work of art tends to become "unobtrusive" for us as regards that work (Stern, 1980). In Cioffi's words, "A reader's response to a work will vary with what he knows; one of the things which he knows and with which his responses will vary is what the author had in mind, or what he intended" (1964, p. 315). Cioffi goes on to make the point I stressed [earlier]: namely, that you cannot know whether remarks are merely biographical or whether they are critical

> until after you have read the work in the light of them. . . . If a critical remark fails to confirm or consolidate or transform a reader's interpretation of a work it will then become for him just evidence of something or other, perhaps the critic's obtuseness. Biographical remarks are no more prone to this fate than any others. (p. 316)

Hence, Cioffi attempts to collapse Wimsatt and Beardsley's distinction between internal and external evidence by translating it into the problematic distinction "between what we can and cannot be expected to know" about a given work of art. He claims that, since art is (importantly) a human product, "there is an implicit biographical reference in our response to [in his example] literature," and that this "is, if you like, part of our concept of literature [art]" (p. 318).

Furthermore, for Cioffi, as for me, interpretation arises in a heterogeneity of contexts.[13] He speaks of throwing a "field of force" around the work of art such that, once certain biographical data are known, it becomes increasingly perplexing to discern the boundaries of the work. An ontological problem now appears: how can we "appeal to the text" when its edges have become blurry? Cioffi's argument runs into difficulties, however, when it comes up against certain sorts of familiar counter-examples in which what we know about the author seems to have minimal or zero effect on our perceptions of the work of art.

Are we justified in assuming "a necessary link between the qualities of the art work and certain states of the artist" is the way the question is put by Tormey (1971, p. 350). He then answers with a resounding "no" but proceeds to draw his examples exclusively from the art of music, a tack also taken by Bouwsma (1954) in his paper on the theory of art as expression. Because music is perhaps the most difficult art to discuss biographically,[14] it well serves the anti-expressionist's cause. In any case, Tormey claims that his arguments hold for the other art forms as well, and I would expect Bouwsma to claim the same. Tormey asserts:

> The expressive qualities of a work of art are logically independent of the psychological states of the artist, and humor (or sadness) in a madrigal is neither necessary nor sufficient for amusement (or despair) in a Monteverdi. . . . The presence of an expressive quality in a work of art is never sufficient to guarantee the presence of an analogous feeling state in the artist. (1971, p. 358)

Tormey bases his argument in part on a distinction he draws between the transitive and intransitive uses of the term "expressive." He points out that performances are noted as ''expressive,'' that ''expressive'' is a commonly met marking on musical scores, that a human face can be called ''expressive,'' in each case without the implication of an intentional object, without in other words an expectation of the further question ''of what?'' His claim is that for a work of art to be expressive, it need not imply a prior act of expression, and that to conflate these two usages is the fundamental error of the Romantic theory of art. For Tormey, ''acts of expression'' are common to all forms of human behavior so that to discuss art in such terms is to say something trivial at best since it is to say nothing that can distinguish a work of art from any other product of human activity. To say, however, that a work of art or a performance is expressive in the former sense is quite different. Expressive in this sense implies that the work in question possesses certain aesthetic qualities our perception of which depends on our ability to discriminate among a ''highly complex set of predicates and . . . their logical relations to one another.''

Tormey offers an example in which knowledge of the personal tragedy of a composer's life ''has little to do with the aesthetically relevant expressive qualities of the music itself.'' If we, for example, should discover that a certain composer was, at the time of writing a certain piece, both anxious and even humiliated though his music when played sounds spritely, carefree, and tuneful (as was so often the case with Mozart), we might infer perhaps that the composer in question was, in relating such a piece, attempting to distance himself from his pain. From a psychoanalytic point of view, we might suggest that the gaiety of the music served as a defense against the fear and depression of the composer. However, what Tormey urges is that we may not claim on that account to *hear* the music differently, to hear it as ''humorous but disguisedly bitter,'' etc. It is not clear, in the case of music at any rate, that, except in cases where music is integrated with a verbal text, extra-musical information of a biographical nature can make us hear the music differently at all. What we hear when we are sensitive to music are the aesthetic qualities of a particular composition in performance.

And performance is important here, especially if, with Susanne Langer (1953), we conceive it as a ''completion'' of the musical work. Langer says that ''real performance is as creative an act as composition . . . a logical continuation of the composition, carrying creation through from thought to physical expression'' (pp. 138–139). Thus, she gives full homage to the ''sonorous imagination'' of the performer who must give ''utterance'' to the "conceptual imagination" of the composer. According to this view, we must extend the notion of expression to cover the feeling-states of performers. Clearly, this is untenable.[15] To say, for example, that a rendition of the Tchaikovsky *Violin Concerto in D* by Jascha Heifetz was more expressive than a performance of the same work by Isaac Stern is to make no psychological statement about either of the two men involved. Tormey's point is that to speak about a work of art is not necessarily to speak about a person and vice-versa. Peter Kivy (1980) has written recently on expression in music and borrows heavily, I feel, from Bouwsma's earlier paper. Kivy quotes Bouwsma to the effect that "the sadness is to the music rather like the redness to the apple, than it is like the burp to the cider" (Bouwsma, 1954, p. 265). Kivy's own images of this difference in the ways we understand expression include a man with a clenched fist, and the face of a St. Bernard dog. Commonly, we would describe the former as "angry," and the latter as "sad." Kivy argues that when we say that the dog has a sad face we do not mean that his face expresses sadness in the same way in which we mean that the fist-clenching man expresses anger. Kivy holds that, similarly, when we refer to a passage in a musical composition as sad, we mean it in the former rather than in the latter sense. His thesis thus involves an effort to divorce biographical reference from musical criticism, though not absolutely, for, as he says, music *can* occasionally express genuine sadness or terror on the part of a composer. What he claims is that, generally speaking, when we characterize a piece of music as "brooding" or "spritely" we do not mean to so characterize its composer, nor do we mean that the music causes us to brood or to caper. We are rather, by using such predicates, Kivy asserts, describing qualities inherent in the music, and he endeavors to offer historical, physiological, and iconographic accounts for such qualities that are not only possible but plausible.

Tormey agrees that there must be some connection between what an artist does and the resulting expressive qualities of the work of art. What he wants to preserve is precisely what Wimsatt and Beardsley want to protect, namely, the uniqueness of the aesthetic object; what these philosophers assert is that there is no simple, logical, or consistent relation between what an artist feels or thinks or knows or does and the resulting expressive qualities of the work of art. The artist, Tormey insists, is, over and above expressing himself, "making an expressive object" (1971), an objective that has the power to make others feel. This may involve even in a nontrivial sense some expression of the artist's state of mind, but to say this is scarcely to begin to address the complexity of the creative act which results in what we perceive as an "expressive" work of art.

Freud himself had some awareness of this problem in the theory of art, as the following quotes will evince. At the end of his *Moses of Michelangelo* (1914a) after initially claiming that "it can only be the artist's intention, in so far as he has succeeded in expressing it in his work and in conveying it to us, that grips us so powerfully" (p. 212), he concludes with doubt:

> What if we have taken too serious and profound a view of details which were nothing to the artist, details which he had introduced quite arbitrarily or for some purely formal reasons with no hidden intention behind? What if we have shared the fate of so many interpreters who have thought they saw quite clearly things which the artist did not intend either consciously or unconsciously? I cannot tell. (pp. 235–236).

In this passage Freud implies that it is not only possible but even likely to find in a work that which the artist did not in some sense intend; he therefore betrays his awareness that intention alone may not provide an adequate theory of art.

There are two issues here: one is whether psychoanalysis can adequately account for the artist's intention, and the other is whether we must allow for aspects in a given work of art that are extra-intentional, even given the psychoanalytic concept of intention, which is far more inclusive than the artist's conscious purpose or design. We are returned here to an ontological question. If, with Wimsatt and Beardsley, we define the work of art as equivalent to the artist's intention, then we must interpret Freud's passage [from *Moses of Michelangelo*] to mean that psychoanalysis simply fails to give a complete account of intention, of the internal workings, dynamics, structure of the work of art. If, on the other hand, we conceive the work of art as a cultural object existing in its own space and time and continuously affected by forces outside the artist's purview (cf. Cioffi), then we can interpret Freud's passage as indicating his awareness not of the limits of psychoanalytic theory to account for works of art as intentional objects but rather its limitations vis-à-vis art seen as that which transcends intention.

Freud's equivocation here has to do partly with his emphasis, in the early stages of the development of psychoanalytic theory, on the investigation of the id. In the years prior to 1923 (with publication of *The Ego and the Id,* which established a new direction for psychoanalytic investigation)—that period in which Freud's major contributions in the direct application of psychoanalysis to the arts were written—his primary focus was on the nature of repressed wishes and drives: he saw this as the "real" material for interpretation. The countervailing forces were acknowledged, but only one side of the intrapsychic conflict was deemed important. Hence, his view of intention was strongly weighted towards id-dominated unconscious factors. Not yet having developed his structural theory into its final form, he was not interpreting from a perspective that included in fair measure accounts of the forces of id, ego, superego, and reality on behavior. Only later, with the work of Anna Freud (1936), Hartmann (1939), Rapaport (1967), and Kris (1952), was a balance established, a more equal distribution of interest, so that some of these issues which seemed so doubtful with respect to art have come more recently to be addressed as somewhat differently by the so-called ego psychologists. (See also Waelder, 1965).

I am suggesting here that, in part, the reason for Freud's view of art as puzzling and for his at times rather baffled attitude towards it lies in the narrowly focused perspective he took on it during the early years of the development of psychoanalytic theory. As this next quote testifies, he seemed to sense this:

> It may be that we have produced a complete caricature of an interpretation by introducing into an innocent work of art purposes of which its creator had no notion, and by so doing have shown once more how easy it is to find what one is looking for and what is occupying one's own mind—a possibility of which the strangest examples are to be found in the history of literature. (1907, p. 91)

A few lines later, however, Freud reasserts his faith in explanatory value of the psychoanalytic notion of unconscious intention, and hence in the deterministic intentionalist theory:

> Our opinion is that the author need have known nothing of these rules and purposes, so that he could disavow them in good faith, but that nevertheless we have not discovered anything in his work that is not already in it. . . . He need not state these laws [of unconscious intention], nor even be clearly aware of them; as a result of the tolerance of his intelligence they are incorporated within his creations. (pp. 91–92).

He again equivocates in his famous line from *Dostoevsky and Parricide* (1928), when he exclaims: "Before the problem of the creative artist analysis must, alas, lay down its arms" (p. 177); and in the same work he refers to the artist's "unanalysable gift."

In yet another work, Freud (1908) again expresses his inability to explain both the artistic (creative) and aesthetic experience but indicates as well his awareness of the transforming power of art. He begins by asking how the artist manages to impress us and arouse in us emotions of which we had not realized ourselves capable. He notes that querying the artist will not result in any satisfactory explanations. Then he offers the following formulation:

> [The artist] creates a world of phantasy which he takes very seriously—that is, which he invents with large amounts of emotion—while separating it sharply from reality. . . . The unreality of the writer's imaginative world, however, has very important consequences for the technique of his art; for many things which, if they were real, could give no enjoyment, can do so in the play of phantasy, and many excitements which, in themselves, are actually distressing, can become a source of pleasure for the hearers and spectators at the performance of a writer's work. (1908, p. 144).

In this passage Freud comes close to a classical view of art as imitation. In the course of this particular work, *Creative Writers and Daydreaming,* he develops a connection between art and children's play, emphasizing the seriousness, the value to the child/artist of his illusory, make-believe world. Thus, he paves the ground for some of the more recent psychoanalytic authors such as Winnicott who have greatly elaborated on the derivation of artistic activity from childhood play.[16]

Having presented these specimens of Freud's shifting views on art, we must return to our original problem, asking now both how psychoanalytic interpretation of art [in the pathographic mode] can respond to the anti-intentionalist and anti-expressionist critiques that have been leveled against it and also what specific contribution psychoanalysis can make to the debate between intentionalists and anti-intentionalists. I have tried in the text to indicate some answers to the first of these questions. The psychoanalytic interpreter must (1) seek to respect the integrity of the work of art, remembering that it is consciously framed and holds a special status within the domain of cultural objects; (2) attend to the way in which it, as an autonomous object, exerts its own pulls upon the artist—pulls that may be technical, aesthetic, and not necessarily traceable to depth psychology; (3) bear in mind that the work of art is a real object apart from the psyche of its creator and that thus to make statements about its creator is not necessarily to make statements about it and vice-versa.

With respect to the second question, clearly the most obvious contribution psychoanalysis can make to the debate on intentionalism is the notion of the dynamic unconscious. This construct significantly broadens the concept of intention. By appeal to unconscious motivation, the most apparently far-fetched intention may be attributed to an artist, his strenuous denial only serving, in the case of resistance, to support rather than disprove the allegation. Theoretically, it becomes possible for the psychoanalyst to claim as the result of intention all aspects of the work of art considered as a psychic product. Since psychoanalytic theory offers no clearly designated limits as to what can and cannot be ascribed to unconscious intention (each case must be treated individually), the analyst is free to press for as inclusive an interpretation as he can supply by, for example, tracing specific imagery to universal unconscious fantasy, etc. Interpretations of this sort cannot be falsified or refuted by recourse to the sorts of confirmatory evidence we would produce in the case of conscious intention. Hence, if we accept it, the concept of unconscious intention adds weight to the old Platonic claim that artists do not stand in any privileged position with respect to the criticism of their own works, while at the same time it supports the intentionalist doctrine. I do not think, however, that psychoanalysis can bolster the intentionalist cause in any other sense than in thus expanding the kinds of intention we may expect to find embodied in works of art. For if, with Wimsatt and Beardsley, we are prone to rule out as critically irrelevant all external evidence of artistic intention, we will be even less apt to be convinced by descriptions of hidden or disguised intention than by that which is openly avowed. On the other hand, Wimsatt and Beardsley's position may be reconciled with other psychoanalytic approaches to art—beyond pathography—which lie outside the scope of this paper.

In the case of expressionism, however, psychoanalysis has perhaps somewhat more to offer. The philosophers (Tormey, Kivy, etc.) who wish to deny simple or direct relations between what, for example, a piece of music expresses and the feeling-state of its composer are nevertheless willing to grant that *some* connection does exist. Psychoanalysis, by giving a complex account of intrapsychic processes, can contribute towards an understanding of the way in which an artist's changing moods, thoughts, and precepts are transformed in the process of creation into what finally emerges in the completed work of art.[17]

Ultimately, the debate turns on the ontological issue. Is the work of art to be seen as a psychic product, the infant-child of its parent-creator whose mind, whose fantasies, we must know in order rightly to fathom it? Or is the work of art to be viewed as semi-autonomous—even, for some critics and philosophers, fully autonomous—an artifact that can and should be judged for itself alone without external reference? Clearly, the pathographer takes the former stance and, although he does not claim exhaustive authority for his interpretations, he is reluctant to define limits for them. What the philosophers point out is that works of art are more than psychic products though they are certainly that. They exist in historical time; they partake of cultural traditions and technical conventions; they frequently outlive their creators and change in response to the new contexts that spring up around them; and they have in some sense a life of their own, a life that grows in part out of the mind of their creator but that may take on overlays of meaning and significance beyond what could ever have been intended either consciously or unconsciously by the artist who created them.

Thus, in conclusion, I suggest the following: although psychoanalytic criticism (pathography) has at least partially fulfilled its tacit promise to penetrate more deeply into the psyche than any previous approach, it seems clear that a serious dialogue with contemporary aesthetics can promise further refinements both of its goals (possibilities and limitations) and possibly even of its methodology. Therefore, it is in the best interests of both disciplines and of the humanities in general to foster this ongoing dialogue.

NOTES

1. See Freud (1894) and Freud and Breuer (1893–95) in which the neurophysiological theory of the mind is presented with its concepts of repression, cathexis, mobile and bound energy, and the splitting of idea from affect. Shortly after this, Freud developed the notion that the repressed idea could be a fantasy rather than a memory and developed the technique of "free association" as opposed to "suggestion."
2. My examples of romantic criticism will be drawn largely from English sources. My point here is not that Freud read these authors (he probably did not) but rather that we can analogize the interests and emphases of these writers with those of Freud. My effort is to draw a parallel rather than merely to make a specifically historical statement.
3. Obviously for a psychoanalytic critic, these categories must somehow expand in meaning to include unconscious intention as well, e.g., the artist's unconscious wish to hide certain things from himself.
4. Apropos of these styles, we might also note the connection between the "stream of consciousness" novel and the psychoanalytic notion of "free association."
5. See Kris and Kurtz (1979) for a fascinating excursion into this topic which traces its roots back to ancient history.
6. For Freud and Romanticism, see Trosman (1976, pp. 46–70).
7. Note also the views of other Romantic critics of the same period, especially Hazlitt, who compared poetry with dreams and even suggested that art may arise from a need to compensate for physical deformity: "Do you suppose we owe nothing to Pope's deformity? He said to himself, 'If my person be crooked, my verses shall be strait' " (in Abrams, 1953, p. 142).

   Note further the following passage by De Quincey: "In very many subjective exercises . . . the problem before the writer is to project his own inner mind; to bring out consciously what yet lurks by involution in many unanalysed feelings; in short, to pass through a prism and radiate into distinct elements what previously had been even to himself but dim and confused ideas inter-mixed with each other'' (in Abrams, 1953, p. 144).

8. To grasp the poet, one must undergo the poem. Note the convergence between this view and Kris's ideas of the progressive identifications in aesthetic experience.
9. Note Stuart Hampshire's (1966) argument against such a notion. Monroe Beardsley rebuts Hampshire on the grounds of what he calls ''critical rationality'' and ''public semantic facts'' that antecede interpretation in ''The Testability of an Interpretation,'' 1970.
10. Freud deals with this issue of determinism and predictability in ''The Psychogenesis of a Case of Homosexuality in a Woman'' (1920), where he points out that although with hindsight the results always seem inevitable, the reverse is not obvious: ''. . . in other words, from a knowledge of the premises we could not have foretold the nature of the result'' (p. 167).
11. Beardsley describes what is admissible as evidence for interpretation of works of art in a later paper (1970): ''. . . public semantic facts, the connotations and suggestions *in* poems, are the stubborn data with which the interpreter must come to terms . . .'' (p. 382, my italics).
12. A classic example of this phenomenon is Freud's mistaking ''vulture'' for ''kite'' in Leonardo's report of his dream. Knowing the word was mistranslated cannot help but affect our attitude towards the interpretation. As Cioffi said, ''There are cases in which we have an interpretation which satisfies us but which we feel *depends* on certain facts being the case'' (1964, p. 311, my italics).
13. On the importance of context, see also B. Lang (1982, p. 411), where he points out that fundamental elements of style are *context-bound,* that they reveal themselves only by acting with and on other units within a (fluctuating) whole or context chosen by creator and then by audience.
14. Although I am not prepared to argue this point here, I would point out the relatively smaller numbers of pathographies of composers and musicians than of writers and artists. One noteworthy pathographer working in the area of music is Stuart Feder, however, and a list of his recent works is included in my references.
15. For a recent, interesting discussion of the way in which biographical knowledge about the composer *can* affect performance, see Rothstein (1983).
16. Bouwsma seemed to have understood this derivation too, for he says: ''In art the world is born afresh, but the travail of the artist may have had its beginnings in children's play'' (1954, p. 265).
17. For an excellent discussion of these issues, see Kris (1952, pp. 302–18).

REFERENCES

Abrams, M. H. (1953). *The mirror and the lamp.* New York: Oxford University Press.

Beardsley, M. (1970). The testability of an interpretation. In J. Margolis (Ed.), *Philosophy looks at the arts.* Philadelphia: Temple University Press, 1978.

Bouwsma, O. K. (1954). The expression theory of art. In M. Philipson & P. J. Gudel (Eds.), *Aesthetics today.* New York: New American Library, 1980.

Cioffi, F. (1964). Intention and interpretation in criticism. In J. Margolis (Ed.), *Philosophy looks at the arts.* Philadelphia: Temple University Press, 1978.

Dutton, D. (1982). Why intentionalism won't go away. Paper read before the American Society for Aesthetics, 40th Annual Meeting, Banff, October 29, 1982.

Eliot, T. S. (1932) Hamlet. In *Selected essays, 1917–32*. London: Faber and Faber.

Feder, S. (1980). Decoration day: A boyhood memory of Charles Ives. *The Musical Quarterly,* 46(2): 234–261.

——— (1978). Gustav Mahler, dying. *The International Review of Psychoanalysis,* 5: 125–148.

——— (1980). Gustav Mahler um mitternacht. *The International Review of Psycho-analysis,* 7: 11–26.

——— (1981). Gustav Mahler: The music of fatricide. *The International Review of Psychoanalysis,* 8: 257–284.

Freud, A. (1936). *The Ego and the mechanisms of defense*. New York: International Universities Press, 1966.

Freud, S. (1894). The neuro-psychoses of defense. *S. E.*, 3: 43–68.

——— (1907). Delusions and dreams in Jensen's "Gradiva." *S. E.*, 9: 3–95.

——— (1908). Creative writers and daydreaming. *S. E.*, 9: 141–153.

——— (1910). Leonardo da Vinci and a memory of his childhood. *S. E.*, 11: 57–137.

——— (1914a). The Moses of Michelangelo. *S. E.*, 13: 211–238.

——— (1914b). On narcicissism. *S. E.*, 14: 73–102.

——— (1920). The psychogenesis of a case of homosexuality in a woman. *S. E.*, 18: 145–172.

——— (1927). Fetishism. *S. E.*, 21: 149–157.

——— (1928). Dostoevsky and parricide. *S. E.*, 21.

Freud, S. & Breuer, J. (1893–95). Studies on hysteria. *S. E.*, 2.

Gay, P. (1976). *Art and act*. New York: Harper & Row.

Hampshire, S. (1966). Types of interpretation. In W. E. Kennick (Ed.), *Art and philosophy*. New York: St. Martin's Press, 1979.

Hartmann, H. (1939). *Ego psychology and the problem of adaptation*. New York: International Universities Press, 1958.

Isenberg, A. (1944). Critical communication. In M. Mothersill, et al. (Eds.), *Aesethetics and the theory of criticism*. Chicago: University of Chicago Press, 1973.

Kivy, P. (1980). *The corded shell*. Princeton, NJ: Princeton University press.

Kris, E. (1952). *Psychoanalytic explorations in art*. New York: International Universities Press.

Kris, E. & Kurtz, O. (1979). *Legend, myth and magic in the image of the artist: A historical experiment*. New Haven & London: Yale University Press.

Lang, B. (1982). Looking for the styleme. *Critical Inquiry,* 9: 405–413.

Langer, S. (1953). *Feeling and form*. New York: Charles Scribner's Sons.

Liebert, R. (1982). Methodological issues in the psychoanalytic study of an artist. *Psychoanalysis and Contemporary Thought,* 5: 439–465.

Mill, J. S. (1833). What is poetry? In J. M. W. Gibbs (Ed.), *Early essays by John Stuart Mill,* London: G. Bell, 1897.

Rapaport, D. (1967). *Collected papers of David Rapaport,* M. Gill (ed.). New York: Basic Books.

Rothstein, E. (1983). Discovering the Beethoven inside the monument. *New York Times* (Jan. 23), 2: 1–24.

Stern, L. (1980). On interpreting. *The Journal of Aesthetics and Art Criticism,* 39, 2: 119–129.

Tormey, A. (1971). Art and expression: A critique. In J. Margolis (Ed.), *Philosophy looks at the arts*. Philadelphia: Temple University Press, 1978.

Trosman, H. (1976). Freud's cultural background. In J. E. Gedo and G. Pollock (Eds.), *Freud: The fusion of science and humanism. Psychological Issues,* Monographs 34/35.

Waelder, R. (1965). *Psychoanalytic avenues to art.* New York: International Universities Press.

Wimsatt, W. K. & Beardsley, M. L. (1954). The intentional fallacy. In J. Margolis (Ed.), *Philosophy looks at the arts.* Philadelphia: Temple University Press, 1978.

Wordsworth, W. (1800). *Preface to the lyrical ballads.*

PART III

NEW PERSPECTIVES

INTRODUCTION

What are the stepping stones in the transition from the classical tradition of "psychoanalysis applied to literature" to the contemporary, more complex and more egalitarian encounter between these two arts? Numerous works, appearing in the 1950s, 1960s, and 1970s, come to mind. We mentioned already Kris's *Psychoanalytic Explorations in Art* (1952), and Winnicott's *Playing and Reality* (1971), two major contributions to a psychoanalytic understanding of art devoid of a pathologizing attitude. Winnicott's work in this area evolved through an interaction with that of Marion Milner (Joanna Field), a British writer turned analyst. Her work has also influenced Norman Holland (1968, p. X), as well as Anton Ehrenzweig's (1957) model of creativity, which reached maturity in his *The Hidden Order of Art* (1971), emphasizing the flexible swings between differentiated and undifferentiated, conscious and unconscious, necessary for the creation and appreciation of art.

Another author who influenced the transition is Jacques Lacan. His "Seminar on 'The Purloined Letter' " became one of the most quoted and debated psychoanalytic studies of literature. Published in French in 1956 (in *La Psychanalyse II*), it was chosen to open Lacan's *Écrits* in 1966, and translated into English by Jeffrey Mehlman in 1973.

The impact of this paper is quite paradoxical, in view of its being described as "a very narrow and one-sided reading of the story" (Phillips, in Kurzweil and Phillips 1983, p. 11), as "an allegory of Lacan's emphatic insistence on the primacy of the Symbolic order" (Benvenuto and Kennedy 1986, p. 90), in which Poe's text "is in many ways a pretext" (Mehlman's introduction to Lacan, in this volume).

To understand Lacan's innovation better, we may compare his discussion of Poe's story to the earlier interpretation of Marie Bonaparte ([1933] 1949, pp. 483–85). The missing letter is seen by her as expressing "regret for the missing maternal penis, with reproach for its loss.'' The struggle between Dupin and the minister is explained in oedipal terms. The minister and the King are seen by Bonaparte as representations of the paternal male figures in Poe's childhood, whereas Dupin represents Poe as a child (all in a pathographic context).

Although traces of this analysis can be found in Lacan's paper (as Derrida 1975, points out) we also notice a basic reversal. Bonaparte subjects literature to an examination based on the clinical understanding of psychopathology. Lacan mobilizes literature for an examination of psychoanalysis (through the equation of Dupin with the psychoanalyst) based on linguistic and literary understanding.

This primacy of linguistic-literary notions may explain Lacan's popularity in academic literary circles, where at times psychoanalysis becomes equated with Lacan's work (a mistaken equation, even in France). Lacan's view that the unconscious is structured as a language, his emphasis on words and verbal nuances in his clinical practice, turned literary scholars into the pioneers of Lacan's thought in the United States and Britain, while practicing psychoanalysts in the English-speaking world were very slow to absorb his work, so different in content and in style from their habitual professional discourse.

Actually, the suspicious attitude of U.S. psychoanalysts towards Lacan is predated by Lacan's animosity and contempt toward the United States and U.S. psychoanalysis. In this context, Gallop (1985, pp. 55–73) points out, it is interesting that he opens his *Écrits* with a study of a U.S. writer, though one admired in France more than in his native country, who places his story in Paris. Lacan identifies with Poe's French protagonist, Dupin, and was criticized by Derrida (1975) for neglecting the figure of the (American?) narrator, another potential psychoanalyst within the text. (Gallop, by the way, criticizes Sheridan, translator of an English selection from *Écrits*, for omitting this ''Franco-American'' paper; but the first two lines of that volume state that the selection was made by Lacan himself; Lacan 1977, p. VII).

At the core of Derrida's (1975) extensive critique of Lacan's paper is his observation, that for Lacan ''literary writing occupies an illustrative position'' (p. 45). ''The formal structure of the work is ignored, quite classically, as soon as, or perhaps whenever, one claims to decipher the 'truth' or the exemplary message'' (p. 53). Derrida suggests that Lacan's repeated discovery of triangles in Poe's story is achieved by excluding the narrator, ''the fourth side,'' as well as by avoiding themes of duality and doubles present in the story.

Barbara Johnson (in Felman 1982), comparing Poe's story, Lacan's seminar, and Derrida's critique, suggests: ''In all three texts, it is the act of analysis which seems to occupy the center of the discursive stage, and the act of analysis of the act of analysis which in some way disrupts that centrality'' (p. 457). She illustrates how, through several inaccurate attributions, ''Derrida is . . . framing Lacan for an interpretative malpractice of which he himself is, at least in part, the author'' (p. 478). The continued debate was later assembled into a book, *The Purloined Poe* (Muller and Richardson 1988).

Evaluations of the contributions of Lacan and Derrida to the psychoanalytic study of literature vary considerably. Phillips, lumping them together, warns that they are encouraging ''the free exercise of the imagination on the part of the interpreter . . . a free-associational form of thinking set up by the work under examination. Lacan spins ideological fantasies as he re-interprets and co-authors the text'' (Kurzweil and Phillips 1983, p. 11). Wright (1984, pp. 104–37), differentiating their positions, offers a much more favorable evaluation, although she also comments: ''Lacan's own example of critical practice is not to be taken as exemplary'' (p. 113). She defines Lacan as part of structural psychoanalysis, and Derrida as part of post structural psychoanalysis:

> Lacan stresses the supremacy of the signifier in determining subjects in their acts. But for Derrida the signifier is not so supreme . . . [Derrida's terms] are designed to show the way any text undermines itself. . . . Words, whether spoken or written, are subject to ''differance,'' differing from and deferring any transient fixation of meaning. . . . Lacan places the emphasis on language's imposition of a mould which creates the unconscious, Derrida places it upon the unconscious's ability to escape the mould. (pp. 133–34)

Felman's paper, ''The Case of Poe,'' originally published in 1980, is another positive evaluation—and explication—of Lacan's position. (Her paper, as well as Mehlman's introduction and notes, may help the reader in understanding Lacan's paper, which is probably more difficult than other papers in this volume). Felman, professor of French and Comparative Literature at Yale University, skillfully demonstrates the implications of Lacan's views for a radical restructuring of the psychoanalysis–literature encounter, including the crucial realization that ''the interpreter is not more immune than the poet to unconscious delusions and errors.''

Felman's own original approach comes into full fruition in her longer paper, "Turning the Screw of Interpretation" (Felman 1982), a study of Henry James's *The Turn of the Screw.*

Felman combines a discussion of the story itself with a study of the stormy debate aroused by Edmund Wilson's "Freudian" interpretation of it, published in 1934. The ghosts haunting the governess, the story's protagonist, do not really exist, suggests Wilson; "they are but figments of the governess' sick imagination, mere hallucinations and projections symptomatic of the frustrations of her repressed sexual desires" (Felman 1982, p. 97). This interpretation aroused a barrage of indignant refutations.

Felman takes no sides in the confrontation between the two views of the ghosts, "psychoanalytic" and "metaphysical," believing "that the *reality of the debate* is in fact more significant for the impact of the text than the reality of the ghosts" (p. 98). She shows how central motives of the story (a danger that must be averted, violent aggression inflicted by an injurious alien force, attack and defense, the enemy's defeat) are all repeated in the polemic against Wilson. The story itself can be seen as questioning (in its rhetoric, thematic content, narrative structure), but Wilson's attempt to reply the text's questions is too literal, and "the literal is 'vulgar' because it *stops* the *movement* constitutive of meaning" (p. 107). She suggests an alternative:

> Our reading of *The Turn of the Screw* would thus attempt not so much to *capture* the mystery's solution, but to follow, rather, the significant path of its flight; not so much to solve or *answer* the enigmatic question of the text, but to investigate its structure; not so much to name and make *explicit* the ambiguity of the text, but to understand the necessity and the rhetorical functioning of the textual ambiguity. The question underlying such a reading is thus not "*what* does the story mean?" but rather "*how* does the story mean?" (Felman 1982, p. 119).

In the process of fulfilling these goals, Felman demonstrates the correspondence between the governess' demand for confession, which leads to her killing the child entrusted to her, and Wilson's attempt to force the text to "a confession," to extort its secret:

> To "grasp" the child, therefore, as both the governess and Wilson do, to press him to the point of suffocating him, of killing or of stifling the silence within him, is to do nothing other than to submit, once more, the silent speech of the unconscious to the very gesture of *repression.* (Felman 1982, p. 193)

The next author in this section, Norman N. Holland, founder of the Institute for Psychological Study of the Arts at the University of Florida in

Gainesville, happens to be another participant in the debate following Lacan's seminar on "The Purloined Letter." Not surprisingly, his contribution (Holland 1980) is the most personally revealing, openly influenced by his own associations, preoccupations, and childhood experiences.

Holland's development as a psychoanalytic literary scholar, as mentioned in my general introduction, follows many different stages of the field. In *The Dynamics of Literary Response* (1968) he already attempts "to build a conceptual bridge from literary texts objectively understood to our subjective experience of them" (p. XIV). He is concerned with the dilemma posed by several different readings of the same text, by varieties of subjectivity:

> If you are a critical relativist (as I am on Mondays, Wednesdays and Fridays), you will simply accept each of these different readings as valid to the extent it brings all the elements of the story together to a single "point." If you are a critical monist (as I am on Tuesdays, Thursdays, and Saturdays), you will carry one step further the process of successive abstraction that led us to these several meanings. (Holland 1968, p. 25)

One of the most innovative chapters was "Form as Defense," where he says: "If I can discover by analysing my own reaction the drives and fantasies the poem stirs up in me and the defensive maneuvers the poem acts out for dealing with these drives, then I can understand the different reactions of others for whom those fantasies and defenses are less congenial or adequate" (p. 117). (The psychoanalytic understanding of artistic form was later elaborated by Rose 1980).

Holland's subsequent work may signify the strengthening of the relativist in him as regarding literary texts, while the monist in him turns his attention from the unity of works of literature to the unity (identity, personality, character) of readers. These are the main issues discussed in "UNITY IDENTITY TEXT SELF" reproduced here. This paper appeared simultaneously with Holland's book *5 Readers Reading* (1975), which he describes briefly in the paper (note 8). *5 Readers Reading* relates the way Faulkner's "A Rose for Emily" is read and understood by five students, to their personalities and emotional patterns as studied independently through projective tests and interviews.

Of Holland's recent work we should mention his useful guide to the literature and psychology field (Holland 1990), as well as his whimsical overview of his twenty-five years of psychoanalytic literary criticism (Holland 1986). In this paper he delightfully parodies several contemporary critical styles. He also includes an interesting discussion of Lacanian critics who "have not yet acknowledged that we do things to texts instead of texts doing things to us or doing things all on their own" and thus contribute to an illusory "blanking out of the reading I" (p. 49). Unveiling "the reading I" appears to be Holland's major influence.

Roy Schafer's paper, "Narration in the Psychoanalytic Dialogue," represents the growing realization of psychoanalysts that literature, rather than supplying them pseudo-patients to analyze, may offer them useful insights for the understanding of their own professional role and professional dilemmas. Schafer is a faculty member of Columbia University's Center for Psychoanalytic Training and Research.

Schafer's interest in narration appears to be rooted in his early work on projective testing (Berman 1988); one of his papers in that area is "How Was This Story Told?" (Schafer 1958). When he attempted to reformulate psychoanlytic theory as an action language (Schafer 1976), the way people talk about themselves caught his attention as a key to their attempt to disclaim action, to view themselves a passive carriers of impulse or emotion, rather than as active agents in their lives:

> Everyday language is not only a record of the fundamental unconsciously maintained desires and conflicts with which people are concerned, but also a record of the many modes that people have developed to ease subjective distress. I particularly have in mind distress felt in connection with being held responsible. (Schafer 1976, p. 144).

This theme is developed and expanded in the present paper, later incorporated into *The Analytic Attitude* (Schafer 1983). The concept of narration becomes, in this book, one of the basic characteristics of the analytic situation, a central activity of both analyst and analysand, who examine potential story lines in exploring the analysand's life and construct multiple histories, which are never seen as an ultimate "discovery," but are constantly subject to challenge, revision, and extension.

Spence (1985), one of those who further developed this conception (e.g., Spence 1987, and chap. 4, this vol.) concludes his survey of Schafer's work with the following lines:

> To emphasize the relational nature of truth is to push back the Ice Age of Positivism and to argue against the traditional subject–object separation of Big Science. The patient's history is no longer an object of study like a bluebird or a molecule, but a constantly changing story that the patient is writing and rewriting, together with the analyst, inside and outside the analytic hour. We are just beginning to listen. (p. 81)

REFERENCES

Benvenuto, B., and R. Kennedy. 1986. *The works of Jacques Lacan: An introduction*. New York: St. Martin's Press.

Berman, E. 1988. Schafer's contribution: Its continuity and development. *Israel Journal of Psychiatry and Related Sciences* 25: 191–97.

Bonaparte, M. [1933] 1949. *The life and works of Edgar Allan Poe: A psycho-analytic interpretation*. London: Imago.

Derrida, J. 1975. The purveyor of truth. *Yale French Studies* 52: 31–113.

Ehrenzweig, A. 1957. The creative surrender: A comment on "Joanna Field's" book *An experiment in leisure. American Imago*, 14: 193–210.

———. 1971. *The hidden order of art: A study in the psychology of artistic imagination*. Berkeley and Los Angeles: University of California Press.

Felman, S., ed. 1982. *Literature and psychoanalysis. The question of reading: Otherwise*. Baltimore and London: Johns Hopkins University Press.

Gallop, J. 1985. *Reading Lacan*. Ithaca and London: Cornell University Press.

Holland, N. N. 1968. *The dynamics of literary response*. New York: Oxford University Press.

———. 1975. *5 readers reading*. New Haven and London: Yale University Press.

———. 1980. Recovering "The purloined letter": Reading as a personal transaction. In *The reader in the text: Essays on audience and interpretation*, edited by S. R. Suleiman and I. Crosman. Princeton: Princeton University Press.

———. 1986. Twenty-five years and thirty days. *Psychoanalytic Quarterly* 55: 23–52.

———. 1990. *Holland's guide to psychoanalytic psychology and literature-and-psychology*. New York and Oxford: Oxford University Press.

Kurzweil, E., and W. Phillips, eds. 1983. *Literature and psychoanalysis*. New York: Columbia University Press.

Kris, E. 1952. *Psychoanalytic explorations in art*. New York: International Universities Press.

Lacan, J. 1966. *Écrits*. Paris: Editions du Seuil.

———. 1977. *Écrits: A selection*, translated by A. Sheridan. New York: Norton.

Muller, J. P., and W. J. Richardson. 1988. *The purloined Poe: Lacan, Derrida and psychoanalytic reading*. Baltimore and London: Johns Hopkins University Press.

Rose, Gilbert J. 1980. *The power of form: A psychoanlytic approach to aesthetic form*. New York: International Universities Press.

Schafer, R. 1958. How was this story told? *Journal of Projective Techniques* 22: 181–210.

———. 1976. *A new language for psychoanalysis*. New Haven and London: Yale University Press.

———. 1983. *The analytic attitude*. New York: Basic Books.

Spence, D. P. 1985. Roy Schafer: Searching for the native tongue. In *Beyond Freud: A study of modern psychoanalytic theorists*, edited by J. Reppen. Hillsdale, N.J.: Analytic Press.

———. 1987. Narrative recursion. In *Discourse in psychoanalysis and literature*, edited by S. Rimmon-Kenan. London and New York: Methuen.

Winnicott, D. W. 1971. *Playing and reality*. London: Tavistock.

Wright, E. 1984. *Psychoanalytic criticism: Theory in practice*. London and New York: Methuen.

12. Seminar on "The Purloined Letter"

Jacques Lacan

INTRODUCTORY NOTE

If "psychoanalytic criticism" is an effort to bring analytic categories to bear in the solution of critical problems, Lacan's text is certainly not an example of that discipline. One has the feeling that, on the contrary, in the confrontation between analysis and literature, the former's role for Lacan is not to solve but to open up a new kind of textual problem. The Poe text then is in many ways a pretext, an exemplary occasion for lacan to complicate the question of *Beyond the Pleasure Principle*. It is indeed a "purloined letter."

The crux of the problem is in the ambiguity of the term *letter* in Lacan's analysis. It may mean either typographical character or epistle. Why?

a) As typographical character, the letter is a unit of signification without any meaning in itself. In this it resembles the "memory trace," which for Freud is never the image of an event, but a term which takes on meaning only through its differential opposition to other traces. It is a particular arrangement of "frayings." The striking image of this situation in the tale is that we never know the *contents* of the crucial letter. Here then is a psychoanalysis indifferent to deep meanings, concerned more with a latent organization of the manifest than a latent meaning beneath it. In its refusal to accord any "positive" status to linguistic phenomena, this might be viewed as Lacan's Sausserean side (see text note 24).

b) As epistle, the letter allows Lacan to play on the intersubjective relations which expropriate the individual. ("To whom does a letter belong?") It is Levi-Strauss (and Mauss) who are no doubt at the source of this effort to think of the Oedipus complex in terms of a structure of *exchange* crucial to the "fixation" of unconscious "memory traces."

These losses—of the plenitude of meaning and the security of (self-) possession—are thus the principal modes of the Lacanian *askesis* in this

Reprinted by permission of Editions du Seuil from *Yale French Studies*, 48 (1972).

parable of analysis. To which we may add a third: that of metalanguage. By which we mean: 1) that the Prefect is already repeating the "events" he recounts at the moment he pretends to view them objectively; 2) even Dupin (as analyst) is trapped in the fantasmatic circuit (repetitive structure, mobile scenario . . .) at the moment of his rage against the Minister. The difference between the Prefect (trapped in the transference) and Dupin (counteracting the countertransference) is that the latter is intermittently aware of his loss.

In translating the text, we found that a large measure of its difficulty was a function of Lacan's idiosyncratic use of prepositions. As a result, the reader has to play with various possibilities of subordination in a number of sentences in order to determine the "proper" one(s). For better or worse, in English we have (necessarily) chosen to normalize the use of prepositions. We have thus occasionally been obliged to chart a course through Lacan's labyrinth rather than reproduce that labyrinth whole. There has no doubt been a concomitant loss (in syntactical richness) and gain (in clarity).

The notes we have added to the text (signed —Ed) are, on the whole, explanations of allusions or clarifications of particularly oblique points.

This text was originally written in 1956 and—along with an introductory postface—is the opening text of the *Écrits*.*

—Jeffrey Mehlman

Und wenn es uns glückt,
Und wenn es sich schickt,
So sind es Gedanken.

Our inquiry has led us to the point of recognizing that the repetition automatism *(Wiederholungszwang)* finds its basis in what we have called the *insistence* of the signifying chain.[1] We have elaborated that notion itself as a correlate of the *ex-sistence* (or: eccentric place) in which we must necessarily locate the subject of the unconscious if we are to take Freud's discovery seriously.[2] As is known, it is in the realm of experience inaugurated by psychoanalysis that we may grasp along what imaginary lines the human organism, in the most intimate recesses of its being, manifests its capture in a *symbolic* dimension.[3]

The lesson of this seminar is intended to maintain that these imaginary incidences, far from representing the essence of our experience, reveal only

* Jacques Lacan, *Écrits*. Paris: Editions du Seuil, 1966.

what in it remains inconsistent unless they are related to the symbolic chain which binds and orients them.

We realize, of course, the importance of these imaginary impregnations *(Prägung)* in those partializations of the symbolic alternative which give the symbolic chain its appearance. But we maintain that it is the specific law of that chain which governs those psychoanalytic effects that are decisive for the subject: such as foreclosure *(Verwerfung),* repression *(Verdrängung),* denial *(Verneinung)* itself—specifying with appropriate emphasis that these effects follow so faithfully the displacement *(Entstellung)* of the signifier that imaginary factors, despite their inertia, figure only as shadows and reflections in the process.[4]

But this emphasis would be lavished in vain, if it served, in your opinion, only to abstract a general type of phenomena whose particularity in our work would remain the essential thing for you, and whose original arrangement could be broken up only artificially.

Which is why we have decided to illustrate for you today the truth which may be drawn from that moment in Freud's thought under study—namely, that it is the symbolic order which is constitutive for the subject—by demonstrating in a story the decisive orientation which the subject receives from the itinerary of a signifier.[5]

It is that truth, let us note, which makes the very existence of fiction possible. And in that case, a fable is as appropriate as any other narrative for bringing it to light—at the risk of having the fable's coherence put to the test in the process. Aside from that reservation, a fictive tale even has the advantage of manifesting symbolic necessity more purely to the extent that we may believe its conception arbitrary.

Which is why, without seeking any further, we have chosen our example from the very story in which the dialectic of the game of even or odd—from whose study we have but recently profited—occurs.[6] It is, no doubt, no accident that this tale revealed itself propitious to pursuing a course of inquiry which had already found support in it.

As you know, we are talking about the tale which Baudelaire translated under the title: *La lettre volée.* At first reading, we may distinguish a drama, its narration, and the conditions of that narration.

We see quickly enough, moreover, that these components are necessary and that they could not have escaped the intentions of whoever composed them.

The narration, in fact, doubles the drama with a commentary without which no *mise en scène* would be possible. Let us say that the action would remain, properly speaking, invisible from the pit—aside from the fact that the dialogue would be expressly and by dramatic necessity devoid of whatever meaning it might have for an audience: in other words, nothing of the drama could be grasped, neither seen nor heard, without, dare we say, the twilighting which the narration, in each scene, casts on the point of view that one of the actors had while performing it.

There are two scenes, the first of which we shall straightway designate the primal scene, and by no means inadvertently, since the second may be considered its repetition in the very sense we are considering today.

The primal scene is thus performed, we are told, in the royal *boudoir,* so that we suspect that the person of the highest rank, called the "exalted personage," who is alone there when she receives a letter, is the Queen. This feeling is confirmed by the embarrassment into which she is plunged by the entry of the other exalted personage, of whom we have already been told prior to this account that the knowledge he might have of the letter in question would jeopardize for the lady nothing less than her honor and safety. Any doubt that he is in fact the King is promptly dissipated in the course of the scene which begins with the entry of the Minister D . . . At that moment, in fact, the Queen can do no better than to play on the King's inattentiveness by leaving the letter on the table "face down, address uppermost." It does not, however, escape the Minister's lynx eye, nor does he fail to notice the Queen's distress and thus to fathom her secret. From then on everything transpires like clockwork. After dealing in his customary manner with the business of the day, the Minister draws from his pocket a letter similar in appearance to the one in his view, and, having pretended to read it, he places it next to the other. A bit more conversation to amuse the royal company, whereupon, without flinching once, he seizes the embarrassing letter, making off with it, as the Queen, on whom none of his maneuver has been lost, remains unable to intervene for fear of attracting the attention of her royal spouse, close at her side at that very moment.

Everything might then have transpired unseen by a hypothetical spectator of an operation in which nobody falters, and whose *quotient* is that the Minister has filched from the Queen her letter and that—an even more important result than the first—the Queen knows that he now has it, and by no means innocently.

A *remainder* that no analyst will neglect, trained as he is to retain whatever is significant, without always knowing what to do with it: the letter, abandoned by the Minister, and which the Queen's hand is now free to roll into a ball.

Second scene: in the Minister's office. It is in his hotel, and we know—from the account the Prefect of police has given Dupin, whose specific genius for solving enigmas Poe introduces here for the second time—that the police, returning there as soon as the Minister's habitual, nightly absences allow them to, have searched the hotel and its surroundings from top to bottom for the last eighteen months. In vain—although everyone can deduce from the situation that the Minister keeps the letter within reach.

Dupin calls on the Minister. The latter receives him with studied nonchalance, affecting in his conversation romantic *ennui*. Meanwhile Dupin, whom this pretense does not deceive, his eyes protected by green glasses, proceeds to inspect the premises. When his glance catches a rather crumpled piece of paper—apparently thrust carelessly in a division of an ugly pasteboard card-rack, hanging gaudily from the middle of the mantelpiece—he already knows that he's found what he's looking for. His conviction is re-enforced by the very details which seem to contradict the description he has of the stolen letter, with the exception of the format, which remains the same.

Whereupon he has but to withdraw, after "forgetting" his snuff-box on the table, in order to return the following day to reclaim it—armed with a facsimile of the letter in its present state. As an incident in the street, prepared for the proper moment, draws the Minister to the window, Dupin in turn seizes the opportunity to snatch the letter while substituting the imitation, and has only to maintain the appearances of a normal exit.

Here as well all has transpired, if not without noise, at least without all commotion. The quotient of the operation is that the Minister no longer has the letter, but, far from suspecting that Dupin is the culprit who has ravished it from him, knows nothing of it. Moreover, what he is left with is far from insignificant for what follows. We shall return to what brought Dupin to inscribe a message on his counterfeit letter. Whatever the case, the Minister, when he tries to make use of it, will be able to read these words, written so that he may recognize Dupin's hand: ". . . *Un dessein si funeste / S'il n'est digne d'Atreé est digne de Thyeste*," whose source, Dupin tells us, is Crébillon's *Atreé*.[7]

Need we emphasize the similarity of these two sequences? Yes, for the resemblance we have in mind is not a simple collection of traits chosen only in order to delete their difference. And it would not be enough to retain those common traits at the expense of the others for the slightest truth to result. It is rather the intersubjectivity in which the two actions are motivated that we wish to bring into relief, as well as the three terms through which it structures them.[8]

The special status of these terms results from their corresponding simultaneously to the three logical moments through which the decision is precipitated and the three places it assigns to the subjects among whom it constitutes a choice.

That decision is reached in a glance's time.[9] For the maneuvers which follow, however stealthily they prolong it, add nothing to that glance, nor does the deferring of the deed in the second scene break the unity of that moment.

This glance presupposes two others, which it embraces in its vision of the breach left in their fallacious complementarity, anticipating in it the occasion for larceny afforded by that exposure. Thus three moments, structuring three glances, borne by three subjects, incarnated each time by different characters.

The first is a glance that sees nothing: the King and the police.

The second, a glance which sees that the first sees nothing and deludes itself as to the secrecy of what it hides: the Queen, then the Minister.

The third sees that the first two glances leave what should be hidden exposed to whomever would seize it: the Minister, and finally Dupin.

In order to grasp in its unity the intersubjective complex thus described, we would willingly seek a model in the technique legendarily attributed to the ostrich attempting to shield itself from danger; for that technique might ultimately be qualified as political, divided as it here is among three partners: the second believing itself invisible because the first has its head stuck in the ground, and all the while letting the third calmly pluck its rear; we need only enrich its proverbial denomination by a letter, producing *la politique de l'autruiche,* for the ostrich itself to take on forever a new meaning.[10]

Given the intersubjective modulus of the repetitive action, it remains to recognize in it a *repetition automatism* in the sense that interests us in Freud's text.

The plurality of subjects, of course, can be no objection for those who are long accustomed to the perspectives summarized by our formula: *the unconscious is the discourse of the Other.*[11] And we will not recall now what the notion of the *immixture of subjects,* recently introduced in our re-analysis of the dream of Irma's injection, adds to the discussion.

What interests us today is the manner in which the subjects relay each other in their displacement during the intersubjective repetition.

We shall see that their displacement is determined by the place which a pure signifier—the purloined letter—comes to occupy in their trio. And that is what will confirm for us its status as repetition automatism.

It does not, however, seem excessive, before pursuing this line of inquiry, to ask whether the thrust of the tale and interest we bring to it—to the extent that they coincide—do not lie elsewhere.

May we view as simply a rationalization (in our gruff jargon) the fact that the story is told to us as a police mystery?

In truth, we should be right in judging that fact highly dubious as soon as we note that everything which warrants such mystery concerning a crime or offense—its nature and motives, instruments and execution; the procedure used to discover the author, and the means employed to convict him—is carefully eliminated here at the start of each episode.

The act of deceit is, in fact, from the beginning as clearly known as the intrigues of the culprit and their effects on his victim. The problem, as exposed to us, is limited to the search for and restitution of the object of that deceit, and it seems rather intentional that the solution is already obtained when it is explained to us. Is *that* how we are kept in suspense? Whatever credit we may accord the conventions of a genre for provoking a specific interest in the reader, we should not forget that "the Dupin tale," this the second to appear, is a prototype, and that even if the genre were established in the first, it is still a little early for the author to play on a convention.[12]

It would, however, be equally excessive to reduce the whole thing to a fable whose moral would be that in order to shield from inquisitive eyes one of those correspondences whose secrecy is sometimes necessary to conjugal peace, it suffices to leave the crucial letters lying about on one's table, even though the meaningful side be turned face down. For that would be a hoax which, for out part, we would never recommend anyone try, lest he be gravely disappointed in his hopes.

Might there then be no mystery other than, concerning the Prefect, an incompetence issuing in failure—were it not perhaps, concerning Dupin, a certain dissonance we hesitate to acknowledge between, on the one hand, the admittedly penetrating, though, in their generality, not always quite relevant remarks with which he introduces us to his method and, on the other, the manner in which he in fact intervenes.

Were we to pursue this sense of mystification a bit further we might soon begin to wonder whether, from that initial scene which only the rank of the protagonists saves from vaudeville, to the fall into ridicule which seems to await the Minister at the end, it is not this impression that everyone is being duped which makes for our pleasure.

And we would be all the more inclined to think so in that we would recognize in that surmise, along with those of you who read us, the definition we once gave in passing of the modern hero, "whom ludicrous exploits exalt in circumstances of utter confusion."[13]

But are we ourselves not taken in by the imposing presence of the amateur detective, prototype of a latter-day swashbuckler, as yet safe from the insipidity of our contemporary *superman?*

A trick . . . sufficient for us to discern in this tale, on the contrary, so perfect a verisimilitude that it may be said that truth here reveals its fictive arrangement.

For such indeed is the direction in which the principles of that verisimilitude lead us. Entering into its strategy, we indeed perceive a new drama we may call complementary to the first, in so far as the latter was what is termed a play without words whereas the interest of the second plays on the properties of speech.[14]

If it is indeed clear that each of the two scenes of the real drama is narrated in the course of a different dialogue, it is only through access to those notions set forth in our teaching that one may recognize that it is not thus simply to augment the charm of the exposition, but that the dialogues themselves, in the opposite use they make of the powers of speech, take on a tension which makes of them a different drama, one which our vocabulary will distinguish from the first as persisting in the symbolic order.

The first dialogue—between the Prefect of police and Dupin—is played as between a deaf man and one who hears. That is, it presents the real complexity of what is ordinarily simplified, with the most confused results, in the notion of communication.

This example demonstrates indeed how an act of communication may give the impression at which theorists too often stop: of allowing in its transmission but a single meaning, as though the highly significant commentary into which he who understands integrates it, could, because unperceived by him who does not understand, be considered null.

It remains that if only the dialogue's meaning as a report is retained, its verisimilitude may appear to depend on a guarantee of exactitude. But here dialogue may be more fertile than seems, if we demonstrate its tactics: as shall be seen by focusing on the recounting of our first scene.

For the double and even triple subjective filter through which that scene comes to us: a narration by Dupin's friend and associate (henceforth to be called the general narrator of the story) of the account by which the Prefect reveals to Dupin the report the Queen gave him of it, is not merely the consequence of a fortuitous arrangement.

If indeed the extremity to which the original narrator is reduced precludes her altering any of the events, it would be wrong to believe that the Prefect is empowered to lend her his voice in this case only by that lack of imagination on which he has, dare we say, the patent.

The fact that the message is thus retransmitted assures us of what may by no means be taken for granted: that it belongs to the dimension of language.

Those who are here know our remarks on the subject, specifically those illustrated by the counter case of the so-called language of bees: in which a linguist[15] can see only a simple signaling of the location of objects, in other words: only an imaginary function more differentiated than others.

We emphasize that such a form of communication is not absent in man, however evanescent a naturally given object may be for him, split as it is in its submission to symbols.

Something equivalent may no doubt be grasped in the communion established between two persons in their hatred of a common object: except that the meeting is possible only over a single object, defined by those traits in the individual each of the two resists.

But such communication is not transmissible in symbolic form. It may be maintained only in the relation with the object. In such a manner it may bring together an indefinite number of subjects in a common "ideal": the communication of one subject with another within the crowd thus constituted will nonetheless remain irreducibly mediated by an ineffable relation.[16]

This digression is not only a recollection of principles distantly addressed to those who impute to us a neglect of non-verbal communication: in determining the scope of what speech repeats, it prepares the question of what symptoms repeat.

Thus the indirect telling sifts out the linguistic dimension, and the general narrator, by duplicating it, "hypothetically" adds nothing to it. But its role in the second dialogue is entirely different.

For the latter will be opposed to the first like those poles we have distinguished elsewhere in language and which are opposed like word to speech.

Which is to say that a transition is made here from the domain of exactitude to the register of truth. Now that register, we dare think we needn't come back to this, is situated entirely elsewhere, strictly speaking at the very foundation of intersubjectivity. It is located there where the subject can grasp nothing but the very subjectivity which constitutes an Other as absolute. We shall be satisfied here to indicate its place by evoking the dialogue which seems to us to merit its attribution as a Jewish joke by that state of privation through which the relation of signifier to speech appears in the entreaty which brings the dialogue to a close: "Why are you lying to me?" one character shouts breathlessly. "Yes, why do you lie to me saying you're going to Cracow so I should believe you're going to Lemberg, when in reality you *are* going to Cracow?"[17]

We might be prompted to ask a similar question by the torrent of logical impasses, eristic enigmas, paradoxes and even jests presented to us as an introduction to Dupin's method if the fact that they were confided to us by a would-be disciple did not endow them with a new dimension through that act of delegation. Such is the unmistakable magic of legacies: the witness's fidelity is the cowl which blinds and lays to rest all criticism of his testimony.

What could be more convincing, moreover, than the gesture of laying one's cards face up on the table? So much so that we are momentarily persuaded that the magician has in fact demonstrated, as he promised, how his trick was performed, whereas he has only renewed it in still purer form: at which point we fathom the measure of the supremacy of the signifier in the subject.

Such is Dupin's maneuver when he starts with the story of the child prodigy who takes in all his friends at the game of even and odd with his trick of identifying with the opponent, concerning which we have nevertheless shown that it cannot reach the first level of theoretical elaboration, namely: intersubjective alternation, without immediately stumbling on the buttress of its recurrence.[18]

We are all the same treated—so much smoke in our eyes—to the names of La Rochefoucauld, La Bruyère, Machiavelli and Campanella, whose renown, by this time, would seem but futile when confronted with the child's prowess.

Followed by Chamfort, whose maxim that "it is a safe wager that every public idea, every accepted convention is foolish, since it suits the greatest number," will no doubt satisfy all who think they escape its law, that is, precisely, the greatest number. That Dupin accuses the French of deception for applying the word *analysis* to algebra will hardly threaten our pride since, moreover, the freeing of that term for other uses ought by no means to provoke a psychoanalyst to intervene and claim his rights. And there he goes making philological remarks which should positively delight any lovers of Latin: when he recalls without deigning to say any more that "*ambitus* doesn't mean ambition, *religio,* religion, *homines honesti,* honest men," who among you would not take pleasure in remembering . . . what those words mean to anyone familiar with Cicero and Lucretius. No doubt Poe is having a good time. . . .

But a suspicion occurs to us: might not this parade of erudition be destined to reveal to us the key words of our drama? Is not the magician repeating his trick before our eyes, without deceiving us this time about divulging his secret, but pressing his wager to the point of really explaining it to us without us seeing a thing. *That* would be the summit of the illusionist's art: through one of his fictive creations to *truly delude us.*

And is it not such effects which justify our referring, without malice, to a number of imaginary heroes as real characters?

As well, when we are open to hearing the way in which Martin Heidegger discloses to us in the word *aletheia* the play of truth, we rediscover a secret to which truth has always initiated her lovers, and through which they learn that it is in hiding that she offers herself to them *most truly.*

Thus even if Dupin's comments did not defy us so blatantly to believe in them, we should still have to make that attempt against the opposite temptation.

Let us track down [*dépistons*] his footprints there where they elude [*dépiste*] us.[19] And first of all in the criticism by which he explains the Prefect's lack of success. We already saw it surface in those furtive gibes the Prefect, in the first conversation, failed to heed, seeing in them only a pretext for hilarity. That it is, as Dupin insinuates, because a problem is too simple, indeed too evident, that it may appear obscure, will never have any more bearing for him than a vigorous rub of the rib cage.

Everything is arranged to induce in us a sense of the character's imbecility. Which is powerfully articulated by the fact that he and his confederates never conceive of anything beyond what an ordinary rogue might imagine for hiding an object—that is, precisely the all too well known series of extraordinary hiding places: which are promptly catalogued for us, from hidden desk draws to removable table tops, from the detachable cushions of chairs to their hollowed out legs, from the reverse side of mirrors to the "thickness" of book bindings.

After which, a moment of derision at the Prefect's error in deducing that because the Minister is a poet, he is not far from being mad, an error, it is argued, which would consist, but this is hardly negligible, simply in a false distribution of the middle term, since it is far from following from the fact that all madmen are poets.

Yes indeed. But we ourselves are left in the dark as to the poet's superiority in the art of concealment—even if he be a mathematician to boot—since our pursuit is suddenly thwarted, dragged as we are into a thicket of bad arguments directed against the reasoning of mathematicians, who never, so far as I know, showed such devotion to their formulae as to identify them with reason itself. At least, let us testify that unlike what seems to be Poe's experience, it occasionally befalls us—with our friend Riguet, whose presence here is a guarantee that our incursions into combinatory analysis are not leading us astray—to hazard such serious deviations (virtual blasphemies, according to Poe) as to cast into doubt that "x^2 plus px is perhaps not absolutely equal to q," without ever—here we give the lie to Poe—having had to fend off any unexpected attack.

Is not so much intelligence being exercised then simply to divert our own from what had been indicated earlier as given, namely, that the police have looked *everywhere:* which we were to understand—vis-à-vis the area in which police, not without reason, assumed the letter might be found—in terms of a (no doubt theoretical) exhaustion of space, but concerning which the tale's piquancy depends on our accepting it literally: the division of the entire volume into numbered "compartments," which was the principle governing the operation, being presented to us as so precise that "the fiftieth part of a line," it is said, could not escape the probing of the investigators. Have we not then the right to ask how it happened that the letter was not found *anywhere,* or rather to observe that all we have been told of a more far-ranging conception of concealment does not explain, in all rigor, that the letter escaped detection, since the area combed did in fact contain it, as Dupin's discovery eventually proves.

Must a letter then, of all objects, be endowed with the property of *nullibiety:* to use a term which the thesaurus known as *Roget* picks up from the semiotic utopia of Bishop Wilkins?[20]

It is evident ("a little *too* self-evident")[21] that between *letter* and *place* exist relations for which no French word has quite the extension of the English adjective: *odd. Bizarre,* by which Baudelaire regularly translates it, is only approximate. Let us say that these relations are . . . *singuliers,* for they are the very ones maintained with place by the *signifier*.

You realize, of course, that our intention is not to turn them into "subtle" relations, nor is our aim to confuse letter with spirit, even if we receive the former by pneumatic dispatch, and that we readily admit that one kills whereas the other quickens, insofar as the signifier—you perhaps begin to understand—materializes the agency of death.[22] But if it is first of all on the materiality of the signifier that we have insisted, that materiality is *odd* [*singulière*] in many ways, the first of which is not to admit partition. Cut a letter in small pieces, and it remains the letter it is—and this in a completely different sense than *Gestalttheorie* would account for which the dormant vitalism informing its notion of the whole.[23]

Language delivers its judgment to whomever knows how to hear it: through the usage of the article as partitive particle. It is there that spirit—if spirit be living meaning—appears, no less oddly, as more available for quantification than its letter. To begin with meaning itself, which bears our saying: a speech rich with meaning ["plein *de* signification"], just as we recognize a measure of intention ["*de* l'intention"] in an act, or deplore that there is no more love ["plus *d'amour*"]; or store up hatred ["*de la* haine"] and expend devotion ["*du* dévouement"], and so much infatuation ["taint *d'*infatuation"] is easily reconciled to the fact that there will always be ass ["*de* la cuisse"] for sale and brawling ["*du* rififi"] among men.

But as for the letter—be it taken as typographical character, epistle, or what makes a man of letters—we will say that what is said is to be understood *to the letter* [*à la lettre*], that *a letter* [*une lettre*] awaits you at the post office, or even that you are acquainted with *letters* [*que vous avez des lettres*] —never that there is *letter* [*de la lettre*] anywhere, whatever the context, even to designate overdue mail.

For the signifier is a unit in its very uniqueness, being by nature symbol only of an absence. Which is why we cannot say of the purloined letter that, like other objects, it must be *or* not be in a particular place but that unlike them it will be *and* not be where it is, wherever it goes.[24]

Let us, in fact, look more closely at what happens to the police. We are spared nothing concerning the procedures used in searching the area submitted to their investigation: from the division of that space into compartments from which the slightest bulk could not escape detection, to needles probing upholstery, and, in the impossibility of sounding wood with a tap, to a microscope exposing the waste of any drilling at the surface of its hollow, indeed the infinitesimal gaping of the slightest abyss. As the network tightens to the point that, not satisfied with shaking the pages of books, the police take to counting them, do we not see space itself shed its leaves like a letter?

But the detectives have so immutable a notion of the real that they fail to notice that their search tends to transform it into its object. A trait by which they would be able to distinguish that object from all others.

This would no doubt be too much to ask them, not because of their lack of insight but rather because of ours. For their imbecility is neither of the individual nor the corporative variety; its source is subjective. It is the realist's imbecility, which does not pause to observe that nothing, however deep in the bowels of the earth a hand may seek to ensconce it, will ever be hidden there, since another hand can always retrieve it, and that what is hidden is never but what is *missing from its place,* as the call slip puts it when speaking of a volume lost in a library. And even if the book be on an adjacent shelf or in the next slot, it would be hidden there, however visibly it may appear. For it can *literally* be said that something is missing from its place only of what can change it: the symbolic. For the real, whatever upheaval we subject it to, is always in its place; it carries it glued to its heel, ignorant of what might exile it from it.

And, to return to our cops, who took the letter from the place where it was hidden, how could they have seized the letter? In what they turned between their fingers what did they hold but what *did not answer* to their description. "A letter, a litter": in Joyce's circle, they played on the homophony of the two words in English.[25] Nor does the seeming bit of refuse the police are now handling reveal its other nature for being but half torn. A different seal on a stamp of another color, the mark of a different handwriting in the superscription are here the most inviolable modes of concealment. And if they stop at the reverse side of the letter, on which, as is known, the recipient's address was written in that period, it is because the letter has for them no other side but its reverse.

What indeed might they find on its observe? Its message, as is often said to our cybernetic joy? . . . But does it not occur to us that this message has already reached its recipient and has even been left with her, since the insignificant scrap of paper now represents it no less well than the original note.

If we could admit that a letter has completed its destiny after fulfilling its function, the ceremony of returning letters would be a less common close to the extinction of the fires of love's feasts. The signifier is not functional. And the mobilization of the elegant society whose frolics we are following would as well have no meaning if the letter itself were content with having one. For it would hardly be an adequate means of keeping it secret to inform a squad of cops of its existence.

We might even admit that the letter has an entirely different (if no more urgent) meaning for the Queen than the one understood by the Minister. The sequence of events would not be noticeably affected, not even if it were strictly incomprehensible to an uninformed reader.

For it is certainly not so for everybody, since, as the Prefect pompously assures us, to everyone's derision, "the disclosure of the document to a third person, who shall be nameless," (that name which leaps to the eye like the pig's tail twixt the teeth of old Ubu) "would bring in question the honor of a personage of most exalted station, indeed that the honor and peace of the illustrious personage are so jeopardized."

In that case, it is not only the meaning but the text of the message which it would be dangerous to place in circulation, and all the more so to the extent that it might appear harmless, since the risks of an indiscretion unintentionally committed by one of the letter's holders would thus be increased.

Nothing then can redeem the police's position, and nothing would be changed by improving their "culture." *Scripta manent:* in vain would they learn from a *de luxe*-edition humanism the proverbial lesson which *verba volant* concludes. May it but please heaven that writings remain, as is rather the case with spoken words: for the indelible debt of the latter impregnates our acts with its transferences.

Writing scatter to the winds blank checks in an insane charge.[26] And were they not such flying leaves, there would be no purloined letters.[27]

But what of it? For a purloined letter to exist, we may ask, to whom does a letter belong? We stressed a moment ago the oddity implicit in returning a letter to him who had but recently given wing to its burning pledge. And we generally deem unbecoming such premature publications as the one by which the Chevalier d'Éon put several of his correspondents in a rather pitiful position.

Might a letter on which the sender retains certain rights then not quite belong to the person to whom it is addressed? or might it be that the latter was never the real receiver?

Let's take a look: we shall find illumination in what at first seems to obscure matters: the fact that the tale leaves us in virtually total ignorance of the sender, no less than of the contents, of the letter. We are told only that the Minister immediately recognized the handwriting of the address and only incidentally, in a discussion of the Minister's camouflage, is it said that the original seal bore the ducal arms of the S . . . family. As for the letter's bearing, we know only the dangers it entails should it come into the hands of a specific third party, and that its possession has allowed the Minister to "wield, to a very dangerous extent, for political purposes," the power it assures him over the interested party. But all this tells us nothing of the message it conveys.

Love letter or conspiratorial letter, letter of betrayal or letter of mission, letter of summons or letter of distress, we are assured of but one thing: the Queen must not bring it to the knowledge of her lord and master.

Now these terms, far from bearing the nuance of discredit they have in *bourgeois* comedy, take on a certain prominence through allusion to her sovereign, to whom she is bound by pledge of faith, and doubly so, since her role as spouse does not relieve her of her duties as subject, but rather elevates her to the guardianship of what royalty according to law incarnates of power: and which is called legitimacy.

From then on, to whatever vicissitudes the Queen may choose to subject the letter, it remains that the letter is the symbol of a pact, and that, even should the recipient not assume the pact, the existence of the letter situates her in a symbolic chain foreign to the one which constitutes her faith. This incompatibility is proven by the fact that the possession of the letter is impossible to bring forward publicly as legitimate, and that in order to have that possession respected, the Queen can invoke but her right to privacy, whose privilege is based on the honor that possession violates.

For she who incarnates the figure of grace and sovereignty cannot welcome even a private communication without power being concerned, and she cannot avail herself of secrecy in relation to the sovereign without becoming clandestine.

From then on, the responsibility of the author of the letter takes second place to that of its holder: for the offense to majesty is compounded by *high treason*.

We say: the *holder* and not the *possessor*. For it becomes clear that the addressee's proprietorship of the letter may be no less debatable than that of anyone else into whose hands it comes, for nothing concerning the existence of the letter can return to good order without the person whose prerogatives it infringes upon having to pronounce judgment on it.

All of this, however, does not imply that because the letter's secrecy is indefensible, the betrayal of that secret would in any sense be honorable. The *honesti homines,* decent people, will not get off so easily. There is more than one *religio,* and it is not slated for tomorrow that sacred ties shall cease to rend us in two. As for *ambitus:* a detour, we see, is not always inspired by ambition. For if we are taking one here, by no means is it stolen (the word is apt), since, to lay our cards on the table, we have borrowed Baudelaire's title in order to stress not, as is incorrectly claimed, the conventional nature of the signifier, but rather its priority in relation to the signified.[28] It remains, nevertheless, that Baudelaire, despite his devotion, betrayed Poe by translating as ''la lettre volée'' (the stolen letter) his title: the purloined letter, a title containing a word rare enough for us to find it easier to define its etymology than its usage.

To purloin, says the Oxford dictionary, is an Anglo-French word, that is: composed of the prefix *pur-,* found in *purpose, purchase, purport,* and of the Old French word: *loing, loigner, longé.* We recognize in the first element the Latin *pro-,* as opposed to *ante,* in so far as it presupposes a rear in front of which it is borne, possibly as its warrant, indeed even as its pledge (whereas *ante* goes forth to confront what it encounters). As for the second, an old French word: *loigner,* a verb attributing place *au loing* (or, still in use, *longé),* it does not mean *au loin* (far off), but *au long de* (alongside); it is a question then of *putting aside,* or, to invoke a familiar expression which plays on the two meanings: *mettre à gauche* (to put to the left; to put amiss).

Thus we are confirmed in our detour by the very object which draws us on into it: for we are quite simply dealing with a letter which has been diverted from its path; one whose course has been *prolonged* (etymologically, the word of the title), or, to revert to the language of the post office, a *letter in sufferance.*[29]

Here then, *simple and odd,* as we are told on the very first page, reduced to its simplest expression, is the singularity of the letter, which as the title indicates, is the *true subject* of the tale: since it can be diverted, it must have a course *which is proper to it:* the trait by which its incidence as signifier is affirmed. For we have learned to conceive of the signifier as sustaining itself only in a displacement comparable to that found in electric news strips or in the rotating memories of our machines-that-think-like men, this because of the alternating operation which is its principle, requiring it to leave its place, even though it returns to it by a circular path.[30]

This is indeed what happens in the repetition automatism. What Freud teaches us in the text we are commenting on is that the subject must pass through the channels of the symbolic, but what is illustrated here is more gripping still: it is not only the subject, but the subjects, grasped in their intersubjectivity, who line up, in other words our ostriches, to whom we here return, and who, more docile than sheep, model their very being on the moment of the signifying chain which traverses them.

If what Freud discovered and rediscovers with a perpetually increasing sense of shock has a meaning, it is that the displacement of the signifier determines the subjects in their acts, in their destiny, in their refusals, in their blindnesses, in their end and in their fate, their innate gifts and social acquisitions notwithstanding, without regard for character or sex, and that, willingly or not, everything that might be considered the stuff of psychology, kit and caboodle, will follow the path of the signifier.

Here we are, in fact, yet again at the crossroads at which we had left our drama and its round with the question of the way in which the subjects replace each other in it. Our fable is so constructed as to show that it is the letter and its diversion which governs their entries and roles. If *it* be "in sufferance," *they* shall endure the pain. Should they pass beneath its shadow, they become its reflection. Falling in possession of the letter—admirable ambiguity of language—its meaning possesses them.

So we are shown by the hero of the drama in the repetition of the very situation which his daring brought to a head, a first time, to his triumph. If he now succumbs to it, it is because he has shifted to the second position in the triad in which he was initially third, as well as the thief—and this by virtue of the object of his theft.

For if it is, now as before, a question of protecting the letter from inquisitive eyes, he can do nothing but employ the same technique he himself has already foiled: leave it in the open? And we may properly doubt that he knows what he is thus doing, when we see him immediately captivated by a dual relationship in which we find all the traits of a mimetic lure or of an animal feigning death, and, trapped in the typically imaginary situation of seeing that he is not seen, misconstrue the real situation in which he is seen not seeing.[31]

And what does he fail to see? Precisely the symbolic situation which he himself was so well able to see, and in which he is now seen seeing himself not being seen.

The Minister acts as a man who realizes that the police's search is his own defence, since we are told he allows them total access by his absences: he nonetheless fails to recognize that outside of that search he is no longer defended.

This is the very *autruicherie* whose artisan he was, if we may allow our monster to proliferate, but it cannot be by sheer stupidity that he now comes to be its dupe.[32]

For in playing the part of the one who hides, he is obliged to don the role of the Queen, and even the attributes of femininity and shadow, so propitious to the act of concealing.

Not that we are reducing the hoary couple of *Yin* and *Yang* to the elementary opposition of dark and light. For its precise use involves what is blinding in a flash of light, no less than the shimmering shadows exploit in order not to lose their prey.

Here sign and being, marvelously asunder, reveal which is victorious when they come into conflict. A man man enough to defy to the point of scorn a lady's fearsome ire undergoes to the point of metamorphosis the curse of the sign he had dispossessed her of.

For this sign is indeed that of woman, in so far as she invests her very being therein, founding it outside the law, which subsumes her nevertheless, originally, in a position of signifier, nay, of fetish.[33] In order to be worthy of the power of that sign she has but to remain immobile in its shadow, thus finding, moreover, like the Queen, that simulation of mastery in inactivity that the Minister's "lynx eye" alone was able to penetrate.

This stolen sign—here then is man in its possession: sinister in that such possession may be sustained only through the honor it defies, cursed in calling him who sustains it to punishment or crime, each of which shatters his vassalage to the Law.

There must be in this sign a singular *noli me tangere* for its possession, like the Socratic sting ray, to benumb its man to the point of making him fall into what appears clearly in his case to be a state of idleness.[34]

For in noting, as the narrator does as early as the first dialogue, that with the letter's use its power disappears, we perceive that this remark, strictly speaking, concerns precisely its use for ends of power—and at the same time that such a use is obligatory for the Minister.

To be unable to rid himself of it, the Minister indeed must not know what else to do with the letter. For that use places him in so total a dependence on the letter as such, that in the long run it no longer involves the letter at all.

We mean that for that use truly to involve the letter, the Minister, who, after all, would be so authorized by his service to his master the King, might present to the Queen respectful admonitions, even were he to assure their sequel by appropriate precautions,—or initiate an action against the author of the letter, concerning whom, the fact that he remains outside the story's focus reveals the extent to which it is not guilt and blame which are in question here, but rather that sign of contradiction and scandal constituted by the letter, in the sense in which the Gospel says that it must come regardless of the anguish of whomever serves as its bearer,—or even submit the letter as document in a dossier to a 'third person' qualified to know whether it will issue in a Star Chamber for the Queen or the Minister's disgrace.

We will not know why the Minister does not resort to any of these uses, and it is fitting that we don't, since the effect of this non-use alone concerns us; it suffices for us to know that the way in which the letter was acquired would pose no obstacle to any of them.

For it is clear that if the use of the letter, independent of its meaning, is obligatory for the Minister, its use for ends of power can only be potential, since it cannot become actual without vanishing in the process,—but in that case the letter exists as a means of power only through the final assignations of the pure signifier, namely: by prolonging its diversion, making it reach whomever it may concern through a supplementary transfer, that is, by an additional act of treason whose effects the letter's gravity makes it difficult to predict,—or indeed by destroying the letter, the only sure means, as Dupin divulges at the start, of being rid of what is destined by nature to signify the annulment of what it signifies.

The ascendancy which the Minister derives from the situation is thus not a function of the letter, but, whether he knows it or not, of the role it constitutes for him. And the Prefect's remarks indeed present him as someone "who dares all things," which is commented upon significantly: "those unbecoming as well as those becoming a man," words whose pungency escapes Baudelaire when he translates: "ce qui est indigne d'un homme aussi bien que ce qui est digne de lui" (those unbecoming a man as well as those becoming him). For in its original form, the appraisal is far more appropriate to what might concern a woman.

This allows us to see the imaginary import of the character, that is, the narcissistic relation in which the Minister is engaged, this time, no doubt, without knowing it. It is indicated as well as early as the second page of the English text by one of the narrator's remarks, whose form is worth savoring: the Minister's ascendancy, we are told, "would depend upon the robber's knowledge of the loser's knowledge of the robber.'' Words whose importance the author underscores by having Dupin repeat them literally after the narration of the scene of the theft of the letter. Here again we may say that Baudelaire is imprecise in his language in having one ask, the other confirm, in these words: ''Le voleur sait-il? . . .'' (Does the robber know?), then: ''Le voleur sait . . .'' (the robber knows). What? ''que la personne volée connaît son voleur'' (that the loser knows his robber).

For what matters to the robber is not only that the said person knows who robbed her, but rather with what kind of a robber she is dealing; for she believes him capable of anything, which should be understood as her having conferred upon him the position that no one is in fact capable of assuming, since it is imaginary, that of absolute master.

In truth, it is a position of absolute weakness, but not for the person of whom we are expected to believe so. The proof is not only that the Queen dares to call the police. For she is only conforming to her displacement to the next slot in the arrangement of the initial triad in trusting to the very blindness required to occupy that place: ''No more sagacious agent could, I suppose,'' Dupin notes ironically, ''be desired or even imagined.'' No, if she has taken that step, it is less out of being ''driven to despair,'' as we are told, than in assuming the charge of an impatience best imputed to a specular mirage.

For the Minister is kept quite busy confining himself to the idleness which is presently his lot. The Minister, in point of fact, is not *altogether* mad.[35] That's a remark made by the Prefect, whose every word is gold: it is true that the gold of his words flows only for Dupin and will continue to flow to the amount of the fifty thousand francs worth it will cost him by the metal standard of the day, though not without leaving him a margin of profit. The Minister then is not *altogether* mad in his insane stagnation, and that is why he will behave according to the mode of neurosis. Like the man who withdrew to an island to forget, what? he forgot,—so the Minister, through not making use of the letter, comes to forget it. As is expressed by the persistence of his conduct. But the letter, no more than the neurotic's unconscious, does not forget him. It forgets him so little that it transforms him more and more in the image of her who offered it to his capture, so that he now will surrender it, following her example, to a similar capture.

The features of that transformation are noted, and in a form so characteristic in their apparent gratuitousness that they might validly be compared to the return of the repressed.

Thus we first learn that the Minister in turn has *turned the letter over,* not, of course, as the Queen's hasty gesture, but, more assiduously, as one turns a garment inside out. So he must procede, according to the methods of the day for folding and sealing a letter, in order to free the virgin space on which to inscribe a new address.[36]

That address becomes his own. Whether it be in his hand or another, it will appear in an extremely delicate feminine script, and, the seal changing from the red of passion to the black of its mirrors, he will imprint his stamp upon it. This oddity of a letter marked with the recipient's stamp is all the more striking in its conception, since, though forcefully articulated in the text, it is not even mentioned by Dupin in the discussion he devotes to the identification of the letter.

Whether that omission be intentional or involuntary, it will surprise in the economy of a work whose meticulous rigor is evident. But in either case it is significant that the letter which the Minister, in point of fact, addresses to himself is a letter from a woman: as though this were a phase he had to pass through out of a natural affinity of the signifier.

Thus the aura of apathy, verging at times on an affectation of effeminacy; the display of an *ennui* bordering on disgust in his conversation; the mood the author of the philosophy of furniture[37] can elicit from virtually impalpable details (like that of the musical instrument on the table), everything seems intended for a character, all of whose utterances have revealed the most virile traits, to exude the oddest *odor di femina* when he appears.

Dupin does not fail to stress that this is an artifice, describing behind the bogus finery the vigilance of a beast of prey ready to spring. But that this is the very effect of the unconscious in the precise sense that we teach that the unconscious means that man is inhabited by the signifier: could we find a more beautiful image of it than the one Poe himself forges to help us appreciate Dupin's exploit? For with this aim in mind, he refers to those toponymical inscriptions which a geographical map, lest it remain mute, superimposes on its design, and which may become the object of a guessing game: who can find the name chosen by a partner?—noting immediately that the name most likely to foil a beginner will be one which, in large letters spaced out widely across the map, discloses, often without an eye pausing to notice it, the name of an entire country. . . .

Just so does the purloined letter, like an immense female body, stretch out across the Minister's office when Dupin enters. But just so does he already expect to find it, and has only, with his eyes veiled by green lenses, to undress that huge body.

And that is why without needing any more than being able to listen in at the door of Professor Freud, he will go straight to the spot in which lies and lives what the body is designed to hide, in a gorgeous center caught in a glimpse, nay, to the very place seducers name Sant' Angelo's Castle in their innocent illusion of controlling the City from within it. Look! between the cheeks of the fireplace, there's the object already in reach of a hand the ravisher has but to extend. . . . The question of deciding whether he seizes it above the mantelpiece as Baudelaire translates, or beneath it, as in the original text, may be abandoned without harm to the inferences of those whose profession is grilling.[38]

Were the effectiveness of symbols[39] to cease there, would it mean that the symbolic debt would as well be extinguished? Even if we could believe so, we would be advised of the contrary by two episodes which we may all the less dismiss as secondary in that they seem, at first sight, to clash with the rest of the work.

First of all, there's the business of Dupin's remuneration, which, far from being a closing *pirouette,* has been present from the beginning in the rather unselfconscious question he asks the Prefect about the amount of the reward promised him, and whose enormousness, the Prefect, however reticent he may be about the precise figure, does not dream of hiding from him, even returning later on to refer to its increase.

The fact that Dupin had been previously presented to us as a virtual pauper in his ethereal shelter ought rather to lead us to reflect on the deal he makes out of delivering the letter, promptly assured as it is by the check-book he produces. We do not regard it as negligible that the unequivocal hint through which he introduces the matter is a "story attributed to the character, as famous as it was excentric," Baudelaire tells us, of an English doctor named Abernethy, in which a rich miser, hoping to sponge upon him for a medical opinion, is sharply told not to take medicine, but to take advice.

Do we not in fact feel concerned with good reason when for Dupin what is perhaps at stake is his withdrawal from the symbolic circuit of the letter—we who become the emissaries of all the purloined letters which at least for a time remain in sufferance with us in the transference. And is it not the responsibility that their transference entails which we neutralize by equating it with the signifier most destructive of all signification, namely: money.

But that's not all. The profit Dupin so nimbly extracts from his exploit, if its purpose is to allow him to withdraw his stakes from the game, makes all the more paradoxical, even shocking, the partisan attack, the underhanded blow, he suddenly permits himself to launch against the Minister, whose insolent prestige, after all, would seem to have been sufficiently deflated by the trick Dupin has just played on him.

We have already quoted the atrocious lines Dupin claims he could not help dedicating, in his counterfeit letter, to the moment in which the Minister, enraged by the inevitable defiance of the Queen, will think he is demolishing her and will plunge into the abyss: *facilis descensus Averni,*[40] he waxes sententious, adding that the Minister cannot fail to recognize his handwriting, all of which, since depriving of any danger a merciless act of infamy, would seem, concerning a figure who is not without merit, a triumph without glory, and the rancor he invokes, stemming from an evil turn done him at Vienna (at the Congress?) only adds an additional bit of blackness to the whole.[41]

Let us consider, however, more closely this explosion of feeling, and more specifically the moment it occurs in a sequence of acts whose success depends on so cool a head.

It comes just after the moment in which the decisive act of identifying the letter having been accomplished, it may be said that Dupin already *has* the letter as much as if he had seized it, without, however, as yet being in a position to rid himself of it.

He is thus, in fact, fully participant in the intersubjective triad, and, as such, in the median position previously occupied by the Queen and the Minister. Will he, in showing himself to be above it, reveal to us at the same time the author's intentions?

If he has succeeded in returning the letter to its proper course, it remains for him to make it arrive at its address. And that address is in the place previously occupied by the King, since it is there that it would re-enter the order of the Law.

As we have seen, neither the King nor the Police who replaced him in that position were able to read the letter because that *place entailed blindness.*

Rex et augur, the legendary, archaic quality of the words seems to resound only to impress us with the absurdity of applying them to a man. And the figures of history, for some time now, hardly encourage us to do so. It is not natural for man to bear alone the weight of the highest of signifiers. And the place he occupies as soon as he dons it may be equally apt to become the symbol of the most outrageous imbecility.[42]

Let us say that the King here is invested with the equivocation natural to the sacred, with the imbecility which prizes none other than the Subject.[43]

That is what will give their meaning to the characters who will follow him in his place. Not that the police should be regarded as constitutionally illiterate, and we know the role of pikes planted on the *campus* in the birth of the State. But the police who exercise their functions here are plainly marked by the forms of liberalism, that is, by those imposed on them by masters on the whole indifferent to eliminating their indiscreet tendencies. Which is why on occasion words are not minced as to what is expected of them: "*Sutor ne ultra crepidam,* just take care of your crooks.[44] We'll even give you scientific means to do it with. That will help you not to think of truths you'd be better off leaving in the dark."[45]

We know that the relief which results from such prudent principles shall have lasted in history but a morning's time, that already the march of destiny is everywhere bringing back—a sequel to a just aspiration to freedom's reign —an interest in those who trouble it with their crimes, which occasionally goes so far as to forge its proofs. It may even be observed that this practice, which was always well received to the extent that it was exercised only in favor of the greatest number, comes to be authenticated in public confessions of forgery by the very ones who might very well object to it: the most recent manifestation of the pre-eminence of the signifer over the subject.

It remains, nevertheless, that a police record has always been the object of a certain reserve, of which we have difficulty understanding that it amply transcends the guild of historians.

It is by dint of this vanishing credit that Dupin's intended delivery of the letter to the Prefect of police will diminish its import. What now remains of the signifier when, already relieved of its message for the Queen, it is now invalidated in its text as soon as it leaves the Minister's hands?

It remains for it now only to answer that very question, of what remains of a signifier when it has no more signification. But this is the same question asked of it by the person Dupin now finds in the spot marked by blindness.

For that is indeed the question which has led the Minister there, if he be the gambler we are told and which his act sufficiently indicates. For the gambler's passion is nothing but that question asked of the signifier, figured by the *automaton* of chance.

"What are you, figure of the die I turn over in your encounter *(tychē)* with my fortune?[46] Nothing, if not that presence of death which makes of human life a reprieve obtained from morning to morning in the name of meanings whose sign is your crook. Thus did Scheherazade for a thousand and one nights, and thus have I done for eighteen months, suffering the ascendancy of this sign at the cost of a dizzying series of fraudulent turns at the game of even or odd.''

So it is that Dupin, *from the place he now occupies,* cannot help feeling a rage of manifestly feminine nature against him who poses such a question. The prestigious image in which the poet's inventiveness and the mathematician's rigor joined up with the serenity of the dandy and the elegance of the cheat suddenly becomes, for the very person who invited us to savor it, the true *monstrum horrendum,* for such are his words, ''an unprincipled man of genius.''

It is here that the origin of that horror betrays itself, and he who experiences it has no need to declare himself (in a most unexpected manner) ''a partisan of the lady'' in order to reveal it to us: it is known that ladies detest calling principles into question, for their charms owe much to the mystery of the signifier.

Which is why Dupin will at last turn toward us the medusoid face of the signifier nothing but whose obverse anyone except the Queen has been able to read. The commonplace of the quotation is fitting for the oracle that face bears in its grimace, as is also its source in tragedy: ''. . . *Un destin si funeste, / S'il n'est digne d'Atrée, est digne de Thyese.*''[47]

So runs the signifier's answer, above and beyond all significations: ''You think you act when I stir you at the mercy of the bonds through which I knot your desires. Thus do they grow in force and multiply in objects, bringing you back to the fragmentation of your shattered childhood. So be it: such will be your feast until the return of the stone guest I shall be for you since you call me forth.''

Or, to return to a more moderate tone, let us say, as in the quip with which—along with some of you who had followed us to the Zurich Congress last year—we rendered homage to the local password, the signifier's answer to whomever interrogates it is: ''Eat your Dasein.''

Is that then what awaits the Minister at a rendez-vous with destiny? Dupin assures us of it, but we have already learned not to be too credulous of his diversions.

No doubt the brazen creature is here reduced to the state of blindness which is man's in relation to the letters on the wall that dictate his destiny. But what effect, in calling him to confront them, may we expect from the sole provocations of the Queen, on a man like him? Love or hatred. The former is blind and will make him lay down his arms. The latter is lucid, but will awaken his suspicions, But if he is truly the gambler we are told he is, he will consult his cards a final time before laying them down and, upon reading his hand, will leave the table in time to avoid disgrace.[48]

Is that all, and shall we believe we have deciphered Dupin's real strategy above and beyond the imaginary tricks with which he was obliged to deceive us? No doubt, yes, for if "any point requiring reflection," as Dupin states at the start, is "examined to best purpose in the dark,"we may now easily read its solution in broad daylight. It was already implicit and easy to derive from the title of our tale, according to the very formula we have long submitted to your discretion: in which the sender, we tell you, receives from the receiver his own message in reverse form. Thus it is that what the "purloined letter," nay, the "letter in sufferance" means is that a letter always arrives at its destination.

NOTES

1. The translation of repetition *automatism*—rather than *compulsion*—is indicative of Lacan's speculative effort to reinterpret Freudian "overdetermination" in terms of the laws of probability. (Chance is *automaton*, a "cause not revealed to human thoughts," in Aristotle's *Physics*.) Whence the importance assumed by the Minister's passion for gambling later in Lacan's analysis. Cf. *Ecrits*, pp. 41–61).—Ed.
2. Cf. Heidegger, *Vom Wesen dar Wahrheit*. Freedom, in this essay, is perceived as an "exposure." *Dasein* ex-sists, stands out "into the disclosure of what is." It is *Dasein*'s "ex-sistent in-sistence" which preserves the disclosure of beings.—Ed.
3. For the meanings Lacan attributes to the terms *imaginary* and *symbolic*, sees entries in *The Language of Psychoanalysis* (Laplanche and Pontalis; N.Y.: Norton, 1973), also reproduced in the appendices, *Yale French Studies*, 48, 1972.—Ed.
4. For the notion of *foreclosure*, the defence mechanism specific to psychosis, see *The Language of Psychoanalysis* (Laplanche and Pontalis) or in the appendices, *Yale French Studies*, 48, 1972.—Ed.
5. For the notion of the signifier (and its relation to the Freudian "memory trace,") see J. Mehlman, "The Floating Signifier: From Lévi-Strauss to Lacan," *Yale French Studies;* 48, 1972.—Ed.
6. Lacan's analysis of the guessing game in Poe's tale entails demonstrating the insufficiency of an *imaginary* identification with the opponent as opposed to the *symbolic* process of an identification with his "reasoning." See *Écrits*, p. 59.—Ed.
7. "So infamous a scheme, / If not worthy of Atreus, is worthy of Thyestes." The lines from Atreus's monologue in Act V, Scene V of Crébillon's play refer to his plan to avenge himself by serving his brother the blood of the latter's own son to drink.—Ed.
8. This intersubjective setting which coordinates three terms is plainly the Oedipal situation. The illusory security of the initial *dyad* (King and Queen in the first sequence) will be shattered by the introduction of a *third* term.—Ed.
9. The necessary reference here may be found in "Le Temps logique et l'Assertion de la certitude anticipée," *Écrits*, p. 197.

10. *La politique de l'autruiche* condenses ostrich *(autruche),* other people (autrui), and (the politics of) Austria *(Autriche).*—Ed.
11. Such would be the crux of the Oedipus complex: the assumption of a desire which is originally another's, and which, in its displacements, is perpetually other than "itself."—Ed.
12. The first "Dupin tale" was "The Murders in the Rue Morgue."—Ed.
13. Cf. "Fonction et champ de la parole et du langage" in *Écrits.* Translated by A. Wilden, *The Language of the Self* (Baltimore; Johns Hopkins University Press, 1968).
14. The complete understanding of what follows presupposes a rereading of the short and easily available text of "The Purloined Letter."
15. Cf. Emile Benveniste, "Communication animale et langage humain," *Diogène,* No. 1, and our address in Rome, *Ecrits,* p. 178.
16. For the notion of *ego ideal,* see Freud, *Group Psychology and the Analysis of the Ego* (1921, Standard Edition, vol. 18).—Ed.
17. Freud comments on this joke in *Jokes and Their Relation to the Unconscious,* (1905, Standard Edition, vol. 8) p. 115: "But the more serious substance of the joke is what determines the truth. . . . Is it the truth if we describe things as they are without troubling to consider how our hearer will understand what we say? . . . I think that jokes of that kind are sufficiently different from the rest to be given a special position: What they are attacking is not a person or an institution but the certainty of our knowledge itself, one of our speculative possessions." Lacan's text may be regarded as a commentary on Freud's statement, an examination of the corrosive effect of the demands of an intersubjective communicative situation on any naive notion of "truth."—Ed.
18. Cf. *Écrits.* p. 58. "But what will happen at the following step (of the game) when the opponent, realizing that I am sufficiently clever to follow him in his move, will show his own cleverness by realizing that it is by playing the fool that he has the best chance to deceive me? From then on my reasoning is invalidated, since it can only be repeated in an indefinite oscillation . . ."
19. We should like to present again to M. Benveniste the question of the antithetical sense of (primal or other) words after the magisterial rectification he brought to the erroneous philological path on which Freud engaged it (cf. *La Psychanalyse,* vol. 1, pp. 5–16). For we think that the problem remains intact once the instance of the signifier has been evolved. Bloch and Von Wartburg date at 1875 the first appearance of the meaning of the verb *dépister* in the second use we make of it in our sentence.
20. The very one to which Jorge Luis Borges, in works which harmonize so well with the phylum of our subject, has accorded an importance which others have reduced to its proper proportions. Cf. *Les Temps modernes,* June–July 1955. pp. 2135–36 and Oct. 1955, pp. 574–75.
21. Underlined by the author.
22. The reference is to the "death instinct," whose "death," we should note, lies entirely in its diacritical opposition to the "life" of a naive vitalism or naturalism. As such, it may be compared with the logical moment in Lévi-Strauss's thought whereby "nature" exceeds, supplements, and symbolizes itself: the prohibition of incest.—Ed.
23. This is so true that philosophers, in those hackneyed examples with which they argue on the basis of the single and the multiple, will not use to the same purpose a simple sheet of white paper ripped in the middle and a broken circle, indeed a shattered vase, not to mention a cut worm.
24. Cf. Saussure, *Cours de linguistique générale,* Paris, 1969, [*Course in general linguistics.* N.Y.: McGraw Hill, 1966. Originally pub. 1916] p. 166: "The preceding amounts to

saying that *in language there are only differences*. Even more: a difference presupposes in general positive terms between which it is established, but in language there are only differences *without positive terms*."—Ed.

25. Cf. *Our Examination Round his Factification for Incamination of Work in Progress,* Shakespeare & Co., 12 rue de l'Odéon, Paris, 1929.
26. The original sentence presents an exemplary difficulty in translation: "Les écrits emportent au vent les traites en blanc d'une cavalerie folle." The blank (bank) drafts (or transfers) are not delivered to their rightful recipients (the sense of *de cavalerie, de complaisance*). That is: in analysis, one finds absurd symbolic debts being paid to the "wrong" persons. At the same time, the mad, driven quality of the payment is latent in *traite,* which might also refer to the day's trip of an insane cavalry. In our translation, we have displaced the "switch-word"—joining the financial and equestrian series—from *traite* to *charge*.—Ed.
27. *Flying leaves* (also fly-sheets) and *purloined letters—feuilles volantes* and *lettres volées*—employ different meanings of the same word in French.—Ed.
28. See discussion of Lévi-Strauss's statement—"the signifier precedes and determines the signified"—in Mehlman, op. cit. (note 5)—Ed.
29. We revive this archaism (for the French: *lettre en souffrance*). The sense is a letter held up in the course of delivery. In French, of course, *en souffrance* means in a state of suffering as well.—Ed.
30. See *Écrits,* p. 59: ". . . it is not unthinkable that a modern computer, by discovering the sentence which modulates without his knowing it and over a long period of time the choices of a subject, would win beyond any normal proportion at the game of even and odd . . ."
31. See note 3—Ed.
32. *Autruicherie* condenses, in addition to the previous terms, deception *(tricherie)*. Do we not find in Lacan's proliferating "monster" something of the *proton pseudos,* the "first lie"of Freud's 1895 *Project:* the persistent illusion which seems to structure the mental life of the patient?—Ed.
33. The fetish, as replacement for the missing maternal phallus, at once masks and reveals the scandal of sexual difference. As such it is the analytic object *par excellence*. The female temptation to exhibitionism, understood as a desire to *be* the (maternal) phallus, is thus tantamount to being a fetish.—Ed.
34. See Plato's *Meno:* "Socrates, . . . at this moment I feel you are exercising magic and witchcraft upon me and positively laying me under your spell until I am just a mass of helplessness. If I may be flippant, I think that not only in outward appearance but in other respects as well you are like the flat sting ray that one meets in the sea. Whenever anyone comes into contact with it, it numbs him, and that is the sort of thing you are doing to me now . . ."—Ed.
35. Baudelaire translates Poe's "*altogether* a fool" as "*absolument* fou." In opting for Baudelaire, Lacan is enabled to allude to the realm of psychosis.—Ed.
36. We felt obliged to demonstrate the procedure to an audience with a letter from the period concerning M. de Chateaubriand and his search for a secretary. We were amused to find that M. de Chateaubriand completed the first version of his recently restored memoirs in the very month of November 1841 in which the purloined letter appeared in *Chamber's Journal*. Might M. de Chateaubriand's devotion to the power he decries and the honor which that devotion bespeaks in him (*the gift* had not yet been invented), place him in the category to which we will later see the Minister assigned: among men of genius with or without principles?
37. Poe is the author of an essay with this title.
38. And even to the cook herself.—J. L.

The paragraph might be read as follows: analysis, in its violation of the imaginary integrity of the ego, finds its fantasmatic equivalent in rape (or castration.) But whether that "rape" takes place from in front or from behind (above or below the mantelpiece) is, in fact, a question of interest for policemen and not analysts. Implicit in the statement is an attack on those who have become wed to the ideology of "maturational development" (libidinal stages *et al*) in Freud (i.e., the ego psychologists).—Ed.

39. The allusion is to Lévi-Strauss's article of the same title ("L'efficacité symbolique") in *L'Anthropologie structurale*.—Ed.
40. Virgil's line reads: *facilis descensus Averno.*
41. Cf. Corneille, *Le Cid* (II, 2): "A vaincre sans péril, on triomphe sans gloire." (To vanquish without danger is to triumph without glory).—Ed.
42. We recall the witty couplet attributed before his fall to the most recent in date to have ralllied Candide's meeting in Venice:

    "Il n'est plus aujourd'hui que cinq rois sur la terre,
    Les quatre rois des cartes et le roi d'Angleterre."

    (There are only five kings left on earth: four kings of cards and the king of England.)
43. For the antithesis of the "sacred," see Freud's "The Antithetical Sense of Primal Words." *S.E.*, 11. The idiom *tenir á* in this sentence means both to prize and to be a function of. The two senses—King and / as Subject—are implicit in Freud's frequent allusions to "His Majesty the Ego."—Ed.
44. From Pliny, 35, 10, 35: "A cobbler not beyond his sole . . ."—Ed.
45. This proposal was openly presented by a noble Lord speaking to the Upper Chamber in which his dignity earned him a place.
46. We note the fundamental opposition Aristotle makes between the two terms recalled here in the conceptual analysis of chance he gives in his *Physics*. Many discussions would be illuminated by a knowledge of it.
47. Lacan misquotes Crébillion (as well as Poe and Baudelaire) here by writing *destin* (destiny) instead of *dessein* (scheme). As a result he is free to pursue his remarkable development on the tragic Don Juan ("multiply in objects . . . stone guest").—Ed.
48. Thus nothing shall (have) happen(ed)—the final turn in Lacan's theatre of lack. Yet within the simplicity of that empty present the most violent of (pre-)Oedipal dramas—Atreus, Thyestes—shall silently have played itself out.—Ed.

13. The Case of Poe: Applications/Implications of Psychoanalysis

Shoshana Felman

Lacan's first collection of published essays, the *Ecrits*, opens with a chapter entitled "The Seminar on *The Purloined Letter*." This so-called "Seminar" is the written account of a year-long course devoted to the exploration of a short literary text, one of Edgar Allan Poe's *Extraordinary Tales*, "The Purloined Letter." The Seminar was offered to trainees in psychoanalysis. Why did Lacan choose to devote a whole year of teaching to this tale? What is the significance of the strategic decision to place this "Seminar" at the opening of the *Ecrits*, as a key work in Lacan's endeavor?

I will approach these questions indirectly, by meditating first on the "case of Poe" in the literary investigations of psychology and psychoanalysis before Lacan. I will then attempt to analyze both the difference that Lacan has made in the psychoanalytical approach to reading and the way in which the lesson Lacan derived from Poe is a lesson in psychoanalysis.

To account for poetry in psychoanalytical terms has traditionally meant to analyze poetry as a symptom of a particular poet. I would here like to reverse this approach, and to analyze a particular poet as a symptom of poetry.

Perhaps no poet has been so highly acclaimed and, at the same time, so violently disclaimed as Edgar Allan Poe. One of the most controversial figures on the American literary scene, "perhaps the most thoroughly misunderstood of all American writers,"[1] "a stumbling block for the judicial critic,"[2] no other poet in the history of criticism has engendered so much disagreement and so many critical contradictions. It is my contention that this critical disagreement is itself symptomatic of a *poetic effect*, and that the

Reprinted by permission from Shoshana Felman, *Jacques Lacan and the Adventure of Insight: Psychoanalysis in Contemporary Culture*, Harvard University Press, 1987.

critical contradictions to which Poe's poetry has given rise are themselves indirectly significant of the nature of poetry.

THE POE-ETIC EFFECT: A LITERARY CASE HISTORY

No other poet has been so often referred to as a "genius," in a sort of common consensus shared even by his detractors. Joseph Wood Krutch, whose study tends to belittle Poe's stature and to disparage the value of his artistic achievement, nevertheless entitles his monograph *Edgar Allan Poe: A Study in Genius.*[3] So do many other critics, who acknowledge and assert Poe's "genius" in the very titles of their essays.[4] "It happens to us but few times in our lives," writes Thomas Wentworth Higginson, "to come consciously into the presence of that extraordinary miracle we call genius. Among the many literary persons whom I have happened to meet . . . there are not half a dozen who have left an irresistible sense of this rare quality; and among these few, Poe."[5] The English poet Swinburne speaks of "the special quality of [Poe's] strong and delicate genius"; the French poet Mallarmé describes his translations of Poe as "a monument to the genius who . . . exercised his influence in our country"; and the American poet James Russell Lowell, one of Poe's harshest critics, who, in his notorious versified verdict, judged Poe's poetry to include "two fifths sheer fudge," nonetheless asserts, "Mr. Poe has that indescribable something which men have agreed to call *genius* . . . Let talent writhe and contort itself as it may, it has no such magnetism. Larger of bone and sinew it may be, but the wings are wanting."[6]

However suspicious and unromantic the critical reader might wish to be with respect to "the indescribable something which men have agreed to call genius," it is clear that Poe's poetry produces what might be called a *genius effect:* the impression of some undefinable but compelling force to which the reader is subjected. To describe "this power, *which is felt,*"[7] as one reader puts it, Lowell speaks of "magnetism"; other critics speak of "magic." "Poe," writes Bernard Shaw, "constantly and inevitably produced magic where his greatest contemporaries produced only beauty."[8] T. S. Eliot quite reluctantly agrees: "Poe had, to an exceptional degree, the feeling for the incantatory element in poetry, of that which may, in the most nearly literal sense, be called 'the magic of verse.' "[9]

Poe's "magic" is thus ascribed to the ingenuity of his versification, to his exceptional technical virtuosity. And yet the word *magic,* "in the most nearly literal sense,'' means much more than just the intellectual acknowledgment of an outstanding technical skill; it connotes the effective action of something that exceeds both the understanding and the control of the person who is subjected to it; it connotes a force to which the reader has no choice but to submit. ''No one could tell us what it is,'' writes Lowell, still in reference to Poe's genius, ''and yet there is none who is not inevitably aware of . . . its power'' (p. 11). ''Poe,'' said Shaw, ''inevitably produced magic.'' Something about Poe's poetry is experienced as inevitable, unavoidable (and not just as irresistible). What is more, once this poetry is read, its inevitability is there to stay; it becomes lastingly inevitable: ''it will stick to the memory of every one who reads it,'' writes P. Pendleton Cooke (p. 23). And Eliot: ''Poe is the author of a few . . . short poems . . . which do somehow stick in the memory'' (pp. 207–8).

This is why Poe's poetry can be defined, and indeed has been, as a poetry of influence par excellence, in the sense emphasized by Harold Bloom: ''to inflow,'' or to have power over another. The case of Poe in literary history could in fact be accounted for as an extreme and complex case of ''the anxiety of influence,'' of the anxiety unwittingly provoked by the ''influence'' irresistibly emanating from this poetry. What is unique, however, about Poe's influence, as about the magic of his verse, is the extent to which its action is unaccountably insidious, exceeding the control, the will, and the awareness of those who are subjected to it. Eliot writes:

> Poe's influence is . . . puzzling. In France the influence of his poetry and of his poetic theories has been immense. In England and America it seems almost negligible . . . And yet one cannot be sure that one's own writing has *not* been influenced by Poe. (p. 205; original italics)

Studying Poe's influence on Baudelaire, Mallarmé, and Valéry, Eliot goes on to comment:

> Here are three literary generations, representing almost exactly a century of French poetry. Of course, these are poets very different from each other . . . But I think we can trace the development and descent of one particular theory of the nature of poetry through these three poets and it is a theory which takes its origin in the theory . . . of Edgar Poe. And the impression we get of the influence of Poe is the more impressive, because of the fact that Mallarmé, and Valéry in turn, did not merely derive from Poe through Baudelaire: each of them subjected himself to that influence directly, and has left convincing evidence of the value which he attached to the theory and practice of Poe himself. (p. 206; original italics)

Curiously enough, while Poe's worldwide importance and effective influence is beyond question, critics nonetheless continue to protest and to proclaim, as loudly as they can, that Poe is unimportant, that Poe is *not* a major poet. Taxing Poe with ''vulgarity,'' Aldous Huxley argues:

Was Edgar Allan Poe a major poet? It would surely never occur to any English-speaking critic to say so. And yet, in France, from 1850 till the present time, the best poets of each generation—yes, and the best critics, too; for, like most excellent poets, Baudelaire, Mallarmé, Paul Valéry are also admirable critics—have gone out of their way to praise him. . . . We who are speakers of English . . . , we can only say, with all due respect, that Baudelaire, Mallarmé, and Valéry were wrong and that Poe is not one of our major poets. (*Recognition,* p. 160).

Poe's detractors seem to be unaware, however, of the paradox that underlies their enterprise: it is by no means clear why anyone should take the trouble to write—at length—about a writer of no importance. Poe's most systematic denouncer, Ivor Winters, thus writes:

The menace lies not, primarily, in his impressionistic admirers among literary people of whom he still has some, even in England and in America, where a familiarity with his language ought to render his crudity obvious, for these individuals in the main do not make themselves permanently very effective: it lies rather in the impressive body of scholarship . . . When a writer is supported by a sufficient body of such scholarship, a very little philosophical elucidation will suffice to establish him in the scholarly world as a writer whose greatness is self-evident. (*Recognition,* p. 177)

The irony here is that, in writing his attack on Poe, what the attacker is in fact doing is adding still another study to the bulk of ''the impressive body of scholarship'' in which, in his own terms, ''the menace lies''; so that, paradoxically enough, through Winters' study, the menace—that is, the possibility of taking Poe's ''greatness as a writer'' as ''self-evident''—will indeed increase. I shall argue that, regardless of the value-judgment it may pass on Poe, this impressive bulk of Poe scholarship, the very quantity of the critical literature to which Poe's poetry has given rise, is itself an indication of its effective poetic power, of the strength with which it drives the reader to an *action,* compels him to a *reading act.* The elaborate written denials of Poe's value, the loud and lengthy negations of his importance, are therefore very like psychoanalytical negations. It is clear that if Poe's text in effect were unimportant, it would not seem so important to proclaim, argue, and prove that he is unimportant. The fact that it so much *matters* to proclaim that Poe *does not matter* is but evidence of the extent to which Poe's poetry is, in effect, a poetry that matters.

Poe might thus be said to have a *literary case history,* most revealing in that it incarnates, in its controversial forms, the paradoxical nature of a strong poetic effect: the very poetry that, more than any other, is experienced as *irresistible* has also proved to be, in literary history, the poetry most *resisted,* the one that, more than any other, has provoked resistances.

This apparent contradiction, which makes of Poe's poetry a unique case in literary history, clearly partakes of the paradoxical nature of an *analytical effect.* The enigma it presents us with is the enigma of the analytical par excellence, as stated by Poe himself, whose amazing institutions of the nature of what he calls "analysis" are strikingly similar to the later findings of psychoanalysis: "The mental features discoursed of as the analytical are, in themselves, but little susceptible of analysis. We appreciate them only in their effects."[10]

Because of the very nature of its strong effects, of the reading-acts that it provokes, Poe's text (and not just Poe's biography of his personal neurosis) is clearly an analytical case in the history of literary criticism, a case that suggests something crucial to understand in psychoanalytic terms. It is therefore not surprising that Poe has been repeatedly singled out for psychoanalytical research, has persistently attracted the attention of psychoanalytic critics.

THE PSYCHOANALYTICAL APPROACHES

The best-known and most influential psychoanalytic studies of Poe are the 1926 study by Joseph Wood Krutch and the 1933 study by Marie Bonaparte, *Edgar Poe: Etude psychanalytique.*[11] Through a brief summary of the psychoanalytic issues raised by these two works, I will attempt to analyze the methodological presuppositions guiding their approaches (their "application" of psychoanalysis), in order to compare them later to Lacan's strikingly different approach in his methodologically unprecedented "Seminar on *The Purloined Letter,*" published in 1966.[12]

Joseph Wood Krutch: Ideological Psychology, or the Approach of Normative Evaluation

For Krutch, Poe's text is nothing other than an accurate transcription of a severe neurosis, a neurosis whose importance and significance for "healthy" people is admittedly unclear. Poe's "position as the first of the great neurotics has never been questioned,'' writes Krutch ambiguously. And less ambiguously, in reply to some admiring French definitions of that position: ''Poe 'first inaugurated the poetic conscience' only if there is no true poetry except the poetry of morbid sensibility.'' Since Poe's works, according to Krutch, ''bear no conceivable relation . . . to the life of any people, and it is impossible to account for them on the basis of any social or intellectual tendencies or as the expression of the spirit of any age'' (p. 210), the only possible approach is a biographical one, and ''any true understanding'' of the work is contingent upon a diagnosis of Poe's nervous malady. Krutch thus diagnoses in Poe a pathological condition of sexual impotence, the result of a fixation on his mother, and explains Poe's literary drive as a desire to compensate for, on the one hand, the loss of social position of which his foster father had deprived him, through the acquisition of literary fame and, on the other hand, his incapacity to have normal sexual relations, through the creation of a fictional world of horror and destruction where he found refuge. Poe's fascination with logic would thus be merely an attempt to prove himself rational when he felt he was going insane; and his critical theory merely an attempt to justify his peculiar artistic practice.

The obvious limitations of such a psychoanalytic approach were very sharply and accurately pointed out by Edmund Wilson in his essay ''Poe at Home and Abroad.'' Krutch, argues Wilson, seriously misunderstands and undervalues Poe's writings, in

> complacently caricaturing them—as the modern school of social psychological biography, of which Mr. Krutch is a typical representative, seems inevitably to tend to caricature the personalities of its subjects. We are nowadays being edified by the spectacle of some of the principal ornaments of the human race exhibited exclusively in terms of their most ridiculous manias, their most disquieting neurosis, and their most humiliating failures. (*Recognition,* p. 144)

It is, in other words, the reductionist, stereotypical simplification under which Krutch subsumes the complexities of Poe's art and life that renders this approach inadequate:

> Mr. Krutch quotes with disapproval the statement of President Hadley of Yale, in explaining the refusal of the Hall of Fame to accept Poe among its immortals: ''Poe wrote like a drunkard and a man who is not accustomed to pay his debts''; and yet Mr. Krutch himself . . . is almost as unperceptive when he tells us, in effect, that Poe wrote like a dispossessed Southern gentleman and a man with a fixation on his mother. (p. 145)

Subscribing to Wilson's criticism, I would like to indicate briefly some further limitations in this type of psychoanalytic approach to literature. Krutch himself, in fact, points out some of the limits of his method in his conclusion:

> We have, then, traced Poe's art to an abnormal condition of the nerves and his critical ideas to a rationalized defense of the limitations of his own taste . . . The question whether or not the case of Poe represents an exaggerated example of the process by which all creation is performed is at best an open question. The extent to which all imaginative works are the result of the unfulfilled desires which spring from either idiosyncratic or universally human maladjustments to life is only beginning to be investigated, and with it is linked the related question of the extent to which all critical principles are at bottom the systematized and rationalized expression of instinctive tastes which are conditioned by causes often unknown to those whom they affect. The problem of finding an answer to these questions . . . is the one distinctly new problem which the critic of today is called upon to consider. He must, in a word, endeavor to find the relationship which exists between psychology and aesthetics. (pp. 234–35)

This, indeed, is the real question, the real challenge that Poe as poet (and not as psychotic) presents to the psychoanalytic critic. But this is precisely the question that is never dealt with in Krutch's study. Krutch discards the question by saying that "the present state of knowledge is not such as to enable" us to give any answers. This remark, however, presupposes that the realm of aesthetics, of literature and art, might not itself contain some knowledge about precisely, "the relationship between psychology and aesthetics"; it presupposes knowledge as a given, external to the literary object and imported into it, and not as a result of a reading-process, that is, of the critic's work upon and with the literary text. It presupposes, furthermore, that a critic's task is not to question but to answer, and that a question that cannot be answered, can also therefore not be asked; that to raise a question, to articulate its thinking power, is not itself a fruitful step that takes some work, some doing, into which the critic could perhaps be guided by the text.

Thus, in claiming that he has traced "Poe's art to an abnormal condition of the nerves," and that Poe's "criticism falls short of psychological truth," Krutch believes that his own work is opposed to Poe's as health is opposed to sickness, as normality is opposed to abnormality, as truth is opposed to delusion. But this ideologically determined, clear-cut opposition between health and sickness is precisely one that Freud's discovery fundamentally unsettles, deconstructs. In tracing Poe's "critical ideas to a rationalized defense of the limitations of his own taste," Krutch is unsuspicious of the fact that his own critical ideas about Poe could equally be so traced; that his doctrine, were it true, could equally apply to his own critical enterprise; that if psychoanalysis indeed puts rationality as such in question, it also by the same token puts itself in question.

Krutch, in other words, reduces not just Poe but analysis itself into an ideologically biased and psychologically opinionated caricature, missing totally (as is most often the case with "Freudian" critics) the radicality of Freud's psychoanalytic insights: their self-critical potential, their power to return upon themselves and to unseat the critic from any guaranteed, authoritative stance of truth. Krutch's approach does not, then, make sophisticated use of psychoanalytic insights, nor does it address the crucial question of the relationship between psychology and aesthetics, nor does it see that the crux of this question is not so much in the interrogation of whether or not all artists are necessarily pathological, but of what it is that makes of art—not of the artist—an object of *desire* for the public; of what it is that makes for art's effect, for the compelling power of Poe's poetry over its readers. The question of what makes poetry lies, indeed, not so much in what it was that made Poe write, but in what it is that makes us read him[13] and that ceaselessly drives so many people to write about him.

Marie Bonaparte: The Approach of Clinical Diagnosis

In contrast to Krutch's claim that Poe's works are only meaningful as the expression of morbidity, bearing "no conceivable relation . . . to the life of any people," Marie Bonaparte, although in turn treating Poe's works as nothing other than the recreations of his neuroses, tries to address the question of Poe's power over his readers through her didactic explanation of the relevancy, on the contrary, of Poe's pathology to "normal" people: the pathological tendencies to which Poe's text gives expression are an exaggerated version of drives and instincts universally human, which normal people have simply repressed more successfully in their childhood. What fascinates readers in Poe's texts is precisely the unthinkable and unacknowledged but strongly felt community of these human sexual drives.

If Marie Bonaparte, unlike Krutch, thus treats Poe with human sympathy, suspending the traditional puritan condemnation and refraining from passing judgment on his "sickness," she nonetheless, like Krutch, sets out primarily to diagnose that sickness and trace the poetry to it. Like Krutch, she comes up with a clinical portrait of the artist that, in claiming to account for the poetry, once again verges on caricature:

> If Poe was fundamentally necrophilist, as we saw, Baudelaire is revealed as a declared sadist; the former preferred dead prey or prey mortally wounded . . . ; the latter preferred live prey and killing. . . .
>
> How was it then, that despite these different sex lives, Baudelaire the sadist recognised a brother in the necrophilist Poe? . . .
>
> This particular problem raises that of the general relation of sadism to necrophilia and cannot be resolved except by an excursus into the theory of instincts. (p. 680)

Can poetry thus be clinically diagnosed? In setting out to expose didactically the methods of psychoananlytic interpretation, Bonaparte's pioneering book at the same time exemplifies the very naiveté of competence, the distinctive professional crudity of what has come to be the classical psychoanalytic treatment of literary texts. Eager to point out the resemblances between psychoanalysis and literature, Bonaparte, like most psychoanalytic critics, is totally unaware of the differences between the two: unaware of the fact that the differences are as important and as significant for understanding the meeting-ground as are the resemblances, and that those differences also have to be accounted for if poetry is to be understood in its own right. Bonaparte, paradoxically enough but in a manner symptomatic of the whole tradition of applied psychoanalysis, thus remains blind to the very specificity of the object of her research.

It is not surprising that this blind nondifferentiation or confusion of the poetic and the psychotic has unsettled sensitive readers, and that various critics have protested against this all too crude equation of poetry with sickness. The protestations, however, most often fall into the same ideological trap as the psychoanalytical studies they oppose: taking for granted the polarity of sickness versus health, of normality versus abnormality, they simply trace Poe's art (in opposition, so they think, to the psychoanalytic claim) to normality as opposed to abnormality, to sanity as opposed to insanity, to the history of ideas rather than that of sexual drives, to a conscious project as opposed to an unconscious one. Camille Mauclair insists upon the fact that Poe's texts are "constructed objectively by a will absolutely in control of itself," and that genius of that kind is "always sane."[14] For Allen Tate,

> The actual emphases Poe gives the perversions are richer in philosophical implication than his psychoanalytic critics have been prepared to see . . . Poe's symbols refer to a known tradition of thought, an intelligible order, apart from what he was as a man, and are not merely the index to a compulsive neurosis . . . the symbols . . . point towards a larger philosophical dimension. (*Recognition*, p. 239)

For Floyd Stovall, the psychoanalytic studies "are not literary critiques at all, but clinical studies of a supposed psychopathic personality":

> I believe this critic should look within the poem or tale for its meaning, and that he should not, in any case, suspect the betrayal of the author's unconscious self until he has understood all that his conscious self has contributed. To affirm that a work of imagination is only a report of the unconscious is to degrade the creative artist to the level of an amanuensis.
>
> I am convinced that all of Poe's poems were composed with conscious art. (p. 183) . . .
>
> "The Raven," and with certain necessary individual differences every other poem Poe wrote, was the product of conscious effort by a healthy and alert intelligence. (p. 186)

It is obvious that this conception of the mutual exclusiveness, of the clear-cut opposition between conscious art and the unconscious, is itself naive and oversimplified. Nonetheless, Stovall's critique of applied psychoanalysis is relevant to the extent that the psychoanalytic explanation, in pointing exclusively to the author's unconscious sexual fantasies, indeed does not account for Poe's outstanding conscious art, for his poetic mastery and his technical and structural self-control. As do its opponents, so does applied psychoanalysis itself fail precisely to account for the dynamic interaction between the unconscious and the conscious elements of art.

If the thrust of the discourse of applied psychoanalysis is, in tracing poetry to a clinical reality, to reduce the poetic to a "cause" outside itself, the crucial limitation of this process of reduction is that the cause, while it may be necessary, is by no means a sufficient one. "Modern psychiatry," judiciously writes David Galloway, "may greatly aid the critic of literature, but . . . it cannot thus far explain why other men, suffering from deprivations of fears or obsessions similar to Poe's, failed to demonstrate his particular creative talent. Though no doubt Marie Bonaparte was correct in seeing Poe's own art as a defense against madness, we must be wary of identifying the necessity for this defense, in terms of Poe's own life, with the success of this defense, which can only be measured in his art."[15]

That the discourse of applied psychoanalysis is limited precisely in that it does not account for Poe's poetic genius is in fact the crucial point made by Freud himself in his prefatory note to Marie Bonaparte's study:

> In this book my friend and pupil, Marie Bonaparte, has shown the light of psychoanalysis on the life and work of a great writer with pathologic trends.
>
> Thanks to her interpretative effort, we now realize how many of the characteris-

tics of Poe's works were conditioned by his personality, and can see how that personality derived from intense emotional fixations and painful infantile experiences. *Investigations such as this do not claim to explain creative genius,* but they do reveal the factors which awake it and the sort of subject matter it is destined to choose.

No doubt, Freud's remarkable superiority over most of his disciples—including Marie Bonaparte—proceeds from his acute awareness of the very limitations of his method, an awareness that in his followers seems most often not to exist.

I would like here to raise a question that has, amazingly enough, never been asked as a serious question: Is there a way around Freud's perspicacious reservation, warning us that studies like those of Bonaparte "do not claim to explain creative genius"? Is there, in other words, a way—a different way—in which psychoanalysis *can* help us to account for poetic genius? Is there an alternative to applied psychoanalysis?—an alternative that would be capable of touching, in a psychoanalytic manner, upon the very specificity of what constitutes the poetic?

Lacan: The Approach of Textual Problematization

"The Purloined Letter," as is well known, is the story of the double theft of a compromising letter, originally sent to the queen. Surprised by the unexpected entrance of the king, the queen leaves the letter on the table in full view of any visitor, where it is least likely to appear suspicious and therefore to attract the king's attention. Enter the Minister D who, observing the queen's anxiety and the play of glances between her and the unsuspicious king, analyzes the situation, figures out, recognizing the addressor's handwriting, what the letter is about, and steals it—by substituting for it another letter he takes from his pocket—under the very eyes of the challenged queen, who can do nothing to prevent the theft without provoking the king's suspicions. The queen then asks the prefect of police to search the minister's apartment and person for the letter. The prefect uses every conceivable secret-police technique to search every conceivable hiding place on the minister's premises, but to no avail.

Having exhausted his resources, the prefect consults Auguste Dupin, the famous "analyst," as Poe calls him (i.e., an amateur detective who excels in solving problems by means of deductive logic), to whom he tells the whole story. (It is, in fact, from this narration of the prefect of police to Dupin and in turn reported by the first-person narrator, Dupin's friend, who is also present, that we, the readers, learn the story.)

On a second encounter, Dupin, to the great surprise of the prefect and of the narrator, produces the purloined letter out of his drawer and hands it to the prefect in return for a large amount of money. The prefect leaves, and Dupin explains to the narrator how he found the letter: he deduced that the minister, knowing that his premises would be thoroughly combed by the police, had concluded that the best principle of concealment would be to leave the letter in the open, in full view; the letter would not be discovered precisely because it would be too self-evident. On this assumption, Dupin called on the minister in his apartment and, glancing around, soon located the letter carelessly hanging from the mantlepiece in a card rack. A little later, a disturbance in the street provoked by a man in Dupin's employ drew the minister to the window, at which moment Dupin quickly replaced the letter with a facsimile.

What Lacan is concerned with at this point of his research is the psychoanalytic problematics of the "repetition compulsion,"[16] as elaborated in Freud's speculative *Beyond the Pleasure Principle*. The thrust of Lacan's endeavor, with respect to Poe, is thus to point out the way in which the story's plot, its sequence of events (as, for Freud, the sequence of events in a life-story), is contingent on, overdetermined by, a principle of repetition that governs it and inadvertently structures its dramatic and ironic impact. "There are two scenes," remarks Lacan, "the first of which we shall straightway designate the primal scene . . . since the second may be considered its repetition in the very sense we are considering today" (p. 273). The primal scene takes place in the queen's boudoir: it is the theft of the letter from the queen by the minister; the second scene—its repetition—is the theft of the letter from the minister by Dupin.

What constitutes repetition for Lacan, however, is not the mere thematic resemblance of the double theft, but the whole structural situation in which the repeated theft takes place: in each case, the theft is the outcome of an intersubjective relationship between three terms; in the first scene, the three participants are the king, the queen, and the minister; in the second, the three participants are the police, the minister, and Dupin. In much the same way as Dupin takes the place of the minister in the first scene (the place of the letter's robber), the minister in the second scene takes the place of the queen in the first (the dispossessed possessor of the letter); whereas the police, for whom the letter remains invisible, take the place formerly occupied by the king. The two scenes thus mirror each other, in that they dramatize the repeated exchange of "three glances, borne by three subjects, incarnated each time by different characters." What is repeated, in other words, is not a psychological act committed as a function of the individual psychology of a character, but three functional *positions in a structure* which, determining three different viewpoints, embody three different relations to the act of seeing—of seeing, specifically, the purloined letter.

> The first is a glance that sees nothing: the King and the Police.
>
> The second, a glance which sees that the first sees nothing and deludes itself as to the secrecy of what it hides: the Queen, then the Minister.
>
> The third sees that the first two glances leave what should be hidden exposed to whomever would seize it: the Minister, and finally Dupin. (p. 275)

I have devised the following diagram as an attempt to schematize Lacan's analysis and to make explicit the synchronic, structural perceptions he proposes of the temporal, diachronic unfolding of the drama.

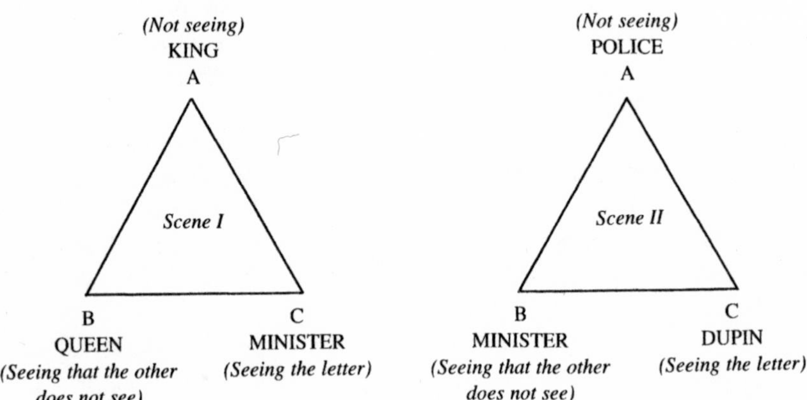

Although Lacan does not elaborate upon the possible ramifications of this structure, the diagram is open to a number of terminological translations, reinterpreting it in the light of Freudian and Lacanian concepts. Here are two such possible translations:

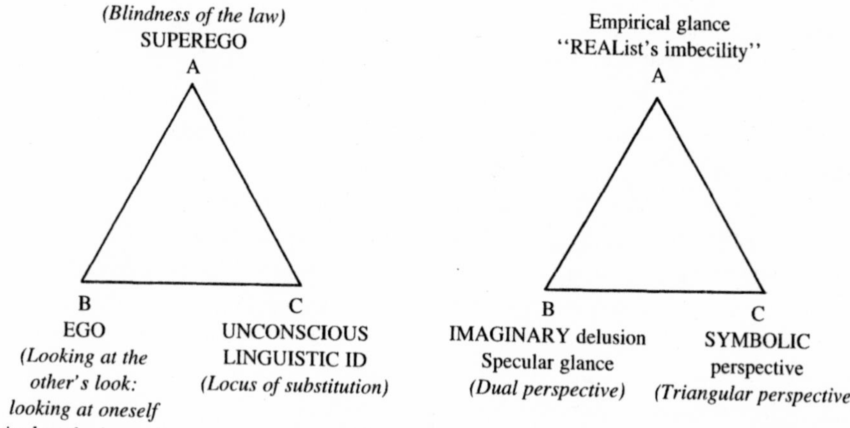

"What interests us today," insists Lacan,

> is the manner in which the subjects relay each other in their displacement during the intersubjective repetition.
>
> We shall see that their displacement is determined by the place which a pure signifier—the purloined letter—comes to occupy in their trio. And that is what will confirm for us its status as repetition automatism. (pp. 275–76).

The purloined letter, in other words, becomes itself—through its insistence in the structure—a symbol or a signifier of the unconscious, to the extent that it is destined "to signify the annulment of what it signifies"—the necessity of its own repression, of the repression of its message: "It is not only the meaning but the text of the message which it would be dangerous to place in circulation" (p. 284). But in much the same way as the repressed *returns* in the *symptom,* which is its repetitive symbolic substitute, the purloined letter ceaselessly returns in the tale—as a signifier of the repressed—through its repetitive displacements and replacements. "This is indeed what happens in the repetition compulsion," says Lacan (p. 286). Unconscious desire, once repressed, survives in displaced symbolic media that govern the subject's life and actions without his ever being aware of their meaning or of the repetitive pattern they structure:

> If what Freud discovered and rediscovers with a perpetually increasing sense of shock has a meaning, it is that the displacement of the signifier determines the subjects in their acts, in their destiny, in their refusals, in their blindness, in their end and in their

fate, their innate gifts and social acquisitions notwithstanding, without regard for character or sex, and that, willingly or not, everything that might be considered the stuff of psychology, kit and caboodle, will follow the path of the signifier. (p. 287)

In what sense, then, does the second scene in Poe's tale, while repeating the first scene, nonetheless differ from it? In the sense, precisely, that the second scene, through the repetition, allows for an understanding, for an *analysis* of the first. This analysis through repetition is to become, in Lacan's ingenious reading, no less than an *allegory of psychoanalysis*. The intervention of Dupin, who restores the letter to the queen, is thus compared to the intervention of the analyst, who rids the patient of the symptom. The analyst's effectiveness, however, does not spring from his intellectual strength but—insists Lacan—from his position in the repetitive structure. By virtue of his occupying the third position—that is, the *locus* of the unconscious of the subject as a place of substitution of letter for letter (of signifier for signifier)—the analyst, through transference, allows at once for a repetition of the trauma and for a symbolic substitution, and thus effects the drama's denouement.

It is instructive to compare Lacan's study of the psychoanalytical repetition compulsion in Poe's text to Marie Bonaparte's study of Poe's repetition compulsion through his text. Although the two analysts study the same author and focus on the same psychoanalytic concept, their approaches are strikingly different. To the extent that Bonaparte's study of Poe has become a classic, a model of applied psychoanalysis, I would like, in pointing out the differences in Lacan's approach, to suggest the way in which those differences at once put in question the traditional approach and offer an alternative to it.

1. What does a repetition compulsion repeat? Interpretation of difference as opposed to interpretation of identity. For Marie Bonaparte, what is compulsively repeated through the variety of Poe's texts is the same unconscious fantasy: Poe's sadonecrophiliac desire for his dead mother. For Lacan, what is repeated in the text is not the content of a fantasy but the symbolic displacement of a signifier through the insistence of a signifying chain; repetition is not of *sameness* but of *difference*, not of independent terms or of analogous themes but of a structure of differential interrelationships,[17] in which what *returns* is always *other*. Thus, the triangular structure repeats itself only through the difference of the characters who successively come to occupy the three positions; its structural significance is perceived only *through* this difference. Likewise, the significance of the letter is situated in its displacement, that is, in its repetitive movements toward a different place. And the second scene, being, for Lacan, an allegory of analysis, is important not just in that it *repeats* the first scene, but in the way this repetition (like the transferential repetition of a psychoanalytical experience) *makes a difference:* brings about a solution to the problem. Thus, whereas Bonaparte analyzes repetition as the insistence of identity, for Lacan any possible insight into the reality of the unconscious is contingent on a perception of repetition, not as a confirmation of identity, but as the insistence of the indelibility of a difference.

2. *An analysis of the signifier as opposed to an analysis of the signified.* In the light of Lacan's reading of Poe's tale as itself an allegory of the psychoanalytic reading, it might be illuminating to define the difference in approach between Lacan and Bonaparte in terms of the story. If the purloined letter can be said to be a sign of the unconscious, for Bonaparte the analyst's task is to uncover the letter's content, which she believes—as do the police—to be hidden somewhere in the real, in some secret biological depth. For Lacan, on the other hand, the analyst's task is not to read the letter's hidden referential content, but to situate the superficial indication of its textual movement, to analyze the paradoxically invisible symbolic evidence of its displacement, its structural insistence, in a signifying chain. "There is such a thing," writes Poe, "as being too profound. Truth is not always in a well. In fact, as regards the most important knowledge, I do believe she is invariably superficial."[18] Espousing Poe's insight, Lacan makes the principle of symbolic evidence the guideline for an analysis not of the signified but of the signifier—for an analysis of the unconscious (the repressed) not as hidden but on the contrary as *exposed*—in language—through a significant (rhetorical) displacement.

This analysis of the signifier, the model of which can be found in Freud's interpretation of dreams, is nonetheless a radical reversal of the traditional expectations involved in the common psychoanalytical approach to literature and its invariable search for hidden meanings. Indeed, not only is Lacan's reading of "The Purloined Letter" subversive of the traditional model of psychoanalytic reading: it is, in general, a type of reading that is methodologically unprecedented in the history of literary criticism. The history of reading has accustomed us to the assumption—usually unquestioned—that reading is finding meaning, that interpretation can dwell only on the meaningful. Lacan's analysis of the signifier opens up a radically new assumption, an assumption that is an insightful logical and methodological consequence of Freud's discovery: that what *can* be read (and perhaps what *should* be read) is not just meaning but the lack of meaning; that significance lies not just in consciousness but, specifically, in its disruption; that the signifier can be analyzed in its effects without its signified being known; that the lack of meaning—the discontinuity in conscious understanding—can and should be interpreted as such, without necessarily being transformed into meaning. "Let's take a look," writes Lacan:

> We shall find illumination in what at first seems to obscure matters: the fact that the tale leaves us in virtually total ignorance of the sender, no less than of the contents, of the letter. (p. 284).

> The signifier is not functional. . . . We might even admit that the letter has an entirely different (if no more urgent) meaning for the Queen than the one understood by the Minister. The sequence of events would not be noticeably affected, not even if it were strictly incomprehensible to an uninformed reader. (pp. 283–84)

But that this is the very effect of the unconscious in the precise sense that we teach that the unconscious means that man is inhabited by the signifier. (p. 291) Thus, for Lacan, what is analytical par excellence is not (as is the case for Bonaparte) the readable but the unreadable and the effects of the unreadable. What calls for analysis is the insistence of the unreadable in the text.

Poe, of course, had said it all in his comment on the nature of what he too—amazingly enough, before the fact—called "the analytical": "The mental features discoursed of as the analytical are, in themselves, but little susceptible of analysis. We appreciate them only in their effects." But, oddly enough, what Poe himself had said so strikingly about the analytical had itself remained totally unanalyzed, indeed unnoticed, by psychoanalytic scholars before Lacan, perhaps because it, too, according to its own analytical logic, had been "a little too self-evident" to be perceived.

3. A textual as opposed to a biographical approach. The analysis of the signifier implies a theory of textuality for which Poe's biography, or his so-called sickness, or his hypothetical personal psychoanalysis, become irrelevant. The presupposition—governing enterprises like that of Marie Bonaparte—that poetry can be interpreted only as autobiography is obviously limiting and limited. Lacan's textual analysis for the first time offers a psychoanalytical alternative to the previously unquestioned and thus seemingly exclusive biographical approach.

4. The analyst/author relation: a subversion of the master/slave pattern and of the doctor/patient opposition. Let us remember how many readers were unsettled by the humiliating and sometimes condescending psychoanalytic emphasis on Poe's "sickness," as well as by an explanation equating the poetic with the psychotic. There seemed to be no doubt in the minds of psychoanalytic readers that if the reading situation could be assimilated to the psychoanalytic situation, the poet was to be equated with the sick patient, with the analysand on the couch. Lacan's analysis, however, subverts not only this clinical status of the poet, but along with it the "bedside" security of the interpreter. If Lacan is not concerned with Poe's sickness, he is quite concerned nonetheless with the figure of the poet in the tale, and with the hypotheses made about his specific competence and incompetence. Both the minister and Dupin are said to be poets, and it is their *poetic* reasoning that the prefect fails to understand and that thus enables both to outsmart the police. "D———, I presume is not altogether a fool," comments Dupin early in the story, to which the prefect of police replies:

> "Not altogether a fool . . . but then he's a poet, which I take to be only one remove from a fool."
>
> "True," said Dupin, after a long and thoughtful whiff from his meerschaum, "although I have been guilty of certain doggerel myself." (p. 334)

A question Lacan does not address could be raised by emphasizing still another point that would normally tend to pass unnoticed, since, once again, it is both so explicit and so ostentatiously insignificant: Why does Dupin say that he too is *guilty* of poetry? In what way does the status of the poet involve guilt? In what sense can we understand the guilt of poetry?

Dupin, then, draws our attention to the fact that both he and the minister are poets, a qualification to which the prefect is condescending. Later, when Dupin explains to the narrator the prefect's defeat, he again insists upon the prefect's blindness to a logic or to a "principle of concealment" which has to do with poets and thus (it might be assumed) is specifically poetic:

> This functionary has been thoroughly mystified; and the remote source of his defeat lies in the supposition that the Minister is a fool, because he has acquired renown as a poet. All fools are poets; this the Prefect feels; and he is merely guilty of a *non distribution medii* in thence inferring that all poets are fools. (pp. 341–42)

In Baudelaire's translation of Poe's tale into French, the word *fool* is rendered, in its strong, archaic sense, as *fou,* "mad." Here, then, is Lacan's paraphrase of this passage in the story:

> After which, a moment of derision [on Dupin's part] at the Prefect's error in deducing that because the Minister is a poet, he is not far from being mad, an error, it is argued, which would consist . . . simply in a false distribution of the middle term, since it is far from following from the fact that all madmen are poets.
>
> Yes indeed. But we ourselves are left in the dark as to the poet's superiority in the art of concealment. (pp. 280–81)

Both this passage in the story and this comment by Lacan seem to be marginal, incidental. Yet the hypothetical *relationship between poetry and madness* is significantly relevant to the case of Poe and to the other psychoanalytical approaches we have been considering. Could it not be said that the error of Marie Bonaparte (who, like the prefect, engages in a search for hidden meaning) lies precisely in the fact that, like the prefect once again, she simplistically equates the poetic with the psychotic, and so, blinded by what she takes to be the poetic *incompetence,* fails to see or understand the specificity of poetic *competence?* Many psychoanalytic investigations diagnosing the poet's sickness and looking for his poetic secret in his person (as do the prefect's men) are indeed very like police investigations; and like the police in Poe's story, they fail to find the letter, fail to see the textuality of the text.

Lacan, of course, does not say all this—this is not what is at stake in his analysis. All he does is open up still another question where we believed we had come into possession of some sort of answer:

> Yes indeed. But we ourselves are left in the dark as to the poet's superiority in the art of concealment.

This seemingly lateral question, asked in passing and left unanswered, suggests, however, the possibility of a whole different focus or perspective of interpretation in the story. If "The Purloined Letter" is specifically the story of "the poet's superiority in the art of concealment," then it is not just an allegory of psychoanalysis but also, at the same time, an allegory of poetic writing. And Lacan is himself a poet to the extent that a thought about poetry is what is superiorly concealed in his Seminar.

In Lacan's interpretation, however, the poet's superiority can only be understood as the structural superiority of the third position with respect to the letter: the minister in the first scene, Dupin in the second, both poets. But the third position is also—this is the main point of Lacan's analysis—the position of the analyst. It follows that, in Lacan's approach, the status of the poet is no longer that of the sick patient but, if anything, that of the analyst. If the poet is still the object of the accusation of being a fool, his folly—if it does exist (which remains an open question)—would at the same time be the folly of the analyst. The clear-cut opposition between madness and health, or between doctor and patient, is unsettled by the odd functioning of the purloined letter of the unconscious, which no one can possess or master. "There is no metalanguage," says Lacan: there is no language in which interpretation can itself escape the effects of the unconscious; the interpreter is not more immune than the poet to unconscious delusions and errors.

5. Implication, as opposed to application, of psychoanalytic theory. Lacan's approach no longer falls into the category of what has been called "applied psychoanalysis," since the concept of application implies a relation of exteriority between the applied science and the field it is supposed, unilaterally, to inform. Since, in Lacan's analysis, Poe's text serves to reinterpret Freud just as Freud's text serves to interpret Poe; since psychoanalytic theory and the literary text mutually inform—and displace—each other; since the very position of the interpreter—of the analyst—turns out to be not outside but inside the text, there is no longer a clear-cut opposition or a well-defined border between literature and psychoanalysis: psychoanalysis can be intraliterary just as much as literature is intrapsychoanalytic. The methodological stake is no longer that of the *application* of psychoanalysis *to* literature but, rather, of their *interimplication in* each other.

If I have dealt at length with Lacan's innovative contribution and with the different methodological example of his approach, it is not so much to set this example up as a new model for imitation, but rather to indicate the way in which it suggestively invites us to go beyond itself (as it takes Freud beyond itself), the way in which it opens up a whole new range of as yet untried possibilities for the enterprise of reading. Lacan's importance in my eyes does not, in other words, lie specifically in any new dogma his "school" may propose, but in his outstanding demonstration that *there is more than one way* to implicate psychoanalysis in literature; that *how to* implicate psychoanalysis in literature is itself a question for interpretation, a challenge to the ingenuity and insight of the interpreter, and not a *given* that can be taken in any way for granted; that what is of analytical relevance in a text is not necessarily and not exclusively "the unconscious of the poet," let alone his sickness or his problems in life; that to situate in a text the analytical as such—to situate the object of analysis or the textual point of its implication—is not necessarily to recognize a *known*, to find an answer, but also, and perhaps more challengingly, to locate an *unknown*, to find a question.

THE POE-ETIC ANALYTICAL

Let us now return to the crucial question we left in suspension earlier, after having raised it by reversing Freud's reservation concerning Marie Bonaparte's type of research: Can psychoanalysis give us an insight into the specificity of the poetic? We can now supplement this question with a second one: where can we situate the analytical with respect to Poe's poetry?

The answers to these questions might be sought in two directions. (1) In a direct reading of a poetic text by Poe, trying to locate in the poem itself a signifier of poeticity and to analyze its functioning and its effects; to analyze, in other words, how poetry as such works through signifiers (to the extent that signifiers, as opposed to meanings, are always signifiers of the unconscious); (2) in analytically informed reading of literary history itself, since its treatment of Poe obviously constitutes a literary *case history*. Such a reading has never, to my knowledge, been undertaken with respect to any writer: never has literary history itself been viewed as an analytical object, as a subject for a psychoanalytic interpretation.[19] And yet it is overwhelmingly obvious, in a case like Poe's, that the discourse of literary history itself points to some unconscious determinations that structure it but of which it is not aware. What is the unconscious of literary history? Can the question of *the guilt of poetry* be relevant to that unconscious? Could literary history be in any way considered a repetitive unconscious *transference* of the guilt of poetry?

Literary history, or more precisely the critical discourse surrounding Poe, is indeed one of the most visible ("self-evident") effects of Poe's poetic signifier, of his text. Now, how can the question of the peculiar effect of Poe be dealt with analytically? My suggestion is: by locating what seems to be unreadable or incomprehensible in this effect; by situating the most prominent discrepancies or discontinuities in the overall critical discourse concerning Poe, the most puzzling critical contradictions, and by trying to interpret those contradictions as symptomatic of the unsettling specificity of the Poe-etic effect, as well as of the contingence of such an effect on the unconscious.

According to its readers' contradictory testimonies, Poe's poetry, let it be recalled, seemed to be at once the most *irresistible* and the most *resisted* poetry in literary history. Poe is felt to be at once the most unequaled master of conscious art *and* the most tortuous unconscious case, as such doomed to remain "the perennial victim of the *idée fixe,* and of amateur psychoanalysis."[20] Poetry, I would thus argue, is precisely the effect of a deadly struggle between consciousness and the unconscious; it has to do with resistance and with what can neither be resisted nor escaped. Poe is a symptom of poetry to the extent that poetry is both what most resists a psychoanalytical interpretation and what most depends on psychoanalytical effects.

But this, paradoxically enough, is what poetry and psychoanalysis have in common. They both exist only insofar as they resist our reading. When caught in the act, both are always already, once again, purloined.

NOTES

1. "Although Poe was not the social outcast Baudelaire conceived him to be, he was, and still is, perhaps the most thoroughly misunderstood of all American writers." Floyd Stovall, *Edgar Poe the Poet: Essays New and Old on the Man and His Work* (Charlottesville: University of Virginia Press, 1969).
2. T. S. Eliot's famous statement on Poe in his study, "From Poe to Valéry," *Hudson Review,* Autumn 1949; reprinted in *The Recognition of Edgar Allan Poe: Selected Criticism since* 1829, ed. Eric W. Carlson (Ann Arbor: University of Michigan Press, 1966) p. 205. This collection of critical essays will hereafter be cited as *Recognition,* with individual essays abbreviated as follows: P. P. Cooke, "Edgar A. Poe," (1848); T.S. Eliot, "From Poe to Valéry" (1949); T. W. Higginson, "Poe" (1879); Aldous Huxley, "Vulgarity in Literature" (1931); J. R. Lowell, "Edgar Allan Poe" (1845); C. M. Rourke, "Edgar Allan Poe" (1931); G. B. Shaw, "Edgar Allan Poe" (1909); Edmund Wilson, "Poe at Home and Abroad" (1926); Ivor Winter, "Edgar Allan Poe: A Crisis in American Obscurantism" (1937).
3. J. W. Krutch, *Edgar Allan Poe: A Study in Genius* (New York: Knopf, 1926).
4. J. M. S. Robertson, "The Genius of Poe," *Modern Quarterly,* 3 (1926); Camille Mauclair, *Le Génie d'Edgar Poe* (Paris, 1925); John Dillon, *Edgar Allan Poe: His Genius and His Character* (New York, 1911); John R. Thompson, *The Genius and Character of Edgar Allan Poe* (privately printed, 1929); Jeannet A. Marks, *Genius and Disaster: Studies in Drugs and Genius* (New York, 1925); Jean A. Alexander, "Affidavits of Genius: French Essays on Poe," *Dissertation Abstracts,* 22 (September 1961).
5. Higginson, "Poe," *Recognition,* p. 67.
6. Swinburne, letter to Sara Sigourney Rice, 9 November 1875, *Recognition,* p. 63. Stéphane Mallarmé, "Scolies," in *Oeuvres complètes,* ed. H. Mondor and G. Jean-Aubry (Paris: Pléiade, 1945), p. 223; my translation. Lowell, "Edgar Allan Poe," *Recognition,* p. 11.

7. Cooke, quoting Elizabeth Barrett, in "Edgar A. Poe," *Recognition*, p. 23; original italics.
8. Shaw, "Edgar Allan Poe," *Recognition*, p. 98.
9. Eliot, "From Poe to Valéry," *Recognition*, p. 209.
10. "The Murders in the Rue Morgue," in *Edgar Allan Poe: Selected Writings*, ed. David Galloway (New York: Penguin, 1967), p. 189; hereafter cited as *Poe*.
11. Bonaparte, *Edgar Poe* (Paris: Denöel et Steele, 1933). English edition: *Life and Works of Edgar Allan Poe*, trans. John Rodker (London: Imago, 1949). All references to Marie Bonaparte will be to the English editions.
12. Lacan, "Le Séminaire sur *La Lettre volée*," in *Ecrits* (Paris: Seuil, 1966); translated by Jeffrey Mehlman in "French Freud," *Yale French Studies*, 48 (1972). All references here to Lacan's Poe Seminar are to this translation [chapter 12, this volume; pages quoted according to the present volume].
13. Edmund Wilson: "The recent revival of interest in Poe has brought to light a good deal of new information and supplied us for the first time with a serious interpretation of his personal career, but it has so far entirely neglected to explain why we should still want to read him" (*Recognition*, p. 142).
14. Mauclair, *Le Génie d'Edgar Poe;* quoted in *Poe*, p. 24.
15. Galloway, Introduction to *Poe*, pp. 24–25.
16. For a remarkable analysis of the way repetition is enacted in the problematics of reading set in motion by Lacan's text, see Barbara Johnson's "The Frame of Reference: Poe, Lacan, Derrida," in *The Critical Difference: Essays in the Rhetoric of Contemporary Criticism* (Baltimore: Johns Hopkins University Press, 1980).
17. "Need we emphasize the similarity of these two sequences? Yes, for the resemblance we have in mind is not a simple collection of traits chosen only in order to delete their difference. And it would not be enough to retain those common traits at the expense of the others for the slightest truth to result. It is rather the intersubjectivity in which the two actions are motivated that we wish to bring into relief, as well as the three terms through which it structures them. The special status of these terms results from their corresponding simultaneously to the three logical moments through which the decision is precipitated and to the three places it assigns to the subjects among whom it constitutes a choice . . . Thus three moments, structuring three glances, borne by three subjects, incarnated each time by different characters." "Seminar on *The Purloined Letter*," pp. 274–75.
18. "The Murders in the Rue Morgue," *Poe*, p. 204.
19. I have attempted, however, an elementary exploration of such an approach with respect to Henry James in my essay, "Turning the Screw of Interpretation," in *Writing and Madness: Literature/Philosophy/Psychoanalysis* (Ithaca: Cornell University Press, 1985).
20. The formula is David Galloway's (*Poe*, p. 24).

14. Unity Identity Text Self

Norman N. Holland

My title has big words, but my essay aims into the white spaces between those big words. Those spaces suggest to me the mysterious openness and receptivity of literature. Somehow, all kinds of people from different eras and cultures can achieve and re-achieve a single literary work, replenishing it by infinitely various additions of subjective to objective. As it turns out, however, to explore the white spaces we need first to bound them, that is, to define the four big words. Then the spaces will—more or less—take care of themselves.

First, *text.* Simply, the words-on-the-page that formalists and "New" critics have been talking about for the last several decades. Evidently, the meaning of the term is so obvious there is scarcely a literary handbook that troubles to mention it. It is just what the writer wrote or, to take the word back to its etymological root, *texere* ("to weave"), what he wove, as in a textile, or what he made, as in words like archi*tect.* In this sense, the writer's emblem is the badger, Old High German *dahs,* an animal who builds; thus, the critic's symbol would be that animal specially bred for ferreting out badgers, the *dachshund,* like so many of my colleagues, long of nose and low of belly.

The notion of literary *unity* involves a good deal more. It first occurs in the *Phaedrus* in connection with oratory, when Socrates argues that a speech should be put together "like a living creature . . . not headless or footless." Aristotle, in a famous passage of the *Poetics,* required that all the arts "must imitate . . . a whole, the structural union of the parts being such that, if any one of them is displaced or removed, the whole will be disjointed and disturbed." And in another famous passage he asked that narratives and, by implication, other works of literature "resemble a living organism in all its unity."[1]

·Reprinted by permission of the Modern Language Association from *PMLA,* 90 (1975).

The idea has, of course, passed through many versions, of which the most energizing came from the German Romantic critics and Coleridge, leading to such emphases and even overextensions of the zoological metaphor as this elegant phrasing by Henry James in "The Art of Fiction": "A novel is a living thing, all one and continuous, like any other organism, and in proportion as it lives will it be found, I think, that in each of the parts there is something of each of the other parts."[2] Our own time is both more analytical and more professional. We heed statements like this by Northrop Frye in a standard handbook for graduate students, suggesting that the first task of the academic critic is to "see the whole design of the work as a unity . . . a simultaneous pattern radiating out from a center" or "central theme," "the unity to which everything else must be relevant."[3]

I find that I arrive at this unity by grouping the particular details of a work together under certain themes, then grouping those particular themes together until I arrive at a few basic terms which constitute a central theme. For example, I might say, "*Hamlet* is a play about the split between the purity of symbolic action and the physicality of real action." Such a theme is not necessarily unique—that is, someone else might arrive at a different theme from mine or, alternatively, I might find that this theme would help me grasp the unity of some other play besides *Hamlet*. All that is implied by the idea of a central theme is that it helps one particular person grasp the unity of one particular work.

Such a theme as this one for *Hamlet* is highly abstract, yet one can quickly move up or down the hierarchy of generality it sets up. One can go from an abstract word in the theme, like "physicality," to the particulars it subsumes, like Gertrude's sensuality or the gravediggers' jokes. One can relate such a detail of speech as the doubling of words in phrases like "the gross and scope of mine opinion," "The expectancy and rose of the fair state," or "You . . . that are but mutes or audience to this act" to a very general term in the theme such as "split" which would link the hendiadys, the "figure of twins" as Puttenham called it, to splittings of characters like Laertes and Ophelia, Horatio and Fortinbras, or the scarcely distinguishable Rosencrantz and Guildenstern whose duality will hardly bear any justification but a thematic one.

As I describe this method of successive abstraction, of induction and deduction around a few general polarities, I realize I am making it sound much more regular and fixed than it is. Obviously, the process is as intuitive and imaginative as it is rational. Each reader groups the details of the play into themes that he thinks important, and if he chooses to press on to a highly condensed central theme it will surely be something that matters to him. Nevertheless, most professional critics assure us that there are right and wrong, better and worse readings, and they insist, often quite fiercely, that the themes and other literary entities they discover have an "objective" validity. Certainly, readings of literary works for their unity can be compared in an almost quantitative way as to how effectively they bring the details of the play into convergence around some central theme. Even more important, however, we compare readings by the extent to which we *feel* we share them. There is, then, a deep question here as to whether literary unities are "subjective" or "objective" or, more exactly, how the subjective and objective parts of a reading for unity interrelate. I think our analysis of the four terms —unity, identity, text, self—will help answer it.

Our second term, *unity,* I realize, has become altogether familiar, even routine, to literary critics. I have lingered with it, though, because it has an important and largely unrecognized use in psychology—not, however, for the first of our two psychological terms: *self.* That is, as the psychological handbooks say, more of a commonsense term than a psychological one—an interesting dichotomy that! It is more easily defined by exclusion, as "one's 'own person' as contrasted with 'other persons' and objects outside [one]self." It is thus "the real total person of an individual, including both his body and his psyche." Freud, for example, sometimes spoke of a *Gesamt-Ich* in contrast to *das Ich* proper, the intrapsychic ego.[4]

The more complex psychological term is *identity.* Erik Erikson, who has done more to make it a byword in and out of psychoanalysis than anyone else, has suggested that it comprises four meanings, any or all of which may be—must be—considered a possibility in any given use: the individual's awareness of the continuity of his existence in space and time and his recognition of others' awareness of his existence; more, his awareness of the continuity in the style of his individuality and its existence and the coincidence of his personal style with his meaning for significant others in his immediate community. Obviously, such a concept is both rich and ambiguous. Indeed, Nathan Leites has recently devoted much of a book to arguing that the word *identity* has been used and abused to the point where it has ceased to have any clear meaning left; that the older word "character" would do just as well.[5]

I would like to restore meaning to the word by turning to the most precise of the modern theorists of identity, Heinz Lichtenstein.[6] When we describe the "character" or "personality" of another person, Lichtenstein shows, we abstract an invariant from "the infinite sequence of bodily and behavioral transformations during the whole life of an individual." That is, we can be precise about individuality by conceiving of the individual as living out variations on an identity theme much as a musician might play out an infinity of variations on a single melody. We discover that underlying theme by abstracting it from its variations.

From a developmental point of view, Lichtenstein holds that such a theme is actually "in" the individual. Out of the newborn child's inheritance of potentialities, its mother-person actuates a specific way of being, namely, being the child that fits this particular mother. The mother thus imprints on the infant, not a specific identity or even a sense of its own identity, but a "primary identity," itself irreversible but capable of infinite variation. This primary identity stands as an invariant which provides for all the later transformations of the individual, as he develops, with an unchanging inner form or core of continuity.

Identity in this developmental sense shows up most graphically, perhaps, in the series of photographs that picture magazines publish at the deaths of famous people. Here is the future President toddling at two, here are his pictures in school and college yearbooks, here as he first began to appear in the news, then the sixty-year-old smiling public man, and finally, "Last scene of all" is "mere oblivion, sans teeth, sans eyes, sans taste, sans everything." And yet, if we look closely we can read back from the careworn visage of the old man at the end and at the height of his career to the soft features of the toddler, finding the same structure, expressions, and frame. In this way, too, identity is like a musical theme on which variations are played: not the notes themselves but their structural relationship to one another remains constant through a lifetime of transformations.

In the developed adult, I can assume such an invariant identity theme (whether or not it coincides with an actual primary identity imprinted in infancy), and by means of it grasp an unchanging essence, a "personality" or "character," that permeates the millions of ego choices that constitute the visible human before me, ever changing and different, yet ever continuous with what went before. I can abstract, from the choices in the life I see, facts as visible as the words on a page, various subordinate patterns and themes until I arrive at one central, unifying pattern in that life which is the invariant sameness, the "identity theme" of the individual living it. In other words, just as I can arrive at a *unity* for the series of choices that is *Hamlet* by means of a central, unifying theme, so I can arrive at an *identity* for a particular self by means of a centering identity theme. And again, it may not be unique: the same identity theme may describe several different people, just as a single literary theme might describe several different texts.

In short, within our four terms, *identity* quite resembles *unity*, so much so that once having defined *unity, identity, text,* and *self,* we can fill in the white spaces between them as follows: unity/identity = text/self. Now my title reads: "*Unity* is to *identity* as *text* is to *self,*" or, by a familiar algebraic transposition, "*Unity* is to *text* as *identity* is to *self.*" Or you could say, "*Identity* is the *unity* I find in a *self* if I look at it as though it were a *text.*"

Now this seems a reasonable enough proportion, I think, something very close to applying the Aristotelian idea of essence both to literary texts and to people. Thus, Aristotle says in his first definition of the term: "What is soul? . . . It is substance in the sense which corresponds to the definitive formula of a thing's essence. That means it is 'the essential whatness' of a body."[7] In more modern terms, we can think of *text* and *self* as data and *unity* and *identity* as constructs drawn from the data. Or we can think of *unity* and *identity* as expressing only sameness or continuity while *text* and *self* show difference or change, or, more exactly, *both* sameness *and* difference, *both* continuity *and* change.

In that sense, *unity* and *identity* are relatively fixed and *text* and *self* relatively variable, as, for example, when I read a novel and decide fairly quickly, within fifty pages or so, what its theme is, although its outcome is as yet quite unknown to me. The same thing happens in human development: one can discern identity, a personal style, within the second or third year of life, yet it is impossible to tell, looking at the three-year-old child, even the simplest things about the adult he will become, whether he will marry, have children, what his profession will be, his health, his location, or any of the most obvious passport data. Because we arrive at identity by considering events apart from their position in time, identity is a purely synchronic concept; it does not help us look diachronically through a life in time and make predictions or retrodictions. Rather, identity defines what the individual brings from old experiences to new ones, and it is the newness of experiences, both those from the world without and those from the biological and emotional world within, by which the individual creates the variations which are his life lived in historical time.

Therefore, the tidy little equation I have offered you, this mathematical neatness matching literary criticism to psychology, must mercifully give way before the essential humanity of both disciplines. *Unity* and *identity,* on the one hand, belong to an entirely different order of factuality from *text* and *self* on the other. *Text* and *self* are very close to experience, while *unity* and *identity* represent quite abstract principles drawn from the experience of *text* or *self.* We sometimes assume, as Aristotle did, that essences such as unity and identity inhere in the physical beings they describe, like a DNA code, but whether or not that is true in some final sense, it is we who have to uncover or decode the surface manifestations to arrive at the informing principle of the text or person. And when I do so, I engage in an act that becomes part of the historical self which grows out of and expresses my own identity theme. To put it another way, when I arrive at the unity in a literary text or the identity theme of a personality I am studying, I do so in a way that is characteristic for me—for my identity theme. And so do you. Otherwise we would all agree about the themes of novels or our understanding of human beings and there would be—o horribile dictu!—no need for *PMLA* or any other forum in which people work out their differing interpretations of texts, selves, and the other events we experience in the world.

Thus, the neat little equation I offered you is not neat at all. The ratio, unity to text, equals the ratio, identity to self, but the terms on the right side of the equation cannot be eliminated from the left side. The unity we find in literary texts is impregnated with the identity that finds that unity. This is simply to say that my reading of a certain literary work will differ from yours or his or hers. As readers, each of us will bring different kinds of external information to bear. Each will seek out the particular themes that concern him. Each will have different ways of making the text into an experience with a coherence and significance that satisfies.

Further, when you actually collect and compare these variations among interpretations, they turn out to be very much larger than one would have expected. For instance, at Buffalo's Center for the Psychological Study of the Arts, I was analyzing readers' taped remarks on Faulkner's "A Rose for Emily." The story contains the following clause describing Colonel Sartoris: "he who fathered the edict that no Negro woman should appear on the streets without an apron." Three readers singled out the word "fathered" for comment. Sandra said: "It's a great little touch of ironic humor . . . using these heroic terms to describe such a petty and obvious extension of bigotry." " 'Fathered,' " said Saul, "is the word you're asking about, I suspect. . . . Sponsored. It means practically the same as 'sponsored,' I think, although I suppose you could talk about paternalism and stuff." "I react to the term, 'fathered the edict,' " said Sebastian when I read him the passage. "That was a strange phrase to use—like fathering the edict seems to in some way be fathering the women, to be fathering that state of affairs. So it implied for me the sexual intercourse that took place between whites and Negroes." [8]

Obviously, since the text presents just the one word "fathered," one cannot explain by means of the text alone why one reader would find that word heroic, another neutral and abstract, and a third sexual. To be sure, differences in age, sex, nationality, class, or reading experience will contribute to differences in interpretation. Yet it is a familiar experience in the world of literary or clinical interpretation to find people similar in age, sex, nationality, class, and interpretive skill nevertheless differing radically over particular interpretations. And one finds the opposite situation: people superficially different agreeing on interpretations. Certainly, the hundreds of psychological experiments inconclusively correlating such variables with interpretation give little hope that they will provide an answer. At the Center for the Psychological Study of the Arts, we have found that we can explain such differences in interpretation by examining differences in the personalities of the interpreters. More precisely, *interpretation is a function of identity*, specifically, identity conceived as variations upon an identity theme.

Merely to state that idea, however, requires an immediate warding off of misunderstandings. The assertion that all interpretations express the identity themes of the people making the interpretations is a statement of fact, not an ethical plea for interpretive Liberty Halls. Nor does that factual statement logically or in any other way imply that all interpretations work equally well as interpretations for people other than the interpreter. On the contrary, I and, I feel sure, you distinguish different readings of a text or personality "objectively" by how much and how directly they seem to us to bring the details of a text or a self into convergence around a centering theme. We also compare them as to whether they "feel right" or "make sense." That is, do we feel we could use them to organize and make coherent our own experience of that text or person?

If, as a factual matter, interpretation is a function of identity, can we be more precise about that function? Recently, at this Center, we have been able to tease out three strands and trace a single overall principle, a figure in the carpet, if you will; in all, four principles that govern the relationship between character or personality or identity and the creation and re-creation of literary and other experiences.[9] Although I present them sequentially, obviously they all go on together.

The overarching principle is: identity re-creates itself, or, to put it another way, style—in the sense of personal style—creates itself. That is, all of us, as we read, use the literary work to symbolize and finally to replicate ourselves. We work out through the text our own characteristic patterns of desire and adaptation. We interact with the work, making it part of our own psychic economy and making ourselves part of the literary work—as we interpret it. For, always, this principle prevails: identity re-creates itself. Then, within that general principle, we can isolate three specific modalities.

First, adaptations must be matched; and, therefore, we interpret the new experience in such a way as to cast it in the terms of our characteristic ways of coping with the world. That is, each of us will find in the literary work the kind of thing we characteristically wish or fear the most. Therefore, to respond, we need to be able to re-create from the literary work our characteristic strategies for dealing with those deep fears and wishes. Imagine, for example, several individuals, all of whom perceive the central desire and danger in their worlds as authority figures. One of these people might characteristically deal with those loved and feared authorities by establishing alternatives in response to their demands; and he might therefore respond to, say, *Hamlet* in terms of the opportunities he found in the play for such alternatives: for him, dualisms, split characters, or the interplay of multiple plots would be primary. Another person might characteristically cope with the authority figures he both fears and is attracted to by establishing limits and qualifications on their authority: he might relate therefore to *Hamlet* by discovering and stressing irony and occasional farce, Osric, Polonius, the gravediggers, and, in general, the contradictions and counterbalance of "purposes mistook / Fall'n on th' inventors' heads." Still another person might customarily deal with authority by total compliance, and he might respond to the tragedy by seeking out and accepting, totally, uncritically, with a gee-gosh, the authority of its author.

The point in this crucial phase of response is that any individual shapes the materials the literary work offers him—including its author—to give him what he characteristically both wishes and fears, and that he also constructs his characteristic way of achieving what he wishes and defeating what he fears. Because his psychological defenses are brought into play, this matching has to take place with considerable exactitude. That is, unless the defense mechanisms are bribed into tranquility, the individual wards off the experience entirely. The defenses, at least, must be matched very closely.

I am, however, talking about much more than defenses: I mean to include the whole, large system by which the individual achieves pleasure in the world and avoids unpleasure, his characteristic pattern of defense mechanisms, methods of coping, or adaptive strategies, including the systems of symbols and values. In the largest sense, I am talking about his whole identity theme considered from the point of view of defense and adaptation. But to the extent the defense mechanisms in a strict sense are included, this matching acts like a shibboleth. The individual can accept the literary work only to the extent he exactly re-creates with it a verbal form of his particular pattern of defense mechanisms and, in a broader sense, the particular system of adaptive strategies that he keeps between himself and the world. This matching is therefore crucial. Without it the individual blocks out the experience. With it the other phases of response take place.

Once someone has taken into himself through his adaptive strategies some literary work, as he had made it fit those strategies, then he derives from it fantasies of the particular kind that yield him pleasure—and he does so very easily indeed. In our observations of readers, the matching of defenses must be very exact, but they can very freely adapt literary works to yield the gratifications of fantasy. Fantasies move in the same "direction" as the continuing pressure from our drives for gratification, while defenses and adaptations have to oppose and redirect those pressures. Hence one matching —the fit to the adaptive strategy—must be quite tight, while the other can be very loose, because the fantasy content we conventionally locate in the literary work is really created by the reader from the literary work to express his own drives.

It is this fantasy content that most psychonalytic studies of particular works of literature, beginning with Freud's discovery of Hamlet's oedipus complex, purport to discover. Such studies, however, raise a difficult question: How is it that readers of widely differing personalities as well as different genders, ages, and cultures can all get pleasure from the same fantasy? Conversely, how can one individual with one dominant mode of fantasy take pleasure in a great range of literary works with widely varying unconscious content? The same man can enjoy the homosexual theme of *Death in Venice* and the intrusive, thrusting masculinity of a Hemingway or Mark Twain. And he can go on to enjoy Scott Fitzgerald's need to be frustrated by a dominant woman and Sylvia Plath's anger at the womanly roles forced upon her. How can one person enjoy such a spectrum? How can many different people from many different cultures and eras enjoy it?

The answer, I believe, is that different readers can all gain pleasure from the same fantasy and one reader can gain pleasure from many different fantasies because *all* readers create from the fantasy seemingly "in" the work fantasies to suit their several character structures. Each reader, in effect, re-creates the work in terms of his own identity theme. First, he shapes it so it will pass through the network of his adaptive and defensive strategies for coping with the world. Second, he re-creates from it the particular kind of fantasy and gratification he responds to.

Finally, a third modality completes the individual's re-creation of his identity or life-style from the literary work. Fantasies that boldly represent the desires of the adult or the more bizarre imaginings of the child will ordinarily arouse guilt and anxiety. Thus, we usually feel a need to transform raw fantasy into a total experience of esthetic, moral, intellectual, or social coherence and significance.[10] Most typically, we seek our own particular version of the esthetic unity Plato and Aristotle first described, but we use other ways as well: comparing this experience to others, associating to it, bringing one's knowledge or expertise to bear, evaluating it, placing it in a tradition, treating it as an encoded message to be decoded, and all the other strategies of professional, amateur, and vulgar literary criticism. All serve to synthesize the experience and make it part of the mind's continuing effort to balance the pressures of the drives for gratification, the restraints of conscience and reality, and one's inner need to avoid emotional and cognitive dissonance. In short, we put the work together at an intellectual or esthetic level as we do in terms of fantasy or defense—according to the same overarching principle: identity re-creates itself.

This description of the way identity finds unity is, I realize, both abstract and long. To ameliorate the length, I can offer a simple mnemonic, the square root sign we learned in school: $\sqrt{}$. We can think of our three steps as the left end of the sign, the bottom tip, and the right end. The small horizontal portion on the left images the tight, narrow process of filtering the literary work through the defensive aspect of one's identity. Once in, the literary experience drops down to "deep," unconscious levels (like the day-residue from which a dream is made) and there becomes transformed into the unconscious wish associated with this person's particular identity theme, a fantasy pushing for gratification, pressing upward toward coherence and significance. And it is at this higher level that we talk about artistic experience to others, passing the work through from left to right and from primitive, "lower" modes of enjoyment to "higher" appreciations. If you prefer a verbal mnemonic for the *de*fense-*f*antasy-*t*ransformation model of the literary experience, the best acronym I can find is DEFT (not, I would insist, "daft").

A mnemonic may help compress the length of the description; it does nothing, of course, for its abstractness. To try to overcome that I would like to talk about one particular reader; and to demonstrate, in so brief a space as this, how one person's identity re-creates itself through literary and other experiences, I have picked a reader well known through his writings, but whom, for the time being, I would like to leave nameless. Let me identify him for you, not by a sketch or portrait, but only by his X-ray, that is, his identity theme. I would like you then to read, not his imaginative works, which you probably know, but informal remarks that reveal the way he constructs his experience of the world, of science, say, or poetry, fiction, politics, and himself. Compare that to his identity theme and, when you come to recognize him, to those of his literary works you know.

As I look over his writings and the facts of his life, this man seems to me to have seen his world as something huge, threatening, unknown, and chaotic, but nevertheless something he could identify with or even master by treating small things (notably words) as magical symbols for those large unknowns. That is, he polarized his world into the big unknown and the familiar small, the big being potentially destructive in aggressive or sexual ways, and the small serving as a way his ego would either master or become part of the big powers. I can put his identity theme (as I see it) in somewhat more precise terms this way: *to be in touch with, to create, and to restrain huge unknown forces of sex and aggression by smaller symbols: words or familiar objects.* Or, more briefly, *to manage great, unmanageable unknowns by means of small knowns.*

As we shall see, one can move from this very abstract formulation to the particular details of the man's life, much as if we were going from a central theme for *Hamlet* to particular details of text. Notice, too, how this statement of an identity theme involves polarities: great and small, known and unknown, creation and restraint, manageable and unmanageable. Such dualisms reflect the paradoxical combinations of love and hate or wish and fear that underlie all human development, permeating every later experience. Notice the way this man in particular finds such polarities in experience and then deals with them by playing off symbols against one another.

For example, in a letter to his daughter after his wife's death, he characterized himself in terms of such a balancing: "No matter how humorous I am, I am sad. I am a jester about sorrow." He saw other writers the same way. "The style is the man," he quoted.

Rather say the style is the way the man takes himself; and to be at all charming or even bearable, the way is almost rigidly prescribed. If it is with outer seriousness, it must be with inner humor. If it is with outer humor, it is with inner seriousness. Neither one alone without the other under it will do.

In fact, as if to carry this balance out, our writer was known to his friends for his anger and rages—he himself called them "my Indian vindictiveness" —but he was known to the public for his folksiness and his gentle, proverbial humor and irony. All his life he needed to make himself into a legend this way, often falsifying the actual facts to do so. "Don't trust me too far . . . don't trust me on my life" was his repeated caution to scholars and biographers. It was as though he needed to put on myth like a mask to help him, not just with his public image but with his far deeper need to cope with an important polarity in himself between the manageable and the unmanageable. The small, cozy mannerisms served to deal with the large, aggressive forces within.

His literary tastes carried out the same defensive strategy. Among his favorite reading he included the *Odyssey* (as I see it, the escape and homecoming rather than the deadlock and entanglement of the grander *Iliad*); Poe and Emerson (both of whom deal with efforts to master supernatural forces by natural ones); and such romances as *The Last of the Mohicans, The Prisoner of Zenda,* and *The Jungle Book.* Romances matched the way he created an exaggerated need for courage as a reaction against the unmanageable in himself. He would set up heroes and worship them, and he constantly tried to build himself up into the sturdy stoicism he admired. Thus, he was especially fond of Kipling; and, he said, "*Robinson Crusoe* is never quite out of my mind. I never tire of being shown how the limited can make snug in the limitless. *Walden* has something of the same fascination. Crusoe was cast away; Thoreau was self-cast away. Both found themselves sufficient."

The same defensive strategy, using the tangible or limited to stand off the unknown and unlimited, emerged as his intellectual style when he came to evaluate science or philosophy.

Greatest of all attempts to say one thing in terms of another is the philosophical attempt to say matter in terms of spirit, or spirit in terms of matter, to make the final unity. That is the greatest attempt that ever failed. We stop just short here. But it is the height of poetry, the height of all thinking, the height of all poetic thinking, that attempt to say matter in terms of spirit and spirit in terms of matter. It is wrong to call anybody a materialist simply because he tries to say spirit in terms of matter, as if that were a sin. . . . The only materialist—be he poet, teacher, scientist, politician, or statesman—is the man who gets lost in his material without a gathering metaphor to throw it into shape and order. He is the lost soul.

He saw science, too, as an attempt to achieve such a gather metaphor and, given his attitude toward superior forces, he was not about to allow that it was any different from poetry as a way of managing the big unknowns. Thus he said of Einstein's theory, "Wonderful, yes, wonderful but no better as a metaphor than you or I might make for ourselves before five o'clock." And in more general terms: "Isn't science just an extended metaphor; its aim to describe the unknown in terms of the unknown? Isn't it a kind of poetry, to be treated as plausible material, not as cold fact?"

He himself took over an idea of Emerson's, that "the world is a temple whose walls are covered with emblems, pictures and commandments of the Deity . . . there is no fact in nature which does not carry the whole sense of nature." That is a nice way of putting it. A rival poet, however, wrote of a man,

To whom every grass-blade's a telephone wire,
With Heaven as central and electrifier.
He has only to ring up the switch-board and hear
A poem lightly pattering into his ear.[11]

That's a bit nasty, but is it really inaccurate?

Our writer himself often implied that poetry was his way of getting in touch with and managing the great unmanageables. "I believe in what the Greeks called synecdoche: the philosophy of the part for the whole; skirting the hem of the goddess. All that an artist needs is samples." "I started called myself a Synecdochist when others called themselves Imagists or Vorticists. Always, always a larger significance. A little thing touches a larger thing." "I am a mystic," he told a reporter. "I believe in change and in changing symbols." And so he should, for by manipulating symbols he achieved not only great poetry and national acclaim but the warding off of his deepest fears. "Every poem is an epitome of the great predicament; a figure of the will braving alien entanglements." "When in doubt there is always form for us to go on with. Anyone who has achieved the least form to be sure of it, is lost to the larger excruciations.'' For him, a poem took on a life and direction of its own, culminating in a sense of mastery or at least an attempt at it:

> The figure a poem makes. It begins in delight and ends in wisdom. . . . It begins in delight, it inclines to the impulse, it assumes direction with the first line laid down, it runs a course of lucky events, and ends in a clarification of life—not necessarily a great clarification, such as sects and cults are founded on, but in a momentary stay against confusion.

Finally, I can comprehend this man as a unity. By seeing him centered around an identity theme, I can interrelate what he says about his own writing, the writing of others, or the relation of science to poetry or matter to spirit. I can, in fact, achieve Yeat's ''fancy that there is some one Myth for every man, which, if we but knew it, would make us understand all he did and thought.''[12] I can understand why Robert Frost's commitment to synecdoche went along with a fondness for Rudyard Kipling or why a man who enjoys ''being shown how the limited can make snug in the limitless'' would also feel ''All that an artist needs is samples.''

Through the concept of identity as an identity theme and variations upon it, I can bring together intellectually the way this particular individual construed experiences of all kinds. But more than that, I can reach him empathically as well. Once I could feel teased, even a bit annoyed, by the cuteness in a remark like

> I never dared be radical when young
> For fear it would make me conservative when old.

Now, I hear in it another note: the need to hold at bay the fear and dare of politics in 1936 by balancing off opposed symbols. I can delight in his description of poetry, for example: ''The figure is the same as for love. Like a piece of ice on a hot stove the poem must ride on its own melting.'' Yet that image of the small object harried by its dangerous and hostile environment (and as a figure of love!) reminds me of the pain Robert Frost knew alongside the marvels of wit and irony that enabled him to tolerate it.[13]

I can share empathically the unity and continuity this man created in his life because, by the very act of experiencing his identity, I mingle his characteristic style with my own. Indeed, the only way one can ever discover unity in texts or identity in selves is by creating them from one's own inner style, for we are all caught up in the general principle that identity creates and re-creates itself as each of us discovers and achieves the world in his own mind. Whenever, as a critic, I engage a writer or his work, I do so through my own identity theme. My act of perception is also an act of creation in which I partake of the artist's gift. I find in myself what Freud called the writer's "innermost secret; the essential *ars poetica*," that is, the ability to break through the repulsion associated with "the barriers that rise between each single ego and the others."[14]

In doing so, I close a dualism that has dominated systematic thought since Descartes: the belief that the reality and meaning of the external world exist alone, independent of the perceiving self, and that therefore true knowledge requires the splitting of the knower from the known.[15] I am suggesting that a larger law subsumes this seventeenth-century epistemology and points rather to experiencing as an in-gathering and in-mixing of self and other as described by Whitehead or Bradley or Dewey or Cassirer or Langer or Husserl. The Cartesian cleaving of *res extensa* from *res cogitans* is a historical and personal strategy governed by a still more all-encompassing principle; and the psychoanalytic psychologist can give precision to what the philosophers adumbrated: *interpretation re-creates identity,* considered specifically as defense, fantasy, and ego style.

As Basil Willey urged some forty years ago,[16] seventeenth-century science itself came into being as a result of a deep psychological change in the kind of assurance people sought from explanations.

> For example, the spots on the moon's surface might be due, theologically, to the fact that it was God's will they should be there; scientifically they might be "explained" as the craters of extinct volcanoes. The newer explanation may be said, not so much to contain "more" truth than the older, as to supply the *kind* of truth which was now demanded. An event was "explained" . . . when its history had been traced and described.

"Interest was now directed to the *how,* the manner of causation, not its *why,* its final cause."

In our own time, we the successors of Freud, Marx, and Durkheim find ourselves amidst cultural anthropology, transactional psychology, the discovery of absolute limits to mathematical axiomatization, the Whorf–Sapir hypothesis in linguistics, relativity, randomness, and uncertainty even in the "hard" sciences, and many other relativizing discoveries, most important for our purposes, psychoanalytic psychology. Psychoanalysis enables us to go *through* science, as it were, to a psychological principle that itself explains science: any way of interpreting the world, even physics, meets human needs, for interpretation is a human act. From a medieval *why* to the *how* that underlay the three great centuries of classical science, we proceed to a psychoanalytic *to whom*. Willey might have been anticipating it when he said, "One cannot . . . define 'explanation' absolutely; one can only say that it is a statement which satisfies the demands of a particular time or place." Or, I would say, person. The claim of objectivity can take the form of experiment in psychology, formalism in literary criticism, or even the universal DEFT principle relating identity to interpretation here put forward. Whatever form it takes, any such toehold into objectivity makes it possible for some human being to feel he has protected his self against falling into some Other, human or inhuman, a fear to which the nonlegendary Robert Frost was no stranger, nor am I. Nor, I suspect, is any literary critic.

I began with assurance, but I sense that I must end with reassurance. Please recognize that in establishing an inextricable proportionality among unity, identity, text, and self, and so denying claims of objectivity that would separate them, I am not positing an isolated, solipsistic self. Just the opposite, in fact. I said I would try to fill in the white spaces in my enigmatic title. Let me now reassure you that I am indeed filling them in, and you are too, and all people are, all the time—including the hardest of "hard" scientists. Every time a human being reaches out, across, or by means of symbols to the world, he reenacts the principles that define that mingling of self and other, the creative and relational quality of all our experience, not least the writing and reading of literature.

NOTES

1. *Phaedrus*, 264C. *Poetics*, Sec. VIII and 1459a20.
2. "The Art of Fiction" (1884), in *The Great Critics*, ed. James H. Smith and Edd Winfield Parks, 3rd ed. (New York: Norton, 1951), p. 661.
3. "Literary Criticism," in *The Aims and Methods of Scholarship in Modern Languages and Literature*, ed. James Thorpe (New York: MLA, 1963), p. 65.
4. *A Glossary of Psychoanalytic Terms and Concepts*, ed. Burness E. Moore and Bernard D. Fine (New York: American Psychoanalytic Association, 1967), s.v. "Self."
5. Erikson, *Identity: Youth and Crisis* (New York: Norton, 1968), p. 50. Leites, *The New Ego: Pitfalls in Current Thinking about Patients in Psychoanalysis* (New York: Science House, 1971), Chs. viii–xiv.
6. Lichtenstein, "Identity and Sexuality: A Study of Their Interrelationship in Man," *Journal of the American Psychoanalytic Association* 9 (1961), 179–260; "The Dilemma of Human Identity: Notes on Self-Transformation, Self-Objectivation and Metamorphosis," *Journal of the American Psychoanalytic Association*, 11 (1963), 173–223; "The Role of Narcissism

in the Emergence and Maintenance of a Primary Identity," *International Journal of Psycho-Analysis*, 45 (1964), 49–56; "Towards a Metapsychological Definition of the Concept of Self," *International Journal of Psycho-Analysis*, 46 (1965), 117–28.

7. *De Anima*, II.1.412b11, trans. J. A. Smith, in *Introduction to Aristotle*, ed. Richard McKeon (New York: Random, 1947), p. 172.
8. The responses of readers to this story are reported and analyzed in detail in my *5 Readers Reading* (New Haven: Yale Univ. Press, 1975). In "A Letter to Leonard," *Hartford Studies in Literature*, 5 (1973), 9–30, I have described how these larger-than-expected differences make the usual explanation of the variability of literary response inadequate. It is usually said that the literary text embodies norms for an infinite number of experiences which its several readers each partially achieve. One can explain the very many and very different readings of a text more economically (or more Occamically), however, by saying the differences comes from the very many and very different readers rather than the text which, after all, remains the same and is demonstrably not infinite.

   Incidentally, it is the close analysis of what readers actually say about what they read that differentiates, on the one hand, the work of what has been called the "Buffalo school of psychoanalytic critics" or the literary use of communiation theory by Elemér Hankiss in Budapest from, on the other, the "affective stylistics" of Stanley E. Fish or more philosophical statements on response by Wolfgang Iser and Hans Robert Jauss of the Universität Konstanz. Compare, e.g., this essay or Hankiss, "Shakespeare's *Hamlet:* The Tragedy in the Light of Communication Theory," *Acta Litteraria Academiae Scientiarum Hungaricae*, 12 (1970), 297–312, with Fish, "Literature in the Reader: Affective Stylistics," *New Literary History*, 2 (1970), 123–62, Iser, "Indeterminacy and the Reader's Response in Prose Fiction," *Aspects of Narrative*, ed. J. Hillis Miller, English Institute Essays (New York: Columbia Univ. Press, 1971), pp. 1–45, or Jauss, "Literary History as a Challenge to Literary Theory," *New Literary History*, 2 (1970), 7–37.
9. These principles are evidenced and more fully stated in my *Poems in Persons* (New York: Norton, 1973) and *5 Readers Reading*.
10. I have described at length this transformational process and the way the reader uses materials from the literary work to achieve it in *The Dynamics of Literary Response* (New York: Oxford Univ. Press, 1968), Chs. i–vi.
11. Amy Lowell, *A Critical Fable* (Boston: Houghton, 1922), p. 22.
12. "At Stratford-on-Avon," *Ideas of Good and Evil* (London: A. H. Bullen, 1903), p. 162.
13. My first quotation is from a letter to Lesley Frost Francis, 1 March 1939, *Family Letters of Robert and Elinor Frost*, ed. Arnold Grade (Albany: State Univ. of New York Press, 1972), p. 210. Most of the rest come from the first 2 vols. of the Lawrance Thompson biography: *Robert Frost: The Early Years, 1874–1915*, I (New York: Holt, 1966) and *Robert Frost: The Years of Triumph, 1915–1938*, II (New York: Holt, 1970). "The style is the man" (II, 421). Reading tastes (I, 549). "Greatest of all attempts" (II, 694 and 364). Two remarks on science (II, 649–50). Emerson (I, 70–71). Synecdoche (II, 693). "I am a mystic" (I, 550). "Every poem is an epitome" (I, xxii). "When in doubt there is always form" (I, xxiii). Quotations that use the phrase, "The Figure a Poem Makes," are from that essay, preface to the 1939 and succeeding editions of his collected poems. "I never dared be radical" is from the poem "Precaution" (1936).

    While this essay was in MS, C. Barry Chabot published a searching and convincing—and confirmatory—formulation of Frost's central theme: the created as a wall against a giant invader ("The 'Melancholy Dualism' of Robert Frost," *Review of Existential Psychology and Psychiatry*, 13, 1974, 42–56).
14. "Creative Writers and Day-Dreaming" (1908), *Standard Edition of the Complete Psy-*

chological Works of Sigmund Freud, ed. James Strachey (London: Hogarth, 1959), IX, 153.

15. In this paragraph, I am drawing on ideas developed in an essay by Murray Schwartz, "The Space of Psychological Criticism," *Hartford Studies in Literature,* 5 (1973), x–xxi.
16. *The Seventeenth Century Background: Studies in the Thought of the Age in Relation to Poetry and Religion* (1934; rpt. Garden City: Doubleday, 1953); pp. 12–14.

15. Narration in the Psychoanalytic Dialogue

Roy Schafer

1. PREFACE: PSYCHOANALYTIC THEORIES AS NARRATIVES

Freud established a tradition within which psychoanalysis is understood as an essentialist and positivist natural science. One need not be bound by this scientific commitment, however; the individual and general accounts and interpretations Freud gave of his case material can be read in another way. In this reading, psychoanalysis is an interpretive discipline whose practitioners aim to develop a particular kind of systematic account of human action. We can say, then, either that Freud was developing a set of principles for participating in, understanding, and explaining the dialogue between psychoanalyst and analysand or that he was establishing a set of codes to generate psychoanalytic meaning, recognizing this meaning in each instance to be only one of a number of kinds of meaning that might be generated.

Psychoanalytic theorists of different persuasions have employed different interpretive principles or codes—one might say different narrative structures—to develop their ways of doing analysis and telling about it.[1] These narrative structures present or imply two coordinated accounts: one, of the beginning, the course, and the ending of human development; the other, of the course of the psychoanalytic dialogue. Far from being secondary narratives about data, these structures provide primary narratives that establish what is to count as data. Once installed as leading narrative structures, they are taken as certain in order to develop coherent accounts of lives and technical practices.

It makes sense, and it may be a useful project, to present psychoanalysis in narrational terms. In order to carry through this project, one must, first of all, accept the proposition that there are not objective, autonomous, or pure psychoanalytic data which, as Freud was fond of saying, compel one to draw

Reprinted by permission of the author and the University of Chicago Press from *Critical Inquiry*, 7 (1980).

certain conclusions. Specifically, there is no single, necessary, definitive account of a life history and psychopathology, of biological and social influences on personality, or of the psychoanalytic method and its results. What have been presented as the plain empirical data and techniques of psychoanalysis are inseparable from the investigator's precritical and interrelated assumptions concerning the origins, coherence, totality, and intelligibility of personal action. The data and techniques exist as such by virtue of two sets of practices that embody these assumptions: first, a set of *practices of naming and interrelating* that is systematic insofar as it conforms to the initial assumptions; and second, a set of *technical practices* that is systematic insofar as it elicits and shapes phenomena that can be ordered in terms of these assumptions. No version of psychoanalysis has ever come close to being codified to this extent. The approach to such codification requires that the data of psychoanalysis be unfailingly regarded as constituted rather than simply encountered. The sharp split between subject and object must by systematically rejected.

In his formal theorizing, Freud used two primary narrative structures, and he often urged that they be taken as provisional rather than as final truths. But Freud was not always consistent in this regard, sometimes presenting dogmatically on one page what he had presented tentatively on another. One of his primary narrative structures begins with the infant and young child as a beast, otherwise known as the id, and ends with the beast domesticated, tamed by frustration in the course of development in a civilization hostile to its nature. Even though this taming leaves each person with two regulatory structures, the ego and the superego, the protagonist remains in part a beast, the carrier of the indestructible id. The filling in of this narrative structure tells of a lifelong transition: if the innate potential for symbolization is there, and if all goes well, one moves from a condition of frightened and irrational helplessness, lack of self-definition, and domination by fluid or mobile instinctual drives toward a condition of stability, mastery, adaptability, self-definition, rationality, and security. If all does not go well, the inadequately tamed beast must be accommodated by the formation of pathological structures, such as symptoms and perversions.

Freud did not invent this beast, and the admixture of Darwinism in his account only gave it the appearance of having been established in a positivist scientific manner. The basic story is ancient; it has been told in many ways over the centuries, and it pervades what we consider refined common sense.[2] But Freud used the old story well. His tale of human development, suffering, defeat, and triumph was extraordinarily illuminating in is psychological content, scientifically respectable in its conceptualization and formalization, dramatically gripping in its metaphorical elaboration, and beneficial in his work with his patients.

Because this archtypal story has been mythologically enshrined in the metaphoric language that all of us have learned to think and live by, it is more than appealing to have it authorized and apparently confirmed by psychological science. At the same time, however, it is threatening to be told persuasively how much it is the beast that pervades, empowers, or at least necessitates our most civilized achievements. Except when we are moralizing about others, human beings do not wish to think consciously of having bestial origins, continuities, and destinies, and so we develop defenses and allow ourselves to think only of certain aspects of our "natures." Through his uncompromising effort to establish a systematic psychoanalytic life story in these terms, Freud exposed our paradoxical attitude toward his fateful story of human lives.

Freud's other primary narrative structure is based on Newtonian physics as transmitted through the physiological and neuroanatomical laboratories of the nineteenth century. This account presents psychoanalysis as the study of the mind viewed as a machine—in Freud's words, as a mental apparatus. This machine is characterized by inertia; it does not work unless it is moved by force. It works as a closed system; that is, its amount of energy is fixed, with the result that storing or expending energy in one respect decreases the energy available for other operations: thus on purely quantitative grounds, love of others limits what is available for self-love, and love of the opposite sex limits what is available for love of the same sex. The machine has mechanisms, such as the automatically operating mechanisms of defense and various other checks and balances.

In the beginning, the forces that move the machine are primarily the brute organism's instinctual drives. Here the tale of the mental apparatus borrows from the tale of the brute organism and consequently becomes narratively incoherent: the mechanical mind is now said to behave like a creature with a soul—seeking, reacting, and developing. The tale continues with increasing incoherence.[3]

Both of Freud's primary narrative structures assume thoroughgoing determinism: the determinism of evolutionary necessity and the determinism of Newtonian forces. No room is left for freedom and responsibility. Those actions that appear to be free and responsible must be working into the deterministic narrative of the beast, the machine, or the incoherent mingling of the two. Freedom is a myth of conscious thought.

Freud insisted on the two narrative structures I have synopsized as the core of what he called his metapsychology, and he regarded them as indispensible. But, as I said at the outset, Freud can be read in other ways. One can construct a Freud who is a humanistic-existentialist, a man of tragic and ironic vision,[4] and one can construct a Freud who is an investigator laying the foundation for a conception of psychoanalysis as an interpretive study of human action.[5] Although we can derive these alternative readings from statements made explicitly by Freud when, as a man and a clinician, he took distance from his official account, we do not require their authority to execute this project; and these alternative readings are not discredited by quotations from Freud to the opposite effect.

That Freud's beast and machine are indeed narrative structures and are not dictated by the data is shown by the fact that other psychoanalysts have developed their own accounts, each with a more or less different beginning, course, and ending. Melanie Klein, for example, gives an account of the child or adult as being in some stage of recovery from a rageful infantile psychosis at the breast.[6] Her story starts with a universal yet pathological infantile condition that oscillates between paranoid and melancholic positions. For her, our lives begin in madness, which includes taking in the madness of others, and we continue to be more or less mad though we may be helped by fortuitous circumstances or by analysis. Certain segments of common speech, for example, the metaphors of the witch, the poisonous attitude, and the people who get under your skin or suck out your guts, or the common recognition that we can all be "crazy" under certain circumstances all support this account that emphasizes unconscious infantile fantasies of persecution, possession,and devastation.

To bypass many other more or less useful narratives that over the years have been proposed in the name of psychoanalysis, we currently have one developed by Heinz Kohut. Kohut tells of a child driven almost instinctlike fashion to actualize a cohesive self. The child is more or less hampered or damaged in the process by the empathic failures of caretakers in its intimate environment. Its growth efforts are consequently impeded by reactive and consoling grandiose fantasies, defensive splitting and repression, and affective "disintegration products" that experientially seem to act like Freud's drives or else to take the form of depressive, hypochondriacal, perverse, or addictive symptoms. In truth, however, these pathological signs are bits and pieces of the shattered self striving to protect itself, heal itself, and continue its growth. The ending in Kohut's story is for each person a point on a continuum that ranges from a frail, rageful, and poverty-stricken self to one that is healthy, happy, and wise.[7]

My schematization of Freudian narration and of Klein's and Kohut's alternatives can be useful. Schematization, when recognized as such, is not falsification. It can serve as a code for comparative reading in terms of beginnings, practices, and possible endings. It can clarify the sets of conventions that govern the constituting and selective organizing of psychoanalytic data. And in every interesting and useful case, it will help us remain attentive to certain commonsensically important events and experiences, such as the vicissitudes of the development, subjective experience, and estimation of the self or the child's struggles with a controlling, frightening, and misunderstood environment. Let us say, then, that some such code prepares us to engage in a systematic psychoanalytic dialogue.

I shall now attempt to portray this psychoanalytic dialogue in terms of two agents, each narrating or telling something to the other in a rule-governed manner. Psychoanalysis as telling and retelling along psychoanalytic lines: this is the theme and form of the present narration. It is, I think, a story worth telling. This much has been my author's preface—if, that is, a preface can be clearly distinguished from the narration that it both foretells and retells.

2. NARRATION IN THE PSYCHOANALYTIC DIALOGUE

We are forever telling stories about ourselves. In telling these self-stories *to others* we may, for most purposes, be said to be performing straightforward narrative actions. In saying that we also tell them *to ourselves,* however, we are enclosing one story within another. This is the story that there is a self to tell something to, a someone else serving as audience who is oneself or one's self. When the stories we tell others about ourselves concern these other selves of ours, when we say, for example, "I am not master of myself," we are again enclosing one story within another. On this view, the self is a telling. From time to time and from person to person, this telling varies in the degree to which it is unified, stable, and acceptable to informed observers as reliable and valid.

Additionally, we are forever telling stories about others. These others, too, may be viewed as figures or other selves constituted by narrative actions.

Other people are constructed in the telling about them; more exactly, we narrate others just as we narrate selves. The other person, like the self, is not something one has or encounters as such but an existence one tells. Consequently, telling "others" about "ourselves" is doubly narrative.

Often the stories we tell about ourselves are life historical or autobiographical; we locate them in the past. For example, we might say, "Until I was fifteen, I was proud of my father" or "I had a totally miserable childhood." These histories are present tellings. The same may be said of the histories we attribute to others. We change many aspects of these histories of self and others as we change, for better or worse, the implied or stated questions to which they are the answers. Personal development may be characterized as change in the questions it is urgent or essential to answer. As a project in personal development, personal analysis changes the leading questions that one addresses to the tale of one's life and the lives of important others.

People going through psychoanalysis—analysands—tell the analyst about themselves and others in the past and present. In making interpretations, the analyst retells these stories. In the retelling, certain features are accentuated while others are placed in parentheses; certain features are related to others in new ways or for the first time; some features are developed further, perhaps at great length. This retelling is done along psychoanalytic lines. What constitutes a specifically psychoanalytic retelling is a topic I shall take up later.

The analyst's retellings progressively influence the what and how of the stories told by analysands. The analyst establishes new, though often contested or resisted, questions that amount to regulated narrative possibilities. The end product of this interweaving of texts is a radically new, jointly authored work or way of working. One might say that in the course of analysis, there develops a cluster of more or less coordinated new narrations, each corresponding to periods of intensive analytic work on certain leading questions.[8] Generally, these narrations focus neither on the past, plain and simple, nor on events currently taking place outside the psychoanalytic situtation. They focus much more on the place and modification of these tales within the psychoanalytic dialogue. Specifically, the narrations are considered under the aspect of transference and resistance as these are identified and analyzed at different times and in relation to different questions. The psychoanalytic dialogue is characterized most of all by its organization in terms of the here and now of the psychoanalytic relationship. It is fundamentally a dialogue concerning the present moment of transference and resistance.

But transference and resistance themselves may be viewed as narrative structures. Like all other narrative structures, they prescribe a point of view from which to tell about the events of analysis in a regulated and therefore coherent fashion. The events themselves are constituted only through one or another systematic account of them. Moreover, the analysis of resistance may be told in terms of transference and vice versa. (I will return to the analysis of resistance in section 3).

In the traditional transference narration, one tells how the analysand is repetitively reliving or reexperiencing the past in the present relationship with the analyst. It is said that there occurs a regression within the transference to the infantile neurosis or neurotic matrix, which then lies exposed to the analyst's view. This is, however, a poor account. It tells of life history as static, archival, linear, reversible, and literally retrievable. Epistemologically, this story is highly problematic. Another and, I suggest, better account tells of change of action along certain lines; it emphasizes new experiencing and new remembering of the past that unconsciously has never become the past. More and more, the alleged past must be experienced consciously as a mutual interpenetration of the past and present, both being viewed in psychoanalytically organized and coordinated terms.[9] If analysis is a matter of moving in a direction, it is a moving forward into new modes of constructing experience. On this account, one must retell the story of regression to the infantile neurosis within the transference; for even though much of its matter may be defined in terms of the present version of the past, the so-called regression is necessarily a progression. Transference, far from being a time machine by which one may travel back to see what one has been made out of, is a clarification of certain constituents of one's present psychoanalytic actions. This clarification is achieved through the circular and coordinated study of past and present.

The technical and experiential construction of personal analyses in the terms of transference and resistance has been found to be therapeutically useful. But now it must be added that viewing psychoanalysis as a therapy itself manifests a narrative choice. This choice dictates that the story of the dialogue and the events to which it gives rise be told in terms of a doctor's curing a patient's disease. From the inception of psychoanalysis, professional and ideological factors have favored this kind of account, though there are some signs today that the sickness narrative is on its way to becoming obsolete. Here I want only to emphasize that there are a number of other ways to tell what the two people in the analytic situation are doing. Each of these ways either cultivates and accentuates or neglects and minimizes certain potential features of the analysis; none is exact and comprehensive in every way. For example, psychoanalyis as therapy tells the story from the standpoint of consciousness: consciously, but only consciously, the analysand presents his/her problems as alien interferences with the good life, that is, as symptoms in the making of which he/she has had no hand; or the analyst defines as symptomatic the problems he/she consciously wishes to emphasize; or both. In many cases, this narrative facilitates undertaking the analysis; at the same time, a price is paid, at least for some time, by this initial and perhaps unavoidable collusion to justify analysis on these highly defensive and conscious grounds of patienthood.

My own attempt to remain noncommittal in this respect by speaking of analyst and analysand rather than therapist and patient is itself inexact in at least three ways. First, it does not take into account the analyst's also being subject to analysis through his/her necessarily continuous scrutiny of countertransferences. Second, during the analysis, the analysand's self is retold as constituted by a large, fragmented, and fluid cast of characters: not only are aspects of the self seen to incorporate aspects of others, they are also unconsciously imagined as having retained some or all of the essence of these others; that is, the self-constituents are experienced as introjects or incomplete identifications, indeed sometimes as shadowy presences of indeterminate location and origin. The problematic and incoherent self that is consciously told at the beginning of the analysis is sorted out, so far as possible, into that which has retained otherness to a high degree and that which has not. A similar sorting out of the constituents of others' selves is also accomplished; here the concept of projecting aspects of the self into others plays an important role. The upshot is that what the analysand initially tells as self and others undergoes considerable revision once the initial conscious account has been worked over analytically.[10] A third inexactness in my choice of terminology is that the division into analyst and analysand does not provide for the increasing extent to which the analysand becomes coanalyst of his/her own problems and, in certain respects, those of the analyst, too. The analysand, that is, becomes coauthor of the analysis as he/she becomes a more daring and reliable narrator. Here I touch on yet another topic to take up later, that of the unreliable narrator: this topic takes in analyst as well as analysand, for ideally both of them do change during analysis, if to different degrees, and it leads into questions of how, in the post-positivist scheme of things, we are to understand validity in analytic interpretation.

If we are forever telling stories about ourselves and others and to ourselves and others, it must be added that people do more than tell: like authors, they also show. As there is no hard-and-fast line between telling and showing, either in literary narrative[11] or in psychoanalysis, the competent psychoanalyst deals with telling as a form of showing and with showing as a form of telling. Everything in analysis is both communication and demonstration.

Perhaps the simplest instances of analystic showing are those nonverbal behaviors or expressive movements that include bodily rigidity, lateness to or absence from scheduled sessions, and mumbling. The analyst, using whatever he/she already knows or has prepared the way for, interprets these showings and weaves them into one of the narrations of the analysis: for example, "Your lying stiffly on the couch shows that you're identifying yourself with your dead father"; or, "Your mumbling shows how afraid you are to be heard as an independent voice on this subject." Beyond comments of this sort, however, the analyst takes these showings as communications and on this basis may say (and here I expand these improvised interpretations), "You are conveying that you feel like a corpse in relation to me, putting your life into me and playing your dead father in relation to me; you picture me now as yourself confronted by this corpse, impressing on me that I am to feel your grief for you." Or the analyst might say, "By your mumbling you are letting me know how frightened you are to assert your own views to me just in case I might feel as threatened by such presumption as your mother once felt and might retaliate as she did by being scornful and turning her back on you." In these interpretive retellings, the analyst is no longer controlled by the imaginary line between telling and showing.

Acting out as a form of remembering is a good case in point.[12] For example, by anxiously engaging in an affair with an older married man, a young woman in analysis is said to be remembering, through acting out, an infantile Oedipal wish to seduce or be sexually loved and impregnated by her father, now represented by the analyst. In one way, this acting out is showing; in another way, it is telling by a displaced showing. Once it has been retold as remembering through acting out, it may serve as a narrative context that facilitates further direct remembering and further understanding of the analytic relationship.

The competent analyst is not lulled by the dramatic rendition of life historical content into hearing this content in a simple, contextless, time-bound manner. Situated in the present, the analyst takes the telling also as a showing, noting, for example, when that content is introduced, for it might be a way of forestalling the emotional experiencing of the immediate transference relationship; noting also how that content is being told, for it might be told flatly, histrionically, in a masochistically self-pitying or a grandiosely triumphant way; noting further the story line that is being followed and many other narrative features as well. The analyst also attends to cues that the analysand, consciously or unconsciously, may be an unreliable narrator: highlighting the persecutory actions of others and minimizing the analysand's seduction of the persecutor to persecute; slanting the story in order to block out significant periods in his/her life history or to elicit pity or admiration; glossing over, by silence and euphemism, what the analysand fears will cast him/her in an unfavorable light or sometimes in too favorable a light, as when termination of analysis is in the air, and, out of a sense of danger, one feels compelled to tell and show that one is still "a sick patient." All of which is to say that the analyst takes the telling as performance as well as content. The analyst has only tellings and showings to interpret, that is, to retell along psychoanalytc lines.

What does it mean to say "along psychoanalytic lines"? Earlier I mentioned that more than one kind of psychoanalysis is practiced in this world, so let me merely summarize what conforms to my own practice, namely, the story lines that characterize Freudian retellings. The analyst slowly and patiently develops an emphasis on infantile or archaic modes of sexual and aggressive action (action being understood broadly to take in wishing, believing, perceiving, remembering, fantasizing, behaving emotionally, and other such activities that, in traditional theories of action, have been split off from motor action and discussed separately as thought, motivation, and feeling). The analyst wants to study and re-describe all of these activities from the standpoint of such questions as "What is the analysand doing?" "Why now?" "Why in this way?" and "What does this have to do with me and what the analysand fears might develop between us sexually and aggressively?"

Repeatedly the analysand's stories (experiences, memories, symptoms, selves) go through a series of transformations until finally they can be retold not only as sexual and aggressive modes of action but also as defensive measures adopted (out of anxiety, guilt, shame, and depression) to disguise, displace, deemphasize, compromise, and otherwise refrain from boldly and openly taking the actions in question. The analyst uses multiple points of view (wishful, defensive, moral, ideal, and adaptive) and expects that significant features of the analysand's life can be understood only after employing all of these points of view in working out contextual redescriptions or interpretations of actions. Single constituents are likely to require a complex definition; for example, sexual and aggressive wishing are often simultaneously ascribable to one and the same personal problem or symptom along with moral condemnation of "self" on both grounds.

The Freudian analyst also progressively organizes this retelling around bodily zones, modes, and substances, particularly the mouth, anus, and genitalia; and in conjunction with these zones, the modes of swallowing and spitting out, retaining and expelling, intruding and enclosing, and the concrete conceptions of words, feelings, ideas, and events as food, feces, urine, semen, babies, and so on. All of these constituents are given roles in the infantile drama of family life, a drama that is organized around births, losses, illnesses, abuse and neglect, the parents' real and imagined conflicts and sexuality, gender differences, sibling relations, and so on. It is essential that the infantile drama, thus conceived, be shown to be repetitively introduced by the analysand into the analytic dialogue, however subtly this may be done, and this is what is accomplished in the interpretive retelling of transference and resistance.

3. DRIVES, FREE ASSOCIATION, RESISTANCE, AND REALITY TESTING

To illustrate and further develop my thesis on narration in the psychoanalytic dialogue, I shall next take up four concepts that are used repeatedly in narrations concerning this dialogue: drives, free association, resistance, and reality testing.

Drives

Drives appear to be incontrovertible facts of human nature. Even the most casual introspection delivers up a passive picture of the self being driven by internal forces. It might therefore seem perfectly justified to distinguish being driven from wishing, in that wishing seems clearly to be a case of personal action. The distinction is, however, untenable. It takes conscious and conventional testimony of drivenness as the last or natural word on the subject;

but to do so is to ignore the proposition that introspection is itself a form of constructed experience based on a specific narration of mind.

The introspection narrative tells that each person is a container of experience fashioned by an independently operating mind and, that by the use of mental eyes located outside this container, the person may look in and see what is going on.[13] Thus the introspector stands outside his/her mind, thinking—with what? A second mind? We have no unassailable answer. The introspection narrative tells us that far from constructing or creating our lives, we witness them. It thereby sets drastic limits on discourse about human activity and responsibility. The uncritical and pervasive use of this narrative form in daily life and in psychological theories shows how appealing it is to disclaim responsibility in this way.

The drive narrative depends on this introspection narrative and so is appealing in the same way. It appeals in other ways as well. As I mentioned earlier, the drive narrative tells the partly moralistic and partly Darwinian-scientific tale that at heart we are all animals, and it sets definite guidelines for all the tales we tell about ourselves and others. By following these guidelines, we fulfill two very important functions, albeit often painfully and irrationally: we simultaneously derogate ourselves (which we do for all kinds of reasons) and disclaim responsibility for our actions. Because these functions are being served, many people find it difficult to accept the proposition that drive is a narrative structure, that is, an optional way of telling the story of human lives.

Consider, for example, a man regarding a woman lustfully. One might say, "He wishes more than anything else to take her to bed"; or one might say, "His sexual drive is overwhelming and she is its object." The wishing narrative does not preclude the recognition that physiological processes may be correlated with such urgent wishing, though it also leaves room for the fact that this correlation does not always hold. In case the physiological correlates are present, the wishing narrative also provides for the man's noticing these stimuli in the first place, for his having to give meaning to them, for his selecting just that woman, and for his organizing the situation in terms of heterosexual intercourse specifically. From our present point of view, the chief point to emphasize is that the wishing narrative allows one to raise the question, in analytic work as in everyday life, why the subject tells himself that he is passive in relation to a drive rather than that he is a sexual agent, someone who lusts after a specific woman.

A similar case for wishful action may be made in the case of aggression.

In one version or theory, aggression is a drive that requires discharge in rages, assaults, vituperation, or something of that sort; in another version, aggression is an activity or mode of action that is given many forms by agents who variously wish to attack, destroy, hurt, or assert and in each case to do so for reasons and in contexts that may be ascertained by an observer. The observer may, of course, be the agent himself/herself.

In the course of analysis, the analysand comes to construct narratives of personal agency ever more readily, independently, convincingly, and securely, particularly in those contexts that have to do with crucially maladaptive experiences of drivenness. The important questions to be answered in the analysis concern personal agency, and the important answers reallocate the attributions of activity and passivity. Passivity also comes into question because, as in the case of unconscious infantile guilt (so-called superego guilt), agency may be ascribed to the self irrationally (for example, blame of the "self" for the accidental death of a parent).

Free Association

The fundamental rule of psychoanalysis is conveyed through the instruction to associate freely and to hold back nothing that comes to mind. This conception is controlled by the previously mentioned narrative of the introspected mind: one is to tell about thinking and feeling in passive terms; it is to be a tale of the mind's running itself, of thoughts and feelings coming and going, of thoughts and feelings pushed forward by drives or by forces or structures opposing them. Again, the analysand is to be witness to his/her own mind. The psychoanalytic model for this narration is Freud's "mental apparatus."

If, however, one chooses the narrative option of the analysand as agent, that is, as thinker and constructor of emotional action, the fundamental rule will be understood differently and in a way that accords much better with the analyst's subsequent interpretive activity. According to this second narrative structure, the instruction establishes the following guidelines: "Let's see what you will do if you just tell me everything you think and feel without my giving you any starting point, any direction or plan, any criteria of selection, coherence, or decorum. You are to continue in this way with no formal beginning, no formal middle or development, and no formal ending except as you introduce these narrative devices. And let's see what sense we can make of what you do under these conditions. That is to say, let's see how we can retell it in a way that allows you to understand the origins, meanings, and significance of your present difficulties and to do so in a way that makes change conceivable and attainable."

Once the analysand starts the telling, the analyst listens and interprets in two interrelated ways. First, the analyst retells what is told from the standpoint of its content, that is, its thematic coherence. For example, the analysand may be alluding repeatedly to envious attitudes while consciously portraying these attitudes as disinterested, objective criticism. By introducing the theme of envy, the analyst, from his/her special point of view on analytic narration, identifies the kind of narrative that is being developed. (Of course, one does not have to be an analyst to recognize envy in disguise; but this only illustrates my point that analytic narration is not sharply set off from refined common sense.) The specific content then becomes merely illustrative of an unrecognized and probably disavowed set of attitudes that are held by the analysand who is shown to be an unreliable narrator in respect to the consciously constructed account. Ultimately, the unreliability itself must be interpreted and woven into the dialogue as an aspect of resistance.

The analysand's narrative, then, is placed in a larger context, its coherence and significance are increased, and its utility for the analytic work is defined. The analyst has not listened in the ordinary way. Serving as an *analytic* reteller, he/she does not, indeed, cannot coherently, respond in the ordinary way: listening in the ordinary way, as in countertransference, results in analytic incoherence; the analyst's retellings themselves become unreliable and fashioned too much after the analyst's own "life story."

In the second mode of listening and interpreting, the analyst focuses on the action of telling itself. Telling is treated as an object of description rather than, as the analysand wishes, an indifferent or transparent medium for imparting information or thematic content. The analyst has something to say about the how, when, and why of the telling. For example, the analyst may tell that the analysand has been circling around a disturbing feeling of alienation from the analyst, the narration's circumstantial nature being intended to guarantee an interpersonally remote, emotionally arid session; and if it is envy that is in question, the analyst may tell that the analysand is trying to spoil the analyst's envied competence by presenting an opaque account of the matter at hand.

In this way, the analyst defines the complex rules that the analysand is following in seeming to "free associate."[14] There are rules of various kinds for alienated discourse, for envious discourse, and so on, some very general and well known to common sense and some very specialized or individual and requiring careful definition in the individual case, but which must still, ultimately, be in accord with common sense. The analyst treats free association as neither free nor associative, for within the strategy of analyzing narrative actions, it is not an unregulated or passive performance.

The analysand consciously experiences many phenomena in the passive mode: unexpected intrusions or unexpected trains of thought, irrelevant or shameful feelings, incoherent changes of subject, blocking and helpless withholdings of thoughts, and imperative revisions of raw content. The analysand consciously regards all of these as unintentional violations of the rules he/she consciously professes to be following or wishes to believe are being followed. But what is to the analysand flawed or helpless performance is not so to the analyst. For the analyst, free associating is a no-fault activity. What is consciously unexpected or incomprehensible is seen rather as the analysand's having unconsciously introduced more complex rules to govern the narrative being developed: the analysand may have become uneasy with what is portrayed as the drift of thought and sensed that he/she was heading into danger, or perhaps the tale now being insistently foregrounded is a useful diversion from another and more troubling tale. In the interest of being "a good patient," the analysand may even insist of developing narratives in primitive terms, for instance, in terms of ruthless revenge or infantile sexual practices, when at that moment a more subjectively distressing but analytically useful account of the actions in question would have to be given in terms of assertiveness, or fun-lovingness, or ordinary sentimentality. Whatever the case may be, a new account is called for, a more complex account, one in which the analysand is portrayed as more or less unconsciously taking several parts at once—hero, victim, dodger, and stranger. These parts are not best understood as autonomous subselves having their say ("multiple selves" is itself only a narrative structure that begs the question); rather, each of these parts is one of the regulative narrative structures that one person, the analysand, has adopted and used simultaneously with the others, whether in combination, opposition, or apparent incoherence. The analyst says, in effect, "What I hear you saying is . . ." or "In other words, it's a matter of . . . ," and this is to say that a narrative is now being retold along analytic lines as *the only narrative it makes good enough sense to tell at that time.*

Resistance

Resistance can be retold so as to make it appear in an altogether different light; furthermore, it can be retold in more than one way. Before I show how this is so, I should synopsize Freud's account of resistance.[15] For Freud, "*the* resistance," as he called it, was an autonomous force analogous to the censorship in the psychology of dreams. The term refers to the many forms taken by the analysand's opposition to the analyst. The resistance, Freud said, accompanies the analysis every step of the way, and technically nothing is more important than to ferret it out and analyze it. The resistance is often sly, hidden, secretive, obdurate, and so on. In the terms of Freud's theory of psychic structure, there is a split in the analysand's ego; the rational ego wants to go forward while the defensive ego wants to preserve the irrational status quo. The analysand's ego fears change toward health through self-understanding, viewing that course as too dangerous or too mortifying to bear. These accounts of resistance establish narrative structures of several pairs of antagonists in the analytic situation: one part of the ego against another, the ego against the id, the analysand against the analyst, and the analyst against the resistance. The conflict centers on noncompliance with the fundamental rule of free association, a rule that in every case can be observed by the analysand only in a highly irregular and incomplete fashion. Presenting the resistance as a force in the mind, much like a drive, further defines the form of the analytic narration: resistance is presented as animistic or anthropomorphic, a motivated natural force that the subject experiences passively.

How does the story of resistance get to be retold during an analysis? In one retelling, resistance transforms into an account of transference, both positive and negative. Positive transference is resistance attempting to transform the analysis into some repetitive version of conflictual infantile love relationship on the basis of which one may legitimately abandon the procedures and goals of analysis itself. In the case of negative transference, the analyst is seen irrationally and often unconsciously as an authoritarian parent to be defied. Through a series of transformations, and with reference to various clues produced by the analysand, the opposition is retold by the analyst as an enactment of the oral, anal, and phallic struggles of infancy and childhood, that is, as a refusal to be fed or weaned or else as a biting; or as a refusal to defecate in the right place and at the right time, resorting instead to constipated withholding or diarrheic expelling of associations, feelings, and memories; or as furtive masturbation, primal scene voyeurism and exhibitionism, defensive or seductive changes of the self's gender, and so on. Thus the distinction between the analysis of resistance and the analysis of transference, far from being the empirical matter it is usually said to be, is a matter of narrative choice. Told in terms of transference, resistance becomes disclaimed repetitive activity rather than passive experience.[16] And it is as activity that it takes its most intelligible, coherent, and modifiable place in the developing life historical contexts.

There is another, entirely affirmative way to retell the story of resistance. In this account, the analysand is portrayed as doing something on his/her behalf, something that makes sense unconsciously though it may not yet be understood empathically by the analyst. The analyst may then press confrontations and interpretations on the analysand at the wrong time, in the wrong way, and with the wrong content. Kohut's account of narcissistic rage in response to such interventions presents the analysand as protecting a fragile self against further disintegration in response to the analyst's empathically deficient interventions. Or the analysand may be protecting the analyst against his/her own anticipated ruthless, destructive, or at least permanently alienating form of love. Matters of personal pride and honor may be involved. In one instance, the analysand's resistance was understood as a form of self-abortion and in another instance as a refusal to be forced into what was taken to be a phallic role.

Whatever the case and whatever the manifestly oppositional attitude, the analysand is portrayed as engaged in a project of preservation, even enhancement, of self or analyst or both. The project is one that the analysand at that moment rightly refuses to abandon despite what may be the misguided efforts of the analyst to narrate the analysis along other lines. In this affirmative narration of resisting, the analyst may be an uncomprehending brute or an unwitting saboteur. One young woman's spontaneously defiant insistence on persistently excoriating her parents had to be retold analytically in two main ways: as a turning away from the unbearable horror of her imagined inner world and as a firm assertion on her part that the problem resided in the family as a system and not merely in her infantile fantasies and wishes. On the one hand, there was a crucial strategy of self-prevention implied in her apparent resistance: as she said at one point, "If I let myself appreciate myself and see what, against all odds, I've become, it would break my heart." On the other hand, there was the analysand's search for the self-affirming truth of parental madness. To have thought of her strident analytic activity simply as resistance would have been to start telling the wrong kind of psychoanalytic story about it.

A third way to retell the story of resistance radically questions the analysand's use of ability and inability words. It is developed along the following lines. Resistance seems to go against the analysand's wishes and resolutions. The analysand pleads inability: for example, "Something stops me from coming out with it," or "My inhibitions are too strong for me to make the first move," or "I can't associate anything with that dream." The narrative structure of inability in such respects is culturally so well established that it seems to be merely an objective expression of the natural order of things. Yet it may be counted as another aspect of the analysand as unconsciously unreliable narrator. In the first example (not coming out with it), the retelling might be developed along these lines: "You *don't* come out with it, and you *don't* yet understand why you *don't* act on your resolution to do so." In the third example (inability to associate), it might be developed like this: "You *don't* think of anything that seems to you to be relevant or acceptable, anything that meets your rules of coherence, good sense, or good manners, and you dismiss what you *do* think of."

In giving these examples, I am not presenting actual or recommended analytic interventions so much as I am making their logic plain. In practice, these interventions are typically developed in ways that are tactful, tentative, circuitous, and fragmentary. For a long time, perhaps, the "don't" element is only implied in order to avoid the analysand's mishearing description as criticism and demand; *exhortation* has no place in the analyst's interventions. Nor am I suggesting that the analyst's initial descriptions are the decisive words on any important subject. They are only the first words on the subject in that they begin to establish the ground rules for another kind of story to be told and so of another kind of experience to construct. These are the rules of action language and the reclaiming of disclaimed action.

Choosing action as the suitable narrative language allows the analyst to begin to retell many inability narrations as disclaimings of action. In order to analyze resistance—now to be designated as resist*ing*—one must take many narrations presented by analysands in terms of *can* and *can't* and retell them in terms of *do* and *don't* and sometimes *will* and *won't*. Usually, the analysand is disclaiming the action unconsciously. That this is so does not make the disclaiming (defense, resistance) any the less an action; nor does it make what is being disclaimed any the less an action. In analytic narration, one is not governed by the ordinary conventions that link action to conscious intent.

So often, the analyst, after first hearing "I can't tell you" or "I can't think about that," goes on to establish through close and sustained consideration of free associations the reasons why the analysand does not or will not tell or think about whatever it is that is troublesome. It may be that the action in question would be humiliating, frightening, or apparently incoherent and therefore too mad to be tolerated. It may be that unconsciously the not telling or not thinking is an act of anal retention or Oedipal defiance that is being presented as innocent helplessness. It may be that an important contention between two events has never before been defined, so that the analysand, lacking a suitable narrative structure, simply does not take up the two in one consciously constructed context; connections and contexts might come into existence only through the analyst's interpretive activity. Interpretation may also give the reasons why the context and connections never have been developed. In all such instances, it is no longer ability that is in question, it is the proper designation of a ruled performance.

The same narrative treatments of action and inaction are common in daily life: one hears, "I couldn't control myself," "I can't concentrate on my studies," "I can't love him," and so on. Implicit in these narrations, as in the resisting narrations, is the disclaiming of the activity in what is being told. This disclaiming is accomplished by taking recourse to the terms of uncontrollable, impersonal forces. These accounts, too, may be retold analytically. For instance, after some analysis, "I can't concentrate on my studies" may become the following (synopsized) narrative: "I don't concentrate on what I resolve to work on. I think of other things instead. I think of girls, of my dead father, of all the failures of my life. These are the things that really matter to me, and I rebel against the idea that I should set them aside and just get through the reading like a machine. It's like shitting on demand. Additionally, by not working, I don't risk experiencing either frightening grandiose feelings if I succeed or the shame of mediocrity if I just pass. On top of which, really getting into the work is sexually exciting; it feels something like sexual peeping to read, as I must, between the lines, and it feels wrong to do that." Retold in this way, "I can't concentrate on my studies" becomes "I don't concentrate for certain reasons, some or all of which I did not dare to realize before now. I told myself I was trying to concentrate and couldn't when actually I was doing other things instead and doing them for other reasons." The narrative has changed from the conscious one of helplessness and failure, designed to protect the consciously distressing status quo, to a narrative of unconscious activity in another kind of reality. The new story, told now by a more reliable narrator, is a story of personal action, and as such it may serve as a basis for change.

Nothing in the immediately preceding account implies that for narrative purposes, *inability* words or, for that matter, *necessity* words are narratively ruled totally out of the analytic court. Rather, these words are now found to be useful and appropriate in a far more restricted set of circumstances than before. These sets of circumstances include unusual physical and mental ability and training and also one's inevitable confrontations with the forceful independent actions of others and with impersonal events in the world. Yet even these necessities become analytically relevant only in terms of how the analysand takes them. In any event, necessity (or happening) does not include mental forces and structures that reduce a person to impotence; much impotence is enacted rather than imposed.[17]

Thus the analyst may retell resisting to the analysand in two ways: as what the analysand *is not doing* and why and as what he/she *is doing* and why. It is a matter simply of how best to retell the actions in question. Both versions are technically useful in the analysis of resisting. Neither depends on a narration composed in terms of autonomous and antagonistic natural forces that are thwarting conscious and wholehearted resolve. Both may be encompassed in a narrative of action. There is nothing in the analysis of resistance that necessarily leads beyond this narrative framework into the one structured in terms of psychic forces or other processes of desymbolization or dehumanization.[18]

Reality Testing

Traditionally, the official psychoanalytic conception of reality has been straightforwardly positivistic. Reality is "out there" or "in there" in the inner world, existing as a knowable, certifiable essence. At least for the analytic observer, the subject and object are clearly distinct. Reality is encountered and recognized innocently: in part it simply forces itself on one; in part it is discovered or uncovered by search and reason free of theory. Consequently, reality testing amounts simply to undertaking to establish what is, on the one hand, real, true, objective and, on the other hand, unreal, false, subjective. On this understanding, one may then conclude, for example, that x is fantasy (inner reality) and y is fact (external reality); that mother was not only loving as had always been thought but also hateful; that the situation is serious but not hopeless or vice versa; and so on.

But this positivistic telling is only one way of giving or arriving at an account of the subject in the world, and it is incoherent with respect to the epistemological assumptions inherent in psychoanalytic inquiry, that is, those assumptions that limit us always to dealing only with *versions* of reality. The account I am recommending necessarily limits one to constructing some version or some vision of the subject in the world. One defines situations and invests events with multiple meanings, which are all more or less adequately responsive to different questions that the narrator, who may be the subject or someone else, wants to answer and which are also responsive to the rules of context that the narrator intends to follow and to the level of abstraction that he/she wishes to maintain. Sometimes, for example, an assertive action of a certain kind in a certain situation may with equal warrant be described as sadistic *and* masochistic, regressive *and* adaptive. In this account, reality is always mediated by narration. Far from being innocently encountered or discovered, it is created in a regulated fashion.

The rules regulating creation of reality may be conventional, in which case no questions are likely to be raised about the world and how we know it; if needed, consensual validation will be readily obtained. But things can be otherwise. Once certain rules are defined, they may prove to violate convention in a way that is incoherent or at least not understandable at a given moment. In this case, the place of these rules requires further investigation and interpretation; those rules that inform truly original ideas may necessitate revision of accepted ideas about the rules that "must" be followed and the kind of reality that it is desirable or interesting to construct. Freud's highly particularized, "overdetermined" accounts of the idiosyncratic systems of rules followed in dreams, neuroses, perversions, psychoses, and normal sexual development showed his real genius.

One may say that *psychoanalytic interpretation tells about a second reality*. In this reality, events or phenomena are viewed from the standpoint of repetitive re-creation of infantile, family-centered situations bearing on sex, aggression, and other such matters. Only superficially does the analytic construction of this second reality seem to be crudely reductive; it is crudely reductive only when it is performed presumptuously or stupidly, as when the analyst says, "This is what you are *really* doing." The competent analyst says in effect, "Let me show you over the course of the analysis another reality, commonsensical elements of which are already, though incoherently and eclectically, included in what you now call reality. We shall be looking at you and others in your life, past and present, in a special light, and we shall come to understand our analytic project and our relationship in this light, too. This second reality is as real as any other. In many ways it is more coherent and inclusive and more open to your activity than the reality you now vouch for and try to make do with. On this basis, it also makes the possibility of change clearer and more or less realizable, and so it may open for you a way out of your present difficulties.''

From the acceptance of this new account, there follows a systematic project of constructing a psychoanalytic reality in which one retells the past and the present, the infantile and the adult, the imagined and the so-called real, and the analytic relationship and all other significant relationships. One retells all this in terms that are increasingly focused and coordinated in psychoanalytic terms of action. One achieves a narrative redescription of reality. This retelling is adapted to the clinical context and relationship, the purpose of which is to understand anew the life and the problems in question. The analysand joins in the retelling (redescribing, reinterpreting) as the analysis progresses. The second reality becomes a joint enterprise and a joint experience. And if anyone emerges as a crude reductionist it is the analysand, viewed now as having unconsciously reduced too many events simply to infantile sexual and aggressive narratives.

At this point we may return once more to the question of the unreliable narrator for it bears on the large question of validity of interpretation. To speak of the unreliable narrator, one must have some conception of a reliable narrator, that is, of validity; and yet the trend of my argument suggests that there is no single definitive account to be achieved. Validity, it seems, can only be achieved within a system that is viewed as such and that appears, after careful consideration, to have the virtues of coherence, consistency, comprehensiveness, and common sense. This is the system that establishes the second reality in psychoanalysis. The analysand is helped to become a reliable narrator in this second reality which is centered on transference and resistance. A point of view is maintained and employed that both establishes a maximum of reliability and intelligibility of the kind required and confirms, hermeneutically, that achievement. The increased possibility of change, of new and beneficial action in the world, is an essential aim of this project and an important criterion of its progress. It must be added at once that the appropriate conception of change excludes randomness or personally ahistorical or discontinuous consequences, such as abrupt and total reversals of values and behavior. The reallocation of activity and passivity is another important aim and criterion. Finally, the analytic accounts achieved may be judged more or less valid by their ability to withstand further tough and searching questions about the story that has now been told and retold from many different, psychologically noncontradictory though often conflictual, perspectives and in relation to considerable evidence constituted and gathered up within the analytic dialogue.

4. THE NORMATIVE LIFE HISTORY

Psychoanalytic researchers have always aimed to develop a normative, continuous psychoanalytic life history that begins with day one, to be used by the psychoanalyst as a guide for his/her participation in the analytic dialogue. Freud set this pattern by laying out the psychosexual stages and defining the instinctual vicissitudes, the stage of narcissism, phase-specific orientations and conflicts (oral, anal, etc.), the origins and consolidation of the ego and superego, and other such developmental periods, problems, and achievements. Yet it is safe to say that in the main, his life histories take shape around the time of the Oedipus complex, that is, the time between the ages of two and five. In his account, earlier times remain shadowy prehistory or surmised constitutional influences, not too accessible to subjective experience or verification.

Today the field of psychoanalysis is dominated by competing theories about these earlier, shadowy phases of mental development. These now include the phase of autism, symbiosis, and separation-individuation; the phase of basic trust and mistrust; the phase of pure narcissism, in which there are no objects which are not primarily part of the self; the mirror phase; and variations on the Kleinian paranoid-schizoid and depressive phases or ''positions'' of infancy. For the most part, these phases are defined and detailed by what are called constructions or reconstructions, that is, surmises based on memories, symbolic readings, and subjective phenomena encountered in the analysis of adults, though some direct observation of children has also been employed. These surmises concern the nature of the beginning of subjective experience and the formative impact of the environment on that experience, an impact which is estimated variously by different theorists. In all, a concerted attempt is being made to go back so far in the individual's subjective history as to eliminate its prehistory altogether.

These projects are, for the most part, conceived and presented as fact-finding. On the assumption that there is no other way to understand the present, it is considered essential to determine what in fact it was like way back when. Whatever its internal differences, this entire program is held to have heuristic as well as therapeutic value. It is not my present intention to dispute this claim. I do, however, think that from a methodological standpoint, this program has been incorrectly conceived.

The claim that these normative life historical projects are simply fact-finding expeditions is, as I argued earlier, highly problematic. At the very outset, each such expedition is prepared for what is to be found: it has its maps and compasses, its conceptual supplies, and its probable destination. This preparedness (which contradicts the empiricists' pretensions of innocence) amounts to a narrative plan, form, or set of rules. The sequential life historical narration that is then developed is no more than a second-order retelling of clinical analysis. But this retelling confusingly deletes reference to the history of the analytic dialogue. It treats that dialogue as though—to change my metaphor—it is merely the shovel used to dig up history and so is of no account, except perhaps in manuals on the technique of digging up true chronologies. The theorists have therefore committed themselves to the narrative form of the case history, which is a simplified form of traditional biography.

Is there a narrative form that is methodologically more adequate to the psychoanalytic occasion? I believe there is. It is a story that begins in the middle which is the present: the beginning is the beginning of the analysis. The present is not the autobiographical present, which at the outset comprises what are called the analysand's presenting problems or initial complaints together with some present account of the past; the reliability and usefulness of both of these constituents of the autobiographical present remain to be determined during the analysis. Once the analysis is under way, the autobiographical present is found to be no clear point in time at all. One does not even know how properly to conceive that present; more and more it seems to be both a repetitive, crisis-perpetuating misremembering of the past and a way of living defensively with respect to a future which is, in the most disruptive way, imagined fearfully and irrationally on the model of the past.

It soon becomes evident that, interpretively, one is working in a temporal circle. One works backward from what is told about the autobiographical present in order to define, refine, correct, organize, and complete an analytically coherent and useful account of the past, and one works forward from various tellings of the past to constitute that present and that anticipated future which are most important to explain.[19] Under the provisional and dubious assumption that past, present, and future are separable, each segment of time is used to set up a series of questions about the others and to answer the questions addressed to it by the others. And all of these accounts keep changing as the analytic dialogue continues.[20]

I said that the analytic life history is a second-order history. The first-order history is that of the analytic dialogue. (This history is more like a set of histories that have been told from multiple perspectives over the course of the analysis and that do not actually lend themselves to one seamless retelling; I shall refer to it as one history, nevertheless, inasmuch as analysts typically present it in that way.) This history is situated in the present: it is always and necessarily a present account of the meanings and uses of the dialogue to date or, in other words, of the transference and resistance. The account of the origins and transformations of the life being studied is shaped, extended, and limited by what it is narratively necessary to emphasize and to assume in order to explain the turns in this dialogue. The analysand's stories of early childhood, adolescence, and other critical periods of life get to be retold in a way that both summarizes and justifies what the analyst requires in order to do the kind of psychoanalytic work that is being done.

The primary narrative problem of the analyst is, then, not how to tell a normative chronological life history; rather, it is how to tell the several histories of each analysis. From this vantage point, the event with which to start the model analytic narration is not the first occasion of thought—Freud's wish-fulfilling hallucination of the absent breast; instead, one should start from a narrative account of the psychoanalyst's retelling of something told by an analysand and the analysand's response to that narrative transformation. In the narration of this moment of dialogue lies the structure of the analytic past, present, and future. It is from this beginning that the accounts of early infantile development are constructed. Those traditional developmental accounts, over which analysts have labored so hard, may now be seen in a new light: less as positivistic sets of factual findings about mental development and more as hermeneutically filled-in narrative structures. The narrative structures that have been adopted control the telling of the events of the analysis, including the many tellings and retellings of the analysand's life history. The time is always present. The event is always an ongoing dialogue.

NOTES

1. See my "On Becoming an Analyst of One Persuasion or Another," *Contemporary Psychoanalysis* 15 (July 1979): 345–60. [Also in *The Analytic Attitude*. New York: Basic Books, 1983]. I will frequently refer the reader to my own books and articles since many brief assertions and discussions here are based on more extended arguments in specialized publications not likely known to most readers of this journal. My great debt to many thinkers in psychoanalysis (especially Freud) and in other interpretive disciplines is acknowledged in these earlier publications.
2. Refined common sense structures the history of human thought about human action. It takes into account the emotional, wishful, fantasy-ridden features of action, its adaptive and utilitarian aspects, and the influence on it of the subject's early experiencing of intimate formative relationships and of the world at large. The repositories of common sense include mythology, folk wisdom, colloquial sayings, jokes, and literature, among other cultural products, and, as Freud showed repeatedly, there are relatively few significant psychoanalytic propositions that are not stated or implied by these products. Refined common sense serves as the source of the precritical assumptions from which the psychoanalytic narrative structures are derived, and these structures dictate conceptual and technical practices. But common sense is not fixed. The common sense presented in proverbs and maxims, for example, is replete with internal tension and ambiguity. Most generalizations have counter-generalizations (A penny saved is a penny earned, but one may by penny-wise and pound-foolish; one should look before one leaps, but he who hesitates is lost, and so on), and just as common sense may be used to reaffirm traditional orientations and conservative values (Rome wasn't built in a day), it may also be used to sanction a challenge to tradition (A new broom sweeps clean) or endorse an ironic stance (The more things change, the more they remain the same). Since generalizations of this sort allow much latitude in their application, recourse to the authority of common sense is an endless source of controversy over accounts of human action. Still, common sense is our storehouse of narrative structures, and it remains the source of intelligibility and certainty in human affairs. Controversy itself would make no sense unless the conventions of common sense were being observed by those engaged in controversy.

   Psychoanalysis does not take common sense plain but rather transforms it into a comprehensive distillage, first, by selection and schematic reduction of its tensions and ambiguities and, second, by elevating only some of these factors (such as pleasure versus reality and id versus ego) to the status of overarching principles and structures. Traditionally, these elevations of common sense have been originated and presented as psychoanalytic metapsychology.

   As more than one such distillation of common sense has been offered in the name of psychoanalysis, there have been phases in the development of psychoanalytic theory, and there are schools of psychoanalysis, each with a distinctive theory of its own. Each distillation (phase or school) has been elaborated and organized in terms of certain leading narrative structures that are to be taken as certain.
3. To sketch this increasing incoherence: In the beginning, the mental apparatus is primitive owing to its lack of structure and differentiated function. Over the course of time, the apparatus develops itself in response to experience and along lines laid down by its inherent nature; it becomes complex, moving on toward an ending in which, through that part of it called the ego, it can set its own aims and take over and desexualize or neutralize energies

from the id. At the same time, the ego takes account of the requirements of the id, the superego, external reality, and its own internal structural problems, and it works out compromises and syntheses of remarkable complexity. When nothing untoward happens during this development, the machine functions stably and efficiently; otherwise, it is a defective apparatus, most likely weak in its ego, superego, or both. A defensive apparatus cannot perform some of the functions for which it is intended, and it performs some others unreliably, inefficiently, and maladaptively, using up or wastefully discharging precious psychic energy in the process. Its effective operation depends on its mechanism's success in restricting the influence of the archaic heritage of infancy. This machine is dedicated to preserving its own structure; it guarantees its own continuity by serving as a bulwark against primal chaos and changes itself only under dire necessity. This mechanic account accords well with the ideology of the Industrial Revolution. We still tend to view the body in general and the nervous system in particular as marvelous machines, and traditional metapsychologists still ask us to view the mind in the same way.

4. See my "The Psychoanalytic Vision of Reality," *A New Language for Psychoanalysis* (New Haven, Conn., and London, 1976), pp. 22–56.
5. See *A New Language for Psychoanalysis* and my *Language and Insight* (New Haven, Conn. and London, 1978).
6. See Hanna Segal's *Introduction to the Work of Melanie Klein* (New York: 1964).
7. For the most part, Kohut remains aware that he is developing a narrative structure. He goes so far as to invoke a principle of complementarity, arguing that psychoanalysis needs and can tolerate a second story, namely, Freud's traditional tripartite psychic structure (id, ego, superego). On Kohut's account, this narrative of psychic structure is needed in order to give an adequate account of phases of development subsequent to the achievement, in the early years of life, of a cohesive self or a healthy narcissim. This recourse to an analogy with the complementarity theory of physics fails to dispel the impression one may gain of narrative incoherence. The problem is, however, not fatal: I am inclined to think that complementarity will be dropped from Kohut's account once it becomes clear how to develop the tale of the embattled self into a comprehensive and continuous narrative—or once it becomes professionally acceptable to do so. See Kohut's *The Analysis of the Self: A Systematic Approach to the Psychoanalytic Treatment of Narcissistic Personality Disorders* (New York, 1971) and *The Restoration of the Self* (New York, 1977).
8. See my "The Appreciative Analytic Attitude and the Construction of Multiple Life Histories," *Psychoanalysis and Contemporary Thought 2,* no. 1 (1979): 3–24. [Also in *The Analytic Attitude,* op. cit.]
9. See my "The Interpretation of Transference and the Conditions for Loving," *Journal of the American Psychoanalytic Association* 25, no. 2 (1977): 335–62. [Also in *The Analytic Attitude,* op. cit.]
10. See my "Self-Control," *Language and Insight,* pp. 67–103.
11. See Wayne C. Booth's *The Rhetoric of Fiction* (Chicago, 1961).
12. See Sigmund Freud's "Remembering, Repeating and Working-Through," *The Standard Edition of the Complete Psychological Works of Sigmund Freud,* ed. James Strachey, 24 vols. (London, 1953–1974), 12:145–56.
13. See Gilbert Ryle's *The Concept of Mind* (New York, 1965). The introspection narrative has been extensively elaborated through a spatial rendering of mental activity, perhaps most of all through the language of internalization and externalization. This spatial language includes: inner world, inwardly, internalize, projection, deep down, levels, layers, and the like. See my "Internalization: Process or Fantasy?" *A New Language for Psychoanalysis,* pp. 155–78.

14. See my "Free Association," *Language and Insight*, pp. 29–66.
15. See, for example, Freud's "The Dynamics of Transference," *Standard Edition*, 12:97–108.
16. See my "The Idea of Resistance," *A New Language for Psychoanalysis*," pp. 217–63.
17. See my "Impotence, Frigidity, and Sexism," *Language and Insight*, pp. 139–71.
18. For a contrasting view, see, for example, Paul Ricoeur's "The Question of Proof in Psychoanalysis," *Journal of the American Psychoanalytic Association* 25, no. 4 (1977): 835–72, esp. sec. 2. Juergen Habermas, working within a purely hermeneutic orientation, has taken what is, from the present point of view, an intermediate position on this matter in his discussion of the contents of the unconscious as deformed, privatized, degrammaticized language. See his *Knowledge and Human Interests*, trans. Jeremy J. Shapiro (Boston, 1971), chaps. 10–12; my discussion owes much to Habermas' penetrating analysis of the linguistic and narrative aspects of psychoanalytic interpretation.
19. See my "The Psychoanalytic Life History," *Language and Insight*, pp. 3–27.
20. Freud's major case studies follow this narrative form. His report on the Rat Man is a good case in point; one has only to compare his notes on the case with his official report on it to see what different tales he told and could have told about this man, that is, *about his work with this man*. See Freud's "Notes upon a Case of Obsessional Neurosis," *Standard Edition*, 10:153–249.

PART IV

RECENT WORK: A MATURE PHASE?

INTRODUCTION

Meredith Anne Skura's book, *The Literary Use of the Psychoanalytic Process,* which appeared in 1981, was praised as "the ablest, most informed, and most complex synthesis of psychoanalysis and literary criticism that we have" (Reed 1983, p. 473). Its subtlety attested to the maturity achieved by this field in the 1980s. Not surprisingly, both Roy Schafer and Norman Holland are listed by the author (p. VII) among those who helped her in formulating her approach. Skura, past trainee of the Western New England Institute for Psychoanalysis, is now a professor of English at Rice University, Houston, Texas.

The book's title conveys Skura's emphasis: not on psychoanalysis as a general theory, but on psychoanalytic method as applied in shaping the psychoanalytic process. "A sensitivity to the delicate changes in consciousness taking place moment by moment in the actual process of an analytic hour can lead to a renewed awareness of the possibilities of language and narrative—an awareness that will increase our range of discriminations rather than reduce them to a fixed pattern, as the theory tends to do" (Skura 1981, p. 5).

She structures her book along a sequence of models used in the psychoanalytic discussion of literature, a sequence that roughly represents a chronological evolution in Freud's thinking: from case studies, to the exploration of fantasy and dream, to the study of transference and a focus on the process of recovery itself. This sequence also expresses a gradual movement away from the search for what "really happened" in the patient's life; "away from the referential to other aspects of a patient's discourse—in particular, to its intrapsychic function (in fantasies); to its mode of representation (in dreams); and to its rhetorical or interpsychic function (in the psychoanalytic exchange)" (p. 9).

Each chapter explores the implications, advantages, and risks of each model for the study of literature, with numerous examples. Discussing literature as case history makes us focus on content, and tempts us to talk about the unconscious mind of specific characters. The limitations of this endeavor are studied by Skura mostly through Shakespeare's plays, and she emphasizes the "tension between characters as characters, and characters as part of a state of mind which pervades the work" (p. 56), requiring a more holistic study of the play or story.

Studying literature as fantasy or daydream suffers from another limitation: its "functional definition of literature as a need satisfier" (p. 63). If literature is therapy, we may be drawn toward "something closer to moral than to aesthetic criticism." We must realize, Skura argues, that fantasies do resonate with the manifest content of stories, but never replace it. Moreover, "any one fantasy is really a series of fantasies from different stages of life" (p. 81):

> In *Jane Eyre,* for example, the manifest story about Jane's progress to adulthood is reinforced by a barely concealed female oedipal fantasy in which growing up means marrying Daddy. But it is also contradicted by a more primitive oral-stage fantasy that repeats its own regressive wish fulfillment in the very events which supposedly show Jane's escape from such infantile indulgences. (Skura 1981, p. 91)

Skura proceeds to discuss Freud's dream interpretation model, and explores attempts to compare it to poetic thinking (e.g., condensation and displacement as metaphor and metonymy, in Lacan's view; the mapping of defensive distortions onto poetic tropes, according to Harold Bloom 1975). She also studies parallels and differences between dream and allegory, and their ways of employing pictorial narratives. Her examples here include Chaucer and Spenser.

When literature is likened to transference, its attempt to move or affect the reader, its rhetorical function, is at the center. Just as we can distinguish between varieties of teller–listener relations in the analytic situation, texts also presume a variety of relationships (generalizing is risky, including defining *all* texts through Winnicott's concept of transitional phenomena). Skura studies rhetorical exchanges within a text through Dickens's *Old Curiosity Shop*.

At this point in Skura's sequence comes the discussion of literature as psychoanalytic process, which we include here. It is followed by a section on "less manifest parallels," in which she discusses the psychoanalytic critic's disregard for literary conventions as a possible springboard for the questioning of such conventions. Skura then provides an extensive study of

Measure for Measure and its contrasting critical interpretations, pointing to the play's basic ambiguity, and concludes: "It is only out of such radical doubt that a new kind of certainty can develop, a certainty based on human exchanges rather than absolute truths" (p. 270).

Gail S. Reed's penetrating critique of Greenacre's work on Swift, quoted earlier in this book, and her enthusiastic reception of Skura's work, give us an orientation to her basic outlook on psychoanalysis and literature. In another paper, she proposed "a methodology which seeks to use psychoanalysis to fathom the unique quality of the literary text without turning the text into a symptom or its author into a patient. Its hypothesis: The literary text evokes an unconscious fantasy in its readers; critics who respond to the text empathically but without conscious understanding re-enact aspects of its organizing fantasy in the way they write their criticism" (Reed 1982, p. 19). This methodology, influenced by Felman's study of James, as well as by clinical studies of parallelism phenomena between therapy and its supervision, is tested in the 1982 paper through a study of Diderot's *Jacques le Fataliste et son Maître*. In the paper we include here, first published in 1983, Reed studies the reader's experience of Voltaire's *Candide*.

In a subsequent paper, Reed (1985) compares two methods of interpretation, which are implied within literature itself. She contrasts a poem by Andrew Marvell, which implies an attitude of certainty toward its language, to a poem by Stéphane Mallarmé, whose poetry defies any "certain" reading. "In the first, the signifier is fixed; in the second, it is always a substitute for something unattainable and a variable one at that" (p. 48). She compares the first approach to the use of psychoanalysis as a fixed theory about the unconscious; this limited, at times dogmatic use, is defined by Reed as "psychoanalysis appropriated." Only the second approach can be a suitable metaphor for the true application of psychoanalysis as an open-ended method of investigation and exploration, approaching the signifier as a condensation of endless multiple meanings. These two strategies, Reed shows, are both found in Freud's work, such as his study of Leonardo da Vinci.

Reed, a literary scholar turned practicing analyst, was an active member of the Interdisciplinary Colloquium on Psychoanalysis and Literature at the New York Psychoanalytic Institute, chaired for several years by Francis Baudry, a member of that Institute's faculty. Baudry's own views are spelled out in a programmatic essay (Baudry 1984), in which he outlines the difficulties in applying psychoanalysis to a text "due to the absence of the unconscious, defenses, or conflicts, which are attributes of persons (authors) not of fictional characters'' (p. 568). He warns against ''substituting general truths of little interest for the specific images and interactions of metaphors of the text'' (p. 571), as well as against the temptation to ''all too quickly equate the manifest content of the work with the author's mental life, relying on a mechanical application of analogy, identification and projection'' (p. 572).

Baudry's concern with the difficulties of validation (''a text will not react to our interpretations,'' p. 577) is evident in his later paper included here. Baudry's caution, his avoidance of speculative and overconfident interpretations typical of the older pathographic tradition, does not prevent him from exploring the biographical context and emotional undercurrents in the poetry of John Keats.

Rivka Eifermann's paper is an excellent example of the potential contribution of a psychoanalytic approach to the enrichment of Reader Response Criticism. She follows Holland's belief in the personal sources and meaningfulness of each individual reading, and explores in depth her own reading of *Little Red Riding Hood* with the aid of meticulous self-analysis. This exploration is continued in a subsequent paper (Eifermann 1987) in which she describes her move from predominantly oral to Oedipal inner material in her memories and associations to the story, thus ''re-discovering'' the most basic psychoanalytic hypotheses anew. Eifermann is a faculty member of the Israel Psychoanalytic Institute and of the Hebrew University in Jerusalem.

Our concluding paper is written by Bennet Simon, a psychoanalyst based in Newton, Massachusetts, author of the highly acclaimed *Tragic Drama and the Family: Psychoanalytic Studies from Aeschylus to Beckett* (Simon 1988). Simon's study of Beckett and Bion combines the two lines of advancement in psychoanalysis, which I mentioned in the introduction to this book: the shift in the conceptualization of clinical psychoanalysis toward a more mutual model of the analyst–analysand relationship, and the shift toward a more egalitarian model of the literature–psychoanalysis encounter. Rather than seeing the writer-analysand (Beckett) as mostly interpreted and influenced by the analyst (Bion), Simon believes that the patient made a profound impact on the analyst, and the imaginary twinship developed by the two shaped a common gestalt of form and content that became central in their subsequent creative work.

The hope for, and the belief in such mutual enrichment and impregnation, characterize much of the work in this book. The papers in this last section convey the range of contributions published in the literature and psychoanalysis field in the 1980s. We have good reasons to expect that the studies of the 1990s will be no less creative, thoughtful, and exciting.

REFERENCES

Baudry, F. 1984. An essay on method in applied psychoanalysis. *Psychoanalytic Quarterly* 53: 551–81.

Bloom, H. 1975. *A map of misreading*. New York: Oxford University Press.

Eifermann, R. R. 1987. Fairly tales: A royal road to the child within the adult. *Scandinavian Psychoanalytic Review* 10: 51–77.

Reed, G. S. 1982. Toward a methodology for applying psychoanalysis to literature. *Psychoanalytic Quarterly* 51: 19–42.

———. 1983. Review of Skura's *The Literary use of the psychoanalytic process. Psychoanalytic Quarterly* 52: 469–73.

———. 1985. Psychoanalysis, psychoanalysis appropriated, psychoanalysis applied. *Psychoanalytic Quarterly* 54: 234–69.

Simon, B. 1988. *Tragic drama and the family: Psychoanalytic studies from Aeschylus to Beckett.* New Haven and London: Yale University Press.

Skura, M. A. 1981. *The literary use of the psychoanalytic process.* New Haven and London: Yale University Press.

16. Literature as Psychoanalytic Process: Surprise and Self-Consciousness

Meredith Anne Skura

The roads by which men arrive at their insights into celestial matters seem to me almost as worthy of wonder as those matters themselves.

—Johannes Kepler

Though everything's astonishment at last,
Who leaps to heaven at a single bound?

—Theodore Roethke, "Four for Sir John Davies"

Each of the models I have described in my book emphasizes only one aspect of the material being considered—content, psychic function, means of representation, or rhetorical function. The psychoanalytic process, however, begins with the assumption that communication has many facets, and the analyst must draw on "all the ways by which one human being understands another"[1] as he tries to put his experience into words; the analyst is as interested in why and how something is said as he is in the words that are actually spoken. The psychoanalytic process provides no special or exotic means of reading the unconscious; its strength derives from two simple strategies: first, it insists on paying attention to everything, and second, it mistrusts the seemingly obvious implications of what it then observes. Freud prescribed "intense but uncritical attention," meaning *uncritical* in the sense of an editorial openness and a suspension of all conclusions. In each case the analytic listener tries to be open to the sudden switches and rearrangements that reveal alternate meanings and expose the dynamic play of meaning behind what may seem to be a simple surface. The analytic process offers a more complete model for literary texts than the other methods we have

Reprinted by permission of Yale University Press from *The Literary Use of the Psychoanalytic Process,* by Meredith Ann Skura, 1981.

examined [elsewhere]; all the ways we understand each other are the ways we understand texts, too.

The analytic model is a better model for another reason too. It is not only more inclusive but also more complex, because it includes, along with a recognition of the separate aspects of discourse, an explicit emphasis on those moments of insight and self-consciousness that organize and take account of the rest. Reservations about using psychoanalytic models for literature usually come from a reluctance to reduce a complex literary text to the model of something much simpler, like a fantasy or a dream—efforts that, according to Paul de Man, "apply to less rigorous modes of consciousness than those at work in literary texts."[2] But the psychoanalytic process is designed to dismantle less rigorous modes of consciousness, to break up the defensively distorted versions of inner and outer reality that cramp a person's life and his language. The blindly symptomatic use of fantasy and dream may constitute a less rigorous mode of consciousness than the ordinary text, but when the psychoanalytic process is used correctly, its elements reflect on one another with the subtlety, rigor and self-consciousness of a literary text. Ernst Kris's description of "the good hour"[3] in an analysis unwittingly comes closer to describing the way a poem works than anything he ever wrote about literature.

This resemblance implies that a study of the minute changes which take place during an analytic hour can not only suggest new meanings for texts but can also suggest how *any* meaning is created within and between people. We can thereby gain a renewed appreciation of the way language and literature work, not only in creating fictional scenes but in creating significance apart from any scene at all; in diverting, displacing, or elaborating meanings, expanding an image into a web of associations or condensing a flow of statements into a single focusing insight; in shifting meanings by shifting perspectives or changing the rules for interpretation. Many analysts themselves are coming to see the exchanges in the psychoanalytic process as the most important part of psychoanalysis, whether their interest is expressed in the continental philosophical terms of discourse with the "other" or in terms of the transference and countertransference that Freud first described. And it is in these exchanges, where analysis is most vital, that it is also most suggestive as a model for other disciplines.[4]

PSYCHOANALYTIC PROCESS: DISORGANIZATION AND REORGANIZATION

The analytic method is a two-part process directed toward the disorganization and reorganization of the ego, as Hans Loewald has described it.[5] Within the bounds of the "therapeutic frame,"[6] analyst and patient agree to ignore all ordinary rules—not only those of decorum but also of logic, common sense, and taste. This dissolution of rules is neither dissolute nor easy. It does not just provide the patient with an "oasis from the desert of reticence," as Philip Rieff says, but is rather a "forced labor," as Lacan has called it, which "the psychologist (not without humor) and the psychiatrist (not without cunning)" have called *free association*.[7] The labor derives from undoing all the habits and expectations that shape a life in civilization, all the frames of reference and schema we use to organize the deluge of inner and outer sensations into manageable form so that we can communicate with others about them.

These schema shape all the levels of discourse discussed in earlier chapters of my book: content, psychic function, representational stratagies, and rhetorical strategies. They have become all the more firmly established insofar as they have been drafted into the service of tendentious motives, to construct the prejudices and automatisms we use to defend ourselves against the intrusion of unwanted realities. As the patient frees himself from these schema in this laborious free association, the analyst responds with a correspondingly "benign curiosity" or "evenly suspended attention,"[8] which we might call *free listening*.

But psychoanalysis is more than an undoing or loosening of codifications, and while one part of the mind is freely associating, the "observing ego" performs the second part of the process as it tries out new forms of organization. The "observer" (whether internal or external) often draws on the resources of logic and secondary process thinking discarded by free association, but its role is not to provide authoritative interpretation, in the sense of diagnosing a symptom or filling in a missing memory. Instead, it provides new perspectives, finds new relationships, reorganizes figure and ground, and changes emphasis. Together, finally, the two processes—loosening and reorganization—lead to those moments of surprise that are the characteristic marks of a good analysis.[9] The surprise in psychoanalysis, however, is not the shock of having something brought up from the alien depths, nor the drama of recalling a secret that only the analyst had guessed at before.

Rather, it is the quiet realignment, the small shift in perspective, the recognition of what was always there but not seen before, or what was almost there.

For an example of the psychoanalytic looseness and reorganization in which every aspect of the analytic material is subject to doubt and to surprising reversals and displacements, let us examine Freud's analysis of his own "disturbance of memory on the Acropolis."[10] As Freud tells the story, he was seeing Athens before him for the first time, after years of longing to visit the city. Suddenly he found himself saying, much to his surprise, "So it really does exist after all!" Could it be that he had doubted the existence of Athens all along? "Nonsense," Freud said, and not tempted into dismissing the statement as a meaningless social interjection, he set out to discover what it really meant.

As he examines the associations he made to the experience, Freud sees that his doubt about Athens was actually an incredulity about his presence there, which, in turn, was based on a sense of guilt at being there. ("It can't be true! [Because] I don't deserve it!") But Freud was not finished. His doubt was "doubly displaced": first, from his presence in the city to the existence of the city itself, and then from the present moment to the past. Why the past? In the past he had never really doubted the existence of Athens, or the fact that he might one day go so far as to visit it. But there *had* been some doubt that he would "go very far" in another sense—in particular, that he would go as far as his father. And yet here he was, in the city his father not only had not seen, but could not appreciate as Freud did.

By the end of the analysis, Freud's expression of doubt about Athens has become an expression of "filial piety." The rearrangement is possible only because he was able to entertain the potential displacements of meaning without holding onto the premature formulations that his exclamation first encouraged. And these displacements affect every aspect of his thinking. The shifts in content are perhaps most familiar from other psychoanalytic anecdotes: Freud's statements float freely from present to past referents (from "I have doubts about myself" to "I have doubts about others"). But all aspects of the psychoanalytic material are subject to shifts, and there are still others, like the shift in the means of representation (from the figurative meaning of "Freud will never go far" to the literal meaning). And finally, there are shifts that draw attention away from one aspect of the material to an entirely new one, at first one and then another of the aspects we looked at in the earlier chapters become important. Thus the seemingly referential judgment about Athens turns out to serve a psychic function as a fear-appeasing offer of filial piety.

Freud's anecdotal report of his detective work makes it sound elementary. But even here, and especially in such a brief example, his sudden shifts of meaning may seem dubiously determined and hard to reproduce. Any example of psychoanalytic reasoning taken out of context is hard to follow, and many of Freud's readers have found his reasoning arbitrary. Even some of Freud's followers have defined the method as "systematic impiet[y]"[11] that belongs to a slightly sinister "school of suspicion,"[12] whose responsibility toward the text is dubious. Their doubts are understandable. There is no denying that the analyst often sounds less like someone who might say something useful about literature than like a hair-splitting pedant, as Freud described himself,[13] a tedious philologist at best, and more often a tone-deaf freshman with a dirty mind. He ignores obvious meanings and disregards the amenities of ordinary conversation ("But I didn't mean that literally, doctor!"); he sees proclivities in Swift's naming a character Master Bates.[14] Like William Empson, he has "erected the ignoring of 'tact' into a point of honour."[15]

In fact, it may sound as if I am invoking Freud to justify the kind of free associational play in interpretation that has recently become familiar in France and elsewhere. When Freud came to America in 1908, with his strange discoveries about sex and about the way the mind works, he warned, "I bring you the plague"; but current literary criticism has plagues of its own, whether caught from Freud or not. Beginning with the recognition of all the nonreferential determinants of meaning, some critics have rejected belief in reference altogether; they regard the name of the father as separate from reference to any particular father and consider all names separate from what they might naively be thought to refer to. Jacques Derrida even goes beyond the *nom de père* to a verbal dadaism and a nihilism, whose current derivatives might seem to infect meaning in the same way Freud seemed to suggest.

Free association and the free play that French theorists describe are not the same, however. In the first place, despite the way the analyst's comments appear out of context, psychoanalytic experience provides evidence that these comments really do express something that is present in what the patient says and are not simply the analyst's own creative reworking of it. The analyst's "polymorphous perceptiveness," to borrow a term Phyllis Greenacre uses elsewhere to describe the artist,[16] opens the analyst to the polymorphous perversity of "unconscious" expression, so that he can see past the indirections of piety, sophistication, and tact beneath which this perversity, like the Emperor's nakedness, hides. Such social and linguistic clichés are often the means for covering up fantasies and dreamlike expressions and making them respectable ("It was only a joke, doctor!"), just as the agent of secondary revision in a dream takes raw material and hastily constructs a covering story to account for its presence. Free association is not without rules but is governed by rules other than the ones we usually observe.

In fact, while Paul Ricoeur says that "the poem means everything it can mean,"[17] the rules governing the psychoanalytic process strongly suggest that the process can*not* mean everything. The process is indeed unpredictable and sometimes outrageous in its course, but it is neither arbitrary nor always interminable. We can know, in the proper context, when an interpretation has succeeded, just as we know when a line of poetry has worked, although all too often we do not know why. Some of the most exciting discoveries in Freud's case histories—and in analysis in general—have begun with a provocative wrong guess about an interpretation and have emerged through a series of corrections. Anyone who has been on either side of the couch knows that there is less free play in interpretations there than in some literary criticism. The interpretations, even the "right" ones, sound odd; but we know when they have gone wild or stale. "I was going to free associate," said the man as he lay down on the couch, "but I'd better tell you what's on my mind."

This candid patient was judging the rightness of his statements by an intuitive feeling, just as the analyst does. But there are other objectives as well, which can determine how any one statement affects and is supported by the others surrounding it. As even the brief example given [previously] shows, psychoanalytic "truth" comes out of a whole process and not out of any one statement extracted from that process. The movements toward disorganization and reorganization take time; they are neither isolated nor strictly sequential but continuously play against one another. The resemblance between psychoanalysis and literature lies in their dynamic interaction: the interaction between the free-ranging play of mind and the organizing response to it, and the continuing play which they contradict or confirm. Ultimately, the interaction leads to those moments of reorganization when a pattern begins to fit together or a final piece is added; when tentative explorations in different directions suddenly condense into one focused moment, and the random remarks of an hour combine to make a revealing joke, or a list of repeated humiliations is suddenly seen as cover for a deeper ambition.

These are the moments of insight and surprise that I have described earlier; they are never isolated moments. They derive from the surrounding play of ideas—or rather, from the surrounding process that brings them "close [enough] to consciousness."[18]

The moment of insight is itself a focused moment, but its power—like the owner of an image or a line or a scene in any literary text—comes from its place in the context of the analysis. The analyst's work, Kris says, is not to make revelations but to find the conditions for them and to make recall possible by recreating them. The actual insight would not take place, the surprising idea would not have its effect, if it were not for the carefully placed—or fortuitously emerging—anticipatory ideas[19] that establish the terms for interpretation and set up the appropriate mood. More significant than any single insight or the recovery of any specific memory in analysis is the whole process of "working through," in which any idea or memory is less important than its gradually revealed relationships with all the rest of the patient's ideas, as the idea or memory appears in new and surprising contexts. Old organizations are exposed and new ones are made possible.

Analysis is effective because of this gradual loosening of larger patterns and relationships, which makes newer and freer ones possible. The most important fact about psychoanalysis—and perhaps the most often misunderstood—is that analysts are not looking for specific things but for *ways of seeing* things. They are not looking for something hidden but for new aspects of what was already there; they are not looking for the past but for all the ways in which the past affects the present, without being recognized as doing so. The analyst does not search for particular sorts of unconscious things, like sexual fantasies or symbols. There is no predictable specific secret revealed in a switch from manifest to latent meaning; there is no inherently explanatory latent content for a manifest symptom or symbol ("We cannot assume that this man must symbolize her father, who's the one she *really* loves"). Instead, the analyst looks at the play between more and less consciously perceived ideas, seeing how the switch from one kind of consciousness to another affects ideas, be they sexual or secular.

When Freud's patient Dora dreamed that her father came to her bedside to rescue her from a fire, Freud—concerned not with some inherently unconscious content ("It must be love for her father") but with the relation between conscious and unconscious ways of seeing the dream—suggested that Dora was using her father to represent another man. The final interpretation depends not on being able to point to the man Dora "really" loves but rather on being able to show how the conscious and unconscious aspects of her love work together (why does she represent the man in terms of her father's being fatherly?).[20]

Just as the analyst looks, not for a particular sort of unconscious content behind the conscious content of his patient's words, but only for the relations between ideas that are revealed by different modes of consciousness, so, too, he does not look for a particular sort of thing that is wish-fulfilling (like sex) behind a particular sort of thing that is defensive (like morality) but rather for the way in which ideas of whatever kind express general psychic conflict. Thoughts have to be judged by their function and context, not by their literal meaning. Wishes can serve as defenses against even more terrifying wishes, and real wish fulfillments are not always attractive. Ideas about oedipal wishes or homosexual wishes are not necessarily the inner-most secrets hidden behind symptoms but may be the symptoms themselves.

One young man, for example, began to fear for his sexual identity when he found himself obsessed by fantasies about homosexual intercourse with his analyst, during the last stages of his analysis.[21] Assuming that he had finally uncovered his darkest secret, he glumly prepared to accept the truth about himself—until further analysis showed that his erotic fantasies expressed his wish to stay in analysis and to continue receiving his analyst's "penetrating" interpretations. Awareness of this wish, it turns out, embarrassed him even more than the idea of homosexuality. Here the supposedly primitive secret actually disguised a more sophisticated wish. In another case, homosexual behavior concealed a still more primitive wish than itself. A seriously disturbed mental patient had been making homosexual advances to his fellow patients, but this no more represented an open wish fulfillment than the case just described; the man was actually searching for a primitive merger with a mirror image of himself.[22]

If wishes are not always wish-fulfilling, neither are defenses always cramping and distorting. One analyst reported a "defense by reality," in which an orphaned girl insisted on facing the facts of her unhappy situation (rather than wishfully distorting them). Her constant reference to her parents' abandonment of her, it turned out, was in the service of her "family romance fantasies" that her real parents were a king and a queen.[23]

In other words, the symptom seldom derives from a simple case of repression, where the trouble is that something is missing and the solution is to replace it. The missing element is almost always present in some relation to the rest of the patient's experience. The analyst, then, is always looking for relationships, not things, and his interpretation takes the form of suggesting a new relationship rather than an answer. Whether the switch he suggests affects the content, the psychic function, the means of representation, or the rhetorical function of the analytic exchange, what he does is reorganize the material rather than produce something new. The examples we have just seen refer to a shift in content, but this reorganization also occurs in the less classically Freudian shifts in means of representation and in the assumed rules for interpreting what we hear, as discussed in chapter 4 of my book. There the latent meaning is even more clearly present in the material but is just not seen by the patient who is locked into one mode of consciousness.

Sometimes the analyst's contribution is nothing more than a reorientation —a simple change in the truth status of the material already present. This happens in parapraxis, when the truth slips out, but is taken for an accident. Similarly, dreams "hide" wishes by presenting them as accomplished facts, and Freud's first patients concealed their fantasies by presenting them as memories. There can even be an evasion by too *much* memory, as well as in the supposedly typical case of too much forgetfulness. This occurs in cases of *déjà vu* or *fausse reconnaissance,* where the patient recognizes what he can never have seen; but this unsettling delusion turns out to be a distraction from what the patient is really remembering. He focuses on the scene itself ("I've been in this office before") and removes his attention from the fantasy that is actually familiar ("I've wanted to kill people before, just the way I want to kill this analyst now"). The relationship between cover and truth can become very complicated indeed, and Freud even reports a "supposed parapraxis," where the patient merely *thought* she had committed a parapraxis and left her umbrella at the doctor's office; when she returned to fetch it she realized that she had been carrying it all along.

In suggesting one of these reorganizations, whatever aspects of the analytic material it may affect, the analyst does not have to reach for the ideal of pure scientific truth; he simply takes account of the data in a new way and sees them from a new point of view. His "interpretation" is not a scientific diagnosis but may even make use of "defensive" indirections; it may be metaphorical or ironic, the way symptomatic speech habits can be. Victor Rosen, for example, tells about one patient who hid his meaning in a conversation by breaking it up and taking his own words literally: on the day after getting his monthly bill, the patient filled the hour with general complaints about the price of living, the shrinking value of the dollar, and so on, in such a rambling manner that the patient himself stopped at one point to ask, "But what has all this got to do with the price of lettuce?" Rosen's interpretation consisted of little more than taking the scattered remarks figuratively and reorganizing them. "Yes," he said, "it takes a lot of lettuce to shrink a head," making explicit the unspoken complaint and incidentally providing the first laugh in an otherwise humorless analysis.[24] The interpretation, in fact, may take any form but one—the one fixed by the patient's own chosen, restrictive defenses.[25] Rosen's joke worked for the humorless patient, but elsewhere the analyst might achieve the same end by taking seriously the patient's "joking." The most important thing an interpretation does is change the way the patient views his symptom and free him to see it in a new way. That is why psychoanalysis is different from shamanism, though critics have employed the latter term when viewing the analyst's interpretation as just another fantastic symptom, merely phrased in new language. (Like the medicine man, Lévi-Strauss says, the analyst substitutes a socially acceptable myth for the patient's private myth—childhood trauma for current paranoia.)[26]

Moving from symptom to symptom may well be an endless journey from myth to myth, but moving from symptom to insight is like moving from Ptolemaic to Copernican systems. It is a movement away from insistence on ocular proof and on the letter away, from the focus on a reductively concrete center that masks complex forces at work. Moving from symptom to insight is not only a shift from one meaning to another but a transcendence of the old stale alternatives and an insight into their ground. For instance, this approach does not involve a switch in the patient's focus from "I don't want to pay anyone" to "I don't want to pay my analyst" but instead involves an escape from niggling about payment altogether and an insight into the more important forces behind such complaints. The patient does not move from "I fear for my wife" to "What's really troubling me is that I hated my mother and was afraid that I'd hurt her," but escapes from needing to think in terms of hate at all. As Stanley Cavell describes the therapy:

> The problems are solved only when they disappear, and answers are arrived at only when there are no longer questions. . . . The more one learns, so to speak, the hang of oneself, and mounts one's problems, the less one is able to *say* what one has learned; not because you have forgotten what it was, but because nothing you said would seem like an answer or a solution: there is no longer any problem or question which your words would match. You have reached conviction but not about a proposition; and consistency, but not in a theory. You are different, what you recognize as problems are different, your world is different. And that is the sense, the only sense in which, what a work of art means cannot be said.[27]

The one difference between what Cavell describes and the psychoanalytic process—and this is the final aspect of the process that I will stress here—is that the latter is more self-conscious. The patient begins to understand more than just the one symptom that brought him to analysis; he begins to understand how he has been making his life symptomatic and to recognize the motives and methods he has been using to deal with experience. The psychoanalytic process is more than a means of achieving isolated insights or retrieving isolated memories; it becomes an end in itself. Freud's original goal in psychoanalysis was to fill in the gaps of his patients' memories; more recently, as one analyst has suggested, the goal has become "to show the patient how his mind works."[28] The whole history of psychoanalysis may be summed up as the change in emphasis from one of these two goals to the other; what Kris called the "vicissitudes of insight" have become more interesting than the location of instincts.[29]

The therapeutic value of analysis, in other words—and its aesthetic value, too—does not lie in specific concrete cures for symptoms. And neither do its most characteristic moments. The moment of surprise that I have described is recognized most often by a peculiar sense of rightness, a "clicking," as Otto Fenichel has called it,[30] which brings emotional as well as intellectual recognition. But the emotion does not result from the content of what has been discovered. The moment of insight is often marked by a giggle or by an inner feeling very like one. But this laughter has little to do with what has just been discovered. Painful recognitions about one's family or about one's flaws are no joke; but still the patient laughs. Freud tried to explain this seemingly automatic phenomenon by talking about the economy of energy: according to him, the patient was releasing some of the energy he formerly spent repressing the uncovered idea, so that it escaped in the form of laughter. But the laughter here, like the triumph at a tragic recognition, has nothing to do with what has been recognized; it is a response to the act of recognition itself. That most narcissistic moment in a narcissistic process, the moment of psychoanalytic insight is also—paradoxically—the most objective, when pain and complaints become building material for a kind of art.

MANIFEST PARALLELS IN LITERATURE

I have suggested that the movement from the psychoanalytic to the aesthetic experience is a natural one. The connection between the psychoanalytic process and the aspect of poetry that makes it *poetry* (rather than paraphrasable statement) is even closer than the more immediately obvious connection between a dream and a "dreamlike" poem. To compare a work of literature to a fantasy is to isolate that aspect of the text which returns us to more primitive levels of experience. To compare it to the psychoanalytic process is to discover those aspects that avoid such a return—but this can be accomplished only by exposing and taking account of the work's own fantasy and dreamlike elements.

The most obvious literary parallels to the reorganizations in analysis are found in relatively primitive works where the switch in how we see things is exaggerated, like the blatantly "surprising" jokes and the uncanny stories Freud studied, and these examples provide a good starting place for a closer look at the relation between the psychoanalytic process and literary texts. Jokes and uncanny stories depend on a single surprising moment of reorganization like the moment of insight in analysis, and they have a curiously similar emotional impact. As Freud suggests, for example, in the following joke, there is a switch in meaning, which makes us laugh:

FIRST JEW: Have you taken a bath?
SECOND JEW: No, is one missing?

And in E.T.A. Hoffmann's uncanny tale "The Sand-Man," there is a switch that makes us shiver, when the nursery tale abut a sandman coming to take out a boy's eyes suddenly seems to come true.[31]

It is significant that jokes and the uncanny are the only genres Freud chose to write about at any length, because they provide the same kind of phenomena that his clinical experience provided. He never connected the two studies, of course; he would not have said that he was using the psychoanalytic process as a model, and he would not have agreed with my analysis of the switch that occurs in both genres.[32] Instead, just as he had defined the goal of analysis as filling in the gaps in memory, he explained the "kinetic" effect of jokes and the uncanny by referring to the specific material which they revealed or "filled in." Freud attributed their power to the simple presence of specific "unconscious" or "wishful" ideas. The joke worked, according to Freud, by making it possible for unconscious material to escape the censor, and our response was not to the joke but to the unconscious material. Normally, we have to suppress the rebelliousness and perversity that makes the second Jew say, in effect, "I'm not listening to you about this civilized business of cleanliness; I'm so far from all of that, I don't even recognize the expression describing it." Similarly, the uncanny story worked, according to Freud, by making it possible for unconscious material—in this case, frightening infantile fantasies about oedipal wishes and the blinding ("castration") that follows as punishment—to escape the censor.

Freud denied that comic or uncanny effect could be explained by a conflict between ideas rather than by the presence of an inherently comic or uncanny idea. Theories defining jokes as the product of sense in conflict with nonsense, Freud said, described only an intellectual conflict, just as theories about the uncanny as the product of conflicting interpretations of events depended only on intellectual confusions. Merely intellectual conflicts, Freud insisted, could not produce the powerful effect a joke or an uncanny story has.[33] These effects depend on the fact that a repressed idea from childhood has returned, only incidentally causing confusion.

With the more recent definition of the psychoanalytic process as a switching between two ways of seeing rather than between the absence and presence of a particular element, we can now take advantage of Freud's contribution to make a composite theory. As in the psychoanalytic process, it is not simply the visible presence or absence of some inherently powerful material that makes the joke, but the way the material makes its presence known. The joke depends not on the return of repressed material but on a change in relationship between manifest and latent significance of the same material: the joke begins when our ordinary interpretation gives way to an old, literal-minded one, and an absurd world emerges in the center of an ordinary landscape. Freud saw the innocent beginning of a joke as a mere disguise for or distraction from the really funny punch line; but without the beginning, the joke would not be funny. The humor lies in the movement from the innocent setup to the punch line. Jokes, at least the ones Freud cites, work by switching the grounds for interpretation. We think we are playing one game when we hear the first Jew ask, "Did you take a bath?" But we know we are playing another when the second answers, "No, is one missing?"

Even Freud, however, recognized implicitly that the joke depends on a general switch in our method of interpretation rather than on the introduction of a particular content. He claimed that what makes the audience laugh is the Jew's taboo motive for switching: the second Jew switches the meaning, not the joke. But even though he tried to locate the power of the joke solely in content and not in a general mode of representation or reading, Freud still felt that he had to take into account the joke's social context. Unlike other fiction, a joke needs an audience, Freud said, and it can only be understood in the rhetorical context of a purposeful exchange between teller and listener. Thus Freud implicitly recognized the joke's switch in narrative and linguistic conventions. Where he said the joke "needs an audience,"[34] we would say that it requires a set of conventional expectations to play with and against.

The same is true in the case of the uncanny. Here, too, Freud attributed a story's power to the mere presence of a forbidden idea, like the idea of castration in Hoffmann's "The Sand-Man"; or to the mere presence of a forbidden "way of thinking," like the fear of magical retaliation in the same story. But in both cases it is the play between two ways of thinking or seeing that causes the effect, as commentators have always noticed. What Freud has added to the understanding of the uncanny, as in the case of the joke, is that the necessary play must be between two different kinds of ideas or two different kinds of thinking, one of which is more primitive than the other. As he pointed out, this is what distinguishes the joke from the merely comic and the uncanny from the merely frightening.

Finally, with the more subtle model of the psychoanalytic process available, we can also use Freud's explanation as a starting point to discriminate between the joke and that which is uncanny. Working with his single-dimensional explanatory model of repression/openness, Freud wound up with the same explanation for both jokes and the uncanny: what makes a joke funny is the same "return of the repressed" that makes the uncanny story uncanny. We can now be more specific and say that each of these genres is defined by a switch in a different aspect of the material. The success of the joke depends on a switch in content or reference, from "washing in a tub" to "stealing a tub." The uncanny, however, depends on a switch in what is accepted as truth. An old nanny's tale suddenly becomes real when the sandman comes after the grown-up Nathaniel's eyes. The uncanny and its related phenomena—*déjá vu, déjá raconté,* and *fausse reconaissance*—are more unsettling than jokes because they disrupt our sense of ourselves and our orientation in the world; these phenomena are what the analyst calls *ego disturbances.* The joke, on the other hand, merely distorts the message and does not affect us significantly.

The exceptions prove this rule that jokes switch content and the uncanny switches truth status; they illuminate material that falls between the categories of jokes and the uncanny. For example, in a now classic psychoanalytic essay on literature, Norman Holland analyzes a *Playboy* joke that actually works like the uncanny in reverse and falls somewhere between the genres of the joke and the uncanny:

A young executive had stolen company money and lost it on the stock market, and was about to jump off a bridge when an old crone appeared, said she was a witch, and promised to replace the money for a slight consideration—which turned out to be a night in a nearby motel. Though revolted, the man agreed. In the morning as he was about to escape, the crone asked how old he was. "Forty two," he answered, "Why?" "Ain't you a little old to believe in witches?" she replied.[35]

Holland explains the joke's effect in fairly strict Freudian terms: we are presented with the desired—but feared—threat of an oedipal encounter between the old hag and the young man, and our laughter follows when we learn, with relief, that we have been saved from it after all. But the joke's effect depends on more than an economy of wishes and fears. It depends on a switch in the joke's status as truth or fictional "truth." We think we are playing one game when the joke begins (a game in which we accept witches as realities), but we realize we are playing another at exactly the moment the executive realizes it. This is the same kind of switch that defines the uncanny. In that case, of course, the switch moves in the opposite direction: in "The Sand-Man," the fantasy sandman turns out to be real, but in the *Playboy* joke, the real witch turns out to be only a fantasy (which is probably why the joke amuses or annoys rather than frightens us). But it affects us in much the same way as the uncanny, challenging us on more levels than Freud's jokes do.

There are moments in his two essays when Freud seems to take all these factors into account and to come around to saying that a joke or an uncanny story is formed not simply by recalled material but also by the way in which this material is brought back. The uncanny, he says, can be generated by the return of even the least uncanny material; and jokes use material that was neither wish-fulfilling nor funny when it was first repressed. The mere resurrection of infantile memories is not enough to explain why we react as we do, even to these primitive forms of literature. One of the most poignant moments in Freud's book on jokes, in fact, is the closing statement, in which he moves away from seeing the joke as a simple return to earlier pleasure and comes closer than he does anywhere else to seeing jokes (and by implication, all the products of our discontented civilization) as something new, designed as a substitute for early experience, perhaps, but not as an imitation of it. Jokes, the comic, and humor, he says, attempt to regain from mental activity a pleasure that has been lost through the development of that activity—a euphoria which is "nothing other than the mood of a period of life . . . when we were ignorant of the comic, when we were incapable of jokes and when we had no need of humour to make us feel happy in life.''[36]

This is not the Freud who saw literature as only a simple escape to a mindlessly literal reproduction of our earliest fantasy worlds. Here Freud sees not simply a return of repressed material but a whole new world that takes account of it. He sees the indirections that move toward new forms of pleasure, the pleasure of insight, the Wordsworthian pleasures of consciousness, and the literary pleasures that escape any simple reflex explanation.

Obviously, the sudden shifts in jokes and uncanny stories move us more crudely than more sophisticated literature does, and their effect has less influence on the way we see the world after we have enjoyed them. The joke and the uncanny story lie at the borders of literature; they are examples of what Stephen Dedalus might call kinetic art, like pornography and propaganda, because, like these two pragmatic genres, they are meant to ''move'' us, though in a different way. They are in fact defined by the giggle and the *frisson.* Yet all literature moves us the same way these trivial texts do—by the way it presents material and not by its content alone. We recognize poetic touchstones by being ''thoroughly penetrated by their power,''[37] and though the punch in a joke's punchline may seem far removed from the finer touch of poetry Matthew Arnold was describing, it belongs in the same category.

The reorganization made suddenly explicit in a joke is related to that which we can find unfolding more slowly and less explosively in every aspect of literary texts—in their content, their function, their language and literary conventions, and their rhetorical dimension. The literary critics who most resemble psychoanalysts are not the ones who talk about fantasies but those who talk about ambiguity and who challenge the assumptions integral to ordinary reading processes, like William Empson, Kenneth Burke, and Sigurd Burckhardt. The alternative readings they point out are not always sexual (though Empson's and Burke's often are), but neither are the analyst's; what they share with the analyst is an eye for the tenuous as well as the tendentious and an appreciation of the way supposedly farfetched alternative readings may be much closer to the meaning of a text than we realize, in a context that shapes our final, ''acceptable'' reading.

In some cases the parallel between the psychoanalytic process and the text is easy to see; the reorganization is quite obviously part of the manifest text and is visible in many separate details. The study of such shifts is in fact one of the most traditional aspects of literary criticism. On the level of individual words and phrases these shifts have been studied as ambiguities of various kinds, the necessary wealth of alternatives that make poetic language. In broader, if vaguer, forms, they have been studied as the "irony" new critics believed to be the necessary condition for poetry. In a very different kind of criticism, Harold Bloom has examined not verbal but rhetorical switches—or "poetic crossings"[38]—in which a poet changes from one to another way of representing and coping with ideas. And more recently, we have begun to hear about a number of more subtly distinguished ways in which a text reveals an interaction between its simultaneous construction and deconstruction of meaning, or in which a text can destroy its own integrity if seen from another perspective.

On a larger scale, traditional critics have studied similar switches and reorganizations. In their studies, the model would no longer be the isolated moment of psychoanalytic insight, which parallels the simple joke or uncanny story; it is instead the entire "good hour" or "good analysis,"[39] as Kris has called it, which Cavell invoked. This larger unit provides a model for the kind of plot movement Aristotle described when he maintained that tragedy depended on a moment of recognition that reorganized an entire world. This model represents a movement toward revelation not only of a specific fact but of a fact that changes everything, that makes us give up one set of values and the belief that the world conforms to them, and shows us how to find another. This manifest movement toward reorganization can make any story resemble a stylized psychoanalysis, or at least the old-style traumatic revelation analysis.

Not surprisingly, nearly all the texts that Freud chose to analyze at length had this kind of plot. *Oedipus* is the most obvious example (its action "can be likened to the work of a psychoanalysis," Freud said),[40] but Wilhelm Jensen's *Gradiva,* which inspired Freud's monograph on dreams and delusion, is another good example; it tells the story of a man who finds that his current love is a figure from his childhood. Even Hoffmann's "Sand-Man" takes the form of a psychological investigation; the author tries to find out what is the matter with Nathaniel, using outside diagnoses and clinical confession, and exploring the return to childhood. Today, of course, with a newer concept of a more subtle kind of revelation—as in Cavell's description which I have quoted—we might find literary analogues not in the plays about revelations but in the stories about failed revelation. Rather than looking for the caricatural "peak-experience" of old-style analysis, we would look to the analogy of the vision that disappears when Spenser's Calidore tries to capture it on Mount Acidale, or the vision that never materializes for Wordsworth in the Alps.

Whether the plot reorganization is sudden or more subtly interfused, however, the movement of thought in the psychoanalytic process takes more into account than that in the other models. It makes a more suggestive model for Shakespeare's plays, for example, than the static character analyses discussed in chapter 2 of my book. What is interesting about Shakespeare's characters is not their diseases but their movement through disease to some kind of curative reorganization. Their proper parallel is not the neurotic but the neurotic in analysis. Freud's patients—neurotics, in general—are caught in stifling, reductive versions of reality, which permit only equally reductive behavior. For example, Frau Cäcilie, mentioned in chapter 1 of my book, was caught in a cliché that was taken literally; she was so obsessed by her facial pains—the only way she acknowledged society's "slap in the face" —that she did not have to cope with anything else or confront any question about her relationships except "Does it make my face hurt or doesn't it?"[41] Every neurotic is caught in a similarly reductive dichotomy, fixated on a question defined by its own terms. Analysis cures by releasing the patient so that he can see the world in new terms.

The parallel between the psychoanalytic process and Shakespeare's plays is easiest to see when a reductive dichotomy affects a character who is trapped in an almost pathologically defensive vision, and the most obvious examples are the several jealous husbands, trapped in obsessive dichotomies that *we* know are beside the point. Othello forgets everything he knows about Desdemona, once he begins his obsessive testing: "Did she or didn't she betray me?" Leontes, in *The Winter's Tale,* hardly bothers to consider the alternatives before he decides that Hermione has betrayed him; and Posthumus Leonatus, in *Cymbeline,* contaminates his marriage the moment he consents even to ask of his wife, "Will she or won't she betray me?" although at first he believes in her. Troilus, who has real cause to feel betrayed, watches Cressida with her new lover and, instead of reactihg directly to the situation, is caught up in the terms of a dichotomy as he asks himself, "Is she or isn't she doing this—is this Cressida?" The movement of each of these plays, however, does not simply answer these obsessive questions but changes the terms in which each man sees his beloved. This redefinition of terms is characteristic of many other Shakespearean plays as well. What makes *Antony and Cleopatra* so strange a play, in fact, is the way in which Antony *starts out* by ignoring such reductive dichtomies, although they pose more appropriate questions for him than for the jealous husbands.

Less obvious but much more characteristic of Shakespeare's plays are the similar changes in characters who are not so blatantly disturbed but are nonetheless caught in their own reductive visions. The young aristocrats in *Love's Labour's Lost,* for example, have to be shaken out of their simplistic view of the world. The men have taken sides in the ancient war between discipline and pleasure, and from the moment they announce their withdrawal to a strict academe, they become caught up in a dichotomous view of the world as blinding as Othello's: "Should I devote myself to books or shouldn't I?"—or rather, "Can I devote myself to books or can't I?" Then the Princess arrives with her women, and the men of course all fall in love. But instead of escaping from their dichotomy, the men simply change it slightly and switch sides: the war becomes a struggle between study and love, and they dedicate themselves with equal extravagance to love. What we begin to see is that the categories have become irrelevant. What matters is neither study nor love, but the way in which the young men go about either one. They have rushed into both like brash, self-confident fools, out to conquer; the women are humbler, mellower, more receptive to what love brings and to forces beyond the control of their individual categorizing wills.

Not only characters but entire societies are sometimes caught up in paralyzing dichotomies. In *Romeo and Juliet,* the war between Montague and Capulet demonstrates such a dichotomy; we can see how irrelevant the categories are, how vital the stars that cut across, but the characters cannot see this until it is too late—and perhaps not even then. In *Troilus and Cressida,* we can at least tell the difference between Greeks and Trojans, but the stalemated war their dichotomous outlook generates is again beside the point. We do not care about their obsessive seven-year-old question as to "who will win, Greek or Trojan." What matters is a question that undermines both sides: what does it mean to win? And elsewhere in the plays we hardly have a chance to compare Roman and Goth, reason and love, Caesar and Brutus, before our comparison is out of date. Initially, we may get caught up in deciding who should be king, Richard or Henry, but before the end of the play we are always asking larger questions, like "What *is* a king?" and "Can there be a king?" The terms have changed, and the change is part of what the plays are about.

But in these cases, as the last examples show, the reorganization affects something more fundamental than the character's experience or the plot alone: it affects the audience as well. If Shakespeare's characters sometimes suffer from clichés, so do we as critics. We may avoid Othello's cage; we may escape the empty distinctions between Montagues and Capulets or Trojans and Greeks, which imprison an entire world. But we fall into other pits. We see beyond the distinction between Montague and Capulet, but elsewhere we find distinctions we think are the true ones. We find, for example, dichotomies between artificial and natural; restraint and freedom; wintry rigidity and spring release; and work world and holiday. These dichotomies have been described often, at least in the comedies, and seem to be embodied in the very geography of the plays: we see them in the contrasts between the city and the forest, the men's academy and the park around it where the women stay, the palace and the heath, Venice and Turkish outlands, and Venice and Belmont.

These dichotomies, however, are not the adequate measure of a play; they are the kind of thing cured by psychoanalysis—the wrong set of terms. And the cure is not simply a compromise between these dichotomous terms (Athenian rationality plus a healthy dose of the forest's irrationality), nor a Hegelian synthesis, nor a paradox beyond our common understanding. Rather, it is a complete reorganization, which shows dichotomy to be beside the point. The opening terms in a Shakespearean play slip away from us as the action moves toward a reorganization not only of characters and action but also of the very way in which we see both. The initial questions no longer remain, because the terms in which they have been defined are no longer relevant.

In Shakespearean criticism, the kind of movement characterizing the psychoanalytic process has also recently become the concern of traditional critics. Much of the Shakespearean criticism of the 1960s and 1970s, though never mentioning psychoanalysis, has traced just such movements in individual plays, though usually implying that the given play is unique in its defiance of categories.[42] It is not in Shakespeare's plays, however, that the literary parallel to psychoanalytic observation is most common. Critics have most often studied this kind of reorganization in works whose slowly elaborated and repetitive movement is even more like psychoanalysis than the swiftly streamlined movement in a Shakespearean play: a major field of study has been the highly self-conscious epic tradition, which culminates in Wordsworth's self-analysis in *The Prelude*. The readers' response, which Stanley Fish has described in Milton and Paul Alpers has noted in Spenser,[43] is a movement from a cramped, constrictive view of the world to a more open and inclusive, if more confusing one—just like the movement from symptom to insight. The symptom, as we have seen, is not a raw eruption of conflict but a rigid, unimaginative way of dealing with conflict by reducing it to a "pseudo-concreteness," such as a paralyzed arm, a horse phobia, or an obsession with clean hands.

At the beginning of his quest, Spenser's Red Cross Knight has a similarly unimaginative idea of holiness, as singly reductive as Frau Cäcilie's idea about human relationships and as closely tied to physical manifestations (such as his armor, for example). He thinks that his enemy is the "dragon" and does not realize that the real enemies in his world are not evils like Unholiness and Intemperance but rather the wrong ideas about holiness and temperance—and the lax attitudes that allow us to slip into them. He—and the reader—must slow down enough in the obsessive pursuit of dragons to be able to redefine the world in other terms. Only then can he escape his partial vision and achieve that wholeness which several critics have associated not only with holiness but with health.[44]

This kind of criticism begins with a bias toward the sensitive but tentative reading necessary in a psychoanalysis. Not surprisingly, the starting point for all later Spenserian critics, William Empson's famous description of the Spenserian stanza, is really a description of the kind of attention needed to read it—the kind of "intense but uncritical" scrutiny Freud prescribed for the analyst's "evenly hovering attention."

> The size, the possible variety, and the fixity of this unit give something of the blankness that comes from fixing your eyes on a bright spot; *you have to yield yourself to it very completely* to take in the variety of its movement, *and, at the same time, there is no need to concentrate the elements of the situation into a judgment as if for action.* [Emphasis added][45]

Paul Alpers elaborates on this description, suggesting that "the condition of Spenser's poetry is an abeyance of the will," which on Spenser's part amounts to a failure to maintain a dramatic identity in relation to his poem.[46] But this is very much like the patient's failure—or, I should say, achievement—in the analytic situation. The failure to maintain a dramatic identity is an escape from the ordinary self that maintains a constant relation to what it sees and says and locates itself firmly in the narrative, whether directly, as opinionated narrator, or indirectly, in the person of a specific character. Whether on Spenser's part or on the reader's part, this "abeyance of the will" is one step further from ordinary reality than the "willing suspension of disbelief" we are familiar with. The latter requires only that we step into a new world, while the Spenserian—or psychoanalytic—stance requires that we give up the idea of any "world" at all, if by that we mean a physical place (however odd) with characters acting within the structure of a plot.

Both in reading and in the psychoanalytic process, the suspension of critical will opens one to moral and perceptual change—to the kind of change occurring in scientific revolutions and in great works of art, which break old schemata or change the way we see them and the way we see the world. Here, again, the analyst and the traditional critic have in common a search for texts that challenge the schemata and rework convention. In particular, they share a sensitivity to all the ways in which a conventional, naturalistic, literal-minded expectation about meaning is defeated; both have become wary of the "referential fallacy,"[47] and they look to other dimensions of a text besides the seemingly obvious literal meaning to which it refers.

Two of the most characteristic concerns of recent criticism, in fact, might be called the defining concerns of modern psychoanalysis; self-consciousness about artistic conventions and fictional status, and a related tendency to see these conventions as ends in themselves—to "find semantic value in formal qualities."[48] In the first case, the critic points to those moments of self-consciousness when we are reminded that "this is only a play"—moments paralleled in analysis by the analyst's habit of calling attention to the patient's defenses and making him self-conscious about them as defenses or fictions. In those moments we see with the eye of the creator, not the audience; means become ends. We experience what George Klein has called a change in mode of consciousness, as we switch from seeing a three-dimensional world on a canvas to seeing a two-dimensional pattern.[49] The power of this change depends of course not only on the way it makes us reexamine artistic conventions of realism (preventing us from accepting, for example, a bare wooden *O* as King Henry's England) but also on the way it calls into question those more insidiously hidden conventions that define "reality." This is precisely what the analyst does when he makes the patient conscious of the conventions he has begun to take for granted in his own role-playing. ("Of course I can't cry in front of my children," the patient may say—a revelation not only about the conventions he has accepted about playing parent but about the ones he may not know he has accepted to define his own feelings.)

In the second case, the critic calls attention to moments in literature that are even more like the reorganization deriving from the suspended will that characterizes analysis. These moments make us self-conscious about convention not simply by naming it but by switching conventions. Shakespeare may call attention to the wooden *O,* diverting us from the thing represented to the means of representation—not England but the barren, wooden boards of the stage. But Samuel Beckett unsettles us in another way when he switches the rules and makes us see the stage as the barren, wooden world. And in Racine's plays, the unities are not mere shapely containers; they become part of the characters' claustrophobic world. Even Shakespeare evokes this queasiness at times, making the audience uncertain about what is a means of representation and what is an end, about what the audience should see and what it is supposed to see through. *The Tempest* observes the unities but is *about* a playwright trying to observe the unities as he presents a drama that spans oceans and stretches from the dark "backward of time" to the future brave new world. And the rude mechanicals in *A Midsummer Night's Dream,* instead of asking that we take the wooden *O,* for a forest, enter a forest for their rehearsal and pretend that *it* is a wooden *O:* "This green plot shall be our stage. . . ." (3.1.3–4).

These switches and their significance are part of what these texts are about, and much of the critical commentary has stressed what we can learn from becoming aware of them: the moral maturity not to be surprised by sin and the perceptual alertness not to be fooled by appearances. But besides instruction there is also delight. Poetry's oldest justifications, it turns out, apply to these switches in mode as well as to its content. The analyst sees in the moment of switching the giggle of insight or the more subtle pleasure and release resulting from cure. And like Aristotle, the critics have found this pleasure too—a delight not only in shapeliness but in a change of shape or a switch from chaos to shape. As Stephen Booth has suggested, in explaining how Shakespeare's play of patterns in the sonnets affects us:

> Perhaps the happiest moment the human mind ever knows is the moment when it senses the presence of order and coherence—and before it realizes the particular nature (and so the particular limits) of the perception. At the moment of unparticularized perception the mind is unlimited. It seems capable of grasping and about to grasp a coherence beyond its capacity.[50]

It is in texts where such self-conscious confrontations become part of the literary work, inseparable from the experience portrayed, that the psychoanalytic process finds its closest parallels. In fact, we can now see why *Oedipus Rex* and *Hamlet* have always been inseparable from conceptions of psychoanalysis. Freud said that this was because of their fantasy content—those secrets that he had just discovered but that the poets had apparently always known. But Freud had discovered the secrets partly by learning to read stories in new ways, and *Oedipus* and *Hamlet* are bound up with the process of discovery as much as with a presentation of facts about the Odeipus complex. They present the reorganizations necessary to incorporate the oedipal fantasy material in a meaningful world. The plays are based on suddenly shifting representations of experience—shifting relations between past and present, fact and fantasy, literal and figurative significance. As in the case of jokes and the uncanny, Freud stressed the importance of certain strong content in these plays, but their effect depends on the way in which that content is presented—on the kind of reorganization of experience that allowed Feud to see in it the secret wishes he was interested in.

The shifts in *Oedipus* in fact make it almost uncanny. Freud locates the play's power in the fact that two desires normally repressed are here presented openly—the wishes for murder and incest. But for anyone seeing the play, the power comes more immediately from the fact that on the literal level the impossible comes true and on another level something which was merely figurative becomes literal. What began as an oracle's pronouncement—which the critic can view as a mere manner of speaking symbolizing our general guilt—comes true. Any attempt to make sense of the events is even more unsettling, particularly if we have just seen Sophocles' play and not merely heard the myth. The play shows a self-confident, ambitious man ruling a city and solving its problems and, after the revelation about what he has done, desperately trying to punish Jocasta and himself. This man and these actions are what the play is about. Behind them we may possibly sense a symbolic murder and an incestuous rape, but only *as* symbols for the onstage drama. They are no more than a projection backward or a reconstruction from Oedipus's current situation, a useful fiction generated solely to explain what is happening on stage. But suddenly the virtual becomes actual, and it is no longer clear what is symbolizing what. The onstage events become symbols for the earlier offstage trespasses. Analysts look at Oedipus confronting the royal couple, Creon and Jocasta, or they look at him breaking into Jocasta's bedroom, waving his sword and crying out on her womb, and they see symbolic displacements of the offstage murder and incest. At first reading, it seems that Oedipus has merely murdered the idea of his father, as we all do; but the second reading shows that in his world the idea is real.

This seamless world generates a confusion that is unlike the simple one in which the past blends imperceptibly into the present (or fantasy blends into reality), as happens in some readings of fantasy material. This is rather a confusion in which the past sometimes seems as if it *were* the present reality; or rather, in which we cannot tell whether the past or the present has priority or whether the fact or the fantasy is "real." The result is a radical doubt about the world that goes beyond moral questions—like Hans Castrop's doubt when his doctor on the magic mountain lectures about "love," but uses

> the word love in a somewhat ambiguous sense, so that you were never quite sure where you were with it, or whether he had reference to its sacred or its passionate and fleshly aspect—and this doubt gave one a slightly seasick feeling. . . .[51]

The uncomfortable reorganization in *Hamlet* works differently but has the same effect of challenging not only our images of ourselves but our ability to perceive and interpret the onstage experience. The play is unsettling on every level; the world of Hamlet is a world of unanswered questions and mystery and has lately been seen as one that upsets the audience with its questions as much as it upsets Hamlet. One critic has called this phenomenon "the tragedy of an audience that cannot make up its mind."[52] We initially see the action the same way Hamlet sees it: he thinks he is a revenge play hero, and is caught in a conflict between what he believes he ought to do—murder Claudius—and his own inability to act.[53] But Hamlet's feeling that "one must kill" is no more adequate to the play's world than was the young men's decision that "one must study" in the world of *Love's Labour's Lost,* and we, along with Hamlet, have to reorganize our conception of Hamlet's problem.

Even more unsettling, the simple events of *Hamlet* are hard to sort out. The content here seems to escape its presentation, almost as Tristram Shandy's subject matter escapes his efforts to set it down. We are accustomed to have the dramatist single out important events and devote time to them on stage; we relax in the expectation that he will allocate the scenes and lines in proportion to their importance and that what matters will take place on stage. But time passes unevenly, and events as important as Hamlet's farewell to Ophelia are almost tossed off as incidental reports, leaving us uncertain how to interpret them. Such confusions we are likely to attribute to our own failures rather than to the play, and so we are likely to ignore them as invalid or irrelevant responses. We feel we must have missed something. Still, such confusions leave a trace of Hans Castorp's seasickness.

Both Hamlet and Oedipus, of course, are dealing with material that is as emotionally explosive as Freud said it was, but their power comes as much from a literary and even a perceptual trespass as from a moral one: they violate our assumptions about what things mean as well as our assumptions about heroic natures. The confusion between latent oedipal fantasy and overt action is only one of several confusions; a play's more general instability is what allows the normally discarded fantasy to claim a place—especially in scenes that seem a little odd anyway, like the scene in which Hamlet speaks daggers to his mother in her closet or the one where Oedipus rushes into Jocasta's bedroom with his sword. But effective as this primitive material may be, it is not the sole challenge to our ordinary assumptions; these plays challenge us in *all* the ways that the tactless and suspicious psychoanalytic process does.

NOTES

1. Rudolph M. Loewenstein, "Some Thoughts on Interpretation in the Theory and Practice of Psychoanalysis," *Psychoanalytic Study of the Child* 12 (1957): p. 132.
2. Paul de Man, *Blindness and Insight* (New York: Oxford University Press, 1971), p. 22.
3. Ernst Kris, "On Some Vicissitudes of Insight in Psychoanalysis," *International Journal of Psychoanalysis* 37 (1956): 445–55.
4. Jacques Lacan's emphasis on the role of language and communication with the "other" naturally finds the exchanges in the psychoanalytic situation central to psychoanalysis, but he even goes so far as to take these exchanges as typical of all other human relationships. Not only the French have been placing more importance on the psychoanalytic situation as a source of or even a replacement for psychoanalytic theory or metapsychology, however. See, e.g., George S. Klein, *Psychoanalytic Theory: An Exploration of Essentials* (New York: International Universities Press, 1976); Hans Loewald, "On the Therapeutic Action of Psychoanalysis," *International Journal of Psychoanalysis* 41 (1960): 16–33; Stanley A. Leavy, "Psychoanalytic Interpretation," *Psychoanalytic Study of the Child* 28 (1973): 305–30; Roy Schafer, *A New Language for Psychoanalysis* (New Haven: Yale University Press, 1976), p. 157.
5. Hans Loewald, "On the Therapeutic Action of Psychoanalysis," *International Journal of Psychoanalysis* 41 (1960): p. 17.
6. M. Masud Khan, "On Freud's Provision of the Therapeutic Frame," in *The Privacy of the Self: Papers on Psychoanalytic Theory and Technique* (New York: International Universities Press, 1974), pp. 129–35.
7. Philip Rieff, *Freud: The Mind of the Moralist* (New York: Doubleday/Anchor, 1961), p. 364; Jacques Lacan, *The Language of the Self: The Function of Language in Psychoanalysis*, trans. Anthony Wilden (Baltimore: Johns Hopkins University Press, 1968), p. 10.
8. Sigmund Freud, "Recommendations for Physicians Practicing Psychoanalysis" (1912), *SE* 12: 111.
9. Such moments of insight have been variously described. Theodor Reik spoke about them in *Surprise and the Psychoanalyst* (New York: E. P. Dutton, 1937). The specifically cognitive

aspects have been described by Ernst Kris, in "Vicissitudes of Insight," and Hans Loewald, in "Therapeutic Action." Others have discussed the more emotional, infantile prototypes for insight; see, e.g., Bertram Lewin, "Some Observations on Knowledge, Belief and the Impulse to Know," *International Journal of Psychoanalysis* 20 (1950): 426–31. Jerome Richfield's "An Analysis of the Concept of Insight," *Psychoanalytic Quarterly* 23 (1954): 390–408, gives an introduction to the different aspects of this phenomenon.

10. Freud, "A Disturbance of Memory on the Acropolis" (1936), *SE* 22: 239–48.
11. Kenneth Burke, "Freud—and the Analysis of Poetry," in *The Philosophy of Literary Form,* rev. ed. (New York: Random House/Vintage, 1961), p. 248, speaks of the "systematic impieties of the clinic."
12. Paul Ricoeur, *Freud and Philosophy: An Essay on Interpretation,* trans. Denis Savage (New Haven: Yale University Press, 1970), pp. 32ff.
13. Freud, "A Seventeenth-Century Demonological Neurosis" (1923), *SE* 19: 83. It is interesting that Freud acknowledges these tendencies in an essay about a pact with the devil and its devilishly pedantic, hair's-breadth loopholes. Such loopholes are also found in pacts with "the unconscious."
14. Phyllis Greenacre analyzes Bates's significance to Jonathan Swift in *Swift and Carroll: A Psychoanalytic Study* (New York: International Universities Press, 1955), p. 99. [See also Chapter 8 in this volume].
15. William Empson makes this claim in the preface to the second edition of *Seven Types of Ambiguity* (New York: Meridian Books, 1955), p. 8.
16. Phyllis Greenacre, speaking of the child, refers to "the inevitable polymorphous character of his perceptiveness" in "Play in Relation to Creative Imagination," in *Emotional Growth, Psychoanalytic Studies of the Gifted and a Great Variety of Other Individuals,* 2 vols. (New York: International Universities Press, 1971), p. 571.
17. Paul Ricoeur, "Metaphor and the Main Problem of Hermeneutics," *New Literary History* 6 (1974): 95–110.
18. Freud, "Wild Psychoanalysis" (1910), *SE* 11: 226.
19. Kris, "Vicissitudes," passim. [See note 3].
20. Freud, "Fragment of an Analysis of a Case of Hysteria" (1905), *SE* 7: 72.
21. Hans Loewald, "Comments on Some Instinctual Manifestations of Superego Formation," reported in *The Bulletin of the Philadelphia Association for Psychoanalysis* 12 (1962): 43–45.
22. Unpublished case report. See also Thomas Freeman et al., *Chronic Schizophrenia* (New York: International Universities Press, 1958), pp. 37ff.
23. Jean Laplanche and J. B. Pontalis, "Fantasy and the Origins of Sexuality," *International Journal of Psychoanalysis* 49 (1968): 2. See also N. Searle, "Flight to Reality," *International Journal of Psychoanalysis* 10 (1929): 280–91.
24. Victor Rosen, "Variants of Comic Caricature and Their Relationship to Obsessive-Compulsive Phenomena," *Journal of the American Psychoanalytic Association* 11 (1963): 719–20.
25. See Rudolph M. Loewenstein, "The Problem of Interpretation," *Psychoanalytic Quarterly* 20 (1951): 9.
26. Claude Lèvi-Strauss, *Structural Anthropology,* trans. Claire Jacobson and Brooke Grundfest Schoepf (Garden City, N.J.: Anchor Books, 1967), pp. 191–200.
27. Stanley Cavell, "Aesthetic Problems of Modern Philosophy," in *Must We Mean What We Say? A Book of Essays* (New York: Charles Scribner's, 1969), pp. 85–86. This parallel was suggested to me by Henry Abelove.
28. Peter L. Giovacchini, "The Influence of Interpretation upon Schizophrenic Patients," *International Journal of Psychoanalysis* 50 (1969): 180.

29. See note 19.
30. Otto Fenichel, *Problems of Psychoanalytic Technique* (New York: Psychoanalytic Quarterly, 1941), p. 8.
31. E.T.A. Hoffmann, *Eight Tales of Hoffmann,* trans J. M. Cohen (London: Pan Books, 1952). Freud retells the story in "The Uncanny" (1919), *SE* 17:226–33.
32. Both in his essay on jokes, *Jokes and Their Relation to the Unconscious* (1905), *SE* 8: 9–226, and in "The Uncanny," written fourteen years later, Freud tried to reduce the text in question to a simpler energic model of disguised wish fulfillment. Each of these genre essays is a spin-off from one of his major theoretical statements and is implicitly offered as a demonstration of it. This is interesting, because while the two essays themselves offer the same explanation for jokes as for the uncanny, the theoretical claims contradict one another. Freud wrote the essay on jokes while working on his monumental "Three Essays on the Theory of Sexuality" in 1905 (*SE* 7: 130–279), which explained behavior solely in terms of the pleasure principle; but he wrote his essay on the uncanny while working on the pivotal essay "Beyond the Pleasure Principle," which suggested that repetition is a motive force for behavior as powerful as wish fulfillment.
33. See Freud, "The Uncanny," *SE* 17: 230–31, and *Jokes, SE* 8: 17–19 and 92–96.
34. Freud, "The Motives of Jokes—Jokes as a Social Process," in *Jokes* (1905), *SE* 8: 140–58.
35. Norman Holland, *The Dynamics of Literary Response* (New York: Oxford University Press, 1968), pp. 3–4. The version given here is only a summary of the original.
36. Freud, *Jokes, SE* 8: 236.
37. Matthew Arnold, "The Study of Poetry," *English Literature and Irish Politics,* The Complete Prose Works of Matthew Arnold, ed. R. H. Super, vol. 9 (Ann Arbor: The University of Michigan Press, 1973), p. 170.
38. Harold Bloom, "Poetic Crossing: Rhetoric and Psychology," *The Georgia Review* 30 (1976): 495–526.
39. Kris, "Vicissitudes," p. 452.
40. Freud, *The Interpretation of Dreams, SE* 4:262.
41. Freud, "Studies on Hysteria" (1893–95), *SE* 2:175–81.
42. Kenneth Burke has suggested in the case of several plays that we must stop evaluating characters simply in terms defined by the content or plot and must switch instead to evaluating them in terms defined by their function: the villain Iago (in the plot's literal terms) then becomes a hero, in a way, for if the play is to work at all it needs both hero and villain playing their interlocking roles. ("*Othello:* An Essay to Illustrate a Method," *Hudson Review* 4 [Summer 1951]: 165–203. See also Burke's "*Coriolanus*—and the Delights of Faction," in *Language as Sumbolic Action* [Berkeley and Los Angeles: University of California Press, 1966], and "*King Lear*: Its Form and Psychosis," *Shenandoah* 21 [Autumn 1969]: 3–18.) A. D. Nuttall suggests a similar reversal in *Measure for Measure,* where in the *plot's* terms the Duke is a hero coping with Angelo's wickedness, but if we think about the characters' *functions,* Angelo is a scapegoat who takes on the Duke's dirty work; like Judas in Borges's version of the Passion, Angelo is the one who makes the real sacrifice, because only he really loses in the end. ("*Measure for Measure:* Quid Pro Quo?" *Shakespeare Studies* 4 [1968]: 231–51. Nuttall cites Borges's "Three Versions of Judas" in *Ficciones* [Buenos Aires: Emace, 1962]). René Girard has proposed several such rereadings, which for him represent a switch from content terms to structural terms (Girard, "Lévi-Strauss, Frye, Derrida and Shakespearean Criticism," *Diacritics* 3 [Fall 1973]: 34–38). At least two new interpretations of *Hamlet* stress the audience's—and the characters'—uncertainty about not only the facts of the play but the terms in which to measure these

facts: Stephen Booth, "On the Value of *Hamlet*," in *Reinterpretation of Elizabethan Drama*, ed. Norman Rabkin (New York: Columbia University Press, 1969); and Howard Felperin, "O'erdoing the Termagant: *Hamlet*," in *Shakespearean Representation: Mimesis and Modernity in Elizabethan Tragedy* (Princeton, N.J.: Princeton University Press, 1977), pp. 44–67. Janet Adelman has proposed a similar uncertainty as the defining quality of *Antony and Cleopatra* (*The Common Liar: An Essay on* Antony and Cleopatra [New Haven: Yale University Press, 1973]). For suggestions that such reversals are characteristic of all Shakespeare's plays, rather than unique qualities defining the nature of a particular play, see Norman Rabkin, "Meaning and Shakespeare," in *Shakespeare 1971*, ed. Clifford Leech and J.M.R. Margeson (Toronto: University of Toronto Press, 1979), and Albert Cook, *Shakespeare's Enactment: The Dynamics of Renaissance Theater* (Chicago: Swallow Press, 1978).

43. Stanley Fish, *Surprised by Sin: The Reader in Paradise Lost* (New York: St. Martin's Press, 1967); Paul J. Alpers, *The Poetry of* The Faerie Queene (Princeton: Princeton University Press, 1967).
44. Stephen Barney discusses this in his chapters on Spenser in *Allegories of History, Allegories of Love* (Hamden, Conn.: Archon Books, 1979), and Isabel MacCaffrey's general remarks on *The Faerie Queene* in *Spenser's Allegory: The Anatomy of Imagination* (Princeton, N.J.: Princeton University Press, 1976).
45. William Empson, *Seven Types of Ambiguity* (New York: Meridian Books, 1955), p. 41.
46. Alpers, *The Poetry of* The Faerie Queene, pp. 95–106. See also Roger Sale's earlier discussion, "Spenser's Undramatic Poetry," in *Elizabethan Poetry: Modern Essays in Criticism*, ed. Paul J. Alpers (New York: Oxford University Press, 1967), pp. 422–46.
47. Michael Riffaterre's term.
48. Jonathan Culler, *Structuralist Poetics: Structuralism, Linguistics, and the Study of Literature* (Ithaca, N.Y.: Cornell University Press, 1975), p. 183; see also Frank Kermode on the verbal medium's potential to be both a "virtual transparency" and something "technically exploited," so that it is seen in its own right: "Novels: Recognition and Deception," *Critical Inquiry* 1 (1974): 103–21.
49. George S. Klein, "The Several Grades of Memory," in his *Perception, Motives and Personality* (New York: Alfred A. Knopf, 1970), p. 303.
50. Stephen Booth, *An Essay on Shakespeare's Sonnets* (New Haven: Yale University Press, 1969), p. 14.
51. Thomas Mann, *The Magic Mountain*, trans. H. T. Lowe-Porter (New York: Alfred A. Knopf, 1951), p. 126.
52. See Booth, "On the Value of *Hamlet*." [Note 42].
53. Booth, *ibid.*, and Felperin, "O'erdoing the Termagant." [Note 42].

17. *Candide:* Radical Simplicity and the Impact of Evil

Gail S. Reed

Several of Voltaire's best known tales are similar in shape and plot, apparent variations on an inner theme. *Zadig* (1741), *Candide* (1750), and *L'Ingénu* (1767) all involve a naïve or idealistic protagonist wandering the world in search of a woman who had been denied him by fate and authority, grappling the while with the frustration imposed by arbitrary and powerful men and carried out through their often impersonal and cruel institutions. At the chronological center of the tales *Candide* has an emotional impact lacking in the others; it has been frequently asserted that it is the product of personal crisis and represents the author's confrontation with the existence of evil.[1] Philosophic and biographical implications aside, for these have been frequently discussed elsewhere, what formal factors, absent in the other tales, compel this impression of the impact of evil?

Like any other attempt to explore the emotional aspect of fiction, this one requires assumptions about a reader, that literary figure who of late has become more controversial than the literature he reads. Critics of several persuasions, while in agreement on the interdependence of reader and text, have been divided over whether the reader should be considered an objective or subjective entity.[2] Such differences threaten to cloud the valuable perspective which the participatory model has opened for us and might best be resolved by recognizing a spectrum of response encompassing both individual differences and (not necessarily conscious) collective experience engendered by a literary text. It is the latter end of the spectrum which will concern me.

The assumption that readers not only react idiosyncratically to a text but also share in a collective experience seems justified on the grounds of their participation both in the human condition itself and in a particular culture

Reprinted by permission of the author.

where, *inter alia,* common educational practices, language, history, mythology, values, and ideals foster a more specific communality. Freud has pointed out the role of unconscious fantasy shared between the creative writer and his audience,[3] and Hanns Sachs has described a community of daydreams.[4] More recently Beres and Arlow have suggested that a reservoir of shared experience as it is elaborated in fantasy forms the basis of empathy, that quality of feeling with another which lies at the root of esthetic participation.[5]

It is not, however, my intention to explore the emotional impact of *Candide* by searching for an unconscious fantasy. The search for latent content raises methodological questions outside the scope of this essay.[6] Rather, I shall follow a suggestion of Hutter,[7] and relate collective response to the structure of the text utilizing psychoanalytic knowledge of normal development as a guide. Accordingly, I shall make no attempt to discern what latent wish or accompanying fantasy might underlie the manifest content of *Candide.* It suffices that the representation of that wish, the hero's pursuit of a woman who combines maternal and sexual qualities, sets in motion a plot characterized by the interplay between the realization of a representation of desire and its frustration. Although the represented wish may conceivably furnish a symbolic structure for several individual wishes, the experience of wish and frustration, which characterizes a reading of *Candide,* is universal.

The problem of defining a collective experience on the basis of an emotional response which will in many be unconscious remains difficult. Not all readers react in the same conscious way to elements in a literary work. For example, the sequence of wish and frustration of wish present in *Candide* tends to evoke anger. The small child will have a tantrum when the frustration of a wish results in an increase of undischarged tension which is experienced as "unpleasure."[8] Some readers, however, may derive gratification from the frustration itself and be consciously immune to the anger it engenders. Others, to avoid experiencing the anger, may idealize the philosophical resolution at the end, concentrate entirely on historical issues, or see only the ironic overlay which minimizes the considerable sadism especially present in the first half of the work. These defensive and characterological responses do not necessarily contradict the assertion of a particular collective experience involving frustration; to the psychoanalytically informed they rather confirm the presence of something consciously unknown.

What is at work in reading is akin to what psychoanalysis calls countertransference in its broadest sense, the emotional responses of the analyst to the patient which, scrutinized, may provide him with valuable information about the patient or, unscrutinized, may interfere with his understanding of and response to the patient. Freud's original description of countertransference was narrower in scope, concerned with interference from the analyst's unconscious exclusively.[9] Gradually, however, definitions have broadened to include the patient's contribution. Several modern theoreticians even hold that in the severer pathologies countertransference reactions are induced, an effort on the part of the patient to recreate his early experiences, or to rid himself of his most fragmenting feelings.[10] The relative merits of these various theoretical developments need not concern us here. What is useful to remember is that certain aspects of countertransference phenomena are not unique to a treatment situation. Conscious response often represents a distortion of the underlying experience and these distorted reactions may occur in all experiences of everyday life, including reading. In fact, such reactions may well account for the strident passion with which rival groups of critics hold fast to contradictory interpretations when the more interesting question remains whether something in the text inspires this disagreement.

The emotional flexibility to explore rather than interpret and hold fast, however, requires the same vigilance to unconscious response as the clinician must exercise: scrutiny of feeling and fantasy, of intense reactions or their absence, of silence or over-talkativeness. Knowledge derived from clinical practice and observations of development shows that certain forms of presentation, certain sequences, certain types of material ought generally to evoke a particular response. Since there is no entirely objective standard by which to identify countertransference reactions, knowledge of hypothetical tendency must be supplemented by self-knowledge, intuition, and experience. We will need, then, to be satisfied with a rather subjective standard after all,, a hypothetical reader whose reading experience represents a hypothetical collective experience.[11] If this uncertainty flies in the face of wishes for scientific rigor, it should be recalled that accepting uncertainty is a necessary corollary to accepting the unconscious.

One may, however, be reasonably certain of the intensity of *Candide*'s emotional impact on the reader,[12] despite both the balance achieved as the second half progresses and the ever present element of ironic distance. To describe this impact in terms of manifest theme, one is drawn to the horrifying—because arbitrary—weight of "civilized" evil. Surely the critical debate over whether Voltaire "solves" the "problem of evil" reflects this impact.[13] Whatever the substance of critics' disagreements, it is much less significant than the fact that they conceive of Voltaire's success or failure in these terms, as though by solving the problem he could in some way protect them from the feeling of vulnerability his work awakens.

What factors in *Candide* could account for this impact of evil? One is the organization of the plot. Beneath the distancing and mitigating ironic tone which characterizes the narrator's presentation, the world of *Candide* is built upon a fundamental rhythm of expectation and betrayal. *Candide* is a dialectic of desire and punishment, of trust and the brutal deception of that trust. The hero, innocently desiring Cunégonde and faithfully believing his tutor, is cast out into a best of all possible worlds which proves a mutilating inferno. Despairing, cold, hungry, and penniless, he finds his flagging faith restored by two strangers who treat him to dinner—then brusquely trick him into military servitude where he is robbed of any modicum of individuality and freedom, and finally stripped of his skin in a beating. His fellow sufferer, the old woman, in her parallel journey through life, is deprived by murder of a princely husband at the moment when she joyously anticipates marriage, then ravished, enslaved, and made witness to the dismemberment of her mother and attendants. A eunuch she believes kind fortunately rescues her from the bloody pile of corpses onto which she has collapsed, then quickly sells her anew into slavery.

These betrayals, rhythmic norms rather than exceptions in *Candide,* frustrate fulfillment; within the fiction they break down the characters' integrity; without, they assault the reader's sense of security through continual frustration of his conventional expectations of the marvelous. The two travelers, so often brutalized and betrayed, withdraw into a state of numbness in which, separate from their bodies, they feel neither physical nor emotional pain; they merely endure. Candide wordlessly traverses a war-torn countryside, objective correlative to his burnt-out inner state; the old woman, less and less desired, becomes first concubine, then slave, than an object dispatched from city to city, until her body is reduced to its most concrete physicality and becomes food. In a final bitter irony, buttock replaces breast in a gruesome parody of the primordial experience of security.

One result of this catastrophic rhythm is the intensified search for warmth and safety. The main characters yearn for protection, for a magic circle of comfort, security, and satiety, as is attested to by their frequent hunger, their stubborn innocence and comic grandiosity, their idealization of Westphalia, and their constant and oft contradicted assertions that they are infallible, perfect, or deserving of the best. Characters and reader are temporarily granted that protection in Eldorado.

Another and parallel result is the release of destructive forces. Indeed the fictional reality of the tale does not permit retreat for long. Outside that magic circle of perfection resides the social world into which the characters are constantly propelled. And this evil outside world is a place where the social institution seeks out the individual to destroy him. Children are castrated to sing in operas, slaves dismembered for disobedience, the military takes brutal possession of Candide's body. In fact, the double row of soldiers poised to club him becomes a giant devouring maw. In this evil social world, rationalized sadism runs rampant. There are, of course, the overt acts of individuals who enslave, rob, rape, and disembowel, but the esthetically pleasing ritual of an auto-de-fé camouflages equally sadistic yet socially sanctioned wishes. When brutality is committed in the name of good, when justice condones robbery and charges a fee, when freedom involves a choice between death by clubbing or firing squad, then language becomes the agent of social deception and the social world beyond the magic circle a place of uncertain perception as well as of danger. Deceiving characters emerge from its midst conferring names on themselves, promising uniqueness and coveting riches, and then merge back into its anonymity. Thus the false Cunégonde is only "a cheat."[14] Candide also becomes part of the universe of shifting forms—separated from his name—stepping back from naïve candor into the socially conferred guise of mercenary. In rapid succession he offers his loyalty to the Spanish, then the Jesuits, avows his German birth and finds Cunégonde's brother, then disguises himself as Jesuit in order to flee, and is held prisoner and threatened with death by the Oreillons because accoutrements designate him as Jesuit. He escapes with his life only by slipping out of the clothing of his assumed identity. This social world, representing the individual's rage at frustration, destroys the self. In becoming part of its spreading insubstantiality, the individual momentarily ceases to exist.

One way in which the evil realm incorporates the self is by undermining the individual's perceptions and thus depriving him of his ability to anticipate, judge, and experience himself as a subjective continuity in time. Encountering Candide, the major characters emerge out of the treacherous social world in continuously changing shapes. The "trembling woman, of a splendid figure, glittering in diamonds, and veiled'' (7, 13) is Cunégonde, though the other veiled woman is a fraud. One of the women ''hanging out towels on lines to dry'' is also Cunégonde, ''her skin weathered, her eyes bloodshot, her breasts fallen, her cheeks seamed, her arms red and scaly'' (29, 71). The Commander, ''his three-cornered hat on his head, his cassock drawn up, a sword at his side, and a pike in his hand,'' is the young Baron (14, 27). He metamorphoses into friend, then into arrogant aristocrat, changes effected with a chameleon-like speed paralleled by Candide's confusion of names: ''Most reverend father . . . my old master, my friend, my brother-in-law'' (15, 29). Pangloss reappears as an ineffective galley-slave, as a corpse dissected back to life, and most frighteningly as that phantom who throws himself on Candide:

> a beggar who was covered with pustules, his eyes were sunken, the end of his nose rotted off, his mouth twisted, his teeth black, he had a croaking voice and a hacking cough, and spat a tooth every time he tried to speak. (3, 6)

The destructiveness represented by the instability of the social realm and of the self here intersect, for Pangloss' ghostly ''disguise'' is a mutilation which ordinarily belongs to nightmare. By making disguise a matter of body, the text turns the possible illusion of the ghost into the fictional reality of a disfigured tutor. As the physical body yields its integrity, the character becomes his disguise, becomes, that is, other.

Both the savageness of the fictional reality and the rhythm of the plot depend on the radical simplicity of the hero for their full effect. An appropriate accompaniment to the cruel and unstable reality which surrounds him, the characteristics united by the name of Candide designate him incomplete. The oscillations of his spirits according to the fullness of his stomach, his taking in of Pangloss' teachings because of the facilitating presence of the beautiful Cunégonde, his profound dependence on her to give his life shape and direction, his belief that a high degree of happiness consists in *being* her, all suggest that Voltaire has constructed a developmentally primitive literary character. So much, in fact, is Candide's simplicity coupled with devices which suggest infantile experience, that it shocks us to discover in the last chapter that as he has reached maturity he has acquired a beard.

Despite this growth—for much of the tale Candide is so lacking in self-definition that he is ''incapable of irony,'' as Coulet aptly notes[15]—he is devoid of judgment. Thus, he is dependent on guides to judge for him. Whether they prove trustworthy, like Cacambo, or treacherous, like Venderdendur, is a hazard of his radical simplicity, for his lack of differentiation manifests itself in uncritical, open-mouthed, passive receptivity.

It is this infantile openness, moreover, that involves the reader in the fictional world and thus in its brutal betrayals. Nothing masks Candide's primitive yearning for Cunégonde, or for that best world promised by Pangloss, and these wishes, emerging contrapuntally against the cruel deceptions of the plot, tend to elicit the reader's empathic wishes for food, warmth, and protection. Thus, when Candide's are abruptly frustrated, so too, our own.

The reader's subjective participation in Candide's desires is facilitated in a number of ways. Among the most important is the adroit use of "internal focus,"[16] Genette's term for the restriction of the reader's field of vision to that of a given character. Of course, internal focus is not the norm of *Candide* where the narration, like that of most tales, is omniscient. Rather, internal focus represents a temporary shift of perspective away from narrative omniscience. Sometimes nearly imperceptible, such a shift may also involve the reader quite dramatically and subjectively in fictional danger. Immediately after the safe arrival in Buenos Aires where Cunégonde and Candide have fled together, new danger supervenes.

> And then she ran straight to Candide:—Get out of town, she said, or you'll be burned within the hour. There was not a moment to lose; but how to leave Cunégonde, and where to go? (8, 25)

Objective description cedes to an internal focus upon Candide's experience of his predicament. At this point, the chapter ends, the danger unresolved and under-distanced.

The reader's vision is reduced to a restricted internal focus that limits his knowledge of the fictional world as severely as Candide's and renders him equally helpless. Thus the reader becomes temporarily one with a character of neither judgment nor knowledge, and the force of that sadistic reality through which the child-hero is deprived of wished-for security increases. The sense of helplessness is complemented by the frustration of the chapter break,[17] a device which, as a formal analogue to Candide's sense of being trapped, places the reader in the same position of powerlessness in relation to the narrator as the hero finds himself in vis-à-vis the causal events of the fiction.

Nor is this the only instance in which a formal analogue furnishes the reader with the fictionally appropriate response. Just as within the fiction the characters' perception of self is threatened by the menacing transformation of the body, so the reader's perception of the fictional world is undermined by the use of an ambiguous signifier. During the carnival in Venice Candide encounters six men who are addressed as kings. "All is but illusion and disaster" (24, 56), he has earlier sighed, preparing to consider the six kings as part of the locally sanctioned disguise. Since Cacambo, so closely allied to Vice and his classical counterpart the slave who manages the comic plot, also appears incognito, the dinner seems designated as theater. What appears to be disguise, however, turns out to be calamity. The kings are exiled and impoverished sovereigns with neither status nor power who cling to meaningless social forms and designations. When one of them actually begs for money, the signifier, "King," becomes dissociated from its conventional connotation of money and power. Fictional reality redefines language.

In this way, the reader shares in attenuated fashion in an experience of disorganization. Fooled by the carnival and Cacambo, then disoriented by the redefinition of the signifier "King," the reader's hold on fictional reality becomes somewhat precarious. The question arises for him: what is real carnival if what appears to be carnival is reality? Although it is not answered, the implied answer is the unsettling one that there is no distinction: fictive illusion and fictive reality merge. Which events are then reliable, asks the reader, the hanging and murder of Candide's friends, either witnessed or committed by Candide, or their existence as galley slaves before his eyes? And if these slaves with disfigured faces are named Pangloss and the Baron, are they, like the kings, Pangloss and the Baron in name only?

What spares the reader too much disorientation is the distancing effect of the omniscient narration. The narrator, reliable, objective, in control, gives a counterbalancing stability to the unstable fictional world and authority to the events he describes. The breadth and scope of his vision creates a distance from fictional event which permits the reader the anticipation of danger, the illusion of safety, and the luxury to appreciate irony. With this broader perspective, the narrator exposes the naiveté of Candide and the self-importance of his companions, enabling us, *Dieu merci,* to find release in laughter.

Yet this relief is not so complete as we might suspect. It alleviates, but does not prevent, our subjective reaction to the dangers of the fictional world. In the presentation of the earthquake, for instance, disaster strikes mimetically:

> Scarcely had they set foot in the town, still bewailing the loss of their benefactor, when they felt the earth quake under foot, the sea . . . burst into the port, and smashed all the vessels. (5, 10)

The restrained description of upheaval in and of itself hardly moves. Rather, its placement in a sequence in which natural disaster and human cruelty follow each other precipitously surprises. When Pangloss and Candide set foot on shore after the death of Jacques and the shipwreck, reader and characters alike prepare for a respite. But safety is accorded only an introductory subordinate clause—in the main clause new disaster shocks.

Only after the reader is startled into subjectivity, does the narrative present the exaggerated and idiosyncratic reactions of the victims: the sailor looks for booty, Pangloss for a way of justifying his philosophic system, Candide for solace. Shock is countered by comedy. Yet these stylized descriptions are dependent on the reader's initial surprise for their comic effect. They afford him release secondarily because they allow him to escape his subjective involvement and to regard the beleaguered characters objectively.

Nor is the earthquake scene an exception. For the first half of the tale, over and over again, deftly and economically, the narrative moves the reader from safety to new danger: Candide and Cunégonde tell leisurely and objectively of the horrors of their lives in the comfort of a sea journey only to be separated the moment they come to port. Further, the narrative moves the reader from safe objectivity to the intimacy of the subjective not only by means of such formal devices as shifts of focus and manipulation of chapter divisions, but also by means of a play with convention which turns the events of the fiction into versions of chance as haphazard and out of control as the fictional world itself.[18]

The rhythm of trust and betrayal, safety and danger thus finds its counterpart in the oscillation of the reader between participation in the danger of the fictional world and a more comfortable sharing of the omniscient narrator's objectivity. Until Candide begins to grow in the second half of the tale, his radical simplicity, evoking as it does a universal infantile defenselessness, emerges as a crucial subjective focus from which objective narration must rescue us before the boundaries of comedy are transgressed.

Through the structure of the text, then, the reader of *Candide* is engaged in a cycle of wish, frustration, and reactive anger which facilitates a transient identification with an infantile hero, on the one hand, and lends the impact of the anger to the arbitrary external authority which assails him, on the other. The plot itself and formal elements such as the ordering of the action, the handling of narrative focus, and the syntax all contribute to the reader's identificatory wishes for warmth, safety, and security. When these wishes, apparently realized, are abruptly frustrated, the resultant anger fosters an experience of outside authority—whether fictional destiny or social institution—as cruel and implacable. The power which anger confers upon frustrating authority, in turn, increases the experience of powerlessness through which the reader, identified with the hero/victim, confronts his own vulnerability. Thus the transient identification with the hero is reinforced and the cycle of wish, frustration, and anger renewed. This reciprocal relationship between literary structure and the affect—conscious or not—that that structure evokes in the reader is an essential and complex element in the esthetic experience of *Candide*.

NOTES

1. Ira O. Wade, *The Intellectual Development of Voltaire* (Princeton, N.J.: Princeton University Press, 1969), pp. 683–84.
2. Among those who objectify response and for whom an objective reader follows logically: Jonathan Culler, *Structuralist Poetics* (Ithaca, N.Y.: Cornell University Press, 1975); Wolfgang Iser, *The Implied Reader: Patterns of Communication in Prose Fiction from Bunyan to Beckett* (Baltimore, Md.: Johns Hopkins University Press, 1974), pp. 274–93; Lowry Nelson, Jr., "The Fictive Reader and Literary Self-Reflexiveness," in Peter Dementz, Thomas H. Greene, Lowry Nelson, Jr., eds., *The Disciplines of Criticism* (New Haven, Conn.: Yale University Press, 1968), pp. 173–91. Among those who hold response and the reader to be subjective: Robert Crosman, "Do Readers Make Meaning?" in Susan R. Suleiman and Inge Crosman, eds., *The Reader in the Text* (Princeton, N.J.: Princeton University Press, 1980), pp. 149–64; David Bleich, *Subjective Criticism* (Baltimore, Md.: Johns Hopkins University Press, 1978); Norman N. Holland, *5 Readers Reading* (New Haven, Conn.: Yale University Press, 1975). For an excellent general survey of varieties of reader-response criticism, see Susan R. Suleiman, "Introduction" in Susan R. Suleiman and Inge Crosman, eds., *The Reader in the Text,* pp. 3–45.
3. Sigmund Freud, "Creative Writers and Daydreaming" (1908), *S.E.*, 9: 143–53.
4. Hanns Sachs, *The Creative Unconscious: Studies in the Psychoanalysis of Art* (Cambridge, Mass.: Science-Art Publishers, 1942), pp. 11–54.
5. David M. Beres and Jacob A. Arlow, "Fantasy and Identification in Empathy," *Psychoanalytic Quarterly* (1974), 43:26–50.
6. See Gail S. Reed, "Towards a Methodology for Applying Psychoanalysis to Literature," *Psychoanalytic Quartrely* (1982), 51:19–42.
7. Albert D. Hutter, "The High Tower of His Mind: Psychoanalysis and the Reader of 'Bleak House,' " *Criticism* (1977), 29:296–316, p. 313.
8. On "unpleasure" see Freud, "Instincts and their Vicissitudes," *The Standard Edition,* edited by James Strachey (London: Hogarth Press and the Institute of Psychoanalysis, 1957), 14:111–40, p. 136.
9. Freud, "The Future Prospects of Psychoanalytic Therapy" (1910), *Standard Edition* 12:144–45.
10. For recent writing about countertransference see, among others, Peter Giovacchini, *Treatment of Primitive Mental States* (New York: Jason Aronson, 1979), pp. 477–95; Otto

Kernberg, *Borderline Conditions and Pathological Narcissism* (New York: Jason Aronson, 1975), pp. 49–69; Robert Langs, ed., *Classics in Psychoanalytic Technique* (New York: Jason Aronson, 1981), pp. 139–347; Harold Searles, *Collected Papers on Schizophrenia and Related Subjects* (New York: International Universities Press, 1965), pp. 192–215, 349–80, 521–59, *passim;* D. W. Winnicott, "Hate in the Countertransference" (1947), in *Through Paediatrics to Psycho-Analysis* (New York: Basic Books, 1975), pp. 194–203.

11. For a suggestion of where more objective evidence of collective response may be found, see Reed, "Towards a Methodology for Applying Psychoanalysis to Literature."
12. See, for example, Amy Marshland, "Voltaire: Satire and Sedition," *Romantic Review* (1966), 57:35–40; Christopher Thacker, introduction to *Candide ou l'Optimisme: Edition Critique* (Geneva: Droz, 1968); Jacques Vanden Heuval, *Voltaire dans ses Contes* (Paris: Armand Colin, 1967), p. 264.
13. For example, Richard A. Brooks, *Voltaire and Leibniz* (Geneva: Droz, 1964), pp. 106–7; William Bottiglia, *Candide, Analysis of a Classic,* 2nd ed. rev. (Geneva: Institut et Musée Voltaire, 1964), pp. 109–10; Henri Coulet, "La Candeur de Candide," *Annales de la Faculté des Lettres et Sciences Humaines d'Aix,* (1960), 34:87–99, p. 95; John Pappas, "*Candide* Rétrécissement ou Expansion?" *Diderot Studies* (1968), 10:241–63, pp. 241–43; Roy S. Wolper, "Candide, Gull in the Garden?" *Eighteenth Century Studies* (1969), 3:265–77.
14. Voltaire, *Candide or Optimism.* Translated and edited by Robert M. Adams (New York: Norton, 1991), 22, p. 53. Further citations will be given in the text and will include chapter and page number.
15. Henri Coulet, "La Candeur de Candide."
16. Gérard Genette, *Figures III* (Paris: Editions du Seuil, 1972), pp. 206ff. Genette's reciprocal term is "zero degree focalization." I have used omniscience in its place for stylistic not theoretical reasons.
17. For a differently oriented discussion of chapter division see Michael Danahy, "The Nature of Narrative Norms in *Candide,*" in Theodore Besterman, ed., *Studies on Voltaire and the Eighteenth Century* (Banbury, Oxfordshire: The Voltaire Foundation, 1973), vol. 114, pp. 113–40.
18. See Martin Price, *To the Palace of Wisdom: Studies in Order and Energy from Dryden to Blake* (1964; rept. Garden City, N.Y.: Doubleday, 1965), p. 314.

18. A Dream, A Sonnet, and a Ballad: The Path to Keats's "La Belle Dame Sans Merci"

Francis Baudry

Here are the poems, they will explain themselves as all poems should do—without comment

—Keats, February 12, 1819, in letter to his brother and sister-in-law

INTRODUCTION

While researching the background of one of the greatest ballads in the English language, "La Belle Dame sans Merci" by John Keats, I uncovered a remarkable sequence of texts which help us to reconstruct certain intermediary steps in the process of creativity and writing.

A personal journal which the English poet Keats kept as a lengthy letter to his brother and sister-in-law, over a period of several months, includes a report of a dream and shortly thereafter a sonnet entitled "On a Dream," and then a poem which has been called the most beautiful ballad in the English language, "La Belle Dame sans Merci." The ballad includes a dream in its content. My interest was aroused in this sequence by the fact that a dream appears to be a "seed" in three different aspects of John Keats's literary output within a very brief period of time. A dream is mentioned in the correspondence; then the same manifest dream is barely transformed as the last lines of a sonnet titled "On a Dream," and finally, a few days later, the great ballad, "La Belle Dame sans Merci," includes a literary dream.

I will consider the flow of material from correspondence to dream, to sonnet, and to ballad as though it were an extended analytic hour. One of my hypotheses is that the sequence—dream, sonnet, ballad—allows for the gradual expression of warded-off depressive affects as though the poems were an "interpretation" of the dream—with the difference that the poet

Reprinted by permission of the author and *the Psychoanalytic Quarterly*, 55 (1986).

may not have listened to or even been interested in the content of the interpretation. This approach to the poems permits us to make certain hypotheses which would not be possible if the poems were simply considered as separate texts unrelated to each other or to elements in the author's life.

I will first try to reconstruct the meaning of the dream experience from information about it in the journal and from its subsequent fate in the poems. The study of meaning will include how the dream is used (its function) in each different fragment—correspondence, sonnet, ballad.

Second, the detailed description of the transformation which the dream experience undergoes as it is incorporated into the poetry will provide a microscopic view of the evolution of the creative process. I will try to show how the various aspects of the dream—its affect, imagery, and probable latent content—emerge and become clarified as the poet's imagination transforms the raw material into verse. I will suggest that the more successful of several poems allows much freer expression of forbidden, threatening, and painful ideas and feelings. It would be tempting to postulate that this free emergence of unconscious elements is a precondition of all great art. Too defensive a stance leads to stilted or less interesting imagery. This is certainly true in the case of the Keats sonnet which I will consider.

In a final section, I will discuss problems of method and validation in applied analysis.

HISTORY

A very few words about Keats's brief and tragic life are in order. Born on October 31, 1795, he was the oldest of four, followed by George (1797), Tom (1799), and Edward (1801); the latter died in infancy. The youngest, Fanny, was born in 1803. The father died as the result of a fall from a horse when John was only nine. At this point the family was thrown into chaos. The mother, unable to manage the family affairs, quickly succumbed to the pleas of a minor clerk in a banking firm, William Rawlings, marrying him in desperation less than four months after her husband's death. The grandmother, who disapproved of the hasty marriage, took over the care of the children who went to live with her. While in boarding school, at age fifteen, Keats lost his mother to tuberculosis, the dreaded disease that was to fell his brother Tom and himself as well. The grandfather had also died by then. The grandmother gave over the care of the boys to a guardian, Abbey, a suspicious and uneducated man who interrupted John's schooling in 1811, having decided he should learn to support himself. The grandmother died in 1814, leaving the children without a home.

After spending several unhappy years in apothecary training, John moved into his brother George's house in 1816, but a stable family life was not destined for him. George, who had played both fraternal and paternal role in the poet's life, married Georgiana Wylie and moved to Kentucky in 1818. There is no doubt that Keats experienced a severe loss at the marriage and departure of his beloved brother and his wife. George had been a stabilizing influence in Keats's life. His marriage had recreated a stable family unit, something Keats had not experienced since the death of his parents. In December 1818, the younger brother, Tom, died of tuberculosis and a few weeks later, shortly before the composition of the poem, Keats developed a sore throat which he correctly diagnosed as an early stage of tuberculosis, the disease that would kill him two years later. During this same period, he first confessed his love to a young woman, Fanny Brawne, a passion that in all likelihood was never consummated even though Keats became engaged to her for a brief period later in the year 1819. Clearly, Keats had many doubts about the wisdom of such a choice. He was beset by persistent financial problems and was encountering poor reviews. He sensed his failing health, and he worried that he might have to give up writing for Fanny Brawne's sake. He was known to suffer chronically from recurrent mood swings and severe depressions.

DATA

I will now turn to Keats's journal[1] to outline the events preceding the dream. In order to maintain a bond with his beloved brother and sister-in-law, now pregnant, he kept this journal from which he sent them passages. The correspondence serves as the backdrop for the works I will consider in detail and for some others I will mention in passing.

The correspondence to George, often addressed to Georgiana, is full of reminiscences, longings, and open expressions of love, as the following excerpt dated March 12, 1819, shows: "I hope you are both now in that sweet sleep which no two beings deserve more than you do. I much fancy you and please myself in the fancy of speaking a prayer and a blessing over you and your lives. God bless you. I whisper good night in your ears and you will dream of me!" (pp. 73–74).[2] An entry dated April 5 informs us that Keats has found a lock of Georgiana's hair in a letter addressed from

Georgiana to George and that he intends to put it in a miniature case of George's. On April 11, Keats discovers a prank which affects him deeply: some love letters written by an alleged Amena Bellefilla addressed to the now deceased Tom turn out to have been written by a common acquaintance, Wells. Keats is furious and swears vengeance.

On April 15, Keats includes in his correspondence a curious bit of writing, an extempore piece entitled "When They Were Come unto the Faeries' Court." Obscure in meaning both comic and nightmarish, this piece deals with the story of a princess lured into fairyland in spite of the warning of her three servants who are three transformed princes. W. Jackson Bate (1963), in his excellent biography of Keats, mentions that the piece could be seen as related to the situation in the strangely beautiful ballad, "La Belle Dame," that Keats was to write five days later. Here is the plot. A fretful princess travels to a fairy court with an ape, a dwarf, and a fool. Finding no one at home, she flies into a rage; the dwarf trembles, the ape stares, the fool does nothing. The princess takes her whip in order to turn on her three attendants, and the dwarf with piteous face begins to rhyme in order to distract her. While the princess is within, her only means of transportation—a mule—manages to get rid of its saddle and escapes. The princess is never seen again. In spite of the comical effect, an eerie sense of warning pervades the piece: after the princess entered the door, "it closed and there was nothing seen but the mule grazing on the herbage green." This anticipates the theme of disappearance in the Belle Dame ballad.

On April 16, having to stay home because of the rain, Keats describes a recent walk with Coleridge and sees fit to list the topics discussed. These include different species of dreams, nightmares, dreams accompanied by a sense of touch, single and double touch, a dream related, a ghost story (p. 89).

The April 16 entry starts out with a passage stressing Keats's wish for revenge against Wells,

> I will hang over his head like a sword by a hair. I will be opium to his vanity. If I cannot injure his interests—he is a rat and he shall have rats bane to his vanity. I will harm him if I possibly can. I have no doubt I shall be able to do so, let us leave him to his misery; alone except when we can throw in a little more. (p. 91)

This passage seems to stress Keats's helplessness in the face of Wells's trickery. Then without transition Keats continues:

> The Fifth Canto of Dante pleases me more and more, it is that one in which he meets with Paolo and Francesca—I had *passed many days in rather a low state of mind,*

and in the midst of them I dreamt of being in that region of Hell. The dream was one of the most delightful enjoyments I ever had in my life—I floated about the whirling atmosphere as it is described with a beautiful figure to whose lips mine were joined [as] it seemed for an age—and in the midst of all this cold and darkness I was warm —even flowery tree tops sprung up and we rested on them sometimes with the lightness of a cloud till the wind blew us away again—I tried a Sonnet upon it—there are fourteen lines but *nothing of what I felt in it—O that I could dream it every night.* (p. 91, italics added)

We do not know the exact date of the dream, save that it was recent. There is little reason to doubt that the dream recorded by Keats was genuine and not made up; it occurs naturally in the context of the passage preceding it and seems an apt commentary on Dante's Fifth Canto—the clear day residue.

The affects aroused by the dream apparently drove the poet to try to capture something of its pleasure by writing a poem on it. "I tried a Sonnet upon it—there are fourteen lines but nothing of what I felt in it." Clearly, an uncontrollable shift in affects intervenes. Here is the sonnet:

On a Dream

As Hermes once took to his feathers light,
  When lullèd Argus, baffled, swooned and slept.
So on a Delphic reed, my idle spright
  So played, so charmed, so conquered, so bereft
The dragon-world of all its hundred eyes;
  And, seeing it asleep, so fled away—
Not to pure Ida with its snow-cold skies,
  Nor unto Tempe where Jove grieved that day;
But to that second circle of sad hell,
  Where in the gust, the whirlwind, and the flaw
Of rain and hail-stones, lovers need not tell
  Their sorrows. Pale were the sweet lips I saw,
Pale were the lips I kissed, and fair the form
I floated with, about that melancholy storm.

The sonnet is immediately followed in the correspondence by more personal passages addressed to Georgiana. "I want very much a little of your wit my dear sister. . . . Are there any flowers in bloom like any beautiful heaths—any street full of corset makers? What sort of shoes have you to fit those pretty feet of yours? . . . Do you ride on horseback? What do you have for breakfast, dinner and supper? Without mentioning lunch and bever and wet and snack and a bit to stay one's stomach'' (p. 92). In a later section Keats amuses himself by giving directions on how Georgiana could employ her day: ''While you are hovering with your dinner in prospect you may do a thousand things—put on a hedge-hog into George's hat—pour a little water in his rifle, soak his boots in a pail of water, cut his jacket round in shreds like a Roman kilt or the back of my grandmother's stays—sow off his buttons'' (p. 93). The mood of these remarks, their jocularity, suggests the pranks a young child would like to play on his father—to make a fool out of him and perhaps reverse the roles.

The next day, April 21, Keats writes, ''I stopped at Taylor with Woodhouse and passed a quiet sort of pleasant day. I have been very much pleased with the panorama of the ships at the north pole with the icebergs, the mountains, the bears, the walrus, the seals, the penguins and a large whale floating [its] back above water. It is impossible to describe the place'' (p. 94). This passage again contains an allusion to floating—a favorite image in Keats's poetry. That evening Keats included in the letter the well-known ballad, ''La Belle Dame sans Merci,'' which ushered in one of his most creative periods, during which he produced odes, sonnets, and a philosophical treatise, ''The Vale of Soul Making.'' The ballad, to which I now turn, was probably written April 19:

La Belle Dame Sans Merci

O what can ail thee, knight-at-arms,
Alone and palely loitering?
The sedge has withered from the lake,
And no birds sing.

O what can ail thee, knight-at-arms,
So haggard and so woe-begone?
The squirrel's granary is full,
And the harvest's done.

I see a lily on thy brow,
With anguish moist and fever-dew,
And on thy cheeks a fading rose
Fast withereth too.

I met a lady in the meads,
Full beautiful—a faery's child,

Her hair was long, her foot was light,
And her eyes were wild.

I made a garland for her head
And bracelets too, and fragrant zone;
She looked at me as she did love,
And made sweet moan.

I set her on my pacing steed,
And nothing else saw all day long,
For sidelong would she bend, and sing
A faery's song.

She found me roots of relish sweet,
And honey wild, and manna-dew,
And sure in language strange she said—
'I love thee true'.

She took me to her elfin grot,
And there she wept and sighed full sore,
And there I shut her wild wild eyes
With kisses four.

And there she lullèd me asleep
And there I dreamed—Ah! woe betide!—
The latest dream I ever dreamt
On the cold hill side.

I saw pale kings and princes too,
Pale warriors, death-pale were they all;
They cried—'La Belle Dame sans Merci
Thee hath in thrall!'

I saw their starved lips in the gloam,
With horrid warning gapèd wide,
And I awoke and found me here,
On the cold hill's side.

And this is why I sojourn here
Alone and palely loitering,
Though the sedge is withered from the lake,
And no birds sing.

In the correspondence following the ballad. Keats adds an amusing light-hearted commentary on one aspect of the poem, selecting one of the more irrelevant details. "Why four kisses—you will say—why four because I wish to restrain the headlong impetuosity of my muse—she would have fain said score without hurting the rhyme—but we must temper the imagination as the critics say with judgement. I was obliged to choose an even number that both eyes might have fair play: and to speak truly, I think two a piece quite sufficient. Suppose I had said seven, there would have been three and a half a piece—a very awkward affair and well got out on my side" (letter of April 19 to Georgiana Keats, p. 98). This is the same chatty, jocular mood we find right after the sonnet—a distancing from the gloom of the poetry.

There follows in the correspondence a poem titled "A Chorus of Fairies." In the third stanza, titled "Zephyr," we find a reminiscence of the imagery of the dream—perhaps a last lingering. Zephyr addresses gentle Brema and beckons her to accompany him "over the tops of trees to my fragrant palace where they ever floating are—beneath the cherish of a star called Vesper—who with silver veil hides brilliance pale" (p. 98).

INTERPRETATION

The setting of the works of Keats that I have just described is not typical of most literary texts. In many ways it fulfills the ideal requirements for analytic interpretation. We are in possession of the author's manifest dream, the context in which it occurred, some of his reactions, and the various creative products which he himself relates to it. To have the correspondence, the dream, and the author's comments as data allows us to approximate more closely his intentions and his states of mind.

From the perspective of an analyst, all the written material presented so far—correspondence, dream, comments on the dream, and the several poems—are to be understood as compromise formations. To be sure, poems are more likely to be influenced by issues of form, they will contain more imagery and metaphors, and they will have been subject to more conscious elaboration than the dream. Similarly, the correspondence will be governed by Keats's style and by his sense of what is appropriate. It should nevertheless be seen as a creative product which will contain seeds of conflicts similar to those found in the dream or in the poetry.

I will begin my interpretation with a close examination of the obvious day residue of the dream, Dante's Fifth Canto. Here are excerpts:

> After I had heard my teacher name the olden dames and cavaliers, pity came over me, and I was as if bewildered.

I began: "Poet, willingly would I speak with those two that go together, and seem so light upon the wind."

And he to me: "Thou shalt see when they are nearer to us; and do thou then entreat them by that love which leads them; and they will come."

Then I turned again to them; and I spoke, and began: Francesca, thy torments make me weep with grief and pity.

But tell me: in the time of the sweet sighs, by what and how love granted you to know the dubious desires?

And she to me: "There is no greater pain than to recall a happy time in wretchedness; and this thy teacher knows.

"But if thou hast such desire to learn the first root of our love, I will do like one who weeps and tells.

"One day, for pastime, we read of Lancelot, how love constrained him; we were alone and without all suspicion.

"Several times that reading urged our eyes to meet, and changed the colour of our faces; but one moment alone it was that overcame us.

"When we read how the fond smile was kissed by such a lover, he, who shall never be divided from me,

"kissed my mouth all trembling: the book, and he who wrote it, was a Galeotto. That day we read in it no farther."

A brief synopsis of the story of Paolo and Francesca as recounted by Dante is relevant to the dream. Francesca was married to a deformed man, Gianciotto of Rimini, and had fallen in love with his brother, Paolo, while reading together the tale of Lancelot. They were discovered by Gianciotto who, in jealous fury, slew them both. The lovers eventually found themselves in the second circle of Hell, reserved for adulterous lovers eternally condemned to swirl about in unending storms.

The relation between the dream and the manifest imagery of the Dante canto is compelling. Dante begins, "Poet, willingly would I speak with those two that go together, and seem so light upon the wind." A bit later, "Then I turned again to them; and I spoke, and began: Francesca, thy torments make me weep with grief and pity.'' In the latter part of the canto which describes the kiss, the last two lines are explicit. ''When we read how the fond smile was kissed by such a lover, he, who shall never be divided from me, kissed my mouth all trembling. . . . That day we read in it no farther.'' I am making the assumption that the dreamer borrowed the imagery of the canto because it resonated with or reflected some of his unconscious wishes or fantasies. What do we find in the canto?

Francesca alludes to the book she and Paolo were reading: ''One day, for pastime, we read of Lancelot, how love constrained him; we were alone and without all suspicion.'' The story of Lancelot is doubly relevant. Lancelot is in love with Guinevere, wife of King Arthur, but he does not dare confess his love to the queen. One day when she is smiling at his embarrasment, Galehaut, her friend and confidant, begs Guinevere to grant Lancelot the forgiveness of a kiss, and the queen kisses Lancelot. Thus, it does not seem farfetched to assume that Galehaut played the kind of role for Guinevere and her knight that the story of Lancelot played for Francesca and Paolo. More important, the Fifth Canto and the written text of the dream and journal may have played such a part for Keats and Georgiana in Keats's fantasy. There is considerable evidence for this imagery of the dream, directly borrowed, as it were, from Dante, and in the details in Keats's correspondence referring to Georgiana. The kiss in the dream could then express both the forbidden impulse and its forgiveness—as the queen's kiss is granted in forgiveness. It is likely, then, that the reading of Dante stimulated in the poet the wish to seduce his sister-in-law as Paolo had seduced Francesca; the consequence of the seduction, represented as a kiss, is a sojourn in hell which reawakens in Keats thoughts of the death of his loved ones and associated depressive affect and mourning.[3]

Pederson-Krag (1951) has referred to the identification of Keats with Francesca and to the poet's guilty love for Georgiana. I would endorse her comment that Keats was, on some level, attempting to seduce his sister-in-law in his correspondence. On the simplest level one could imagine one of the core dream thoughts to be, ''If only I could be kissed by Georgiana the way Francesca was kissed by Paolo, I would find it an ecstasy and would be willing to sojourn in Dante's second circle of Hell.''

Although I have so far focused on the erotic aspects, there is another implication of the Dante canto: its location is hell, and so the role of death has to be considered. We do not know why the canto ''pleases'' Keats ''more and more,'' but it is conceivable that the poet is primarily concerned about death and illness and thus may be mourning both his brother, buried four months previously, and his mother, felled by tuberculosis. Keats may have had a premonition that he would join them in the not too distant future. The theme of love may be a defense against the anticipation of death, or there may be various complicated relationships between the two—for example, "Since I will soon die, I might as well enjoy myself," or "Why worry about death? I will be reunited with my mother." There are several plausible hypotheses which we cannot effectively prove or disprove because of the paucity of evidence.

I will now turn to the function of the dream for Keats and as used by him in the correspondence with George and Georgiana. This will preface a similar examination of the function of the dream in the sonnet and in the ballad. On a simple level, we can postulate that one function of the dream is to minimize Keats's unhappiness and foreboding of death ("it is not true") and to present as fulfilled certain wishes both current and infantile. But what of the fate of the warded-off affects? They reveal themselves ever so briefly in the manifest content—"in the midst of all this cold and darkness"—and are replaced by their opposites in the line, "O that I could dream it every night." What about the function of the dream in the letter, the first creative product? I have already suggested that the dream serves as a veiled (or not so veiled) hint of Keats's guilty attachment to Georgiana. It allows a clear expression of his wish in such a way that it does not take an objectionable form. The dream, as it is used in the correspondence then, is a solution to a conflict arising in Keats's relation to George and Georgiana. Keats can use the manifest dream as a carrier of his secret (or not so secret) longings, expressed with sufficient ambiguity to free him from taking direct responsibility for the affects that are revealed. He may have also used the sharing of the dream and what we see as its day residue to communicate, in an ambiguous manner, his concerns about death to those he loved the most. This use of the dream may be quite secondary to the conflicts which ended up in dream form, or to the purpose of the dream.

Next, I will turn to the sonnet, "On a Dream." Keats was right to be dissatisfied with it. It has a contrived quality. The manifest, barely altered dream is appended in the last six lines, and the first eight lines, full of mythological allusions, are largely intellectual and stilted. A reader with no knowledge of the occurrence of the dream would have no way of understanding the title or of appreciating that the last six lines are the almost literal representation of the poet's personal experience. As we are in possession of the day residue, however, a closer examination of the symbolism and allusions contained in the first eight lines will enrich the examination of the fate of the original dream. I will consider these as modified associations.

The first line, "As Hermes once took to his feathers light," clearly mirrors the sensations of floating and flying in the dream. The next line, "When lullèd Argus, baffled, swooned and slept," is explained by Pederson-Krag (1951) as follows: "The hundred eyed Argus servant by Juno was guarding Io from Jove's attention when Hermes, Jove's messenger, played so sweetly to him that all his hundred eyes closed at once, at which point Hermes murdered him" (p. 275). Keats makes an analogy between Hermes and his own spirit which, unlike Jove, is not interested in Io. Note the implied negation which recurs more forcefully in the next two lines: Keats's idle spright fled away, "Not to pure Ida with its snow-cold skies" (Ida was the mountain where the page Ganymede had been raped by Jove), "Nor unto Tempe where Jove grieved that day" (Tempe was the valley in which Apollo was frustrated by the transformation of Daphne, daughter of a river God; fleeing from the amorous Apollo, she escaped by being changed into a laurel).

As analysts, we might see the "Not" as an attempted escape from the cold (snow-cold skies) and from grief (Jove grieved that day). Indeed, this view is strengthened by a consideration of the last six lines. Keats has implied that he is not tempted even in sleep (or fantasy) to relive scenes of masculine love, or rape, but rather he is drawn back to return to the scene of his dream—now transformed in several ways. In contrast to the original dream's oceanic, manic-like quality, here the grief, depression, sadness, and death break through—"sad" hell, "lovers need not tell their sorrows." The adjective "pale," clearly an allusion to death, occurs twice, and the heaviness is again emphasized by the word "melancholy" describing the storm. Thus, the first poetic "associations" to the dream reveal, perhaps in spite of the poet's wishes, his depressive affect; the form Keats's "spright" floats with is no longer a beautiful figure but a barely disguised representation of death. In the sonnet, Keats tells us, there was "nothing of what I felt in [the dream]." On a manifest level Keats was unable to convey the ecstatic quality of the dream in his poem. From the point of view of defensive operations, we could say that the poet could not maintain the cheerful mood that was initiated by the dream and that interrupted a depressed mood of some days' duration.

I will now examine the ballad in some detail. There is a lengthy tradition associated with La Belle Dame starting in the middle ages and re-emerging with particular strength in the German Romantic movement. Keats's title itself is ambiguous. It can signify "the fairy's lack of pity for the mortal she lures from the world or her own deprivation since she exists without hope of divine grace" (Fass, 1979, p. 43). Keats made prior use of the title of the ballad, derived from a poem by the French medieval writer, Alain Chartier. A month before the dream, Keats wrote the lovely ode, "The Eve of St. Agnes." In the poem an ardent lover, Porphyro, introduces himself by a stratagem into the bedroom of the sleeping Madeleine on the eve of St. Agnes. Madeleine, according to an old tradition, was waiting for a dream to show her the features of her future betrothed. In effect, Porphyro is able to seduce Madeleine while she is still half asleep while singing to her "an ancient ditty, long since mute / In Provence called, 'La belle dame sans merci'." The main themes deal with love awakened and seen in a dream. Love and death are intertwined. Sleep, dream, and awakening are confused, blurring the reality of vision. "Her eyes were open, but she still beheld, / Now wide awake, the vision of her sleep."[4] It is perhaps no accident, then, that Keats should have seized upon "La Belle Dame" as an extraordinary means of representation of the complicated feelings associated with his own dream in which, like Madeleine, he had a vision. "How changed thou art! How pallid, chill, and drear! / Give me that voice again, my Prophyro, / Those looks immortal, those complainings dear! / O leave me not in this eternal woe, / For if thou diest, my Love, I know not where to go" ("The Eve of St. Agnes," Stanza XXV).

The ballad, in contrast to the earlier sonnet, is full of ambiguity. There is a dreamlike quality to the entire poem. This is consonant with the idea that the form of the ballad could have been stimulated in part by the dream—and represents a return of the original form after the distancing of the sonnet. The first three stanzas are spoken by an unidentified narrator, which suggests an analogy with an inner voice. The fourth stanza, starting with "I met a lady in the Meads," is in all likelihood spoken by the knight at arms. There is a complex shift from waking to sleeping which is then interrupted by the knight as narrator telling his dream to an unidentified audience. He then awakens either as a result of the horrible dream or simply after it is ended. The last stanza, purporting to be an explanation ("this is why I sojourn here"), explains nothing. Its form is reminiscent of the activity of the mind during the process of secondary revision.

There are multiple levels of confusion in both content and form, which are perhaps associated with the unclear boundary between fantasy and reality. There is confusion about what ails the knight, though the issue is clearly one of bondage. Does he remain on the hillside because of the dream or because of the experience, and why should such a poetic encounter, full of love, be followed by the warning dream? Is the fairy equated with La Belle Dame? There is confusion regarding the nature of the fairy. Does she represent an "evil fantasy, luring the hero away from the real world or does she represent the sinful world—materialism, keeping the hero away from the path to his real home—heaven in this instance"? (Fass, 1979, p. 27).

It is tempting to see the fairy as the transformed figures from the original dream. From a blissful oceanic fusion emerges a being whose identity is still obscure but who is now both comforter and comforted in the dual role of mother and child. No words are exchanged between the Knight and the fairy, which adds to the sense of mystery and other-worldliness. There seems to be a willed obscurity in the lines, "And there I dreamed—Ah! woe betide!—/ The latest dream I ever dreamt / On the cold hill side." It is not clear whether latest should be understood as "last" or whether it should be taken literally, meaning that the knight at arms had had many previous dreams in the location. There is a puzzling use of time in this sequence—"latest" refers to past and "ever" refers to future in a strange juxtaposition, from the vantage point of the present observer standing outside of the narrative time.

Although the ballad is full of ambiguity concerning the characters and their motives, one aspect is not ambiguous: its somber, almost unrelieved depressed quality, with themes of starvation, cold, desolation, illness, and death. The eruption of the depressive affects clearly continues the process initiated by the sonnet but in a much richer, more poetic vein. In the ballad, love is alluded to but the fairy, without explanation, "wept and sighed full sore." It is not clear who is the comforter and who the comforted. In the rough draft of the ballad the poet clearly struggled (either for poetic or for personal motives) against too direct an expression of the theme of death.

The first draft of the third stanza ran thus:

I see death on thy brow
  With anguish moist and fever dew
And on thy cheek's death a fading rose
  Fast withereth too.

In the printed version, death is omitted in each case. Thus, "I see a lily on thy brow . . . / And on thy cheeks a fading rose."[5]

I will now turn to a closer examination of the "dream" contained in the latter part of the ballad. In contrast to the sonnet which included the original dream imagery without clearly identifying its source, in the ballad we now find a literary dream. As in the sonnet, the dream occurs toward the latter part of the work. It is no longer a "beautiful dream" but more a nightmarish vision, a spoken warning, oracular in nature, of death, bondage, starvation, and cold. It is integrated in the poem and clearly marked off as a literary dream. And yet it flows smoothly, connected both to what precedes it and to what follows it. As Bate (1963) puts it, "He [the knight] does not actually witness the horrid warning of starvation that this attempted union may bring. That anticipation, which may be genuine or primarily the expression of his own uneasiness, has come to him only in a dream—a dream that has also banished 'la Belle Dame.' And if the dream is now proving to be prophetic, it is again through his own divided nature, how own act, his persistence in continuing to loiter on the cold hillside even though the autumn is about to become winter" (p. 481).

It is expedient to study the separate transformation of the content of the original dream by tracing the fate of the affects and of the complex imagery. In the original dream experience the dreamer found ecstasy and hoped that he could dream it every night—that is, return in fantasy to the experience. In the sonnet the poet's "idle spright" fled away to the second circle of Hell, the scene of the dream. In the ballad the situation is reversed; the knight for unclear reasons cannot or will not escape from the desolate scene including the dream. The core image portrays the union between the dreamer and the beautiful figure. Though the sex of the figure is not identified in the original dream, it makes sense to assume it is female. The dream is unchanged in the sonnet but is expanded in the ballad into a story from the fourth to the ninth stanza. The form is that of a dreamlike fantasy which expands the original imagery and etches out a more complete, if somewhat mysterious portrait, giving it the identity of a fairy. The tableau, "I floated about the whirling atmosphere . . . with a beautiful figure to whose lips mine were joined," is transformed into "I set her on my pacing steed / And nothing else saw all day long / For sidelong would she bend and sing." The oral imagery of the dream is expanded to being fed "roots of relish sweet" and being told "sure in language strange . . . / 'I love thee true' "; it is expanded to being taken to "her elfin grot / . . . And there I shut her wild wild eyes / With kisses four." The other part of the manifest dream indicating depression and death finds its own representation but is split off from the tale—in the introductory three stanzas—and projected onto the fairy in one line, "And there she wept and sighed full sore." It emerges encapsulated in the literary dream. This lengthy elaboration can be contrasted to the condensation achieved in the form of the real dream.

Can we say anything about the function of "the dream" in the ballad? This literary dream encapsulates the dreaded inner voice of conscience, doom, and foreboding of death. Yet the poet is able to convey these affects while still preserving the ambiguity of the characters' reactions, thus enriching the multiple meanings and displaying his ambivalence. The function of the dream in the ballad could be considered analogous to that of a dream within a dream. The ballad represents a poetic fantasy on the original dream. The literary dream could be seen in the nature of a superego injection, until then warded off by the dreamer and poet. In the [previous explanation] I am blurring the distinction between "real dream" and "literary dream," which, of course, oversimplifies the issue. We are not sure why Keats included a literary dream as part of the ballad, or whether it was in any way related to the original dream experience. We do know, however, that dreams had profound significance for Keats. As I will show later, Keats contrasted dreams (which he mistrusted) with poetic vision (which was equated with true insight). On this level, then, a literary dream is an ambiguous product and might reflect the author's wish that the nightmarish vision be "only a dream."

There is still another level of possible interpretation of the ballad which I have carefully avoided up to this point because it is so fraught with danger—the symbolic area. However, a certain transparency and fitting together of the themes of the ballad suggests the following.[6] If we heard a patient tell us a dream with a similar manifest content, how many of us would almost preconsciously formulate the story of the ballad as the encounter between a lover and his lady's more private anatomy (the grotto) with dreaded consequences following consummation. The image of "starved lips . . . / With horrid warning gapèd wide" sounds very much like a castration threat. This reading suggests that the lips in the original dream represented a multiple condensation and that in the ballad death and castration are fused—a not uncommon clinical finding. The dream within the ballad then contains the most repressed level—that of castration at the hands of the lover which becomes fused with the representation of the mother. From the point of view of method, this last interpretation is consistent with the previous formal interpretation. Indeed, a professor of literature, Vera Jiji, reading the poem, commented spontaneously that some of the truncated lines ("And no birds sing") could represent the theme of castration in a formal way. There is support for the existence in the poet of castration anxiety in his avoidance of women as sexual objects and in his selection of an unavailable woman with whom to share at a distance his most personal outpourings.

The lure of symbolic interpretation is evident in Williams's (1966) treatment of the ballad. His paper, subtitled "The Bad-Breast Mother," is more an example of the application of Kleinian concepts than a clarification of the poem. Williams states that "the turning of the idealized breast into 'La Belle Dame sans Merci,' the daemonified breast mother, may well have been felt unconsciously to have been due to [Keats's] own devouring greed, complicated and intensified by its being mixed with envy" (p. 70). The evidence Williams offers to buttress such conclusions is rather flimsy. "We can see that a greedy component of his personality existed by the frequency of his allusions to and preoccupation with food and drink and their pervasiveness in his imagery and in his letters. The envy may be linked with his very considerable ambition" (p. 71). Williams made even more fanciful use of the theory in stating that the word " 'Garland' . . . would refer to the halo of idealization or alternatively could represent the arms of the baby Keats twined round his mother's neck, imprisoning her in his embrace and trying to keep her for himself" (p. 71). Such reductionism does justice neither to the theory nor to the poem.

DISCUSSION

My efforts at a psychoanalytic interpretation of the poem led me first to rely on the more traditional method of relating the poem to the mental life of its author. I accumulated as much relevant outside information about the author as possible to try to recreate a context and to insert the personal and poetic products within a fictional mind. This makes it possible to reconstruct some of the more plausible connections and meanings. However, such an effort has its obvious limitations since the valence of any particular element is hard to assess.

I then pursued a second line of investigation, a type of structural analysis, limiting myself largely to a description of the manifest content, particularly the stated affects, the imagery, and the metaphors. This approach initially avoids any dynamic formulations. As there were three different products, I examined the shift and transformations from the dream to the sonnet and finally to the ballad. From such a description one hopes to be in a position to draw some inferences about the meaning of the transformations and their psychological underpinnings.

Finally, I alluded to the reader's reaction to the sonnet and the ballad as additional data on which to base inferences about the creative process.

We are faced with an interesting issue in the case of the sonnet and the ballad. The stimulus for their composition is the dream and its lingering effect upon the poet. We cannot view this stimulus as ordinary day residue, to be sure, as it includes both the manifest content and imagery of the dream and its reverberations in the unconscious. Hamilton (1969) has suggested that "object loss leads to a regressive fusion with the lost object and that the dream becomes an integral part of this process, having originally been utilized by the infant to cope with the loss of direct oral gratification from the mother during sleep. . . . Keats resorted to poetry in an attempt to complete the mourning process and to make restitution for the lost object, most importantly his mother, by externalizing his dreams in the forms of poems" (p. 529).

In the material I have discussed here the role of the dream is complex. In addition to the potent stimulus of the content, the form of the dream becomes a carrier of the lost past. The conflicts which gave rise to the dream involve a struggle against awareness of depressive affects; because of their painful nature, these affects found only marginal expression in the dream. The same defensive stance, however, need no longer be maintained in the poem. It is not clear whether Keats was conscious of the intrusion of the depressive affects in his work and whether his humorous gloss in the correspondence following the ballad ("Why four kisses") reflected a defensive stance made necessary by the poem's depressive affects, or whether the depression expressed in the poem was cathartic and allowed the poet to regain distance from what was, after all, a rather dismal set of circumstances. The gloss is a healthy reminder for us to be extremely cautious in our reconstruction of the author's conscious state of mind. It is conceivable that Keats wrote the ballad without being at all interested in or even aware of its personal meaning or its connection with the dream.

I noted earlier that the ecstatic mood of the dream could not be maintained in the sonnet, being replaced by a depressive mood like the one that had plagued the poet for some days prior to the dream. Perhaps the inability to maintain the ecstasy can be viewed as a failure of defense, which interfered with the poet's creativity and led to a stilted, uninteresting poem. Indeed, the inclusion of the barely transformed manifest dream might then represent a failed attempt to recapture the ecstatic mood of the dream. Thus the reader's reaction to this poem might be an indicator of the incomplete assimilation by the poet of the conflicts aroused by the dream.

Something must be said about the several hypotheses suggested by the data and their varying levels of plausibility. The description of the process of transformation from dream to sonnet and ballad does not initially require the importation of psychological hypotheses. This last step is necessary at the point at which I compared the process with dreamwork and alluded to defensiveness, implying the presence of conflict. The affect of depression is mentioned by the poet and is clearly more evident in the ballad than in the sonnet or the dream. In comparison to the ballad the sonnet appears to be too close to the original dream experience. It has not yet been integrated by the poet, and defensive needs have the upper hand. The sonnet incorporates the real content of the manifest dream without identifying it as such, representing it instead as a flight of imagination. It is hardly transformed and the subtle shifts from waking to sleeping which lend an aura of mystery and beauty to the ballad are missing. Three days later, Keats's creative imagination had a chance to play with both the form and content of the experience, and he produced a haunting work of art.

If we compare the contents and affects of the dream passages, we find remarkable shifts. In the "real" reported dream, there is barely an allusion to death except indirectly, via the words "in the midst of all this cold and darkness." In the sonnet, we move closer to depression and to hints of death, first in the form of denial: Keats's idle sprite does not flee to "pure Ida" with it snow-cold skies or to Tempe where Jove grieved. The imagery of the last four lines refers to lovers not needing to tell their sorrows. The lips of the figure are referred to twice as "pale" and the storm is "melancholy." It is as though the sonnet begins the process of undoing of the manic-like defense of the real dream.

In the process of transformation, then, the poet had first to distance himself from too personal an intrusion; he finds a proper poetic mode in order to give free rein to the expression of his feelings in a different register. However, the defense against the depressive affects is still partly maintained in the ballad, through the use of ambiguity, the attribution of weeping to the fairy, and finally the encapsulation of the frightening warning in a literary dream. Perhaps we could consider these devices as successful (formal) defenses allowing the emergence of a creative solution. Finally, the ballad amplifies the theme of death through the emergence of one of its childhood antecedents—castration—which is absent from the manifest dream.

Concerning the personal meaning of the various products—dream, sonnet, ballad—in the context of the author's life situation, some hypotheses are better supported by data than others. From the point of view of the study of creativity, this is clearly the less interesting part of my discussion as we discover once more the everyday conflicts, frustrations, and anxieties which take their toll of even the most gifted. The themes of love and death are intertwined. The attachment of the poet to Georgiana—his guilt about it and his identification with Paolo—do not require much speculation. The similarity between the manifest content of the dream and the Dante canto suggest than an analogy on some other level is present. The reconstruction of the parallels between Lancelot/Guinevere/Galehaut, Paolo/Francesca/Lancelot, and Keats/Georgiana/journal allows the reconstruction of the nature of Keats's attachment to his sister-in-law. The identification of the fairy with the lost mother is commonplace in fairy tales. What I termed the symbolic interpretation dealing with castration is less well supported by the data. The relationship between object loss and creativity is not a new concept. Certainly, Keats had more than his share of losses and setbacks.

Even though the data are rich, there are a number of unexplained features. It is not clear why certain affectively laden episodes do not obviously find their way into the poetry or the dream. To take but one example, Keats's discovery of the prank played on his deceased brother aroused in him very strong feelings, yet I could detect no obvious representation of that incident. Here I am in disagreement with Pederson-Krag (1951), who felt that the slaying of Argus by Hermes in the sonnet was sufficient evidence for Keats's murderous wishes. The dead brother, Tom, is most likely represented in the third stanza of the ballad, starting with "I see a lily on thy brow." The absence of data hampers our inquiry about the more general meaning of Dante to Keats, surely an interesting aspect.

An issue that needs to be considered is whether the imagery in the poetry following the dream is necessarily dynamically related to it, or whether it could be explained on some other basis—e.g., it is simply characteristic of Keats's fondness for images of floating. I think the inclusion of the dream in the sonnet and the indication by Keats that he wrote the sonnet with a dream in mind is clear evidence. None of Keats's other poems have detailed dreams as content (as does the ballad), although images of sleep and dreaming are frequent throughout his sonnets and other poems. His poetry is full of allusions to fusion with a loved woman, breast imagery, and references to states of dreaming, sleeping, dying, and transition to waking (Hamilton, 1969). The imagery contained in the ballad and other poems examined here cannot, of course, be attributed only to the effects of the dream. It is in many ways typical of Keats's style, including the style of his correspondence, which I will illustrate briefly. The central image in the dream—the two figures floating in the air—is not unrelated to one of Keats's favorite themes, "indolence," the power of passivity. "If I had teeth of pearl and the breath of lilies, I should call it languor, but as I am I must call it laziness. In this state of effeminacy, the fibers of the brain are relaxed in common with the rest of the body and to such a happy degree that pleasure has no show of enticement and pain, no unbearable frown" (p. 78). The association of love and death takes this form in a letter to Fanny Brawne in July 1819: "I have two luxuries to brood over in my walks—your loveliness and the hour of my death. O, that I could have possession of them both in the same minute. I hate the world: it batters too much the wings of my self-will and would I could take a sweet poison from your lips to send me out of it. From no others would I take it" (Baker, 1962, p. 71).

This passage returns to the original image of the dream, which can then be seen to express not only a fantasy of love but also of *Liebestodt,* of dying together, or at least of the lover being the beloved executioner. Dying together in the act of love may also have been charged with other meanings for the poet. It should be noted that Georgiana was pregnant during all of this time. Keats, very much concerned with surviving and immortality, may have yearned for a child.

I have said relatively little about the cultural setting of Keats's works. It would be reductionistic to imply that "La Belle Dame" and the sonnet are nothing but elaborations of the dream thoughts and imagery. Many of their elements need to be placed in the context of the romantic movement and its various favorite clichés and their particular expression in the poetry of Keats. To take one example, a recurrent theme in Keats's poetry is the abandonment of the narrator/hero by a woman who leaves him perhaps while he was asleep. A famous example[7] of this theme is to be found in the long narrative poem, *Endymion* (composed April–November 1817), where a pair of winged horses carry Endymion and his Indian bride aloft, but as he turns to her she dissolves, Eurydice-like, in the moonlight leaving him alone: ". . . I have clung / To nothing, loved a nothing, nothing seen / Or felt but a great dream!"

The blurring of distinction between dreaming and reality is a recurrent theme of Keats. The last two lines of the "Ode to a Nightingale" express this.

Was it a vision, or a waking dream?
  Fled is that music—Do I wake or sleep?

The related concern with the potential disappearance of the loved one is expressed in its negative in the "Ode on a Grecian Urn":

        Bold Lover, never, never canst thou kiss,
Though winning near the goal—yet, do not grieve:
    She cannot fade, though thou hast not thy bliss,
        For ever will thou love, and she be fair!

The dread of awakening, which is related to the knight's loitering, is a common theme. The poem "On Death" contains many other themes of the Belle Dame ballad:

Can death be sleep, when life is but a dream,
  And scenes of bliss as a phantom by?
The transient pleasures as a vision seem,
  And yet we think the greatest pain's to die.
How strange it is that man on earth should roam,
  And lead a life of woe, but not forsake
His rugged path; nor dare he view alone
  His future doom which is but to awake.

The relation between dreaming, waking, sleeping, and poetry always fascinated Keats. In an early work, "Sleep and Poetry," written in 1816, Keats explored the relation between dreams and artistic insight. Sleep is presented as motherly comforter!

Soft closer of our eyes!
Low murmur of tender lullabies!
Light hoverer around our happy pillows!

Some of the same functions are attributed to poesy: it should be a friend to sooth the cares and lift the thought of man.

In his "reworking" of the poem "Hyperion" into the "Fall of Hyperion—A Dream'' shortly before his death, Keats differentiates escapist dreams from the imaginative vision of the poet:

The Poet and dreamer are distinct,
Diverse, sheer opposites, antipodes.
The one pours out a balm upon the world,
The other vexes it.

In the same poem he came back to the issue.

For Poesy alone can tell her dreams,
. . . Who alive can say,
'Thou art not Poet—may'st not tell thy dreams'?
Since every man whose soul is not a clod
Hath visions, and would speak, if he had loved,
And been well nurtured in his mother tongue.
Whether the dream now purposed to rehearse
Be Poet's or Fanatic's will be known
When this warm scribe my hand is in the grave.

Thus it seems that Keats was concerned with the survival of his works after his death but also doubted his right to consider himself a creator. Are his visions those of the ''fanatic''? Is he deceiving himself? In this light he might have taken particular delight in trying to transform the ''fanatic's dream'' into a poetic vision. That it took him more than one attempt is understandable. This same concern was expressed in the lovely ''Ode to a Nightingale'' in the line quoted earlier: ''Was it a vision [i.e., a true discovery worthy of being conveyed, a real insight], or a waking dream?'' [i.e., a personal product of no value].

In addition to being interested in the relation between dreams and poetry, Keats took great pains to elaborate his own theories about creativity. These have been studied by Leavy (1970). His paper, however, fails to go beyond the manifest content of the poet's statements. Leavy says that the ''use of Keats's ideas on creativity depends on our willingness to concede that the poet possessed an exceptional access to the workings of his own mind permitting him to know what he was doing and how he did it. I am therefore quite deliberately using Keats's ideas as if they were themselves, so to speak, 'psychoanalytic interpretations' of the data of experience. I am making almost no attempt to 'analyze' Keats by uncovering the unconscious intentions of his ideas'' (p. 176). While we may admire the ability of the poet to share with us his experience, I believe we do not do him justice to treat him as a theoretician without understanding the many meanings of the terms he uses.

My efforts have been in the direction of a limited descriptive approach to the transformation of imagery and affects. This may be disappointing to readers looking for explanations of creativity. It is, however, in line with my belief that applied psychoanalysis is far too burdened with speculations and too devoid of data close to observation. Ideally, such data as I have provided could generate further hypotheses capable of testing. What emerges is a greater respect for the complex process leading to the selection of a title in a foreign language to express the myriad of meanings contained in a very brief dream which closely mirrors a few lines in an acknowledged master's poem.

Before closing, I wish to remind you of Keats's discontent with the sonnet's failure to capture the mood of the dream. Was he any more satisfied with the ballad? Perhaps the [earlier] analysis will help answer this question. If Keats was still trying to recapture the ecstatic quality of the original dream, the answer would have to be an unqualified "no"; if the poet were to judge the result in terms of the poetic effect and beauty of the ballad, the answer would have to be an unqualified "yes!" Finally, what would Keats's reaction have been to the [previous] analysis if I could have sent him my paper, as Freud did with Jensen? Could the answer be found in the quotation I have put at the beginning of my article? It is relevant, as it is included in the letter to George and Georgiana: "Here are the poems, they will explain themselves as all poems should do—without comment" (p. 58). In light of my reconstructions about the possible meaning of their content I can well sympathize with Keats's emphatic statement.

NOTES

1. Page numbers for all quotations from Keats's journal are from Volume 2 of the edition of his letters edited by Rollins (1958).
2. I mention this entry because of its similarity to the theme of the poem. "The Eve of St. Agnes," which contains the first direct allusion to the "Belle Dame" story.
3. I shall not concern myself in this paper with the deeper meanings of the dream, including the nature of the wish expressed toward Georgiana, now pregnant. There are additional complexities; for example, there is some evidence that Keats has also identified both with Francesca, thus expressing longings for his brother, and with the jealous husband who murders the guilty lovers. The further day residue of rage at Wells who wrote the fake love letters to Tom must also be kept in mind.

4. Note the similarity with the earlier correspondence with George and Georgiana.
5. It should be mentioned that there are two versions of the ballad included in Keats's collected works. Keats undertook relatively minor revisions in some four of the stanzas at the suggestion of Hunt, at a time when he was quite ill. It is difficult to attribute psychological significance to these changes.
6. This reading was suggested by Harry Trosman.
7. I am grateful to M. Frank Alweis for this example.

REFERENCES

Baker, C., Editor (1962). *Keats' Poems and Selected Letters.* New York: Scribner & Sons.

Bate, W. J. (1963). *John Keats.* Cambridge: Harvard Univ. Press.

Dante (1944). *The Divine Comedy.* Translated by M. B. Anderson. New York: Heritage Press.

Fass, B. (1979). *La Belle Dame sans Merci. The Aesthetics of Romanticism.* Detroit: Wayne State Univ. Press.

Hamilton, J. W. (1969). Object loss, dreaming and creativity. The poetry of John Keats. *Psychoanal. Study Child,* 24:488–531.

Leavy, S. A. (1970). John Keats's psychology of creative imagination. *Psychoanal. Q.*, 39:173–197

Pederson-Krag, G. (1951). The genesis of a sonnet. *Psychoanal. Soc. Sci.*, 3:263–276.

Rollins, H. E., Editor (1958). *The Letters of John Keats 1814–1821, Vol. 2.* Cambridge: Harvard Univ. Press.

Williams, A. H. (1966). Keats' "La belle dame sans merci": the bad-breast mother. *Amer. Imago,* 23:63–81.

19. Interactions between Textual Analysis and Related Self-Analysis

Rivka R. Eifermann

In a paper entitled 'Varieties of denial: The case of a fairy tale' (Eifermann 1989b),[1] I presented a partial textual analysis, in psychoanalytic terms, of the Grimms' tale *Little Red Riding Hood,* as well as of a revised version of that tale. For purposes of the present investigation I re-examined everything I had written that directly related to the tale: (1) my notes and comments upon reading it and also upon reading Bettelheim's (1976) interpretation; (2) a reconstruction of the tale which I had put down from memory, and my comments on that. Through this re-viewing, and the concomitant self-analysis, I became aware of, and could eventually work through—aided by two childhood recollections that emerged as connecting links—some of the unconscious conflicts, motives and defences which were, again unconsciously, emotional driving forces in writing this particular paper. Of course, the textual analysis presented in the paper retains its independent status as interpretative narrative, prototype or paradigm, and its value depends on public judgement. It should also be mentioned that not all aspects of the self-analysis were linked to the underlying motives which I had uncovered. None the less, it was only later in this analysis that I could see that some of the more original ideas in that paper—indeed, those which seemed to expand upon the ways in which *Little Red Riding Hood* had been viewed up to then—had been inspired, unconsciously, by personal preoccupations.

My steps toward working through these preoccupations now made it possible for me to reflect back on the textual analysis and to become aware of ways in which I could improve upon it; now I was able to recognize where, and why, unconscious motives had affected the style, atmosphere and content of my paper in ways that did not accord with my original aim. At the

Reprinted by permission of Methuen and Co. from *Discourse in Psychoanalysis and Literature,* edited by S. Rimmon Kenan, 1987.

same time, the process of self-analysis which had been evoked in re-examining my own data made aspects of my inner life, internalized objects and unconscious conflicts, accessible to me from new angles, and in ways not available before this undertaking. Making use of this accessibility through further self-analysis has taken me a step further in the unending process of gaining expansion, continuity and integration of my self-experience. Thus self-analysis can contribute to textual analysis, as the latter can evoke and enrich the former.

It is to this process of reciprocal enrichment, and to some difficulties that may arise through the interactions, that I shall devote this paper, using illustrations from my work. My purpose here is not to present a piece of personal analysis, with all its numerous, intimate and intricate details. I shall be able to present here only a rough outline, leaving out a great many connecting threads and even whole areas of experience. Indeed, this is all that is needed for my present, illustrative purposes. Of course, for purposes of my own progress and eventual gains, short-cuts in time, range and intensity of emotional experiencing—or in mental efforts and processing and working through—were not possible. I therefore hope that the brief outline of this undertaking presented here will not offer a misleadingly simplistic view of the extremely elaborate and complex processes involved. In any case, and for a variety of reasons—some of them inevitably unconscious—I evidently consider it worth the attempt.

I shall, then, begin with a short piece of textual analysis from my paper on denial. When describing and interpreting Little Red Riding Hood's encounter with 'grandmother' (the wolf) upon entering 'her' cottage and finding 'her' in bed, basing myself on the Grimms' original text of *Rotkäppchen,* this is what I wrote:

> According to the Grimms' original tale (1819), when Little Red Riding Hood drew the curtains of her grandmother's bed, she was facing a grandmother who was 'looking very strange': 'Oh, grandmother,' she exclaimed, 'what big ears you have!' And hearing the gentle reply: 'The better to hear you with', she persisted with 'Oh, grandmother, what big eyes you have!' Again, the gentle reply—'The better to see you with'—only leads to a further anxious enquiry, 'Oh, grandmother, what large hands you have,' which calls forth: 'The better to seize *[packen]* you with.' The child, at this point horrified, insistently and, it seems desperately, still demands reassurance, 'Oh! but, grandmother, what a *terribly [entzezlich]* big mouth *[Maul*] you have!' (my italics). [*Maul,* the German word used here for mouth, is only applied with reference to *animals*]. 'The better to devour you with' comes the reply.

And, the tale continues, the wolf had scarcely said this, than, with one bound he was out of bed and swallowed up Little Red Riding Hood.

In the large variety of drawings of 'grandmother' in bed which I have examined, it is the wolf that lies there, quite unmistakably. And children who look at these drawings unhesitantly recognize him for what he is. Thus, it is Little Red Riding Hood's *denial* of the 'reality' in front of her (once we combine picture with tale), that drives her to seek help and reassurance from the very source of her terror—and that leads to her (temporary) doom.

In my personal analysis related to this paragraph of my paper, I shall not begin at the beginning except to say that I know my mother told me the tale of *Rotkäppchen* and other of the Grimms' tales, in German, when I was a small child, and that I do not recall any specific occasion on which she related this tale to me. Nor do I specifically recall having heard or read it in the original German, or in any other version or language, since my childhood. I am aware, however, that I must have encountered other versions because some of its contents quite surprised me when I did, eventually, turn back to the original tale.

It was in one of my graduate seminars on dream analysis (Shanon and Eifermann 1984; Eifermann 1984) that one of my student's dreams, reminiscent of *Little Red Riding Hood,* triggered my conscious interest in the tale. I then read the tale in the original, as well as Bettelheim's (1976) interpretation of it. As I was making some notes on the tale, I sensed increasingly that the child within me was still preoccupied with it—encapsulated and untouched as it had been for many years—and that it retained many of its early unconscious associations and meanings. Nevertheless, since I was analysing the text of the tale (and not myself), these associations remained largely dormant. I was making some notes on Bettelheim's interpretative narrative when it suddenly occurred to me, in a flash, that Little Red Riding Hood's behaviour when confronted with the wolf in her grandmother's bed 'is precisely my *Tümmel* tale!' *Tümmel* is my little girlish way of pronouncing *Kümmel,* the German word for caraway seed, and I was referring to an event from my early childhood, often told by my mother. I did not stop to consider the personal emotional meanings and implications of my discovery at the time or when I applied it in attempting to construct a coherent narrative of Little Red Riding Hood's behaviour.

I had often heard my mother tell my *Tümmel* tale during my childhood, and I sometimes used to ask her to relate it to me, since it always delighted me and filled me with pride: she related it with warmth and joy, implying that I was a sweet little girl. As I retold it to her some years ago, my mother corrected my recollection (of tale, or event—I no longer know) on two points, to which I shall return later. Here is my *Tümmel* tale.

I (aged 3 or 4) had just stepped out of my home on my way to kindergarten. I opened my leather lunch-bag, which was hanging from my neck, and unwrapped the neatly packed sandwich to see what Mummy had prepared for me today. (This curiosity I recall as being in anticipation of pleasure, for my mother's food was attractively prepared and tasty.) As I looked I suddenly saw something on the bread and cried out to my mother, 'Mummy come! Look what's on the bread!' (there was a little insect there). My mother came, looked, and said, 'It's nothing, it's just a caraway seed' (it was caraway seed bread), and turned back. But soon I was screaming, *'Mamy Mamy tom snel, der Tümmel tan laufen!'*, 'Mummy, Mummy come quick, the *caraway* can *run.'* The parallel with, 'But *grandmother,* what a horrible *Maul* you have!' (my italics), seemed overwhelming.

Until I began work on *Little Red Riding Hood* my conscious retention of my own *'Tümmel* tale' was that of the warmth and joy my mother had conveyed to me in telling it. It was through indirect (re)view, as adult, on 'another' little girl's behaviour, that I suddenly and still indirectly, gained new insight into my own. Indeed, perhaps it could only occur while its implications for myself remained unprovoked, for it was Little Red Riding Hood who was paramount in my mind at the time, and I did not stop to pursue my personal discovery. My own tale served merely as a means for gaining new insight into Little Red Riding Hood's behaviour. To me she was extremely obedient to her mother, *had* to see things through her mother's eyes, and that, therefore, since mother had instructed her to go to *grandmother* (and did not mention any wolf), it *had* to be grandmother lying in the bed in her cottage. This was parallel to my perception of the insect as caraway seed. At the time it did not emerge into my consciousness, however, that my perception of my own mother in that context, and my unconscious motives for seeing an insect as *Tümmel,* were at least partly those I had attributed to Little Red Riding Hood in my analysis.

When I had related my recollection of the tale to my mother some years ago she said that it had all occurred at home and that no lunch-bag had been involved. My reconstruction, of having been sent off by my mother, and with food (in a bag), suggests that I connected Little Red Riding Hood's tale with my own quite early in life.

The relevant sequence in my notes, in which the connection emerged as insight, begins as follows: 'To step off the main path from mother to grandmother'; this was my way of referring to Little Red Riding Hood's act of *dis*obedience, when she had walked off the path to pick flowers for her grandmother. It is significant that, in Hebrew, the language in which my notes are written, my expression, *em-hadérech:* 'main path', means 'motherpath'. I had selected the expression without being aware of its implications, which I had in fact made explicit when I continued with: 'The danger lay [not in walking off the path, but] precisely in *returning* to this path of absolute obedience to mother. [Once she was again acting in accord with mother's instructions.] It then *had* to be grandmother who was lying in bed [since it was no one other than grandmother to whom mother had sent her]. Little Red Riding Hood could do no more than wonder about how strange her 'grandmother' looked. *This is precisely my* Tümmel *tale!*'

When I went over the notes I had made as I was reading the original tale of *Little Red Riding Hood,* it became evident to me that I had picked up various signs in the text indicating that Little Red Riding Hood, who was 'loved by everyone', was not loved and not adequately cared for by her mother. It was only much later that I had connected my perception of her as having to obey her mother with not being loved, and that to obey was a condition for being loved. But at this juncture, in writing my paper on denial, I was focusing on mother. My anger about her is rather explicit. This is what I say in the original draft of that paper.

It was quite a revelation for me to discover how unprotective mother is in the original Grimms' tale: She is concerned enough about 'ill and weak' grandmother to send her little girl to her, with a piece of cake and a bottle of wine which 'will do her good.' (Mind you, she does not see to her mother herself.) She does tell her little girl to 'set out before it gets too hot,' but other than that, her rather long-drawn instructions reveal more concern about the child's manners than about her well-being. She does not warn Little Red Riding Hood against talking to strangers (as is the case in later versions of the tale, as well as in Perrault's French version), nor of wicked wolves. She just says, '. . . walk nicely and quietly, and do not run off the path, or you may fall and break the bottle, and then your grandmother will get nothing, and when you go into her room, don't forget to say, "Good-morning", and don't peep into every corner before you do it.' Even when alone in the wood the little girl is to behave like a little lady (indeed the wolf observes, '. . . you walk gravely along as if you were going to school'); Mother prohibits running, 'or you may fall and break the bottle' (not, 'hurt yourself'!); And curiosity (or perhaps even suspiciousness), which would have been quite appropriate under the circumstances encountered by the child upon entering her grandmother's home, is altogether discouraged: 'Don't peep into every corner' before you say 'Good Morning' are mother's instructions. Again, proper manners above all. Yet, had she followed her feelings upon entering the cottage, Little Red Riding Hood may have saved herself from being swallowed by the wolf. 'She was surprised to find the cottage-door standing open, and when she went into the room, she had such a strange feeling that she said to herself, "Oh dear! How uneasy I feel today, and at other times I like being with grandmother so much." ' One may indeed conclude that Little Red Riding Hood's need to deny what she saw, to ignore her feelings and to refrain from peeping anywhere or checking anything, may well have been encouraged by her mother's demand for strict obedience.

The inadequacy, indeed irrelevance (or worse) of mother's instructions are quite striking. They certainly turn out not to be good enough to ensure the child's safe passage through the wood. As the Grimm brothers put it, 'Little Red Riding Hood did not know what a wicked creature he [the wolf] was.'

These observations were coloured by my feelings about mother, my own *Tümmel* tale looming somewhere in my mind. Though reluctantly, I eventually left this paragraph out of my denial paper after it was pointed out to me that it was irrelevant to a discussion of denial, since nowhere in the paper had I even suggested that Little Red Riding Hood's mother was denying.

On re-examination I discovered that the final version of my denial paper still bears the marks of my complaint against mother, though subtly. Almost unaware, I protested too much and too often against any possibility that readers might misinterpret my statements as being directed personally at (against) the mother whose behaviour I presented in the paper. My major argument was 'that a story comes alive only as an *interactive process* going on between story teller and receiver—*both* of whom have needs, wishes, conflicts, fantasies, and defences that draw them together with the story as their common focus'. Specifically, I argued that 'amongst many other things, often protective and loving, that she does by the act of reading the story, mother also exposes her child (who is a willing partner) to a tale of cruelty and fright'. I thereby aimed to illustrate that, 'for whatever reasons, conscious and unconscious, mothers will at times expose their children to more gruesomeness than the tale, or the child, invites', and that denial could be operative in the exposing mother. (Rami Bar-Giora, 1985, has made similar, independent, observations with regard to lullabies.)

Let me quote just one such illustrations from my paper.

Dvora Omer, an Israeli writer in her own right, has revised and published (1978) a collection of the Grimms' Tales in Hebrew. She introduces her collection with the following words (translated from Hebrew):

'[This is] a personal and true story of a writer who is also a mother (of three) and an educator (by profession). . . . I have tried to remain as true to the original as my motherly conscience would allow. I exclude most cruel descriptions and emphasize positive motives. . . . I also emphasize the distance of the world of fairy tales from reality—in the characters, in time and in name—so as to enable the children to cope more easily with contents that may be frightening.'

In what follows I shall demonstrate that Dvora Omer is not successful in her attempt. While she excludes some of the frightening details and the cruelty from the tale, she introduces and elaborates on other such features, ending up with a story no less gruesome than the original. In Omer's (unsuccessful) attempt one may discern denial of some of her unwanted feelings.

One of these unsuccessful attempts which I describe in the paper is the following:

The Grimm brothers describe the events after the wolf had swallowed up Little Red Riding Hood as follows: 'When the wolf had appeased his appetite, he lay down again in bed, fell asleep and began to snore very loudly. The huntsman was just passing the house. . . .' Thus, the brief scary description is immediately relieved through the happy coincidence of a rescuer appearing on the scene right-away. But Omer chooses, instead, to dwell on the horror and agony of it all:

'Since his stomach was full, it was no wonder that the wolf felt tired. After the delicious and voluptuous meal, he returned to grandmother's bed and fell into heavy sleep, snoring loud long snores.'

'And thus, an hour passed, two hours passed. Grandmother and Little Red Riding Hood were caught in the dark, narrow stomach of the wolf. While the wolf lay in the soft and comfortable bed of the old woman, sleeping deeply and snoring loudly. Then a huntsman passed near grandmother's house. . . .'

The slow passage of a long agonizing time is thus described in detail, and in quite realistic terms—contrary to our reviser's declared intention 'to emphasize the distance of the world of fairy tales from reality'.

I sum up my analysis of Omer's revisions, by writing:

Omer finds it difficult, in terms of her conscience as a mother, to expose [her] children to the excessive cruelty and threat which she finds in the original Grimms' tale. In this she denies some other, contrary, aspect of her feelings, which nevertheless finds direct expression in her revision of the tale.

Many readers who have found the analysis of Omer and other mothers in my denial paper convincing, have nevertheless commented that I had been overcautious and unnecessarily apologetic in discussing the implications of my findings. Indeed, I was vaguely aware of this when, again, I said, with regard to Omer:

> *At the risk of repeating myself,* I would like nevertheless to add that this is not a personal analysis of the writer, which I would in any case consider inappropriate. I do not have access to the personal constellation necessary for any statement regarding Omer's general motives, predominant defenses, or indeed any aspects of her as a person. (Italics not in the original)

At the time of my writing the [aforementioned] I could not see that I was overstressing this point, because I was not then aware that the mother(s) I was thereby protecting from being misperceived and misjudged, were strongly connected with my own internalized mother, as perceived in the context of the Grimms' tale. Rather than present them (her) mercilessly, as I had presented Little Red Riding Hoods' mother, I turned to overprotecting her (them). Encapsulated and preserved in my own unconscious version of *Little Red Riding Hood* there remained, amongst other things, aspects of my mother which I had internalized not only as 'often protective and loving' but also as the mother who had sent me off, quite unprepared, cruelly exposing me to a most frightening wolf (insect), who might swallow me up / I might swallow.

I shall shortly turn to another piece of data related to *Little Red Riding Hood* which will lead me back to the [previous] data. However, before doing this I would like to summarize the points from my denial paper. Unlike previous analyses of fairy tales, which deal exclusively with the child's unconscious needs in listening to the tale, such story-telling is, in fact, an interactive process, through which the mother expresses her own unconscious wishes, needs and defences regarding her child. One such need, consciously denied, is to sometimes expose the child to a certain degree of cruelty and fright through the tale. With regard to the text of *Little Red Riding Hood* itself, I interpreted the behaviour of mother as unprotective and inadequate and that of Little Red Riding Hood as overobedient and denying.

When I put down my reconstruction of the tale a few months after having read the German version, my aim was to be as true to the original as I could. (My purpose in this was quite other than that of Holland, 1975, of whose work I did not then know. In any case, other than a very preliminary looking-over of the material and comparing of it with the original, I had left it lying.) But in turning back to it now, once more I was puzzled by the same two deviations from the original tale that had caught my attention at the time: in my reconstruction I had repeatedly referred to the '*Körbchen*' (little basket) into which Little Red Riding Hood's mother placed 'bread, a bottle of wine, and?' But this description was not accurate. To my surprise there was no mention of a basket in the original. (Of course, a basket *is* referred to in many later versions of the tale, and Little Red Riding Hood does appear with a basket in her hand in many drawings. But this is begging the question.) Why did I choose to introduce this detail, rather than another, from later versions? It must have had a very specific personal significance, since I had repeatedly inserted the German *'Körbchen'* into my reconstruction, which was otherwise written in Hebrew, and since I can hardly write German, having come to Israel before I was three and having communicated with my mother almost exclusively in Hebrew, so that German words, when they do occur to me, have the ring of early childhood. As for 'bread, a bottle of wine, and?'—I kept inserting that question mark because I was certain that there *was* something else, which I could not recall. Unlike other details of whose accuracy I was uncertain, I remained with the vague feeling that it was something of particular significance and therefore felt compelled to make special note ('?') of it. I recall my amazement when I realized that there *was* nothing else in the basket! (Besides, I had written down *'bread* [and] a bottle of wine', when the original said *'cake* and a bottle of wine'. But this slight difference did not preoccupy me at the time.) When I returned to the *Körbchen* and question-mark for purposes of my present re-examination, the feeling of surprise and puzzlement returned. Then, at some point when I was looking at the text, only vaguely attentive, I recalled an incident from childhood, in which the *Körbchen* loomed large. But any connection with the Grimms' tale or my reconstruction of it still remained opaque. Then, a few days later, it suddenly hit me, that the something ('?') that was missing from my basket was the essential connecting link between my childhood memory and my recollection of the Grimms' tale. For in the incident that I remembered, my mother had sent me off with an *empty* basket, quite inadequately equipped for my trip.

I had just turned 6, and we had moved to a house in the village only two months before. That day at school (I was in first grade) the festival of Pentecost *[Shavuót/Bikurim]* was to be celebrated. It was a tradition in the village that every child come to school dressed in white, wearing a floral wreath and carrying a basket filled with seasonal fruits and vegetables from their own gardens. The produce was then sold at the school and the profits donated to a worthy cause. My mother, however, quite new from the city, was not aware that the sale was a serious event. As was her way, she prepared lovely wreaths and prettily decorated baskets, for me and for my brother but with nothing inside, feeling that this was surely not necessary for a performance. What I recall, and very distinctly, is that when we were on the path in our garden, already on our way out my brother, two years my senior, insisted that his basket must be filled. As he was crying and screaming, my mother, suddenly and in exasperation stepped into the vegetable garden, pulled out a whole bunch of very young carrots, and threw them furiously into his basket. The next scene that I remember is me sitting in class, hardly able to contain my tears: all the other children had their loaded baskets in front of them, while I had my pretty but empty basket. Our teacher, Tzipora, went around from child to child, looking over their baskets. By the time she reached me I was crying, then she clasped her hands, saying something (which I still do not recall), and kindly and gracefully taking a fruit from one child's basket and a vegetable from another, until nothing was missing anymore in my basket. But all I recall distinctly is that there was one somewhat rotten apricot lying there in the basket, and that I thought, 'Mummy would *never* have given me *that!*' I had to restore her to perfection.

The two tales from my childhood may already have set the reader thinking that, in my mind, my reconstruction of Little Red Riding Hood and my own personal tales have become strongly associated and intertwined, objects and events belonging to one, having been displaced to another. Like mixing metaphors, I *mistakenly* recalled that my encounter with the *Tümmel* had occurred just as I stepped out of my home on the way to kindergarten, whereas that had been the case in my *Körbchen* tale; I had also, and again mistakenly, recalled that I was carrying a lunchbag ('food-bag' in Hebrew, and in my home the German expression used was *Brot-Täschchen,* 'bread-little-bag'), whereas in reality (or my recall of it) the basket for food was part of my *Körbchen* tale. In my reconstruction of *Little Red Riding Hood,* I had mistakenly placed bread (the sandwich in the lunch-bag of my distorted *Tümmel* tale) in the basket instead of the cake in the Grimms' original. (As if all this were not enough, my editor, Norma Schneider, pointed out to me that in writing this paper I consistently added a 't' to the word sandwich. Thus it seems that I was condensing a witch from yet other fairy tales: sand*witch.*)

There are, moreover, quite evident parallels between the manifest content of both my childhood tales, which support one another, and which lend support to, and fill gaps in, tracing unconscious motives that guided my textual interpretation of the Grimms' tale: my putting so much emphasis on Little Red Riding Hood's need to be obedient, on her being unloved by her mother, and so on; and it even throws light on my preoccupation with 'denial'. Without going into any furthur details of my self-analysis, I will offer just one very crude outline of a narrative that combines the two tales, as they cojoined in my mind with 'my' *Little Red Riding Hood* echoing in the background: Mummy has sent me off with a pretty basket containing tasty things that she has prepared for me; but something is very wrong—an insect on the sandwich, nothing in the basket—and she *denies* it! When I was little, just 3 or 4, I still cried out to her, while at the same time joining in her denial ('the caraway can run!'). By age 6 I had become a mere onlooker, at my brother's protests. And I saw that while he did get his way, it was not lovingly. On the contrary, I had witnessed an event that for me acquired the meaning that when something other than the good she chose to offer was demanded of her, my mother might eventually give, but of her rage as well. I therefore chose to be sent away inadequately equipped, exposed to fright, pain and shame.[2]

As I was putting down the [previous information], with considerable feeling of discomfort and increasing doubts as to whether I would ever so crudely and unfairly expose my (internalized) mother in public, I was suddenly shocked by the realization that precisely this has been the unconscious driving force behind the enterprise. At that time the angry, hurt, vengeful child within me still wished to do something through which I would expose my mother to shame, for all to see, just as she had exposed me to my whole (rather new) class of school-children. But I would overcome my pain and disgrace actively by telling my tale rather than being a passive victim. And in so doing I would place the blame where it is due! I did not follow my first impulse, to stop with the paper. For I knew that an additional stretch of self-analysis would enable me to alter that tone and style of this paper by using my vengefully motivated insights, but relegating that motive to a less prominent place because it is better understood and integrated.

I have not altered this paper. With further processing I have gradually become more in touch with the child within me, the child to whom the shock of awareness, the accompanying shame and guilt—and the vengeful intentions—belonged. Going through these early childhood experiences once again, I could be more in touch not only with my own distress as a little girl but also with my mother's, and now better tolerate and accept her imperfections and my own doubts about her. Inner processing such as I have undertaken, motivated as it was by genuine distress, has led to greater tolerance towards the child within and to progress in acceptance and integration of those aspects of the internalized 'good' and 'bad' mother that are still unintegrated. Thus, what I might otherwise have thrown out in shock, shame and guilt I can now offer to my readers, being fully aware that remnants of vengefulness, punishment through self-exposure and other motives unacceptable to my adult conscience, may still be mildly active in the deed.

It is my stance that has changed. And it is with delight that I have come to realize, and could only now come to realize, that a rare opportunity has come my way in the process of writing this paper. For I have inadvertently, 'before your very eyes', while creating a text—and this time an analysis of a textual analysis—reached an unanticipated inner realization. This has driven me to a stretch of self-analysis, which has affected my self-experience and, in turn, the direction and fate of my text. That such processes exist, and can be reciprocally enriching, for both text and self—is the main thesis of this paper!

But while such processes can lead to an examination of one's inner world, and one's work, unless one persists in working through the difficulties encountered, they can also impede or—as almost happened in my case—even entirely hold up writing. It is not unknown that people tear up many month's work in disgust, or put it away, never to be completed. Yet it is also true that one may return to work that was put away and out of mind for a while and fare better with it then. It is not always neccessary or even worthwhile, in terms of time and energies required, to undertake, as I have done, a piece of self-analysis related to one's work, in order to recognize blind spots, overvaluations or misrepresentations of particular points one has made, or even in order to get over a writing block. I have presented my own case in order to demonstrate that there are interactions between writing and unconscious processes and that these may be revealable through self-analysis.

What I hope to offer through this demonstration is a general *procedure for investigating* such interactions, for I believe that such phenomena deserve the careful attention of psychoanalysts, and not only where our analysands are concerned. Further, while we can learn a great deal about the processes involved during sessions, when they are worked on and through during the therapeutic process, such observations have their limitations. There is the need to respect confidentiality, the fact that the records of sessions are inevitably incomplete, and lack accuracy even if they are written down or tape-recorded (procedures which, in any case, I would not recommend)—in addition to the truism that a great deal remains implicit and the analysands' statements will always be partially opaque (Spence 1982). The procedure which I have tried to open up here is therefore a complementary method for investigating, using psychoanalysts as object and subject. For the analyst's own notes and drafts are records preserved exactly as originally made and are more directly accessible in terms of their implied meanings than the associations of our analysands. (I have endeavoured to illustrate this in the elaborations on my own notes, which I put in brackets.)[3] Combined with self-analysis, for which our training, experience and interest make us particularly well suited, psychoanalysts could, I believe, offer a body of data and findings not otherwise obtainable.

My presentation has been concerned throughout with ways in which textual and related self-analysis, *whose aims and methods differ,* may interact and even entirely overlap in terms of the *products*—a 'narrative' in either case. This has sometimes led psychoanalysts to apply aims and methods appropriate for textual analysis in their clinical therapeutic work or in self-analysis; it has led to even greater confusion among non-professionals, who often assume that the aims or methods of work in self-analysis or with analysands are the same as those brought to bear in textual analysis. Unless it is one's own, one cannot do a self-analysis directly from a text. Recollections or dreams, on the other hand, lend themselves to *both* self- and textual analysis. There is no distinction in principle to my mind between a psychoanalytically oriented textual analysis of literary texts, communal tales or such personal material as recollections, reconstructions, dreams or phantasies. The aims of all such analyses are similar: to further an understanding of the psychodynamics of the characters or behaviours presented. But while many psychoanalytically oriented literary analyses offer primarily paradigms of characters and of behaviour—beginning with Freud's Oedipus (1955 [1900]) and [more] recently, for example, Green (1979), Nevo (1985) and Segal (1987)—many analyses of private texts primarily aim at unravelling the psychodynamics of a particular person. Because this distinction is essential for my presentation, I shall try to make it as explicit as I can by returning to my illustrations.

Though unconsciously inspired by personal preoccupations related to the tale of Little Red Riding Hood, my intention in the analysis of her denial was to interpret *her* (not my) behaviour. Motivated by intellectual curiosity, I was in fact expanding on Anna Freud's (1936) hypothesis regarding 'denial in word and act' and testing its applicability. In the process of examining various aspects of Little Red Riding Hood's behaviour, I had even subjected my own personal experience with the *Tümmel* to that purpose. My narrative regarding Little Red Riding Hood's denials (and I have only presented a section of that narrative here) emerged following a process of exciting discoveries of various signs in the text which gradually built, in my judgement, into a coherent, consistent and quite comprehensive interpretation of certain aspects of her behaviour. The purpose and methods in my self-analysis were, however, quite different.

The analysis of my *Tümmel* tale was motivated by the feeling of great emotional discomfort upon discovering that it was not simply the lovely tale that it had consciously been for so many years. As my aim was to come to grips with whatever it was that I had not previously faced in relation to that experience, I did not, and could not know, the direction in which my inner exploration would lead me. In this case, therefore, I was associating, rather than looking for signs. And while I can look for signs in any direction I choose, the more unselective my associations, the less choice and control I have over the thoughts and emotions that emerge. For example, following the realization that it was related to my *Körbchen* tale, my feeling of puzzlement regarding the question-mark in my reconstruction of *Little Red Riding Hood* had changed into upset and pain. Such feelings were not unfamiliar in the context of that recollection, although this time they were more poignant and focal—and I aimed to resolve them. If then I, let alone someone not emotionally involved in my tales, were to examine them as *texts,* we would soon recognize parallels between them, and might even reach, through numerous signs in them, a narrative not very different from that which I eventually constructed. But the route would be quite different: *I* had made *no* connection between my two childhood experiences for a considerable time. As a matter of fact, I became preoccupied with my *Tümmel* experience—first, the thoughts and feelings about and around my experience wandering in and out of my consciousness, hitting me emotionally one way and another, and then new closures and insights occurring from time to time. It was only after a few days of a 'mental block' that the *Körbchen* memory came to mind, and even later, after a very intensive preoccupation with it, that my further insight (the meaning of the question-mark for me) followed. There was a considerable period of working through before I began to see (albeit the realization dawned on me suddenly and felt like an immense discovery) that the two experiences were connected, even intertwined, in my inner world.

Thus also, if my personal tales were treated as texts, they could be expanded around the theme of my 'internalized mother' and my responses to her, in a way that would make good narrative sense by commonly accepted criteria. They could help the *analyser understand* something about my psychodynamics, and it could then be 'explained' to me, or if I were that analyser, I might then understand more about myself. But while such a narrative might make good sense to me, without the inner processing it would not affect my self-experience in anywhere near the way that self-analysis does. (If I were in psychoanalysis proper while the tales were coming up, and appropriately tuned analyst might help me along my path if he did not offer me his ready-made narrative on a platter. This complex analytical task has been variously described, e.g. by Arlow 1980, Schafer 1983; Hrushovski-Moses 1985).

Returning to my two childhood tales, it should be evident from what I have said thus far that I do not have the freedom in self-analysis (nor could I in a parallel situation with my analysands) to pursue any aspect of the tales that I might choose. It is whatever emerges, unselectively, that is its product. At the time of my self-analysis I could of course see that personal issues, other than that regarding my internalized mother, were probably hidden in these tales. Indeed, in the process of that analysis I did wander in and out of some of these issues.[4] But they were not at the focus of what was occurring to me at the time, nor of my feelings. In other words, turning to them then because they might make a good narrative would not at all have served my personal aims. On the other hand, had I, or anyone else trained in such an undertaking, treated my personal tales as texts, I (or they) would have had the freedom to pursue various aspects and might have attempted (on the basis of various signs in the texts) to construct a range of narratives, for example around 'my' curiosity, 'my' feeling of emptiness and being filled, indeed, 'my' penis envy: the 'empty basket', my mother who 'inadequately equipped' me, my brother who, after all, got his 'carrots'. Yet, while such psychoanalytically oriented constructions might make good narrative sense, expand the texts, even offer some prototypes of human behaviour—and while such narratives *might* even describe aspects of my psychodynamics, more or less accurately—they would not serve the same purpose as inner processing. For in order for any narrative to become part of the self-experience, one must first be in touch with its emotive specificity and meanings for oneself; the meanings of private metaphors (Arlow 1979)—such as the 'wolf', 'empty basket', 'carrots', and so on—must emerge and become connected.

Finally, the *interactions* as well as the distinctions that I have drawn between textual and self-analysis, lead to a particularly intriguing question: in what sense, and in what ways, can there be interactions between the two types of analyses when one conducts a textual analysis on a personal text? But this is a subject for another discussion.

NOTES

1. I would like to thank Dr Erich Gumbel for his fruitful comments on an earlier version of this paper. The research quoted in this paper was made possible with the aid of a grant from the Sturman Center for Human Development of the Hebrew University of Jerusalem.
2. Further expansions on these and other associative links appear in Eifermann (1984, 1987a, b, c, d, 1989a, b, in press).
3. Spence (1982) refers to such elaborations, in clinical reporting, as 'naturalizing' a text.
4. In 'proper' analysis the analyst would recognize in some of these moves aspects of resistance and could then help me remain with the issues I had brought up (Eifermann 1987a).

REFERENCES

Arlow, Jacob A. (1979) 'Metaphor and the psychoanalytic situation', *Psychoanalytic Quarterly*, 48, 363–85.

———(1980) 'The genesis of interpretation', in H. P. Blum (ed.) *Psychoanalytic Explorations of Technique: Discourse on the Theory of Therapy*, New York, International Universities Press.

Bar-Giora, Rami (1985) 'Lullabies and the psychology of parenthood: a psychoanalytic contribution to the understanding of a problem in the first literary text in the child's life', paper presented at conference on 'Discourse in Literature, the Arts and Psychoanalysis,' the Hebrew University, Jerusalem.

Bettelheim, Bruno (1976) *The Uses of Enchantment*, New York, Knopf.

Eifermann, Rivka R. (1984) 'Teaching psychoanalysis to nonanalytical students through work on their own dreams', *Psychoanalysis in Europe*, 22, 38–49.

———(1987a) 'Fairy tales—a royal road to the child within the adult', *Scandinavian Psychoanalytic Review, 10*, 51–77. Also in German, in Stork, J. (ed.) *Das Märchen—Ein Märchen? Psychoanalytische Betrachtungzu Wesen, Deutung und Wirkung der Märchen*, Stuttgart-Bad Constatt, Frommann-Holzboog, pp. 165–206.

———(1987b) ' "Germany" and "the Germans": acting out fantasies and their discovery in self-analysis', *International Review of Psychoanalysis*, 14, 245–62. Also in German: *Jahrbuch der Psychoanalyse*, 20, 38–55.

———(1987c) 'Children's games, observed and experienced', *Psychoanalytic Study of the Child*, 42, 127–44. Also in *La psychiatrie de l'enfant*, 33, 457–78, 1990.

———(1987d) Zustande von Uberwaltigung im Umgang mit "Verrucktheit" (oder Psychose). *DPV Informationen*, 2, 19–28.

———(1989a) "It suddenly came to me"—on the "occurrence" of ideas and their sequel. *International Journal of Psycho-Analysis*, 70, 115–26.

———(1989b) 'Varieties of denial: the case of a fairy tale', in Edelstein, E., D. L. Nathanson, & A. Stone (eds.) *Denial,* New York, Plenum, pp. 155–70.

———(in press) 'Discovery of real and fantasized audiences of self-analysis', in J. W. Barron (ed.) *Self-Analysis,* Hillsdale, New Jersey, The Analytic Press.

Freud, Anna (1936) *The Ego and the Mechanisms of Defense,* London, Hogarth Press.

Freud, Sigmund (1955) [1900] *The Interpretation of Dreams,* in *The Standard Edition of the Complete Psychological Works,* London, Hogarth Press, vols. 4 and 5.

Green, André (1979) *The Tragic Effect,* Cambridge, Cambridge University Press.

Grimm, J. and W. (1949) [1819] *Kinder-und Hausmärchen,* Munich, Winkler Verlag.

Holland, Norman N. (1975) *Five Readers Readings,* New Haven, Conn., Yale University Press.

Hrushovski-Moses, Rena (1985) 'Discussion of the paper "Past and present in interpretation" by E. Torras de Beà and J. Rallo Romero', *Psychoanalysis in Europe,* 25, 15–24.

Nevo, Ruth (1985) 'The perils of Pericles', paper presented in a seminar on 'Discourse in Literature, the Arts and Psychoanalysis', at the Center of Literary Studies, the Hebrew University, Jerusalem.

Omer, Dvora (ed. and trans.) (1978) *Fairy Tales of the Magical Palace: A Selection of the Brothers Grimm Tales,* Tel-Aviv, Joseph Schreberk (in Hebrew).

Segal, Ora (1987) 'Joyce's interpretation of dreams', *Hebrew University Studies in Literature and the Arts,* 14, 106–33.

Schafer, Roy (1983) *The Analytic Attitude,* London, Hogarth Press.

Shanon, B. and Eifermann, Rivka (1984) 'Dream-reporting discourse', *Text,* 4, 369–79.

Spence, Donald P. (1982) *Narrative Truth and Historical Truth: Meaning and Interpretation in Psychoanalysis,* New York, Norton.

20. The Imaginary Twins: The Case of Beckett and Bion

Bennett Simon

Hamm: We're not beginning to . . . to . . . mean something?
Clov: Mean something! You and I, mean something! (Brief laugh.) Ah that's a good one!

—Samuel Beckett, *Endgame*

'I cannot promise communication of pure non-sense without the contamination by sense'

—W.R. Bion.

INTRODUCTION AND HYPOTHESES OF THE STUDY

This paper is a study of an intriguing relationship between two unusual men, the playwright Samuel Beckett, still alive, now 80, and the psychoanalyst, Wilfred R. Bion, who died in 1979 at age 82. Their paths crossed during the years 1934–35, when Beckett was in psychoanalysis with Bion. There appears to have been literally no contact between the two men subsequent to the termination, or rather, interruption of the analysis. Bion, we have reason to believe, followed the career of Beckett; Beckett probably had little or no knowledge of Bion's career after 1936. Yet the contact had profound and continuing impact on the two of them. I will argue that in the years of their work together, something happened, or something 'clicked', in their interaction and in the intersection of their life-histories and temperaments. The work with Beckett, in an important sense, helped set up a certain *programme* for Bion's psychoanalytic concerns over the next forty years of his life. Moreover, I will argue that in regard to certain themes and to certain forms of presenting these themes, the works of Beckett and Bion can be shown to run

Reprinted by permission of the author and the Institute of Psychoanalysis from the *International Review of Psycho-Analysis,* 15 (1988).

in parallel course, with Beckett struggling with certain problems about meaning, communication, affect, the origins and fate of human connectedness, in his literary work and Bion pursuing these themes in his psychoanalytic writings and in his autobiographical-psychoanalytic writings.

There are several implications of the thesis that I here present. First, in terms of psychoanalysis, I believe we have an instance where a patient made a profound impact on an analyst, and the analyst spent the rest of his professional career working on, or working out, those personal and theoretic (or theoretic-clinical) issues posed by the work with the patient. I believe this is, in fact, not a rare event in the lives of analysts, particularly with patients they have encountered early in their careers. Something unfinished, unsatisfying, unresolved, but intriguing and attractive, gets into 'the system' of the analyst, and does not let him alone. In the happier instances, the analyst is not merely puzzled or traumatized, but creatively works out some of the implications of the only partially successful therapeutic encounter. It seems to me that Freud's 'classic cases' can be seen as serving this function, namely as the seed-bed and the scaffolding of certain issues to which he kept returning.

The second main interest in this study is in terms of the larger cultural questions about the relationship between psychoanalysis and art, and psychoanalysis and the ambient culture. To state this point briefly, let us say that both Beckett and Bion presented and represented to their audiences major issues of concern in the latter part of the twentieth century: psychic numbing, schizoid ways of being, and a self that must hide out in a bomb-shelter as it were, to protect itself against catastrophe, or even worse, a self that is huddling in the shelter after the castastrophe has taken place. Art and clinical psychiatry and psychoanalysis may deal with similar issues that reflect important cultural and political pressures. Such similarities may arise not only out of the *zeitgeist* common to artists and clinicians, but also by means of particular contacts, between artists and psychoanalysts.[1]

A third point of this study, alluded to in the title, is to examine the question of discovering and discerning formal similarities between two thinkers, or between two realms, namely a question of interpretation. It takes an act of imagination on the part of the one who sees and elaborates on such similarities, but is the construction 'valid', or is it wholly in the 'imagination' of the interpreter? Did Bion, who wrote his first clinical psychoanalytic paper on 'The imaginary twin', find in Beckett such a twin (and vice-versa) or is the twinship created primarily in the mind of the interpreter of the works of these two men? The question of the nature and validity of my construction of a 'twinship' between Beckett and Bion is all the more pressing, because my 'discovery' was in the form of an 'aha' experience, or more precisely, an 'of course' experience. Such experiences lend an intense sense of conviction to the discoverer, but we know we are also likely to be prone to be shaped by ongoing unresolved or unarticulated issues in the mind of the interpreter. Pragmatically, the readers must be the final judges of whether or not the constructions put forward carry conviction or whether they bear the hallmark of a personal 'axe to grind'.

This study arose by serendipity. I have been studying and writing on tragic drama for the past six or so years, developing certain ideas about form and content that define the genre of tragedy (Simon, 1987). My thesis involves a study of the death or murder of children in tragic drama and a concomitant examination of how tragic dialogue 'kills', 'aborts' or 'renders sterile'. In the course of this work, I had finished an investigation of one major modern playwright, Eugene O'Neill, and decided to test out some of my formulations on another modern playwright whose works I scarely knew, namely Samuel Beckett. I had seen several Beckett plays produced in the fifties and early sixties, namely, *Waiting for Godot, Endgame,* and *Krapp's Last Tape.* I had read little of and little about Beckett, and had scarcely any knowledge of his prose works, which I had from time to time tried to read and then put down in boredom or frustration. In the course of now starting to read Beckett's work, especially the drama, and especially *Endgame,* I found not only confirmation of my particular hypotheses, but found plays written as if they were intended for clinical illustrations of some of the major psychoanalytic writings about psychosis, such as the works of Klein, Fairbairn, Searles, Rosenfeld, and Segal. I was particularly struck by the salience in Beckett's works of issues about meaning and connexion, the interplay of logical connexion and of human connexion, and of how both kinds of connexion seemed intertwined and highly problematic for Beckett's characters. His characters seemed to be undermining, attacking, ridiculing and terrified of the act of making a meaningful connexion.

Though it had not been my intention to relate the dramatic oeuvre to the life and psychology of the playwright, I could not help but be curious about the man who was writing such material. All I knew about Beckett was that he is an Irishman who eventually settled in France. When I was able to locate biographical material, especially the 1978 biography by Deirdre Bair, I was astonished to find that the themes I could read out of the two Beckett plays,

Waiting for Godot and *Endgame,* were indeed the stuff of his recurrent personal preoccupations. Specifically, it became clear at once that Beckett, in his late twenties, came to conceptualize his own (rather extensive) personal difficulties as the result of having been born improperly, or not completely born, of terrible experiences in the womb, or of having been born at all. For example, Beckett, according to his friend and lover, Peggy Guggenheim, is said to have been haunted by a pre-natal memory. 'Ever since his birth he had retained a terrible memory of life in his mother's womb. He was constantly suffering from this and had awful crises, when he felt he was suffocating' (Chevigny, 1969, p.3).

I then learned from Bair's biography (1978) that Beckett had been in analysis with Wilfred Bion. When I read Bair's account of the analysis several inter-related thoughts sprung to mind: I have never been able to understand Bion's writings at all—they have appeared to me weird, hyper-involuted or hyperabstract—he and Beckett must have really hit it off; I would have loved to have been a fly on the wall in that analysis, where I think the principals would have understood each other and I neither of them; no wonder so many people (the detractors, obviously) experience or describe a Bion-group as if an experience of a Beckett play. Now I understand—Beckett analysed Bion! In sum, in a moment I had the conviction that now I understood both Beckett, whom I had just been reading, and Bion, whom I had scarcely ever read.

With some trepidation, I began to read Bion's works, and found them indeed much more meaningful than in my previous attempts. I realized how much of what I had taken for granted as a common fund of clinical-psychoanalytic knowledge of schizophrenic communication had either originated with Bion, or had been developed in relation to his work. With great excitement, I read for the first time what is now probably Bion's most widely read, or at least widely cited paper, 'Attacks on linking' (1959). For, in the paper, I found Bion articulating about several severly disturbed patients what I had formulated about the nature of the relationships and communications among the characters in Beckett's plays. Bion wrote of patients who attack the analyst for the *act of interpretation,* not for the contents of the interpretation, for the act implies establishing a link, a connexion between two thoughts, and then may lead to the analyst implying a link or connexion between two people. Bion's patients and Beckett's characters seemed invested in having no union or a sterile union.

Among my preliminary formulations was that Bion had first 'learned' about 'attacks on linking', from his work with Beckett, but had not been able to articulate the concept until he had done a great deal more clinical work. Some twenty years after his work with Beckett, he published a piece that represented his understanding, integration, and assimilation of what had been so salient and so troubling in his work with Beckett. I shall interrupt the tale of my discovery and of my various formulations, to present in more or less narrative form, important facts and constructions about the two men and their contact.

RESUMÉ OF BECKETT'S LIFE

Beckett was born in the spring of 1906, in a suburb of Dublin, the second son of thoroughly respectable and reasonably prosperous Protestant parents. The exact date of his birth is not clear, but he later took on Good Friday, 13 April of that year as his birthday. The limited information we have suggests a very difficult mother who we might label with various diagnostic epithets such as borderline and/or extremely narcissistic. Recurrent unpredictable rages and extremely controlling behaviour were the mother's stock in trade with her two sons, especially with Sam. The father seemed to provide some sort of buffer against the mother, helping to normalize the lives of his sons. At about the age of 10, two orphaned cousins came to live with the family, and they provided an enduring positive relationship. School and friends, and the world of athletics seemed to help provide some core of sanity and normality for the sons. Music was also an important activity, especially from his secondary school years onwards. It appears that at least until the university days, he lived outwardly a normal enough life for a young man of his background and talents.

An indifferent student through secondary school, Beckett seems to have discovered both his academic talents and the excitement of the intellectual life at Trinity College, Dublin, concentrating on French language and literature. It appears that a sense of life, or his life, as difficult, and the perception of others of him as odd, or struggling, or in some way abnormal began during his years at Trinity. His friends knew about his bouts of depression, talk about suicide and his difficulty or unwillingness to get out of bed.

After graduation, an aborted stint as a secondary school teacher, and some continental travelling, he settled in France for several years to take up a teaching fellowship at the prestigious École Normale Supérieure. He began some writing, poems, critical pieces and novels, but did not consider himself as a writer by vocation until several years later, when he returned to teach at Trinity in Dublin, and then soon decided an academic career was not for him.

He returned to Paris in 1932 to pursue his writing, and renewed his association with various literary and artistic people, including James Joyce and some of his circle. He had published some important critical essays and a few poems, and Beckett scholars have been able to show that the seeds of most of Beckett's major characteristics and themes as a mature writer were present in the early 1930's. Among his intellectual attitudes were the instability of the 'I', or self, over time, the inadequacy of language to express and communicate, and a rejection of the possibilities of language and literature adequately conveying anything except negativity and impossibility.

His love life during his young adult years seems to have included some sexual involvement with women, at least with prostitutes, but certainly he became involved in a number of affairs sometime after 1932. Reclusive and difficult in some ways, he was admired and pursued by a number of women, some of whom became lovers, some friends, a few both, a few, enemies.

He was involved in interminable conflict with his mother, May Beckett, who controlled the purse-strings and was not enthusiastic about Beckett's career plans (and lack of career success). During a trip back to Dublin in 1933, his father died of cancer and Beckett lost a person who had helped buffer for him the intrusiveness and control of his mother.

According to information gathered by Bair (1978), information gathered with Beckett's permission from interviews with Beckett's friends and from contemporaneous correspondence, during 1934–35 Beckett was in treatment with Bion in London. He sought treatment because of a combination of long-standing interpersonal difficulties in close relationships; he had to be absolutely in control of the relationship and had profound difficulties in establishing a full intimacy with a woman. He had great problems in separating from a very difficult mother, and, perhaps most serious for a young and aspiring writer, he had a terrible writing block. He also had crippling and puzzling somatic symptoms, which included terrible sleep disturbances requiring his brother to sleep with him, immobilizing lethargy that would keep him in bed for extended periods, and severe recurrent cysts, including a painful anal cyst. He wandered around Dublin, unproductive, uncreative, and getting more and more symptomatic.

His mother was most reluctant to have him leave Dublin, but agreed he was really sick and acceded to his requests for medical help, that is, for psychoanalysis. Apparently, she was so ashamed of his requiring this help, that she did not want him treated in Dublin, lest the community somehow find out, and agreed that he could go to London for treatment and she paid the fees.

Analysis for artists at that time was not a totally alien concept, and both Beckett and his circle could accept, in principle, the potential value of psychoanalysis. The match with Bion was an interesting one, and unfortunately, we have no record of what Beckett's friend Thompson had in mind in selecting Bion. Bion was nine years older than Beckett, and had switched around 1930 from beginning a career in surgery into psychiatry. It is not clear exactly what Bion's clinical-psychiatric experience had been at that point. On the basis of present (incomplete) information, it appears that Beckett had to have been one of his early intensive psychotherapeutic or psychoanalytic cases, and perhaps his first. Bion was not yet accepted for psychoanalytic training (he was in 1937). We do not know if the case was supervised, formally, informally or not at all. We do not know the frequency, or if Beckett sat or lay on the couch. My guess is that the treatment took place three or four times a week.

There are hints from Beckett's comments to his friends that the procedure was difficult, but that he experienced some relief. He made one trip back to Dublin in August of 1934 and indeed had a serious relapse, or regression, hastening his return to London and to Bion. The analysis, in the fall of 1935, seemed stalemated and Bion suggested that he and Beckett go to hear a lecture by Jung, who was delivering a series of lectures at the Tavistock Clinic (where Bion worked); a lecture on Psychopathology and Creativity. In the course of that lecture a number of points that seemed pertinent to Beckett about psychopathology and literary creativity were raised. One important one was Jung's description of the multiple selves amd personages within the psyche of the artist. But, it seemed that a comment by Jung during the question and answer period struck a really deep chord in Beckett. Jung commented about the dreams of a 10-year-old-girl who had died only a year later that her dreams had a premonition of her death. Jung concluded from these premonitory dreams that, 'She had never been born entirely'. To quote Bair:

> Beckett seized upon this remark as the keystone of his entire analysis. It was just the statement he needed to hear. He was able to furnish detailed examples of his own womb fixation, arguing forcefully that all his behavior, from the simple inclination to stay in bed to his deep-seated need to pay frequent visits to his (extremely difficult)

mother, were all aspects of an improper birth. . . . With Jung's words, Beckett finally found a reasonable explanation of his relationship with his mother. If he had not been entirely born, if he did indeed have prenatal memories and remembered birth as 'painful', it seemed only logical to him that the aborted, flawed process had resulted in the improper and incomplete development of his own personality. (1978, pp. 209–10)

Bair goes on to discuss how these themes of blighted birth, the dangers of being born, recur throughout Beckett's work—'Birth was the death of him . . . At suck first fiasco' is a line typical of Beckett's characters (Ben-Zvi, 1986, p. 7). Specific references to Jung's lecture show up many years later in his radio play, *All That Fall* (1957). My construction of this sequence of events—the impasse, Bion's invitation to Jung's lecture, the impact of the contents of that lecture, being there with Bion, and Beckett's leaving of treatment a few months later—represented something incompletely articulated and incompletely worked through both in Beckett and in Bion, and whatever that was, it stuck with both men, incompletely metabolized as it were, for many years. Jung's presentation about being incompletely born and Beckett's response to it represented something like, 'the therapeutic effect of inexact interpretation'. For Bion, as we shall see, a preoccupation with the state of the psyche before birth developed as he grew older, especially in the last decade of his life. For both Beckett and Bion I hypothesize that Jung's comments served as a kind of shared creation, a transitional object that allowed them to separate and yet remain in touch via the theme and fantasy of intra-uterine psychic life.

The treatment ended shortly thereafter, with Beckett announcing that he would terminate at Christmas, 1935 and return to Dublin. Bion warned him of the dangers of returning to live in his mother's house, but Beckett did terminate and return to live with his mother. All of Bion's dire predictions turned out to be true and by 1937, after some travelling back and forth to the continent, Beckett returned to France, never again to take up residence in Ireland. Clearly the results of treatment were far from totally satisfactory. The analysis apparently was of some benefit to Beckett, especially in regard to his writing block for he was able to complete *Murphy,* a novel he began during the analysis (his first published novel, which appeared in 1938). A marvellous line in *Murphy,* suggests something of Beckett's, and perhaps Bion's experience. Murphy, the eponymous hero, begins to work in an insane asylum, Magdalen Mental Mercyseat, where he feels perfectly comfortable, feeling he had at last found a place among his own kind. One reason for Murphy's pleasure was, 'the absolute impassiveness of the higher schizoids, in the face of the most pitiless therapeutic bombardment' (Beckett, 1938, p. 180). I suspect that part of Beckett's attempt to work through the relationship can be seen in various characters in his works. The relationship between Murphy, the attendant, and Endon, the 'amiable schizophrenic' in *Murphy* (and perhaps the absent but omnipresent Godot) may reflect Beckett's feelings about Bion and about their therapeutic work. Treatment may not only have helped Beckett complete the book, but the writing of the book may have been in part a treatment (see Bair, 1978, and Ben-Zvi, 1986, for useful discussion of *Murphy*). Clearly the analysis was difficult for patient and analyst, but years later Beckett looked back with gratitude to Bion, whom he felt had helped him through a difficult period (Beckett, 1985).

There are obviously many questions about the treatment that cannot be answered. Bion is dead and as far as can be told, scrupulously observed the code of professional confidentiality—not a word about his work with Beckett in his extant writings though I believe there are disguised references and allusions. It is not clear how much Beckett would be interested in or willing or able to talk in detail about this treatment of over fifty years ago—probably not much. As for mutual subsequent influences, I have learned from both Mrs Bion and from Beckett that there was no further contact between the two men, professional or personal, after 1935. Beckett did not follow Bion's career, though I believe Bion kept track of, at the least, Beckett's major writings, especially his plays that brought him fame and success.

Beckett settled into life in Paris, but it was clear that the political situation was very unsettling. In early 1938, he was almost stabbed to death in the street, probably a gratuitous assault by someone he did not know. Around the time of that incident, he met and then became involved with Suzanne Deschevaux-Dusmenil, with whom he lived for many years and eventually married in 1961. When the war broke out in 1939, though home in Dublin on a visit, he decided to cast his lot with France and return to his life there. As a citizen of neutral Ireland, he would have some measure of freedom and security in occupied Paris.

During the years of occupation, Beckett worked in an underground resistance cell, a group devoted to gathering information about German military affairs, and he worked at considerable personal risk. In August 1942, about to be arrested, he and Suzanne fled Paris and after several months of difficult and secretive travel arrived in the south of France, at Rousillon, a small village in the Vaucluse. Life was precarious in many ways, there being only a degree of relative safety from the Germans, and the Vichy government. According to Bair's account, he had a major recurrence of symptoms in 1943–44, perhaps a psychotic episode. He undertook the writing of *Watts,* in part as an attempt at self-cure, and it seemed to be effective, perhaps in the same way that *Murphy* may have also been a part of Beckett's therapy. It is a strange book, perhaps his most Kafka-like novel (it has been compared to *The Castle*) but an interesting, at times funny, and successful novel (successful artistically, not commercially).

With the end of the war, Beckett returned to Dublin to visit his ailing mother—she was ill with Parkinsonism and would die of it in 1950—and to see his brother, married and with two children. He stayed only a short time in Dublin, returned to France, at first working with the Irish Red Cross in the Normandy area. He returned to live in Paris in 1946, at the age of 40, and then began the most productive period of his writing, from 1946–50. He produced a novelistic trilogy, *Malone, Molloy,* and *The Unnameable,* and wrote *Waiting for Godot,* the play that would make him world-famous as a writer, as well as stories, poems, and criticism. His life started to become more public in important ways around the theatre, particularly after 1953 when *Godot* was produced. He opted to be deeply involved in problems of staging, directing and acting of his plays and as recently as 1985 he was personally involved in a threatened law suit against the American Repertory Theater for producing his *Endgame* in a manner that he claimed made it not his play.

During this period he switched to writing in French and then did all his own translations (and transformations) into English versions. He later did more writing in English and also did the French versions himself. Literary critics and a few psychoanalysts have commented on the significance of his change of writing, and Beckett himself has provided several different reasons, but the true explanation, as with so much else in Beckett's life, is elusive (Ben-Zvi, 1986, pp. 17–18; Casement, 1982; Anzieu, 1983).

His mother died in 1950, soon after he visited her in a nursing home in Dublin. He destroyed all his personal belongings that were in the family home, and took nothing with him back to Paris. The sickness and death of his mother, including overtones of guilt and neglect, are registered in a number of his works, such as in *Krapp's Last Tape.* But the period between 1950 and 1954 marked the return of a (relative) writing block as he was unable to produce a major new work. The block was ended, paradoxically, with his writing *Endgame,* a play about the ending of everything—the human race, stories, writing, acting, feeling, meaning and caring.

He gained increasing public recognition, won a number of prizes and then won the Nobel Prize in 1969. He has continued to be a prolific writer, and, paradoxically, as many critics have noted, the man whose characters are always professing their inertia, their immobility, their post-catastrophic state of being unable, unwilling or ignorant of how to go on—that man goes on! He celebrated his eightieth birthday 13 April 1986, and [at that time was] still at work. [Beckett died in 1989.]

BION'S LIFE: 1897–1979

The bare facts of the life of Wilfred R. Bion are as follows:[2] he was born to British parents in India, where his father was a civil engineer. At about the age of 8, like many children of his background, he was sent to boarding school in England, never to visit that India again. He was educated at Bishops Stortford College from 1906 to 1915. He was not especially distinguished as a young student, but went on in the higher grades to excel in athletics and do well in his studies.

Soon after graduation, he enlisted in the Army and joined the Royal Tank Regiment on the Western Front, won a DSO for his courage and leadership at Cambrai, and eventually fought at all the major tank battles of the war. His experiences in the war, and especially in the tanks, take up an enormous portion of autobiography—one can imagine an 18-year-old suddenly thrust into an awful war, mastering a brand new technology that was frequently ineptly and disastrously managed by the 'cavalry' generals who were deeply ambivalent about tanks. Various aspects of the horrors of war reverberate, I believe, throughout much of his writing, not only his autobiographical but also his clinical and theoretical writings.

After the war he read Modern History at Oxford and also studied philosophy. Upon graduation he returned to his school, Bishops Stortford College, to teach and to coach rugby and swimming. He left there in 1924 and entered medical training, qualifying in 1929, and seemingly interested primarily in surgery. He had worked closely with Wilfred Trotter, a distinguished surgeon with a passionate interest in individual and group psychology, author of *Instincts of the Herd in Peace and War* (1916). Between 1929 and 1932, his interests shifted to psychiatry and psychoanalysis, and by 1932 he was working at several institutions in the field, joining the Tavistock Clinic in 1933. During the early 1930's he met John Rickman, who was established as an analyst, and in 1937 became Bion's training analyst. Bion had had some sort of eclectic, or eccentric psychotherapy during the late 1920's. Thus, his work with Beckett, from 1934–35, had to have taken place rather early in his psychiatric career, and before Bion had any psychoanalytic experience either as a patient or as an analyst.

During World War II, he did important work in the use of group process and group therapy for the rehabilitation of RAF fliers, doing some of that work with his former analyst, and then friend, John Rickman. That work became the basis for studies on group process for which he became most famous, as his 'Tavistock groups' have become very well known among educators, business and government people, as well as therapists.

He married during the war, his wife became pregnant towards the end of the war, and then died in childbirth in 1945, leaving him with an infant daughter, Parthenope. He somehow picked up the pieces, resumed his profession as a psychiatric practitioner, his association with the Tavistock, and took up analytic training again, this time going to Melanie Klein for analysis.

He qualified as an analyst in 1947, though it appears he continued in analysis with Melanie Klein some time beyond that, and read his first psychoanalytic paper 'The imaginary twin' in 1950 as part of the requirement for membership in the British Psycho-Analytical Society. His career as an analyst continued until his death in 1979, with many important contributions, as a writer, as a teacher, and as a clinician. He was president of the British Psycho-Analytical Society from 1962–65, and in 1968 he moved to Los Angeles where he was a controversial, but important, teacher and analyst. He seems to have exerted a particularly strong influence on Latin American psychoanalysis, expecially in Brazil where he lectured, taught and consulted.

In 1951 he met and soon married Francesca, and they had two children, Julian and Nicola, the former now a physician, and the latter a linguist working in publishing. His first child Parthenope, is working as a psychoanalyst. They had a very durable and loving marriage and Francesca Bion has continued to assist in the publication of any works partially completed at the time of his death in 1979.

He was indeed a rather complex man, and no attempt here will be made to characterize him in the fullness of his life. Rather, I will emphasize some aspects of his style and defences, especially as revealed in his autobiographical prose works, that seem especially relevant to understanding the encounter with Beckett.

His childhood, as recalled in his autobiography (the material was probably assembled when he was in his seventies) has some characteristics of an inner turmoil and at times nightmare. It is not clear whether he was an especially sensitive and perceptive child, or if he perhaps also had some breaks with reality, or both. The account of childhood years appears to me as if a combination of the early parts of James Joyce's *Portrait of the Artist as a Young Man* and Jung's *Memories, Dreams, Reflections*. It also has echoes of some of Bion's clinical case reports of work with disturbed patients. He was a man who seems to have struggled with what might be called schizoid issues, especially with schizoid defences against strong affect, including rage. It is likely that Bion understood something of having a very difficult mother, from whom separation was difficult and with whom closeness was dangerous. Representative of these trends, that is, his defences against wishes for closeness, and his style of damping down strong affect, are statements such as:[3]

> One night when I was lying on my bed with pyjamas on waiting for Dudley [his school chum—age 10 or so] to get into his bed, he suddenly discarded the towel he had around his waist and jumped astride me as if challenging me to wrestle. '*Now* how do you feel?' he said. I felt nothing physically; mentally a sense of boredom and anti-climax, which soon communicated itself to Dudley who, after a few futile attempts to provoke a struggle, got off—Dudley and I continued to duel and wrestle with a growing sense of pointlessness. The only overt and unmistakable emotional experience was when futility flared into mutual dislike, or more correctly, hate. (p. 74)

Or speaking of his loneliness and missing his mother after he went off to preparatory school in England:

> Thus, when I found myself alone in the playground of the Preparatory School in England where I kissed my mother a dry-eyed goodbye, I could see, above the hedge which separated me from her and the road which was the boundary of the wide world itself, her hat go bobbing up and down like some curiously wrought millinery cake carried on the wave of green hedge. And then it was gone. Numbed stupefied, I found myself staring into a bright, alert face. (p. 33)
>
> I learned to treasure that blessed hour when I could get into bed, pull the bedclothes over my head and weep. As my powers of deception grew I learned to weep silently till at last I became more like my mother who was *not* laughing, and was *not* crying. (p. 34)

Or (Bion is about to enlist in the army in 1916; he has just finished at his public school):

[My parents] were glad to see me—that I knew. But I could feel that her boy's precocious departure for the war left my mother kissing a chitinous semblance of a boy from whom a person had escaped. (p. 104)

The most striking examples of reactions that involve schizoid defences and/or extreme depersonalization, and those that consume the most space in the autobiography, are Bion's accounts of tank and trench warfare in France. He was a tank commander and was decorated for bravery, but felt that it was a most extraordinary dehumanizing experience. He knew, both by observation of his men and of his fellow officers, and by his own direct experience, the terror, the loneliness and isolation, and the defensive numbness and depersonalization that came with mechanized warfare. He describes his relief at being shot at by a German soldier, a discrete human being, rather than a machine. He describes the defensive withdrawal of caring too much about another soldier, for you know he may well be killed. And, finally, he describes traumatic states and post-traumatic states that overlap considerably with schizoid defences. This was a man for whom the experience of the war crystallized out what were probably schizoid trends and available defences earlier in his development.

There is good reason to believe that much of Beckett's sense of non-communication and the absurdity of letting something or someone mean too much has been profoundly shaped by his awareness of man's inhumanity to man, especially in relation to his own World War II experiences and his knowledge as a young student in Dublin of the returning wounded and maimed young war veterans (Mushatt, 1985). Reverberations of the war are felt throughout his work, as with Nell and Nagg in ashcans in *Endgame,* having lost their legs in a bicycle accident, 'in the Ardennes, on the way to Sedan'.[4]

There is a palpable 'Beckettian flavour', a theatre of the absurd quality to some of Bion's accounts of the war casualties. A fellow officer:

He has lost both eyes, his right arm and both legs. He didn't know who I was though the nurse told him. He's simply—just has a silly grin. The nurse told me afterwards that every now and then he becomes terrified, cowers down in a corner of the room and sucks his thumb. Once he told his doctor that at these times he could see a patch of lawn open up, his mother rise out of her grave and walk slowly towards him. Otherwise he told no one—just went into a corner, scuttling on his stumps with astonishing speed, stuffed his left thumb into his mouth and waited trembling. When the fit was over he would go back to his silly giggling. (p. 186)

After reading Bion's accounts of the incredible destructiveness of the war, one can see the irony in technical psychoanalytic terms 'part objects', 'splitting', 'fragmentation', and 'projection'.[5] It seems to me that Bion's understanding of psychosis, of psychotic inner catastrophe, must have formed in connexion with the perception of the war as psychic as well as physical catastrophe.

Bion did not lack passion, impetus, strong desires or will—he was not a character out of a Beckett novel or play, but he clearly could mobilize stances and defences cut from the same mould as those characters. In important respects, he and Beckett must have experienced considerable temperamental similarity. It is my speculation that in the analysis both Beckett and Bion profoundly influenced each other. Bion must have been struggling to articulate his personal issues, to understand within himself and with his patients the nature of early defects in object relations, early issues around closeness and its dangers. At that time he encountered Beckett who probably presented such issues in 'pure culture', in his personal turmoil, and who in his literary work and creative thinking had already picked up and developed themes that could help express in words and literary form his inner turmoil and dilemmas. Beckett's skills in expression of these states related to early objectal problems and dilemmas may well have helped Bion formulate these issues in psychoanalytic terms.

BION'S WORK[6]

For this reader, Bion's written works present considerable problems in reading and understanding. Both his devotees and critics speak of the difficulties in comprehending what he meant, and it seems one must take seriously the quip cited as an epigram at the beginning of the paper—'I cannot promise communication of pure non-sense without the contamination by sense' (Bion, 1979). He is cryptic, elliptic, overly abstract, and at times his clinical illustrations barely seem to illustrate his points at all. At times he teases with obfuscation, and at times he earnestly struggles to express clearly some very difficult to express emotional states, or only half-articulated concepts. If Bion began his psychiatric and then psychoanalytic work in the early 1930's, it seems that it was at least ten years or more before he wrote papers in the field. Bion, by his own account, seems to have had some difficulty in writing.

He seems to have derived substantial benefit for his problems with writing from his analysis with Klein.

(1) During and shortly after World War II, he wrote some short papers on his experiences in groups, work which became the foundation of more substantial and quite influential publications on groups. These are reprinted and collected in a 1961 volume, *Experiences in Groups*. His classification of groups according to their 'basic assumptions', became important not only in studies of group therapy and group process, but have also influenced his views of the 'group process' in the analyst–analysand relationship.

(2) His first psychoanalytic papers began to appear in the fifties, hearlded by his presentation in 1950 to the British Psycho-Analytical Society of 'The imaginary twin' (later published). These papers dealt primarily with clinical issues arising in the setting of the treatment of very difficult, schizoid and/or schizophrenic patients. An exceedingly important one for our purposes is his 1959 paper, the last in this series, 'Attacks on linking'.

External evidence points to the fact that the patient reported in his first (1950) paper had to have been treated either just after the war or else it had to do with a patient treated in the 1930's. Internal evidence suggests that the patient was either Beckett, or another patient that shared important features with Beckett. Later comments of Bion indicate that the patient's identity is heavily disguised, lest 'the patient' see himself in the paper (in *Second Thoughts: Selected Papers on Psycho-Analysis,* 1977).

More important for our purposes than the identifying of the patient is to grasp some of the main points Bion is struggling to articulate in his first psychoanalytic clinical paper. Actually, there are three patients, A, B, C, though the bulk of the material concerns A, who was a very sick patient, no matter what the degree of disguise, and his discourse for a long time represented speech without prominent affect or strong commitment to communication. The title, 'The imaginary twin', refers to a transference interpretation by Bion, that the patient treated him, Bion, as if he were the patient's imaginary twin. The other two patients were involved in 'twinning' as well: B was one of identical twins and C was quite concerned and attuned to twins. Twinning and splitting of the person into sub-persons, or replication, cloning of the person, are recurrent themes in Beckett's works, as we shall see later.

Patient A had, in fantasy, according to Bion's construction, prevented an 'imaginary twin' from being born and the patient was now being punished by the unborn imaginary twin. Bion was to understand the patient's communications as if a twin was supposed to know that he was 'imaginary', and was also standing in opposition to the patient. Bion further thought that this fantasy represented an early objectal or pre-objectal problem in relationship, and was reflected in the patient's inability to tolerate an object not under his control. The function of the imaginary twin was to deny a reality different from himself.

In his 1967 'Commentary' on the case, Bion wondered why he had given such central importance to this construction of an imaginary twin, and thought in retrospect that the notion was important as an affective realization of something in the communicative process. I would guess that Bion needed this patient, or this construction, as his own 'imaginary twin', a kind of transitional experience and thought, to assist him in articulating an experience he had had in his own life and in treating sicker patients. As he later developed a schema and conceptual apparatus for describing communicational blocks and problems in analysis, he jettisoned, or discarded the 'twin'. In short, I would argue that he used these Beckett-like patients as his twin in the process of expressing, and gaining control over experiences in treatment and in his own life that were difficult to manage and difficult to communicate.

In his 1959 paper, 'Attacks in linking', Bion presents material from patients who strenuously object to the analyst's act of interpreting, even more than to the contents of the interpretations. 'Linking' of one thought or feeling, or one situation to another, is viewed as a profound threat by these patients because it implies the possibility of the patient and the analyst meaning something to each other, and having some links between them. He cites several examples (stating that they represent merged material from two different patients).

(i) I had reason to give the patient an interpretation making explicit his feelings of affection and his expression of them to his mother for her ability to cope with a refractory child. The patient attempted to express his agreement with me, but although he needed to say only a few words his expression of them was interrupted by a very pronounced stammer which had the effect of spreading out his remark over a period of as much as a minute and a half. The actual sounds emitted bore resemblance to gasping for breath; gaspings were interspersed with gurgling sounds as if he were immersed in water. I drew his attention to these sounds and he agreed that they were peculiar and himself suggested the descriptions I have just given. (p. 308)

(vi) Half the session passed in silence; the patient then announced that a piece of iron had fallen on the floor . . . I said that he felt so envious of himself and of me for being able to work together to make him feel better that he took the pair of us into him as a dead piece of iron and a dead floor that came together not to give him life but to murder him . . . he felt he could not go on because he was either dead, or alive and so envious that he had to stop good analysis. There was a marked decrease of anxiety, but the remainder of the session was taken up by isolated statements of fact which again seemed to be an attempt to preserve contact with external reality as a method of denial of his phantasies. (pp. 309–10)

In discussing the patient who experienced iron falling, Bion wrote that what is important is:

the patient's envy of the parental couple had been evaded by his substitution of himself and myself for the parents. . . . The couple engaged in a creative act are felt to be sharing an enviable, emotional experience; as well . . . a *hatred of emotion, and therefore, by a short extension, of life itself.* This hatred contributes to the murderous attack on that which links the pair, on the pair itself and on the object generated by the pair . . . the patient is suffering the consequences of his early attacks on the state of mind that forms the link between the creative pair and his identification with both the hateful and creative states of mind. (my italics) (p. 311.)

The interpretation threatens to link patient and analyst in a creative and fecund relationship and this cannot be tolerated by the patient:

If my interpretation was correct, and subsequent events suggested that it was, it meant that the experience of being understood had been split up, converted into particles of sexual abuse and ejected. (p. 309)

In my fourth example . . . my understanding and his agreeable state of mind have been felt as a link between us which could give rise to a creative act. The link had been regarded with hate and transformed into a hostile and destructive sexuality rendering the patient-analyst couple sterile. (p. 310)

Bion closes with:

The main conclusions of this paper relate to that state of mind in which the patient's psyche contains an internal object which is opposed to, and destructive of, all links whatsoever from the most primitive (which I have suggested is a normal degree of projective identification) to the most sophisticated forms of verbal communication and the arts. . . . These attacks on the linking function of emotion lead to an over-prominence in the psychotic part of the personality of links which appear to be logical, almost mathematical, but never emotionally reasonable. Consequently the links surviving are perverse, cruel and sterile. (pp. 314–5)

When I read this paper it brought home to me how much I had been interpreting Beckett's plays, especially *Endgame,* using, implicitly, models that Bion makes explicit (and that, I believe had entered into a certain common fund of knowledge in the psychodynamics of seriously ill patients). Each of these clinical vignettes or commentaries suggests a character or situation or dynamic in a Beckett work. Another aspect of the similarity between the clinical material and Beckett's works resides in the paradox that along with, or even despite, the push to break all meaningful links, there is a persistent push to keep trying, to keep communicating. To read either Bion's patients' or Beckett's texts as *only* efforts at thwarting communication is to be complicit in the defences used by the patient, and by the 'texts' (Cavell, 1969).

My knowledge of Beckett and his works also suggests to me very strongly that Beckett is the 'modal' patient in those clinical vignettes; or rather, that if it is not Beckett himself, it is a few patients whose issues and presentations overlap considerably with Beckett's. It is with this paper that Bion essentially concludes his clinical-case writing, and for all intents and purposes, forgoes extensive case reporting.

My hypothesis is that Bion waited fifteen years to begin to write up material from his treatment with Beckett, not only because of reasons of confidentiality, but also because it took him this long to begin to find a framework and to conceptualize this difficult and torturing clinical material. Beckett, I believe, sensitized Bion to these issues, and Bion continued to struggle with them, only being able more fully to articulate them in the years after World War II, either by dint of personal analysis and growth and/or by dint of more clinical experience and exposure to other psychoanalytic viewpoints (especially Klein and Fairbairn). Over the decade or so from 1950 to 1959, when Bion wrote this series of clinical papers on schizoid and psychotic phenomena in analysis, he was 'working through' the impact, perhaps even the trauma, of doing intensive analytic work with Beckett and with similar patients.

I would also hypothesize that Beckett's verbal and artistic gifts allowed him to articulate more vividly than some other patients the nature of his disturbed and disturbing inner experiences and perhaps touch something personal in Bion's inner struggles. My guess is that Beckett's writing of his highly successful plays, *Waiting for Godot* (first performed in 1952) and then a few years later, *Endgame,* was in part facilitated by his working through, some fifteen years after his treatment with Bion, enough of these themes to articulate them in a way that could reach a wide public.

The next phase of Bion's writings is heralded by *Learning from Experience* in 1962 and is followed over the next eight years by three more works, *Elements of Psycho-Analysis* in 1963; *Transformations* in 1965; and *Attention and Interpretation* in 1970 (Green, 1973). In these works, (now collected in Bion, 1977), Bion moves to writing more abstractly, with symbolic notation, about issues of the genesis and fate of meanings and connexions, genesis ontologically and also within the psychoanalytic setting (including within the mind of the analyst). My hypothesis is that he begins to grapple theoretically and systematically with issues that Beckett is grappling with artistically.

Following are some impressions, largely derived from *Learning from Experience,* of the issues that I believe are central in Bion's theoretical treatises. Bion, it seems to me, is struggling with problems of how we know —people, things, feelings, thoughts, and how we can transmit, teach, explain, communicate to others (and others to us). In particular, he is concerned with the problem of knowledge within the psychoanalytic situation—knowledge between patient and analyst, and, then, the problem of how to transmit more generalizable knowledge to others, to other analysts, in particular, so that the field of analysis may be built up. He is concerned lest the field remain a solipsistic enterprise of individual analysts with individual patients and with no accrual of knowledge.

Bion tries to isolate *elements,* such as 'factors', 'functions' and the like. A part of this strategy is to label these functions, with alphabetic notations. He is aware of two 'dangers'—the one of reducing complex human feelings and thinking states, human interchanges, to only a skeleton of their richness. The other danger is that of using scientific, mathematical, formalistic terms in ways other than their denotations within scientific fields, or scientific frames of thinking. To this objection he confesses (Bion, 1962, Introduction, paragraph 5):

> It may seem that I am mis-using words with an established meaning, as in my use of the terms function and factors. A critic has pointed out to me that the terms are used ambiguously and the sophisticated reader may be misled by the association of both words with mathematics and philosophy. I have diliberately used them because of the association, and I wish the ambiguity to remain. I want the reader to be reminded of mathematics, philosophy and common usage, because a characteristic of the human mind I am discussing may develop in such a way that it is seen at a later stage to be classifiable under those headings—and others. . .

His ultimate goal, he claims, is to advance psychoanalytic thinking, by which he means do his methods and ideas promote *development*—of the field and of the individual patient.

In effect, what Bion is saying is that this cultivated ambiguity in the terms he uses replicates something of the operations of the human mind, particularly the mind as viewed from the perspective of psychoanalysis. Hence, he claims his use of symbols and abstractions does not dessicate or constrict the psychoanalytic field, but is an attempt to get a handle on describing the mental life of analyst and patient.

From another perspective, what we are seeing is that Bion is starting out from his struggles with a small number of highly challenging and interesting patients, but puzzling and frustrating individuals, who are psychotic or near psychosis. They do not seem to have adequate 'alpha-function'—the capacity to render 'alpha-elements'—feelings, proto-thoughts, experiences—into symbols that can enter dreams, thinking or reverie. Such patients are filled with 'beta-elements'—concretized things, experiences, undigestable, unmetabolized experiences that he can only take in or evacuate—the stuff of which certain kinds of acting out are made. Story telling and narrative, in the conventional sense of stories as vehicles for symbolizing, expressing, communicating and linking of teller and audience, of linking of the generations —such telling with sequence, plot, motivation and affect is seriously defective in these severely schiziod or schizophrenic patients. (See Grotstein, 'Who is the dreamer?' in Grotstein, 1983c, especially pp. 373–89).

Bion describes, for example (Bion, 1962) failures in early development and relationship to the breast (and to the mother!) that:

> makes breast and infant appear inanimate with consequent guiltiness, fear of suicide and fear of murder, past, present and impending. The need for love, understanding and mental development is now deflected, since it cannot be satisfied, into the search for material comforts. Since the desires for material comforts are reinforced the craving for love remains unsatisfied and turns into overweening and misdirected greed . . . his pursuit of a cure takes the form of a search for a lost object and ends in increased dependence on material comfort; quantity must be the governing consideration, not quality. He feels surrounded by bizarre objects, so that even the material comforts are bad and unable to satisfy his needs. (p. 11)
>
> The fact that the patient uses an equipment suited for contact with the inanimate to establish contact with himself helps to explain the confusion produced by the patient's awareness that he is in fact alive. (p. 12) The attempt to evade the experience of contact with live objects by destroying alpha-function leaves the personality unable to have a relationship with any aspect of itself that does not resemble an automaton. (p. 13)
>
> The scientist whose investigations include the stuff of life itself finds himself in a situation that has a parallel in that of the patients I am describing. The breakdown in the patient's equipment for thinking leads to dominance by a mental life in which his universe is populated by inanimate objects . . . We assume the psychotic limitation is due to an illness: but that of the scientist is not. (p. 14)

Hence, Bion's theory-making is instigated by the problems posed by patients who cancel out the distinction between animate and inanimate by making everything inanimate and concrete. These patients practice the opposite of primitive animism—they infuse all living things with the quality of death.

Thus, by chapter 15, he has introduced 'functions', 'factors', 'alpha-functions' and 'alpha-elements', beta-functions and beta-elements, and a notation about the relationship of 'objects' to each other: 'L = x loves y; H = x hates y; K = x knows y'.

The relationships among these three terms are complex, but at the least any attempt of a person to articulate L or H for himself, let alone to communicate something about that love or hate, entails K, that is, knowing. He grants that the clinical situation he describes (a patient knows a therapist who botched up the treatment of one of the patient's friends, ruined his marriage, etc.) contains a large number of permutations and combinations. If one takes into account all of these (including hetero- and homo-sexual currents) the printed page would be replete with a huge number of these alphabetic combinations. Bion's writing would then uncannily resemble the caricature in Borges' novel *Chronicles of Bustos Demecq* (1967) (Albright, 1981, p. 3).

> There will be no plot, no chronicle of events, no logic of discourse, but two themes, the Descent into Hades from Homer, a Metamorphosis from Ovid, and, mixed with these, medieval or modern historical characters . . . He has scribbled on the back of an envelope certain sets of letters that represent emotions or archetypal events—I cannot find any adequate definition—ABCD and then JKLM, and then each set of letters repeated, and then ABCD inverted and this repeated, and then a new element XYZ, then certain letters that never recur, and then all sorts of combinations of XYZ and JKLM and ABCD and DCBA, and all set whirling together. (pp. 4–5 of Borges)

One could describe Bion as having a few themes (or 'stories')—the bad breast, the movement back and forth between the paranoid–schiziod position and the depressive position, mother, or analyst, as 'container' or as failed container for infant or for patient—and then there are the permutations and combinations of the letters, English and Greek, and finally the great 'periodic table' that is on the inside cover of his books.

Borges' caricature of modernist writing also highlights a serious problem in art and in psychoanalytic theory: presenting in an organized way the chaotic and the unorganized, perhaps even the unorganizable. Can one communicate the uncommunicable without either premature obsessive and schizoidal systematization that distances one emotionally from dread and chaos? Can one achieve such communication without enough organization to prevent the audience from being utterly confused or overwhelmed? *The Shape of Chaos,* a title of a book on Beckett, epitomizes the problems faced by both Beckett and Bion.

Another important strand of Bion's writing, generally know only to serious students of his work, is a three volume work entitled, *A Memoir of the Future* (the three parts are *Book One: The Dream* (1975); *Book Two: The Past Presented* (1977); *Book Three: The Dawn of Oblivion* (1979).[7] These volumes are in form poetic, imagistic, dialogue, free-associational, and, in spirit, serious, yet often quite funny. They constitute a kind of autobiography, and become more intelligible when combined with the two volume prose autobiography.

In these three imagistic dialogue volumes, several features are striking in relation to the connexions between Beckett and Bion. They are essentially dialogues among parts of the self including (especially Book Three) dialogues among parts taking place in utero, or, as if somehow, extra-utero, embryological parts of the self are dialoguing with various later life stages. They resemble, quite remarkably to me, a number of Beckett's later plays, that is, plays written after *Godot* and *Endgame. Krapp's Last Tape,* for example, exploits the technology of the tape-recorder to establish a kind of dialogue among the selves at different ages and life-stages. Other, shorter plays, especially some for radio, present disembodied voices, or 'mouth', or 'listener' and 'reader', and other parts of people or 'part objects'. (See, for example, *Words and Music, Cascando, Breath, Not I, A Piece of Monologue*—in *The Collected Shorter Plays of Samuel Beckett.)*

Chapter 1 of Book Three includes a dialogue among 'Em-mature', 'Premature', 'Eight Years', 'Four somites', 'Twenty months', P.A. (which presumably stands for psychoanalyst but might also be 'pain in the ass') and various other 'characters'.[8] Em-mature begins by asserting:

> This book is a psycho-embryonic attempt to write an embryo-scientific account of a journey from birth to death overwhelmed by pre-mature knowledge, experience, glory and self-intoxicating self-satisfaction. I acknowledge dependence on sensible and experienced transcriptions; I cannot promise communication of pure non-sense without the contamination by sense. I shall not repeat my apology for having to borrow the language of experience and reason despite its inadequacy. (p. 1)

After a fairly raucous and rowdy bit of dialogue the cast proclaims:

THE GRID

	Definitory Hypotheses 1	ψ 2	Notation 3	Attention 4	Inquiry 5	Action 6	. . . n.
A β-elements	A1	A2				A6	
B α-elements	B1	B2	B3	B4	B5	B6	. . . Bn
C Dream Thoughts Dreams, Myths	C1	C2	C3	C4	C5	C6	. . . Cn
D Pre-conception	D1	D2	D3	D4	D5	D6	. . . Dn
E Conception	E1	E2	E3	E4	E5	E6	. . . En
F Concept	F1	F2	F3	F4	F5	F6	. . . Fn
G Scientific Deductive System		G2					
H Algebraic Calculus							

ALL: I don't know what you are talking about.
P.A. You think it's *about* something. It has already been said by Shakespeare—'It is a tale told by an idiot, signifying nothing'.

Or, in a dialogue between Mind and Body:

MIND: . . . do you get them [words] through the diaphragm?
BODY: They penetrate it. But the meaning does not get through . . .
MIND: . . . The meaning does not get through whether it is from you to me, or from me to you.

The themes of the difficulty of representation of one level of experience in the language of another, of the pain of life in the uterus, of the impossibility of ascribing and maintaining meaning, the difficulties of establishing and maintaining connexions among people, parts of the person, or among people—all these themes are redundantly represented artistically in the works of Beckett. The inadequacy of language to convey experience is also central to Beckett. What we see in Bion, I believe, is that the issues about communication, the inadequacy of language, meaning, attachment, thinking and symbolizing, and the hatred, avoidance, or inability in these functions, are first articulated in his 1950–59 clinical papers. Then various aspects of these problems get elaborated over the last two decades of his life in two different kinds of treatise, namely the hyperabstract and symbolically overloaded treatises, and the imagistic and imaginary dialogue version of autobiographical issues and struggles. Both of these forms mirror, replicate, or incorporate aspects of both the form and content of Beckett's writing during these decades.

Finally, there is the 'work' that is largely unrecorded in writing, namely Bion's extensive psychoanalytic practice. Apart from Bion's own comments on 'technique', (a word he disliked) there are accounts by several analysands who are now analysts (Grotstein, 1986a, b; Tustin, 1981). One impression, among many, is that he had a way of offering interpertations, but would also convey irony, some sarcasm, or scepticism about his interpretation, lest the patient hypostasize or worship his interpretation, and the patient sell short his or her own capacity to make interpretations. He did not attack or undermine the effort to make meanings and links, but it is as though he learned from his patients who mounted 'attacks on linking', and from his own analysis with Klein, that 'links' as forged by the analyst, or by the patient's rush for closure could become 'chains'.

THEMES AND ASPECTS OF BECKETT'S WORK

As a brief example, however, of some of the issues Bion considers both in theory and in these imagistic autobiographical dialogues, let us glance at some characteristics and recurrent themes in Beckett's work (Albright, 1981).

(1) The problematic of the 'I': This can be conveyed in several different aspects. First, in many of his works, especially the novelistic trilogy, *Molloy, Malone Dies, The Unnameable,* there is a persistent 'I', a narrator of sorts, but what one learns about that 'I' or persona is astonishingly little, mostly about some very peculiar or unstable sense of the 'I', the self. Or, particularly in the later plays, there are parts of the self, loosely or poorly integrated, organs with autonomy, or aspects of the self, different ages and stages, that do not convey a coherent, agent-centred sense of self. The instability of the image of the self is epitomized in *The Unnameable* (pp. 305–6) where the hero describes himself with a ceaseless abundance of images—a talking ball, a hairless wedgehead, a skull made of solid bone, a tympanum, a red-mouthed half-wit; his genitals, hair and nose have all fallen off. No single image is held longer than an instant; each image drives out the image before it, as if the imagination's perfection consisted not in creating images but in extinguishing them. The view that various characters in a story are parts of the self is at times explicit in Beckett. The narrator in *Murphy* proclaims, in regard to a cryptic allusion about Job and his comforters (p. 70):

> But what is Bildad but a fragment of Job, as Zophar and the others are fragments of Job.

Twinning, splitting, and fragmenting of the self are recurrent in Beckett's works. One of the more poignant examples, a child creating imaginary companions, is found in *Endgame*. Hamm, terrified of finally having driven away everyone so that no one is left to hear his story, exclaims (Beckett, 1958a, p. 70):

> All kinds of fantasies! That I'm being watched! A rat! Steps! Breath held and then . . . (He breathes out.) The babble, babble, words, like the solitary child who turns himself into children, two, so as to be together, and whisper together in the dark.

The passivity, indeed sloth, and immobility of the self also repeatedly stands out in Beckett's work, as epitomized in the images of Murphy, the 'hero' of *Murphy,* tying himself into a rocking chair and endlessly rocking. In *Words and Music* (1961; in Beckett, 1984, p. 127) we find sloth praised:

the most powerful passion and indeed no passion is more powerful than the passion of sloth, this is the mode in which the mind is most affected . . .

(2) Characters cannot learn, they cannot grow, as if they have no apparatus for assimilating, transforming and representing symbolically. They have no memory and no formed desires. The characters in *Waiting for Godot,* or in *Endgame,* go round and round, in ever decreasing concentric circles, with no sense of progression or growth. Whatever growth and learning take place is by evasion, guile, or by the most roundabout and indirect movements.

(3) The symbol-making capacities of Beckett's characters are severely impaired. In *The Unnameable* (pp. 407–8) we find vivid examples of the 'meaninglessness' of words, the kind of phenomena that Bion is describing in psychotic patients, where words are only 'beta-elements', not alpha-elements that are capable of being rendered into the realm of the symbolic.[9]

that's all words they taught me, without making their meaning clear to me, that's how I learnt to reason, I use them all, all the words they showed me, there were columns of them, of the strange glow all of a sudden, they were on lists, with images opposite, I must have forgotten them, I must have mixed them up, these nameless images I have, these imageless, names, these windows I should perhaps rather call doors, at least by some other name, and this word man which perhaps not the right one for the thing I see when I hear it . . . I call that the dark, perhaps it's azure, blank words, but I use them, they keep coming back, all those they showed me . . . it's a lie, a score would be plenty, tried and trusty, unforgettable, nicely varied, that would be palette enough . . . that's how it will end, in heartrending cries, inarticulate murmurs, to be invented as I go along, improvised, as I groan along, I'll laugh, that's how it will end, in a chucke, chuck chuck, ow, ha, pa, I'll practice, nyum, hoo, plop, psss, nothing but emotion, bing bang, that's blows, ugh, pooh, what else, oooh, aaah, that's love, enough, it's tiring.

Related to the difficulty of symbolizing and connecting is an urge towards a mechanized, or arithmetic mode of experiencing passion or pleasure. Conversely, passion and human preference threaten the 'system' of permutations and combinations. In the first part of *Molloy,* there are sixteen sucking stones —they must be arranged in the right order. In *Murphy,* the hero becomes aware of the fact that he could eat his five different biscuits in one hundred and twenty different orders, if only he were not bothered by his preferences!

it struck him for the first time that these prepossessions reduced to a paltry six the number of ways in which he could make his meal . . . Even if he conquered his prejudice against the anonymous, still there would be only twenty-four ways in which the biscuits could be eaten.

(4) 'Nothing' and 'no meaning' point to some of the most important values for Beckett's characters, and, to some degree, for Beckett himself. In his critical writings, he announces his preference for:

> the expression that there is nothing to express, nothing with which to express, nothing from which to express, no power to express, no desire to express, together with the obligation to express (Cohn, *Disjecta,* 1984, p. 139).

From an aesthetic viewpoint, from a perspective within literary history, Beckett is attacking the notion that art is an attempt to 'express oneself' or express a feeling, or even to make a point. From a more personal viewpoint —as is often articulated by his characters—art is 'the art' of carrying on, knowing there is nothing. It also became apparent from statements that Beckett had made about what his works 'mean' that Beckett had at best an ambivalent, and at worst a decidedly negative and hostile view to any attempts at ascribing meaning or significance to his work, i.e. part of his credo involves the folly, or perhaps danger, of seeking to find connexions and meanings. In a now much quoted statement about *Endgame* he derides interpreters, and says that the play is only a matter of 'fundamental sounds' [no joke intended] and the only thing it is 'about' is *nec tecum, nec sine te,* 'not with you and not without you' (Cohn, 1984, p. 109), which is a succint statement of the schizoid dilemma.

(5) The impossibility of, indeed the attack on, story telling is central to Beckett's art (Morrison, 1983). 'Hell roast this story', said Mr Kelly, 'I shall never remember it' (*Murphy,* p. 15). In novels and in his plays, especially in *Endgame,* story telling is repeatedly mocked, undermined, made more and more involuted; when not mocked, the act of story telling appears as an impossible task, for which there is no incentive and no energy. In many different contexts, for Beckett's characters, the fundamental linking entailed in one person telling a story to another, in one person linking events together in meaningful sequence—that activity is derided. The fundamental distinctions among story, story-teller, and audience are impossible to maintain. Yet, there is, by implication, an urge to keep telling, even, if the tale told is a tale of how nothing is there, and nothing can happen and nothing can emerge! There is an awareness, however perversely perceived and presented by Beckett's characters, that without stories there is death, degeneration, and total sterility.

(6) The attack on birth and generation:

Neary leaned against the Pillar railings and cursed, first the day in which he was born, then—in a bold flash-back—the night in which he was conceived.

This parody of Job's curse (Job 3) exemplifies the unmistakable hallmark, 'birthmark', personal signature of Beckett. Earlier we noted the 'revelation' in the Jung lecture, a kind of understanding of his personal plight that was reflected in Beckett's earlier writings (e.g. *Whoroscope*) and became a central theme, indeed preoccupation in virtually all his later writings. *Endgame,* of course, makes most explicit how terrible it is to be born, to be on earth, and how generation is the worst crime of all. Stillbirth or non-conception appear as yearnings of his characters; life in the uterus is problematic, indeed a torture, and being born is even worse. The ancient dirge of the chorus in Sophocle's *Oedipus at Colonus,* 'Best is never to have been born' becomes central in these modern works. For example, *Not I* (1973), a stage play relating the lonely death of a lonely old woman, opens with Beckett's 'Mouth' speaking:

out . . . into this world . . . this world . . . tiny little thing . . . before its time . . . in a godfor- . . . what? . . . girl? . . . yes . . . tiny little girl . . . into this . . . out into this . . . before her time . . . godforsaken hole called . . . no matter . . . parents unknown . . . unheard of . . . he having vanished . . . thin air . . . no sooner buttoned up his breeches . . . she similarly . . . eight months later . . . almost to the tick . . . so on love . . . spared that . . . no love such as normally vented on the . . . speechless infant . . . in the home . . . no . . .

The death of children and indeed the murder of children, as in so much of modern drama, (e.g. O'Neill, Pinter, Sam Shepard), is a related recurring motif in Beckett's works. *All That Fall,* (1957) a play referred to above because it seems to incorporate twenty years later so much of Beckett's experience of Jung's lecture, deals with the disdain of the male protagonist for birth and for children, and with the possibility that he deliberately pushed a young boy off a moving train.

(7) Among the characteristics of his work in the sixties, seventies and eighties that are of interest for our purposes, is a tendency to write plays and poems, or prose poems, in increasingly geometricized, mathematicized form. His TV and radio play scripts consist largely of diagrams and permutations and combinations of letters and numbers. On the printed page, the ratio of geometry to words is startling. In some of his less well known works, such as *Lessness* (1970) and *Imagination Dead Imagine* (1965) one sees that both the process and product of composition involve laying out bleak, painful and

barren scenes or prospects, and then imposing a geometric or mathematical arrangement upon them. The latter work opens:

> No trace anywhere of life, you say, pah, no difficulty there, imagination not dead yet, yes, dead, good, imagination dead imagine. Islands, waters, azure, verdure, one glimpse and vanished, endlessly, omit . . . No way in, go in, measure. Diameter three feet, three feet from ground to summit of the vault. Two diameters at right angles AB CD divide the white ground into two semicircles ACB BDA. Lying on the ground two white bodies, each in its semicircle.

On the one hand the process can be seen as a kind of musical composition of themes and variations, but on the other as 'the mathematizing of pain' (my own phrase). The earliest version of *Lessness* is a series of sentences, conveying, certainly, great bleakness and destruction. Beckett progressively makes combinations and systematic arrangements that at once make the distress more remote and more formal—distancing the pain—but simultaneously makes the pain more intense by virtue of its being crafted and shaped. The effect is similar, in a way, to the attempt to disguise horrible death and destruction associated with war, or with nuclear destruction, by citing statistics, percentages, and 'acceptable losses' of say forty to fifty percent of the population of the United States.

Let us, then, consider a possible motive for Bion's attempts at formalizing the varieties of thought, affect, and experience. Did he need to master and control the pain of human isolation, degradation and destructiveness, whether associated with collective behaviour, as in war, or with individual and dyadic settings, such as in psychosis, profound disturbances in infant-mother relationships, or pained and unworkable psychoanalytic relationships? Does the 'grid' attempt to synthesize and reintegrate that which has been torn asunder by 'catastrophe' (one of Bion's favorite terms), whether in development or in communication, or, even in the making of theories and assumptions about disturbed human behaviour? In short, the comparison with Beckett raises the possibility that there are such aspects of Bion's theorizing, namely attempts at mastery and restitution.

THE METHOD OF INTERPRETATION AND ITS RESULTS

I have, in this work, attempted to understand two difficult and problematic thinkers by comparing them with each other. I have minimized, indeed neglected, many important issues of differences between the two. I have not, in this work, provided expositions of the line of development for Beckett and for Bion as totally independent and separate, developments which have a history in terms of the field where each was working. Bion's writings have to be viewed in the complex multiple contexts of problems in psychoanalytic thinking, clinical work, and even psychoanalytic organizations. Some of his students and commentators have begun that task, though I believe there is much more to be mined in the totality of his works. A good biography of Bion would constitute a major contribution to understanding trends and conflicts in psychoanalysis in the second half of the twentieth century. Similarly, Beckett's work has an internal development in terms of aesthetic and compositional issues that Beckett has worked on for over fifty years. Such work also has to be seen in the context of twentieth-century literary movements and issues, an aspect of interpreting Beckett that has attracted and elicited some superb literary criticism and literary history.

My claim is that there is an important gestalt, a gestalt of form and content common to Beckett and Bion. I also suggest that in the encounter between the two during the years 1934–35, that each intuitively apprehended the presence of that gestalt in the other, though neither could conceptualize or formalize it. I would assume that the decision to go to the Jung lecture represented a subliminal awareness that they needed someone to catalyze or crystallize their inchoate understanding, and that over the remaining years each in his own way would work out and work in the implications of and exposition of that gestalt.

What is that gestalt, that complex? In very compressed language, the term 'schizoid', especially as elaborated by Fairbairn and Guntrip, applies. It is a mixture of a certain kind of conflict and defence, an encounter or encounters with psychic disruptions of at times psychotic or near psychotic proportions; a certain interwined view of the difficulties of human communications and yet a deep regard for the struggle to maintain that communication; an insistence on honestly owning up to the implications of a profound unwillingness or inability, or dread of making deep connexions with another human being. At a somewhat more cognitive level, the two men shared, or gradually evolved, a view of the problematic nature of language, and the necessity of exploring the implications of those problems. The gestalt includes, or subsumes, a capacity to utilize and blend two seemingly contrasting styles—the construction of primitive dialogue among primitive objects and part objects, 'names without words and words without names', (a Beckettian phrase) and the construction of highly ordered, mathematical grids and algebraic combinations. The *style* implicit in the gestalt includes a willingness to experiment, to 'play', to outrage, to push to the limits, and a deep conviction of the absolute necessity to spell out and play out all the implications of their ideas.

Now this gestalt, or aspects of it, can certainly be considered as part of the *zeitgeist* of the twentieth century, as part of the modernist spirit. Students of Beckett have done much to locate Beckett within such currents in European cultural history (e.g. Kern, 1970, in existentialism; Ben-Zvi, 1980 on aspects of linguistic philosophy; Cavell, 1969, in terms of problems common to sceptical philosophy, and to Austin and Wittgenstein). Commentators on Bion have tended to look more to certain 'classical' or pre-modern influences on Bion, e.g. Greek and Latin literature, Kantian philosophy, William Blake (e.g. Grotstein, 1983b; Williams, 1985) as well as to modern philosophy of science and mathematics. Beckett himself, of course, played an important role in bringing to light the nature and existence of this 'gestalt', to some extent in his own critical works, and even more so in the way his plays and novels elicited a kind of commentary that clarified his underlying assumptions. Bion has not been a major intellectual influence in twentieth-century culture, but he has played a role, and perhaps his expositors will enlarge that role, in articulating for psychoanalysis the problems for understanding mental life in general that are posed by the existence of psychotic levels of experience and of communication. He has, starting out with a clinical base, recursively come upon a particular twentieth-century mode of dealing with the coexistence of the most primitive and the most abstract. His expositions indirectly highlight the 'pre-modernist', or 'classical' nature of Freud's distinction between primary and secondary process, and of the hierarchical assumptions built into the model. Bion's models and Bion's style import more of the anarchy and the flirtation with the inchoate that characterizes much of twentieth-century art and literature.

Have I constructed a valid schema of what these two men have in common, or have I constructed a procustean bed into which I insist on fitting them? My own answer is: there is a dialectical process, of which I am only one participant and commentator. The dialectic involves creative thinkers and artists in the twentieth century, including a few psychoanalysts, who have tried to make sense of the non-sensical and further tried to show how much of art, science, and psychoanalysis, is devoted to portraying and critiquing the processes by which we try to make sense. My excitement with both Beckett and Bion in part has to do with my responsiveness to their ability to 'play' with this dialectic, and thereby both clarify for me what my struggles are in this regard and also enhance my ability to think more freely, more loosely, and more playfully. At various points, and this the reader will have to judge, I believe I 'cycle' through a stage of critical exposition, on my way from and to the more exotic and chaotic universes described by Beckett and Bion. This quest has helped clarify for me a certain vision of what is the psychoanalytic process, and more broadly speaking, what is the task of art. I am neither Beckettian nor Bionian, but I hope I have borrowed, incorporated and then transmitted to others something durable that emerges from the struggles which they have undertaken.

ACKNOWLEDGEMENTS

I want to thank Prof. Deidre Bair, Drs James Grotstein and Hanna Segal for encouragement and several specific suggestions; Miss Pearl King for information from the Archives of the British Psycho-Analytical Society; and Drs Roberta Apfel, Francis Baudry, Lynne Layton, John Looper, and Himal Mitra for critical reading of the manuscript.

NOTES

1. See the important study by Sass (1985) who examines several possible modes of interrelationship between modernist culture and theories in psychiatry and psychoanalysis, including that important twentieth century artists and writers were themselves psychotic.
2. These facts are excerpted from James Grotstein's memoir (Grotstein, 1983a; Lyth, 1980). Autobiographical material (with some substantial editing after his death) is found in Bion, 1982 and 1985.
3. The page numbers following these excerpts refer to Bion, 1982.
4. See Bair (1978, p. 520) for an account of a transient breakdown in Beckett's own usual detached way of dealing with memories of terrible incidents in World War II.
5. For another example of the overlap between the disasters of war and the theatre of the absurd see Bion (1985, pp. 47-8). It seems to me that Bion's account of World War I, in its emphasis on detachment, depersonalization and grotesque absurdity resembles, in literary terms, some of the post-World War II writing about war more than it does the great World War I classics, such as *All Quiet on the Western Front*. On 'Theatre of the absurd', see Barchilon (1973).
6. In the extensive psychoanalytic literature on Bion (much of which I have not read, or only perused), I will single out several works which I have found most helpful: Boris, 1986; Eigen, 1985; Grotstein, 1983a, b; Meltzer, 1978; Williams, 1985.
7. I have only been able to obtain the last, but have read excerpts from the first two—see Williams (1985).
8. That Bion seems to take the question of pre-natal psychology seriously is suggested, however, perversely, obscenely and impishly, in his brief paper, 'On a quotation from Freud' (Bion, 1977a). Freud's work introduce this somewhat weird paper, 'There is much

more continuity between intra-uterine life and earliest infancy than the impressive caesura of the act of birth would have us believe'.

9. See Ben-Zvi (1980) for an elegant discussion of Beckett's views on the total inadequacy of language to communicate, and his relationship to the linguistic philospher, Mauthner.

REFERENCES

I do not list the original dates and titles of those works written in French and then later translated into English by Beckett. The interested reader can refer to either Bair or Ben-Zvi for a complete bibliographical listing.

Albright, D. (1981). *Representation and the Imagination: Beckett, Kafka, Nabokov, and Schoenberg*. Chicago: Univ. Chicago Press.

Anzieu, D. (1983). Un soi disjoint, une voix liante: l'écriture narrative de Samuel Beckett. *Nouvelle Rev. Psychanal.*, 28: 71–86.

Bair, D. (1978). *Samuel Beckett: A Biography*. New York: Harcourt Brace Jovanovich.

Barchilon, J. (1973). Pleasure, mockery and creative integrations: their relationship to childhood knowledge, a learning defect and the literature of the absurd. *Int. J. Psychoanal.*, 54: 19–34.

Beckett, S. (1938). *Murphy*. Reprint, New York: Grove Press, 1957.

——— (1957). *All That Fall*. New York: Grove Press.

——— (1958a). *Endgame, Followed by Act Without Words*. New York: Grove Press.

——— (1958b). *The Unnameable*. In *Three Novels by Samuel Beckett*. New York: Grove Press.

——— (1961). *Words and Music*. In *The Collected Shorter Plays of Samuel Beckett*. New York: Grove Press, 1984.

——— (1965). *Imagination Dead Imagine*. London: Calder and Boyars.

——— (1970). *Lessness*. London: Calder and Boyars.

——— (1973). *Not I*. In *The Collected Shorter Plays of Samuel Beckett*. New York: Grove Press, 1984.

——— (1984). *The Collected Shorter Plays of Samuel Beckett*. New York: Grove Press.

——— (1985). Personal Communication.

Ben-Zvi, L. (1980). Samuel Beckett, Fritz Mauthner, and the limits of language. *PMLA*, 95: 183–200.

——— (1986). *Samuel Beckett*. Boston: Twayne Publishing.

Bion, F. (1985) Personal Communication.

Bion, W. R. (1950). The imaginary twin. In *Second Thoughts*. New York: Jason Aronson, 1977, pp. 3–23; Commentary, pp. 120–38.

——— (1959). Attacks on linking. *Int. J. Psychoanal.*, 40: 308–15.

——— (1962). *Learning from Experience*. In Bion, 1977.

——— (1977). *Seven Servants: Four Works by Wilfred R. Bion*. New York: Jason Aronson.

——— (1977a). On a quotation from Freud. In *Borderline Personality Disorders*, ed. P. Hartocollis. New York: Int. Univ. Press, pp. 511–15.

——— (1979). *Memoir of the Future: Book Three: The Dawn of Oblivion*. Perthshire: Clunie Press.

——— (1982). *The Long Week-End, 1897–1919: Part of a Life*. Abingdon: Fleetwood Press.

——— (1985). *All My Sins Remembered: Another Part of a Life and The Other Side of Genius: Family Letters*, ed. F. Bion. Abingdon: Fleetwood Press.

Boris, H. N. (1986). Bion re-visited. *Contemp. Psychoanal.*, 22: 159–84.

Casement, P. J. (1982). Samuel Beckett's relationship to his mother-tongue. *Int. Rev. Psychoanal., 9: 35–44.*

Cavell, S. (1969). Ending the Waiting Game: A reading of Beckett's *Endgame*. In *Must We Mean What We Say?* ed. S. Cavell. Cambridge: Cambridge Univ. Press, 1977.

Chevigny, B. G. (1969). Introduction. In *Twentieth Century Interpretations of ENDGAME: A Collection of Critical Essays,* ed. B. G. Chevigny. Englewood Cliffs: Prentice-Hall.

Cohn, R. (1984). *Disjecta; Miscellaneous Writings and a Dramatic Fragment: Samuel Beckett.* New York: Grove Press.

Eigen, M. (1985). Towards Bion's starting point: between catastrophe and death. *Int. J. Psychoanal.,* 66: 321–30.

Green, A. (1973). On negative capability: a critical review of W. R. Bion's *Attention and Interpretation. Int. J. Psychoanal.,* 54: 115–19.

Grotstein, J. ed. (1983a). *Do I Dare Disturb the Universe: A Memorial to Wilfred R. Bion.* (Reprinted 1983 with corrections by H. Karnac Ltd, London. Original is 1981, Caesura Press.)

——— (1983b). Wilfred R. Bion: The man, the psychoanalyst, the mystic. A perspective on his life and work. In Grotstein, 1983a.

——— (1983c). Who is the dreamer who dreams the dream and who is the dreamer who understands? [Revised]. In Grotstein, 1983a.

——— (1986a). Personal Communication.

——— (1986b). Making the best of a bad deal: On Harold Boris' 'Bion Revisited'. *Contemp. Psychoanal.,* 23: 61–76.

Kern, E. (1970). *Existential Thought and Fictional Technique.* New Haven: Yale Univ. Press.

Lyth, O. (1980). Obituary: Wilfred Ruprecht Bion (1897-1979). *Int. J. Psychoanal.,* 61: 269–74.

Meltzer, D. (1978). *The Kleinian Development: Part III. The Clinical Significance of the Work of Bion.* Perthshire: Clunie Press.

Morrison, K. (1983). *Canters and Chronicles: The Use of Narrative in the Plays of Samuel Beckett and Harold Pinter.* Chicago: Univ. Chicago Press.

Mushatt, C. (1985). Personal Communication.

Sass, L.A. (1985). Time, space and symbol: a study of narrative form and representational structure in madness and modernism. *Psychoanal. Contemp. Thought,* 8: 45–84.

Simon, B. (1987). Tragic drama and the family: the killing of children and the killing of story-telling. In *Discourse in Psychoanalysis and Literature,* ed. S. Rimon-Kenan. London: Methuen.

Tustin, F. (1981). A modern pilgrim's progress: reminiscences of personal analysis with Dr Bion. J. *Child Psychother.,* 7: 175–92.

Williams, M. H. (1985). The tiger and 'O': a reading of Bion's *Memoir* and Autobiography. *Free Associations,* 1: 33–57.

Name Index

Subject Index

About the Editor

EMANUEL BERMAN studied in Israel and the U.S. He is Associate Professor of Psychology at the University of Haifa, training and supervising analyst at the Israel Psychoanalytic Institute, and Visiting Associate Professor at New York University's postdoctoral program in Psychoanalysis and Psychotherapy. His papers have appeared in psychoanalytic and psychological journals in the U.S., Israel, and Europe.

Printed in the United States
1389100001B/398